ROUTLEDGE HANDBOOK OF DESCRIPTIVE RHETORICAL STUDIES AND WORLD LANGUAGES

The *Routledge Handbook of Descriptive Rhetorical Studies and World Languages* offers a useful collection of papers that presents rhetorical analysis of the discoursal practice in different cultural settings.

Covering issues from America to Europe and Asia, and topics from politics to media, education to science, agriculture to literature, and so on, the handbook describes how language can guide listeners' interpretations, alter their perceptions and shape their worldviews. This book offers a solid foundation for rhetorical studies to become an essential discipline in arts and humanities, engendering innovative theory and applications in areas such as linguistics, literature, history, cultural studies, political science and sociology.

This handbook will be crucial for students and researchers in areas such as literature and linguistics, communication studies, political science and arts and humanities in general. This book will also be useful to social science, education, business, law, science and engineering departments due to its coverage of rhetoric in a multidisciplinary and multilingual context.

Weixiao Wei has been working as a lecturer at the College of Foreign Languages and Literatures, Taiyuan University of Technology, China, for 12 years since she obtained her MA degree in 2010. In July 2017, she received a visiting scholarship from the China Scholarship Council (CSC) to undertake research projects at Swansea University, UK, for a year. Since then, she has published two monographs and six book chapters with Routledge. She is currently the chief editor of the *Routledge Handbook of Descriptive Rhetorical Studies* and is planning another handbook of language learning in a global context. She is also the editor of the Chinese language studies section in the upcoming *Routledge Research Encyclopedia of Chinese Studies*. In addition to preparing research papers, a monograph and an edited volume for further publication, she has been pursuing her PhD study in rhetoric and composition at the University of Houston, USA.

James Schnell, PhD (Ohio University), is an Assistant Professor in the Defense Critical Languages & Culture Program at the University of Montana, USA. He is a three-time Fulbright Scholar (Cambodia, Myanmar and Kosovo) and has published widely on matters having to do with cross-cultural communication, most specifically focusing on China. Schnell has taught in the USA at Cleveland State University, Ohio State University, University of Cincinnati, and Miami University and in China at Beijing Jiaotong University. He was a visiting scholar at Fudan University, China, in 2017.

ROUTLEDGE HANDBOOK OF DESCRIPTIVE RHETORICAL STUDIES AND WORLD LANGUAGES

Edited by Weixiao Wei and James Schnell

LONDON AND NEW YORK

Designed cover image: Andyworks via Getty Images

First published 2023
by Routledge
4 Park Square, Milton Park, Abingdon, Oxon OX14 4RN

and by Routledge
605 Third Avenue, New York, NY 10158

Routledge is an imprint of the Taylor & Francis Group, an informa business

© 2023 selection and editorial matter, Weixiao Wei and James Schnell; individual chapters, the contributors

The right of Weixiao Wei and James Schnell to be identified as the authors of the editorial material, and of the authors for their individual chapters, has been asserted in accordance with sections 77 and 78 of the Copyright, Designs and Patents Act 1988.

With the exception of Chapter 16, no part of this book may be reprinted or reproduced or utilised in any form or by any electronic, mechanical, or other means, now known or hereafter invented, including photocopying and recording, or in any information storage or retrieval system, without permission in writing from the publishers.

Chapter 16 of this book is available for free in PDF format as Open Access from the individual product page at www.routledge.com. It has been made available under a Creative Commons Attribution-Non Commercial-No Derivatives 4.0 license.

Trademark notice: Product or corporate names may be trademarks or registered trademarks, and are used only for identification and explanation without intent to infringe.

British Library Cataloguing-in-Publication Data
A catalogue record for this book is available from the British Library

Library of Congress Cataloging-in-Publication Data
Names: Wei, Weixiao, editor. | Schnell, James A., 1955– editor.
Title: Routledge handbook of descriptive rhetorical studies and world languages / edited by Weixiao Wei and James Schnell.
Other titles: Descriptive rhetorical studies and world languages
Description: Abingdon, Oxon ; New York, NY : Routledge, 2023. |
Includes bibliographical references and index.
Identifiers: LCCN 2022056695 (print) | LCCN 2022056696 (ebook) |
ISBN 9781032049441 (hardback) | ISBN 9781032049458 (paperback) |
ISBN 9781003195276 (ebook)
Subjects: LCSH: Rhetoric. | LCGFT: Essays.
Classification: LCC P301 .R68 2023 (print) |
LCC P301 (ebook) | DDC 808–dc23/eng/20230313
LC record available at https://lccn.loc.gov/2022056695
LC ebook record available at https://lccn.loc.gov/2022056696

ISBN: 978-1-032-04944-1 (hbk)
ISBN: 978-1-032-04945-8 (pbk)
ISBN: 978-1-003-19527-6 (ebk)

DOI: 10.4324/9781003195276

Typeset in Times New Roman
by Newgen Publishing UK

CONTENTS

Editorial Board	*ix*
List of Figures	*x*
List of Tables	*xi*
List of Contributors	*xii*

Introduction   1
Weixiao Wei

PART I

Historical Dimension of Rhetorical Studies   7

1   Mandate of Heaven at the Root of Chinese Political
Rhetoric: Origin, Transformation and Legacy   9
Weixiao Wei and Yuqian Wei

2   Gods of the Thresholds: Liminality and the Origins of Rhetorical
Theory in Ancient Global Myth   24
Shawn D. Ramsey

3   Rhetoric and Silence in Corporate America: Ending the Patent War
between Google and Microsoft   38
Joshua Welsh

4   From the Learning of Classical Rhetoric to the Learning of
Communication: The Evolution of Rhetoric in the Secondary
Education Systems of Spain and Portugal   53
Gracia Terol Plá

Contents

5 Evolution of Arabic Rhetoric: From Classical *Balāgha* to Modern
   Concepts of Persuasion   69
   Marcin Styszyński

PART II
Descriptive Rhetorical Studies: Regional Diversity   87

6 Rhetorical Devices in Japanese: The Case for Onomatopoeia   89
   Massimiliano Tomasi

7 Rhetoric of Russian Civilizational Identity: A Case Study of
   Patriarch Kirill's Discourse   101
   Natalia Bruffaerts

8 Media Sensationalism of the West and the Rhetoric of Poverty
   Porn in India   116
   Sony Jalarajan Raj and Adith K. Suresh

9 Rhetoric of Protest, Tradition and Identity: Polish Songs of
   Freedom and Resistance   131
   Agnieszka Kampka

10 A Descriptive Study of Arabic Rhetorics   148
    Rabeea Al-Mubarak and Ian E. J. Hill

PART III
Descriptive Studies of Political Rhetoric   163

11 The Democrat's Linguistic Stance towards Migration in Electoral
    Campaigns: *Ethos, Logos*, and *Pathos* in Barack Obama's and
    Joe Biden's Discourses   165
    Teresa Fernández-Ulloa and María del Carmen López-Ruiz

12 Political Rhetoric in Jonathan Swift's *Conduct of the
    Allies*: Boosting and Hedging as Persuasive Devices   178
    Rosa María López-Campillo

13 The Rhetoric of the Immigration Discourse of Far-Right Parties in
    Spain and France   198
    Isabel Negro

14 Rhetoric of Polish Political Discourse on Family   218
    Ewa Bogdanowska-Jakubowska and Nika Bogdanowska

Contents

15 Multimodal Nationalist Rhetoric in Finland: From Banal to
Extreme Political Persuasion 234
Eemeli Hakoköngäs and Inari Sakki

16 Between Adversariness and Compromise: A Rhetorical Analysis of
Greek Political Discourse in Times of Crisis 249
Assimakis Tseronis and Dimitris Serafis

PART IV
Rhetorical Analysis of Academic and Professional Texts 265

17 The Failing Essay: Broadening the "Composition" of Critical
Pedagogy in the Age of Digital Literacy 267
Bradley A. Hammer

18 Diverse Voices? A Rhetorical Analysis of First-Year Composition
Textbooks and Open Education Resources 284
Mary F. McGinnis

19 Demonstrating and Debating Climate Change: The Function of
Rhetoric from Science to the Public 310
Ferenc Jankó and Priszcilla Hafenscher

20 A Descriptive Study of Rhetoric in South Korean Business Texts:
CEOs' Quality Management Rhetoric and Audience Responses 325
Mansup Heo

21 Discursive Strategies of Persuasion in the Film Review Genre: The
Case of the Reviewer's Ethos 345
Dominika Topa-Bryniarska

PART V
The Visual and Affective Domains of Descriptive Rhetorical Analysis 365

22 Visual Rhetoric of Otherness in Newspaper Photographs of the
European Refugee Crisis 367
Jari Martikainen

23 Visual Representation of Food in Italian Cinema 380
Fatma Nazlı Köksal and Ümit İnatçı

vii

Contents

24 The Ethos-Pathos Continuum in the Portuguese "Obrigado"
Advertising Campaign 391
Samuel Mateus

25 Emotional Rationality as an Indicator of Rhetoric Discourse in
Polish Agricultural Texts 403
Maria Joanna Gondek and Paweł Nowak

26 Rhetoric in Travel Writing: A Tool to Enhance Verisimilitude and
Persuade Readers 421
David Taranco

27 Ethos, Pathos, and Logos in Culture: An Analysis and Visualization
of the Rhetorical Structure of Narrative in Japanese 440
Tetsuta Komatsubara

Index 462

EDITORIAL BOARD

Kyle Mattson, University of Central Arkansas, USA
Randy Allen Harris, University of Waterloo, Canada
Amy Lipke, San Jacinto College (Central Campus), USA
Laura Filardo-Llamas, Universidad de Valladolid, Spain
Garima Singh, Himgiri Zee University, India
Tanupriya, CHRIST (Deemed to be University) Delhi NCR, India
Islam M. Farag, University of Pittsburgh, USA

FIGURES

14.1	The poster of the anti-abortion campaign: I am dependent [on you]. I trust you	229
14.2	The poster of the anti-abortion campaign: I am 11 weeks old	229
18.1	Coding breakdown	291
18.2	Number of codes per text type	292
18.3	Percentage of codes per type	293
18.4	Difference and multiple marginalizations per text	294
18.5	Race codes per text and text type	296
18.6	Gender/sex codes per text and text type	298
18.7	Class codes per text and text type	299
18.8	Sexuality codes per text and text type	301
18.9	Immigration codes per text and text type	302
18.10	Religion codes per text and text type	304
18.11	Language codes per text and text type	305
18.12	Disability codes per text and text type	306
27.1	The notations of visualization	445
27.2	Examples of visualization	446
27.3	Rhetorical organization of the introduction	451
27.4	Rhetorical organization of the statement	454
27.5	Rhetorical organization of the proof	456
27.6	Rhetorical organization of the conclusion	457
27.7	Visualization of the rhetorical organization of the narrative	458

TABLES

1.1	Six public speeches in ancient China: summary of contents	11
1.2	Four public speeches in Western Zhou: summary of contents	15
13.1	Research corpus	202
13.2	Structures and strategies in Abascal's and Le Pen's immigration discourse	203
18.1	Corpus information	288
18.2	Coding scheme	290
18.3	Percentages of readings addressing difference and with multiple codes	295
20.1	*Samsung* CEO Lee Kun-hee's quality management rhetoric	331
20.2	Descriptive statistics about the audience's perceptions	334
20.3	T-test on the audience's gender and perceptions	334
20.4	Correlation analysis between the audience's perceptions	335
20.5	Multiple regression analysis of the audience's perceptions	336
21.1	Four different genre types according to Maingueneau's classification	350

CONTRIBUTORS

Rabeea Al-Mubarak is a PhD candidate in the Department of English Language and Literatures at the University of British Columbia, Canada. His dissertation focuses on transgressive forms of verbal and non-verbal communication. With a cross-disciplinary academic background in law and applied linguistics, his interests include interdisciplinary research and rhetorical criticism across the fields of rhetoric, discourse studies, critical legal studies, and psychoanalysis.

Ewa Bogdanowska-Jakubowska received her PhD and DLitt in Linguistics from the University of Silesia in Katowice, Poland. Her research interests include pragmatics, critical discourse studies, (im)politeness and face. Her recent works include "Work Ethos in American Ceremonial Discourse Addressed to the Young" (*Discourse and Communication*, 2020) and "The Discursive Representation of Places Significant for an Individual: An Analysis of Polish Academic Year Inauguration Speeches and American Commencement Addresses" (Wydawnictwo Uniwersytetu Śląskiego, 2021).

Nika Bogdanowska received her PhD in Literary Studies from the University of Silesia in Katowice, Poland. Her research interests include discourse studies and rhetoric. She has published a monograph about commentary as a text type, *Komentarz i komentowanie. Zagadnienia konstrukcji tekstu* (Wydawnictwo Uniwersytetu Śląskiego, 2003). Her recent publications include "Addressing the Other in Poland (the 20th and 21st Centuries): Different Times, Different Contexts, Different Meanings" (*Journal of Pragmatics*, 2021).

Natalia Bruffaerts teaches at the Marie Haps Faculty of Translation and Interpreting, Université Saint-Louis – Bruxelles. She holds a PhD in Comparative Linguistics. Her main fields of research comprise rhetoric, discourse analysis and translation studies.

María del Carmen López-Ruiz holds a PhD in Translation and Interpreting at the University of Córdoba, Spain. Her research interests in Translation Studies encompass different domains: translation of political discourse, discourse analysis, and didactics of translation.

Contributors

Teresa Fernández-Ulloa has a PhD in Spanish Language and Linguistics at the University of Deusto, Bilbao, Spain. She has worked at the University of Cantabria, Santander, Spain, and East Carolina University, North Carolina, USA. She has been a Professor at California State University, Bakersfield since 2003. Her areas of teaching and research are sociolinguistics, discourse analysis, and language teaching methodologies.

Maria Joanna Gondek, PhD, is an Assistant Professor in the Faculty of Social Sciences of the John Paul II Catholic University, Lublin. Her academic interests concern the philosophical foundations of rhetoric and the philosophy of culture. She is the author of several books as well as numerous articles, and she is a lecturer at the National School of Judiciary and Public Prosecution.

Priszcilla Hafenscher, MSc in Biology, is a PhD student in the Department of Social and Economic Geography at Eötvös Loránd University, Hungary. She plans to pursue a doctoral degree in climate change communication. Her research interests include human environment interactions and media representation of the environment.

Eemeli Hakoköngäs, D.Soc.Sci., title of Docent, University of Helsinki, is a Lecturer in Social Psychology at the University of Eastern Finland, Finland. His research interests include visual rhetoric, collective memory and political psychology.

Bradley Hammer studied at Columbia University, USA, and, since the fall of 2007, has been on Faculty at the University of North Carolina, Chapel Hill, USA. With almost 30 years of experience teaching academic writing, he has received numerous teaching awards and helped direct writing programs at both UNC and Duke University. Additionally, Dr. Hammer has lectured throughout China on the teaching of "critical thought" while serving as a visiting professor at Shanghai University. His recent book, *The Elements of Composition*, examines the teaching of academic writing in the age of digital literacy.

Mansup Heo is a Professor in the Division of Liberal Arts & General Education at Gangneung-Wonju National University, South Korea. He received his PhD from the School of Media & Communication at Korea University and also worked as a newspaper reporter. His main areas of interest are rhetoric, communication, and digital media. His books and articles include *Presidential Rhetoric of South Korea and the U.S.*, *Abused Metaphors in Political Communication*, and *A Study on Social Media Usage, Helplessness, and Loneliness*.

Ian E. J. Hill is an Associate Professor in the History and Theory of Rhetoric at the University of British Columbia, Canada, where he is also affiliated faculty with the Graduate Program in Science and Technology Studies. His research focuses on rhetoric, technology, and comparative rhetoric, and he teaches courses in rhetorical history and theory, the rhetoric of technology, textual criticism, argumentation, brevity, and memes. He published *Advocating Weapons, War, and Terrorism: Technological and Rhetorical Paradox* in 2018.

Ümit İnatçı, Professor, completed his higher education at Pietro Vannucci Academy of Fine Arts in Perugia, Italy. He has written art criticism and essays in various journals, and has published his own art magazine. He has worked in the field of documentary film, and has produced and directed TV and radio programs. He has been a writer and editor for various newspapers and magazines.

Sony Jalarajan Raj is an Assistant Professor in the Department of Communication, MacEwan University, Edmonton, Canada. Dr. Raj is a professional journalist turned academic who has worked in different demanding positions as a reporter, special correspondent, and producer for several news media channels such as the BBC, NDTV, Doordarshan, AIR, and Asianet News.

Ferenc Jankó is an Associate Professor at Eötvös Loránd University, Budapest, and the University of Sopron, Hungary. He received his PhD in Human Geography from Eötvös Loránd University, Hungary, in 2007. His main field of research is climate change and environmental controversies, climate change adaptation, and the history of geographical knowledge with a special focus on Burgenland, Austria. He has published articles on the topic in *Geoforum, Scientometrics, Environmental Education Research* and *Journal of Cleaner Production*, and others.

Agnieszka Kampka is an Assistant Professor at Warsaw University of Life Sciences, Poland. She is a Sociologist (PhD, Habil.), Philologist (MA) and Art Historian (MA). Her research interests include the rhetoric of politics, visual rhetoric and debate, and public discourse. She is the author and editor of several visual and political rhetoric books. She is also on the board of the Polish Rhetoric Society and the chief editor of the international open-access journal *Res Rhetorica*.

Tetsuta Komatsubara received his PhD in Linguistics from Kyoto University, Japan, in 2015, and teaches and researches rhetoric and cognitive linguistics at Kobe University, Japan. Special attention goes to creative meaning, grammatical constructions, and communicative effects of figurative language. He is the author of the volume *Rhetoric and Creativity in Meaning: Linguistic Deviation and Cognitive Linguistics* (2016) and has published articles on rhetoric and intercultural studies.

Rosa María López-Campillo studied at Murcia and Castilla-La Mancha universities, Spain, and has worked at Castilla-La Mancha University, Spain, since 1990. She teaches English and English Phonetics and researches in linguistics, ELT and public opinion. She is particularly interested in discourse analysis and political propaganda in early modern Britain and language education in bilingual schools.

Jari Martikainen studied Art History at the University of Jyväskylä, Finland, and Social Psychology at the University of Eastern Finland, Finland, and holds PhD degrees in both disciplines. He works as a university lecturer in Social Psychology in the Department of Social Sciences at the University of Eastern Finland, Finland. His interdisciplinary research combining social scientific and visual approaches focuses on migration, populism and issues related to leadership and teachership.

Samuel Mateus is Professor of Communication Studies at Madeira University, Madeira, and a researcher at Labcom. He researches in the fields of communication theory, political communication and rhetoric. He is the author of *Introduction to Rhetoric in the 21st*

Century (2018, in Portuguese), editor of *Media Rhetoric: How Advertising and Digital Media Persuade Us* (2021), and co-editor of *From Multitude to Crowds: Collective Action and the Media* (2015).

Mary F. McGinnis is an Assistant Professor of English at the College of Coastal Georgia, USA. She holds a PhD in Rhetoric & Composition from Ball State University, USA; an MA in Training & Development and an MA in Women's and Gender Studies from Roosevelt University, USA; and an MA in English & American Literature from Indiana State University, USA. Her research focuses on cultural rhetorics, transformative pedagogies, and multimodal literacy in the composition classroom. Her research is deeply entwined with her teaching.

Fatma Nazlı Köksal, PhD, completed her higher education at Eastern Mediterranean University, Famagusta, Turkish Republic of North Cyprus, and has worked at İstanbul Aydın University, Turkey, since 2020. She teaches and researches in visual communication and representation and is particularly interested in the use of visual images for communication, visual rhetoric and semiology. She has published articles in various international journals, and book chapters.

Isabel Negro is an Assistant Professor at Complutense University in Madrid, Spain, where she teaches Business English. She has published many articles in international journals (including *English Studies, Metaphor and the Social World, Journal of French Language Studies, Visual Communication Quarterly*). Her research fields are discourse analysis, English for specific purposes, cognitive semantics and contrastive linguistics.

Paweł Nowak is a Professor at Maria Curie-Skłodowska University, Poland, a communicologist, media expert and pragmalinguist, an employee of the Department of Media Communication at Maria Curie-Skłodowska University in Lublin, Poland, Head of the Department of Linguistics and Psychology of the Institute of Forensic Expertise "Analityks" and Chairman of the Scientific Council of the Institute, and a lecturer at the National School of Judiciary and Public Prosecution and the National School of Public Administration. Paweł Nowak is author and co-author of more than 100 publications.

Shawn Ramsey received his PhD in Rhetoric and Writing from Bowling Green State University, USA. He is an Assistant Professor at the University of Doha for Science and Technology, Qatar, who generously supported this research. He has taught many genres of writing at almost every skill level as well as the history and theory of writing, rhetoric and argumentation on three continents. His work has appeared in scholarly journals such as *RSQ, Rhetoric Review, Rhetorica*, and the *Journal for the History of Rhetoric*.

Inari Sakki, D.Soc.Sci., title of Docent, University of Helsinki, is a Professor in Social Psychology at the University of Helsinki, Finland. Her research interests include political communication, nationalism, populism, national and European identity, collective memory, social representations, discourse and multimodality.

Dimitris Serafis is an SNSF Postdoctoral Research Fellow currently based at USI – Università della Svizzera italiana, Switzerland, and Adjunct Lecturer at the Panteion University of Social and Political Sciences, Greece. His research interests lie at the intersection of critical discourse studies, social semiotics and multimodality, and argumentation studies, with his current focus being on topics such as migration, racism and hate speech, authoritarianism and populism, and communication in times of crisis.

Marcin Styszyński, PhD, is an Associate Professor in the Faculty of Arabic and Islamic Studies at Adam Mickiewicz University in Poznan, Poland. He focuses in his research on Arabic rhetoric and political language as well as media and advertisement in the Arab world. Dr Styszynski is also the author of several books.

Adith K. Suresh is currently working as a Research Assistant in the Department of Communication, MacEwan University, Edmonton, Canada. Adith holds a Master's degree in English Language and Literature from Mahatma Gandhi University, India. His research interests include film studies, literary criticism, and South Asian cultural studies.

David Taranco holds a doctoral degree from Universitat de València, Spain. He currently teaches Spanish at Doshisha University, Kyoto, Japan. His research focuses on travel writing, translation, and modern Japanese poetry. He is exploring travel accounts by foreign visitors in Meiji and Taisho Japan as well as journals written by early Japanese travellers to Europe. As a translator, he has rendered into Spanish Tanikawa Shuntarō's *minimal* (2019) and a collection of poems by Nakahara Chūya (2021).

Gracia Terol Plá is a PhD candidate at University of Almería, Spain. Her research, supported by the Spanish Ministry of Universities (ref. FPU 18/01386), explores the relationship between classical rhetoric and communicative skills in secondary education. Her main field of research is the teaching of rhetoric in Spain and Portugal during the nineteenth century and the practical application of the discipline to current communicative learning. She has published articles on the topic in Spanish and Portuguese journals, among others.

Massimiliano Tomasi has a PhD in Japanese from Nagoya University, Japan. He is currently Professor of Japanese and Director of the Center for East Asian Studies at Western Washington University, USA. Research interests include modern Japanese literature and rhetoric. He is the author of *Rhetoric in Modern Japan: Western Influences on the Development of Narrative and Oratorical Style* (2004); *The Literary Theory of Shimamura Hōgetsu and the Development of Feminist Discourse in Modern Japan* (2008); and *The Dilemma of Faith in Modern Japanese Literature: Metaphors of Christianity* (2018). He has also edited a volume titled *Religion and Spirituality in Japanese Literature*.

Dominika Topa-Bryniarska, PhD, is an Assistant Professor at the University of Silesia in Katowice, Poland. Her main area of interest is French linguistics, with a particular focus on journalistic persuasion, rhetoric and pragmatics. She is the author of a monograph on the discursive universe in journalistic opinion genres. Additionally, she has participated in many international conferences and given presentations on argumentation and journalistic rhetoric.

Assimakis Tseronis is Associate Professor in the section of Rhetoric at Örebro University, Sweden. He teaches courses on rhetoric and argumentation as well as on visual and multimodal communication. His research interests fall under the areas of discourse analysis, multimodal rhetorical argumentation, and pragmatics. He has published on both the verbal and visual dimensions of argumentative communication, focusing on argumentation markers and the expression of stance and disagreement in deliberations, as well as on the argumentative reconstruction of printed advertisements, magazine covers, and documentary films.

Joshua Welsh earned his PhD in Rhetoric and Scientific and Technical Communication from the University of Minnesota, USA, in 2013. Since then, he has taught technical and professional writing courses in the English Department at Central Washington University, USA. His research focuses on rhetoric, writing, and pedagogy.

INTRODUCTION

Weixiao Wei

Rhetoric started as an art of persuasion in Greek and Roman times, survived through the Middle Ages in various didactic and religious forms, enjoyed a resurgence of interest in the Renaissance, and became a transnational and multidisciplinary subject in the contemporary world, with Europe and North America maintaining a stronghold for this extremely valuable and yet somewhat underrepresented academic discipline. So far, most research and debate on rhetoric is to a large extent confined to the aforementioned historical background and inherited tenets, and the progression of rhetorical studies within the academic sphere is relatively slow. Wiley-Blackwell's *Handbook of Rhetoric and Public Address* (2010) made a valiant attempt to connect public address to civil engagement and democratic citizenship, but the genre of public speech restricted the dialogue to the historical framework. *The Oxford Handbook of Rhetorical Studies* (2014) follows the Greco-Roman rhetoric model and is therefore prescriptive in nature, with three-quarters of the book dedicated to the elaboration of rhetorical conventions from ancient Greece to the Modern and Enlightenment periods. The remaining chapters largely follow the 'find and match' methodology and do not offer adequate material for generating new insights and theory for research in contemporary rhetoric.

In view of the rapidly changing landscape of the world in the twenty-first century due to pandemic, warfare, climate change, food shortages, political confrontation, ideological conflict and false information, it is increasingly important for rhetoric scholars worldwide to consolidate their research findings and formulate a new body of rhetorical theory to enable critical distinction between rhetoric and reality (for example, will nuclear war be an option or is this merely a rhetorical trick at work?), develop an updated rhetorical framework for identifying new genres of speech such as provocative diplomatic talks and fake news, and offer abundant space and resources to work with other disciplines where rhetoric touches the discourse specific to the genre (e.g. scientific discourse, legal documents, medical reports, social media posts). The editors of this volume hope to draw from the historical insights of rhetorical studies without being confined by its theoretical framework (going beyond the conventional Rhetorical Triangle model, for example) or constrained by existing theory and terminology, while, at the same time, introducing innovative ideas and approaches that may update and enrich rhetorical studies for the

DOI: 10.4324/9781003195276-1

academic disciplines to cope with contemporary discourses permeated with a bewildering variety of rhetorical tricks and strategies.

The current handbook gives a relatively comprehensive coverage of rhetorical ideas across many subjects and disciplines. We aim to introduce a new research and presentation rationale in the study of rhetoric which we call Descriptive Rhetorical Studies. This is essentially a 'bottom up' approach where we gather evidence of the use of rhetoric (defined broadly here as the human perceptible symbols or signs that demonstrate a strong intention to achieve something important to the initiator) in multilingual and multidisciplinary settings in the hope of identifying patterns and regularities in genre-specific rhetorical practice for a given geographic region or virtual community at a given time. The approach we take is descriptive rather than prescriptive, the method inductive rather than deductive, which we hope can contribute to the formation of a useful referential framework for conceptualizing current practice of rhetoric in a diversity of cultural settings and interpersonal contexts.

This handbook offers a collection of articles which, while revealing the authors' knowledge and training in classical rhetoric theory, conscientiously flag newly-spotted developments in rhetorical studies which may help conceptualize the directions current trends of research in rhetoric are heading and point out ways forward. With the escalation of the global situation in aspects of war, hunger, disease and ideology, and the increasingly diversified use of rhetorical means to persuade, deceive or unnerve, we believe the time is ripe to bring out a ground-breaking handbook showcasing innovative ideas and new findings in uncharted territories. In compiling this book, we undertake the responsibility of uncovering the truths behind deceptively innocent talks and seek solutions to defend ourselves against cognitively invasive rhetorical tricks.

The first section of the handbook marshals five chapters to set the tone of the book and connect the present to the past in respect of rhetorical ideas and studies. Chapter 1 provides ammunition to the main argument of the book for presentation of new rhetorical evidence and conceptualization of new rhetorical theory by introducing a rhetorical concept which ran through the entirety of Chinese history. It demonstrates a research methodology that may broaden the concerns and findings of rhetorical enquiries to prevent contemporary rhetoricians from being painted into a corner due to lack of new insights. In this chapter, rhetorical properties and cultural implications associated with the concept of Heaven are discussed, which elaborate into the Chinese rhetorical convention of utilizing Heaven as the source of legitimacy in overthrowing existing regimes and establishing new political entities. Rhetoric in this context has a temporal dimension that extends beyond the audience in a fixed setting. Chapter 2 applies von Gennep and Turner's theory of liminality in exploring the conceptual origins of rhetoric in ancient myths. The author offers a fascinating account of how these myths operate by implicating mythic entities and their liminal nature as a means of making analogical arguments about the nature of rhetoric. Chapter 3 provides a useful overview of the history of silence in rhetoric. A cohesive theoretical framework centering heavily on context is offered by the author for the study of silence, which is illustrated with an interesting case study regarding the settlement of a long-standing patent dispute between Google and Microsoft where, according to the author, silence was used to manipulate the audience. Chapter 4 analyzes how classical rhetoric has evolved into the modern concept of communication, focusing on the history of education in Spain and Portugal in the nineteenth and twentieth centuries. The author explains how the learning of first languages in this region has adopted a communicative approach based on the contributions of pragmatics and the precepts and didactic methods inherited from classical rhetoric. Chapter 5 directs readers' attention to the evolution of Arabic rhetoric (*balāgha*), from classical theories during the Abbasid era to modern concepts of persuasion. The main finding of the study is that the modern concept of Arabic rhetoric still relies on classical criteria formulated by Abbasid rhetoricians despite significant influence from the West such as Perelman's argumentative and legal rhetoric, Peirce's pragmatics, Lakoff's metaphors and so on.

The second section of the handbook brings more diversities into the grand picture of rhetorical studies in respect of geographic regions, touching upon rhetorical ideas or practices adopted in Japan, Russia, India, Poland and the Arab states. Chapter 6 provides a timely input, ranging from the booming of Japanese language education around the globe to the understanding of mimetic words as a rhetorical device in Japanese. In particular, it examines the use of colloquial language in literature, which leads to the rediscovery of onomatopoeia as a distinctive rhetorical feature of modern Japanese. Chapter 7 elucidates the idea of Russkiy Mir ('Russian World') promoted by the church in cooperation with the state on the basis of common religious, linguistic and historical heritage of the Eastern Slavs. It examines the evolution of rhetorical mechanisms as seen in the speeches of Patriarch Kirill from 2009 until 2021 which represented Russkiy Mir as a transcendental concept of unifying supranational force. Chapter 8 sets out to investigate how the rhetoric of 'poverty porn' sensationalizes the economically and socially vulnerable aspect of the Indian public sphere in both national and international visual media. Based on Edward Said's notion of Oriental 'Othering', the authors discuss how Western depictions of the East sensationalize poverty porn and encourage the West to imagine and represent poverty as an Asian phenomenon. The study attempts to challenge the logic of poverty porn as an international media practice and responds to the call for the de-Westernization of media discourses. Chapter 9 discusses the multimodality of protest rhetoric using selected examples of songs that have become symbols of resistance and struggle for freedom. It describes chosen pieces that have been considered exceptionally significant in the public sphere in Poland in recent decades, songs that are sung and shouted during street demonstrations and protests. Chapter 10 describes Arabic rhetoric as a multifaceted space of theological, social, cultural, and political trends, characterized as a unified yet also dispersed body of rhetorical practice, criticism, and knowledge production. The chapter revolves around four themes, from the Qur'an's reputation as the peak of Arabic eloquence to contemporary application of Western rhetorical theories to Arabic discourses.

The third section of the handbook focuses on political rhetoric and examines presidential talks, immigration discourse, nationalistic rhetoric, political discourse on the topic of family and Greek political discourse in times of crisis. Chapter 11 compares the different rhetorical mechanisms used in political speeches by Barack Obama and Joe Biden when dealing with the topic of immigration. This study demonstrates how a cutting-edge corpus-based discourse analysis tool can bring new light to a classical rhetoric theory. Chapter 12 follows with a turn to a rhetorical analysis of literary texts. Adopting Fairclough's social-theoretical approach to discourse within the tradition of Critical Discourse Analysis and the face theory developed by Brown and Levinson, the author draws attention to the boosting and hedging verbal devices employed by Jonathan Swift to convince his audience of the necessity to put an end to the war. Working within a theoretical framework which integrates the tenets of Critical Discourse Analysis into the classical rhetorical approach, Chapter 13 seeks to explore the way immigration discourse is built by right-wing parties in Europe. The study analyzes a corpus of public discourse

produced by the respective leaders of the Spanish and French right-wing parties to identify the constructive and dismantling strategies employed in the far-right immigration
discourse and show how such strategies pertain to the logos, ethos or pathos in the classical model. Chapter 14 employs the principle of triangulation and approaches discourse
from a variety of methodological and theoretical perspectives taken from various disciplines. The author analyzes the rhetoric of Polish right-wing populist discourse aimed at
imposing on society the 'only acceptable' model of family which subsumes conservative
values, a heteronormative worldview, traditional gender roles, and so on. Chapter 15
intends to show how the analysis of multimodal material can enrich understanding of
the different structures and tools of current nationalist rhetoric. It argues that analysis
of both banal and novel nationalist rhetoric cannot focus merely on spoken and written
narration. Instead, it is necessary to broaden the scope to multimodal communication to
reach a more diverse understanding of the form and function of persuasion. Chapter 16
assesses the extent to which contemporary Greek scholarship in humanities and social
sciences makes use of rhetorical categories as relevant descriptive and analytical tools.
It revisits two classical rhetorical concepts, topoi and endoxa, in order to illustrate their
descriptive and explanatory potential for the analysis of political discourse characterized
by adversariness, polyphony and the need to create communion.

The fourth section of the handbook focuses on academic and professional texts as
they are presented to students, teachers and the general public. Chapter 17 attempts to
deconstruct the key rhetorical elements of the traditional college essay and examine the
growing irrelevancy of print-forms and other academic compositional modes. By analyzing the changing spaces of university discourse modes and the evolving formulations of
multimodal discourse within the academy, the author looks for a new critical pedagogy to
reimagine first-year writing courses through the formulation of a new, multimodal genre
of 'e-composition'. Chapter 18 conducts a corpus study of 12 first-year composition
textbooks and finds that diversity is not adequately represented in these first-year composition course materials. The author argues that textbook choosers have a responsibility
to engage diversity more often in the classroom in an effort to prepare students to become
more active and sympathetic citizens in a democratic society. Chapter 19 aims to provide
an overview of the linguistic practices and rhetorical strategies employed in offline and
online communications to transmit climate change science to the public. It goes deep
into the heart of analyzing rhetoric, increasingly significant in climate change communication research, and the role it plays to transmit relevant scientific findings to the public.
Chapter 20 explains how Korean CEOs' rhetoric is composed and perceived, suggesting
that the more conservative the audiences are and the more they perceive the CEO's charm
and expertise, the more they support the CEO's quality management rhetoric. Korean
audiences also expect CEOs to reflect Confucian virtues such as benevolence, righteousness, propriety, wisdom, and sincerity. Chapter 21 demonstrates the breadth and diversity
of the journalistic film review genre by applying Aristotle's theory of ethos elements, i.e.,
practical wisdom (phronêsis), moral virtue (aretê) and goodwill (eunoia), as components
of a speaker's character. The findings show that different discursive persuasion strategies
fulfill the ethotic appeal to instill particular views and concepts.

The final section of the handbook shows some trailblazing fruits pertinent to the visual
and affective domain of rhetoric. Chapter 22 introduces the visual rhetorical approach
and applies it to analyze news photographs depicting refugees. It offers a summary of
visual rhetorical strategies used in the photographs to position refugees in the realm of
Otherness, and discusses their social functions. Chapter 23 envisions our concerns in food

and food-related practices in film scenes. Based on the methodological approach of visual rhetoric, the author identifies the strengths and potential for the communicative function of food in terms of cinematic language and pertinent cultural identity discussions. Chapter 24 analyzes the 'Obrigado' (Thank you) campaigns in Portugal according to the MELCA model of rhetorical analysis, aiming to demonstrate the functioning of a pathetic ethos. Chapter 25 provides a rich history of the many recent and not-so-recent rhetorical studies in Polish agriculture by rhetoric categories. The authors consider persuasion in agricultural texts as a key theme for the organization of the message. Chapter 26 sets out to show how rhetorical devices are used in travelogues to persuade readers of the faithfulness of the traveller's descriptions, to shorten the distance between the act of reading and the reader, and to conceal writers' cognitive deficiencies and/or their lack of hermeneutic ability. The author aims to prove how traveller-writers rely on rhetorical devices to win the reader over by making sure that their arguments and descriptions are likely and consistent. Finally, due to the marginality of the field of cultural influences in how persuasive modes are selected and arranged in discourse, the author of Chapter 27 takes pains to develop a descriptive framework for analyzing and visualizing culturally motivated rhetorical organization consisting of ethos, pathos, and logos.

Rhetoric is an old concept and term that may require updating as communication methods and interactional purposes diversify with the advancement of time and technology. This handbook offers a collection of 27 articles that present rhetorical analysis of the discoursal practice of many facets of social lives from a variety of cultures. Covering issues from America to Europe and Asia, and topics from politics to media, education to science, agriculture to literature and so on, we trust the handbook has something to offer to everyone interested in knowing how language works to guide listeners' interpretation, alter their perception and shape their worldviews. As a result of reading this book, we hope more and more people will become interested in reading about rhetoric research, and even become 'part-time' rhetoric researchers themselves within their respective professions. The outcome will be a huge number of publications describing the rhetorical conventions and innovations in many walks of life in the global setting. Eventually, a body of knowledge and theory about rhetoric will be formed as a result of increasingly pervasive descriptive rhetorical studies around the globe. By that time, rhetoric will have acquired abundant resources and built solid foundations to become an essential discipline in arts and humanities from which to develop formidable theory and applications in linguistics, literature, history, cultural studies, political science, sociology, and so on, just as AI means to many science and engineering disciplines. In that sense, this relatively small handbook will have taken a giant step in the world of rhetorical studies.

PART I

Historical Dimension of Rhetorical Studies

1
MANDATE OF HEAVEN AT THE ROOT OF CHINESE POLITICAL RHETORIC

Origin, Transformation and Legacy

Weixiao Wei and Yuqian Wei

Introduction

A widely formed impression about Chinese rhetoric is that there are no public speeches in ancient China due to the absence of such suitable environment as seen in the public debates of ancient Greece. One of the purposes of this chapter is to reveal direct evidence regarding the origin of Chinese rhetoric and present a more accurate picture of ancient, de-Westernized Chinese rhetorical practice. In doing so, we draw from an important historical document noted by Rawson (1989), that is, 'the theories and arguments presented in the *Book of Documents* [尚书]' which, according to Rawson, is 'the earliest surviving discussions in Chinese of the nature of kingship and the state' (p. 74). As a first step, this chapter analyzes the earliest public speeches in the *Book of Documents* by summarizing the vital role played by the Mandate of Heaven in Chinese rhetoric, so far mentioned only by a handful of researchers (e.g., Schwartz 1985, Ching 1997, Marshall 2002, Wei 2021). The formulaic features present in the public speeches epitomize the characteristics of early ancient Chinese rhetoric. That is, the rhetoric when first put to use in the Chinese context was to justify a king's claim to power often by speaking publicly to soldiers right before the war. Next, we examine the rhetorical shift in the Zhou dynasty where the morality of emperors was added as an essential quality of rulers on top of the Mandate of Heaven. Evidence comes to light in the form of bronze inscriptions which carry forward this political rhetoric embedded in religious and ceremonial texts. We then continue to trace the development of this rhetorical convention and examine the political discourse based broadly on Mandate of Heaven including the spawning of the 'people-based' political philosophy. We conclude with a critical look at the influence of the concept of Mandate of Heaven and its associated discourse and rhetoric on subsequent dynasties in the political dimension.

DOI: 10.4324/9781003195276-3

The Origin of Chinese Rhetoric

The root of Chinese rhetoric can be traced back to the Xia dynasty which lasted from about 2070 BC to 1600 BC and left a great number of ritual vessels made of bronze and jade. As only some fragmentary texts have been found so far in these remnants, this dynasty seems to exist on the borderline of history and mythology. If the historical records about this period are correct, the earliest public speech is Ganshi (甘誓),[1] recorded both in the *Book of Documents* (尚书 see Wei 2021 for more details) and *Records of the Grand Historian* (史记), which served as a military mobilization order given by Xia Qi (夏启) soon after his ascendancy to the throne. Rhetoric, like its carrier language, could not have originated at a single point full-fledged in human history. Rather, as noted by Enos (1993), 'it was an evolving, developing consciousness about the relationship between thought and expression' (p. xvii). China's rhetorical tradition certainly does not pale in face of the West in respect of the creation of rhetoric when consciousness traverses from thought to language. In particular, there is plenty of neglected evidence of public speeches which perform a rhetorical function in their original contexts. For example, in the mobilization order Ganshi, Emperor Qi reportedly said the following to justify his crusade against a rebelling tribal commander Youyi: 有扈氏威侮五行，怠弃三正，天用剿绝其命，今予惟恭行天之罚 (Youyi tribe acted against the Mandate of Heaven and violated traditional rituals and practice. Heaven has ordered their livelihood be terminated. We are now empowered by Heaven to dish out this punishment). In the same way, other such public speeches with similar rhetorical elements have been recorded: Yinzheng (胤征 Yin campaigns against Yi and He)[2] in the Xia dynasty; Tangshi (汤誓 a speech made by Tang, the first king of the Shang dynasty)[3] in 1600 BC; Taishi (太/泰誓 a speech made by King Wu)[4] in 1084 BC; Mushi (牧誓 the speech at Mu)[5] on January 20, 1046 BC; and Qinshi (秦誓 a speech made by Qin Mugong)[6] in 627 BC, etc. Table 1.1 offers a brief summary of the contents of these oaths in relation to the use of Mandate of Heaven prior to military action. As a specific type of public speech and noted by Kirkpatrick and Xu (2012), 'shi (誓 oath) was performed by a ruler before a war to encourage morale, and is a type of deliberative rhetoric' (p. 19). In the ancient Chinese world, the emperor appealed to the Mandate of Heaven to unite his army and justify his conquering mission. A similar behavior, to evoke deity for rhetorical purposes, was observed recently by Thorpe (2013) in the West, who discussed the phrase 'under God' being added into the middle of the Pledge of Allegiance on June 14, 1954 by President Eisenhower as a rhetorical symbol to unite Americans against the Communists.

The absence of research on the aforementioned public speeches has led to the imperfect conclusion that ancient rhetoric in China aimed mainly to persuade the emperor or warlords in private settings (e.g. Graham 2004). While Kao (1993) offered a more general characteristic of Chinese rhetorical practice by emphasizing the factor of pathos, or the hearer's psychology where the art of rhetoric 'consists in subtly manipulating the ego of the auditor' (p. 150), he nevertheless also followed the overall trend and commented that 'the object of persuasion, the addressee, is normally the monarch of a state' (ibid.). It seems, then, that the majority of researchers on Chinese rhetoric are not aware of the existence of Chinese rhetoric on mass audience occasions, i.e. the public speeches made in front of solders prior to war, resembling those seen in the court systems of ancient Greece.

As previously mentioned, *shi* (oath) was a type of public speech delivered by an ancient Chinese ruler before sending the troops to war. Five out of the six public speeches recorded in the *Book of Documents* and shown in Table 1.1 were military mobilization orders which shared a bundle of features: accusations of moral corruption against the

Table 1.1 Six public speeches in ancient China: summary of contents

Title	Length in Chinese characters	Reference to Mandate of Heaven	Cause of war	Relevance to the audience/soldiers
Ganshi	94	Heaven's retribution on Youyi	YouYi's contempt for Heaven and the loss of mandate	Reward for obedience; death for defiance
Yinzheng	315	Heaven's retribution and command from the Son of Heaven	Negligence of duty and violation of law by the descendants of YiHe	Appeal to solders to fight hard
Tangshi	190	Mandate of Heaven granted to Tang to end calamities caused by Jie	Jie's demand for unpaid labor from people and his exploitation of state properties	Reward for obedience and penalty for disobedience
Taishi	88	Execution of Heaven's retribution by King Wu	King Zhou's indulgence in women and abandonment of traditional rites	Appeal to soldiers to be brave and fight hard
Mushi	332	Execution of the orders of Heaven to terminate King Zhou	King Zhou's indulgence in women and abandonment of traditional values	Appeal to soldiers to march valiantly forward
Qinshi	315	none	none mentioned	Moral lessons to be learned from loss of battle

person being targeted, reason for going to war, reference to Mandate of Heaven to justify the action, promised rewards or punishment for soldiers based on their actions, morale-boosting words for troops, and so on. The discussion here focuses on the first five speeches with regard to the most grandiose term in the speeches, Heaven, or more precisely, the Mandate of Heaven, which is repeated consistently in subsequent classical texts for the same political purposes and implications.

Before entering a decisive battle which can seal the fate of an independent state in ancient China, the commander-in-chief must make the soldiers understand why they should fight. The importance of this assembly speech and its rhetorical effect prior to war is pointed out by Clarke (1996) who commented that 'a good general would have to know how to address his troops, and if he was not an orator he would also, like Marius, find himself disadvantaged in the political arena' (p. ix). Among the many pretexts for going into war, the most irrefutable in that era was probably to follow the Mandate of Heaven (天命 *tianming*) which played a key role in the overthrow of the Xia dynasty by the Shang clan. The Shang people defeated Xia because of their cohesive force and combat effectiveness, but a compelling reason is required to justify the ousting of the previous regime.

Thus, in that highly religious era, it was relatively easy and undisputable for the winning troops to claim that the destiny of Heaven had descended upon them.

As a result, in that early period of China, the will of Heaven in the political context came to be known as a force for 'rewarding the good and punishing the evil' and for 'the preservation and destruction of states' (Clarke 1996, p. 16). The target of invasion – for example, YouYi, King Jie and King Zhou as listed in Table 1.1 – had disobeyed Heaven and deserved to be punished with the demise of their dynasty. In general, the Mandate of Heaven was used as a vindication throughout the history of China, especially in the Xia, Shang and Zhou dynasties, the earliest periods of Chinese history. Starting from slave owners and aristocrats, this heavenly decree was used to inculcate the idea that the masters' and the elite's command is the manifestation of divine will on earth which all commoners should unconditionally obey. The orator of the first five speeches in Table 1.1 went one step further to associate the regime with the Mandate of Heaven in order to legitimize their military actions against their opponents, and all too obviously to claim that the current regime was blessed by Heaven, thus victory would be on their side. This rhetorical idea based on the reference to Heaven went on to become a central theme of Chinese political rhetoric in China's putative four thousand years of history.

The Rhetoric of Mandate of Heaven

The meaning of *tian* (天 sky/heaven/cosmos) in Chinese philosophy can be interpreted in many different ways. Zeng (2013) identifies five senses of *tian*: the material sky, the personified Heaven with a divine character, the destiny or karma of humans, the cosmos system, and the cardinal principle guiding the universe. The Mandate of Heaven (hereafter abbreviated to MoH) used as a key element of war rhetoric in the five public speeches summarized in Table 1.1 is largely based on a 'personified heaven' like God in Western culture. The concept of MoH has at least four layers of meaning which exerted decisive influence on subsequent development of Chinese culture.

1. Explanation of natural phenomena
2. Legitimation of an invasion
3. Appointment of kings
4. Creation of a tradition

According to historical books, the initiator of MoH, especially when attempting to depose the existing ruler, often made reference to some kind of natural phenomenon, be it real or fabricated, and interpreted it as a sign for heavenly instruction to take action. Although this rhetorical trick was not utilized in the earliest five speeches, it is seen in the narrative of many ensuing military actions taken by usurpers to overthrow existing regimes. For example, historical books record that on the eve of the war waged by Emperor Gaozu of Tang against the last general of the Sui dynasty, purple air like rainbows was seen to shoot across red sky towards the Big Dipper asterism (紫氣如虹，橫繚火中，上衡北斗) (see Li 2013, p. 129). A similar story is also told about Nurhaci, the founding father of the Qing dynasty, who allegedly saw two beams of blue-yellow light shooting from the ground to the moon on the eve of his military uprising (Liu 2013, p. 371). This kind of superstitious account of natural phenomena (or the fabrication of such stories) offers 'physical evidence' to the abstract concept of MoH, making it more convincing by integrating the material sky and the deified Heaven as two of the five senses of *tian* identified by Zeng (2013).

Mandate of Heaven and Chinese Political Rhetoric

Having a reason for launching an invasion is arguably the most important prerequisite for calling for or justifying such an action. MoH served this purpose well due to the lofty, mysterious and unchallengeable nature of the entity or system the word *tian* refers to, including the God interpretation, the organizer of human destiny and the underlying principle of the cosmos (Zeng 2013, p. 70). Among the early five public speeches, in addition to the previously mentioned case of Ganshi, two other examples are noted by Li, Liu and Wei 2013) where MoH was used as a pretext to legitimize an impending war waged against a failing regime:

> Tangshi: King of Xia has committed multiple crimes and shall be deposed by the order of Heaven (有夏多罪，天命殛之)
>
> Qinshi: King of Shang has perpetrated heinous crimes and shall be eliminated by Heaven (商罪贯盈，天命诛之)

This utilization of MoH is a unique feature in Chinese culture in relation to war narrative, for the purpose of legitimizing a military action, especially one used to fight against a failing regime. If the assumed years of the Xia dynasty's existence (2070–1600 BCE) were correct, the recorded Ganshi alleged to happen at the beginning of that dynasty would have been repeated by Hong Xiuquan (1814–1864), the Taiping Heavenly King, nearly four thousand years later in respect of using MoH to fight against a corrupt regime (see Wang 2002). This function of MoH to legitimize a calling for war was later absorbed into a 'unification discourse' (正统观) in Chinese history which according to Yang (2020) consists of three elements:

- Space constraint: To establish a new dynasty, a vast territory must be conquered by the incoming commander-in-chief.
- Time constraint: The new dynasty must be subsumed into a temporal cycle of MoH assigned on the basis of the rotation of 'five virtues' (Wood, Fire, Earth, Gold, Water).
- Ethnic constraint: Han people are preferred in this discourse to be the leader of a Chinese regime; other peoples in and around China are to be excluded and closely watched.

According to Yang, the founding kings of the Qing dynasty, being of Manchu origin and unable to be subsumed into the Chinese unification model by failing to satisfy the second and third criteria (i.e. not belonging to Han or within the MoH cycle), had to create their own discourse of justification, playing down both the second and third elements and emphasizing their territorial conquest and a newly established moral system which did have some connection with MoH.

Concurrent with the appeal to Mandate of Heaven for military action, the commander-in-chief who made the call often assumed the position of the Son of Heaven, who was here to serve as the ultimate ruler of human affairs and represented 'a special relation to Heaven' (Wei 2021, p. 12), and who was also the sole beneficiary of this heavenly authority who can both command the troops and enjoy the major benefits of the victory. To begin with, the first five speeches in Table 1.1 bear the mark of *Heaven* as a token of respect to raise the possibility of winning the war and to raise the political status of the speaker. These five orators then claimed that they inherited the Mandate of Heaven for the establishment of a new regime or to carry out a punitive attack. In the Yinzheng speech, the speaker additionally declared that his military action was taken under the direct order of the Son of Heaven. In other words, Heaven is the ultimate ruler of the universe and the sole arbitrator of mundane business including deciding whose reign has come to an end and who is to succeed. On that basis, Wei (2021) suggests that Heaven plays a key role in the creation of Chinese ethos, and that the significance of Heaven in its role as a defining attribute of Chinese ethos 'is reflective of a unique cultural heritage that carries its own historical complexities and philosophical intricacies' (p. 1). Thus, Heaven was to the Chinese like God to Christians in the West (see Goldin 1999). As Wei (2021) put it, Heaven 'was thought to be responsible for various natural phenomena, to have control over human affairs, and to have emotions and the capacity to act' (p. 6). This concept of Heaven applies to the entirety of ancient Chinese history starting from the five public speeches made in the early Xia-Shang-Zhou period, setting the tone for future development of Chinese rhetoric, extending from political discourse to all walks of life.

The Rhetorical Shift in the Zhou Dynasty

The last king of the Shang dynasty, Emperor Zhou, was said to be unspeakably cruel and dissolute; he constructed a pool filled with wine surrounded by trees hung with all sorts of meat and had fun all day, ignoring affairs of the state. His tyrannic rule made the continuation of the Shang dynasty impossible. In time, King Wu of Zhou led his army to defeat the Shang army in Muye in 1066 BC. After the establishment of the Western Zhou dynasty, the Zhou elite considered how to strengthen their rule by reflecting on the failure of the previous dynasty. The demise of the Shang dynasty made it abundantly clear that the Mandate of Heaven was not only a gift but also a duty that should not be breached. In other words, the failure to respect the MoH is a moral failure of the ruler and directly leads to his fall. Therefore, the succeeding emperors started to notice the issue of morality and highlight the importance of virtue in ruling the country to avoid the mistakes made by the last regime of the Shang dynasty. Thus, when discussing state affairs, the Zhou elite not only made reference to the mysterious power of the MoH but also to political virtues as a critical part of legitimacy and governance.

Within the relatively primitive context of that period, however, the introduction of any new idea was not readily acceptable and a process of religious conversion was mandatory. The official discourse was that only through the mediation of virtue can people successfully pray for the continuous blessing of Heaven. In this way, Zhou people combined MoH with the concept of virtue in a seamless fashion. The shift of focus in governing policy from Mandate of Heaven alone to the support of virtue can be captured in four so far undervalued public speeches, shown in Table 1.2. This kind of speech, like many other classic Chinese literary styles, was given the name *gao*, for which Kirkpatrick and Xu (2012) offered a useful definition:

> A gao (诰 announcement/proclamation) was performed by the king at mass gatherings such as the celebration of a harvest and is a type of epideictic rhetoric, and which could also be offered by ministers to the king in order to inspire him to follow the examples of Wen and Wu, the wise, benevolent and virtuous founders of the dynasty.
>
> *p. 19*

The public speeches shown in Table 1.2 clearly indicate the Zhou dynasty's divergence from the Shang's orthodox belief in Heaven's unconditional blessing, to the emphasis of

Mandate of Heaven and Chinese Political Rhetoric

Table 1.2 Four public speeches in Western Zhou: summary of contents

Title	Length in Chinese characters	Reference to Mandate of Heaven	Ancestral spirit	Reference to de (virtue 德)
Kanggao (Proclamation to Kang 康诰; Kangshu is the brother of King Wu)	1084	Help me follow the Mandate of Heaven; Beware that the Mandate of Heaven is not a permanent endowment.	Follow the example of your deceased father, the great prophet; Remember and carry forward the virtues of the former king.	You must always remember to be virtuous; win people by de; Rule by de; publicly display your de.
Jiugao (Proclamation on Alcohol 酒诰)	293	Heaven sent a decree; Heaven descended punishment; Yin lost their Mandate due to unbridled lust and abusive behavior.		Heaven descended punishment for the loss of morality; You have to discipline yourselves with morality.
Zicai (梓材)	320	The Mandate of Heaven is unfathomable; Heaven has entrusted the territory and population to my late king.		King Wen has tried his best to rule the kingdom with virtue.
Shaogao (Proclamation to Shao 召诰)	879	Heaven terminated the fortune of Yin; King Cheng accepted the Mandate of Heaven; May the king and people retain eternal Mandate of Heaven.	Many of the sage kings of Yin were in heaven, so later kings of Shang could uphold the Mandate of Heaven.	Our king must respect virtue and conscientiously implement the policy of virtue; Xia dynasty and Shang dynasty did not pay attention to virtue and lost their heavenly blessing.

the ruler's virtue. In the newly embraced political ideology, the Zhou kings represented a moral authority recognized as universal and binding for its populations all under the gaze of Heaven. In other words, the Zhou king now acted as an elected leader empowered by divine authority instead of being just a high priest as was the Shang king who had inherited the kingdom as a purely religious endowment. Under this new ideology, Heaven had the power to choose a ruler based on political virtues and sovereign grace and to bless the good or punish the bad. Thus, two important political

15

principles of 'respecting Heaven (敬天)' and 'protecting people (保民)' took form in the Zhou dynasty. Eventually, the moral precept 'matching virtue with Heaven (以德配天)' was formulated, which prescribed a stable political structure composed of 'Heaven', 'King' and 'its people'. This structure is elaborated by Wang (1959) in the following way:

> These principles have been devised with the aim to integrate all people, above and below, within *de*. Thus, the Son of Heaven, the vassal governors, the officials, the high ministers, the intelligentsia and the commoners form a society of morality.
>
> *p. 453*

Thus, the responsibility to govern the country was devolved down from Heaven to people on all levels of the social hierarchy and this created a shared, group accountability. According to Luo (2020), this political philosophy incorporating the unpredictability of Heaven and the supplementation of virtue became the direct source of ideology in the formation of the grand unification discourse for the forthcoming Chinese dynasties.

The speeches in Table 1.2 also include some references to ancestral spirit, in the form of advice for listeners to pay respect to 'former kings'. For Kennedy (1998), this represents a 'tradition of the ancestors who continue to watch the living' (p. 151). Mo (2011) also notes that Shang and Zhou people both thought their deceased ancestors rose to the heavenly kingdom and resided with God. Tang (2020) suggests that God and the ancestors maintain a king–minister relationship in which God gives ancestors the right to govern the mundane world. Zhang (2021) informs us that Shang people personized God/Heaven and deified their ancestors at the same time. Zhang also notes that God was thought to be the dominator of the universe who controlled the wind, the rain and everything else. People, however, could not pray directly to God and must invoke the ancestors to help influence the decisions of God. Ancestors, therefore, assume a mixture of parental and religious authority in Chinese culture. That is to say, not only the highly elusive concept of Heaven but also the more tangible category of ancestors plays a part in determining the ongoing development of political culture in Chinese society. Indeed, most Chinese are irreligious but they do worship ancestors. In a way, the ancestors work on the same plane as Heaven and provide moral guidance to Chinese people, many of whom go tomb sweeping at least once a year; while many keep an ancestor altar at home and pray to them on a daily basis.

Barnwell (2013) explains that *de* 'seems to denote the admirable character, ethos, and probably conduct of revered ancestors. Their descendants (ritually) pledged to grasp, follow and model both them and their De' (p. 77). That is to say, *de* represents the sum of all virtues possessed by the ancestors and handed down to their descendants. As generations of Chinese create and walk into history, more and more distinguished characters with high morality are integrated into history and the anthropomorphous lineage merged with the divine essence to become a complicated web of hybrid deity that involves superstition and familial connections, both of which emphasize the importance of virtue.

The Rhetorical Idea of *De* Shown in Bronze Inscriptions

More concrete evidence is available about the early existence of Chinese rhetoric in terms of MoH and the later supplement of *de* (virtue). The earliest copper smelting technology in China appeared in the late Neolithic period. China had effectively entered the bronze age civilization as early as in the Xia dynasty. Bronze wares serving as ritual paraphernalia were regarded as a symbol of kingship and a medium of communication between man and Heaven. They were instrumental in conveying awe and worship of Heaven and ancestral spirits. There are over 14,000 bronzes with inscriptions discovered so far, including records of sacrifices, ancient letters of appointment, words of admonition and instruction, blessings, inscriptions on dowries, documents and bonds, and so on. Bronzes in Shang before DiYi (帝乙 the 29th king) and DiXin (帝辛 the last king, also known as Zhou) had no graphs except a few pieces with lineage emblems (族徽), date notations or vessel donor, some vessels inscribed with only ten characters describing the casting procedures or expressing gratitude to the king's bestowment. From mid- to late Western Zhou onwards, the graph numbers increased vastly, especially appointment inscriptions. These lengthy historical documentary records, if considered from the rhetorical instead of historical perspective, reveal the essence of ancient Chinese rhetoric that is of incalculable value.

The current authors did a manual calculation of the aforementioned bronze inscriptions to identify writings relevant to MoH and the additional idea of *de* (virtue). It was found that among the inscriptions were a myriad of writings with accompanying graphs recording why and in what form the king gave rewards, inscriptions about land sales and litigation, and routine script to thank and promote the good will of the King of Zhou. Excluding these less relevant records, the bronze inscriptions which highlight the Mandate of Heaven or Heaven itself are listed in the Appendix, including some references to *de* (德 virtue) which are mistakenly believed to have originated from the Spring and Autumn or Warring States periods.

The contents summary of bronze inscriptions shown in the Appendix indicates that Zhou people inherited the concept of MoH from previous dynasties and used it as a foundation for constructing political rationality and legitimacy. For that purpose, Zhou people devised various means to mold public opinion, such as kings being assigned the MoH to rule the commoners etc. To reinforce the impression of the ultimate destruction of Shang, King Wu created a series of auspicious signs indicating that the MoH had been transferred from Shang to Zhou. A manifestation of this effect is the often-repeated phrase in bronze inscriptions, 'The highly distinguished King Wen and King Wu accepted the Great Mandate' (丕显文武 膺受大命). Also, as previously mentioned, the ruling class of Zhou realized that it was not enough for kings to rule by order of Heaven. Thus, the concept of *de* was engendered to address this inadequacy. The newly created phrase 'Match Heaven with *de*' signified the vulnerability of the divine power, ushering in the (partial) transfer of authority from the divinity onto the human representatives, or in Schwartz's (1985) terms, from a 'combination of ancestor worship and nature religion' (p. 16) to a 'religious-ethical transcendence' (p. 55). Personal accountability appeared to work in tandem with the MoH. As Grundmann (2018) notes, 'the king and the vessel donor together with his forebear [now act] as two separate social entities who relate to each other through their common commitment to a third factor, the theo-political command of Heaven' (p. 245). A compelling piece of evidence to this effect is that the logogram *de* inscribed on these vessels, bells, and the like, was first seen in Western Zhou and not before it.

Further Development of Mandate of Heaven in the Political Context

The evolution of MoH did not stop with the addition of morality on top of the power conferred by the divine mandate. Gu and Yu (2014) offered a comprehensive review of the subsequent schools of thought in relation to MoH immediately after the Zhou dynasty. According to them, the Duke of Zhou (周公 Zhou Gong) was responsible for transforming the original MoH popularized in the Xia and Shang dynasties by 'playing down MoH and emphasizing human affairs' (轻天命 重人事). Confucius, who held Zhou Gong in high respect, further made a connection between Heaven and humans by introducing the element of rituals (礼 *li*). Gu and Yu explained that Confucius regarded MoH as the ultimate authority, while humans cultivate their virtues to connect with Heaven and carry out the divine will. The well-known age-achievement scheme devised by Confucius incorporates his understanding of and engagement with MoH by suggesting that a person should 'know the MoH' (知天命) by the age of 50. According to Gu and Yu, the final target Confucius set at age 70, 'Do what you want without breaking the rules' (从心所欲不逾矩), denotes that by the age of 70, the person's thought and behavior should be perfectly synchronized with the MoH.

The MoH-based political philosophy continued to evolve after the input of Confucius. A prominent fourth generation disciple of Confucius, Mencius, elaborated on the humanitarian side of MoH and advocated the integration of people's hearts (民心) with Heaven's will (天意), hence the well-known phrase, 'Heaven and humans as one' (天人合一). Following this logic, if the king is able to govern the country well and win people's hearts, it means his reign is approved by Heaven. Therefore, Mencius proposed the famous 'people-based' (民本) theory, which was to become the basis of the 'people at the center' (以人民为中心) approach pursued in contemporary China.

Not all ancient Chinese thinkers followed the mainstream approach to MoH, however. According to Gu and Yu (2014), Mozi and Xunzi, two thinkers living consecutively in the Spring and Autumn period and Warring States period, both considered heaven only a term related to natural phenomena. Mozi used the key words 'emphasizing labour' (尚力) and 'not destiny' (非命) to encourage people to break away from the limitations of MoH and improve their own life with hard work; while Xunzi proposed the idea of 'harnessing the natural power for people's use' (制天命而用之). Nevertheless, these innovative thoughts at that time were unable to be incorporated into mainstream thinking about MoH which still regarded Heaven as a divinity that wields absolute power over mundane existence.

Recall Yang's (2020) unification discourse which subsumes a temporal cycle of MoH assigned to a succession of Chinese rulers as one of three key elements in the model (the other two being territory and ethnicity). The founding kings of the Qing dynasty were certainly not the first to recognize the importance of establishing the relevance of MoH to legitimize the regime. According to Yang (2015), the founding father of the Ming dynasty, Zhu Yuanzhang, also found it difficult to integrate the newly established regime into the historical trend of MoH since Zhu himself originated from a bandit group and not from a regular army. He too introduced a new theory to modify the meaning of MoH in an attempt to legitimize his regime. Incorporating the idea of karma in Buddhism, Zhu first invented the term 'Rewarding and retribution in the way of Heaven' (天道报施), referring to a vicious cycle of someone killing the existing ruler and being killed by the next one himself, to explain away his own usurping of the throne. In addition, Zhu pointed out that Heaven will not give the world to the first gang who overthrow the current regime (天不与首乱者) as they are only instrumental in paving the way for the real ruler intended by Heaven to come next.

Hong Xiuquan, leader of the Taiping Rebellion against the Qing dynasty, appears to be the last commander of a Chinese rebellion force to use MoH as a pretext to initiate a revolutionary act; according to Wang (2002), he had a bizarre dream of ascending to Heaven and confirming his identity as the second son of God. Wang explained that

Hong Xiuquan's idea of using religion to initiate a revolution actually originated from Christian missionaries, who supposedly could have brought accompanying modern political thought to update the structure and ideology of the regime. However, Wang claims, due to Hong's insistence on clinging to the authoritarian nature of MoH, the opportunity of learning from Western politics through the mediation of religion was lost, as well as the chance to modernize his regime.

It would appear then that the MoH has gone through many transformations in the history of China, changing form periodically as political philosophy changed or as a function of the needs of the current regime in response to the origin of the rebellious force and the political context it found itself in. Correct calculation and ingenious manipulation of MoH leads to the successful establishment of legitimacy by exploiting the thousand-year-old tradition where a personified Heaven-God is used to provoke feelings of fear, reverence and reliance on the part of those being ruled. But a total reliance on an unmodified image of MoH as a basis for staging an armed uprising, as in the case of Hong Xiuqian, can directly cause the fall of a revolutionary regime.

Conclusion

The previous sections have shown that the concept of Mandate of Heaven had created a long-lasting Chinese rhetorical convention developed uniquely on the soil of China since ancient times. The MoH rhetoric was first used to legitimize wars waged against rivaling regimes. In later dynasties, in addition to being a pretext for overthrowing declining regimes, MoH was also used as an empowering divine force to help maintain smooth and productive governance. From a descriptive rhetoric point of view, it is desirable to find comparable rhetorical practice elsewhere in the world to explore the rhetorical power of language in similar contexts and to facilitate the study of international relations, for example, by moving from idiosyncratic rhetorical behavior to political ideology of individual countries and to compare and contrast such practice across the globe. That is, however, beyond the scope of this chapter which nevertheless may have offered adequate material to conceptualize the nature of Chinese political discourse based on the ancient rhetoric of MoH for further descriptive studies.

Notes

1 Ganshi (甘誓): Gan (甘) is the name of a place. Shi (誓 oath) means the covenant before sending armed forces to suppress You Hu (有扈氏), a tribe of the Xia dynasty, which was not satisfied with Qi who was in power at that time. The whole mobilization order for war has 102 characters including the causes of war, military discipline, rewards and punishments.
2 Yinzheng (胤征 Yin campaigns against Xi and He) has 126 characters. Xi and He indulged in sexual immorality, and Yin (胤) went to war, making this mobilization order to boost morale.
3 Tangshi (汤誓 oath made by Tang): When Tang (汤), the first ruler of the Shang dynasty, was conquering Jie (桀 the last king known for his brutal rule), Tang's army and people were unwilling to go to war. His words, around 180 characters, were a clear call to arms against this tyrant by first explaining the reason for the campaign and then stating the method of reward and punishment.
4 Taishi (太/泰誓 oath made by King Wu): In the ninth year of King Wu's accession to the throne, before he attacked Zhou (纣 the last king of the Shang dynasty), he summoned all the vassal states to Mengjin (孟津 name of place) and made this speech.
5 Mushi (牧誓 the oath at Mu) was the mobilization order for war on January 20, 1046 BC. King Wu of the Zhou dynasty commanded three hundred chariots and three thousand men to fight

with Zhou (纣) in Muye (牧野). King Wu enumerated King Zhou's main charges, and then talked about how to attack, how to deal with the surrenders of the enemy.

6 Qinshi (秦誓 Qin oath): In 627 BC, the Lord of Qin refused Jian shu's (蹇叔 c. 690–610 BC) remonstrance and began to repent and blame himself after the failure of the surprise attack on the state of Zheng (郑), and summarized the lessons. Jianshu kushi (蹇叔哭师 crying remonstrance by Jianshu) was a well-known essay describing the last attempt by Jianshu who made every effort to stop this losing battle.

References

English References

Barnwell, Scott A. (2013). 'The Evolution of the Concept of De 德 in Early China.' *Sino-Platonic Papers*. 235: 1–83.

Ching, Julia. (1997). *Mysticism and Kingship in China: The Heart of Chinese Wisdom*. Cambridge University Press.

Clarke, M. L. (1996). *Rhetoric at Rome: A Historical Survey*. Routledge.

Enos, Richard Leo. (1993). *Greek Rhetoric before Aristotle*. Waveland.

Goldin, Paul Rakita. (1999). *Rituals of the Way: The Philosophy of Xunzi*. Open Court.

Graham, A. C. (2004). *Later Mohist Logic, Ethics and Science*. The Chinese University of Hong Kong Press.

Grundmann, Joern P. (2018). 'Command and Commitment: Terms of Kingship in Western Zhou Bronze Inscriptions and in the *Book of Documents*.' PhD thesis, University of Edinburgh, Edinburgh.

Kennedy, George. (1998). *Comparative Rhetoric: An Historical and Cross-Cultural Introduction*. Oxford University Press.

Kirkpatrick, Andy and Zhichang Xu. (2012). *Chinese Rhetoric and Writing: An Introduction for Language Teachers*. Parlor Press.

Kao, K. (1993). 'Recent Studies of Chinese Rhetoric'. *Chinese Literature: Essays, Articles, Reviews*. 15: 143–154.

Marshall, S. J. (2002). *The Mandate of Heaven: Hidden History in the I Ching*. Columbia University Press.

Rawson, Jessica. (1989). 'Statesmen or Barbarians? The Western Zhou as Seen through Their Bronzes.' *Proceedings of the British Academy*. 75: 71–95.

Schwartz, Benjamin I. (1985). *The World of Thought in Ancient China* (revised edition). The Belknap Press of Harvard University Press.

Thorpe, M. E. (2013). '"Under God": An Epideictic Weapon in the Fight against Communism.' In M. Ballif (Ed.), *RelFraming National Identity* (pp. 28–40). Waveland.

Wei, Yong-Kang. (2021). 'Ethos in Early Chinese Rhetoric: The Case of "Heaven".' *Humanities*. 10(7): 1–21.

Chinese References

Gu, Kansheng and Yu, Degang 辜堪生，余德刚 (2014). 'Duke of Zhou's Mandate of Heaven Idea and Its Impact on Later Philosophers of Various Schools' 论周公的"天命"哲学思想及其对后世的影响. *Journal of Sichuan University (Social Science Edition)* 四川大学学报(哲学社会科学版). 190: 43–50.

Li, Danjie 李丹婕 (2013). 'Inheritance or Revolution: The Establishment of Tang Dynasty and Its Historical Narrative' 承继还是革命 – 唐朝政权建立及其历史叙事. *Journal of Chinese Literature and History* 中华文史论丛. 111: 123–156.

Li, Jianqun, Liu, Xiaoyong and Wei Jingyu 李建群，刘晓勇，魏靖宇 (2013). 'Humanitarianism and Utilitarianism: The Differences and Similarities in War Theory between Confucianism and the Bing School' 人本主义与功利主义——先秦儒家与兵家战争观的歧异与会通. *Theory Journal* 理论学刊. 236: 89–92.

Liu, Zheng 刘铮 (2013). 'The Influence of Nurhaci's *Tianming* Thought on Post-Jin Society' 努尔哈赤天命思想对后金社会的影响. *Academic Exchange* 学术交流. (October): 371.

Luo, Xinhui 羅新慧. (2020). 'The Evolution of the Concept of Destiny in the Spring and Autumn Period' 春秋時期天命觀念的演變. *Social Sciences in China* 中國社會科學. 12: 99–118.

Mo, Fasong 牟發松. (2011). 'On *Tianxia*: Centering on the Social Meaning of *Tianxia*' 天下論——以天下的社會涵義為中心. *Jianghan Luntan* 江漢論壇. 6: 114–124.

Tang, Mingliang 唐明亮. (2020). 'On *Di* and the *Tianming* Perspective of Zhou People It Reflects' 說"帝"及其反映的周人天命觀. *Journal of Beijing Normal University (Social Sciences)* 北京師範大學學報（社會科學版）. 282: 143–150.

Wang, Guowei 王国维. (1959). 殷周制度论 (A Treatise on the Institutions of Yin and Zhou). 观堂集林 (Guantang Jinlin). Taipei: 中华书局.

Wang, Licheng 王立诚. (2002). 'The *Tianming* Theory of Hong Xiuquan and the Power Structure of the Heavenly Kingdom' 洪秀全的天命论与太平天国的政权建构. *Fudan Journal (Social Sciences Edition)* 复旦学报(社会科学版). 1: 60–64.

Yang, Nianqun 杨念群. (2020). 'How the *Tianming* Is Transferred: The Reinterpretation of "Great Unification" in Qing Dynasty' '天命'如何转移：清朝'大一统'观再诠释. *Journal of Tsinghua University (Philosophy and Social Sciences)* 清华大学学报（哲学社会科学版）. 35(6): 21–46.

Yang, Yongkang 杨永康. (2015). 'Zhu Yuanzhang's Theory in the Replacement of Yuan Dynasty by Ming and His Belief in Manifest Destiny' 朱元璋的元明易代观及其天命论. *Nankai Journal (Philosophy, Literature and Social Science Edition)* 南开学报(哲学社会科学版). 5: 70–79.

Zeng, Xueling 曾雪灵. (2013). 'The Initial Exploration of the Justice War Theory of Xunzi: Including Its Difference from Mencius' Same Theory and Reasons for Difference' 荀子正义战争理论初探——兼论荀孟正义战争理论的差异及其原因. *Morality and Civilization* 道德与文明. 2: 68–71.

Zhang, Fang 張芳. (2021). 'From the Mysterious Universe to the Moral Universe: The Ethical Turn of *Tianming* in Ancient China' 從神秘宇宙到道德宇宙：中國上古"天命"觀的倫理學轉向. *Jin Gu Wen Chuang* 今古文創. 37: 72–73, 85.

Appendix

The snippet inscriptions from the total number of verbatim texts in bronzes regarding the Mandate of Heaven and/or *de*

Name of the bronze	Length in Chinese characters	Reference to Heaven	Reference to de (virtue)
Feng gui (丰簋) or TianWang gui (天亡簋) gui (a food vessel, similar to a tureen)	76	King Wu hopes that King Wen can win the favor of Heaven and care for Zhou under the help of Heaven.	
The Xing Hou gui (邢侯簋)	68	Di will not bring an end to the Mandate of the Zhou. I will complete my duties to the ancestors, and not dare to be remiss.	
MiBo gui (羋伯簋)	149	King Wen and King Wu accepted such Mandate of Heaven wholeheartedly.	
Xun gui (询簋)	131	Great and wise King Wen and King Wu accepted the Mandate of Heaven.	

Ban gui (班簋)	197	The mighty Heaven has always blessed success in everything; Rong disobeyed the Mandate of Heaven and thus brought about its demise.	Ban, you must possess virtue and love people.
Hu gui (胡簋)	124	Day and night King Li has been diligent in managing the state left by my father, worthy to the heavens; King Li offers sacrifices to the Mandate of Heaven.	
Guai Bo fui (乖伯簋)	149	Three previous kings accepted the Heaven-given tasks; according to the will of Heaven, your ancestors came here to assist the Zhou King.	
ShiXun fui (师询簋)	213	Heaven is satisfied with King Wen and King Wu's virtue, and we heartily accept the great Mandate of Heaven.	
DaYu Tripod (大盂鼎)	291	Great and wise King Wen accepted the Mandate of Heaven; Heaven protected the king with love and blessed him with power; Shang King lost the Mandate of Heaven; revere the majesty of Heaven.	King Kang will follow the decrees and virtues of King Wen.
DaKe Tripod (大克鼎)	290	Ke thanked Heaven wholeheartedly.	The intellectual virtue of my grandfather
Duke Mao Tripod (毛公鼎)	499	Heaven is satisfied with King Wen and King Wu's virtue, and we heartily accept the great Mandate of Heaven; Heaven unremittedly protected our Zhou, greatly consolidating the former king's mandate; Tell me (King Xuan) often of the virtues of my father, so that I may continue to strive to maintain the Mandate of Heaven in accordance with its will.	Tell me often of the virtues of my father (King Li).
ZongZhou Bell (宗周钟)	121	King Li thanked Heaven and the gods for their blessings; King Li reveres Heaven.	
ShanBo haosheng Bell (单伯昊生钟)	34	My ancestors followed the Mandate of Heaven to assist the King.	ShanBo will uphold the virtues of his ancestors.
HeZun (何尊 ritual wine vessel)	122	King Wen accepted the Mandate of Heaven to rule the state.	

SuiGong Xu (遂公盨 food vessel)	98	Heaven made Yu implement the policy of virtue.	Cultivate virtue; implement virtue; It is only right for the people to firmly carry out this moral policy; The standard of reward is virtue; virtue won the support of the people; propagandize virtue, make virtue deeply rooted in the people.
ShiKe Xu (师克盨)	148	The great King Wen and King Wu accepted the Mandate of Heaven.	
Qiang Basin (墙盘)	284	Heaven governs the affairs of the imperial court, and protects the son of Heaven and grants him the Mandate.	Qiang's father YiGong possesses the great virtue.
Qiu Basin (逨盘)	360	ShanGong helped King Wen and King Wu and received the Mandate of Heaven; My glorious GongShu, who assisted the King Cheng in his full acceptance of Mandate of Heaven; The great and prominent King Wen and King Wu inherited the Mandate of Heaven and conquered vast territories. Your holy ancestors served the king and worked hard for the Mandate.	Qiu's forebears' upright *de*; ShanGong had intellectual *de*; my father PangShu was just and had great *de*.

2
GODS OF THE THRESHOLDS
Liminality and the Origins of Rhetorical Theory in Ancient Global Myth

Shawn D. Ramsey

Introduction

Plato, Cicero, and rhetoric's early chroniclers have offered narratives for the origin of rhetoric from the time of its first systematic development. Sometimes these narratives are essentially mythic, such as Cicero's *fabula* of the First Orator at the outset of *De Inventione* (1949) and Plato's myth of Theuth in *Phaedrus* (1972). But contemporary scholars have questioned the origin of the term "rhetoric", as well as the origins of rhetorical theory, since Edward Schiappa (1999) began to interrogate rhetoric's origin in the traditional narrative of Corax and Tisias. Jeffrey Walker has argued that the mythopoetic prefigured rhetoric, and was embedded in discourse as a force that could bring peace and accord to the *polis*. The poet permits in his ability to "recall, interpret, and apply to" questions a communal answer from the past to present dilemmas (2000: 7). This stands in stark relief to many modern historians who have characterized Greek thought as a transition from mythos to logos, characterizing the two as a transition from "irrational" to "rational" thought, a largely simplistic view now widely debunked (Fowler 2011: 45). Following Walker, Christopher Johnstone has rejected previous views that characterize "the 'transition from *mythos* to *logos*'" in Hellenic thought as being a turn from the irrational to the rational (28). Johnstone points out that this transition was not linear, nor was it sudden or final, and associated with the development of alphabetic systems (2012: 37). This argument illustrates that myths are also a vital source for understanding the rhetorical theories that hinged on the concept of liminality in the ancient world on a global scale. It illustrates that myth depicted figures, spaces and personae associated with rhetoric that were liminal in nature; by way of these depictions, one can extrapolate that part of ancient rhetorical theory was to convey that rhetoric was a form of liminal discursive action.

To do so, this argument expands on previous authority by applying the theory of liminality of van Gennep (2019) and Turner (2018) to rhetorical myths. These myths are one locus of the recorded articulation of abstract rhetorical concepts in multiple ancient world cultures. To show this, it is necessary to examine the nature of the personae in these myths and the narratives related to the origins of writing in which they are intimately involved.

These myths operate by implicating mythic entities and their liminal nature as a means of making analogical arguments about the nature of rhetoric. This essay first describes the scholarly background on the role of myth in relation to rhetoric, and then examines the nature of non-Western liminars, and the spaces they occupy and their relationship to symbols. In so doing, I demonstrate that ancient liminars are narrative embodiments in non-Western rhetorical theory, who represent the liminal nature of rhetoric itself across cultures. I will show how mythic liminars, in their occupancy of these conceptual spaces, convey ancient beliefs in a conceptual, rhetorical "presence" that occurs in the "cultural cycles" which cannot be adequately described by coining new terminology. The rhetorical act operates outside the "classificatory nets" of their "routinized spheres of action" through liminal action (Turner, Abrahams, and Harris 1986: vii).

Myth and Rhetoric

Philologists, philosophers, and psychologists have critically examined the nature of myth for sub-structural insights into their respective fields. A cursory examination of intellectual history confirms this contemporary fascination in the works of Giambattista Vico, Friedrich van Schelling, Friedrich Nietzsche, Karl Jung, Sigmund Freud, Claude Levi-Strauss, and countless others (see generally Doty 2000). Scholars have long remarked that myths across cultures exhibit an eerie similitude, while wildly varying in their fine details. Likewise, to see the theories of what is commonly described as "rhetoric" from the perspective of ancient people, one key lies in the liminal nature of their myths about the inventors of writing. These myths fundamentally spurred the development of their rhetorical culture. These liminal myths often concern the invention of writing, and it is apparent that in traditional stories about writing's origins, ancient rhetorical theories emerge. Previous authorities have suggested that the origin of rhetorical theory in ancient Greece followed a pivotal transformation that was attributable to the importation of the Phoenician writing system, following Enos (2011), Havelock (1986) and Ong (1982). These origins owe not wholly to a cultural transition from oral to literate societies. Rather, the relationship of writing and myth demonstrates an ancient recognition that writing was a physical manifestation analogous to purposeful, rhetorical symbolic action. Therefore, myths that treat writing as a subject strongly reveal conceptual assumptions about rhetorical theory. This qualification permits insights into patterns of development across the history of rhetoric in multiple cultures, and in so doing, as Turner suggested, "History will of course unpack its latent structure, especially as experience encounters traditional structures of culture and thought" (1986: 293). As I illustrate below, likewise, in ancient China, the rhetorical theory of *wen* as proper discursive action derived from the liminal nature of the myth of the invention of writing by Cangjie. In Sumeria, theories of the origins of the first writing were intimately related to the telos of rhetorical action between persons and city-states in myths such as *Enemerkar and the Lord of Aratta* (Vanstiphout 2004). Ancient myths implicate many aspects of formalized rhetorical theory in the Greco-Roman world, but in other cultures, deploy these stories as analogical rather than systematic articulations of those theories. One way they do so is by deploying mythic liminars as the principal actors in those narratives.

The concept of liminality in Arnold van Gennep and Victor Turner's model refers to a transitory phase of human *rites de passage*. Liminality is one of a large number of concepts that are used as a heuristic tool by mythographers, and is a fitting lens to examine rhetorical myths. Liminality is an anthropological concept that refers to a quality of ambiguity or "in-between-ness" in the middle stage of human rites of passage. A ritual participant in human society first undergoes separation or detachment from the social structure and enters a margin (or limen), as a transformative period, then is reincorporated into the social unit. But liminality need not refer to a religious ritual in all circumstances, as Turner includes "liminars" and "marginals" who can enter a liminal space that is indeterminate and fluid. But the liminal actor is also in a state of fluidity in his union with the in-between space. These hallmarks of liminality pervade ancient narratives related to writing and personae associated with it. The anthropomorphic figure in ancient myth is a liminal messenger between fixed *conceptual* realms. Turner notes that in the ritual of preliterate societies, "In liminality resides the germ not only of religious askesis, discipline, and mysticism, but also of philosophy and pure science" – and, as I shall show, rhetoric (Turner 2018: 242). Ancient mythic figures analogically articulate the theory of liminality as an element of ancient rhetorical theory.

Writing myths provide not only theories of writing but theories of rhetoric that would pervade non-Greco-Roman cultures in the ancient world. Myths have been established as containing the germinal origin of rhetorical theory across cultures by Walker (2000), Johnstone (2012), and most recently Ramsey (2021a, 2021b), unlimited by an Eastern or Western divide; and the recordation of these myths shapes rhetorical theory and culture. The Hellenic corpus cites at least three different mythic originators of writing, including Prometheus, the Muses, and Palemenides (Ceccarelli 2013: 65–68). In the classical cultures with which Western scholars are most intimate, the invention of rhetoric is attributed to the figures of Corax and Tisias to contend with an explosion of litigation in ancient Sicily (Schiappa 1999: 4); influential progenitor myths are also found in ancient Roman rhetoric in Cicero's *De Inventione* in the myth of the first rhetor. To recapitulate *De Inventione*'s opening: once there was a time in prehistory when humans were "like animals" wandering the fields, without religious, political, or other systems to determine the paternity of children (1.2.2). It was through teaching the art of eloquent speech, according to Cicero who was writing well after the development of rhetoric in ancient Greece, that one anonymous human ascertained the latent power in rhetoric and gave people the basic tools of civilization. Plato's account of the invention of writing by Theuth (*Phaed.* 274c) is likewise familiar.

While rhetorical theory was expressed in non-mythic and, eventually, formal and systematic terms in ancient Greece, other ancient cultures set forth elements of their theories of rhetoric in mythic terms through analogical reasoning (Ramsey 2021a). As in the case of the sophists who linguistically "stretched" existing terminology to describe abstractions (Johnstone 2012), mythic figures were analogical representations recorded to preserve and disseminate these concepts through their personifications and attendant narratives. Just as contemporary speakers might draw an analogy like "the sun lights up the morning sky just as a great idea clears the mind", the Egyptians might say Thoth conveys the hidden meaning of the sign as the speaker reveals his thoughts to a listener. As one basic example among many demonstrated below, Thoth is an Egyptian mythological messenger and is intimately associated with the word; but on a still deeper level his cult believed he had a fundamentally epistemic role between signifier and signified. Thoth is the personified hermeneutic act in his central role as conceptual liminar. Thoth is also the medium through which a lifeless sign becomes a meaning. Thoth existed between worlds and between sign and signified and was thus liminal. Thoth is just one of the prolific examples of liminars that pervade the mythic cultures of the ancient world and are associated with writing. This phenomenon occurred in geographically pervasive patterns: examples can be seen in ancient Mesopotamia, India, Egypt and China. The evidence suggests that the origin of ancient rhetorical theory was intimately related to the ancient cultural imaginal through their expression of liminal myth.

Evidence that a similar tendency existed to express rhetorical theory through myth has been established elsewhere. Walker has argued that the origin of rhetoric could be found in mythopoetic discourse, which in many ways could move a hearer as effectively as reasoned argument (2000: 23, 5–7). He observed that Homer and Hesiod reveal "that rhetoric's characteristics were evident in early Hellenic discourse long before rhetoric was recognized as a discipline" (23). Building on the observations of Walker, Johnstone has noted that in ancient Greece, proto-scientific and philosophical writings had analogical thinking fundamentally embedded into the arguments they advanced (2012: 9). Johnstone tends to advance the terms analogical and metaphorical interchangeably, and under-standably so, as there exists a great deal of interplay between the two modes of analysis; it was this analogical capacity that permitted the ancient Greeks to linguistically "stretch" existing ideas into abstraction (10). Indeed, Johnstone concludes his entire work with an observation about the presocratic use of analogical thinking to explain abstract universal principles, in his example, a sense of universal interconnectedness (217). This "leap" of presocratic thinking, Johnstone contends, was dependent on analogical reasoning (217). Johnstone likewise advances that myth in ancient Greece was key in the development of analogical reasoning, but suggests that the anthropomorphic gods possessing arbitrary characteristics had to be "stripped of … association" for such analogical reasoning to assert itself in ancient culture, permitting rhetorical theory to emerge (38).

These authorities have identified Greco-Roman myth as an "origin" of rhetorical theory, but in many cultures the expression of rhetorical theory was not a prologue to the expression of their rhetorical theory but foundationally sufficient in its analogical expression. Thus, a key to understanding mythic rhetorical theory lies in the tendency of mythic narratives to make conceptual propositions by way of analogical reasoning. Ames and Hall (2010) have identified analogical reasoning in ancient Chinese Confucian discourse and Volkov (1992) and Graham in Daoist literature (1989); it has been iden-tified in ancient Talmudic literature by Douglas (2000), and in Sumerian myth by Averbeck (2003); and Egyptian sources likewise show hallmarks of analogical thinking even in their medical texts (Wee 2017). Ramsey (2021a) has advanced that analogical reasoning is fundamental to the interpretation of non-Western mythic narratives and arguments. These arguments advanced their insights into the nature of writing and rhet-oric. Additionally, Ramsey has noted that in at least two non-Greco-Roman cultures, the advent of literacy and the recordation of myth shaped subsequent rhetorical theories over time (2021b). This leap in analogical reasoning was not confined to ancient Greek culture; analogical reasoning to explain human phenomena in mythic terms – including in ancient Greece – both prefigured and persisted throughout the development of rhet-orical theory, and was an integral link in the chain of intellectual development in many cultures. Thus, it seems logical that a clue to the development of rhetorical theory might be found in myths concerning the creation of writing or the role of writing in relation to the supernatural world in antiquity. If myths in cultures outside of Greece are examined in multiple instances, the recordation of myths *about* writing seems to be a pivotal piece of textual evidence from which the origins of rhetorical theory begin to emerge.

As noted above, the figures in ancient rhetorical myths are liminal: they represent transitory personae or perform transitory and mediating acts between the human, divine, and intellectual world. This personification is a way of discussing a theory about the nature of rhetoric itself. Many mythical liminars are tasked with traveling between the world of the gods and men, and have an instrumental role for the transition from life to death. In this process they act as the mediators between deliberation and forensic judgment. Other mythical liminars act as transitional figures between sign and signifier and are a personification of epistemological action. Still others represent the transitional agent between invention and cognitive realization. Thus, the personae and their activities become analogical for the theory of rhetorical concepts in ancient non-Western cultures. The persistent liminality of these figures, and the narratives they participate in, are not mere stories but analogies for cognitive and creative states that are allied to classical concepts in rhetoric. Turner hypothesizes the concept of liminal spaces, conceived as sometimes social and conceptual. These liminal territories are themselves occupied by liminal personae. It is within these spaces and among these actors that "suppositions, desires, hypotheses, possibilities, and so forth, all become legitimate" (Turner, Abrahams and Harris 1986: vii). Turner explains that "to live, to breathe, and generate novelty, human beings have had to create – by structural means – spaces and times in the calendar or, in the cultural cycles of their most cherished – groups which cannot be captured in the classificatory nets of their quotidian, routinized spheres of action" that he defines as "liminal areas of time and space" (Turner, Abrahams and Harris 1986: vii).

But the nature of the liminal entity in liminal space is not, alone, the most vital part of their relation to writing – and by extension the rhetorical concepts they are related to. Rather, the liminar's "attributes" are consistently associated with or identified by "a rich variety of symbols" in societies that ritualize transitions (Turner 2018: 84). Turner states that the subject of liminal processes "must be a tabula rasa, a blank slate, on which is inscribed the knowledge and wisdom of the group" (103–104). Liminal figures "elude or slip through the network of classifications" in the conceptual space of a culture (95). I posit that rhetoric can be found in a germinal state through myth and associated symbol, as in many preliterate societies; but evidence also supports its conceptual presence in myth after the development of literacy. Those symbols are associated with ritual and mythic processes whereby "mentalities of neophytes, generative rules, codes, and media" are employed. Thereby, they can "manipulate the symbols of speech and culture to confer some degree of intelligibility on an experience that perpetually outstrips the possibilities of linguistic (and other cultural) expression" (Turner 2018: 240). Turner notes that in some cultures, in fact the "maker" of "myths and symbols" can also become a symbol themselves (99).

Turner's contention that symbols are central to the function of liminal personae represents further reason to employ it as a key to a mythic conception of rhetoric. Written characters are the central preoccupation of many narratives about liminal beings. Therefore, these characters are mythically-expressed theories of rhetoric, and often concern writing; they answer fundamental conceptual questions about what humans do when they write or use speech for a purpose. Rhetorical processes, assemblies, and genres arguably originate in such ritual processes; judicial proceedings held to determine if the sequence of events in the past, assemblies for deliberation about the future, and funerary ceremonies and orations are all rituals and mirror the ancient genres of rhetoric. The manipulation of symbols, be they spoken or written, is central to all of them. Ancient myths related to rhetoric are often myths about the nature of symbols, and the symbols are associated with a liminal exponent. Thus, myth is a symbolic extension of conceptual thought in many ancient cultures in which their rhetorical precepts can be found, particularly in myths about writing. Ancient myths and the liminars within them often signify theories of the way we employ rhetorical action, and are a rich source of global rhetorical theories. To advance this argument, I now move to specific illustrations of liminars, myths of spatial liminality related to rhetoric, and the relationship of mythic liminars to symbols in ancient cultures.

Liminars as Personae in Ancient Rhetorical Myths

To recapitulate, by personifying rhetorical concepts in myths, ancient cultures "stretched" the idea of writing to fit an un-named art of rhetoric long before the Greeks systematized or classified it. While some previous authorities have identified Greco-Roman myth as prologue to a mature expression of rhetorical theory, in many cultures rhetorical theory was sufficiently expressed in its mythic form for them through analogy. Other, often far older, ancient cultures expressed their complex rhetorical theories by making the figures in their mythic narratives liminal in nature to thereby illustrate the nature of rhetoric theory; in this narrow example, about the liminal nature of rhetorical action. The personae in these myths, by way of their identities, can be seen to be neither "here nor there" in the sense that they have transitional and unfixed settings and movements when connected to writing. Personification was one means of linguistic "stretching" that Johnstone (2012) has described. It occurred as cultures "manipulated the symbols of speech and culture" that outstripped their linguistic expression. None of the liminars are precisely human, and they are diverse in gender. But all have a liminal relationship to writing, rhetoric, or are responsible for its supervision or invention. Still others have a relationship to rhetorical processes in the ancient world, and rhetorical spaces. In effect, ancient myth states that rhetoric is like these liminars; rhetorical power happens on the way to speaking as, analogically, meaning is created between the word and the mind. In these cases, the identifying details of both the personae and their stories *are* often ancient theories of rhetorical action. The theme conveys the theory in multiple myths: that rhetorical action, and thereby its actors, are liminal in nature. This quality is intended to conceptually convey that rhetoric is a liminal force.

The Egyptian god Thoth is a primary example of a liminal persona because much is known about the way his persona was conceived by his ancient followers. On the other hand, nearly no myths consisting of narratives about him have come down to us from the Egyptological corpus, and certainly not any resembling Plato's narrative in *Phaedrus* at 275sa-e. Thoth is generally known as a messenger god and the famed scribe who records the acts of a soul in the afterlife (itself a liminal place); and of course, he is the inventor of hieroglyphics. But what is thus far known about Thoth mostly can be found in inscribed appellations and titles where he is mentioned, and not narrative myths. Jennifer Westerfield (2019) has most recently summarized Thoth's relationship to the invention of writing, for which there is no account bearing similarity to Plato's in the existing corpus. Westerfield points out the many epithets related to writing reserved for Thoth:

> In the Egyptian sources, Thoth is reckoned as "excellent of speech (ı̓k̟ r ḏd)," "lord of script (nb sẖ)," "lord of books (ḥk mḏt)," "excellent scribe (sẖ ı̓k̟ r)," and "he who gave words and script (rdı̓ ʾ mdw drf)," among other titles.
>
> *2019: 36*

Westerfield, too, concludes that Thoth was "lord of hieroglyph (nb mdw nṯr)" (36). Thoth as exemplar can be found in the book eponymous with Thoth's name, lately assembled and translated into English by Richard Jasnow and Karl-Theodor Zauzich (2005). *The Book of*

Thoth is a set of what appear to be scribal initiations into the cult of the House of Life, which was an area appointed for scribes and scribal activity adjacent to the Library of Alexandria (2005: 35). Jasnow notes that it will "obviously deal with the hieroglyphs and writing in general" (Jasnow 2011: 297). It thus contains numerous allusions to Thoth, his relationship to writing, and the liminal relationship of writing and Thoth to knowledge itself.

Jasnow provides reference to writing imagery, where Thoth acts as a liminal force within the text itself, and connects this force to writing. However, the collective textual evidence also suggests that Thoth was a necessary actor in deriving meaning from writing as a mediating force between signifier and signified. Thoth's indispensability to rhetorical operations in these liminal spaces partly explains his omnipresence in ancient Egypt. At one point, Thoth states, "The document is a nest. The books [*possible tr.* 'Signs'] are its/his young ones" (Jasnow 2011: 298). Thoth continues, "I desire to make an explanation (or 'be a fisherman/bird-catcher') of the signs" (300). Thoth is depicted as a fowler whose quarry is the hieroglyphic *signs*. When Thoth captures the fugitive signs, he bridges the gap between signifier and signified like the fibers of a net that catches birds in flight. Thoth exists, in other words, as a god of liminal spaces and processes, the power of the net of meaning that gathers the birds together in one place.

To a certain extent, Thoth's "netting" role aligns with ancient views of the process of invention, and not just comprehension; as Mary Carruthers pointed out, a fullness of understanding akin to the netting, or gathering together of signs, is similar to one "fundamental assumption about the nature of 'creativity' in classical culture" (2000: 11–12). The net as a symbol of this structure occurs not only in Plato's *Theaetetus* but in other extremely ancient sources such as the Sumerian *Enmerkar and the Lord of Aratta*, as metaphor for complex notions of epistemology and the theory of writing. Thoth, as the messenger god and the scribe of the judgment of the dead, is a liminal persona representing the rhetorical process itself. Thoth is not only the patron of all signs, but the messenger that carries the meaning between the symbol and the meaning of signs, and the idea of what is spoken between speaker and listener. Thoth exists in the conceptual *space between* speaker and hearer, and without him all meaning is lost in the art of persuasive speech. To the Egyptians, therefore, Thoth was somewhat akin to the idea of logos found in Greek culture. He was the pervasive living force that conferred meaning to mere symbols and sounds, and conveyed them "in-between" the liminal space that exists between two minds. But apart from the conceptual liminal space of the symbol and page, Thoth, to Egyptian initiates, represented a conceptual liminar between the word and the mind. Jasnow has pointed out that the *Book of Thoth* seems to be an initiatory book intimately related to initiation as ritual. The adept of Thoth seemed to have been asked and heard to answer the questions therein to reform the social *communitas* of his priesthood. It is in this way that Thoth is an exemplar of the liminal nature of rhetorical mythic figures more than almost any other: he moves in the space between participants, ideas, and worlds with total conceptual fluidity. His domain is neither the word nor the meaning of the symbols he controls, but the liminal spaces between.

Other gods, goddesses, and cultural heroes can properly be styled liminars, whether in their attributes or in details arising from their mythic narratives. Enmerkar acts as mediating figure between goddesses and his rival in the narrative of *Enmerkar and the Lord of Aratta*. It is important to note that it is commonly known as a narrative about the invention of writing from Sumeria; but the inventor of written characters in a far older epoch of Mesopotamia (c. 2300) was the goddess of Nisaba, discussed below (Meador 2011: 1). In *Enmerkar* might be the earliest narrative in which a human employs writing for a *rhetorical purpose*. In *Aratta*, Enmerkar issues challenges and accepts counter challenges from his rival, first using a personal messenger, and finally a writing. But the nature of writing is perhaps a secondary purpose of the narrative: it is the story of a rhetorical contest over the disposition and exchange of resources. The entire contest begins at the bidding of the goddess Inana who directs Enmerkar to send a messenger to Aratta: "Come Enmerkar, I shall advise you – let my advice be heeded! – I shall speak a word – let it be heard! Having chosen among the troops a messenger, clever of speech and hardy" (Vanstiphout 2004: I.A.69–71). That the narrative is framed by the dispatch of one "clever of speech" is a strong indicator that its topic concerns rhetorical action. Enmerkar acts as the conduit between the supernatural world and his rival, Aratta, just as Thoth fulfills the same function in Egyptian cosmology. The contest notably begins with threats of warfare before the ultimate culmination of the creation of writing. Enmerkar threatens to destroy Aratta (191–195) at the beginning of the contest, but ultimately seems to resolve it with the invention of writing in his ultimate victory over Aratta. Yet in the end, Enmerkar praises both Inana and his rival because they have brought writing and persuasion between kingdoms, unifying them: "They are a nation Dumuzid selected among the other nations, One that firmly establishes the holy word of Inana!" (I.A.566–568). Rather beautifully, in the story, both contestants win: Aratta fulfills his desire to unite the languages of humankind with writing and rhetoric, and a terrible plague visited on Aratta's kingdom is lifted. Enmerkar is a liminal entity and a liminal social figure, moving between the spoken and written medium.

The moral of the story, or lesson of the *fabula*, is that writing deployed for rhetorical action will bring peace and prosperity. It is a testament to the liminal power of both rhetoric and the written word, all deployed analogically in a kind of play full of liminal actors. *Enmerkar and the Lord of Aratta* deserves an important role in the history of rhetoric, because it is the Sumerian gospel of rhetorical action, and a true hymn to the power of rhetoric at least 1000 years before Plato's *Phaedrus*. Enmerkar's narrative creates multiple levels of mediation in a conflict that is essentially persuasive in nature. In so doing, Sumerian myth conveys analogically that rhetoric is a culturally organizational practice, much as it was conceived as a "civilizing force" in Isocrates and Cicero. This civilizing force, similar to the concept of logos in ancient Greece, is further illustrated in *Enmerkar*. In *Enmerkar's* narrative, a contest of persuasion and communicative exchange first begins with threats of violence. But *Enmerkar's* resolution is one of an explosion of prosperity: in creating or implementing writing, a famine lifts from Aratta and the fields explode in abundant harvest. The power of mediation is personified by narrative actors in ancient Sumerian tradition. The mediating power of these liminal actors thus illustrates their theory of teleology in relation to their theory of rhetoric. To the Sumerians, rhetorical processes, particularly in writing, were as one with security and agricultural prosperity, and this was part of rhetoric's purpose or *telos*. What is suggested by this evidence is that the liminars were a personified assertion about rhetorical theory; Greco-Roman culture, by contrast, removed their rhetorical theory from analogically-embedded myth, to read differently by systematizing and categorizing rhetoric as an insular field of human knowledge.

Liminal Space in Ancient Myth and Rhetorical Theory

Turner argues that liminal personae also occupy liminal spaces as part of their conceptual, rhetorical "presence". This presence occurs in "cultural cycles" which cannot be adequately described by coining new terminology. Turner and Harris describe them as the "classificatory nets: of their routinized spheres of action" (Turner, Abrahams and Harris 1986: vii). The occupation of liminal space by the rhetorical personae of the liminars is a commentary about where rhetoric itself exists. In non-literate cultures liminal roles are sometimes memorialized by rites and liminal initiates; myth allowed these cultures to represent rhetorical action symbolically in conceptual space. Ancient mythic figures also occupy a liminal space that is largely conceptual to the cultures that venerated them. The most notable of these are the civilizations of ancient China and Egypt. In China, the myth of Cangjie was integral in the development of rhetorical theory relating to rhetoric and writing. Cangjie's myth has a long history of commentary by subsequent generations of rhetoricians, philosophers, and ethicists (Ramsey 2021b). This tradition reflects his enduring and pervasive cultural influence on the art of proper rhetorical action. His myth had a tremendous resonance for future generations and can be authoritatively assembled from diverse accounts. A synthesis of the myth of Cangjie's creation of writing can be aggregated from major details from sources such as the *Shuowen Jiezi* (說文解字), *Lunheng* (論衡), *Huainanzi* (淮南子), and *Hanfeizi* (韓非子), as the primary texts we possess that mention him. Cangjie was scribe to the Yellow Emperor, who was in legend the first Emperor of China. The *Hanfeizi* explains that Cangjie created the Chinese system of characters (*guwen*), and later discussions explain that he modeled the system of characters through observations of the tracks of birds; in some accounts he observed the movement of stars as well. The *Xunzi* explains that Cangjie's script was the first to be passed down in complete form from ancient times. Because of this, *Lunheng* explains, humans were at last able to improve or better themselves. The *Huainanzi* adds that when Cangjie had finished, the ghosts wept in the night, and the sky rained millet.

In the myth of Cangjie, the connection between agricultural prosperity, literacy, and liminality can likewise be found. In China, one literacy myth demonstrated a distinct connection between the means of persuasion and nature, and as in Sumerian culture, very overtly connected the presence of liminal beings and writing to social organization. Through these limited details, it is apparent that Cangjie, too, is a liminar, as he wanders in the wilderness, and is temporally in a space that is neither related to his ordained social position nor to anything else. Like ritual liminars in preliterate society, he must travel to discover and manipulate symbols to return to the Yellow Emperor. He is sent as an agent for another, like Enmerkar, making him the messenger or agent between the mind of his principal, and the world of symbols. But more significantly, he occupies conceptual space as a mediating figure between nature and civilization. Indeed, later commentators expressed the theory that human speech should analogically follow the example of Cangjie. In interpreting the story, a commentator in the *Shuowen Jiezi* notes that because Cangjie modeled the letters on the tracks of birds, then others who wish to follow suit must subscribe to the concept of "*wen* 文 'cultured pattern' (writing)". It shows that *wen* "is a means to disseminate education and illuminate ethical influence for the king at court, it is also a means ... for storing up virtue and making clear what is prohibited" (tr. O'Neill 2013: 259). Garrett (1991) has discussed the significance of *wen* to Chinese rhetoric, explaining that *wen* was a concept with primacy in "education and language training" and thus Chinese written rhetorical traditions. These traditions began at a much later date than the myth of Cangjie itself, which is so antique that its precise provenance likely cannot be known. Thus, the analogical argument the commentator makes is that Cangjie developed a cultured pattern of written signs from nature; therefore humans should speak in accordance with their own nature when discharging their civic duties. Cangjie, as a mythic figure, bridges the liminal, conceptual gap between signs of human nature – and nature itself – and human society. The aspect of calligraphic writing as an unbroken tradition in Chinese culture, even to this day, has been noted by Zhang et al. (2008: 531) who have cited it as, by definition, fitting UNESCO's standards for "intangible cultural heritage" because of its relationship to "performance, ritual, craftsmanship, and as concerned with man and nature" (531). The shadow of myth is very long.

A related Sumerian example of a deity of liminal space deeply associated with rhetorical knowledge and literacy is Nisaba of Eresh. Extensive references to her character and nature litter the written record of ancient Sumeria. Her role in the creation and organization of letters and society is documented in ritual hymns and invocations from a period beginning approximately 2600 BCE (Meador 2011: 5). Nisaba was, in addition to a goddess of letters, intimately associated with grain, recordation, and measurement, which Sumerian civilization viewed as synchronically linked to provide them with the tools of survival. But Nisaba is a persona who is a liminal entity that unifies culture and the written word. Her relationship to these aspects of human survival suggests the beginning of rhetorical theory in a non-Greco-Roman context. She is described in the Hymn of Gudea as "she who opens the doors of the house of understanding" and who "knows the inmost secrets of numbers" (Meador 2011: 19). Yet in none of these descriptions is she seen to be either in one place or the other: Nisaba opens the door of the house of understanding for humanity. Her role as a gatekeeper, neither on one side nor the other, is thus fundamentally liminal, and is depicted as thus to convey the fundamentally rhetorical nature of her persona. She is not precisely in the Sumerian script but keeps possession of it. In creating a mythic precedent for the organization of symbolic patterns, the narrative demonstrates Sumerian belief that civic development can occur without rhetorical activity. The "Hymn to King Isbi-Erra of Isin" from the third millennium contains a reflection of how the Sumerians perceived the fundamentally civilizing and life-sustaining force of language in organized patterns. These patterns closely align to the much later Greco-Roman rhetorical traditions whose earliest formulation can be found in Isocrates. The hymn states that wherever Nisaba approaches, "There is writing!" (Reisman 1976: 359). This line is prefatory to her liminal associations with other concepts in the hymn, but is important because Nisaba is not characterized as where writing is or elsewhere: Nisaba approaches an earthly location and causes writing to appear. Neither here nor there, her action is one of liminal delivery and in liminal space. Just as she exists between spaces where "humanity is not established", and "cities are not built", and, significantly, rites to the gods are not performed (359). "Kings are not raised" without Nisaba, and thus there is no basis of government.

The hymn implies, however, that on the opposite end of this liminal spectrum it is Nisaba that provides the basis of all these things; where there is grain and milk is churned (359). Yet nowhere in this excerpt is Nisaba said to *be* anywhere. She is a liminal goddess whose instruments are agricultural and literate. She establishes the rites that permit human existence in the spaces between wilderness and civilization, the divine world and the human – liminal connections from liminal space. Sumerians employed writing for nearly every rhetorical purpose; Kennedy states that it wholly subsumed the spoken rhetorical medium (Kennedy 1998: 198). Typically, if the Sumerians discussed rhetoric theoretically it was through the manipulation of symbols, particularly mythic symbols; an exception would be their perceptual handbook lists. The liminal spaces occupied by their gods were yet another way ancient cultures thereby asserted propositions about their perspective of rhetorical concepts.

Liminars: Their Symbols and Rhetorical Processes

Rhetorical liminars also manipulate and organize signs and symbols as part of their innate nature in ancient myth, which in Turner's terminology allows them to create "webs of classification" which connect the germinal theories of rhetoric to their narratives. In so doing, the narratives they act in convey a liminal theory of symbolic action that stands at the foundation of rhetorical theory. There are many liminars associated with writing in the myths of the ancient world who also have a relationship to the transition of humans to the afterlife, and also the recordation in judgment. Thoth records the acts of the dead to establish a true record of the past, as do figures in ancient India, such as Chitragupta, and in ancient China, the Lord of Hell Yan Wang. But often liminars have a relationship to *time* through the organization of symbols, as well. In contemporary human society, we make decisions about the future and findings about the past by mobilizing symbols, and so did the ancient liminal deities. Across global culture, we hold trials to determine past facts, and organize action in the future by mobilizing a whole host of symbolic data: speeches, graphs, charts, document, and legislation, to name a few. Some of the most ancient deities of which we are aware had a liminal relationship to the mobilization of symbols. Ancient liminars mobilized these symbols in order to bring order to society and to the soul of human beings. Some even employ their powers to order the cosmos itself, which underscores the pervasiveness of rhetoric across ancient cultures.

Perhaps the most famous liminar in this respect is Thoth, not only the liminal lord of transit between life and death, but the mobilizer of symbols in the trial of the dead. Thoth is famously pictured holding the writing instruments in illustrations of The Judgment of the Dead. During this process, he is often depicted holding the reed and the palette of a scribe; there is some scholarly disagreement about whether he merely recorded the result of the judgment or was, himself, judge (Stadler 2012: 1). Most important, however, is the fact that throughout the entirety of the process Thoth is present and active. Every part of the judicial fact-finding process is subject to his introduction, interrogation, or finding of fact and recordation of events (Nagel 1942). Jasnow writes, the author or compiler of *The Book of Thoth* seems to "conceive, implicitly, if not explicitly, of writing as 'capturing' signs and, in a sense, subduing or 'domesticating' them" (306). To use the parlance of Jasnow's argument, Thoth the fowler is a mediator, catching and organizing the fugitive signs, and his role as fowler stands as a personified metaphor for the way language operates as an intangible force in the Egyptian rhetorical imagination. Jasnow explains that "Thoth has strong associations with trapping and nets" and cites several examples outside the *Book of Thoth* found as funerary art in discovered tombs (306). One might conceive of a "net" or web as a connective piece of Egyptian technology but, in this instance, for the mediating power of written signs and understanding. But Thoth's organizing rhetorical power is not merely between words, but between and among humans and their associations. While Thoth himself is described as a connective force, or invisible net of meaning and organization that orders the cosmos, the scribes themselves are described as birds in that net while their fitness to serve as his agents is tested. From all of these details, it can be inferred the "net" could be the social practice of hermeneutic and rhetorical training associated with entering the service of Thoth. In fact, in the *Book of Thoth*, one of Thoth's epithets is "he who has ordered the earth with his scribal palette" (Butler 2013: 233), conveying the organizing principle at work not just in writing but reality itself, with a very unambiguous connection to a tool of writing. But most importantly Lipson points out that the deities can represent an interpersonal and social force, as in the case of the Goddess Ma'at, "connective justice" that involves "a collection of social norms that govern how individuals should interact with others to form communities" (2004: 81). This is an important step, because it demonstrates how gods can represent connective or mediating forces in Ancient Egyptian thought that operate between people and rhetorical systems. By his instruction, Thoth again mediates between persons and words, just as he is depicted organizing and interpreting writings in other roles throughout Egyptian literature.

The goddess Nisaba's most relevant narrative to the inquiry of the role of symbol is her role in the creation of the Sumerian characters. The central connection to rhetorical theory is her role as the goddess of the conceptual "net" – the connective and organizing principle that she is responsible for, like Thoth. Nisaba gathers the symbols together for the gods to create meaning. Nisaba's net has many functions, but in relation to stories of the gods, certain invocations of her, or *āšipu*, derive from ritual practices to gain favor or remedy disfavor between people and their gods (Meador 2011: 73). In one such *āšipu* the invoker beseeches Nisaba to "net against" angry supernatural forces (2011: 71). I offer this example of Nisaba's association with the "net" as binding not only humans and gods, but humans to one another in a kind of social fabric which is enacted ritualistic-ally. Nisaba is the actor in the divine world who is analogical in function to Enmerkar, whose acts of "netting" meaning together in the human world led to the establishment of rhetorical action. It is Nisaba's intimate and progenitive relationship to language and symbols that is the basis of this invocation, itself a rhetorical act. Nisaba is not only said to have created the discrete symbols of the Sumerian writing system, but she is said to have "netted" together these symbols. According to a very early version of the Kesh Hymn, discovered at Abu Sulabik, Nisaba created written language by capturing the words of a hymn by the chief god, Enlil (Meador 2011: 3). In so doing she then placed the words on a tablet she held, establishing a "standard" lexicon. "She spun, as it were, a web/of those words" laying them "ready to hand" for the human world (4). Nisaba is one of the eldest rhetorical patrons and progenitors not only because she personifies the cre-ation of language, which is her popular attribution; she orders and arranges language to mediate between the human and divine world. The image of the "net" represents Nisaba's intercessional rhetorical power to the Sumerians that is embodied in language.

Like Thoth, the Sumerians analogically posited that Nisaba made meaning for the gods, and Nisaba perhaps was the first liminar to be given overt credit in the textual record for such. Nisaba is thus the net maker – the primal force that gathers the symbols together. To the Sumerians, Nisaba personified rhetorical process in her role as symbol creator, organizing and assembling the symbols into meaning. By contrast, in *Emerkar and the Lord of Aratta*, Enmerkar *casts the net*. But more significantly, Enmerkar's net is intended to represent an organized message from one person to another in a "contest" that was rhetorical in nature. The "net" image in Thoth's myth, Enlil's myth, and the story of Enmerkar, represents a force that binds people together in rhetorical exchange, and functions as a substitute for persuasion by physical compulsion. The message of many of the aforementioned myths is that language is a liminal force that derives from the gods. The gods themselves, as liminars, are thus an analogical argument about the nature of rhetoric in these cultures. The implication is multifold, but it underscores that liminars, as personifications or analogical exempla, were themselves a way of theorizing rhetoric. But in terms of the symbols they employ, the liminars associated with writing in its component parts are themselves analogical arguments about rhetoric, for cultures who may not have had comparable linguistic units to describe rhetoric. The liminal symbols they control are not decontextualized marks on wood, paper, or stone but an abstract process of organization.

The Webs of the Liminars

Ancient myths are frequently offered as argumentative propositions to convey rhetorical theory expressed in an analogical manner. The very nature of the agents and actors in those myths can be analogical expressions of complex theories related to rhetoric within their own culture and in their own historical milieu. These analogical arguments take shape in the liminal nature of the persons, symbols, and spaces within mythic systems. The liminars at work in these systems, first, can be observed to personify qualities that are liminal in their relationship to humans, concepts, symbols, and even reality itself. The liminars act as agents in liminal spaces, much the way that rhetoric operates in-between persons, such as speakers and listeners. Likewise, liminars use symbols to convey meaning between actors, and are responsible for processes between minds and persons. In ancient Sumeria, Egypt, and China, these liminal acts, processes, and personae reflected the conceptual relationship of humans to rhetorical processes. All of these myths represent one stage of time in the life of ancient civilizations where myth provided insight into culturally pervasive concepts surrounding the role of discursive communication. In non-Greco-Roman cultures, these myths and the figures within them operated analogically to convey rhetorical theory in ways distinct from Greco-Roman counterparts that functioned as a descriptive set of rhetorical theories: they provide insights not only into ancient rhetoric outside Greece and Rome but into the ways rhetorical theory was differently shaped in the ancient world.

References

Ames, R., & Hall, D. (2010). *Dao de jing: A Philosophical Translation*. Ballantine Books.
Averbeck, R. E. (2003). Myth, Ritual, and Order in "Enki and the World Order". *Journal of the American Oriental Society, 123*(4), 757–771.
Butler, E. P. (2013). Opening the Way of Writing: Semiotic Metaphysics in the Book of Thoth. In *Practicing Gnosis: Ritual, Magic, Theurgy and Liturgy in Nag Hammadi, Manichaean and Other Ancient Literature. Essays in Honor of Birger A. Pearson*. April D. DeConick, Gregory Shaw, John D. Turner, editors. Brill, 215–247, 233.
Carruthers, M. (2000). *The Craft of Thought: Meditation, Rhetoric, and the Making of Images, 400–1200* (Vol. 34). Cambridge University Press.
Ceccarelli, P. (2013). *Ancient Greek Letter Writing: A Cultural History (600 BC–150 BC)*. Oxford University Press.
Cicero. (1949). *De Inventione. With an English translation by HM Hubbell*. Harvard University Press.
Doty, W. G. (2000). *Mythography: The Study of Myths and Rituals*. University of Alabama Press.
Douglas, M. (1999). *Leviticus as Literature*. Oxford University Press.
Enos, R. L. (2011). *Greek Rhetoric before Aristotle*. Parlor Press LLC.
Fowler, Robert L. (2011). Mythos and Logos. *The Journal of Hellenic Studies, 131*, 45–66.
Garrett, Mary. (1991). Asian Challenge. In *Contemporary Perspectives on Rhetoric*. Sonja Foss, Karen Foss, and Robert Trapp, editors. Waveland, 1991, 295–306.
Graham, A. C. (1989) *Disputers of the Tao: Philosophical Argument in Ancient China*. Open Court.
Havelock, E. A. (1986). *The Muse Learns to Write: Reflections on Orality and Literacy from Antiquity to the Present*. Yale University Press.
Jasnow, R. (2011). "Caught in the Web of Words" – Remarks on the Imagery of Writing and Hieroglyphs in the Book of Thoth. *Journal of the American Research Center in Egypt*, 297–317.
Jasnow, R., & Zauzich, K. (2005) *The Ancient Egyptian Book of Thoth: A Demotic Discourse on Knowledge and Pendant to the Classical Hermetica, Volume 1*. Otto Harrassowitz Verlag,

Johnstone, C. L. (2012). *Listening to the Logos: Speech and the Coming of Wisdom in Ancient Greece*. University of South Carolina Press.

Kennedy, George. (1998). *Comparative Rhetoric: An Historical and Cross-Cultural Introduction*. Oxford: Oxford University Press.

Lévi-Strauss, C. (2013). *Myth and Meaning*. Routledge.

Lipson, Carol S. (2004). Ancient Egyptian Rhetoric: It All Comes Down to Maat. *Rhetoric Before and Beyond the Greeks*, 79–97. At 80.

Meador, Betty De Shong. (2011). Nisaba of Eresh: Goddess of Grain, Goddess of Writing. In *Goddesses in World Culture, Volume 2*. Patricia A. Monaghan, editor. Praeger, 3–17.

Nagel, G. (1942). Le dieu Thot d'après les textes égyptiens. *Eranos Jahrbuch*, 9, 109–140.

O'Neill, T. (2013). Xu Shen's Scholarly Agenda: A New Interpretation of the Postface of the Shuowen jiezi. *Journal of American Oriental Society*, 133(3), 413–440.

Ong, W. J. (1982). *Orality and Literacy: The Technologizing of the Word*. London: Methuen.

Plato. *Plato: Phaedrus*. Reginald Hackforth, Ed. No. 119. Cambridge University Press, 1972.

Ramsey, S. (2021a). From Sunlight to Shadow and Back Again: Enmerkar and the Lord of Aratta and the Function of Analogical Reasoning in Mesopotamian Rhetoric. *Rhetoric Society Quarterly*, 51(1), 42–54.

Ramsey, S. (2021b). Mythic Progenitors in Chinese and Sumerian Rhetorical Culture: A Short Primer. *Rhetoric Review*.

Reisman, D. (1976). A 'Royal' Hymn of Isbi-Erra to the Goddess Nisaba. In *Kramer Anniversary Volume*. Barry L Eichler, editor. Verlag Butzon and Berckler.

Schiappa, E. (1999). *The Beginnings of Rhetorical Theory in Classical Greece*. Yale University Press.

Stadler, M. A. (2012). Thoth. *UCLA Encyclopedia of Egyptology*, 1(1).

Turner, V. G. (2018). *Dramas, Fields, and Metaphors: Symbolic Action in Human Society*. Cornell University Press.

Turner, V., Abrahams, R. D., & Harris, A. (1986). *The Ritual Process: Structure and Anti-Structure*. Routledge.

Van Gennep, A. (2019). *The Rites of Passage*. University of Chicago Press.

Vanstiphout, H. H. L. (2004). *Epics of Sumerian Kings: The Matter of Aratta* (Vol. 20). Brill.

Volkov, A. (1992). Analogical Reasoning in Ancient China: Some Examples. *Extrême-Orient Extrême-Occident*, 15–48.

Walker, J. (2000). *Rhetoric and Poetics in Antiquity*. Oxford University Press.

Wee, J. Z. (Ed.). (2017). *The Comparable Body-Analogy and Metaphor in Ancient Mesopotamian, Egyptian, and Greco-Roman Medicine*. Brill.

Westerfield, Jennifer Taylor. (2019). *Egyptian Hieroglyphs in the Late Antique Imagination*. University of Pennsylvania Press.

Zhang, J., Tang, W., Shi, C., Liu, Z., & Wang, X. (2008). Chinese Calligraphy and Tourism: From Cultural Heritage to Landscape Symbol and Media of the Tourism Industry. *Current Issues in Tourism*, 11(6), 529–548.

3

RHETORIC AND SILENCE IN CORPORATE AMERICA

Ending the Patent War between Google and Microsoft

Joshua Welsh

Introduction

In Amor Towles's novel *A Gentleman in Moscow*, set in Soviet Russia, the protagonist's old friend, Mishka, has a job editing a multi-volume collection of the letters of Anton Chekhov. The senior editor of the project calls Mishka to his office and tells him that one of the letters, which was written from Berlin in 1904, needs a single sentence to be cut: "People who have never travelled abroad don't know how good bread can be" (2016, p. 264). Mishka complies but comes to deeply regret his acquiescence. Years later, the protagonist reflects on the excised sentence: "Given the hardships of the 1930s ... he supposed he could understand why [the senior editor] (or his superiors) had insisted upon this little bit of censorship – having presumed that Chekhov's observation could only lead to feelings of discontent or ill will" among the Russian people (p. 374). This omission provides a telling illustration of what rhetorician Thomas Huckin describes as *manipulative silences*, and without drawing too strong an analogy between Soviet Russia and Corporate America, such silences are common in press releases and other corporate communications. Huckin lists manipulative silences along with several other types of textual silences: "speech act silences ... presuppositional silences ... discreet silences ... [and] genre-based silences" (Huckin 2002, p. 348). While each of these types of silence has its own set of characteristics, Huckin argues that manipulative silences are different from the others in that they leave out "relevant information ... to the benefit of the writer or speaker" (p. 351).

In this chapter, I relate a case study that involves a similar sort of manipulative silence. The silence I analyze comes in the form of a joint statement released by Microsoft and Google at the end of a four-year patent dispute. The press release consists of just a few lines of plain and terse text, announcing the settlement of all pending patent litigation and the intention to collaborate in the future. Such terseness may be expected in a press release, but I analyze the statement within the context of the larger patent dispute. I argue that the statement constitutes a manipulative silence, benefiting the rhetors by leaving out

38

DOI: 10.4324/9781003195276-5

a great deal of what could have been said at the end of such a long, drawn-out conflict, which both sides often characterized as a "war." Furthermore, I argue that the companies' choice of genre itself helps support this manipulation: by selecting a genre (the press release) for which terseness is often expected, the two companies make it less likely that the reader will notice what is missing. In the rest of this chapter, I offer a brief overview of the history of rhetorical silence, a theoretical lens for studying silence, a description of the methodology I used for my case study, and the case study itself.

History

Speech has long been seen as a key distinction that separates people from animals, or even as a gift from or a connection to the gods (Glenn 2004, p. 3). As writing was developed, it came to be seen as a storehouse for culture and civilization, and even as a way to cross time and communicate with later generations (Ong 1982). But as powerful and important as speech and writing are, silence has always played a role in communication.

Since at least the time of ancient Egypt, thinkers and scholars have been interested in the role that silence plays in the power of language. As Fox tells us, "The first canon of Egyptian rhetoric is silence. Silence is both a moral posture and a rhetorical tactic" (Fox 1983, p. 12). For the Egyptians, silence was considered a virtue and a "strategy for success, one that will help you get your own way by improving your ethos and allowing your opponents to destroy their own" (p. 12). This tactic was generally employed as a response to an argument initiated by someone else.

Moving forward to the time of classical Athens, Plato seems to view silence differently. Given the elevated status that Plato gives to the art of dialectic (talking and debating with others to find the Truth of a matter), it should be no surprise that silence was viewed with some suspicion. In fact, silence constitutes one aspect of Plato's famous critique of writing in *Phaedrus* (2003). Among writing's failings was the fact that written speeches are silent and "cannot protect themselves from others." Nevertheless, that same critique shows that, for Plato, the appropriate use of silence was crucial to effective dialectic, as Plato's Socrates asks rhetorically about the power of speech over writing: "Is there not another kind of word or speech far better than this [i.e., writing]? ... I mean an intelligent word graven in the soul of the learner, which can defend itself, and knows when to speak and when to be silent" (lines 275–276). Silence played a philosophical role in Platonism and eventually early Christianity.

During the time of Quintilian, silence was seen as an important component of the dangerous work of challenging authority: "In summarizing the use of figured speech in direct attacks on tyrants, Quintilian refers to it as *silentium*, 'silence', an appropriate term for speech in which what is meant is not said, but left for the listener to discover" (Ahl 2010, p. 8). This was also known as speaking or writing "*aperte*, 'openly,' in that [the writer's] meaning, though not declared forthrightly, can be detected by anyone who looks for it: it is 'figured' speech" (Ahl 2010, p. 5). Stylistically, speech that is delivered *aperte* can be contrasted with speech that is *palam*, in other words stated directly. For Quintilian, the figurative *aperte* style, which used silence to avoid directly criticizing authority, could be used to criticize tyrants indirectly, since the meaning is left open to discovery by the audience. Nevertheless, according to Ahl, arguments in law courts did not require silence in the same way as public writing critical of tyrants themselves (Ahl 2010, p. 8). As with other aspects of persuasion, the appropriateness and effectiveness of rhetorical silence depended heavily on context. As we will see below, context continues to be especially important for those interested in determining the meaning and effectiveness of rhetorical silences.

As Christian thinking developed, silence began to emerge as something more than a rhetorical tactic. According to Mazzeo, "a philosophical theology of silence was present in both Platonism and Christianity, and the latter began to develop it quite early" (Mazzeo 1962, p. 192). By the time of Augustine, Christian theology had imbued silence with a more transcendental meaning: "For St. Augustine all dialectic, true rhetoric, and thought itself were but attempts to reascend to that silence from which the world fell into the perpetual clamor of life as fallen men know it" (ibid.). Furthermore, St. Augustine explicitly contrasted inner silence with the language created by people:

> There are two kinds of *verba*, those which are man-made and conventional, what we customarily call language in the broadest sense of the term, and which contrast with the second category of internal, silent words by which the inner teacher, Christ, teaches us the truth.
>
> *Ibid.*

This distinction, according to Mazzeo's reading of Augustine, is essentially the difference between "eloquence and truth, words and realities" (ibid.). Modern scholars of rhetoric may find it interesting that, for Augustine, answers to age-old questions that pit rhetoric against reality were to be found in silent contemplation. According to Jerrold Seigel, Renaissance scholar Petrarch held a view of silence that followed Augustine's closely at times: "*Veritas in silencio* [i.e., truth in silence] represented for Petrarch an ideal of life on a higher plane than the one the orator occupied" (Seigel 1968, p. 45). Nevertheless, much of Petrarch's work deals with the tensions between philosophy and oratory, and much of his work had the goal of combining the two.

My purpose in this brief overview has been to highlight a range of historical perspectives that Western rhetoricians have taken to silence. Even this short summary can demonstrate the fact that understanding the meaning of silence, as with any other rhetorical device, depends on understanding the rhetorical situation. Ultimately, silence will mean different things for different authors, to different audiences, and in different contexts.

Theory

In this section I outline a cohesive theory consisting of four key claims:

1. Silence is shaped by its context.
2. Silence can be used to communicate.
3. Silence can be used rhetorically.
4. Silence can be analyzed and critiqued by studying its context.

By approaching the theory of silence through these claims, I intend to provide a theoretical framework for students and scholars to use when analyzing instances of silence.

Silence Is Shaped by Its Context

The first claim I want to make here is that silence is shaped by its context. For example, as I type these words, the room I am in is quiet, but not silent. My keyboard clicks with each letter, breaking the silence. If I stop typing for a moment, a silence seems to take shape, only to be pushed away as other background sounds claim my attention – a fan in the next room, birds in the backyard, or cars on a nearby road. Some would argue that there is rarely any space on earth that is truly silent, that is devoid of all sound, but this ebb and flow demonstrates the relationship between silence and context: my perception of any particular "silence" depends heavily on the sounds that surround it. This inter-dependence between silence and perception is equally true for the relationship between silence and discourse, including both speech and writing.

Zembylas and Michaelides summarize various philosophical perspectives on the relationships between silence and speech nicely:

> While the common assumption is that silence is the opposite of speech, many thinkers throughout history, including Eastern and Western mystics, Martin Heidegger, Maurice Merleau-Ponty, and Ludwig Wittgenstein, have emphasized that silence is not the mere absence of speech. Heidegger, for example, claimed that silence is constitutive of discourse, and Merleau-Ponty argues that something exists beyond what is said, a silence and implicit language; they both emphasized that in order to be silent, one must have something to say.
>
> *Zembylas and Michaelides 2004, p. 193*

Zembylas and Michaelides also point us towards a perspective of silence connected to context: "Although there are different kinds of silence, what seems to be important is *how* silence works in specific contexts" (p. 194). In other words, we can under-stand silence better by focusing less on what it is and more on what it does and how it works. Rather than thinking about what makes up the ebb and flow of silence that surrounds me, I can consider how it affects my mood or my ability to concentrate. This relationship between silence and context can be helpful to rhetoricians interested in understanding the potential meanings and impacts of a given silence, as I hope to dem-onstrate below. But first it is necessary to make a second claim regarding silence: silence can be communicative.

Silence Can Be Used to Communicate

Silence as communication is demonstrated through any number of common interactions. My son might ask me if he can have a sugary snack. If I remain silent long enough, he might understand my silence as a "no." But as this example illustrates, the communicative intent of a given silence depends as much on the receiver as it does on the sender. Scholars of silence have understood this for decades, even arguing that the communicative intent of a given silence depends *more* on the receiver than it does on the sender.

For example, nearly 50 years ago, Johannesen made it clear that the meanings created through silence depend heavily on the audience: "Silence communicates because listeners and observers will attach meaning to the silence whether the sender wishes so or not" (Johannesen 1974, p. 29). Robert Scott makes a similar point in the epigraph to his 1972 study of rhetoric and silence: "*You cannot not communicate*" (Scott 1972, p. 146, emphasis in original). In other words, it does not matter if my silence in response to my son's request for a snack was not intended as a negative response but was instead a result of me pausing to consider how close it is to dinnertime. If my son interprets the silence as communicating a negative response, then that is what the silence means to him.

This is not to say that every scholar interested in silence agrees with this position. Attaching meaning to silence may contradict common-sense definitions of communication, including Edwin Black's somewhat restrictive requirements for communicative messages and his warning against seeing meaning in instances where no message is intended:

> To interpret something as a communication requires that the "message" exhibit certain linguistic conventions that qualify it as a message. Erring in this interpretation in a chronic way by overdetermining the meanings that can be attributed to events is as truly paranoidal as is the conviction that hostile conspiracies rule the world.
>
> *Black 1988, p. 138*

Here Black seems to be concerned with attaching meaning to events where none is intended. However, the same warning can be made to people who consistently read malicious intent into silence. And seeing hostility in every silence would certainly exhibit a paranoid style similar to the conspiracy theorists described by Hofstadter (1964). Furthermore, anyone who has waited for a response to a job application would do well to listen to Black's caution, even without falling into the trap of hostile conspiracy theories. For example, when I was applying for jobs in my final year of graduate school, I sent out many applications, most of which garnered no response. I applied to one particular institution in early January and when I hadn't heard anything back by late February, I assumed that I had not been selected to be interviewed. I interpreted (wrongly as it turned out) that the silence following my application was intended to communicate "no," when, in fact, the hiring committee had simply not screened applicants as quickly as I expected. I had attached meaning to silence even though the sender had not intended the silence to be communicative, and indeed had probably not even perceived the delay as a silence. However, this type of misinterpretation on the part of the audience does not mean that silence itself cannot communicate. It simply points to the potential for miscommunication in the absence of specific linguistic conventions. But such miscommunication is possible and common in instances where messages are conveyed discursively as well.

Silence Can Be Used Rhetorically

The third claim I want to make is that silence can be used rhetorically. Scholars and students of rhetoric will hopefully agree that if silence can be used to communicate, then it must follow that silence can be used to persuade. Nevertheless, it is worth considering some of the ways that silence as rhetoric can fit into existing rhetorical theory. A rhetoric of silence can be built from Aristotle's fundamental definition of the term: "Rhetoric may be defined as the faculty of observing in any given case the available means of persuasion" (Aristotle 2007, 1.2, 1355b27–28), since "means of persuasion" can include symbolic and non-symbolic communication.

Much more recently, Sonya Foss's description of rhetorical criticism leaves room for analyzing and critiquing silence as well: "Any action, whether intended to communicate or not, can be interpreted rhetorically by those who experience or encounter it" (Foss 2018, p. 5). The rhetorical intent of a given silence is determined by the receiver. This makes sense, given that the communicative intent of a silence is also determined by the receiver. But more than having the ability to persuade, some scholars argue that silence (at least silence created by humans) cannot help but be rhetorical. Cheryl Glenn argues that "listeners and observers attach various and individualized meanings to ... silence, regardless of the silent person's intent" (Glenn 2004, pp. 15–16). For example, if I am explaining a difficult concept to a student during office hours, the student may sit in silence. I might interpret that silence as an indication that the student does not understand the concept and wants me to explain it in a different way. Another person in the room might interpret the silence as an indication that the student does understand the concept and wants to end the meeting. These different examples illustrate the various rhetorical meanings that can be attached to a given silence. As with spoken or written rhetoric, the purpose of a given silence is determined (and possibly misinterpreted) in large part by the audience. Also, like other forms of rhetoric, context is important to understanding the rhetorical implications of silence, which leads to the final theoretical aspect I outline in the next section.

However, before considering silence in context, it is important to note that there is a difference between choosing to be silent and being forced into silence. A great deal of scholarship deals with rhetorical silencing, where those in power have forced silence upon those with less power. In *Unspoken: A Rhetoric of Silence* (2004), Glenn analyzes several cases of rhetorical silencing, such as that of Lani Guinier, who was nominated by Bill Clinton to lead the Civil Rights Division of the Department of Justice in 1993. Guinier was considered highly qualified for the job, but "following White House protocol" (p. 68) was not allowed to speak to the press to answer her critics in advance of her confirmation hearings. Glenn contrasts this silencing with Clinton's own choice to remain silent himself, rather than to speak up on her behalf:

> The White House was saying very little, thereby exerting its masculinist power through silence. Resisting her professional training as a speaker, writer, and arguer, Lani Guinier was saying nothing, thereby inhabiting a traditionally feminine im/position of silence. Clinton on the other hand, used his silence to deliver his power.
>
> *Glenn 2004, p. 69*

Similar instances of rhetorical silencing have been outlined by Fleckenstein (2011), Haviland (2008), and Brown (2009), to name just a few examples.

Silence Can Be Analyzed and Critiqued by Studying Its Context

The first three components of this theory of silence may seem obvious to scholars of rhetoric. The interplay between context, communication, and persuasion is fundamental to our field. But there may still be a conceptual gap between recognizing these relationships and developing a coherent method for studying silence. The reason for this gap is that it is difficult to study the absence of a phenomenon. Nevertheless, if silence is rhetorical, then it ought to be able to bear the burden of analysis and critique. Since silence as absence leaves little to study, however, the study of silence relies even more heavily on context than other forms of rhetorical analysis do.

Numerous case studies serve as examples and illustrations that support this claim. For example, Watson uses the context provided through contemporary accounts of Denmark Vesey's silence during his trial for conspiring to start a revolt of the enslaved people of Charleston, South Carolina (Watson 2011). Watson argues that Vesey's silence, which seems uncharacteristic for a man described by contemporaries as a skillful orator, may have been his best rhetorical choice, given that his "rhetorical problem was confounding: silence would make him look guilty, but so would eloquence, since reports of his impassioned appeals among Charleston's slaves were used as some of the most damning evidence against him" (Watson 2011, p. 79). In a similar fashion, Mack looks at the meanings of women's silence in the transition to post-apartheid South Africa by focusing on the effects of those silences rather than the silences themselves. Mack argues that focusing on effects, including institutional and literary effects, provides one way to study silence in spite of its immateriality. This is because of the role that effects can play in understanding the broader cultural context of a situation: "A cultural rhetoric approach, which understands all texts to be rhetorical participants in a 'cultural conversation' ... broadens the range of materials that scholars can access to understand the workings of silence in a given context" (Mack 2011, p. 211). A final example comes from Huckin's analysis of textual silence found in an extensive corpus of newspaper writing concerned with the issue of homelessness. Huckin's analysis demonstrates that such textual silence can be used manipulatively. He argues that "manipulation occurs when the writer uses framing in a restricted way to intentionally mislead a reader for the writer's benefit" (Huckin 2002, p. 369). Huckin's method for analyzing silence through context is compelling, so much so that it forms the basis of the methodology I outline in the next section.

Methodology

The method I use in this case study is based on two of Huckin's publications on silence: "Textual Silence and the Discourse of Homelessness" (2002) and "Propaganda by Omission" (2019). In both publications, the importance of context is made clear. For example, in "Propaganda by Omission," he describes "wide reading about the topic" as a crucial step in determining which subjects or terms are being omitted from a given piece of discourse (2019, p. 193). In "Textual Silence," Huckin makes the importance of context quite explicit: "Analyzing the context in sufficient detail should enable the analyst to determine what *could* have been said yet *wasn't*" (2002, p. 353, emphasis in original). My method below follows Huckin closely – I combine context modeling with the typology of silences he outlines in "Textual Silence" to determine what kind of silence is represented by Google and Microsoft's joint press release, as well as what the statement seems to be leaving out.

Huckin defines textual silences as instances where relevant information is left out of a text. He categorizes such silences into five groups: "*speech act silences* ...; *presuppositional silences* ...; *discreet silences* ...; *genre-based silences* ...; and *manipulative silences*" (Huckin 2002, p. 348, emphasis in original). Speech act silences are those in which the sender "*intends* the silence to be perceived as having communicative import, [and] the listener or reader can arrive at this understanding only via shared expectations" (2002, p. 349). For example, when a teacher is explaining a difficult concept to a student, if the student remains silent at the end of the explanation, the teacher may interpret the silence to mean that concept is still unclear to the student.

In the case of presuppositional silences, Huckin argues that information is left out by the author when they assume that the information is "already known to the reader, and ... can easily be reconstructed by consulting immediate context" (2002, p. 350). This is essentially the information left out in enthymematic statements or in passive constructions. In some cases the missing information is not needed or is easily recognized by the speaker, but in other cases leaving out such information can be manipulative. A sign left on a classroom door saying "Professor Smith's Class Today Has Been Cancelled" assumes that the students reading the sign will reconstruct a context in which the professor is sick and was not able to come to work. This may be the case, or Professor Smith may be canceling the class to take a personal day. It's easy to see how this message will be affected by context; depending on whether this is the first time or the sixth time the class has been canceled, the audience may read the missing information differently.

Huckin describes discreet silences as those where the author leaves out "sensitive information." Such silences share three characteristics: first the topic must by "socially, legally, or culturally sensitive"; second, the rhetor "does not intend the silence to be perceived as having communicative import other than perhaps reinforcing community norms"; finally, the "effectiveness of the silence is not dependent on whether the silence is noticed" by the audience (2002, p. 351). Huckin puts omissions involving "confidentiality, tactfulness, and taboo topics" in this category. Examples may range from removing identifying information from sample student papers to avoiding discussing why a professor abruptly resigned.

Another type of omission that involves cultural norms can be found in what Huckin calls "genre-based silences," which are "omissions that are conventional to a particular genre," and for which "the author may be aware of the omission, but is not using the omission for either communicative or manipulative purposes" (Huckin 2002, p. 351). Huckin gives the example of "formal obituaries [which conventionally] omit any negative comments or facts about the deceased" (2002, p. 351).

Lastly, Huckin describes a type of silence intended to control or exploit people, "manipulative silences." Examples of such silences are easy to find in documents including "advertisements, journalism, campaign rhetoric, press releases" and many more. Manipulative silences are omissions "that intentionally conceal relevant information from the reader or listener, to the advantage of the writer or speaker; unlike other types of silence, these silences depend for their success on not being noticed by the reader or listener" (2002, p. 351). One familiar example can be found in the teenager who asks to go to a party but does not mention that the host's parents are out of town. Huckin describes more systematic manipulative silences such as journalistic omissions involving military conflicts abroad or the debate over affirmative action in the United States (2002, p. 352). As such these silences are similar to what Huckin describes as topical silences in "Propaganda by Omission," arguing that topical silences are especially effective at manipulating people "because they escape the attention of many if not most audience members ... Given no option to choose from, many audience members will be induced to 'go with the flow' and agree with the speaker's pitch, especially if it conforms to their own beliefs" (2019, p. 187).

To help understand context systematically, Huckin (following Van Dijk) describes the concept of a *context model*. Context models include "such factors as social or professional domain, genre, purpose, location, date, time, circumstances, participant role, and affiliation" (Huckin 2002, p. 353). Students of rhetoric will find helpful parallels between many of these factors and well-known categories of rhetorical analysis. For example, purpose, participant role, and circumstances might be thought of as various components of the rhetorical situation. Location, date, and time might be considered aspects of *kairos*. Social or professional domain and affiliation could fall under the umbrella of discourse communities. Lastly, understanding genre is considered crucial to effective communication. In other words, rhetorical analysis is a broad discipline that is well situated to help establish a context model when studying a given omission or silence.

That said, context modeling is not without its limitations. As Huckin points out, attempts to understand context are necessarily "subjective and personal." Nevertheless, he argues that "much public discourse is ideologically shaped, drawing on well-established social orientations, attitudes, values, and other group beliefs" (2002, p. 354). Thus, such discourse is well suited to rhetorical analysis, which concerns itself heavily with these aspects of communication.

Lastly, it should be noted that Huckin's method involved corpus analysis. Such an approach is very compelling for cases in which a corpus of texts can be reasonably constructed. However, for many cases (such as my own analysis below), no body of texts exists, and so corpus analysis is less applicable. In such cases, understanding context becomes even more crucial to making a reasonable estimation of the meaning of a given silence.

Case Study

I begin this section by constructing a context model of the case at hand. To do this, it makes sense to start with the circumstances that led to the settlement of a complex set of lawsuits between Microsoft and Google, often referred to as "The Patent War." These lawsuits involved patents covering a range of technologies built into smart phones. The dispute itself began in October of 2011, but in order to fully understand the context of this case it is necessary to look at the circumstances that preceded that lawsuit. By the mid- to late 2000s smart phones began to include technologies such as Wi-Fi and video – two of the key capabilities which set apart today's pocket-sized computers that happen to make phone calls from the relatively simply devices of 30 years ago, and two of the technologies which figured heavily in the patent war.

In 2007, Apple released the first iPhone (Burgess 2012). The following year, the first Android phone was released (Levy 2011). Around that same time, Microsoft released the Windows Phone operating system, which had similar technological features to iPhone and Android devices (Warren 2013). Android and Apple soon became the dominant mobile operating systems, and Windows Phone's share of the market dwindled to the low single digits (van der Meulen and Rivera 2016, n.p.). But even as fewer and fewer phones were being built using the Windows Phone operating system, Microsoft owned patents on technologies that were often built into iOS (Apple's operating system) and Android. In many cases, these patented technologies were written into technological standards and shared under Reasonable and Non-Discriminatory (RAND) licensing agreements. Such agreements are intended to strike a balance between the property rights of a patent holder and the public good, which can benefit when technologies are built upon shared standards. In October of 2011, Microsoft sued Motorola Mobility (which would soon be purchased by Google) for patent infringement. As discussed below, the conflict between Microsoft and Motorola/Google involved a great deal of rhetorical language, issued in a range of genres: press releases, blog postings, tweets, and so on. But in the fall of 2015, Microsoft and Motorola abruptly announced that the dispute had been settled; in contrast to the vast amounts of highly rhetorical blog posts, tweets, U.S. Securities and Exchange Commission (SEC) filings, and court briefs that were produced during the conflict, the settlement was announced with just a few lines of text, and then both companies fell silent on the question. The rest of the context model outlined below is offered to try to help better understand that silence.

Patents, Standards, and Licensing Agreements

To understand the context surrounding these lawsuits, it is important to flesh out the fundamental purposes of patents and of licenses. Patents are intended to support inventors and foster the public good, which is believed to benefit when ideas are shared. Inventors receive a limited-term monopoly on profiting from their ideas in exchange for full disclosure of how the invention works. This trade is intended to give inventors an incentive for sharing their inventions. However, when a technology involves a high number of patented technologies, the danger of a "patent thicket" arises – the tangle of patented technology becomes too thick to cut through, and innovation suffers (Shapiro 2001, p. 119).

Standards are also meant to foster innovation, but they do so through a different mechanism. Rather than incentivizing individual inventions and the disclosure of how those inventions work, standards are formed through community consensus. Standards-setting organizations work to determine which technologies will be built into standards. Often those technologies are themselves patented, but the owners of the patents agree to allow others to use the technology. In many ways, standards are in tension with patents. Patents give the owner a monopoly on the technology (albeit one of limited duration); standards are created to make it easier to implement shared technologies. RAND agreements help ease this tension. RAND agreements can be made to govern the contribution of a technology to a standard. For an agreement to be considered RAND, the owner of a technology must charge a reasonable royalty for its use, and they may not give some companies better rates than others (Welsh 2016a, p. 115).

Another important aspect of how circumstances play into this context model can be seen in the specific technologies at issue in this dispute. Although the minutiae of standards and licensing language might seem contrary to rich rhetorical language, the technologies that formed the basis of the lawsuits are common and fundamental to producing smart phones that people will want to buy and upgrade. A significant portion of the legal dispute between Microsoft and Motorola involves two key standards: the 802.11 standard, which makes Wi-Fi connections work, and the H.264 standard, which involves digital video encoding. Although these technologies may seem ubiquitous and even mundane to those of us that are accustomed to phones that easily connect to our home Wi-Fi networks to watch online videos, they also speak to the necessity of standards. It is easy to imagine a phone that connects to the internet using a more efficient technology than Wi-Fi, but if my home router doesn't use the same technology, then the increased efficiency is useless. By the same token, a developer could create a phone that uses a cleverer video encoding scheme, providing sharper video with smaller file sizes, but if content producers don't use the same scheme, then the crisper, more efficient files can't be downloaded or viewed. By agreeing to standards, technology producers can create devices that are more useful to more people. Many of the lawsuits between Microsoft and Motorola involved RAND-covered technologies, and much of the rhetoric surrounding the lawsuits demonstrates that the companies see defending these technologies and the means by which they are developed and shared to be a high-stakes proposition.

A third important piece of context is found in Google's purchase of Motorola Mobility. Microsoft sued Motorola Mobility in the fall of 2011. Motorola Mobility counter-sued shortly thereafter. Before long, the web of lawsuit and counter lawsuit grew to include 50 patents and seven legal jurisdictions (Mueller 2011). In 2011, Google entered talks with Motorola Mobility, with the intent of purchasing some of the latter's immense patent portfolio, but the Motorola executives did not think the company would fare well in the contentious cellphone marketplace without a large collection of patents to defend itself in court (Welsh 2016b, p. 349). Ultimately, Google bought Motorola Mobility outright, patents and all, for $12.5 billion. In the spring of 2014, Google sold most of Motorola Mobility to Lenovo for just $2.9 billion, but the search giant kept Motorola Mobility's patents. Larry Page, who was CEO of Google at the time, indicated that the purchase of Motorola Mobility was intended to give the company access to a large patent portfolio (Page 2011). An SEC filing supports this assertion (Motorola Mobility 2011). Clearly, not every patent involved in the deal was subject to the lawsuits brought by Microsoft. But the purchase and subsequent sale of Motorola Mobility point to the high value that Google put on intellectual property related to mobile phones, and the lengths to which the company would go to defend itself in this area.

The last piece of the context model for this case involves the participants' choices of genre when communicating about the dispute. During the dispute, the parties involved made use of a wide range of genres, including official documents such as court briefs and SEC filings as well as more informal platforms such as blog posts and tweets. This stands in contrast to the single, poorly publicized press release that was used to announce the settlement. Although it may seem a natural choice to issue a brief statement at the settlement of such a dispute, the choice itself carries rhetorical implications. Given the wide range of genres and platforms used throughout the dispute, it is remarkable that neither party took the opportunity to celebrate the end of the lawsuits with more fanfare. In the next section of this chapter, I look at what *was* said, and compare it with what *could have been* said.

Analysis: Silence vs. Rhetoric

Microsoft and Google announced the settlement with little fanfare and comment. In fact, the announcement itself is difficult to locate and neither company responded to a request I made for the press release that accompanied the settlement announcement. Therefore, we are forced to rely on passages quoted in the press. The longest available snippet of the joint press release issued by Google and Microsoft consists of the following lines:

> Microsoft and Google are pleased to announce an agreement on patent issues.
> As part of the agreement, the companies will dismiss all pending patent infringement litigation between them, including cases related to Motorola Mobility.
> Separately, Google and Microsoft have agreed to collaborate on certain patent matters and anticipate working together in other areas in the future to benefit our customers.
>
> *Lee 2015*

The relatively plain language used to announce the settlement contrasts sharply with the rich use of metaphor and other rhetorical devices deployed in other documents throughout the conflict.

For example, when announcing the sale of Motorola Mobility to the Chinese company Lenovo, Larry Page made use of the well-known "level playing field" metaphor in a blog post: "Motorola's patents have helped create a level playing field, which is good news for all Android's users and partners" (Page 2014, n.p.). Page is reassuring his audience that the patents purchased from Motorola are intended to be used to benefit Google's customers and others involved in creating Android devices. Such reassuring language could easily have been expected in the press release announcing the settlement. Although the release does inform the reader that the two companies "anticipate working together in other areas to the future benefit of our customers," much more could have been said about the fundamental values that would support such a partnership.

Rhetorical language used to establish and reinforce common values was a regular feature in communications from the companies throughout other phases of the dispute. For example, Google often used rhetorical devices to create what I describe as a sense of "faux" technological holism, while Microsoft used its own set of devices that focus on consumption, profits, and consumer choice as the proper purpose of technology and intellectual property. In blog postings and corporate statements published during the dispute, company executives make rich use of metaphors such as the Android "ecosystem," intellectual property as an "economic engine," the idea of patents being used as "bullets," and of course, the over-arching metaphor of the "Patent War" itself. In other public writings, Google executives make use of allusion, referencing the U.S. Constitution as well as founding father and inventor Benjamin Franklin to create a sense of solidarity within their community.

The settlement press release, on the other hand, gives no sense of either company's overall philosophical understanding of intellectual property, as emerged from some of the rhetorical discourse surrounding the dispute itself. Gone are the allusions that call to mind Benjamin Franklin and the notion of invention as the work of geniuses working in isolation. Instead we are left with relatively dry statements such as "Separately, Google and Microsoft have agreed to collaborate on certain patent matters and anticipate working together in other areas to the future benefit of our customers" (Lee 2015).

Perhaps the most striking aspect of the settlement statement is its lack of metaphor. Some may read the corporate names "Google" and "Microsoft" in the first sentence as metonymy, but if the names are being used metaphorically, the effect is likely to be lost on the reader, since corporations are personified so often in this way. Another possible metaphor may be found in the word "agreement," which with a bit of stretching could be read as a euphemism for settlement. But aside from these two relatively weak possibilities, the statement seems to be devoid of metaphorical language. Compare this to the important role that metaphor played in earlier language used in the dispute: two very common metaphors involve the idea of technology as an "ecosystem" and the lawsuits themselves as a "war." The range of metaphors and rhetorical language used throughout the conflict should come as no surprise, since both sides were working diligently to build and support arguments aimed at gaining an edge in the patent dispute. What is surprising is the lack of such language when announcing the settlement.

Another helpful comparison comes in the form of an announcement made by Microsoft when the company settled a similar patent dispute with phone maker Samsung. This statement was issued by Microsoft's General Counsel Brad Smith and Deputy General Counsel Horacio Gutierrez:

> Intellectual property continues *to provide the engine that incentivizes* research and development, leading to inventions that put new products and services in the hands of millions of consumers and businesses.
>
> Put in this context, today's announcement does not yet represent the *beginning of the end* for this industry-wide assortment of issues. But to borrow a well-known phrase, perhaps we've now reached the *end of the beginning*.
>
> *2011, paras 4–5, emphasis added*

Here again we see the "intellectual property as engine" metaphor, which helps establish fundamental values for the lawsuits and settlement. We also see the use of antimetabole ("not ... the beginning of the end, ... but the end of the beginning") to look towards the future in the other patent disputes involving Android. The fact that this well-known phrase also can be read as an allusion to Winston Churchill speaking at the end of the Blitz in the midst of World War II also points to the kind of metaphors, stylistic devices, and allusions that *could* have been used to celebrate the final end of the patent war between Microsoft and Google.

It is easy to imagine war-like metaphors that could have been used to describe the settlement: truce, ceasefire, and treaty spring to mind. Similarly, the ecosystem concept is completely absent from the statement. Instead of a metaphor that implies technology as something that grows and evolves of its own accord, the companies themselves seem to be the only actors, as seen in this sentence: "The companies will dismiss all pending patent infringement litigation between them, including cases related to Motorola Mobility" (Lee 2015). The statement could have combined end-of-war metaphors with the ecosystem metaphor to describe the kind of peaceful cooperation and growth that the two companies envisioned for the future.

Finally, given the importance that genre plays in establishing a context model, it is worth considering the choice of genre itself. It could be argued that the lack of figurative language in a press release is simply a function of the genre – such releases are usually terse and direct. But a press release would be a natural choice of genre for executives and lawyers at all phases of a patent dispute. Yet for years the leaders of both companies chose to take their messages to the public through genres that invite rhetorical language: blog posts, open letters posted to the web, and even tweets. All of these genres invite engaging rhetorical language, and many of them invite direct feedback from the audience, whether the opposing side or the general public. In one exchange between Google's Chief Legal Officer and two of Microsoft's executives, the two sides went back and forth between blog posts and tweets, each replying to the other in escalating fashion, as is common on social media platforms. Outside observers would be forgiven if they thought that the participants were enjoying the highly public nature of the fight. The two sides could have easily chosen to celebrate the settlement with similar gusto on various social media platforms, but instead chose the terseness of a non-interactive press release.

Conclusion

Ultimately, the choice of genre combined with the absence of rhetorical language gives the impression of a manipulative silence. Recall that, according to Huckin, manipulative silences are those "that intentionally conceal relevant information from the reader or listener, to the advantage of the writer or speaker; unlike other types of silence, these silences depend for their success on not being noticed by the reader or listener" (2002, p. 351). Although it could certainly be argued that the omissions left by the press release are simply characteristics of the genre itself, accepting that argument would let speakers and writers off the hook for their manipulations, simply because they are skillful rhetors who know which genre to pick to maximize effectiveness in a given situation. If the companies had treated developments throughout the patent war with similarly terse press releases, then the choice of genre would not be remarkable and would not rise to the level of manipulation. However, when viewed through the lens of a fully developed context model it becomes clear that the choice of genre was deliberate.

Furthermore, comparing what was said in the press release with what was said throughout the rest of the dispute brings to light what *could* have been said but wasn't. The companies could have staked out the shared values that would undergird their collaborations in the future. Doing so might have given the audience a sense of the future the companies see for technological development and how intellectual property – patents, standards, and licensing agreements – would play into that future. Why the two companies chose not to take that opportunity remains a mystery. Nevertheless, I hope that identifying the press release as a manipulative genre choice can serve as a model to future scholars interested in understanding corporate communications. The difference between a non-manipulative genre choice and a manipulative one seems to lie in the intent of the author. Puzzling out authorial intent is always risky, but by developing a context model it becomes possible to make reasonable assumptions about what *could* have been said but wasn't.

References

Ahl, F. (2010) 'Quintilian and Lucan', in *Lucan's Bellum civile: Between Epic Tradition and Aesthetic Innovation*, Berlin, New York, De Gruyter, pp. 1–16.

Aristotle (2007) *Aristotle: On Rhetoric: A Theory of Civic Discourse* (trans. G. Kennedy), 2nd ed., New York, Oxford University Press.

Black, E. (1988) 'Secrecy and Disclosure as Rhetorical Forms', *Quarterly Journal of Speech*, vol. 74, no. 2, pp. 133–150.

Brown, M. T. (2009) 'LGBT Aging and Rhetorical Silence', *Sexuality Research and Social Policy Journal of NSRC*, vol. 6, no. 4, pp. 65–78 [Online]. DOI: 10.1525/srsp.2009.6.4.65.

Burgess, J. (2012) 'The iPhone Moment, the Apple Brand, and the Creative Consumer: From "Hackability and Usability" to Cultural Generation', in Hjorth, L., Burgess, Jean, and Richardson, I. (eds.), *Studying Mobile Media Cultural Technologies, Mobile Communication, and the iPhone*, Routledge Research in Cultural and Media Studies, New York, Routledge, pp. 28–42.

Fleckenstain, K. S. (2011) 'Out of "Wonderful Silence" Comes "Sweet Words": The Rhetorical Authority of St. Catherine of Siena', in *Silence and Listening as Rhetorical Arts*, Carbondale, Southern Illinois University Press, pp. 37–74.

Foss, S. K. (2018). *Rhetorical Criticism: Exploration and Practice*, 5th ed. Waveland.

Fox, M. V. (1983) 'Ancient Egyptian Rhetoric', *Rhetorica*, JSTOR, vol. 1, no. 1, pp. 9–22.

Glenn, C. (2004) *Unspoken: A Rhetoric of Silence*, Carbondale, Southern Illinois University Press.

Haviland, V. S. (2008) ' "Things Get Glossed Over": Rearticulating the Silencing Power of Whiteness in Education', *Journal of Teacher Education*, vol. 59, no. 1, pp. 40–54 [Online]. DOI: 10.1177/0022487107310751.

Hofstadter, R. (1964) 'The Paranoid Style in American Politics', *Harper's Magazine*, November, pp. 77–86.

Huckin, T. (2002) 'Textual Silence and the Discourse of Homelessness', *Discourse & Society*, vol. 13, no. 3, pp. 347–372 [Online]. DOI: 10.1177/0957926502013003054.

Huckin, T. (2019) 'Propaganda by Omission: The Case of the Topical Silence', in Murray, A. J. and Durrheim, K. (eds.), *Qualitative Studies of Silence: The Unsaid as Social Action*, New York, Cambridge University Press.

Johannesen, R. L. (1974) 'The Functions of Silence: A Plea for Communication Research', *Western Speech*, vol. 38, no. 1, pp. 25–35 [Online]. DOI: 10.1080/10570317409373806.

Lee, D. (2015) 'Google and Microsoft in Lawsuit Truce', *BBC News*, London, October 1 [Online]. Available at www.bbc.com/news/technology-34409077 (accessed April 16, 2019).

Levy, S. (2011) *In the Plex*, New York, Simon & Schuster.

Mack, K. (2011) 'Hearing Women's Silence in Transitional South Africa: Achmat Dangor's *Bitter Fruit*', in *Silence and Listening as Rhetorical Arts*, Carbondale, Southern Illinois University Press, pp. 195–213.

Mazzeo, J. A. (1962) 'St. Augustine's Rhetoric of Silence', *Journal of the History of Ideas*, vol. 23, no. 2, pp. 175–196 [Online]. DOI: 10.2307/2708154.

Meulen van der, R. and Rivera, J. (2016) *Gartner Says Worldwide Mobile Phone Sales Declined 1.7 Percent in 2012* [Online]. Available at http://archive.fo/Kpvst (accessed January 25, 2022).

Motorola Mobility (2011) 'Preliminary Special Proxy Statement', Motorola Mobility [Online]. Available at www.sec.gov/Archives/edgar/data/1495569/000119312511246952/d224940dprem14a.htm (accessed September 17, 2012).

Mueller, F. (2011) 'Microsoft vs. Motorola: The Patent Battlefield as of 11 Dec 11', Scribd [Online]. Available at www.scribd.com/doc/75443115/MicrosoftVsMotorola-11-12-11 (accessed December 27, 2012).

Ong, W. J. (1982) *Orality and Literacy: The Technologizing of the Word*, London; New York, Methuen.

Page, L. (2011) 'Supercharging Android: Google to Acquire Motorola Mobility', *Google: Official Blog* [Online]. Available at http://googleblog.blogspot.com/2011/08/supercharging-android-google-to-acquire.html (accessed August 27, 2012).

Page, L. (2014) 'Lenovo to Acquire Motorola Mobility', *Official Google Blog*, Corporate Blog [Online]. Available at http://googleblog.blogspot.com/2014/01/lenovo-to-acquire-motorola-mobility.html (accessed May 7, 2014).

Plato (2003) *Plato's Phaedrus* (trans. S. Scully), Newburyport, MA, Focus Pub./R. Pullins Co.

Scott, R. L. (1972) 'Rhetoric and Silence', *Western Speech*, vol. 36, no. 3, pp. 146–158 [Online]. DOI: 10.1080/10570317209373743.

Seigel, J. E. (1968) *Rhetoric and Philosophy in Renaissance Humanism: The Union of Eloquence and Wisdom, Petrarch to Valla* [Online]. Available at https://ebookcentral.proquest.com/lib/cwu/reader.action?docID=4071129.

Shapiro, C. (2001) 'Navigating the Patent Thicket: Cross Licenses, Patent Pools, and Standard Setting', in *Innovation Policy and the Economy*, vol. 1, Cambridge, MA, MIT Press, pp. 119–150 [Online]. Available at www.nber.org.ezp2.lib.umn.edu/chapters/c10778.pdf (accessed November 12, 2012).

Smith, B. and Gutierrez, H. (2011) 'Our Licensing Deal with Samsung: How IP Drives Innovation and Collaboration', *Microsoft on the Issues: News and Perspectives on Legal, Public Policy and Citizenship Topics* [Online]. Available at http://blogs.technet.com/b/microsoft_on_the_issues/archive/2011/09/28/our-licensing-deal-with-samsung-how-ip-drives-innovation-and-collaboration.aspx (accessed December 4, 2012).

Towles, A. (2016) *A Gentleman in Moscow*, New York, Viking.

Warren, T. (2013) *Xbox Video App Finally Arrives on Windows Phone* [Online]. Available at www.theverge.com/2013/12/18/5223842/xbox-video-windows-phone-app-download (accessed January 24, 2022).

Watson, S. (2011) 'Trying Silence: The Case of Denmark Vesey and the History of African American Rhetoric', in *Silence and Listening as Rhetorical Arts*, Carbondale, Southern Illinois University Press, pp. 75–93.

Welsh, J. (2016a) 'The Rhetoric of Reasonable and NonDiscriminatory: Conflicting Visions of Innovation in the Smart Phone Patent Wars', *Journal of Contemporary Rhetoric*, vol. 6, no. 3/4, pp. 112–126.

Welsh, J. (2016b) 'Patent Wars and Ecosystems: Metaphor and "Black Boxes"', *Rhetoric Review*, vol. 35, no. 4, pp. 348–360 [Online]. DOI: 10.1080/07350198.2016.1215003.

Zembylas, M. and Michaelides, P. (2004) 'The Sound of Silence in Pedagogy', *Educational Theory*, vol. 54, no. 2, pp. 193–210 [Online]. DOI: 10.1111/j.1741-5446.2004.00014.x.

4

FROM THE LEARNING OF CLASSICAL RHETORIC TO THE LEARNING OF COMMUNICATION

The Evolution of Rhetoric in the Secondary Education Systems of Spain and Portugal

Gracia Terol Plá

Introduction

During the twentieth century, rhetoric has been revitalized as a technique of persuasive discourse production and analysis (López Eire 1995: 10–11; Pujante 2022). The history of linguistic and literary education in Spain and Portugal from the nineteenth century until today constitutes an appropriate framework for describing this phenomenon. This chapter focuses on Spain and Portugal because their historical and educational similarities allow a comparative study of the development of rhetorical instruction in the two countries.

This process can be divided into two periods. First, in the nineteenth century, rhetorical instruction was reconfigured due to the dissemination of new philosophical perspectives and the consolidation of liberal regimes in the Iberian Peninsula. Modern philosophy contributed to the understanding of rhetoric as the art of expression charged with transmitting the knowledge discovered by other disciplines (Conley 1994: 167–171). At the same time, in the Anglo-Saxon context, "Belletristic Rhetoric" – which united the study of rhetoric and *Belles Lettres* – was being promoted to cover all genres of prose and poetry (Howell 1971: 442). Consequently, within the sphere of Spanish and Portuguese liberal education, classical rhetoric was no longer oriented towards the development of communicative skills. Rhetoric, combined with poetics, became a belletristic rhetoric, which was conceived for the transmission of national values through literary study. Deprived of its original functions, rhetoric gradually declined in study programs until its definitive substitution by the history of national literature, a discipline more suitable for meeting the political interests of the respective regimes.

DOI: 10.4324/9781003195276-6

As for the second period, the birth of pragmatics in the middle of the twentieth century encouraged attempts to integrate rhetorical theory into modern communication studies (Chico-Rico 2020; Pujante 2022) and to include communication skills learning as an essential part of education. In the Iberian Peninsula, such an educational reorientation was disdained by the dictatorial regimes of Francisco Franco in Spain (1939–1975) and António de Oliveira Salazar in Portugal (1926–1974). However, the emergence of democracy in both countries brought to light the necessity of providing citizens with tools for participating in public life.

During this second stage, learning first languages was oriented towards acquiring communicative competence. As Backlund and Morreale noted (2015: 13), this concept, which covers the necessary skills for effective discourse production, has its early roots in rhetoric, which is considered the most ancient discipline dedicated to the study of the phenomenon of communication. In fact, due to the adoption of this communicative approach, the study programs of *"Português"* and *"Lengua castellana y literatura"* incorporated discursive production techniques that represent a modern version of the five rhetorical operations.

This chapter analyses rhetoric's trajectory in Spanish and Portuguese education from the nineteenth century to date, attending to the countries' educational legislation and school manuals. The first sections are devoted to the common similar development of rhetorical instruction which is, in both cases, influenced by the liberal governments of the nineteenth century and the dictatorial and democratic regimens of the twentieth century.

The last sections focus on the precepts and didactic methods that current linguistic and literary education in both Spain and Portugal have inherited from classical rhetoric. These sections devote more space to the study of Portugal due to two particularities of its educational system: the Portuguese program includes practical methodological strategies related to traditional rhetorical training and the school manuals offer explicit rhetorical contents through the literary study of the Jesuit preacher, Father António Vieira (1608–1697), one of the great authors of Portuguese literature.

From Classical Rhetoric to Belletristic Rhetoric in Portuguese and Spanish Education

The Diffusion of Belletristic Rhetoric in Portugal and Spain

From the sixteenth century onwards, the secondary education systems of Spain and Portugal were monopolized by the Jesuits, whose teachings had spread the knowledge of classical rhetoric. By the middle of the eighteenth century, the expulsion of Jesuits from both countries presented an opportunity for the renovation of rhetorical theory. The Scottish Protestant preacher Hugh Blair, a member of the Scottish Enlightenment, played a fundamental role in the dissemination of belletristic rhetoric. Through his work *Lectures on Rhetoric and Belles Lettres*, published around 1783, his doctrine reached all of Enlightenment Europe and influenced the rhetorical theory of Spanish and Portuguese school manuals (Abbott 1989; Conley 1994: 220–223; Kennedy 1999: 282–285).

In Portugal, the first move to adapt rhetoric to the philosophy of the belletristic approach started in 1819 with the publication of the *Theoria do discurso Applicada á Lingoa Portugueza* by professor António Leite Ribeiro. In *Theoria*, the understanding of reason was driven by uniting ideology, grammar, logic, and rhetoric. Each discipline represented a particular function that would reach the common goal of developing the judgement of students. Ideology and logic focused on the content and formation of ideas; grammar considered their expression; and rhetoric, reduced to the theory of *elocutio*, was concerned with the stylistic manifestation of the qualities of thought.

In Spain, José Luis Munárriz translated Blair's *Lectures* in 1798 and, in 1815, published an abridged translation, *Compendio de las lecciones sobre la Retórica y Bellas Letras de Hugo Blair*, which was presented in three parts. The first described the general principles for the study of literature, i.e. the aesthetic aspects of taste and criticism and stylistic theory taken from the classical *elocutio* (1815: 7–178). Meanwhile, the second part discussed prose genres (1815: 180–308). When talking about oratory, the *Compendio* did include the rest of rhetorical theory – albeit a version suppressed by changes and critiques. In the *dispositio*, it remarked that it was preferable to prepare the composition following a clearer and more rational method. The *inventio* was considered useless since what was essential was knowing the speech's subject matter, and the three *genera causarum* were substituted by legal, political, and religious eloquence. Lastly, the third part of the *Compendio* explored verse genres, taking poetics into consideration (1815: 309–444).

In Portugal and Spain the wish to put an end to the rhetorical excesses resulting from the previous scholastic tradition led to the dissemination of a more philosophical belletristic rhetoric that was tailored to the ascendant literature theory (Agnew 1998: 25–33).

The new rhetorical current reached the educational sphere with the educational reforms of the Spanish and Portuguese liberal governments. The purpose of the liberal reforms was to create the first state educational systems which were adapted to the new class society. Secondary education had as its goal the promotion of national and liberal values that would ensure the stability of the regime as well as fulfill the aspirations of an emerging middle class that would be in charge of leading societal roles (Ávila de Azevedo 1972: 365; De Puelles Benítez 1998: 78).

Humanistic disciplines were becoming tools for the creation of a national spirit, reducing the pedagogical presence of classical humanities and turning the focus towards the history of Spanish and Portuguese literature respectively (García Jurado 2005). In this respect, rhetoric and poetics ceased to complement the classical languages in order to acquire a new function as auxiliaries to the study of literature.

In Portugal, the educational reforms of the liberal government of Passos Manuel (1936) established in secondary schools the subject of "*A Oratoria, a Poetica, e a Litteratura Classica, especialmente a Portugueza*". In Spain, the consolidation of the liberal educational model began with the *Ley de Bases* of 1857, a law promulgated by the minister Claudio Moyano that merged rhetoric and poetics into "*Principios de Literatura*". In both countries, rhetoric and poetics were perceived as precedents of the study of the history of national literature. In the new subjects, rhetorical content is divided first into "common rules to all of the discourse genres" – which concerned style and expression, hence reflecting the theory of *elocutio* – and, secondly, into "particular rules to prose literature genres". In this second division, amongst other genres, we find oratory and a brief explanation of the five rhetorical operations (*inventio, dispositio, elocutio, memoria* and *actio*) (Terol Plá 2020a).

The Reorientation of Rhetoric Reflected in the School Manuals of Father Jeronymo d'Andrade and Raimundo de Miguel

Soon, it was understood that what benefited the new social order the most was the study of the history of national literature rather than any classical precepts. Although in the next few decades the structure of literary education remained as previously described, rhetorical and poetic content were both gradually decreasing in favor of literary history. While rhetoric and poetics were associated with the educational program of an old regime whose upheaval was desired, the history of national literature favoured the transmission of national values and could meet the interests of the liberal regimes. The decrease of rhetorical and poetic content influenced contemporaneous school manuals.

An example hereof is *Primeiros elementos de Literatura Classica, Oratoria, e Poetica* (1847) written by Father Jeronymo Emiliano d'Andrade. This brief manual covered the five rhetorical operations, simplifying their theory as much as possible (1847: 41–83) in order to specifically offer the most basic notions necessary for students to memorize. It was not about teaching a communicative technique but rather about offering the general characteristics of the oratory genre for its later use in literary analysis. Over the course of the century, the contents in literary history were amplified until the latter's own manuals appeared; in the meantime, treatises on rhetoric started to shorten and shift their focus, in particular towards the *elocutio*.

In Spain, the "rhetoric and poetics" manuals adopted a similar scheme to the Portuguese ones. A good example can be found in the *Curso elemental teórico práctico de retórica y poética*, which Raimundo de Miguel, Professor of Rhetoric and Poetics at the San Isidro Secondary School of Madrid, published in 1857 (we consulted the fourth edition of 1875). Much like other school treatises, the *Curso* was divided between an explanation of the rules common to every literature composition in which we find the classical *elocutio* (1875: 5–70), and the particular rules extracted from rhetoric and poetics with regard to each literary genre. Rhetoric and poetics were applied to the verse and prose genres, respectively. Since oratory was found among the prose genres, the rest of the rhetorical operations were given a similar treatment to that in Munárriz's *Compendio* (1875: 70–94).

Therefore, the classical *elocutio* was set apart from the rest of the rhetorical doctrines to become a sort of general stylistic literary feature. The rest of the rhetorical operations endured as part of the historical study of the three oratorical genres then known as sacred, forensic and parliamentary oratory. However, the rhetorical operations experienced a progressive reduction when the discovery and disposition of contents – *inventio* and *dispositio* – were associated with logic, while *memoria* and *actio* also lost their place in this mostly theoretical education (Aradra Sánchez 1997).

Unlike ecclesiastic rhetoric, which stayed much more loyal to the classical scheme due to its practical purpose of training future preachers, the civil school treaties tended to be closer to Blair's postulates. Increasingly subordinate to the teachings of literature, rhetoric in state secondary education increased its theoretical focus and lessened its practical aspects (López-Muñoz and Terol Plá 2021: 660). If previously rhetoric had been deprived of any oratorical exercises, in the end, it also stopped being oriented towards composition or other practical purposes.

Although liberal governments entailed new social liberties, rhetoric was not presented as a communication technique for future citizens. This was also the case in the Anglo-Saxon countries: "Several developments in the nineteenth century undermined the association of rhetorical skills with civic participation, perhaps most notably the decline of oratorical rhetoric" (Love 2006: 29).

Oratorical training took place in higher education studies aimed at a select minority designed to be the future leading elites who would also need the skill of eloquence to intervene in public life. In Spain and Portugal, political rhetoric developed outside of the classrooms in parliamentary, popular, or ecclesiastic spaces. Yet, secondary schools spread a theoretical and literary rhetoric destined to train a middle class that was aware of its social role and detached from public controversies – a tendency, as highlighted by Miller (1993: 12), that also appeared in the Anglo-Saxon context:

> From the outset, such ideals were more conducive to the study of belletristic literature than to rhetoric, and the rhetoricians who first institutionalized modern cultural studies helped to establish a tradition that would gradually but programmatically eliminate political rhetoric as an area of study in the humanities, leaving rhetoric confined to skills-oriented composition courses that were as far removed from public controversies as basic courses in learned languages had traditionally been.

The confusion of rhetoric and poetics with the simple *elocutio* – a trend dating back centuries – marked the culmination of the "literaturization" of rhetoric, a process whereby rhetoric became distanced from public eloquence, with its orientation towards literature studies leading to the consequent loss of its original identity (Kennedy 1999: 3). In Spain and Portugal, rhetoric and poetics reached the end of the nineteenth century in a mutilated state, practically expelled as independent disciplines from the education system (López-Muñoz and Terol Plá 2021: 665).

From Belletristic Rhetoric to Communication in Portuguese and Spanish Education

In the second half of the century, an increasing interest in the field of discourse contributed to two parallel phenomena: the revitalization of rhetoric through the so-called "new rhetorics", and the arrival of pragmatics.

The resurgence of rhetoric was encouraged by linguists and philosophers in Liège (Groupe μ), Cambridge (Stephen Toulmin), Brussels (Chaïm Perelman), and Frankfurt (Jürgen Habermas) (Conley 1994: 285–304). However, the attempts to revise rhetoric as an argumentative theory (Perelman and Olbrechts-Tyteca 1958) or a figurative language theory (Groupe μ 1970) did not imply recovering the entire rhetorical system. The fragmentation of the discipline hindered the adoption of a wider perspective which considered the whole of rhetoric as a discursive theory.

This wider perspective of the phenomenon of communication would start to emerge out of new pragmatic theories. In the European context, pragmatics was understood as "a functional perspective on every aspect of linguistic behaviour" (Huang 2007: 4). The development of pragmatics led to the emergence of new disciplines (textual linguistic and discourse analysis) that took discourse as a sample to be analyzed attending to contextual factors in order to determine its meaning.

These theoretical advances eventually influenced the educational field. Out of the concept of "communicative competence" coined by D. H. Hymes (1972), and from Anglo-Saxon studies in didactics and applied linguistics, a new communicative approach in the teaching of languages started to be shaped under the influence of pragmatics, philosophy of language (Austin 1962; Searle 1969), and systemic functional linguistics (Halliday et al. 1964; Halliday 1985). Also known as "communicative language teaching", this approach understood language learning as a functional appropriation of the knowledge and skills needed to use the language in an efficient way in different communicational contexts (Canale and Swain 1980).

Nevertheless, in both countries (Spain and Portugal), the adoption of this approach was delayed as a consequence of the educational principles established during the dictatorships of Francisco Franco (1939–1975) and António de Oliveira Salazar (1926–1974). During this period, the linguistic-literary education in both countries focused on the study of the grammar and history of national literature in order to disseminate a patriotic and Christian morality in line with the ideals of the respective regimes. The Spanish language and literature questionnaires recommended to analyse literary works related to "temas de formación moral, religiosa y patriótica" (themes for moral, religious, and patriotic education) (Ministerio de Educación Nacional 1939: 12). Likewise, the "*Português*" program in the *Decreto n° 27:058 de 14 de outubro de 1936* prescribed the study of national authors as a "pretexto para a reflexão moral e cívica" (pretext for moral and civic reflection) (Ministério da Educação Nacional 1936: 1244).

By the end of the twentieth century, the official secondary educational structures in Spain and Portugal had still not established a systematic education for developing communicative skills. In two political systems that tried to reduce behavior to a number of absolute truths, there was no real interest in developing the expressive skills of students, let alone their argumentative capacity. Whilst education was designed as a program for ideological inculcation and not as the enlightenment of citizens for the purpose of participation in public life, there was no place to develop communicative competencies. In the same way, rhetoric's origins and prosperity were linked to the democratic period and experienced a decline with the loss of civic liberties (López Eire 2007: 60–63).

The advent of democracy in Spain and Portugal and the emergence of more opportunities for participating in public life increased interest in the study of discourse. New works regarding the development of rhetoric in Spanish and Portuguese educational history appeared (Pinto de Castro 1973; Vieira Mendes 1989; Marques 1989; Artaza 1989; López Grigera 1994; Luján Atienza 1999).

Although rhetoric is not considered as an antecedent of pragmatics (Schlieben-Lange 1975: 28–29), another set of works identified several similarities between the two disciplines from the fields of philosophy, linguistics and literary theory (as we see in Pozuelo Yvancos 1988; Albaladejo 1991; López Eire 1995; López-Muñoz and Salazar García 1998). Despite their differences, the origins of rhetoric and pragmatics were connected with a similar perception of the distance between reality and language, between a message and its implicit meaning. Rhetoric and pragmatics share a common view of communication as an exchange of information and influence. Considering that discourse does not transmit neutral meanings and its interpretation depends on the context, both disciplines analyse communicative techniques and propose strategies to use language in an efficient way. In addition, rhetoric and pragmatics understand *logos* as an action unable to reflect objective reality, but useful for modifying such reality (López Eire 1995: 150; Terol Plá 2020b: 236–238).

Different disciplines interested in the phenomenon of communication (pragmatics, textual linguistic or discourse analysis, among others) encouraged new attempts to recover rhetoric, now understood as a set of communicative techniques that allowed for the elaboration and analysis of discourse. In the field of literary theory, Antonio García Berrio (1984) suggested the creation of a general rhetoric that would incorporate contemporary knowledge about discourse. From then on, rhetoric would continue to influence linguistics and literary theory (Albaladejo 1991) and would apply its contents to discursive analyses of specific areas, such as publicity (López Eire 1995), politics (López Eire and De Santiago Guervós 2000), and mass media (Gonçalves Herédia 2008;

Gutiérrez-Sanz 2022). Furthermore, García Berrio's general rhetoric led to two different approaches in rhetorical studies: cultural rhetoric, proposed as a methodological system to analyse the cultural dimensions of various kinds of discourse (Albaladejo 2013: 4–16), and constructivist rhetoric, conceived as an analytical model based on constructivist positions that study the construction of meaning through communicative practices (Pujante 2022: 52–54).

At the same time, communication studies reached both countries' educational spheres. The dictatorships having ended, educational reforms in Portugal (1986) and Spain (1990) took place in an attempt to "democratize" their systems by establishing as a general goal of secondary education the education of free, critical and independent citizens. That goal implied providing students with the tools that would help them manage themselves in an interconnected global structure in which the autonomy of individuals entailed producing, interpreting, and exchanging information (Castells 1996).

Accordingly, the study programs of *"Português"* (Ministério de Educação 1991: 8–25) and *"Lengua castellana y literatura"* (Ministerio de Educación y Ciencia 1991: 53) adopted a communicative approach promoting an efficient use of language as the main objective of the subjects. Since then, the acquisition of communicative skills has been included among the specific ends of secondary education, as seen in both countries' recent educational legislation – the *Decreto-Lei n.º 55/2018* (Article 19.º) in Portugal (Ministério da Educação e Ciência 2018) and the *Ley Orgánica 3/2020, de 29 de diciembre, por la que se modifica la Ley Orgánica 2/2006, de 3 de mayo, de Educación* (Article 2.2) in Spain (Ministerio de Educación y Formación Profesional 2020).

Nowadays, communication education remains closely linked to the learning of the mother language in the subjects *"Português"* and *"Lengua castellana y literatura"* whose objectives are set in the *Perfil dos alunos à saída da escolaridade obrigatória* (D'Oliveira Martins 2017) and in the *Real Decreto 217/2022, de 29 de marzo* (Ministerio de Educación y Formación Profesional 2022) respectively. In both cases, the teaching of the mother tongue implies, above all, the acquisition of communicative competence. Due to influential factors such as the technological revolution and the consolidation of democracy, "communicative competence" has reached new dimensions that overtake the purely discursive, pragmatic, and socio-linguistic aspects.

Beyond covering the linguistic and didactic contributions of languages, the concept of "communicative competence" now explicitly points to the development of a critical mindset and the exercise of active citizenship, two dimensions related to rhetoric since its origins in the fifth century BC (López Eire 2007: 50–51). In addition, the connection between rhetoric and communicative competence had been previously highlighted by Backlund and Morreale (2015: 14): "Without a doubt, modern conceptions of communication competence have a solid foundation in the study of rhetoric." Spanish and Portuguese educational legislation already suggests a "rhetorical competence" that involves communicative, critical, and civic training, in other words: (1) communicative skills that allow for the efficient use of the language; (2) the critical capacity to handle information and argue in a substantiated way; and (3) the involvement of the latter skills in the active exercise of democratic citizenship (D'Oliveira Martins 2017: 21–25; Ministerio de Educación y Formación Profesional 2022: 27).

According to the relation between this rhetorical competence and the learning of first languages, it would be interesting to analyze how the subjects of *"Português"* and *"Lengua castellana y literatura"* are structured to achieve these goals. This curricular approach has led to the inclusion of some precepts and didactic methods related to rhetoric in the teaching of the mother language. In this sense, the current linguistic and literary education of both countries reflects a rhetorical inheritance, which is more noticeable in the Portuguese case, as we will see in the next sections.

The Current Learning of Communication in the Study Programs and School Manuals of Portuguese and Spanish

The Learning of Communication in the Study Programs of Portuguese and Spanish

Rhetorical training is reflected in the study programs of *"Português"* (Buescu et al. 2014) and *"Lengua castellana y literatura"* (Ministerio de Educación y Formación Profesional 2022). The two study programs share several features, organizing the subject into four sections: "grammar", "literary education", "written communication" (reading comprehension and written expression), and "oral communication" (oral comprehension and expression). In both cases, all of these elements aim to develop the student's communicative competence as the ultimate end of the discipline.

The "communication" sections promote skills that enable the comprehension and interpretation of texts as well as a critical assessment of their form and content. In addition, they include oral and written production techniques that constitute a modern version of the five rhetorical operations. The first step of "planning the text" is connected with invention (*inventio*) and arrangement (*dispositio*) because it entails strategies for selecting information, finding arguments, and organizing the speech into different parts. The process of "textualization" relies on the principles of correctness, clarity, ornamentation, and propriety, which are specific characteristics of elocution (*elocutio*). Lastly, the "declamation" of the speech attends to some aspects of "memory" (*memoria*) and "delivery" (*actio*), such as mnemonic devices or the control of nonverbal communication.

These discursive production techniques are included in the previously mentioned study programs of both countries (Buescu et al. 2014: 45–47; Ministerio de Educación y Formación Profesional 2022: 126–129). The fundamental difference between the programs consists in the methodological strategies proposed by the Portuguese document to systematically train concrete abilities. Furthermore, review of these strategies reflects some parallels between the Portuguese program and classical instruction in rhetoric.

All of the Portuguese language's instruction is based on the students' direct contact with a selection of representative works of Portuguese literature studied in chronological order to illustrate each literary period. The selected works represent various literary genres (drama, epic, novel, and so on) associated with certain textual typologies (i.e. dialogue, narrative text, descriptive text, etc.). For example, the unit focused on the Jesuit preacher António Vieira and his most representative sermon, the *Sermão de Santo António aos peixes* (1654), studies the literary genre of oratory and the features of political discourse (Buescu et al. 2014: 17).

Each unit of the subject is focused on an author's work and begins with activities that include reading aloud and analyzing the literary work in detail. The analysis addresses the work's historical-literary context and some aspects of its content (the theme, the structure, or the development of ideas) or form (the style or the use of rhetorical figures), evaluating the suitability of these elements to the context, literary genre, and authorial intention (an example of the case of Father António Vieira's sermon is provided in the next section) (Buescu et al. 2014: 19).

Moreover, the analysis also examines grammatical and pragmatic issues in the text. In this respect, the study of grammar is conceived of as a preliminary stage to the acquisition of discursive skills; thus, lower educational levels touch on grammar lessons while learners' secondary education is limited to the revision of grammatical content through the study of literary texts. The latter level's meticulous literary analysis aspires to stimulate the communicative skills of the student by offering them different models for imitation. Later, the student is expected to adapt the resources employed by the authors to their own compositions (Buescu et al. 2014: 5–10).

Likewise, in the classical education system, the secondary level of instruction began with grammatical studies and commentaries on literary texts. The *praelectio* included reading aloud and analyzing the texts in terms of grammatical issues, features of the literary genre, and historical context. Since the exposition of these authors implicated a preparation for the rhetorical stage, the analysis concentrated on literary aspects such as the style, structure, or adaptation of the content and expressions to the genre and the author's intentions. The objective was to provide pupils with *exempla* for the stylistic and literary *imitatio* (Clark 1957: 59–66; Bonner 2012: 212–249).

In Portuguese language teaching, the literary study is characteristically followed by students' training in written and oral expression. The training method is composed of a series of exercises in composition for improving such discursive skills as summarizing, explaining, describing, and arguing. First, the students' assignments entail the modification of a given text by amplifying, compressing, and reformulating its topic. At a later stage, the curriculum prescribes practices based on concrete textual genres, namely synthesis, exposition, critical description and commentary, and an argumentative essay. For instance, the program establishes as a goal of the first level of a student's secondary education: "Produzir os seguintes géneros de texto: síntese e apreciação crítica" (To produce the following textual genres: synthesis and critical description and commentary) (Buescu et al. 2014: 45). Also, the curriculum sets these objectives for the last level of secondary education: "Produzir os seguintes géneros de texto: texto de opinião e diálogo argumentativo" (To produce the following textual genres: argumentative essay and argumentative dialogue) (Buescu et al. 2014: 53).

These practices are graded in order of difficulty, so that the students start performing simple tasks like synthesis and finish with the successful completion of complex exercises that combine a number of the communicative skills trained throughout the preceding genres. For example, an argumentative essay could require an exposition and a description, in addition to an argument.

> Começa-se pela capacidade de sintetizar textos, essencial na aquisição de conhecimentos; passa-se, seguidamente, para o aprofundamento da capacidade de expor temas de forma planificada e coerente; finalmente, elegem-se a apreciação crítica e o texto de opinião como géneros que representam, neste nível, o coroar do desenvolvimento da expressão escrita.

> (It begins with the ability of summarizing texts, essential in the acquisition of knowledge; immediately, it follows with the development of the ability of explaining topics in a planned and coherent way; finally, it selects critical description and commentary, and the argumentative essay as genres which represent, at this level, the highest point of the development of facility in written expression.)
>
> *Buescu et al. 2014: 9*

In this way, the method involves a wide range of practices, from the production of different parts of speech to the elaboration of complete argumentative speeches which, in most instances, must be delivered orally. Furthermore, these compositions must develop a theme associated with the analyzed literary work.

Likewise, in classical instruction, oral and written exercitation started by modifying passages of the studied works. These practices were followed by a sequence of preliminary exercises in composing of increasing difficulty called *progymnasmata* or *praeexercitamenta*. The program included simple compositions designed to train basic communicative skills that would be necessary for the production of discourse (i.e. synthesis, narration, and description, among other abilities). The exercises were preliminary to the elaboration and declamation of complete argumentative speeches in the judicial and deliberative genres. In addition, topics for such compositions were extracted from the literary works that had been previously commented upon (Clark 1957: 177–261; Bonner 2012: 250–276).

The analysis of these strategies reflected in the Portuguese program suggests the existence of an "implicit rhetorical tradition" – a concept proposed to designate the set of similarities detected between the Portuguese model and the rhetorical program taught in ancient times and perpetuated by the Jesuit educational system. It seems that the study program of *"Português"*, by abandoning the grammatical approach and encouraging a rhetorical education for future citizens, in an indirect way has recovered teaching methods related to the rhetorical program for literary analysis and the learning of communicative skills.

However, in the Spanish study program *"Lengua castellana y literatura"*, this "implicit rhetorical tradition" is reduced simply to the discursive production techniques due to a lack of methodological strategies for connecting the four sections' theories and practices. For instance, the training in written expression involves the processes of "planning", "textualization" and "revision" of the text, without offering a set of particular exercises in composition (Ministerio de Educación y Formación Profesional 2022: 129). Likewise, the sections focused on oral expression determine as a general objective the performance of planned oral tasks with different levels of formality. These sections mention some exercises (for example, the declamation of argumentative discourse) and establish several standards of evaluation, such as the correct pronunciation or the control of nonverbal communication (Ministerio de Educación y Formación Profesional 2022: 126).

Nevertheless, the program fails to offer the gradual and systematic method that we find in the Portuguese model. The Spanish program treats the different parts of the subject separately and pays significant attention to the content and standards of evaluation, omitting specific recommendations about methodology.

The Learning of Rhetoric through Father Vieira's Sermons in Portuguese School Manuals

Apart from the pedagogical techniques described above, the subject of *"Português"* explicitly presents content concerning rhetoric; this is imparted in the second level of students' secondary education, corresponding to the eleventh academic year of compulsory education attended by students between the ages of 16 and 17. We will see examples of such content in two of the school manuals used in the subject produced by the publishing houses Asa (Vilas-Boas and Vieira 2016) and Areal (Pereira and Delindro 2016).

The explicit teaching of rhetoric in Portugal stems from one of the great authors of Portuguese literature in the seventeenth century – the Jesuit preacher António Vieira (1608–1697), the greatest exponent of Portuguese baroque oratory. The presence of this author in the subject's curriculum effectively requires school manuals to teach rhetorical content in order to adequately study his most representative sermon, the *Sermão de Santo António aos peixes* (1654). In the case of Father António Vieira's sermon, the program recommends that one analyzes the following aspects: the author's historical-literary context, his intention, and the sermon's persuasive mechanisms (the argumentative structure or the use of different rhetorical figures to express social critiques) (Buescu et al. 2014: 19).

In the first unit, both manuals focus on the *Sermão de Santo António aos peixes* and, before the literary analysis, they contextualize it by portraying in different sections the author and his work's historical context. This literary-historical contextualization interprets the persuasive intention of the sermon as well as the social function of preaching as a political act and form of performance intended to delight the audience (Pereira and Delindro 2016: 34; Vilas-Boas and Vieira 2016: 13). Through Vieira's work, the unit tackles the literary genre of oratory and the characteristics of argumentative text. Its explanation of this genre includes the objectives of eloquence (*docere, delectare, movere*) and the three means of persuasion (*logos, ethos, pathos*) (Vilas-Boas and Vieira 2016: 12). In addition to highlighting the particular features of baroque oratory, the manuals present other content associated with the rhetorical operations of *inventio, dispositio,* and *elocutio.*

Meanwhile, different sections focus on argumentation theory and address the use of syllogisms and different types of arguments (quantity or quality arguments, analogy arguments, authority arguments, etc.) (Pereira and Delindro 2016: 46; Vilas-Boas and Vieira 2016: 34). The treatment of *dispositio* consists of a description of the discourse's components and their identification in the sermon structure:

> Em Vieira, autor de um impressionante número de *Sermões* (cerca de duzentos) e *Cartas*, "o plano do sermão corresponde sempre, de modo geral, ao plano clássico, constituído por um *exórdio* (em que [o pregador] geralmente termina com uma breve oração invocando a Virgem), *desenvolvimento* (argumentação, demonstração, confirmação) e *peroração* ou conclusão.

> [In Vieira, author of an impressive number of *Sermões* (two hundred, approximately) and *Cartas*, "always the sermon's plan generally corresponds to the classical structure, composed by an *introduction* (in which [the preacher] generally ends with a brief invocation of the Virgin), *development* (argumentation, demonstration, confirmation) and *peroration* or conclusion.]
>
> *Pereira and Delindro 2016: 34*

Lastly, the theory of *elocutio* is reflected in the explanation of the main rhetorical figures of speech and the use of humor and allegories as a means for conducting social and political critique. In this way it highlights the validity of the rhetorical doctrine in contemporaneous oratory:

Na oratória barroca de Vieira, mas também no discurso político da atualidade, a **argumentação** e a **alegoria**, ou a **metáfora**, têm lugar de destaque. A argumentação consiste na organização estratégica de um conjunto de razões com o intuito de persuadir e transformar. A alegoria é um recurso expressivo que consiste na expressão de uma ideia ou conceito através de uma representação figurativa, convocando-se assim dois planos: o sentido literal e o sentido figurado. A eloquência não dispensa também a **ironia** e a **sátira**, poderosos instrumentos de persuasão em todas as épocas.

[The **argumentation, allegory** or **metaphor** play a fundamental role in Vieira's baroque oratory as well as in modern political oratory. The argumentation consists in the strategic organization of a set of reasons with the purpose of persuading and transforming. The allegory is an expressive resource which consists in the expression of an idea or concept through a figurative representation, combining two levels: the literal and figurative meaning. In addition, eloquence does not exclude the use of **irony** and **satire**, powerful means of persuasion in all the epochs.]

Pereira and Delindro 2016: 65; the bolded words appeared in the original text

The aforementioned knowledge must be applied in the manual's suggested activities in order to analyze the literary work. These activities may entail identifying the rhetorical figures of speech, the components of the discourse, the cited arguments, or the biblical passage which is the central thread of the sermon. In other cases, the student is asked to assess the persuasive efficiency of some fragments, as we see in the next example:

Sabendo que a eloquência barroca tinha como objetivos *docere* (ensinar), *delectare* (encantar) e *movere* (persuadir), apresenta, justificadamente, uma opinião sobre a função deste momento do sermão.

[Taking into account that baroque eloquence had as its objectives *docere* (to instruct), *delectare* (to delight) and *movere* (to persuade), you must present a justified opinion about the function of this sermon's moment.]

Vilas-Boas and Vieira 2016: 29

In accordance with the views expressed above, rhetorical theory can also be used for the analysis of other non-literary argumentative texts such as political speeches or opinion articles in the field of journalism.

Rhetorical content is described in order to be applied to both the textual analyses as well as the communicative exercises of the students. To do so, the manuals prescribe formulating argumentative texts and academic debates about topics related to the work of Father Vieira – for instance, the use of allegory as a means of social criticism or the influence of the doctrine and the natural gifts in the orator's training (Pereira and Delindro 2016: 53, 70).

The Communicative Approach of Spanish School Manuals

In the subject *"Lengua castellana y literatura"*, the stage of learning argumentation takes place in the fourth course of compulsory secondary education attended by students between 15 and 16 years of age. The plan for this argumentative teaching is reflected in the school manuals of the publishing houses Casals (Reina 2021) and Anaya (Gutiérrez et al. 2021).

Unlike the Portuguese case, the Spanish model does not present any study of rhetoric because the curriculum of the course includes neither the study of oratory as a literary genre nor a representative orator in Spanish literature. Due to the lack of an explicit rhetorical tradition, this analysis of Spanish manuals will be shorter and will only focus on highlighting the content and exercises suggested for the communicative education of Spanish students in secondary school.

The organization of the Spanish school manuals reflects the approach of the discipline's program. As the program does not include defined methodological strategies, the manuals address, in different segments, grammar, literature, and communication, without making any explicit connection between the fields. Notably, the influence of pragmatics is present in the units dedicated to communication; here, the principles of relevance, courtesy, and cooperation, conversational precepts, and the importance of adequacy in the communicative context are all referred to. For instance, a definition of the principles of courtesy and cooperation can be consulted in Gutiérrez et al. (2021: 112).

Meanwhile, we find the study of argumentation in the communication segment. This skill is covered by the sections in which the types of arguments and fallacies, the structure of the argumentative text, and the characteristics of the debate genre are presented (Reina 2021: 87–90; Gutiérrez et al. 2021: 178–181). With the intention of putting into practice what has been learned, brief texts are added; the students must identify the thesis, types of arguments, and argumentation structure of the texts. In order to exercise their oral and written skills, students are asked to compose an oral exposition and are offered a number of guidelines for choosing the topic, the discourse's planning, and its declamation (Gutiérrez et al. 2021: 150). Finally, the manuals suggest conducting an academic debate that is adjusted to the following framework: thesis presentation, argumentation, conclusion, and time for replies and counter-arguments (Reina 2021: 83; Gutiérrez et al. 2021: 184–187).

Conclusion

In both Spain and Portugal, the evolution of education in terms of communicative techniques was dependent on the contributions of the respective countries' academic fields as well as the interests of consecutive governments. In this process, we can distinguish two important stages.

On the one hand, in the nineteenth century, philosophical ideas encouraged the "literaturization" of rhetoric. This tendency coincided with the aim of the countries' liberal governments to use literary study as a means of disseminating national values and culminated in the exclusion of rhetoric from the field of secondary education.

On the other hand, throughout the twentieth century, pragmatics, also initiated within the philosophical domain (specifically, in the philosophy of language), boosted the recovery of rhetoric as the science of discourse. With the fall of the dictatorships in Spain and Portugal, advances in the educational field promoted a rhetorical training that combined the communicative approach, developed from linguistics and didactics, with the democratic values linked to rhetoric since the latter's origin. These values are reflected in the relation between the concept of "communicative competence" and the exercise of active citizenship, as previously seen in both countries' recent educational legislation.

While the two countries have to date followed similar paths, the main difference between them lies in the pedagogical approach towards students' communicational training when learning their mother tongue. The teaching of both languages assumed a new approach through the contributions of pragmatics. However, "*Português*" also resorted to didactic methods related to the traditional instruction of rhetoric, especially practices that involved the production of different parts of a speech and the elaboration of complete argumentative speeches. Furthermore, content regarding rhetorical theory was added because of the presence of Father Vieira in the canon of main authors in the subject's curriculum. Unlike the Spanish model, the Portuguese system currently offers a practical rhetorical training that is oriented towards literary analysis as well as the acquisition of communicative techniques.

References

Abbott, D. P. (1989) 'The Influence of Blair's Lectures in Spain', *Rhetorica: A Journal of the History of Rhetoric* 7(3), 275–289.

Agnew, L. (1998) 'The Civic Function of Taste: A Re-Assessment of Hugh Blair's Rhetorical Theory', *Rhetoric Society Quarterly* 28(2), 25–36.

Albaladejo, T. (1991) *Retórica*, Madrid: Síntesis.

Albaladejo, T. (2013) 'Retórica cultural, lenguaje retórico y lenguaje literario', *Tonos digital: Revista de estudios filológicos* 25, 1–21.

Aradra Sánchez, R. M. (1997) *De la Retórica a la Teoría de la Literatura (siglos XVIII y XIX)*, Murcia: Universidad de Murcia.

Artaza, E. (1989) *El 'ars narrandi' en el siglo XVI español. Teoría y práctica*, Bilbao: Universidad de Deusto.

Austin, J. L. (1962) *How to Do Things with Words*, Oxford: Clarendon Press.

Ávila de Azevedo, R. (1972) *Tradição educativa e renovação pedagógica (Subsídios para a História da Pedagogia em Portugal – Século XIX)*, Porto: Oficinas Gráficos Reunidos.

Backlund, P. M. and Morreale, S. P. (2015) 'Communication Competence: Historical Synopsis, Definitions, Applications, and Looking to the Future', in A. F. Hannawa and B. H. Spitzberg (eds.), *Communication Competence*, Berlin: De Gruyter, 11–38.

Bonner, S. (2012) *Education in Ancient Rome. From the Elder Cato to the Younger Pliny* (first published in 1977), London/New York: Routledge.

Buescu, H. C., Maia, L. C., Silva, M. G. and Rocha, M. R. (2014) *Programa e Metas Curriculares de Português. Ensino Secundário*, Lisboa: Ministério da Educação e Ciência.

Canale, M. and Swain, M. (1980) 'Theoretical Bases of Communicative Approaches to Second Language Teaching and Testing', *Applied Linguistics* 1, 1–47.

Castells, M. (1996) *The Information Age: Economy, Society and Culture. Volume I: The Rise of the Network Society*, Cambridge, MA: Blackwell Publishers Inc.

Chico-Rico, F. (2020) 'Desarrollos actuales de los estudios retóricos en España: la Retórica desde la Teoría de la Literatura', *Rétor* 2, 133–164.

Clark, D. L. (1957) *Rhetoric in Greco-Roman Education*, Morningside Heights, NY: Columbia University Press.

Conley, E. T. (1994) *Rhetoric in the European Tradition*, Chicago: University of Chicago Press.

D'Andrade, J. E. (1847) *Primeiros elementos de Literatura Classica, Oratoria, e Poetica para uso das lições de cór dos estudantes da quinta cadeira do Lyceo Nacional da cidade D'Angra do Heroismo*, Angra do Heroismo: Typographia Do Angrense.

De Miguel, R. (1875) *Curso elemental teórico-práctico de retórica y poética: acomodado a la índole de los estudios de la segunda enseñanza, conforme al programa oficial*, 4th ed., Madrid: Agustín Jubera.

De Puelles Benítez, M. (1998) *Textos sobre la Educación en España (Siglo XIX)*, Madrid: Universidad Nacional de Educación a Distancia (UNED).

D'Oliveira Martins, G. (coord.) (2017) *Perfil dos Alunos à Saída da Escolaridade Obrigatória*, Lisboa: Ministério da Educação/Direção-Geral da Educação (DGE).

García Berrio, A. (1984) 'Retórica como ciencia de la expresividad: presupuestos para una retórica general', *ELUA: Estudios de Lingüística. Universidad de Alicante* 2, 7–59.

García Jurado, F. (2005) 'La Literatura como historia. Entre el pensamiento ilustrado y la reacción romántica', in F. García Jurado (coord.), *La historia de la literatura grecolatina en el siglo XIX español: espacio social y literario*, Málaga: Universidad de Málaga, 47–65.

Gonçalves Herédia, L. C. (2008) 'A Retórica do Jornalismo', *Rhêtorikê: revista digital de retórica* 1, 1–15.

Groupe µ (1970) *Rhéthorique génerale*, Paris: Larousse.

Gutiérrez, S., Luna, R., Pérez, D. and Serrano, J. (2021) *4 ESO. Lengua y Literatura*, Madrid: Grupo Anaya.

Gutiérrez Sanz, V. (2022) 'El terrorismo en el discurso público: ¿la construcción retórica de un «mal natural»?', in D. Pujante and J. A. Alonso Prieto (eds.), *Una retórica constructivista. Creación y análisis del discurso social*, Castellón de la Plana: Universitat Jaume I, 73–82.

Halliday, M. (1985) *An Introduction to Functional Grammar*, London: Edward Arnold.

Halliday, M., McIntosh, A. and Strevens, P. (1964) *The Linguistic Sciences and Language Teaching*, London: Longman.

Howell, W. (1971) *Eighteenth-Century British Logic and Rhetoric*, Princeton: Princeton University Press.

Huang, Y. (2007) *Pragmatics*, Oxford: Oxford University Press.

Hymes, D. H. (1972) 'On Communicative Competence', in J. B. Pride and J. Holmes (eds.), *Sociolinguistics. Selected Readings*, Harmondsworth: Penguin, 269–293.

Kennedy, G. A. (1999) *Classical Rhetoric and Its Christian and Secular Tradition from Ancient to Modern Times*, 2nd edn, Chapel Hill/London: University of North Carolina Press.

Leite Ribeiro, A. (1819) *Theoria do discurso Applicada á Lingoa Portugueza; em que se mostra a estreita relação, e mutua dependencia das quatro Sciencias intellectuaes, a saber: Ideologia, Grammatica, Logica, e Rhetorica*, Lisboa: Impressão Regia.

López Eire, A. (1995) *Actualidad de la retórica*, Salamanca: Hespérides.

López Eire, A. (2007) 'Política y ética de la Retórica', *Noua tellus* 25(1), 41–91.

López Eire, A. and De Santiago Guervós, J. (2000) *Retórica y Comunicación política*, Madrid: Cátedra.

López Grigera, M. L. (1994) *La retórica en la España del Siglo de Oro: teoría y práctica*, Salamanca: Universidad de Salamanca.

López-Muñoz, M. and Salazar García, V. (1998) 'Antecedentes de las máximas conversa-cionales en la retórica antigua', in F. Delgado León, F. Osuna García and M. L. Calero Vaquera (coords.), *Estudios de lingüística general: actas del II Simposio de Historiografía Lingüística (Córdoba, 18-20 de marzo de 1997)*, Córdoba: Universidad de Córdoba, 315–326.

López-Muñoz, M. and Terol Plá, G. (2021) 'Retórica y poética (tradición de la)', in F. García Jurado (dir.), *Diccionario Hispánico de la Tradición y Recepción clásica. Conceptos, personas y métodos*, Madrid: Guillermo Escolar Editor, 657–666.

Love, R. (2006) 'The Relevance of Nineteenth-Century Rhetoric: The Decline and Revival of Civic Rhetoric', *South Atlantic Review* 71(4), 26–44.

Luján Atienza, A. L. (1999) *Retóricas españolas del siglo XVI: el foco de Valencia*, Madrid: Consejo Superior de Investigaciones Científicas.

Marques, J. F. (1989) *A parenética portuguesa e a Restauração, 1640–1668: a revolta e a mentalidade* (2 vols.), Lisboa: Instituto Nacional de Investigação Científica.

Miller, T. (1993) 'The Rhetoric of Belles Lettres: The Political Context of the Eighteenth-Century Transition from Classical to Modern Cultural Studies', *Rhetoric Society Quarterly* 23(2), 1–19.

Ministério de Educação (1991) *Português. Organização curricular e programas. Ensino secundário*, Lisboa: Ministério de Educação; Direcção Geral dos Ensinos Básico e Secundário.

Ministério da Educação e Ciência (2018) 'Decreto-Lei n.º 55/2018 de 6 de julho', *Diário da República, I Série, N.º 129, 6 de julho de 2018*, 2928–2943.

Ministério da Educação Nacional (1936) 'Decreto n.º 27:058 de 14 de outubro de 1936', *Diário do Govêrno, I Série, N.º 241, 14 de outubro de 1936*, 1243–1283.

Ministerio de Educación y Ciencia (1991) 'Real Decreto 1007/1991, de 14 de junio, por el que se establecen las enseñanzas mínimas correspondientes a la Educación Secundaria Obligatoria', *Boletín Oficial del Estado* núm. 152, de 26 de junio de 1991, 21193–21195.

Ministerio de Educación y Formación Profesional (2020) 'Ley Orgánica 3/2020, de 29 de diciembre, por la que se modifica la Ley Orgánica 2/2006, de 3 de mayo, de Educación', *Boletín Oficial del Estado* núm. 340, de 30 de diciembre de 2020, 122868–122953.

Ministerio de Educación y Formación Profesional (2022) 'Real Decreto 217/2022, de 29 de marzo, por el que se establece la ordenación y las enseñanzas mínimas de la Educación Secundaria Obligatoria', *Boletín Oficial del Estado* núm. 76, de 30 de marzo de 2022, 41571–41789.

Ministerio de Educación Nacional (1939) 'Orden de 14 de abril de 1939 aprobando los Cuestionarios de Enseñanza Media', *Boletín Oficial del Estado de 8 de mayo de 1939, suplemento del Núm. 128*, 1–36.

Munárriz, J. L. (1815) *Compendio de las lecciones sobre la Retórica y Bellas Letras de Hugo Blair*, Madrid: Imprenta de Ibarra.

Pereira, M. J. and Delindro, F. B. (2016) *Palavras 11º Ano*, Lisboa: Areal Editora.

Perelman, C. and Olbrechts-Tyteca, L. (1958) *Traité de l'argumentation: La nouvelle rhétorique*, Paris: Presses Universitaires de France.

Pinto de Castro, A. (1973) *Retórica e teorização literária em Portugal. Do Humanismo ao Neoclassicismo*, Coimbra: Centro de Estudos Românicos.

Pozuelo Yvancos, J. M. (1988) *Del formalismo a la neorretórica*, Madrid: Taurus.

Pujante, D. (2022) 'La retórica constructivista. Perspectivas teóricas e históricas', in D. Pujante and J. A. Alonso Prieto (eds.), *Una retórica constructivista. Creación y análisis del discurso social*, Castellón de la Plana: Universitat Jaume I, 19–59.

Reina, A. (ed.) (2021) *Lengua castellana y Literatura. 4º E.S.O.*, Barcelona: Editorial Casals.

Schlieben-Lange, B. (1975) *Pragmática Lingüística*, trans. E. Bombín, Madrid: Gredos (original work published in 1975).

Searle, J. R. (1969) *Speech Acts. An Essay in the Philosophy of Language*, Cambridge: Cambridge University Press.

Terol Plá, G. (2020a) 'La herencia clásica en la enseñanza de la retórica en el siglo XIX: El caso de Portugal y España', *eClassica* 6: 193–207.

Terol Plá, G. (2020b) 'Decorum retórico y teoría pragmática', *Minerva. Revista de Filología Clásica* 33, 233–249.

Vieira Mendes, M. (1989) *A oratória barroca de Vieira*, Lisboa: Caminho.

Vilas-Boas, A. and Vieira, M. (2016) *Entre palavras. 11 Português*, Lisboa: Asa.

5

EVOLUTION OF ARABIC RHETORIC

From Classical *Balāgha* to Modern Concepts of Persuasion

Marcin Styszyński

Introduction

The main objective of Arabic rhetoric (*balāgha*) reflects persuasion and influence on emotions, thoughts and expectations of the audience. The word *balāgha* is derived from the verb *balagha*, which means to achieve or to succeed. Arabic rhetoric aims at reaching excellent standards in language and style called sophisticated speech (*kalām balīgh*) or pure and eloquent discourse (*faṣāḥa*) (Styszyński 2008: 42). Likewise, aesthetic and stylistic features lead to effective communication and persuasion.

Moreover, *balāgha* also involves *khaṭāba*, which is related to Islamic jurisprudence (*fikh*) and preaching or liturgical sermons (*khuṭba*) (Halldén 2005: 19–38). *Khuṭba* is one of the oldest narrative and oratory forms in the Arab and Muslim world. It is usually presented by religious scholars called *khaṭīb* in mosques during Friday prayer or on special occasions of feasts and holidays. Alongside poetry, the Qur'ān or hadiths (tradition of sayings and deeds attributed to the Prophet Muhammad), *khaṭāba* became an important literary source for Arab philologists who analyzed different rhetorical devices adopted in liturgical speeches. *Khuṭba* consists of a unique model that is different from *balāgha*'s structure, and it usually refers to theological skills of *khaṭīb* as well as religious content of the speech. The narrative of the sermon consists of two parts. The first usually starts with religious invocations followed by the expression *wa ba'd* (and then, afterwards), which begins the second part of the speech. The second part is delivered after a short break of *khaṭīb* (Qutbuddin 2008: 176–273).

Study on Arabic *balāgha* developed during the Abbasid caliphate (750–1258) that witnessed significant social and economic progress, and integrated different cultures from ancient Greece, Persia and India. The caliphate differed from the Umayyad era (661–750), which conserved the Arabic character of the empire. The Abbasids appealed to non-Arab Muslims to resist against the Arab dynasty and to establish a new caliphate. They also moved the capital from Damascus to Baghdad, which became a cultural centre

DOI: 10.4324/9781003195276-7

for philosophy, theology, astronomy, medicine and mathematics as well as literature and philological studies (El-Hibri 2021: 28–68).

Furthermore, philologists such as Abū ʿUthmān al-Jāḥiẓ (d. 869), ʿAbd al-Qāhir al-Jurjānī (d. 1078), Abū Hilāl al-ʿAskarī (d. 1005) and Yusūf Ibn Abū Bakr al-Sakkākī (d. 1229) responded to the new intellectual environment and started study on literary criticism, poetry and rhetoric. The philologists also frequented the Muʿtazila school, which conducted speculative theology (*kalām*) and disputes over rationalism, empiricism, human freedom, as well as creation of the Qurʾān or the oneness and justice of Allah. The doctrine opposed the conservative traditions arguing that the Qurʾānic text is divine and eternal. Muʿtazila claimed that Allah has gifted sanity, free will and reason to people that stimulate their behaviors and actions. The philologists also classified and systematized literary sources such as pre-Islamic poetry, prose and sermons, the Qurʾān and hadiths, and they conducted further studies on rhetorical principles (Heemskerk 2000: 1–11). Despite multicultural conditions in the Abbasid empire, Greek rhetoric did not significantly affect Arabic *balāgha*, and classical rhetoricians have formulated a unique model that affected further research on eloquence. Moreover, Aristotle and Plato's philosophy was popularized by Ḥunayn Ibn Isḥāq (d. 873) who translated Greek works from Syriac into Arabic in the eighth and ninth centuries (Vagelpohl 2015: 76–91). However, Greek thought had a major impact on Muslim philosophers such as Al-Kindi (d. 873), Al-Farabi (d. 951), Avicenna (d. 1037) and Ibn Rushd (d. 1198), who referred to Aristotle's logic and syllogism including ethos, pathos and logos. Hence ethos demonstrates credibility of the speaker, and it appeals to his authority, skills and professionalism; pathos convinces the audience by emotions and sentiments as well as rhetorical embellishments; and logos is defined as logical arguments based on deductive and inductive reasoning (Al-Osaimi 2000: 121–124).

This chapter deals with the evolution of Arabic rhetoric from classical *balāgha* to modern interpretations of rhetorical principles in the twentieth century as well as the most recent objectives of Arabic rhetoric in the frame of Western influences in the twenty-first century. The research argues that despite modern reinterpretations and Western influences, Arabic rhetoric has retained its classical model based on three main criteria: *ʿilm al-maʿānī* (semantics, word order), *bayān* (clear expression) and *badīʿ* (embellishments). However, the study also demonstrates that rhetorical conceptual apparatus creates new scope for further research because some rhetorical devices remain theoretically unspecified.

Thus, the research is divided into four sections. The first part reflects the traditional concept of Arabic rhetoric, and the second part refers to theories demonstrated by modern Arab philologists such as Amīn al-Khūlī (d. 1966), Aḥmad Ḥasan al-Zayyāt (d. 1968) and Salāma Mūsa (d. 1958) who developed new interpretations of classical *balāgha*. The third section reflects the most recent studies in the twenty-first century regarding Western influences of pragmatism, hermeneutics and intertextuality. The fourth section involves research on rhetorical conceptual apparatus.

Methodology

The methodology implemented in this project relies on critical analysis, which consists of description and evaluation of data, including qualitative data. The data will be collected through literature reviews. Moreover, the critical analysis also relies on appropriate arrangement of data according to sources published in Arabic and Western languages, which demonstrate different perspectives of rhetoric.

Evolution of Arabic Rhetoric

The methodology adopted in the chapter also refers to comparative analysis that involves research on similarities and differences between classical Arabic rhetoric, Greek rhetoric, as well as modern rhetoric in the West. This methodology aims at discovering common features and formulating a modern concept of *balāgha*.

The Traditional Concept of Arabic Rhetoric

Classical rhetoricians identified different criteria of *balāgha*, and Al-Jāḥiẓ was one of the first philologists who determined rhetorical principles in his book *Kitāb al-bayān wa al-tabyīn* (Book of clarity and clarification). Apart from rhetoric, Al-Jāḥiẓ focused in his works on zoology, philosophy, theology, and morals and habits of the Abbasid society. He also cooperated with Abbasid's administration during caliph Al-Ma'mūn's reign (786–833) who supported Mu'tazila philosophy.

Al-Jāḥiẓ's rhetorical approaches highlight the concept of *bayān* (clear expression) that refers to exact words corresponding to current meanings and appropriate argumentation based on the Qur'ān, hadiths or liturgical speeches and poetry ('Āṣī 1981: 181). Al-Jāḥiẓ's briefness is demonstrated by various neologisms coined in the Abbasid caliphate. For example, a hot and wet day is called *ghumq*. A starry night without clouds is referred to the word *idhiyāna*. A cold night, during which water does not freeze, is called *ṣanbara*. And a winter season with strong winds and heavy snowfalls is defined by the term *damq* (Al-Shadhr 1998: 310). In addition, when Al-Jāḥiẓ observed unknown species of fish, he proposed the word *biyāḥ*, which included distinctive features regarding the lake where the fish lived (Ibn Imbīrīk 1985: 23).

In addition, the significance of semantic features in rhetoric is reinforced by the statement of Ibn Rashīq al-Qayrawānī (d. 1070): 'The word is a body, and the meaning is its soul. Their relations are like relations between the soul and the body.' The philologist also encourages people to avoid words considered as strange (*gharība*) or rough (*waḥshiyya*) because they hide essential meanings and separate the audience from the context of discourse (Badawī 1979: 37).

Furthermore, Al-Jāḥiẓ's study on meanings and words had an impact on the concept of scholasticism (*jadal*) that reflected Mu'tazila philosophy and assignment of appropriate arguments and details. Al-Jāḥiẓ usually briefly discusses specific topics in his works, and then he highlights various details based on precise words. In the work *Kitāb al-ḥayawān* (The book of animals) he starts one of the chapters with the following words: *Ismu ṭā'irin yaqa'u 'ala thalāthati ashyā'in ṣūratin wa ṭabṭ'atin wa janāḥin, wa laysa bi-al-rīshi wa al-qawādimi wa al-abāhiri wa al-khawāfī yusamma ṭā'iran* (Name of a bird consists of three elements: appearance, nature and wings. It is called the bird not only because of its features or the front part of the wings, the shortest features and the features visible after the wing fold) (Styszyński 2008: 51–52). Al-Jāḥiẓ adopts precise and single words, which include specific ornithological terminology. The English translation involves additional descriptive forms that describe the meanings of the Arabic words *qawādim* (the front part of the wings), *abāhir* (the shortest features) and *khawāfī* (the features visible after the wing fold). In addition, Al-Jāḥiẓ's briefness is followed by further arguments that combine examples of animal nature and different ornithological species with human behaviors and other philosophical or theological topics illustrating the greatness of Allah or hierarchy of the surrounding environment.

Unlike Al-Jāḥiẓ, Ibn Qutayba (d. 889), who served as a judge in the Abbasid caliphate, argues that rhetorical embellishments such as similes or metaphors are just as important as clear and precise words. Moreover, rhetorical discourse should be phonetically and semantically well-formed, and any disturbances within both fields affect the final version of discourse. Ibn al-Mu'tazz (d. 908) shares similar opinions. He was a representative of the Abbasid dynasty, and he concentrated in his study on literary criticism. He was the first rhetorician who formulated the notion *badī'* in the work *Kitāb al-badī'* (The book of the embellishment). However, *badī'* was further elaborated by Persian Muslim scholar Al-Sakkākī.

Furthermore, classical rhetoricians agreed on communicative features of *balāgha* as well as pragmatic factors between the communicator and the addressee. Al-Jāḥiẓ indicates the idea of condition (*ḥāl*) which refers to emotions and thoughts of the audience. He states: 'The word should not be ordinary or strange. Rhetorical discourse relies on different platforms as people belong to various social classes.' He elaborates that analysis of words and meanings attributed to particular social groups affects persuasive factors of discourse. In his opinion, people who live in the desert usually use words describing the heat, fire and elements of the Bedouin camp. However, residents of mountains express meanings concerning snow, cold and winds. Al-'Askarī, who was a poet, lexicographer and literary critic of Persian origin, demonstrates similar opinions and he states that the communicator must attribute appropriate words to certain groups of the audience because Arabs, foreigners or villagers and Bedouins are usually familiar with different meanings. Besides, effective eloquence and persuasion rely on word order and special arrangement of discourse. Al-Jurjānī, who was a philologist and rhetorician of Persian origin, compares rhetorical values of words to a necklace, which contains the same beads symbolizing sound and semantic balance of rhetorical discourse (Sallūm 1986: 94).

Al-Jāḥiẓ and Al-Jurjānī also refer to inimitability of the Qur'ān (*I'jāz al-Qur'ān*), which focuses on traditional exegesis considering the Qur'ān as sacred text sent to the Prophet Muhammad. The rhetoricians adopted new hermeneutic approaches that focused on the Mu'tazila doctrine and literary research on the Qur'ānic text. In the work *Dalā'il al-i'jāz* (The Arguments of inimitability) Al-Jurjānī examines linguistic and rhetorical phenomena of the Qur'ān, and he highlights figures of speech applied in the Qur'ānic text and determines particular rhetorical notions (Nasr 2003: 8–47). However, further research on *i'jāz* was developed by Abū al-Qāsim al-Zamakhsharī (d. 1144) and his work *Al-Kashshāf 'an ḥaqā'iq at-tanzīl* (The Discoverer of revealed truths). He represented the Mu'tazila doctrine, and focused on theological and linguistic commentary on the Qur'ān. Al-Zamakhsharī remarks that the Qur'ānic text relies on perspicuous and ambiguous verses that need logical reasoning and interpretation, as in the fragment *Fa-man shā'a fal-yu'min wa man shā'a fal-yakfur* (Whosoever wishes, let him believe, and whosoever wishes, let him disbelieve) (Ullah 2017: 68). The verse is considered by Al-Zamakhsharī as perspicuous due to the Mu'tazila philosophy of free will. In addition, stylistic analysis is evident in the Qur'ānic verse of the chapter *Al-Baqara* (The Cow) *Khatama Allāhu 'ala qulūbihim wa 'ala sam'ihim wa 'ala abṣārihim ghishawatun wa lahum 'azābun 'aẓīmun* (God has sealed their hearts and their hearing, and on their sight is a veil. For them is a great punishment) (Ullah 2017: 73). Al-Zamakhsharī elaborates that the word *ghishawa* (veil) contains a metaphorical sense related to unbelievers who are excluded from the faith because their eyes are covered and veiled, and they reject the signs of God.

I'jāz led to further studies on order system (*naẓm*) that is concerned with arrangement of sentences due to particular contexts and connotations. *Naẓm* is also divided into true or false statements or exaggeration, rebuke, warning, remorse and praising (Raof 2006: 100–103). For example, Al-'Askarī refers to the phrase *halakat al-shajā'atu wa māta al-jūdu* (The bravery and generosity have died), which designates mourning and sorrow after the death of a close person. However, the equivalent refers to the sentence *māta jawādan wa shujā'an* (He has died as a brave and proud person). The appropriate form of the words eliminates the predicative in the first sentence, and it enables praise of the deceased. His death annihilates entirely the sense of bravery and generosity (Salām 1982: 307).

Moreover, Al-Sakkākī also developed the concept of *nazm*, which involves linguistic devices to persuade sceptical and suspicious audiences, as in the sentence *Samīrun marīḍun* (Samīr is ill). Additional affirmative tools such as the particle *inna* and the preposition *la* are needed in this regard. The final version is as follows: *Inna Samīran la-marīḍun* (Verily, Samīr is, indeed, ill). Furthermore, oath words are another important method of persuasion, as in the sentence *Aqsimu bi-Allāhi lam aqul dhalika* (I swear by God, I did not say that). It includes the expression *Aqsimu bi-Allāhi* (I swear by God) which reinforces the statement *lam aqul dhalika* (I did not say that) (Raof 2006: 107–109).

Further studies headed by rhetoricians such as Al-Sakkākī and Al-Jurjānī clarified and specified rhetorical theories that became final patterns of classical *balāgha*. In the work *Miftāḥ al-'ulūm* (Key to the disciplines) Al-Sakkākī proposes consolidated criteria of Arabic rhetoric that include three categories: *'ilm al-ma'ānī* (semantics, word order), *bayān* (clear expression) and *badī'* (embellishments). Al-Sakkākī's analysis was commented on by Jalāl al-Dīn al-Qazwīnī (d. 1338) in his work *Talkhīṣ al-miftāḥ* (Summary of *al-miftāḥ*), in which he concentrates on rhetorical principles presented by Al-Sakkākī. Al-Qazwīnī accepts the three categories, *'ilm al-ma'ānī, bayān* and *badī'*, but he includes some comments explaining the significance of rhetorical devices that acknowledge how to speak and express in order to achieve and persuade different audiences (Ullah 2017: 70).

Thus the category of *'ilm al-ma'ānī* is concerned with various semantic and structural aspects related to the predicate and relations between the subject (*musnad ilayhi*) and the verb (*musnad*). The position of the subject in the sentence *Allah anzala min al-samā'i mā'un* (Allah has sent water from the sky) modifies traditional grammatical structure of Arabic verbal sentences that reflects priority of the verb, and the normal word sentence is verb-subject-object. The initial position of the subject at the beginning of the sentence emphasizes and expresses the greatness of Allah. Moreover, the modification in syntactic structure of Arabic is also evident in the phrase *Zaidun mā qatala al-rajula* (Zaid did not kill the man). The subject *Zaid* is placed before the negation *mā* (not) and the verb *qatala* (to kill) emphasizes a denial of the killing attributed to *Zaid* (Raof 2006: 107–109).

However, *'Ilm al-ma'ānī* also implies informative and affirmative utterances (*khabar*) as well as performative emotional utterances (*inshā'*), which reflect different techniques of composition based on imperative, prohibition or interrogative and vocative sentences. The structure of discourse relies on clear, lucid words and sentences, which express different semantic features of particular meanings. *'Ilm al-ma'ānī* is also related to concision (*ījāz*) and prolixity (*iṭnāb*) as well. The first notion regards briefness and condensation of words and sentences in order to express and specify main ideas presented in orations. *Iṭnāb* is the opposite notion, which reflects application of additional arguments in discourse (Siwiec 2008: 128–143).

Furthermore, the second category *bayān* is different from Al-Jāḥiẓ's perspectives that considered *bayān* as lucid and clear expressions. According to Al-Sakkākī, *bayān* consists of rhetorical tropes such as simile (*tashbīh*) and different types of metaphorical expression (*majāz*), including metaphor (*isti'āra*), metonymy (*kināya*) and synecdoche (*majāz mursal*). *Majāz* is the opposition of the truth (*ḥaqīqa*), and primarily it reflected replacement of meanings by different words, which preserved some semantic similarities with the replaced meaning. Further studies on rhetoric clarified different types of metaphors, and *majāz* became a theoretical term, which generalized a variety of metaphorical devices applied in the Arabic language.

Likewise, rhetorical figures are elaborated by Al-Jurjānī who indicates that simile reflects combination of the likened to (*mushabbah*) and the likened (*mushabbah bihi*), which are connected with the particles *ka* or *ka-anna* (like). The phrase *Zayd ka al-asadi* (Zaid is like a lion) identifies the bravery and courage of Zaid, and it relies on the noun *Zaid* that represents the likened-to, and the noun *asad* that regards the likened, including the particle *ka* (Al-Jārim and Amīn 1979: 23–24). Al-Jurjānī analyzes various types of comparative epithets and argues that simile should correspond to realistic and natural features to persuade local audiences. Al-Jāḥiẓ also shares this idea and gives the examples of running gazelle or walking cat that describe women's alluring moves. Women's beauty is also symbolized by the moon, which evokes positive associations with a pleasant evening and breeze instead of the heat during the daytime. However, friendship and loyalty are defined by the image of a camel that is resting on the fertile land after a long journey (Ibn Imbīrīk 1985: 48).

Furthermore, the metaphor (*istiʿāra*) stands for a shortened version of simile that excludes one of its elements. The metaphor *Zaidun asadun* (Zaid is a lion) eliminates the particle *ka*, and the word *asad* (lion) determines the metaphorical sense of this rhetorical figure. In addition, revival of abstract or inanimate objects is another important aspect of this metaphor. For example, the phrase *ḍaḥika al-ṣubḥu* (the morning has laughed) is attributed to the abstract meaning of the morning, and the metaphorical context reflects the joy and optimism of sunshine. The revival of the abstract meaning is also evident in the metaphor *dhabaḥanī al-ʿaṭashu* (the thirst has butchered me) (Al-Jārim and Amīn 1979: 76). The verb *dhabaḥa* (to butcher) is attributed to a person who suffers from thirst and his feelings are compared to slaughtering and killing (Balmalīḥ 1984: 216).

In addition, *kināya* is concerned with literal interpretation that contributes to metaphorical meanings. For example, the metonymy *huwa naqiyyu al-thawbi* (he has clean clothes) literally reflects a person who wears clean clothes. However, it also refers to a person who stands out with spiritual purity that is visible and evident like clean clothes exposed on public display (Abbas 2002: 123). Literal and metaphorical meanings are also evident in the phrase *huwa ṭawīlu al-nijādi rafīʿu al-ʿimādi kathīru al-ramādi* (He is tall and he has sublime position and he is covered with a lot of ash) (Al-Jārim and Amīn 1979: 123–124). The expression *kathīru al-ramādi* (he is covered with a lot of ash) may be interpreted literally, but the ash on the person described in the example also refers to his generosity and hospitality. The ash is associated with a fireplace, a kitchen or cooking. The generosity and hospitality become in this context additional features that reinforce the high qualities of the person.

Synecdoche (*majāz mursal*) is another innovative form of metaphor. This term reflects cause and effect relations between a substituted meaning and its metaphorical equivalent. In the synecdoche *yanazzilu lakum min al-samāʾi rizqan* (he sends you blessed food from the sky), the food stands for rainfall that determines a good harvest. *Majāz mursal* is also evident in the similar phrase *raʿaynā al-ghaytha* (we cultivated the rain), which indicates the cause and effect between the rain and agriculture (Abbas 2002: 133). Moreover, *majāz mursal* also involves partial and entire metaphorical forms, as in the phrases *kam baʿathnā al-jaysha jarran wa arsalnā al-ʿuyūnā* (so many fortified armies and eyes have been sent) and *wa innī kullamā da'awtuhum li-taghfira lahum ja'alū aṣābi'ahum fī adhānihim* (whenever I invite them to be forgiven by you, they press their fingers into their ears) (Al-Jārim and Amīn 1979: 108–109). In the first synecdoche the word *'uyūn* (eyes) replaces the essential meaning that refers to significance of spies on the battlefield. Perceptivity and careful looking are important attributes in spy work, and the synecdoche reflects a partial characteristic of the replaced meaning. The second phrase refers to the Qur'ān and it encourages believers to follow Islam. The word *aṣābi'* (fingers) is a substitute for fingertips. In fact, the believers cannot put their whole fingers in their ears, and the synecdoche designates an entire characteristic of the replaced meaning.

The third category of Arabic rhetoric regards *badī'* and it includes, among others, rhetorical devices like antithesis (*muqābala*) and antonym (*ṭibāq*) or homonymy (*tajnīs*). For example, the sentence *laysa lahu ṣadīqun fī al-sirri, wa lā 'aduwwun fī al-'alāniyati* (he has not a secret friend and a public enemy) includes opposite meanings in the second part of the sentence, and each word contains its opposite equivalent arranged through antonyms. Unlike antonyms, homonymy regards words containing the same or similar sound and form, but different meanings. The words *qahara* (to conquer) and *nahara* (to humiliate) can serve as an example. The letters *q* and *n* become distinctive phonological features, and the words include different meanings. This type of homonym is called incomplete homonym (*jinās ghayr tāmm*). However, complete homonym (*jinās tāmm*) is concerned with the same sound and form of words, but different meanings. For example, the word *sā'a* (hour) designates simultaneously time measuring and the Last Judgement (Al-Jārim and Amīn 1979: 263–264).

Furthermore, *badī'* also contains chiasmus (*'aks*), which deals with reversal of lexical structure in phrases or cross-shaped arrangement of words, as in the fragment of the Qur'ānic verse *yakhruju al-ḥayya min al-mayyiti wa yakhruju al-mayyita min al-ḥayyi* (he brings out the living from the dead, and brings out the dead from the living). The cross-shaped arrangement of the words *ḥayy* (living), *mayyit* (dead) and the verb *yakhruju* (to bring out) emphasizes Allah's almightiness and greatness because he can revive or put to death human beings (Al-Hshim 2012: 313–314).

In addition, *badī'* involves the term *taṭrīz* (a decorative embroidery), which reflects segmental arrangement of words in sentences including narrative without linking words, which reminds us of a decorative embroidery. *Badī'* also includes anaphora (*takrār*) which consists of repetition of particular words or expressions at the beginning of each sentence or passage. The rhetorical figures also include an interesting term called *iqtibās*, which concerns appeal to Qur'ānic verses or hadiths to diversify the style and lend credence to discourse, as in the poem of Ibn Sina' al-Mulk (d. 1212), *Raḥalū fa-lastu musā'ilan 'an dārihim anā bākhi'un nafsī 'ala āthārihim* (They have gone so I'm not asking about their homes, and I will kill myself in grief over their footsteps). The poet quotes the fragment of the Qur'ānic chapter *Kahf* (The Cave), *fa-la'allaka bākhi'un nafsī 'ala āthārihim in lam yu'minū bi-hādha al-ḥadīthi asafan* (Perhaps, you, would kill yourself in grief over their footsteps because they do not believe in this narration) (Al-Jārim and Amīn 1979: 269–270). The footsteps refer to evil deeds that leave tracks, and the poet reinterprets the verse, which is attributed to his personal experiences regarding sorrow for departure of loved ones. The appeal to Qur'ānic verses or hadiths also allows to modify original versions according to specific content. Ibn Sina' al-Mulk ignores the ending of the verse *in lam yu'minū bi-hādha al-ḥadīthi asafan* (because they do not believe in this narration) to avoid religious connotations of his poem.

During the eleventh and twelfth centuries Arabic rhetoric was affected by a stagnation period and a lack of innovative critics. Rhetorical studies usually concentrated on sophisticated forms praising the Prophet Muhammad as well as poems called *badī'iyyāt*, which relied on various embellishments (Raof 2006: 51–52).

Arabic Rhetoric in the Twentieth Century

During the 1940s and 1950s, study on Arabic rhetoric was focused on theories presented by Salāma Mūsa, Aḥmad Ḥasan al-Zayyāt and Amīn al-Khūlī who presented new perspectives of rhetoric and adapted them to the new social, cultural and political context of the Arab world. The rhetoricians also considered innovative perspectives of eloquence as heritage of classical *balāgha*. The research on rhetoric was also affected by Western stylistics that expanded analysis of different linguistic forms in texts, and unlike *balāgha*, stylistics did not rely on a restricted model of Arabic rhetoric. However, persuasive and communicative values of texts have become common features for stylistics and rhetoric (Al-Muṭṭalib 1994: 106).

Furthermore, Salāma Mūsa formulated new approaches of semantics in the Arabic language. Mūsa was an Egyptian intellectual and journalist from a Coptic family who expressed his theories in the work *Al-Balāgha al-'aṣriyya wa al-lugha al-'arabiyya* (Modern rhetoric and the Arabic language). The Arab world needed, in his opinion, to reform the Arabic language in the frame of social, economic and political changes that modified traditional structures of local societies (Ibrahim 1979: 346–357). He also advocated for Egyptian socialism and national identity as well as modernization of the country and economic growth. Incorporation of new meanings from science and technology as well as Western terminologies is a consequence of these tendencies (Suleiman 2019: 181–186). Mūsa claims that the words *taṭawwur* (development), *mas'uliyya* (responsibility) and *dustūr* (constitution) did not exist previously in a modern context and they gained semantic features from Western languages (Mūsa 2012: 73–82). In addition, interpretations of new meanings in the Arab world must represent current laws and regulations as well as particular context. Mūsa also refers to the example of a factory, which was considered in the past as an unhealthy and unfriendly place for workers by traditional Egyptian institutions. However, this meaning does not correspond to modern perceptions regarding industrial development, trade or profits and the labour market (Mūsa 2012: 92).

Mūsa also claims that, historically, Arabic designated multiple-meaning words or inimical significations. He gives an example of the word *thu'bān*, which designates the eel. However, Egyptian society dislikes this kind of fish because literal interpretation of *thu'bān* refers to the snake (Mūsa 2012: 46). Mūsa also stresses that Arabic does not include sufficient words to express precise meanings. He quotes the verb *aḥabba* (to love), which refers to a general sense of love. Mūsa remarks that this verb cannot distinguish love between a man and a woman or love of a mother toward her child as well as ordinary love for cinema or sweets (Mūsa 2012: 60–61). Mūsa argues that English, in contrast to Arabic, can separately specify these meanings by using the verbs 'to love' and 'to like'. Thus Arabization of Western vocabulary should be postponed and replaced by Latinization of loan words (Mūsa 2012: 10–14). However, Mūsa does not specify phonological or graphic aspects of the Latinization process in Arabic.

Musa's opinions are quite problematic because the rhetorician ignores important semantic features of Arabic synonyms that provide hierarchy in degree of love, and they contain emotional character of specific words. For example, the word *hawā* implies falling into a trap due to being in love. However, *ṣabāba* symbolizes deep and strong love. Moreover, *walaʿ* literally means catching fire, and in regard to love it conveys the sense of obsession. *Huyām* defines in turn burning thirst, which is compared to love. In addition, desire is designated by the word *ʿishq* (Obeidat 2017: 300–314).

Musa's negative perspectives of Arabic are a result of his personal views regarding modernization of the Arabic language as well as his educational and cultural experiences, raised in the book *Tarbiyat Salāma Mūsa* (The education of Salāma Mūsa). He was inspired by Western literature, culture and liberty during his stays in France and England. He confronted new experiences with traditional Egyptian society and poor conditions of life (Mūsa 1961: 37–44). The synonyms of love were in this context too archaic and insufficient for Mūsa who preferred English equivalents.

According to Mūsa's theories, language is a way of thinking, and human minds are able to distinguish and compare different words and meanings. He states that the Arabic language still consists of archaic words demonstrating rural, Bedouin or aristocratic backgrounds (Mūsa 2012: 10–14). He also indicates the problem of diglossia that combines colloquial forms with classical Arabic. The colloquial corresponds to social environment in Egypt, and classical Arabic becomes more and more artificial for the audience. In addition, there are various difficulties in expression of new meanings, including foreign terminology. Thus, the Arab world cannot resist Western influences that affect various semantic equivalents (Suleiman 2019: 181–186).

However, Mūsa also presents some critical opinions about *bayān* and *badīʿ*. Arabic eloquence preserves its traditional principles and replaces, in his opinion, logic argumentation and exact words with stylistic devices, which are pointless and rely on emotions and sentiments. For example, he classifies metaphors as unclear figures of speech that distract persuasion (Mūsa 2012: 63–65). However, Mūsa appreciates Al-Jāḥiẓ's theories that reflect appropriate analysis of meanings and words as well as logical thinking (Mūsa 2012: 104).

Furthermore, rhetorical theories were studied by Aḥmad Ḥasan al-Zayyāt who was an Egyptian intellectual and writer. He studied at Al-Azhar University in Cairo, and in 1922 he was appointed head of the Arabic department at the American University in Cairo. He also established the literary magazine *Al-Risāla* (The Letter) (Sheyhatovitch and Kasher 2020: 208–225).

Al-Zayyāt published his research in the book *Difāʿ ʿan al-balāgha* (Defence of rhetoric) in 1945. Al-Zayyāt indicates three main patterns of rhetoric: originality (*aṣāla*), concision (*wijāza*) and harmony (*talāʾum*) (Al-Muṭṭalib 1994: 102–103). Thus, *aṣāla* corresponds to author's credibility, and it appeals to his authority, literary skills and professionalism. In addition, every author stands out with his own style that is hard to transmit or translate into other languages, including Arabic. Al-Zayyāt mentions in this regard the literary works of Shakespeare or Émile Zola (Al-Zayyāt 1967: 86–87).

However, *wijāza* is the main topic in Al-Zayyāt's concept of rhetoric. It is a combination of *ʿilm al-maʿānī* and French literary criticism. Al-Zayyāt refers to the French novelist Gustave Flaubert (d. 1880), and highlights his remarks regarding application of explicit words, which are created initially in human minds and then expressed in a certain way by concise words and brief arrangement of discourse. According to Al-Zayyāt's theories, many words exist only in dictionaries, and novelists or poets revive them in their literary works (Al-Zayyāt 1967: 86–95). Al-Zayyāt also combines Flaubert's ideas with those of classical Arabic rhetoricians and their concept of *ījāz* coinciding with concision of expression. Al-Zayyāt reinforces his statement by the proverbial saying 'Style is the man himself' declared by the French naturalist Buffon (d. 1788). He also mentions Ibn Rashīq's comparison of words and meanings to the body and soul (Al-Zayyāt 1967: 76–77).

Al-Zayyāt also refers to the anecdote of Ibn Hamra (d. 792) who was a poet from Medina during the Umayyad and Abbasid eras, and he often praised representatives of both dynasties in his poems (Salhi and Alqarni 2016: 56–89). Al-Zayyāt cites Ibn Hamra who has heard a poet reciting: *Bi-Allāhi rabbika in dakhalta fa-qul lahā hādha Ibn Hamra qā'iman bi-al-bābi* (O Allah, if you enter, say Ibn Hamra is standing in the doorway). Al-Zayyāt then proceeds to the dialogue between Ibn Hamra and the poet. Ibn Hamra said that he was not begging or urinating, but he had just stood up (Al-Zayyāt 1967: 97–98). Ibn Hamra adopts the adjective *wāqif*, instead of the adjective *qā'im* applied in the poem. In fact, the English equivalents do not include the specific character of Arabic semantics, and the words may be considered initially as synonyms. However, the word *qā'im* reflects duration of standing caused by specific activities, and *wāqif* concerns spontaneous reactions. Al-Zayyāt emphasizes the significance of semantic details in words that affect the final sense of texts. The specification and application of certain words play a fundamental role in Arabic rhetoric for Al-Zayyāt.

Furthermore, Al-Zayyāt underlines the importance of the Qur'ān, prose or poetry, which facilitate eloquence of discourse. However, *badī'* is criticized because of exaggeration in descriptions instead of appropriate arguments and exact significations. As an example, Al-Zayyāt mentions daily newspapers that contain long reports and columns without a certain goal or further discussion. Readers can perceive, in this context, the main sense of the article after reading the first passages (Al-Zayyāt 1967: 108–110).

Talā'um indicates in turn phonological features such as rhymes or tonal balance of discourse. Al-Zayyāt compares *talā'um* to homonymy and phonological or semantic relations between words with identical forms, but different meanings. He also refers to the rhymed prose (*saj'*) used in the Qur'ān. *Saj'* reflects artistic composition, symmetry and balance in the structure of the text as well as brief sentences and particular rhyme at the end of each phrase (Al-Zayyāt 1967: 31–32).

Rhetorical principles were also formulated by Amīn al-Khūlī who was a Muslim scholar from Al-Azhar University in Cairo. He was appointed head of the faculty of Arabic studies at Cairo University, and cooperated with the publishing house *Dār al-kutub* (The house of books) as well as various intellectual associations (Abū Zayd 2006: 53–59). Theological approaches of Al-Khūlī's study reflect the inimitability of the Qur'ān. His literary exegesis corresponds to the Mu'tazila doctrine, and he underlines the importance of the historical, religious or social and cultural context of the Qur'ānic text, including linguistic structure and nonverbal aspects (Nasr 2003: 8–47).

Al-Khūlī's perspectives of Arabic rhetoric were published in the book *Fann al-qawl* (Art of the speech) in 1947. He states that Arabic demonstrates dynamic changes and vitality that encourage further studies on rhetoric and effective persuasion (Al-Khūlī 1996: 116–117). However, he focuses on literary skills and stylistic features that play an important role in outstanding literary works and effective persuasion. Thus, he designates three categories: creativity (*ijād*), arrangement (*tartīb*) and literary expression or style (*ta'bīr*). Creativity concerns discovering particular topics, data collection and appropriate arguments and storylines that correspond with interests and needs of readers. Al-Khūlī also indicates willingness and motivations that stimulate all activities and literary skills as well as stylistic capacities. Moreover, perception and literary imagination play an important role as well. He gives examples of natural phenomena such as seashores, rivers, mountains or deserts and gardens. Al-Khūlī argues that perception of the surrounding world enables us to understand, reinterpret and finally allows us to express feelings and specific meanings. Besides, this process generates imagination that affects the literary taste of the author and his audience (Al-Khūlī 1996: 101–103). In addition, *tartīb* reflects structure of discourse, including introduction and narrative that concerns facts, evidence, and finally, conclusions.

Furthermore, *ta'bīr* deals with different figures of speech that convince the audience (Al-Khūlī 1996: 101–108). Al-Khūlī states that personal and linguistic skills are insufficient to achieve rhetorical excellence, and meanings can be reached equally by *'ilm al-ma'ānī, bayān* and *badī'* (Al-Khūlī 1996: 237–242). He also remarks that the main rhetorical objective of *balāgha* is concerned with achieving meaning by various stylistic forms such as concision or embellishments. *Bayān* and *badī'* play a crucial role in this context because they contain effective figures that reinforce the persuasion process. Al-Khūlī argues that metaphors are more authentic and convincing than literal expressions (Al-Khūlī 1996: 249).

It should also be noted that Al-Khūlī's theories are similar to the five canons of Aristotle's rhetoric: invention (*inventio*), arrangement (*dispositio*), style (*elocutio*), memory (*memoria*) and delivery (*pronuntatio*). Unfortunately, these terms are not specified in Al-Khūlī's theories, although theoretically *inventio, dispositio* and *elocutio* correspond to Al-Khūlī's concepts of *ijād, tartīb* and *ta'bīr*. In addition, Al-Khūlī's perspective of Aristotle's philosophy is limited to his logic and syllogism, which rely on deduction and cognitive process based on empiricism and sensual recognition as well as arguments from the particular to the universal and probative or impossible proofs. In fact, Al-Khūlī combines Aristotle's logic with *'ilm al-ma'ānī* and clear or lucid words and meanings (Al-Khūlī 1996: 130–132). He focuses on theoretical aspects, and he does not refer to any particular examples demonstrating application of Aristotle's logic in Arabic rhetoric.

In addition, Al-Khūlī refers to Italian philologist Luigi Valmaggi (d. 1925) from the University of Turin who focused in his research on Greek and Latin grammar and poetry. He was also the editor of *Bolletino di filologia classica* (Classical Philology Bulletin) (Carlucci 2013: 80–83). Al-Khūlī mentions Valmaggi's book *Stilistica e metrica* (Stylistics and metre) from 1910, and he refers to antonomasia, which is considered as a sort of *kināya*. Al-Khūlī refrains from further studies on this type of rhetorical device, and he does not give any examples of antonomasia in the Arabic language. In fact, the short reference to Valmaggi leads Al-Khūlī to individual remarks about *ta'bīr* and different stylistic features (Al-Khūlī 1996: 108–109). It is worth mentioning that in Western literary criticism, antonomasia is a sort of synecdoche, which replaces a proper name by an epithet or a descriptive phrase. For example, the epithet 'the philosopher' is the equivalent of the name 'Aristotle' (Fenves 2001: 32–36). Al-Khūlī's definition of antonomasia as metonymy is misleading in this context.

Furthermore, Al-Khūlī's research demonstrates some inaccuracies. Classical *balāgha* remains the main methodological corpus, and Western influences constitute separate and exceptional references. Thus, most rhetorical devices correspond to *'ilm al-ma'ānī, bayān* and *badī'*, and antonomasia represents an exception in Al-Khūlī's conceptual apparatus. Similarly to Al-Zayyāt, Al-Khūlī refers to the proverbial saying 'Style is the man himself' declared by Buffon. However, he does not mention the name of the French naturalist (Al-Khūlī 1996: 153–154). The selective methodology proposed by Al-Khūlī also concerns the definition of rhetoric, which is called *fann al-qawl* (the art of the speech) (Al-Khūlī 1996: 89). Al-Khūlī refers to French literary criticism and the idea of *art de dire* (art of

Marcin Styszyński

speech), which is derived from Quintilian's concept of rhetoric, *ars bene dicendi* (the art to speak well) (Klifman 1992: 64–66).

Arabic Rhetoric in the Twenty-First Century

In the twenty-first century Arab philologists such as Emad Abdul Latif, Muḥammad Miftāḥ, Muḥammad al-Ṭalaba, Ḥamādī Ṣumūd and Ṣalāḥ Faḍl have continued research on classical *balāgha* elaborated by previous rhetoricians, and they have concentrated on Western influences.

For example, Ḥamādī Ṣumūd indicates that until the 1990s, the study of Arabic rhetoric was concerned with reinterpretation of norms formulated by classical philologists. Yet in the twenty-first century Arabic eloquence implies study on argumentation that reflects effective communication and expression of thoughts. Ṣumūd also underlines three sorts of arguments: first, tangible proofs, which are impossible to undermine by the addressee. The second type refers to separate arguments addressed to each part of discourse in order to convince the audience. The third component involves appropriate stylistic devices applied to arguments in order to reinforce the effectiveness of discourse. He compares the third type to Aristotle's *elocutio*, and he advocates for further studies on Greek philosophy that affects, in Ṣumūd's opinion, modern discourse and persuasion methods (Al-Ṭalaba 2008: 276–277).

Hence Ṣumūd divides modern *balāgha* into poetic rhetoric that refers to classical principles, and argumentative rhetoric. Ṣumūd also states that study on Arabic rhetoric should rely on different aspects of everyday communication and a changing world that is experiencing new technologies, globalization and economic challenges (Al-Ṭalaba 2008: 288).

Furthermore, Muḥammad Miftāḥ is inspired by Charles Peirce's pragmatism and his study on relations between languages and their users or semantic interactions between the communicator and the interpreter, as well as Peirce's analysis on how context contributes to meanings. Muḥammad Miftāḥ focuses on intuitive interpretation that involves intentional meanings created in the interpreter's mind following messages transferred by the communicator. Miftāḥ also indicates direct interpretation which generates meanings based on analysis of stylistic devices included in texts and speeches. In addition, he proposes hierarchy in the interpretation process. He distinguishes sources that do not need additional interpretation because they are clarified through their titles. He also highlights sources that contain interpretations which require further analysis leading to appropriate understanding of meanings (Al-Ṭalaba 2008: 244–254). Miftāḥ's study on pragmatism and hermeneutics corresponds to John Austin's theories concerning explicit performatives and inexplicit utterances that contain explicit patterns decoding the text or inexplicit forms that need additional signs and analysis to decode the sense. However, Miftāḥ does not mention Austin's study in his works.

Furthermore, Ṣalāḥ Faḍl also refers to Western hermeneutics and he argues that modern Arabic rhetoric should focus on linguistic analysis of texts according to their historical, social or cultural sense, and stylistics becomes an important rhetorical tool, which enables us to evaluate literary, communicative and persuasive values of certain texts (Al-Ṭalaba 2008: 221–236).

Faḍl also emphasizes traditions of classical *balāgha*, and he states that *ʿilm al-maʿānī* is the main pattern of new rhetoric in the Arab world. However, Al-Jāḥiẓ's concepts of *bayān* and *jadal* are attributed to argumentation (*hijāj*) that appeals to logic, empiricism and common sense in order to persuade the audience of particular content (Al-Ṭalaba 2008: 221–236).

Moreover, Faḍl combines classical *balāgha* with Perelman's argumentation in legal rhetoric. Perelman remarks that arguments are addressed to universal, particular or composite audiences that participate in legal proceedings (Al-Ṭalaba 2008: 221–236). The universal audience is the most effective as it relies on reason, facts, presumptions and truth during evaluation of legal cases. The particular audience involves in turn selective groups that recognize certain arguments due to their preferences and expectations. However, the composite audience recognizes diverse addressees. In addition, argumentation scheme is a common feature of various types of audiences. It is composed of arguments by association that link separate entities into a consolidated form. Arguments by dissociation introduce separate proofs considered previously as an entire scheme (Feteris 2017: 63–75).

Likewise, Faḍl shares Perelman's opinions and he states that classical *jadal* corresponds to legal rhetoric because the argumentation process presented by Al-Jāḥiẓ is also concerned with appropriate arguments that explain and justify certain topics and cases. However, Faḍl does not refer to any particular examples demonstrating implementation of Perelman's theories in Arabic rhetoric. This might be explained by the fact that Faḍl designates argumentation to everyday communication that reflects family conversations, professional debates or political rallies (Al-Ṭalaba 2008: 228–230).

Western influences in Arabic rhetoric are also evident in Faḍl's research on George Lakoff and Mark Johnson's cognitive linguistics and conceptual metaphors, which facilitate, in his opinion, perception and recognition of texts. However, Faḍl states that many metaphors became ordinary in everyday communication. Metaphors often describe abstract ideas such as love and hate, and the abstract meanings are classified according to their semantic compilations evoked by audiences. For example, marriage is often compared to a difficult journey, a car or a boat (Al-Ṭalaba 2008: 236–242).

Furthermore, Abdul Latif proposes interesting methodological perspectives that combine classical rhetorical principles with cognitive linguistics, sociolinguistics or media studies and psychology. He argues that Arabic rhetoric is concerned mainly with literature, and application of rhetorical devices in other fields such as politics, advertisement or media is often marginalized by rhetoricians ('Abd al-Laṭīf 2021: 264–265).

Abdul Latif also highlights that persuasion is the main goal of *balāgha*. Thus, this goal can be achieved by different rhetorical standards such as intertextuality, which becomes one of the most important methodological features in modern rhetorical studies. Abdul Latif also focuses on Norman Fairclough's theories regarding interpretation process based on intertextual relations between literary texts and historical, cultural and social contexts (Abdul Latif 2011: 53–54). Intertextuality is also concerned with relations between a basic text and its literary, historical or cultural and social references based on citations, allusions or dialogs. Intertextual transfers affect audience's perception, recognition and persuasion (Mason 2019: 1–22).

Thus Abdul Latif applies intertextuality to stylistic devices and historical, political or cultural context of president Sadat's speeches in Egypt, as in the fragment, *aqūlu li-sha'bīnā zay rabbinā subḥānahu wa ta'āla mā khāṭabanā wa qāla: lā taḥzanū wa antum al-a'lawna, iḥnā muntaṣirīna bi-idhni Allāhi was sa-naṣilu ila ahdāfinā bi-idhni Allāhi* (I say to our people as our Lord the exalted and high spoke to us and said: 'Do not be sad, you are the superiors', we will be victorious by God's will and will reach our goals God willing) (Abdul Latif 2011: 58–62).

Sadat's speech was released in 1977 after mass protests against high prices called the Egyptian bread riots. Sadat interrupts his oration, and refers to the Qur'ānic chapter *'Imrān family* and verse 139, *lā taḥzanū wa antum al-a'lawna* (do not be sad, you are the superiors). The historical and religious context of the verse is attributed to ongoing social and political conditions in order to reduce tensions among society and encourage people to overcome economic difficulties in the country. In addition, religious references aim to create a positive image of a devoted Muslim and strong leader of the state. Abdul Latif also highlights colloquial words such as *zay* (like) or *iḥnā* (we) as well as possessive or personal pronouns, *sha'binā* (our people), *rabbinā* (our Lord) or *ahdāfinā* (our goals), that demonstrate identification of the president with the audience's feelings and expectations (Abdul Latif 2011: 58–62).

In his book *Al-Balāghat al-ḥurriyya, ma'ārik al-khiṭāb as-siyāsī fī zamān al-thawra* (Rhetoric of freedom, political disputes during the revolution time), Abdul Latif deals with political discourse presented by different political and social groups during the Arab Spring in 2011. He also refers to various slogans, demands and political campaigns during the Egyptian revolution against Hosni Mubarak's regime ('Abd al-Laṭīf 2013).

Furthermore, Abdul Latif's research is concerned with Perelman's argumentation and the universal audience (*balāghat jumhūr*). Abdul Latif states that *balāghat jumhūr* focuses on the audience that participates in common events such as political debates, rallies, religious gatherings, sports matches or cultural festivals ('Abd al-Laṭīf 2021: 349–386). Abdul Latif also argues that effective discourse relies on the competence, credibility and skills of the speaker who convinces his audiences. However, *balāghat jumhūr* also includes nonverbal features such as applause, chanting or gestures ('Abd al-Laṭīf 2021: 313–325).

Complex Rhetorical Terms

Recent studies on Arabic rhetoric are facing new challenges regarding terminology of particular figures which remain unidentified in Arabic rhetoric. The complex character of rhetorical devices was evident in the case of Al-Khūlī's research on antonomasia presented in the second section of this chapter.

Modern Arab philologists often incorporate Western equivalents into the Arabic context and adopt different definitions and translations, as in the Arabic translation of the *Encyclopedia of Rhetoric* (Sloane 2001) and the glossary *Al-Balāgha al-'arabiyya fī ḍaw' al-balāghāt al-mu'āṣira* (Arabic rhetoric in the frame of modern rhetoric) (Nuwaywāt 2013). However, the *Encyclopedia of Rhetoric* refers to English rhetorical terminology ('Abd al-Laṭīf and Labīb 2016), and *Al-Balāgha al-'arabiyya fī ḍaw' al-balāghāt al-mu'āṣira* focuses on French literary theory. Terminological aspects create in this context scope for further research.

For example, apostrophe is usually called unreasonable speech (*mukhāṭaba ghayr al-'āqil*) because it appeals to non-human objects that cannot respond to the message. The notion usually consists of the vocative particle *yā* (O!) or the exclamation noun *ayyuhā* (oh!), as in: *Yā ayyuhā al-nāṣu!* (Oh people!) (Raof 2006: 246–247). However, the vocative utterances refer to the category of *'ilm al-ma'ānī* that recognizes different forms of narrative based on imperative, prohibition or interrogative and vocative sentences.

Paradoxically, rhetorical conceptual apparatus does not correspond to practical application of certain figures. For example, euphemism and dysphemism are considered as understatements (*tahwīn*), and in classical *balāgha* they are classified as metaphorical expressions. Euphemism designates more pleasant substitutes for offensive meanings, and dysphemism is a contrary term, which involves negative or offensive equivalents attributed to particular meanings. Both terms are often applied in political discourse in the Arab world, especially in propaganda of radical Islamist groups such as Al-Qaeda or ISIS, which usually call their opponents *salibiyyūn* (crusaders), *taghūt* (Satan, oppressor) or *kuffār* (sinners) and *murtaddūn* (apostates). The historical and religious context of the words is applied to modern political environments in the Arab world to humiliate local authorities and their allies in Western countries. Application of dysphemism also aims at intensifying political, religious or ideological tensions within Muslim communities. However, the expression *usūd al-ḥaqq* (the lions of truth) minimizes and relieves negative connotations related to terrorist groups which are compared to lions' bravery, courage and victory. Therefore, pleasant meanings minimize brutal and tragic consequences of terrorist acts, and glorify insurgents (Styszyński 2009: 144–160).

Moreover, oxymoron is called *irdāf khulfī* (proximity of contraries), and it concerns two antonyms placed next to each other. This notion is examined by Muḥammad Matwally in his article *Bayna irdāf khulfī wa al-ṭibāq* (Between proximity of contraries and antonyms). Matwally highlights chaotic conditions of rhetorical terminology, and he states that many terms are derived from Western cultures and they do not correspond with Arabic equivalents. He also advocates for terminology based on classical *balāgha*, and proposes the notion *ṭibāq* as the equivalent for oxymoron (Matwally 2020). Despite difficulties in theoretical frames, oxymoron is used by Al-Jāḥiẓ in his works. When Al-Jāḥiẓ explains the sense of good manners and education, he adopts the expression *habā'il thiqf* (trap of good manners) (Styszyński 2008: 86–87). The word *habā'il* designates negative meaning of a trap that symbolizes slavery, weakness or helplessness. Unlike *habā'il*, the word *thiqf* refers to positive meanings of education or good behavior. Al-Jāḥiẓ combines semantically opposite meanings to emphasize the significance of good manners, which should be attached to human beings like a trap.

The notion *iltifāt* also gains various meanings as well. It is literally concerned with change of addressee or turning from one person to another, as in the fragment of the Qur'ān from the chapter *Ya-Sin Wa mā liya lā a'budu al-ladhī fataranī wa ilayhi turja'ūn* (and why should I not worship the One who has originated me, and to whom you will be returned). The first part of the verse is switched suddenly from the first person singular into the second person plural. The transposition of the persons aims at demonstrating that the Prophet Muhammad and his believers share common values (Al-Ṣa'īdī 2009: 137–145).

Iltifāt was also studied by Al-'Askarī who defined it as expression of meaning by different linguistic tools. *Iltifāt* was often called substitution (*tatmīm*) and it designated modifications of pronouns, persons and numbers ('Abd al-Laṭīf 2010: 146–175). Nevertheless, classical rhetoricians disagreed on definition and classification of *iltifāt* in *'ilm al-ma'ānī*, *bayān* or *badī'*. In fact, an approximated equivalent reflects enallage, which concerns interchange and modifications of grammatical forms as well as substitution of tense, number or persons for incorrect versions that are intended because they aim at additional messages. *Iltifāt* is also compared to parenthesis that reflects insertion of additional words or sentences into a paragraph in order to qualify and explain certain meanings ('Abd al-Laṭīf 2010: 146–175).

Conclusion

The study argues that Arabic rhetoric still relies on the classical model identified and classified by Al-Jāḥiẓ, Al-Jurjānī and Al-Sakkākī during the Abbasid era. In fact, modern interpretations in the twentieth century as well as Western influences in the twenty-first century did not modify the core paradigm of *'ilm al-ma'ānī*, *bayān* and *badī'*. The concept of meanings and exact words or relations between the speaker and his audiences as well as the persuasion process became the main features of classical *balāgha*. However, the research demonstrates that Al-Sakkākī and al-Qazwīnī proposed consolidated criteria such as *'ilm al-ma'ānī*, *bayān* and *badī'*. The first category refers to syntactic and lexical regulations that include concision (*ījāz*) and prolixity (*iṭnāb*) as well as affirmative utterances (*khabar*) and performative emotional utterances (*inshā'*). However, *bayān* consists of different forms of metaphorical expression (*majāz*). The embellishments (*badī'*) are concerned with antithesis (*muqābala*) and *ṭibāq* (antonym) or homonymy (*tajnīs*).

Furthermore, the theories of the classical rhetoricians affected modern objectives of *balāgha*. It should be noted that most of the rhetoricians in the twentieth century were from Egypt which experienced social, political and cultural transformations from a rural society into urbanized populations living in Cairo or Alexandria. The rhetoricians appreciated the new environment and they combined classical *balāgha* with Western influences.

However, the research also demonstrates that the rhetoricians focus on modern Western influences. For instance, Al-Zayyāt combines *'ilm al-ma'ānī* with stylistics or French literary criticism, and he refers to Buffon's statement 'Style is the man himself' to emphasize the importance of relations between the speaker and the audience. In addition, Al-Zayyāt combines Gustave Flaubert's ideas with those of the classical rhetoricians and their concept of *ījāz* coinciding with Western concision of expression. Al-Zayyāt distinguishes three main patterns of rhetoric: originality (*aṣāla*), concision (*wijāza*) and harmony (*talā'um*). However, *wijāza* is the main topic in Al-Zayyāt's concept of rhetoric.

The modern rhetoricians also present some critical opinions about classical Arabic. For example, Mūsa supports colloquial Arabic because it facilitates persuasion practices. The research argues that negative approaches reflect *bayān* and *badī'*. According to Mūsa and Al-Zayyāt, embellishments distract the persuasion and logical principles of *'ilm al-ma'ānī*. However, Al-Khūlī demonstrates exceptional perspectives arguing that Arabic rhetoric aims at achieving persuasion by various means, including embellishments. Thus he designates three categories: creativity (*ijād*), arrangement (*tartīb*), and literary expression or style (*ta'bīr*).

The study also argues that the rhetoricians in the twentieth century did not modify the traditional model of *balāgha*, and their reinterpretations or theoretical criteria did not include practical application of their principles in the Arabic language.

Furthermore, innovative approaches are presented in the twenty-first century by philologists such as Emad Abdul Latif, Muḥammad Miftāḥ, Ḥamādī Ṣumūd and Ṣalāḥ Faḍl. For example, Ṣumūd relies in his research on Perelman's argumentative and legal rhetoric, and Miftāḥ refers to Peirce's pragmatism. However, Faḍl focuses on hermeneutics and Lakoff's metaphors. Yet similarly to the rhetoricians in the twentieth century, the philologists do not demonstrate processing of those theories in practice. Moreover, they rather focus on classical *'ilm al-ma'ānī* which determines, in their opinion, the main pattern of modern Arabic rhetoric.

However, Abdul Latif is one of the few philologists who adapt Western concepts of intertextuality, argumentation or universal audiences to the Arabic language, especially to political discourse. His research on Sadat's speeches and political and social demands during the Arab Spring is a good example in this context.

The research also demonstrates that rhetorical terminology creates new scope for further research. The study argues that oxymoron, euphemism, dysphemism and apostrophe remain unclarified in Arabic rhetoric. Analysis of some examples argues that these terms are recognized practically in the Arabic language but the conceptual apparatus needs additional study.

Thus provisional findings lead to a conclusion that classical *balāgha* provides a sufficient model that may be applied to the persuasion process, and it corresponds to needs of audiences in the Arab world. In fact, Western concepts of argumentation, hermeneutics and pragmatism have already been studied and defined by Abbasid rhetoricians who formulated certain communicative and persuasive regulations in *'ilm al-ma'ānī*. Therefore, only the criteria of *bayān* and *badī'* require further study in order to define additional rhetorical figures applied in practice.

References

Abbas, A. (2002) *Arabic Poetic Terminology*. Poznań: Wydawnictwo Naukowe UAM.
Abdul Latif, E. (2011) 'Interdiscursivity between Political and Religious Discourses in a Speech by Sadat', *Journal of Language and Politics* 10 (1): 50–67.
'Abd al-Laṭīf, 'I. (2021) *Al-Balāgha al-'arabiyya al-jadīda: masārāt wa muqārabāt* (Modern Arabic rhetoric: distances and proximities). 'Ammān: Dār kunūz al-ma'rifa.
'Abd al-Laṭīf, 'I. (2013) *Al-Balāghat al-ḥurriyya, ma'ārik al-khiṭāb as-siyāsī fī zamān al-thawra* (Rhetoric of freedom, political disputes during the revolution time). Lubnān: Dār al-tanwīr.
'Abd al-Laṭīf, 'I. and Labīb, M. (2016) *Mawsū'at al-balāgha* (Encyclopedia of rhetoric). Al-Qāhira: Al-Markaz al-qawmī li-al-tarjama.
'Abd al-Laṭīf, 'I. (2010) 'Madhkhal balāghī li-taḥlīl al-khuṭab as-siyāsī' (Rhetorical introduction to analysis of political discourse), *Alif* 30: 146–175.
Abū Zayd, N. Ḥ. (2006) *Reformation of Islamic Thought: A Critical Historical Analysis*, Amsterdam: Amsterdam University Press.
'Āṣī, M. (1981) *Mafāhīm al-jamāliyya wa al-naqd fī adab al-Jāḥiẓ*, (Perception of embellishments and critics in al-Jāḥiẓ's works). Bayrūt: Muassasat Nawfal.
Badawī, A. (1979) *Usūs an-naqd al-adabī 'ind al-'arab* (Principles of literary critic within Arabs). Al-Qāhira: 'Ālim al-kutub.
Balmalīḥ, I. (1984) *Al-Ruya al-bayāniyya 'ind al-Jāḥiẓ* (Al-Jāḥiẓ's expression perspective). Al-Dār al-Bayḍā': Dār al-Thaqāfa.
Carlucci, A. (2013) *Gramsci and Languages: Unification, Diversity, Hegemony*. Leiden/Boston: Brill.
Fenves, P. D. (2001) *Arresting Language: From Leibniz to Benjamin*. Stanford: Stanford University Press.
Feteris, E. T. (2017) 'Perelman's New Rhetoric', in E. T. Feteris, *Fundamentals of Legal Argumentation*. Dordrecht: Springer.
Halldén, Ph. (2005) 'What Is Arab Islamic Rhetoric? Rethinking the History of Muslim Oratory Art and Homiletics', *International Journal of Middle East Studies* 37 (1): 19–38.
Heemskerk, M. T. (2000) *Suffering in the Mu'tazilite Theology: 'Abd Al-Jabbār's Teaching on Pain and Divine Justice*. Leiden: Brill.
El-Hibri, T. (2021) *The Abbasid Caliphate: A History*. Cambridge: Cambridge University Press.
Al-Hshim A. (2012) *Jawāhir al-balāgha*, (Treasures of rhetoric). Bayrūt: Dār al-Kutub al-'Ilmiyya.
Ibn Imbīrīk, A. M. (1985) *Ṣurat bakhīl al-Jāḥiẓ al-fanniyya min khilāl khaṣāiṣ al-uslūb fī kitāb Al-Bukhalā* (Artistic image of a miser in the frame of stylistic principles in Al-Jāḥiẓ's Book of misers). Tūnis: Al-Dār al-Tūnisiyya li-al-Nashr.
Ibrahim, I. A. (1979) 'Salama Musa: An Essay on Cultural Alienation', *Middle Eastern Studies* 15 (3): 346–357.
Al-Jārim, 'A. and Amīn, M. (1979) *Al-Balāgha al-wāḍiḥa* (Clear rhetoric). Bayrūt: Dār al-Ma'ārif.
Al-Khūlī, A. (1996) *Fann al-qawl* (Art of the speech). Al-Qāhira: Dār al-kutub.
Klifman, H. (1992) 'Dutch Language Study and the Trivium: Motives and Elaborations', in J. Noordegraaf, K. Versteegh, and E. F. K. Koerner (eds.), *The History of Linguistics in the Low Countries*. Amsterdam/Philadelphia: John Benjamins Publishing.

Mason, J. (2019) *Intertextuality in Practice*. Amsterdam: John Benjamins Publishing.

Matwally, M. (2020) 'Bayna irdāf khulfī wa al-ṭibāq' (Between oxymoron and antonym), *Ḥamāsa*, 8 July 2020, www.hamassa.com/ (accessed 13 April 2022).

Mūsa, S. (1961) *The Education of Salāma Mūsa*. Amsterdam: Brill.

Mūsa, S. (2012) *Al-Balāgha al-ʿaṣriyya wa al-lugha al-ʿarabiyya* (Modern rhetoric and Arabic language). Al-Qāhira: Hindāwī.

Al-Muṭṭalib, M. (1994) *Al-Balāgha wa al-uslūbiyya* (Rhetoric and stylistics). Lubnān: Maktabat Lubnān nāshirūn.

Nasr, A. Z. (2003) 'The Dilemma of the Literary Approach to the Qur'ān', *Alif: Journal of Comparative Poetics* 23: 8–47.

Nuwaywāt M. (2013) *Al-Balāgha al-ʿarabiyya fī ḍaw' al-balāghāt al-muʿāṣira* (Arabic rhetoric in the frame of modern rhetoric). Al-Jazāir: Dār Hūma.

Obeidat, A. Z. (2017) 'The Semantic Field of Love in Classical Arabic: Understanding the Subconscious Meaning Preserved in the *Ḥubb* Synonyms and Antonyms through Their Etymologies', in A. Korangy, H. Al-Samman, and M. Beard (eds.), *The Beloved in Middle Eastern Literatures: The Culture of Love and Languishing*. London: I.B.Tauris.

Al-Osaimi, M. (2000) *The Politics of Persuasion. The Islamic Oratory of King Ibn Abdul Aziz*. Riyadh: King Faisal Center for Research and Islamic Studies.

Qutbuddin, T. (2008) 'Khutba. The Evolution of Early Arabic Oration', in B. Gruendler and M.Cooperson (eds.), *Classical Arabic Humanities in Their Own Terms: Festschrift for Wolfhart Heinrichs on His 65th Birthday*. Leiden: Brill.

Raof, H. (2006) *Arabic Rhetoric, A Pragmatic Analysis*. New York: Taylor & Francis.

Al-Saʿīdī, ʿAbd al-Mutaʿāl (2009) *Bughyat al-īḍāḥ li-talkhīṣ al-miftāḥ* (Goal of the clarity in the summary of *al-miftāḥ*). Al-Qāhira: Maktabat al-Adāb.

Salām, M. Z. (1982) *Tārīkh al-naqd al-adabī wa al-balāhga* (History of the literary critic and rhetoric). Al-Iskandariyya: Manshaat al-Maʿarif.

Salhi, Z. S., and Alqarni, H. M. (2016) 'New Images in Old Frames: Ibn Harma (d. ca. 176/792) between Classical Poetry and Abbasid Modernity', *Journal of Abbasid Studies* 3 (1): 56–89.

Sallūm, D. (1986) *Al-Naqd al-manhajī ʿind al-Jāḥiẓ* (Al-Jāḥiẓ's methodological critic). Bayrūt: Maktabat al-Nahḍa al-ʿArabiyya.

Al-Shadhr, Ṭ. Ṣ. (1998) *Alfāẓ al-ḥaḍāra al-ʿabbāsiyya fī muallafāt al-Jāḥiẓ* (Words from Abbasid civilization in Al-Jāḥiẓ's works). Al-Qāhira: Dār Qabā li-al-Ṭabʿ wa al-Nashr wa al-Tawzīʿ.

Sheyhatovitch, B. and Kasher, A. (eds.) (2020) *From Sibawayhi to ʿAhmad Hasan al-Zayyat: New Angles on the Arabic Linguistic Tradition*. Leiden: Brill.

Siwiec, P. (2008) *Zarys poetyki klasycznego wiersza arabskiego*. Kraków: Księgarnia Akademicka.

Sloane T. O. (2001) *Encyclopedia of Rhetoric*. Oxford: Oxford University Press.

Styszyński, M. (2008) *Retoryka arabska w twórczości Al-Dżahiza*. Poznań: UAM.

Styszyński, M. (2009) 'Wpływ klasycznej retoryki arabskiej na współczesne społeczeństwo', *Forum Artis Rhetoricae* 3–4 (18–19): 144–160.

Suleiman, Y. (2019) *Arabic Language and National Identity: A Study in Ideology*. Edinburgh: Edinburgh University Press.

al-Ṭalaba, M. (2008) *Al-Hijāj fī al-balāgha al-muʿāṣira* (Argumentation in modern rhetoric). Bayrūt: Dār al-kitāb al-jadīd.

Ullah, K. (2017) *Al-Kashshaf: Al-Zamakhshari's Muʿtazilite Exegesis of the Qur'an*. Berlin/ Boston: Walter de Gruyter.

Vagelpohl, U. (2015) 'The Rhetoric and Poetics in the Islamic World', in A. Alwishah and J. Hayes (eds.), *Aristotle and the Arabic Tradition*. Cambridge: Cambridge University Press.

Al-Zayyāt, A. Ḥ. (1967) *Difāʿ an al-balāgha*, (Defense of rhetoric). Al-Qāhira: ʿĀlim al-kutub.

PART II

Descriptive Rhetorical Studies: Regional Diversity

6

RHETORICAL DEVICES IN JAPANESE

The Case for Onomatopoeia

Massimiliano Tomasi

Introduction

Japanese is a language extremely rich in mimetic expressions. These expressions are known as *giongo* 擬音語 (words that imitate sounds) and *gitaigo* 擬態語 (words that imitate conditions and psychological moods), but are increasingly referred to as *onomatope* オノマトペ (onomatopoeia). The strong interest in these forms witnessed among scholars overseas in recent years is a significant new development, as it was not until the 1990s that more attention began to be paid to the cognitive and linguistic mechanisms that regulate them.[1] The causes of this disregard are likely rooted in the peripheral role that onomatopoeia plays in Western languages and in the resulting marginal fashion in which it has traditionally been discussed. Saussure, it may be recalled, had in fact stated in his notable work at the beginning of the twentieth century that "onomatopoeic formations are never organic elements of a linguistic system . . . not only they are limited in number, but also they are chosen somewhat arbitrarily, for they are only approximate and more or less conventional imitations of certain sounds" (1974: 69). The Japanese academic community was influenced by these early deliberations, but onomatopoeia had already caught researchers' attention well before the introduction of Western linguistics. Albeit not to the same extent of modern times, the usage of mimetic words can in fact be found across a wide range of texts from the classical period, and scholars were fully aware of their existence and distinctive features. Indeed, the theories of language dominating the scientific world in premodern Japan stemmed in part from the very belief in an intrinsic connection of necessity between words and what they represented. Early nineteenth-century scholar Suzuki Akira (1764–1837) drew significantly from these convictions: his distinction between words that are phonetically motivated and that are not, coupled with his awareness of language change and of the universal character of phonosymbolism, is reminiscent of the theoretical premises that later led Saussure to deliberate on the arbitrariness of the linguistic sign.

Following the establishment of linguistics and its methodology, Japanese scholars began to pay increased attention to the properties of their native language. Seminal

DOI: 10.4324/9781003195276-9

essays by Kobayashi (1933), Kobayashi (1937) and Sakuma (1943) analyzed the morphological and phonological structure of Japanese onomatopoeia, whereas Kojima Kōsaburō's *Gendai bungaku to onomatope* (Modern Literature and Onomatopoeia, 1972) later became the first monograph to discuss the use of these forms in literature, providing extensive evidence of the expressive potential of the Japanese imitative system and setting the stage for further investigations at the intersections of rhetoric and stylistics. Interestingly, parallel developments in the field of rhetoric did not reflect these important findings; although the last decades of the twentieth century witnessed a proliferation of scholarly works that centered on the study of tropes and other rhetorical figures, with the partial exception of Nakamura (1977) and Nakamura (1991), none of these studies covered onomatopoeia in any significant fashion.[2] This is surprising if one considers that it is indeed the ability to generate infinite combinations of meaning – its rhetoricity – that stands out as Japanese onomatopoeia's most unique trait, and that it was exactly the field of rhetoric that a century ago had sanctioned its importance as a distinctive rhetorical feature of the Japanese language.

The cohesiveness and systematic nature of the Japanese sound-symbolic system is at the root of its rhetorical potential. While these traits have yet to be adequately discussed in non-Japanese scholarly circles, early references to these properties of Japanese mimetic words can be found in Samuel Martin's *A Reference Grammar of Japanese*. Martin noted that "although dictionaries carry a good many of the mimetic adverbs that are in common use, new ones keep turning up, as well as unexpected variants of older forms" (1975: 1023). He then went on to point out that

> the phonetic system utilizes syllables and moras in ways that facilitate the creation of new variants from established forms; that is one reason dictionaries do not cover this part of the vocabulary comprehensively. Phonetic symbolism helps make connotational variants that differ only in vowels or in choice of initial consonant.

1975: 1024

Shoko Hamano's seminal study, *The Sound-Symbolic System of Japanese*, ratified the existence of such cohesiveness, positing in fact "the autonomous linguistic structure" (1998: 211) of the entire imitative apparatus. Acknowledging the possibilities of "novel or artistic expressions with irregular phonological shapes," Hamano also emphasized that, as one should expect, "the majority of mimetic words conform to rigid structural constraints" (1998: 2), and it is indeed the existence of such a rigid and established set of norms that provides the premises for the deviations that typically occur in figurative language.

As is known, mimetic adverbs and mimetic nominal adjectives constitute the core of the Japanese sound-symbolic system. Possible formations include single-syllable occurrences followed by an elongated vowel ("waa," a loud clamor or commotion), by a glottal stop and the particle "to" ("patto," suddenly) or by the termination -n ("pan," a bang), as well as disyllables, often in a reduplicative pattern and with various expansions that include among others the termination -ri ("pittari," tight, perfect). Four-syllable reduplicative forms are among the most common (for example, "goro goro," a sense of idleness, and "ira ira," a feeling of annoyance or irritation) and are often used in conjunction with the verb "suru" (to do) in a typical syntactic pattern that is related to the semantic under-differentiation of Japanese verbs (Hamano 1998: 1). The following four examples – the first one imitating sounds, the remaining three psychological moods and manners – illustrate how onomatopoeia can be used in a Japanese sentence.

Example 1
Kodomo wa soto de *waa waa* sawaide asonde iru.
The children are playing loudly outside.

Example 2
Kinō uchi de *goro goro* shita.
Yesterday I relaxed at home.

Example 3
Watashi wa *katto* shita.
I got upset.

Example 4
Kodomo wa *nikkori* waratta.
The child smiled cheerfully.

Consonants and vowels are perceived to carry distinctive phonosymbolic connotations – such as quickness, softness and heaviness – that help speakers recognize nuanced variations in meaning, and repetition itself can convey further semantic nuances. The following examples, all from Hamano (1998: 104–105), show the slight difference in meaning resulting from the combination of this latter mechanism with each single phonosymbolic element present in the sentence.

Example 5
Shio o *para para* to futta.
I sprinkled salt.

Example 6
Shio o *para paratto* futta.
I gave a quick sprinkle of salt.

Example 7
Shio o *para para paratto* futta.
I gave a quick sprinkle of salt (all over).

The ability to generate special effects by virtue of these variations or by other types of cognitive associations across different semantic domains is a distinctive trait of the entire imitative system, and the impractical task of compiling a dictionary that is inclusive of all possible occurrences is not only reflective of these properties, it is also indicative of the rhetorical potential these forms exercise across the semantic continuum they represent. The increased visibility and attention they have garnered in recent years stem from the popularization of graphic texts and narratives – like *anime* and *manga* – that exploit exactly the existence of this continuum. It should be noted however that, as mentioned earlier, the current linguistic and pedagogical relevance of Japanese onomatopoeia is rooted in literary developments that occurred more than a century ago. This study examines the details of those developments, unveiling the crucial role played by the field of rhetoric in the legitimization of onomatopoeia as a distinctive rhetorical feature of written Japanese.

Onomatopeia and the Vernacular

Although, as briefly mentioned earlier in this study, the employment of mimetic expressions is not rare in pre-modern texts, it is only in relatively recent years that their use in writing has become more common and universally sanctioned. The written language of mid- to late nineteenth-century Japan was in fact still a classically-based mode of expression that differed greatly from the spoken tongue and did not allow for this type of expression. The gap between the two mediums reflected in essence the linguistic changes that had caused the vernacular to shift away from the literary language employed in the masterpieces of the classical period; as classical language continued to be revered as permanent and changeless, the vernacular was seen as mutable and devoid of refinement and regularity. The wide discrepancy between the two domains was emblematically captured by Jesuit missionary Alessandro Valignano (1539–1606) in his *Historia del Principio*:

> They have but one language and it is the best, the most elegant and the most copious tongue in the known world; it is more abundant than Latin and expresses concepts better ... The written and spoken languages are very different, and men and women also differ in their way of speaking. There is no less diversity in their way of writing; they write their letters, for example, in one style but their books in another. Finally, it takes a long time to learn the language because it is so elegant and copious. To speak or write in a way other than their accustomed manner is impolite and invites ridicule, just as if we were to speak Latin backwards and with many solecisms.
>
> *Cooper 1981: 171*

The development of *genbun itchi* 言文一致 (unification of the spoken and written language), a written style that could serve as an acceptable compromise between the vernacular and classical modes of literary expression, became one of the major achievements of the modern period. Spanning several decades, from the 1870s to the 1910s, the process transcended the purely linguistic boundaries of the debate, acquiring political overtones that are outside the purview of this study. In the field of literature, the continued tension between the two mediums reinforced the notion of two different levels of signification: an elegant and elitist higher level that was unintelligible to most, and a vulgar and verbose lower one – the sphere of everyday communication. Writers strove to create a new written form that could bridge these realities by satisfying the prerequisites of intelligibility on the one hand and being sufficiently refined for artistic expression on the other. Celebrated writer Mori Ōgai's (1862–1922) works exemplified the metamorphosis that occurred in the transition between the two styles; whereas his novel *Maihime* (The Dancing Girl, 1890) was replete with old linguistic conventions, in his work *Gan* (The Wild Geese, 1911–1913), written two decades later, those conventions had given way to contemporary linguistic features, as exemplified, in particular, by the employment of the "de aru" termination. These writers' efforts were however met by another consequential development: the concurrent call for a simple and unadorned style made by the proponents of Naturalism – the early twentieth century's most influential literary coterie. Naturalism's call for a literary language devoid of rhetorical embellishments but capable of depicting reality faithfully and effectively added a layer of complexity that would have significant implications in the quest for a new written medium.

Rhetorical Devices in Japanese

The progressive increase of the spoken language in literature seen at the turn of the century was thus a reflection of these developments. Because depicting reality faithfully and without exaggerations required a direct and unadorned language, the shift to a more colloquial form of writing was to an extent organic, and that this shift may in turn have led to a wider use of mimetic words is intuitively possible. Indeed, this assumption is consistent with the conventional wisdom that "using onomatopoeia appeals directly to the senses and is extremely effective in the case of descriptive prose" (Jugaku 1983: 186); that these forms "tend to be used sparsely in formal literary styles" (Yamaguchi 1972: 13); that "[they] are highly colloquial" (Kisaka 1977: 113); and that, "as far as Japanese literature is concerned, phonosymbolic words are more widely used now than in the past" (Ōtsubo 1982: 234). Futabatei Shimei's (1864–1909) *Ukigumo* (Drifting Clouds, 1886–1887), for example, considered by many to be Japan's first modern novel, made extensive use of authentic colloquial speech, and it should not be surprising that this included a large quantity of mimetic expressions. Futabatei's deliberate usage of such onomatopoeic expressions as "chonbori" (little), "mukkuri" (plump), and "pacchiri" (wide) helped provide a vivid description of the physical traits of his characters, rendering his prose more colorful and real.[3]

It was not the first time that these expressions had appeared in literature. Many works of the pre-modern period employed the vernacular, and there clearly was already an awareness of its importance which, on a lexical level, led in some cases to a deliberate use of colloquialisms, including mimetic adverbs. These words were however often confined to the dialogical part of the text, and the notion that classical literary conventions were more prestigious than contemporary speech was still highly prevalent. Futabatei Shimei's own 1906 recounting of how he came to the decision of employing everyday language in his novel is revealing:

> At the time, Tsubouchi advised me to make my writing a little more elegant, but I had no wish to do so. Indeed, it might be closer to the mark to say that I did my utmost to keep elegance out of my work, endeavouring instead to polish commonplace words.
>
> *Twine 1991: 138–139*

Futabatei strove to provide the vernacular with a new platform, and using onomatopoeic expressions extensively "was for him directly tied to the creation of a *genbun itchi* style, and as such more importantly than we can ever imagine" (Ozaki 1967: 144). Despite these important early developments, there were many in academic and intellectual circles who opposed the process of vernacularization of literary language. The 1890s saw for example the rise of nationalism in many areas of political and social discourse, which in literature translated into an advocacy for a return to classical themes and diction. The proponents of this movement criticized the spoken language for lacking in rhetorical flavor, melody and elegance, and its employment in writing was considered an oddity at best. As late as 1916, Waseda University professor and prominent literary critic Tsubouchi Shōyō (1859–1935), who had advised Futabatei Shimei and had also been instrumental in providing a theoretical framework for the modern novel, still regarded the excessive use of mimetic words as one of the major defects of the new style (Tsubouchi 1977: 587).

Author and scholar Yamada Bimyō (1868–1910) is known to have provided one of the most effective counterarguments to these theories. In a series of articles written at the turn of the century, Yamada challenged the notion that the vernacular was vulgar and inferior to classical language, and refuting the widespread idea in literary circles that it lacked a grammar of its own, he posited instead that it even had its own rhetorical features (Tomasi 2004). That in a rarely mentioned work titled *Genbun itchi bunrei* (Sample Writings in *Genbun itchi*) he also maintained that "onomatopoeia is an essential rhetorical element of the *genbun itchi* style" (Yamada 1901: 90) is indicative of his strong support for the use of mimetic expressions as a first critical step towards a (re)discovery of the rhetorical potential of the vernacular.

Given the highly controversial nature of the debate, a theoretical framework capable of supporting Yamada's notion that the vernacular had a rhetorical apparatus of its own was critical. The field of rhetoric itself provided such a framework by sanctioning the use of the colloquial in literature, thus spurring language experimentation and the exploration of onomatopoeia's rhetoricity in the written medium.

Rhetoric and the Case for Onomatopoeia

Western rhetoric was first introduced to Japan in the 1870s. Although the literary world developed at first a rather reductive notion of the discipline as an obsolete and anachronistic field of study that merely taught the use of elaborate expressions, rhetoric did eventually play a critical role in the quest for a modern literary language (Tomasi 2004). Its role in providing a framework for the theoretical reappraisal of the vernacular and in the ratification of onomatopoeia as a distinctive rhetorical feature of the new style was highly consequential, especially in light of the skepticism with which this had been discussed even among recent rhetorical treatises in the West. Eighteenth-century philosopher George Campbell (1719–1796) had written in *The Philosophy of Rhetoric* that "this trope, the onomatopoeia, in any form whatever, hath little scope in our tongue, and is hardly admissible except in burlesque" (1963: 301). Likewise, rhetorician Richard Whatley (1787–1863) had stated in his *Elements of Rhetoric* that "it may be worth remarking that an evident effort after this kind of excellence, as it is offensive in any kind of composition, would in prose appear peculiarly disgusting" (1963: 292). Other renowned works that were more readily available to Japanese rhetoricians at the beginning of the twentieth century did not discuss onomatopoeia either, although it is true that they, to some extent, recognized the special status of this class of words, particularly as poetic language. Thus, for example, Alexander Bain acknowledged that "it is possible to make the Sound of the language an echo to the Sense" (1888: 291), and this effect was in his view "a special and notable instance of the pervading principle of Harmony" that was "most easily attained when the subject-matter is sound … [as in] 'whizz,' 'buzz,' burr, hiss …" (1888: 291). John Genung noted that

> a great many words in the language were evidently formed as the result of an effort to make sounds correspond with sense, and be a kind of audible picture of it. Poetry deals with such words, and especially with combinations wherein movement and articulation produce this result together, more largely than does prose.
>
> *1890: 168–169*

Finally, discussing the "words of which the sound suggests the meaning," Adams Sherman Hill stated that these were "clear and forcible, both because they are specific and because they are so familiar that they may be accounted natural symbols rather than arbitrary signs; but when they become a mere trick of style, they lose their value" (1895: 122–123).

Despite the influence of these works in their intellectual circles, many Japanese scholars included onomatopoeia in their discussion of tropes and other rhetorical figures. Among these scholars, Waseda University professor Igarashi Chikara (1874–1947) was perhaps one of the first to acknowledge its importance in the new written language. In his work *Shinbunshō kōwa* (New Lectures on Composition) Igarashi noted a new trend in writing that shunned embellishment and favored a plain and direct style. Such a new style, he argued, made extensive use of colloquial speech, which now appeared not only in the dialogical, but also in the discursive portions of the text. Igarashi advanced the notion that the difference between the classical and contemporary styles did not lie in the presence or absence of rhetorical devices, but in the distinctive character of those devices. He then discussed the "elocutio" and noted that "many of these rhetorical figures are rejected by the new literary style that advocates unadorned writing; only onomatopoeia is however used more frequently in this new style than in the past" (1909: 440–441). Poet and scholar of national literature Utsumi Kōzō (1872–1935), who taught at Meiji University, similarly wrote in support of phonosymbolic words. In his *Bunshō jūkō* (Ten Lectures on Composition), he discussed the *shaseibun* (literary sketches) style in vogue in those years. He ascribed four essential traits to it, citing the reproduction of sounds as one of the most important: "These adverbs are extremely effective in the *shaseibun* style ... in other words, to write well in the *shaseibun* style one has to excel at these mimetic adverbs" (1910: 152–153).

Another scholar of national literature to sanction the importance of onomatopoeia was Haga Yaichi (1867–1927). In his *Sakubun kōwa oyobi bunpan* (Lectures on Composition with Model Examples), Haga, a prominent faculty member at Tokyo Imperial University, discussed a total of 23 rhetorical figures. Touching upon onomatopoeia, he defined it as the most necessary trope in order to portray things vividly, arguing that its use alone would guarantee a written style of the highest standard (1912: 177). He also noted that onomatopoeia was much more common in Japanese than in Chinese and Western languages, and after stating that all famous writers and poets of the past had made use of it, he added: "[this] and simile are the most commonly used rhetorical figures by the naturalist school that advocates unembellished writing" (1912: 183). He then postulated that

> in order to be able to display the full potential of our national written language, it is necessary to become conversant with the use of these two tropes. The naturalist school's advocacy for an unadorned and plain written style is a rejection of the elaborate rhetorical embellishments of the past and should be seen as a call for a return to the origins of rhetorical language. Onomatopoeia and simile are exactly that.
>
> *1912: 183*

Other individuals who placed substantial weight on the importance of mimetic expressions in the Japanese language included Buddhist scholar Katō Totsudō (1870–1949) and scholar of aesthetics Watanabe Kichiharu (1894–1930). Katō, who is known for the important role he played in the popularization of oratory in modern Japan, defined onomatopoeia as an essential rhetorical figure both in writing and speechmaking (1905: 73). Watanabe, on the other hand, noted that "onomatopoeia is frequently used in daily exchanges in which one does not have the time to think of elaborate expressions. For this reason, it is commonly used in spoken-language based written

Japanese" (1926: 221). Meanwhile, as these and other intellectuals engaged in such debates, and naturalism gained significant ground in the literary world, author Futabatei Shimei's own style had shifted further towards the employment of colloquial speech. His novel *Heibon* (Mediocrity, 1908) reflected this transition and was incidentally replete with mimetic expressions, and so were a large number of contemporary novels – such as Nagatsuka Takashi's *Tsuchi* (The Soil, 1910), Naka Kansuke's *Gin no saji* (The Silver Spoon, 1913) and Kasai Zenzō's *Ko o tsurete* (With the Children in Tow, 1919) – that were similarly written in the vernacular.[4] The increased employment of onomatopoiea in these works added significantly to the already highly descriptive character of their naturalist prose style, lending a vividness of detail that appealed to readers by virtue of the directness and richness of the imagery.

The shift towards the employment of the vernacular facilitated the use of colloquial expressions that had until then been barred from serious literature. It was however the field of poetry that provided the most fertile ground for additional meaningful experimentations and for the further ratification of mimetic expressions as a distinctive rhetorical trait of modern Japanese. The first significant steps towards the employment of the vernacular and a meter-free poetic diction were taken in 1882 with the publication of *Shintaishishō* (A Selection of Poetry in the New Style), a collection of five original Japanese poems and 14 translations from English that included such works as Thomas Gray's "Elegy Written in a Country Church-Yard" and Henry Wadsworth Longfellow's "The Psalm of Life." The collection widened the lexical gamut of poetic language to include common speech, which opened up the possibility of exploring old and new themes through a modern sensibility. Most importantly, it challenged the rigid metrical structure of traditional genres like *waka* 和歌, *haiku* 俳句 and *kanshi* 漢詩, sanctioning in the process the use of multisyllabic linguistic tokens – onomatopoeic reduplicative forms, for example – that had until then been precluded due to such restrictions. Of course, the shift from a classical to a vernacular-based poetic language was not immediate. In many cases, however, this transition took place from one anthology to the other, and as it did, the increase of mimetic expressions became further noticeable. For example, after shifting away from classical diction, Hagiwara Sakutarō (1886–1942), one of modern Japan's most celebrated poets, made a large and deliberate use of onomatopoeia in his poetry. In a poem titled "Niwatori" (Rooster) and included in his famous collection *Aoneko* (Blue Cats, 1923), the imitation of the rooster's cry "towotekuu, toworumou, toworumou" is used rhythmically at the end of each stanza, generating an additional rhetorical effect of epiphora. Similarly, in "Guntai" (The Army), another poem from the same collection, the words mimicking the marching soldiers – "zushiri zushiri patari patari" and "zakku zakku zakku zakku" – are employed together at the end of the first stanza, then separately at the end of the second and third, and then used again with some variations in the final two stanzas of the poem. Kusano Shinpei (1903–1988), another famous twentieth-century poet, also employed this device in conjunction with onomatopoeic expressions, as in his poem "Yoru no umi" (Night Sea) from the collection *Manmosu no kiba* (The Mammoth's Tusk, 1966) where the words recurring at the end of each stanza – "zuzuzu wa'ru, zuzuzun zuwa'ru, gunun uwa'ru" – capture the roaring sound of the ocean waves, generating a sensorial experience that lends vividness and power to his verses.

Repetition is indeed central to Japanese onomatopoeia's ability to systematically generate new tokens. Among the rhetorical figures generally attributed to this linguistic mechanism, gemination, the repetition of a single word, was especially common in Hagiwara's poems: in "Hibari no su" (The Skylark's Nest) from the collection *Chō o yumemu* (Dreaming of Butterflies, 1923), for example, the crying sound of the skylark – "piyo" – is repeated eight times in one single verse. Other cases included reduplicative tokens generating additional alliterative effects, such as in "Haru no jittai" (The Essence of Spring) from the collection *Tsuki ni hoeru* (Howling to the Moon, 1917) in which the glittering properties of the wings of moths and butterflies are captured through the eight-syllable mimetic expression "pika pika pika pika" followed by the verb "hikaru" (to shine). Kusano Shinpei's use of this type of repetition is especially emblematic: the fourth and final stanza of his poem "Hanshinron ni yuki ga furu" (Snowing on Pantheism) from the collection *Dekoboko* (Uneven, 1974) consists of nine lines where the mimetic expression "shin shin" – the conditions and sound of the falling snow – is repeated a total of 28 times in a virtually untranslatable text that is a reminder of the richness and associative semantic power of Japanese onomatopoeic expressions. Alliteration is not the only rhetorical effect present in this composition; there is a melodic, rhythmic cadence in this nine-line onomatopoeic sequence that adds substantially to the sensorial experience generated by the work.

The employment of onomatopoeia is not however limited to the reproduction of sounds, psychological moods or conditions. As a cohesive and autonomous linguistic structure, onomatopoeia also lends itself well to the exploration of the heuristic potential of figurative language. In the final lines of the poem "Yopparai no shi" (Death of an Alcoholic) from the collection *Tsuki ni hoeru*, for example, Hagiwara uses the unusual simile "kusa no yō ni *bira bira* warau" (to laugh like fluttering grass) in order to describe the smiling face of the murderer. Similarly, and in a much more light-hearted composition titled "Asa no shi" (Morning Poetry) from his collection *Kaze wa kusagi ni sasayaita* (The Wind Whispered over Trees and Plants, 1918), poet Yamamura Bochō (1884–1924) compares a small rock skipping over an icy surface to the inquisitiveness ("kyoro kyoro," i.e. "looking around") of a chirping bird in the expression "ishikoro wa *kyoro kyoro* to kotori no yō ni saezutte subetta" (the pebble skipped along [the surface] *looking around* like a chirping bird). Finally, in one of his most well-known poems titled "Neko" (Cats), Hagiwara's onomatopoeic rendering of two cats' meowing makes their short conversation on top of a roof more real, adding a distinctive rhetorical effect of personification. The poet's creative use of the mimetic tokens "owaa" and "ogyaa," as opposed to the more standard "nyaa," seems to confer a uniquely personable character on the cats who thus become compassionate and sympathetic observers of the landlord's sorrow.

As this discussion has shown, the use of onomatopoeia became widespread not only among fiction writers but also among poets who could now exploit the rhetorical potential of their native language without the metrical constraints of traditional poetic genres. Indeed, as had been the case in the realm of prose, for many of these authors the shift to a vernacular-based mode of expression resulted in an increase of onomatopoeic words. Takamura Kōtarō (1883–1956), for example, began to move away from classical literary conventions in the middle of his collection *Dōtei* (The Journey, 1914), and as he did, the number of mimetic expressions appearing in his poems increased. The same can be said about Ishikawa Takuboku (1886–1912) as he transitioned from his collection *Akogare* (Yearning, 1905), written in classical diction, to *Kokoro no sugata no kenkyū* (A Study of the Soul, 1909), which was instead rich in colloquial language. The call for a more direct and immediate medium accompanied by the stylistic changes that were taking place in the area of prose led to a renewed awareness of the expressive potential of the vernacular, which, to put it in one scholar's words, "[in turn] conferred upon onomatopoeia the status of poetic language in the poetry of the new style" (Tsukahara 1974: 4).

Conclusion

As stated earlier in this study, the notion that a shift towards the vernacularization of the literary language may have led to an increase of mimetic expressions in writing is intuitively demonstrable, and scholars generally agree that the widespread employment of this class of words and otherwise uncommon colloquialisms was a reflection of this transition. The importance of the language debates and the role that rhetorical research played in this process has however been largely overlooked. The highly influential Western scholarly tradition had relegated onomatopoeia to the margins of linguistic investigation, and the centuries-long diglossia at the root of the tensions between the written and the spoken mediums had further reinforced the belief in the incompatibility of mimetic expressions as a mode of literary signification. Reclaiming onomatopoeia's rightful place as a distinctive rhetorical and stylistic feature of the Japanese language required a concerted effort on various fronts. A condition was a theoretical appraisal of the vernacular, which took place through long and strenuous debates but also thanks to the decisive role played by prominent scholars of rhetoric and literature alike who were instrumental in setting attitudes and trajectories on matters of literacy and language policy. As can be evinced by the examples discussed in this study, in fact, these scholars clearly acknowledged a link of necessity between the prerequisites of the new written style – simplicity, authentic speech, immediacy – and the use of mimetic expressions. Their endorsement of the use of onomatopoeia in literature contributed to a rediscovery of the rhetorical potential and the distinctive nature of this largely dismissed linguistic device. The attention the Japanese language imitative system has been receiving in recent years is therefore a reflection of the fierce debates and deliberations at the intersection of language and literature that took place over a century ago.

Notes

1 The growing number of available dictionaries and illustrated textbooks intended to facilitate their acquisition is the most direct and unequivocal evidence of this recent popularity. See, for example, Fujita and Akiho (1984), Gomi (1989), and Fukuda (2012).
2 For a brief survey of rhetorical research in Japan, see Tomasi (2021). Although outside the field of rhetoric, Ōtsubo (1989) provides extensive evidence of how onomatopoeic forms have been used effectively across a variety of genres, from literature to advertising. Other recent important works on the Japanese mimetic system include Kakehi and Tamori (1993) and Nakazato (2017).
3 See, for example, Futabatei (1984: 10) and Futabatei (1984: 25).
4 See, for example, Futabatei (1984: 436), Nagatsuka (1976: 11), Naka (1989: 53), and Kasai (1974: 165).

English References

Bain, Alexander (1888) *English Composition and Rhetoric*, vol. 2, New York: American Book Company.
Campbell, George (1963) *The Philosophy of Rhetoric*, Carbondale: Southern Illinois Press.
Cooper, Michael (ed.) (1981) *They Came to Japan: An Anthology of European Reports on Japan, 1543–1640*, Berkeley, University of California Press.
Fukuda, Hiroko (2012) *Jazz Up Your Japanese with Onomatopoeias*, New York: Kodansha.
Genung, John F. (1890) *Practical Elements of Rhetoric*, Boston: Ginn & Company.
Gomi, Tarō (1989) *An Illustrated Dictionary of Japanese Onomatopoeic Expressions*, Tokyo: The Japan Times.

Hamano, Shoko (1998) *The Sound-Symbolic System of Japanese*, Stanford: Center for the Study of Language and Information.

Hill, Adams Sherman (1895) *The Principles of Rhetoric*, New York: American Book Company.

Martin, Samuel (1975) *A Reference Grammar of Japanese*, New Haven and London: Yale University Press.

Saussure, Ferdinand de (1974) *Course in General Linguistics*, English translation by Wade Baskin, London: Peter Owen.

Tomasi, Massimiliano (2004) *Rhetoric in Modern Japan: Western Influences on the Development of Narrative and Oratorical Style*, Honolulu: University of Hawai'i Press.

Tomasi, Massimiliano (2021) "The Study of Rhetoric in Japan: A Survey of Rhetorical Research from the Late Nineteenth Century to the Present," in K. Loyd (ed.), *The Routledge Handbook of Comparative World Rhetorics*, London and New York: Routledge.

Twine, Nanette (1991) *Language and the Modern State: The Reform of Written Japanese*, London and New York: Routledge.

Whatley, Richard (1963) *Elements of Rhetoric*, Carbondale: Southern Illinois Press.

Japanese References

Fujita, Takashi 藤田孝 and Akiho Shin'ichi 秋保慎一 (1984) 和英擬音語・擬態 語翻訳辞典 (A Japanese-English Dictionary of Onomatopoeia), Tokyo: Kinseidō.

Futabatei, Shimei 二葉亭四迷 (1984) 二葉亭四迷全集 (The Collected Works of Futabatei Shimei), vol. 1, Tokyo: Chikuma shobō.

Haga, Yaichi 芳賀矢一 (1912) 作文講話及文範 (Lectures on Composition with Model Examples), Tokyo: Fuzanbō.

Hagiwara, Sakutarō 萩原朔太郎 (1966) 日本詩人全集 (The Collected Works of Japanese Poets), vol. 14, Tokyo: Shinchōsha.

Igarashi, Chikara 五十嵐力 (1909) 新文章講話 (New Lectures on Composition), Tokyo: Waseda daigaku shuppanbu.

Jugaku, Akiko 寿岳章子(1983) 室町時代語の表現 (The Language of the Muromachi Period), Tokyo: Seibundō.

Kakehi, Hisao 筧寿雄 and Tamori, Ikuhiro 田守育啓 (1993) オノマトピア・擬音・擬態語の楽園 (A Paradise of Onomatopoeia), Tokyo: Keisō shobō.

Kasai, Zenzō 葛西善三 (1974) 葛西善三全集 (The Collected Works of Kasai Zenzō), vol. 1, Tokyo: Bunsendō shoten.

Katō, Totsudō 加藤咄堂 (1905) 応用修辞学 (Applied Rhetoric), Tokyo: Kokkōsha.

Kisaka, Motoki 木坂基 (1977) '論説的言文一致文章の用語法' (Word Usage in the Argumentative *Genbun itchi* Style), 近世文芸稿 (Papers on Premodern Literature) 22, 104–115.

Kobayashi, Hideo 小林英夫 (1933) '国語象徴音の研究' (A Study of Japanese Phonetic Symbolism) 文学 (Literature) 1:8.

Kobayashi, Yoshiharu 小林好日 (1937) '音義説と音声象徴' (The Theory of the Meaning of Sounds and Phonetic Symbolism) 国語国文 (Language and Literature) 7:3.

Kojima, Kōsaburō 小嶋考三郎 (1972) 現代文学とオノマトペ (Modern Literature and Onomatopoeia), Tokyo: Ōfūsha.

Mori, Ōgai 森鴎外 (1953) *Maihime* 舞姫, 現代日本文学全集 (The Collected Works of Modern Japanese Literature), vol. 7, Tokyo: Chikuma shobō.

Mori, Ōgai 森鴎外 (1953) Gan 雁, 現代日本文学全集 (The Collected Works of Modern Japanese Literature), vol. 7, Tokyo: Chikuma shobō.

Nagatsuka, Takashi 長塚節 (1976) 長塚節全集 (The Collected Works of Nagatsuka Takashi), vol. 1, Tokyo: San'yōdō.

Naka, Kansuke 中勘助 (1989) 銀の匙 (The Silver Spoon), Tokyo: Iwanami shoten.

Nakamura, Akira 中村明 (1977) 比喩表現の理論と分類 (Theory and Classification of Rhetorical Expressions), Tokyo: Shūei shuppan.

Nakamura, Akira 中村明 (1991) 日本語レトリックの体系 (The Rhetorical System of the Japanese Language), Tokyo: Iwanami shoten.

Nakazato, Michiko 中里理子 (2017) オノマトペ語義変化研究 (A Study of the Semantic Change of Onomatopoeic Words), Tokyo: Bensei shuppan.

Ōtsubo, Heiji (1982) '象徴語彙の歴史' (The History of Phonosymbolic Words), in Morita Kenji 森田健二et al. (eds.), 講座日本語学 (Studies of Japanese Language Series), vol. 4, Tokyo: Meiji shoin.

Ōtsubo, Heiji 大坪伴治 (1989) 擬声語の研究 (A Study of Onomatopoeia), Tokyo: Meiji shoin.

Ozaki, Satoakira 尾崎知光 (1967) 近代文章の黎明 (The Dawn of the Modern Written Style), Tokyo: Ōfūsha.

Sakuma, Kanae 佐久間鼎 (1943) 日本語の言語理論的研究 (A Theoretical Linguistic Analysis of the Japanese Language), Tokyo: Sanshōdō.

Tsubouchi, Shōyō 坪内逍遥 (1977) '文章上の挙国一致' (On the Unity of the Written Style), 逍遥選集 (Selected Works of Tsubouchi Shōyō), Tokyo: Daiichi shobō.

Tsukahara, Tetsuo 塚原鉄雄 (1974) '近代詩人とオノマトペ' (Modern Poets and Onomatopoeia) 言語生活 (Communication) 273, 4.

Utsumi, Kōzō 内海弘蔵 (1910) 文章十講 (Ten Lectures on Composition), Tokyo: Bunseisha.

Watanabe, Kichiharu 渡邊吉治 (1926) 現代修辞法要 (Essentials of Modern Rhetoric), Tokyo: Jinbo shoten.

Yamada, Bimyō 山田美妙 (1901) 言文一致文例 (Sample Writings in *Genbun itchi*), Tokyo: Naigai shuppan kyōkai.

Yamaguchi, Nakami 山口仲美 (1972) '今昔物語集の象徴詞' (Phonosymbolic Lexicon in *Konjaku Monogatari*) 王朝 (Dynasty) 5, 7–44.

Yamamura, Bochō 山村暮鳥 (1989) 山村暮鳥全集 (The Collected Works of Yamamura Bochō), vol. 1, Tokyo: Chikuma Shobō.

7

RHETORIC OF RUSSIAN CIVILIZATIONAL IDENTITY
A Case Study of Patriarch Kirill's Discourse

Natalia Bruffaerts

Introduction

The idea of *Russkiy Mir*, literally meaning the "Russian World", as a supranational cultural milieu united by a common language began to gain traction after the collapse of the USSR, when Russian lost its dominance in the former republics. At the same time, a lot of Russians continued to live beyond the boundaries of the Russian Federation. Besides, the discourse of identity has emerged with new vigor in Russia itself against a background of social disintegration. In the 1990s, members of the Institute of Philosophy at the Russian Academy of Sciences were tasked to elaborate the concept of the "Russian idea" (Petro 2015). One of the ideas was *Russkiy Mir*, a "networked structure of large and small communities that think in and speak the Russian language" (Tishkov 2008: 5). However, this concept was not largely promoted further at that moment. The choice of the word *mir* was not fortuitous. It has two root meanings in Russian: "world", or "community", and "peace". Before the reform of orthography after the revolution of 1917, the two words were even spelt differently. The term was reinvigorated in 2006, when President Putin declared during a speech in Derzhavin's House in St. Petersburg on the eve of the Year of the Russian Language that "*Russkiy Mir* can and must unite everyone who cherishes the Russian word and the Russian culture, wherever they live – in Russia or abroad". He called upon the audience to use this term as often as possible (Sycheva 2007: 2–3). In June 2007, Putin established the Russkiy Mir Foundation for the purpose of "promoting the Russian language as Russia's national heritage and a significant aspect of Russian and world culture as well as supporting Russian language teaching programs abroad" (Putin 2007).

The enthronement of Patriarch Kirill took place in 2009, and that very year he delivered a speech at the Third Assembly of the Russkiy Mir Foundation, where he gave an extensive description of the Church's vision of the eponymous concept implying that *Russkiy Mir* as Russian civilizational space goes beyond the boundaries of the Russian Federation and covers other territories where the Russian Orthodox Church is present, in particular Ukraine and Belarus (Kirill 2009). In 2015, selected speeches by Patriarch

DOI: 10.4324/9781003195276-10

Kirill dedicated to *Russkiy Mir* were published in the form of the book *Sem' slov o russkom mire* ("Seven Speeches about *Russkiy Mir*") (Kirill 2015c). The title of the book alludes to the genre of *slovo*, establishing continuity between the old Russian art of oratory and modern rhetoric. However, the outbreak of the Ukrainian conflict in 2014 and the schism within the Russian Orthodox Church, which resulted in the granting of a *Tomos* to the Ukrainian Orthodox Church–Kyiv Patriarchate by Constantinople in 2019, triggered changes in the Patriarch's rhetoric concerning *Russkiy Mir* in terms of the choice of arguments, lexical means and rhetorical devices.

Theoretical Premises

The symbolic importance of religion in discourses of national self-definition has already been discussed in a number of studies (see, for instance, Haskins 2007; Richters 2013; Naydenova 2016; Stoeckl 2020). The purpose of this chapter is to examine how the concept of *Russkiy Mir* is represented in Patriarch Kirill's discourse and what rhetorical mechanisms are used for this purpose. The research is based on the analysis of 23 speeches, interviews and messages by Patriarch Kirill from 2009 until 2021 touching upon *Russkiy Mir* and Russia's civilizational identity.

The analysis will be focused on two canons of rhetoric: *elocutio* and *inventio*. Rhetorical techniques and figures used in the *elocutio* stage will be identified on the basis of linguistic analysis of the texts, in particular, the choice of lexical means, which comprise the use of proper nouns (onyms) used to designate the components of Russian civilizational space in the speeches.

The model devised by Stephen Toulmin (2003) will be used to study *inventio* (invention). The Toulmin model comprises six elements. It is based on the claim (hereinafter in the examples, "C"), which represents the conclusion to be proved. The ground ("G") is used to sustain the claim, and is connected with it through an inferential leap called the warrant ("W"). Additional proof of the warrant is provided through the backing ("B"). The rebuttal ("R") expresses the conditions restricting the claim. Words indicating the speaker's certainty in respect of the claim are called the qualifiers ("Q"). Qualifiers add explicit reference to the degree of force which is conferred on the claim or the warrant (Toulmin 2003: 93).

Frans H. van Eemeren notes that Toulmin's model is imbued with notions found in classical rhetoric (2018: 171). The Toulmin model resembles an enthymeme, the "substance of rhetorical persuasion" according to Aristotle (1354a14–15), and "an argument that is expressible as a categorical syllogism but that is missing a premise or a conclusion" (Hurley 2003: 289). The warrant in the Toulmin model is the major premise of an enthymeme, while the claim is the conclusion, and the ground is the minor premise. Besides, the role of warrants in his model is similar to that of the classical topoi. Topoi and enthymeme play an important role in Lomonosov's theory of *inventio* as well (Gorbounova 2009: 446). Thus, over 2,500 years, rhetoric has developed a set of ideas and practices that changes reality through the mediation of thought and action (Bitzer 1968: 4; Ramsey 2016: 341; Ilie 2018: 90).

The qualifiers in the Toulmin model may express different modality and therefore nuance arguments and produce diverse kinds of discourse effects. Jan Nuyts distinguishes three kinds of modality: deontic, epistemic, and dynamic. In this chapter, we are going to dwell on the first two kinds. Deontic modality is "an evaluation of the moral acceptability, desirability or necessity of a state of affairs, i.e. it crucially involves notions such as 'allowance', 'permission' and 'obligation'" (Nuyts 2006: 25). Epistemic modality refers to "an indication of the estimation, typically, but not necessarily, by the speaker, of the chances that the state of affairs expressed in the clause applies in the world" (Nuyts 2006: 6). It concerns an estimation of the likelihood that (some aspect of) a certain state of affairs is, has been, or will be true (or false) in the context of the possible world under consideration (Nuyts 2001: 18). This estimation of likelihood is situated on the "epistemic scale" going from certainty that the state of affairs applies, via a neutral or agnostic stance towards its occurrence, to certainty that it does not apply (Nuyts 2001: 21–22). Akatsuka (1985) proposes an epistemic scale ranging between the two poles – "Irrealis" (surprise, uncertainty and negative conviction) and "Realis" (positive conviction).

Russia and *Russian* as Objects of Nomination in the Patriarch's Rhetoric

Russia

Before delving into the analysis of the speeches dwelling on *Russkiy Mir* ("Russian World"), it is essential to specify what Patriarch Kirill means by "Russia" and "Russian". In his discourse, these terms are imbued with connotations which play an important role in the strategy of argumentation, as we are going to see later. The Patriarch's speeches comprise a panoply of toponyms denoting Russian civilizational space at different stages of its development: *drevnyaya Rus'* (Ancient Rus'), *istoricheskaya Rus'* (historical Rus'), *svyataya Rus'* (Holy Rus'). While Ancient Rus' and historical Rus' mean Kievan Rus', which existed from the late ninth until the mid-thirteenth century, Holy Rus' is a kind of archetype: "a spiritual tradition" (2010a), "a community of people in which right-eousness is the main dominant of life" (2010b), "a system of spiritual values" (2011) (for more detailed analysis of how the concept of Holy Rus' functions in Patriarch Kirill's discourse, see Naydenova 2016).

The following passage illustrates the use of the toponyms denoting Russia:

> Russia (*Rossiya*) should be understood as a cultural multinational territory in very specific historical and geographical dimensions, which is associated with Ancient Rus'. To a certain extent, Russia is a synonym for Rus' (G). Today we have a different geopolitical reality, when independent states arose on the territory of this historical Russia, many of which are also the heirs of this historical Rus'. Therefore, when I speak about Russia, I always mean this great civilizational space (C).
>
> *Kirill 2013a*

According to the Toulmin model, the ground is "Russia (*Rossiya*) equals Rus'", while the claim is "Independent states are part of Rus'". The unstated warrant is that "Independent states are part of Russia", which apparently contradicts the current geopolitical reality. However, the abundance of toponyms used by the Patriarch to denote Russia as a civilizational space contribute to glossing over the fallacious warrant.

A discrepancy in toponyms denoting Belarus should also be noted – the Patriarch often names this country *Belorussiya*, which is the term officially used during the Soviet period up to 1991, instead of the current official *Belarus*. As for Ukraine, he continues to use the preposition *na*, when saying "in Ukraine" (for both cases see, for instance, Kirill 2015a). Although this is totally compliant with the rules of the Russian language,

Russian People

The adjective "Russian" has two equivalents – *russkiy*, which is more frequently used in the Patriarch's discourse, and *rossyiskiy*. According to the Dictionary of the Russian Language (Kuznetsov 2014), *russkiy* is an adjective derived from *Rossiya* (Russia) and *Rus'* and means something belonging to, created by, or typical for Russians (*russkiye*), while *rossiyskiy* is an adjective derived only from *Rossiya* (Russia) and typical for it.

To strengthen the thesis of the historical unity of Russians, Ukrainians and Belarusians, the Patriarch also uses the ethnonym *Ross*:

> Russian culture is one of the foundations that unites the peoples of historical Russia (C). Its formation was largely facilitated by the choice made by the Holy Prince Vladimir, who in 988 baptized the Ross, as the Greeks called our people at that time, in the waters of the Dnieper (B).
>
> *Kirill 2014b*

In the example above, the warrant is based on the ethnonym and would be that the Ross, i.e. Russians, Ukrainians and Belarusians, remain one and the same people as they were baptized as such. By applying a historical term to the contemporary situation, the speaker creates a warrant, which does not reflect the current state of affairs.

The term *narod* (people) is used by the Patriarch either in singular or in plural. Dating back to 2009, we can encounter its use in singular to denote Russians, Ukrainians and Belarusians taken as a whole: "spiritually, we continue to be one and the same people, mainly pastored by the Russian Orthodox Church" (Kirill 2009). In his later speeches, Patriarch Kirill gives a more detailed explanation: "at the beginning – the single people of Kievan Rus', and now – all peoples which succeeded to that very civilization …" (Kirill 2013b). As the examples demonstrate, "people" in singular is used when speaking about Kievan Rus', and "peoples" in plural denote Russians, Ukrainians and Belarusians as citizens of the respective countries. However, sometimes the use of the term in singular sounds ambiguous. For instance, during his speech commemorating St. Peter of Moscow, Patriarch Kirill evoked "the Church of the great people on the territory of historical Rus'" (Kirill 2019b). This may be explained by the fact that Metropolitan Peter transferred the Church headquarters to Moscow, thus consolidating the Russian Orthodox Church through strengthening the role of this city. However, without further explanation, the use of the term in singular implies that all countries where the Russian Orthodox Church is present today are inhabited by one and the same people.

The choice of grammatical number also varies subject to the addressee of the message. Thus, on 28 July 2021, the day of the baptism of Rus', Patriarch Kirill delivered a homily and sent messages to several heads of states and public officials, including the Presidents of Russia, Ukraine and Belarus. In the homily, the speaker uses the singular: "our historical people, now living in different states" (Kirill 2021a). It should also be noted that in the transcript of the speech on the official website of the Moscow Patriarchate, the term

"Russian land" is spelled with the majuscule "*R*" (*zemlya Russkaya*), which is formally against the rules of the Russian language but aims at highlighting the difference between *russkiy* pertaining to Russia and *Russkiy* pertaining to Rus' (Kirill 2021a).

The message of congratulations addressed to President Putin speaks about the "peoples" in plural:

> Having found spiritual unity in the Dnieper font, the East Slavic peoples carried through the centuries the testimony of Christ and the Gospel, preserved and passed on the traditions of faith and piety to their descendants.
>
> *Kirill 2021b*

The same term in the same form is used in the message addressed to the Ukrainian President Vladimir Zelensky:

> The fateful choice of the Holy Prince Vladimir became a turning point in the history of the East Slavic peoples, predetermined the further path of their social and cultural development, laid the foundations of the spiritual unity of our countries for centuries.
>
> *Kirill 2021c*

In both messages, "people" in plural is accompanied by modifiers (East Slavic), and in the text addressed to the President of Ukraine, it is also followed by "our countries" (*nashy strany*). The latter is done to evoke the spiritual unity of the two nations, thus echoing Putin's article "On the Historical Unity of Russians and Ukrainians" published earlier in July 2021, where the President of Russia states the following:

> Russians, Ukrainians, and Belarusians are all descendants of Ancient Rus', which was the largest state in Europe. Slavic and other tribes across the vast territory – from Ladoga, Novgorod, and Pskov to Kiev and Chernigov – were bound together by one language (which we now refer to as Old Russian), economic ties, the rule of the princes of the Rurik dynasty, and – after the baptism of Rus – the Orthodox faith. The spiritual choice made by St. Vladimir, who was both Prince of Novgorod and Grand Prince of Kiev, still largely determines our affinity today.
>
> *Putin 2021*

As demonstrated by the examples above, the choice of lexical means and their grammatical categories is determined by such factors as the context and the addressee of the message, or intertextual relations that the speaker intends to establish. Their use in the speeches under study is not impartial and varies subject to the speaker's objectives and target audience.

Russkiy Mir: Evolution of the Concept from the Rhetorical Perspective

It was in his speech delivered before the Third Assembly of the Russkiy Mir Foundation in 2009 that Patriarch Kirill set out his in-depth view of *Russkiy Mir*:

> it is necessary to understand clearly what *Russkiy Mir* is today. It seems to me that (R) if we consider the Russian Federation within its modern borders to be

its only centre, we will thereby sin against the historical truth and artificially cut off from ourselves many millions of people who are aware of their responsibility for the fate of *Russkiy Mir* and consider its creation as the main goal of their life.

(C) Russia, Ukraine, Belarus constitute the core of *Russkiy Mir* today, and (B) Saint Reverend Laurentius of Chernigov expressed this idea with his famous phrase: "Russia, Ukraine, Belarus – this is Holy Rus'". (G) It is this understanding of *Russkiy Mir* that lies in the modern self-designation of our Church. The Church is called Russian not on ethnic grounds. This name indicates that the Russian Orthodox Church performs its pastoral mission among peoples who accept the Russian spiritual and cultural tradition as the basis of their national identity, or at least as an essential part of it. That is why, in this sense, we also consider Moldova to be part of this *Russkiy Mir*. At the same time, the Russian Church is the most multinational Orthodox community in the world and seeks to develop its multinational character.

Kirill 2009

In accordance with the Toulmin model, the claim of the passage establishes that Russia, Ukraine, Belarus and Moldova belong to *Russkiy Mir*. This claim is supported by the ground stating that the Russian Orthodox Church has a supranational nature and pastors all peoples assuming "the Russian spiritual and cultural tradition as the basis of their national identity". Therefore, the implied warrant of this passage would be that Russia, Ukraine, Belarus and Moldova as parts of the supranational *Russkiy Mir* have assumed Russian cultural identity. This evidences authoritarian aspirations of the rhetor to produce discourse in the Foucauldian sense, i.e. as a practice that forms the objects of which it speaks (Foucault 1972: 49). The speaker also gives a backing in the form of *argumentum ad verecundiam* by quoting an Orthodox saint. The rebuttal at the beginning of the passage warns the audience against contradicting historical truth and neglecting people belonging to *Russkiy Mir* in their own right. At the same time, the claim is limited by such epistemic qualifiers as "it seems to me", "if we consider", and "we consider". All of them contain personal pronouns, and two of them (those formulated with the conditional) are close to the "Irrealis" pole of Akatsuka's scale.

Going forward, Patriarch Kirill makes a reservation concerning his idea of the borders:

My words do not mean that the Russian Church is questioning the current state borders. Of course, one cannot but admit that these borders, at least for today, create unnecessary obstacles between the peoples of *Russkiy Mir* in view of the current nature of all these border situations.

Kirill 2009

When speaking about the borders, the Patriarch uses predominantly negative constructions and lexical means. He begins with prolepsis consisting in refuting anticipated objections (Lanham 1991: 120) followed by a statement containing an epistemic modal operator ("one cannot but admit"). This rhetorical strategy allows him first to refute possible accusations of neglecting the fact that Ukraine and Belarus are independent states and then to underscore the disadvantages of the state borders.

The speech also contains a detailed description of *Russkiy Mir*, which has, according to the Patriarch, three characteristics: Orthodoxy, Russian culture and language as well as common history and mentality.

Patriarch Kirill recurs to a panoply of arguments, the first one being *argumentum ad antiquetatum*, when he calls the baptism of Kievan Rus' "a historical choice of Saint Prince Vladimir" (in later speeches, this choice will be called "civilizational" – see, for instance, Kirill 2016).

To underpin the unity of the Russian Church, Patriarch Kirill recurs to *reductio ad absurdum*:

> It is inconceivable for a Russian person to oppose the "Ukrainian" Prince Vladimir to the "Russian" (*russkiy*) Reverend Sergius of Radonezh (when I say "Russian" I use of course quotation marks), the "Russian" Prince Alexander Nevsky, the "Belarusian" Reverend Euphrosyne of Polotsk, the "Moldavian" Reverend Paisius to the "Russian" (*rossiyskiy*) Saint Ignatius (Bryanchaninov). It just looks like an anecdote, like a joke. All these are the saints of the Russian land, therefore we must preserve the unity of the Russian Church, honor our common saints, and visit the holy places of *Russkiy Mir*.
>
> *Kirill 2009*

The speaker devises a grotesque clash of opposites based on the places of origin of different Orthodox saints. He also plays on the words *russkiy* and *rossiyskiy*, both translated as "Russian". As St. Sergius was canonized in the fifteenth century, and St. Ignatius during the late Soviet era in 1988, we can suppose that the use of different adjectives is aimed at creating continuity between different periods of Russian history: from Kievan Rus' to modern Russia. This strategy will be more explicitly used by the Patriarch in his later speeches (see, for example, Kirill 2015b). The speaker employs epistemic modality ("it is inconceivable") to highlight the grotesque effect of *reductio ad absurdum*.

While speaking about Russian culture, the Patriarch uses prolepsis again:

> Russian culture is a phenomenon that does not fit into the boundaries of one state and one ethnic group and is not associated with the interests of one state, which is very important to understand today; like this foundation, "Russkiy Mir", is not an instrument of political influence of the Russian Federation ... First of all, Russian culture is the original way and form of expressing values, the historical experience of the people of Rus' ...
>
> *Kirill 2009*

Prolepsis is combined with the figure of analogy, drawing a parallel between Russian culture and *Russkiy Mir* and at the same time refuting possible accusations of hegemony.

The third characteristic of *Russkiy Mir* is also presented through analogical reasoning:

> (C) independent states that exist on the territory of historical Rus' and are aware of their common civilizational affiliation could continue to create *Russkiy Mir* together and regard it as their common supranational project. It would even be possible to launch such a concept as "the country of *Russkiy Mir*" ... In this case, I am not proposing something new, because (B) such associations as the

British Commonwealth of Nations, the Francophonie and the Lusofonia, Ibero-America are built on more or less the same principle.

Kirill 2009

This choice of the backing gives ambiguous colonial connotations to the concept of *Russkiy Mir* as the organizations named by the speaker largely comprise former colonies of Great Britain, France, Portugal and Spain, respectively, and were established by former metropoles not only with cultural but also with political objectives. However, the effect of this connotation is subdued by the use of "would", "could", and "more or less" as qualifiers.

At the Fourth Assembly of the Russkiy Mir Foundation, in 2010, Patriarch Kirill returned to his previous speech:

> it is necessary to clearly define the role of the Orthodox Church and the Russian Orthodox tradition in *Russkiy Mir*. Some of the critics of my speech at the previous assembly accused me of allegedly identifying *Russkiy Mir* exclusively with the Russian Church, while people of other religions and beliefs belong to *Russkiy Mir*. But this interpretation of my words is erroneous. There is no doubt that (G2) Russian civilization is open to different cultures and traditions. However, it is also indisputable that (G1) the Russian Church played a pro-active role in inception and development of *Russkiy Mir*. The Russian Church is also its vital source. (C1) Therefore, the Russian Church's spiritual experience, religious thought, shrines, spiritual centers, saints and outstanding personalities are an integral part of *Russkiy Mir*. It is also indisputable that (C2) the representatives of Islam, Buddhism, Judaism and traditional Christian confessions as well as secular thinkers have made, and continue making an important contribution into the creation of Russian civilization.
>
> *Kirill 2010a*

In order to refute the allegation set forth by his unnamed opponent, the Patriarch recurs to enthymematic reasoning reinforced by epistemic modality, which dominates the passage ("there is no doubt", "it is indisputable"). In fact, the passage constitutes an epicheirema comprising two enthymemes with two claims, two grounds and, consequently, two warrants. The first claim is that the Russian Church is an integral part of *Russkiy Mir*, and the second claim is that the representatives of other religions contribute to the development of Russian civilization. The ground of the first claim is that the Russian Church plays the key role in the development of *Russkiy Mir*, while the ground of the second claim is that Russian civilization is open to different cultures and traditions. Therefore, the warrants would be that those religious groups, which play the key role in the development of *Russkiy Mir*, are its integral part; and that the Russian Church is open to all cultures and traditions, which contribute to its development. The purpose of both enthymemes is to refute the erroneous interpretation of the concept of *Russkiy Mir*. However, the term *Russkiy Mir* itself is found only in the first enthymeme – in the second one, it is replaced by "Russian civilization". This terminological discrepancy entails a hierarchical presentation of the claims: the first claim deals with the "integral part of *Russkiy Mir*", while the predicate of the second is reduced to the contribution to "the development of Russian civilization". Besides, the second claim contains the adverb *takzhe* "also", which means "in addition". The first warrant implies

Rhetoric of Russian Civilizational Identity

that only those groups, which played the key role in the inception of *Russkiy Mir* (i.e. the Russian Orthodox Church), are considered its integral part, thus leaving the others ("contributors" to the development) on the periphery.

The Patriarch's rhetoric about *Russkiy Mir* changed in the aftermath of the outbreak of the Ukrainian conflict. An interview dating back to 2015 is indicative of this rhetorical shift:

> Unfortunately, our opponents use the words *Russkiy Mir* as a bogeyman, as a scarecrow, claiming that this is some kind of doctrine that serves exclusively the foreign policy interests of the Russian Federation ... However, there is nothing further from the truth than identifying *Russkiy Mir* exclusively with the Russian Federation. (C) *Russkiy Mir* [the Russian world] is at the same time the Ukrainian world and the Belarusian world. This is the world of all Rus'. (G) This is the world that was created through the Baptism in the Dnieper, this is the world of Prince Vladimir, this is a system of values that has penetrated the culture, the life of our people.
>
> As for the Russian language, I can only say that this language is the language of our communication. (R) And if the role of this language is weakened, communication between Ukrainians, Russians, Belarusians as well as many other peoples will become much more complicated, because language is a natural means of maintaining relationships between people belonging to the same cultural and spiritual community.
>
> (C) Despite the fact that just to mention *Russkiy Mir* has already become almost a crime in Ukraine within the framework of the current political doctrine, we will continue – quietly, calmly, but persistently – to testify about this truth, about the truth of the Kievan Baptismal font, about the creation of a whole East Slavic civilization, the so-called *Russkiy Mir* ...
>
> (B) Open *The Tale of Bygone Years*, and at the very beginning of this chronicle you read about "the origin of the land of Rus'". There is no mention of Ukraine, Russia, Belarus – there is the Russian land. And do we really have the right to abandon our history, our ideals, our saints, our monasteries, our worship, our common language, to please political sentiments?
>
> *Kirill 2015a*

The figures of repetition abound in the passage. The speaker begins again by refuting the arguments of his unnamed opponents. This is done by first quoting them and then giving his definition of *Russkiy Mir* in the form of epimone, "frequent repetition of a phrase or question, in order to dwell on a point" (Lanham 1991: 68). The expression "This is the world ..." is repeated three times. This excessive repetition is aimed at backing the arguments that prove the unity of *Russkiy Mir*: the claim that Ukraine, Russia, Belarus stem from Rus' and share the same religion, values and culture. Other figures of repetition used in the passage include anadiplosis, when the expression "about this truth" is repeated as the first item in an enumeration, and anaphoric repetition of the pronoun "our" in the rhetorical question closing the passage.

The claim has a complex structure. Its first part is worded as an enumerative definition that lists relevant attributes or parts of the term to be defined (Crowley 1994: 336): "*Russkiy Mir* [the Russian world] is at the same time the Ukrainian world and the Belarusian world. This is the world of all Rus'". Sharon Crowley remarks that

109

enumerative definition has "the persuasive advantage (noted by Aristotle) of making the whole seem greater than it is" (1994: 73). The Patriarch names the constituent parts of *Russkiy Mir* – the Ukrainian world and the Belarusian world. The claim is continued further in the text with the declaration of intention to testify about "a whole East Slavic civilization, the so-called *Russkiy Mir*". It should be noted that the Patriarch had previously spoken about the East Slavic civilization mainly to non-Russian interlocutors such as former Prime Minister of Ukraine Yulia Timoshenko (Yakovleva 2009). However, from 2015 onwards, this term would become omnipresent in the Patriarch's discourse.

The ground is constituted by the statement that Russia, Ukraine and Belarus were baptized by Prince Vladimir and share the same values. Therefore, the implied warrant would be that the countries, whose baptism dates back to Kievan Rus', belong to *Russkiy Mir*. The warrant is underpinned by the backing in the form of *argumentum ad verecundiam* referring the audience to an ancient Russian chronicle, which mentions the Russian land as an indivisible space. The rebuttal concerns the threat of weakening of the use of the Russian language as the main means of communication of *Russkiy Mir*.

The argumentation is based on antithetical reasoning, with the speaker focusing mainly on refuting the arguments of his never named opponents, whether he dwells on the perception of *Russkiy Mir*, the role of the Russian language, or the situation in Ukraine.

The analysis reveals the declarative nature of the argumentation. This is evidenced, in particular, by the repetition of the expressions introducing definitions ("this is"), the choice of lexical means used to formulate the claim ("to testify about the truth"), and the absence of connectors of cause and consequence. However, the term *Russkiy Mir* is for the first time accompanied by the qualifier "so-called", and a synonym – East Slavic civilization.

The choice of lexical means used to describe the constituent parts of *Russkiy Mir* has also changed. From 2009 until 2013, the terms used included "the countries, which are the backbone of historical Rus'" (Kirill 2009), "peoples of *Russkiy Mir*" (Kirill 2010a), "heirs of Holy Rus'" (Kirill 2011). Starting from 2014, although the above terms were still used, the focus shifted more to underlining the fraternity of Russians, Ukrainians and Belarusians: "fraternal Slavic peoples" (Kirill 2014a), "members of the united family of peoples coming from the Baptismal font of Kiev" (Kirill 2017). *Russkiy Mir* is now frequently named through paraphrase: "historical Rus' – Russia, Ukraine, Belorussia and other countries" (Kirill 2017), "heirs of Kievan Rus' – Russians, Ukrainians, Belarussians" (Kirill 2019a), "our Slavic peoples, including the peoples that make up historical Rus'" (Kirill 2021d).

Since 2014, the figure of definition has been more frequently applied to *Russkiy Mir*. For instance, statements concerning the boundaries and composition of *Russkiy Mir* are structured around enumerative definition, which finds various ways of verbal representation. This may be, for instance, enumeration of the names of the capitals:

> Today, the day of the Baptism of Rus' is celebrated in Moscow, Kiev, Minsk and other cities. Millions of people offer their prayers to Prince [Vladimir] for prosperity and peace in the countries of historical Russia, and mutual grievances, disputes and divisions are forgotten in this common prayer. This prayer strengthens the solid spiritual ties that exist between our peoples. These connections do not depend on nationality, culture or changing state borders.
>
> *Kirill 2018b*

Note also the use of anadiplosis ("this common prayer ... this prayer"). The threefold repetition of the term "prayer" is aimed at underscoring the "spiritual ties", which prevail over the "changing borders".

Definition based on the use of historical toponyms can be found in the speech pronounced by Patriarch Kirill in 2019:

> Almost always, when there was a question about the unity of our people, about the unity of Rus' – Great (*Velikaya*), Little (*Malaya*), White (*Belaya*), – it was the Church, its principled stand that largely determined the future.
>
> *Kirill 2019d*

(where Great Rus' stands for Russia, Little Rus' for Ukraine, and White Rus' for Belarus).

The figure of definition is now also commonly employed by other Russian Orthodox Church hierarchs in respect of the concept of *Russkiy Mir*. For instance, when discussing the role of the Crimea as the place of baptism of Kievan Rus', Lazar, the Metropolitan of Simferopol and of the Crimea, says: "The Crimea is the spiritual cradle of Russians, Ukrainians and Belarussians" (2021: 34).

As the schism within the Russian Orthodox Church started escalating in 2018, the statements concerning civilizational space and civilizational identity generally became more cautious due to the use of qualifiers:

> The question of civilizational identity is not a question of some kind of isolationism, or superiority, or opposition to the rest of the world. This is, first of all, the issue of the unity of our civilizational space, which largely coincides with the canonical territory of our Church, where representatives of different states, nationalities and religions live.
>
> *Kirill 2018a*

Although the traditional antithetical reasoning prevails, there appears an adverb, "largely", when speaking about the coincidence between the canonical territory of the Russian Orthodox Church and the territory of "Russian civilizational space".

The Patriarch's speech of 2019 is indicative of the rhetorical shift which took place during the elapsed decade:

> Today we have gathered at the monument to the Baptizer of Rus' to turn our minds again to the events that are at the very foundation of our history, our culture. (G) When we say "our", we mean all peoples who have adopted faith, culture, and language from the Kievan baptismal font ...
>
> (R) A person cannot exist without what is now called identity, that is, without realizing who he is, where his place is, where he is at home, and where he is a stranger. But it also happens that people try to reject their true identity for the sake of a false one, when they try to break the connection with their real roots, when their true identity is replaced by ideological constructions that seem to them more attractive and successful. The consequences are usually very sad both for an individual and for the society, for the state. (C) In order to grow and develop, we cannot but feed on our own origins, the origins of our East Slavic civilization, common for Russians, Ukrainians, Belarusians, the civilization that originates in the Kievan baptismal font ...

> Once again, I cordially congratulate all of you on the great holiday for all the peoples of Russia – on our common Baptism, performed by the grace of God by Holy Prince Vladimir of Kiev, whom we glorify today with full understanding of the greatness of what this prince did for our peoples, for our countries.
>
> *Kirill 2019c*

The claim of the argument resides in the statement that East Slavic civilizational identity is common for Russians, Ukrainians and Belarusians. The ground underpinning the claim is that all these three peoples were baptized by Prince Vladimir of Kiev. Therefore, the warrant linking the claim and the ground would be that all peoples baptized in the era of Kievan Rus' have East Slavic civilizational identity. The rebuttal containing deontic modality ("one cannot ...") warns the audience against losing their true identity.

If we make a comparison with the speech of 2009, we see that the predicate of the claim has changed from *Russkiy Mir* to *East Slavic civilization*. Both passages contain rebuttals, but that of 2009 is based on epistemic modality, close to the "Irrealis" pole of the epistemic scale, while that of 2019 is based on deontic modality. The modifier of the noun "identity" in the implied warrant has changed from "Russian" to "East Slavic". The replacement of a hyponym by a hypernym follows the need for a change of rhetoric in the aftermath of the Ukrainian conflict and the rise of the new independent church of Ukraine, which was vehemently contested by the Moscow Patriarchate as the autocephaly undermined its already weakened influence in the country. As a consequence, the focus of the ground has shifted from the supranational nature of the Russian Orthodox Church to the common roots of East Slavic peoples, which reflects close connections between the civilizational discourse and political events.

Conclusion

The rhetoric of Russian civilizational identity attempts to construct reality rather than document it. The analysis of the *inventio* canon with the help of the Toulmin model has revealed the implied warrants based on the projection of archaic concepts, not applicable to the actual state of things, onto contemporary reality. Analogical reasoning also sometimes turns out to be fallacious as the underlying items sometimes turn out to be incomparable. The authoritarian nature of the rhetoric of *Russkiy Mir* explains the frequent recourse to arguments from authority and from antiquity *ad verecundiam* and *ad antiquetatum* as well as the use of epistemic and deontic modality. It also comes out at the *elocutio* stage through the extensive use of figures of repetition, such as epimone, anaphora, anadiplosis, aimed at emphasizing the edifying aspect of the rhetor's discourse.

The argumentation is frequently built on antithetical reasoning as the Patriarch typically begins his speeches with prolepsis in order to refute the arguments of always unnamed opponents. This choice of reasoning signals the speaker's awareness of the arguments voiced by his opponents, which he prefers to declare untrue from the outset rather than to recur to persuasive argumentation. The choice of lexical means and argument structure is contingent both on the current political events and on the addressee of the discourse.

Therefore, rhetorical argumentation behind the idea of uniting the peoples separated by state borders under the auspices of *Russkiy Mir* nourished by common religion and language has experienced considerable changes during the past decade. After the events in Ukraine, with an armed conflict breaking out in 2014 and the nationalist church being granted a *Tomos* in 2019, the term *Russkiy Mir* has more and more often been replaced by "East Slavic civilization", and the focus shifts from the dominance of *Russkiy Mir* to the fraternity of Slavic peoples. Moreover, the concept of Russian civilizational space has been lately presented by using the figure of enumerative definition: listing the constituent parts of *Russkiy Mir* as well as putting the word "people" in plural underlines its multi-faceted nature and suits the current political situation.

Acknowledgments

The author would like to thank the anonymous peer reviewer, Svetlana Vogeleer-Aloushkova and Paul Arblaster for their valuable comments and advice.

References

English-Language References

Akatsuka, N. (1985) 'Conditionals and the Epistemic Scale', *Language* 61(3): 625–639.

Aristotle (1995) 'Rhetoric', in J. Barnes (ed.), R. Roberts (trans.), *The Complete Works of Aristotle* II, Princeton: Princeton University Press, 2152–2169.

Bitzer, L. (1968) 'The Rhetorical Situation', *Philosophy and Rhetoric* 1(1): 1–14.

Crowley, S. (1994) *Ancient Rhetoric for Contemporary Students*, Boston: Allyn & Bacon.

van Eemeren, F. H. (2018). *Argumentation Theory: A Pragma-Dialectical Perspective*, Cham: Springer.

Foucault, M. (1972) *The Archaeology of Knowledge*, New York: Pantheon Books.

Haskins, E. (2007) 'Religion, Cultural Memory, and the Rhetoric of National Identity in Russia', *Forum Artis Rhetoricae* 8(9): 44–58.

Hurley, P. J. (2003) *A Concise Introduction to Logic*, 8th edn, Belmont: Wadsworth.

Ilie, C. (2018) 'Pragmatics vs Rhetoric: Political Discourse at the Pragmatics-Rhetoric Interface', in C. Ilie and N. R. Norrick (dirs.), *Pragmatics and Its Interfaces*, Amsterdam and Philadelphia: John Benjamins Publishing Company, 85–120.

Lanham, R. A. (1991) *A Handlist of Rhetorical Terms: A Guide for Students of English Literature*, Berkeley and Los Angeles: University of California Press.

Naydenova, N. (2016) 'Holy Rus: (Re)construction of Russia's Civilizational Identity', *Slavonica* 21(1–2): 37–48.

Nuyts, J. (2001) *Epistemic Modality, Language, and Conceptualization: A Cognitive Pragmatic Perspective*, Amsterdam: John Benjamins.

Nuyts, J. (2006) 'Modality: Overview and Linguistic Issues', in W. Frawley (ed.), *The Expression of Modality*, Berlin: De Gruyter, 1–26.

Petro, N. (2015) 'Russia's Orthodox Soft Power', Carnegie Council for Ethics in International Affairs. Available from: www.carnegiecouncil.org/publications/articles_papers_reports/727 (accessed 26 August 2021).

Putin, V. (2007) Decree 796 dated 21 June 2007. Available from: https://russkiymir.ru/en/fund/dec ree.php (accessed 26 August 2021).

Putin, V. (2021) *On the Historical Unity of Russians and Ukrainians*. Available from: http://en.krem lin.ru/events/president/news/66181 (accessed 26 August 2021).

Ramsey, S. (2016) 'A Reevaluation of Alcuin's *Disputatio de rhetorica et de virtutibus* as Consular Persuasion: The Context of the Late Eighth Century Revisited', *Advances in the History of Rhetoric* 19(3): 324–343.

Richters, K. (2013) *The Post-Soviet Russian Orthodox Church: Politics, Culture and Greater Russia*, Abingdon and New York: Routledge.

Stoeckl, K. (2020) 'Russian Orthodoxy and Secularism', *Religion and Politics* 1(2): 1–75.

Tishkov, V. (2008) 'The Russian World – Changing Meanings and Strategies', *Carnegie Papers* 95: 3–55.

Toulmin, S. (2003) *The Uses of Argument*, updated edition, Cambridge: Cambridge University Press.

Natalia Bruffaerts

Other-Language References

Gorbounova, R. (2009) 'L'enthymème entre la philosophie et le style dans la *Rhétorique* de Mixail Speranskij' (The Enthymeme between Philosophy and Style in Mixail Speranskij's Rhetoric), *Revue des études slaves* 80(4): 443–457.

Kirill (2009) Vystuplenie Svjatejshego Patriarha Kirilla na torzhestvennom otkrytii III Assamblei Russkogo mira (Statement by His Holiness Patriarch Kirill at the inaugural ceremony of the IIIrd Assembly of the Russkiy Mir Foundation). Available from: www.patriarchia.ru/db/text/ 928446.html (accessed 26 August 2021).

Kirill (2010a) Vystuplenie Svjatejshego Patriarha Kirilla na otkrytii IV Assamblei Russkogo mira (Statement by His Holiness Patriarch Kirill at the inaugural ceremony of the IVth Assembly of the Russkiy Mir Foundation). Available from: www.patriarchia.ru/db/text/1310928.html (accessed 26 August 2021).

Kirill (2010b) Slovo Svjatejshego Patriarha Kirilla za Bozhestvennoj liturgiej v Kievo-Pecherskoj lavre v Den' Kreshhenija Rusi (Homily by His Holiness Patriarch Kirill after the Divine Liturgy at Kievo-Pechersky Monastery on the Day of Baptism of Rus'). Available from: www.patriarc hia.ru/db/text/1232510.html (accessed 26 August 2021).

Kirill (2011) Slovo Svjatejshego Patriarha Kirilla posle molebna u pamjatnika Krestitelju Rusi na Vladimirskoj gorke (Homily by His Holiness Patriarch Kirill after the prayer at the monument to the Baptizer of Rus' at Vladimirskaya Gorka). Available from: www.orthedu.ru/news/3352- 11.html (accessed 26 August 2021).

Kirill (2013a) Slovo Svjatejshego Patriarha Kirilla na XVII Vsemirnom Russkom Narodnom Sobore (Statement made by His Holiness Patriarch Kirill at the XVIIth World Russian People's Council). Available from: https://vrns.ru/documents/slovo-svyateyshego-patriarkha-kirilla-na-xvii-vsemirnom-russkom-narodnom-sobore/ (accessed 26 August 2021).

Kirill (2013b) Slovo Svjatejshego Patriarha Kirilla posle Bozhestvennoj liturgii na Minskom Zamchishhe (Homily by His Holiness Patriarch Kirill after the Divine Liturgy at Minskoye Zamchische). Available from: www.patriarchia.ru/db/text/3133929.html (accessed 26 August 2021).

Kirill (2014a) Propoved' Svjatejshego Patriarha Kirilla v den' pamjati svjatogo ravnoapostol'nogo velikogo knjazja Vladimira v Hrame Hrista Spasitelja v Moskve (Homily by His Holiness Patriarch Kirill delivered on the occasion of commemoration of Saint Prince Vladimir in Christ the Saviour Cathedral in Moscow). Available from: www.patriarchia.ru/db/text/3697740.html (accessed 26 August 2021).

Kirill (2014b) Privetstvie Svjatejshego Patriarha Kirilla uchastnikam VIII Assamblei Russkogo mira (Message addressed by His Holiness Patriarch Kirill to the participants of the VIIIth Assembly of the Russkiy Mir Foundation). Available from: www.patriarchia.ru/db/text/3823 040.html (accessed 26 August 2021).

Kirill (2015a) Svjatejshij Patriarh Kirill: "Net nichego bolee dalekogo ot istiny, chem otozhdestvljat' Russkij mir iskljuchitel'no s Rossijskoj Federaciej" (His Holiness Patrirach Kirill: "There is nothing further from the truth than identifying Russkiy Mir exclusively with the Russian Federation"). Available from: www.patriarchia.ru/db/text/4164499.html (accessed 26 August 2021).

Kirill (2015b) 'Segodnja nasha strana nahoditsja na poroge novogo istoricheskogo vybora. Vystuplenie Svjatejshego Patriarha Kirilla na otkrytii III Rozhdestvenskih parlamentskih vstrech' (Today, our country stands on the eve of a new historical choice. Statement made by His Holiness Patriarch Kirill at the opening of the IIIrd Christmas Parliamentary Meetings), *Zhurnal Moskovskoj Patriarhii* 2: 49–57.

Kirill (2015c) *Sem' slov o Russkom mire (Seven Speeches about Russkiy Mir)*, Moscow: World Russian People's Council.

Kirill (2016) 'Knjaz' Vladimir. Civilizacionnyj vybor. Slovo Svjatejshego Patriarha Kirilla na otkrytii mezhdunarodnoj nauchno-prakticheskoj konferencii' (Prince Vladimir. Statement made by His Holiness Patriarch Kirill at the opening of the scientific conference), *Zhurnal Moskovskoj Patriarhii* 1: 39–45.

Kirill (2017) Slovo Svjatejshego Patriarha Kirilla v Den' Kreshhenija Rusi posle Liturgii v Troickom sobore Aleksandro-Nevskoj lavry (Homily by His Holiness Patriarch Kirill after the liturgy at the Trinity Cathedral of St. Alexandre Nevsky Monastery). Available from: www.patriarchia.ru/ db/text/4970003.html (accessed 26 August 2021).

Kirill (2018a) Slovo Svjatejshego Patriarha Kirilla na XXII Vsemirnom Russkom Narodnom Sobore (Statement made by His Holiness Patriarch Kirill at the XXIInd World Russian People's Council). Available from: www.patriarchia.ru/db/text/5295249.html (accessed 26 August 2021).

Kirill (2018b) Slovo Svjatejshego Patriarha Kirilla posle molebna u pamjatnika svjatomu ravnoapostol'nomu knjazju Vladimiru v Moskve (Homily by His Holiness Patriarch Kirill after the prayer at the monument to Saint Prince Vladimir in Moscow). Available from: www.patriarc hia.ru/db/text/5244437.html (accessed 26 August 2021).

Kirill (2019a) Slovo Svjatejshego Patriarha Kirilla na plenarnom zasedanii XXIII VRNS (Statement made by His Holiness Patriarch Kirill at the XXIIrd World Russian People's Council). Available from: www.patriarchia.ru/db/text/5515451.html (accessed 26 August 2021).

Kirill (2019b) Slovo Svjatejshego Patriarha Kirilla v den' pamjati svjatitelja Petra Moskovskogo posle Liturgii v Uspenskom sobore Kremlja (Homily by His Holiness Patriarch Kirill on the day of commemoration of St. Peter of Moscow after the liturgy at the Assumption Cathedral of the Kremlin). Available from: www.patriarchia.ru/db/text/5335892.html (accessed 26 August 2021).

Kirill (2019c) Slovo Svjatejshego Patriarha Kirilla posle molebna u pamjatnika svjatomu ravnoapostol'nomu knjazju Vladimiru v Moskve (Homily by His Holiness Patriarch Kirill after the prayer at the monument to Saint Prince Vladimir in Moscow). Available from: www.patriarc hia.ru/db/text/5478751.html (accessed 26 August 2021).

Kirill (2019d) Svjatejshij Patriarh Kirill: Edinstvo Svjatoj Rusi osnovano prezhde vsego na edinstve Russkoj Pravoslavnoj Cerkvi (His Holiness Patriarch Kirill: The unity of Holy Rus' is first of all based on the unity of the Russian Orthodox Church). Available from: www.patriarchia.ru/db/text/5508869.html (accessed 26 August 2021).

Kirill (2021a) Patriarshaja propoved' posle Liturgii v Den' Kreshhenija Rusi (Patriarch's homily after the liturgy on the day of the Baptism of Rus'). Available from: www.patriarchia.ru/db/text/5832500.html (accessed 26 August 2021).

Kirill (2021b) Pozdravlenie Svjatejshego Patriarha Kirilla Prezidentu RF V.V. Putinu s Dnem Kreshhenija Rusi (Message addressed by His Holiness Patriarch Kirill to the President of the Russian Federation V.V. Putin on the day of the Baptism of Rus'). Available from: www.patriarc hia.ru/db/text/5831870.html (accessed 26 August 2021).

Kirill (2021c) Pozdravlenie Svjatejshego Patriarha Kirilla Prezidentu Ukrainy V.A. Zelenskomu s Dnem Kreshhenija Rusi (Message addressed by His Holiness Patriarch Kirill to the President of Ukraine V.A. Zelensky on the day of the Baptism of Rus'). Available from: www.patriarchia.ru/db/text/5830968.html (accessed 26 August 2021).

Kirill (2021d) Patriarshaja propoved' v den' pamjati ravnoapostol'nyh Mefodija i Kirilla (Patriarch's homily on the day of commemoration of St. Methodius and St. Cyril). Available from: www.patriarchia.ru/db/text/5813130.html (accessed 26 August 2021).

Koryagin, V. (2014) 'Predlog dlja ssory' (A proposition of a quarrel), *Gazeta.ru.* Available from: www.gazeta.ru/science/2014/03/22_a_5958681.shtml (accessed 26 August 2021).

Kuznetsov, S. (2014) *Bol'shoj tolkovyj slovar' russkogo yazyka (Dictionary of the Russian language).* Available from: http://gramota.ru (accessed 26 August 2021).

Lazar (2021) 'Mitropolit Simferopol'skij i Krymskij Lazar': Krym – kolybel' duhovnosti russkogo, ukrainskogo i belorusskogo narodov' (Lazar, the Metropolitan of Simferopol and of the Crimea, says: "The Crimea is the spiritual cradle of Russians, Ukrainians and Belarussians"), *Zhurnal Moskovskoj Patriarhii* 3(952): 34–39.

Sycheva, L. (2007) 'Russkij jazyk, russkaja kul'tura, russkij mir' (Russian language, Russian culture, Russian world), *Rossijskaja Federacija segodnja* 14: 2–3.

Yakovleva, E. (2009) 'Patriarh Kirill podaril prem'eru Ukrainy Julii Timoshenko ikonu' (Patriarch Kirill offered an icon to Ukrainian Prime Minister Yulia Timoshenko), *Rossijskaja gazeta.* Available from: https://rg.ru/2009/04/29/kirill-timoshenko-anons.html (accessed 26 August 2021).

8

MEDIA SENSATIONALISM OF THE WEST AND THE RHETORIC OF POVERTY PORN IN INDIA

Sony Jalarajan Raj and Adith K. Suresh

Introduction

The impact of media in everyday life affects the way real-life events become representations. The communicative discourse of representation involves the rhetoric of the image, which serves as a signifier that describes the meaning it intends to disseminate to a range of receivers. Image construction is a process that often disregards authenticity as a quality and seeks those interpretive elements that sensationalize a particular subject. Robert Hariman and John Louis Lucaites (2016) in their work *The Public Image: Photography and Civic Spectatorship* argue that photographs and photojournalism play a crucial role in creating public perception and critical engagement by exposing collective realities through visual rhetoric. In a technologically advanced environment where it is hard to distinguish reality from fiction, the media's role in the process of constructing stories about "what happens in the world" influences the public in their understanding of the world and its many problems. In closer analyses, narratives that paint a particular picture about incidents and regions, geopolitical contexts and cultures, and demographics and social structures reveal the bias ingrained in our views.

Popular media operates on the basis of sensationalism; the ideology that emphasizes strategies and methods of attention-seeking through which public interest on a certain topic is exploited. The spontaneous reactions and responses from a large population of audiences are the result of popular media's interactive communication with the public which covers those events, issues, and themes that can generate a high emotional appeal among the masses. Portraying these stories in a highly exaggerated and dramatic fashion can trigger strong emotions of pain, empathy, shame, guilt, fear, and aversion through which people are able to identify or make connections with media narratives. The tactics of media sensationalism through the sharing of images that highlight human suffering and weakness are referred to as "poverty porn", a phenomenon familiarized by charity organizations that seek donations and help by "showing exploitative imagery of people living in destitute conditions" (Dortonne 2016).

116

DOI: 10.4324/9781003195276-11

The media sensationalism that feeds on human suffering and its marketability through different modes is based on "viewer guilt" that compels one to "choose between sharing the hurtful images of exploitation or 'turn a blind eye' to what they have seen" (Hamilton, Tokpa, McCain, and Donovan 2021: 2). This genre of "poverty porn" explicitly narrates tragedies and miseries of marginalized groups from developing countries as a means to divert popular attention to the romanticized images of tragedy. It paints a generalized picture of geographical regions as less progressive to a global media audience. In this context, regions like India, which are still defined by the vestiges of a colonial past, become subjects of the Western gaze that operates as an ideological tool for the dissemination of poverty porn discourses to the mainstream. Here, media representation of poverty porn specifically includes the overfocusing on tragedies and miseries of marginalized groups in a manner that highlights India as a representation of the "Third World". The use of poverty porn images in media helps the privileged to distinguish the idea of progress by the strategic exclusion and exposition of certain problems. In India, the notion of poverty porn is part of the popular culture, and news agencies, social media, political parties, religious organizations, film, and television take part in a collective discourse of sensationalizing "weakness" using advertisements and public relations where information is manipulated through emotional rhetoric.

This chapter analyzes how the visual representation of poverty porn in India gives rise to a discourse of sensationalism through which social structures maintain their divisive political and cultural intentions. It investigates how the rhetoric of "poverty porn" sensationalizes the economically and socially underprivileged sections of the Indian public sphere in both national and international visual media. In India, the discourses on a range of serious problems such as rape, political martyrdom, sexual abuse, natural disasters, caste violence, and gender inequality focus on nourishing a victim culture rather than objectively addressing deep-rooted problems. Poverty porn representations narrow the boundaries between myth and reality to present facts as emotional reality. The shocking and pervasive images of the victims are ubiquitous in visual media formats as they find news value and political significance. They are used as a form of rhetoric to either maintain the status quo of power relations or to achieve a momentary power transfer through democratic elections. Edward Said's notion of Oriental 'Othering' is used to discuss how Western depictions of the East sensationalize poverty porn. The way poverty porn is portrayed as an Asian phenomenon through media framing and agenda-setting dismisses the universality of human misery by restricting it to regional contexts only. We argue that the benefits of "keeping it sensational" are not long-term, and therefore the strategies of poverty porn must be repeated at regular intervals. Discussing how visual media uses the interpretive aspects of images that embody human misery in a regional context, this chapter focuses on the media rhetoric that negatively frames particular geographical spaces and their people. The attempt to challenge the logic of poverty porn as an international media practice responds to the call for the de-Westernization of media discourses.

Media Ecosystem and Power Production

Western media have always played a major role in controlling the power structure of the world through narratives that aim to establish a distinguishable dominant-submissive dichotomy. The bipolar political conditioning in the Cold War era was perfect for media discourses to find propagandist methods to frame stories in ways that help set special agendas. This was not only an opportunity for global media to take part in international affairs with vested interests but to create a homogenized narrative space in an increasingly globalized environment. In other words, media intervention in the form of agenda-setting rather than reporting events of reality is reflected in this new phase of multimedia-integrated journalistic practices where the spirit of globalization appears as Westernization.

The construction of narratives through a Western angle was prominent in the colonial era where conflicting images of the colonizer and the colonized subject were used to assert a power equation that normalized inequality as the natural order. These narratives favored a colonial perception of the colonized countries as lands of low culture and barbaric practices. The colonizer's curiosity for the indigenous and ritualistic cultural forms of these lands was a sign of exploitation rather than inclusion; the looting and importing of natural resources and artistic assets from colonized regions attest to the desire for things that had pure materialistic value. The disregard for the exotic and exquisite expressions of the native people showed the colonial resentment ingrained in this essential power relationship. For instance, the cultural differences in the culinary and cutlery practices between the Western colonizer and the Oriental colonial subject reflect the colonizer-colonized resentment that negatively brands certain spaces in terms of cleanliness, hygiene, and filth. The revulsion associated with the visual perception of these "outside spaces" is fundamental to the construction of power dominance as it signifies notions of social acceptance and rejection. As a result, the notion of "disgust" gets associated with the body of the colonized Other, and the representations of the "disgusted other" essentialize cultural identities.

Poverty porn as a concept has been used to understand creative works in the way they represent the conditions of places that are generally considered backward (see Stobie 2020). Western literary works have used India as a context that portrays a mysteriously exotic land of spirituality and superstitions, a place of poor development and poverty-stricken households. The novels of E. M. Forster have been criticized for the Orientalist angle used to represent India. The historical depictions in the works of Dominique Lapierre and Larry Collins have presented a picture of India to Westerners as a land of social, economic, and political conflicts. Similarly, stereotypical images of India have appeared in Western news media which often emphasized its Third World status. In the 2014 controversial *New York Times* cartoon, which depicted India's successful Mars Mission in an offensively negative way, an Indian man with his bull is shown knocking on the doors of the "Elite Space Club" (BBC 2014). The picture was criticized for its attempt to portray the West as a group of intelligent elites and the Indian as a stereotyped Third World farmer. India's postcolonial struggles to achieve modernity and autonomy were belittled by such media representations that fail to go beyond what has been established as the 'Other' since colonial times. Manisha Basu (2010) notes that:

> The resulting battles between tradition and modernity, nation and empire, east and west, and self and other were however soon to be rendered even more complex with India's emerging prominence in the global information revolution, its spectacular drive toward complete economic liberalization, and its emerging status as a subaltern military power central to US imperial interests in Asia.
>
> *Basu 2010: 98*

Western media's refusal to acknowledge India as an emerging power has exposed their priorities that only glorify the dominant power positions of the West. Both national and international media disseminate narratives in a way that defines an inexplicable power difference between those who create such narratives and those who are featured in them. It denotes how the production and reinforcement of narrative images and their interpretations are significant in establishing a particular point of view in society. The construction of "image-worlds" affects the existing structural aspects of society and they contain "the ability to reterritorialize and transcode the sordid conditions of a third-world metropolis" (Basu 2010: 95). Media influences the way a particular image gets associated with a region and becomes its most popular defining signifier. Once such pictures are transnationally disseminated, they establish a concrete reality and facilitate further identifications of the region through similar images that refer to such a collective reality.

The Logic of Slums: The Construction and Concealment of "Other" Spaces in Poverty Porn

The concept of the Third World has been characterized as a geopolitical category which contains restricted urban regions that provide poor quality of life to inhabitants. For instance, the notion of "slums" has been a popular trope in media discourses that telecast the conditions of a "Third World" as the conditions of the non-Western world. The self-declaration of countries that mark themselves as a Third World or developing nation implies their acknowledgment of Western superiority (Hall 1996). To make the Third World a symbolic representation of the non-Western, the media frequently used hand-picked regional spaces from countries like India and used them as an example to define a large and complex geographical structure. David Simon (2011) argues that:

> Even where individual slums are occasionally depicted photographically or in words in the media, they tend to be iconic images of particularly large, problematic, complex or resilient examples that seem somehow to outweigh the ability of municipalities, government ministries and NGOs to foster improvements. Dharavi in Mumbai, Kibera and Mathare Valley in Nairobi, Soweto in Johannesburg and the almost ubiquitous favelas of Rio de Janeiro fall into this category.
>
> *Simon 2011: 680*

The generalized perception of slums defines them as "alienating and alienated spaces of deprivation, despair and danger to both their residents and the wider urban population" (Simon 2011: 680). The term "slum" frequently appears in discussions of poverty and development, but more significantly it acquired a popular cultural notion as derogatory rhetoric for emphasizing the deterioration of regional space. Alan Gilbert (2009) observed that the use of slum terminology affected the views on urbanization:

> Critically, many cities are no longer desirable places in which to live; they contain too many slums, are centers of crime and violence and are increasingly polarized into rich and poor areas. With the "discovery" that half the world's population now lives in cities and that there are now one billion slum dwellers, cities have once again become areas of poverty and danger.
>
> *Gilbert 2009: 35–36*

The real problem of using slums as a dominant parameter for measuring social conditions refers to how media shift their focus to particular aspects of these regions to single out what they desire to frame as reality. The type of Othering that operates in this conditioning is through the exclusion of all undesirable realities that exist both inside and outside our mainstream public space. Here, poverty's universality is not considered while making narratives of the slum. Western media's strategic exclusion of their own problems of poverty and suffering shows this fundamental difference in approaching general issues with the same characteristics. Western narratives that construct the Third World as an image of a collective downtrodden do not consider their own ghettos as a sign of a collective problem. It is not natural that Western countries are known for their advanced metropolitan cities where progress and possibility lead the way while the so-called Third World countries are known for their dirty slums and streets. This differentiation ultimately enunciates what it is like to be an Indian and a European as these national identities are an embodiment of the geographical picture they get associated with. The racial stereotypes such as "India is a land of snake charmers and beggars" come from such picturizations that devalue the quality of the land by framing it against a set of overstretched backgrounds.

The ideology of the ghetto emerges out of misconceptions that fail to recognize the multifaceted variables contributing to a particular problem. According to Gilbert (2007), "the very word 'slum' confuses the physical problem of poor quality housing with the characteristics of the people living there" (710). In the case of poverty, the confusion between "place poverty" and "people poverty" is explicit where "the inhabitants of places like slums that appear poor in terms of their physical fabric are assumed to be uniformly poor by virtue of where they live" (Simon 2011: 683). When the slums become sites of human activity, they also provide an opportunity for the Westernizer to gaze upon them. Their desire to visit the slums, often called "slum tourism", is motivated by an exploitative voyeuristic pleasure that seeks to capture the experience of the poor as "poverty porn" (Frenzel 2012: 57; Weiner 2008). Slum tourism involves the act of slumming, which Tony Seaton (2012) defines as a "contact between rich and poor in the territory of the latter" (21).

Since slums are inextricable from India's urban landscape, they often become a central theme and cultural backdrop of Bollywood cinema, India's popular film industry (Basu 2012). The Dharavi slums in Mumbai are infamous for being a subject in films and documentaries. The representation of Dharavi in global media has been criticized as a typical manifestation of the poverty porn discourse centralizing India as a land of poverty and overpopulation. BBC 4's 2010 documentary on Dharavi slums by Kevin McCloud was controversial for broadcasting everyday life in Dharavi, which highlighted footage of dirty sewage and dead rats, children living in unhealthy circumstances and congested housing colonies (Indian Express 2010). The two-part documentary, called *Slumming It*, described Dharavi as a "hellhole" through images and narration that try to brand it as a disturbing "grand design". The documentary film shows how the narrator's encounter with situations such as people living in dwellings near sewage pipes, defecating in public, and picking stuff from large waste pits, etc., makes him uncomfortable, bewildered and mesmerized at the same time. The overwhelmed Western observer is an integral part of the poverty porn spectacles to make sense of the sequence of shocking images shown on screen. The characteristics of the slum present a sense of an outer world to the foreigner, who is anyone living in better conditions than the slum. This outer world exposes a context where the daily struggles of a population are perceived as part of a romanticized impossibility. The narrator's amusement at the operation of the slums is a sign of his desire to explore the uncomfortable realities that are alien to the privileged life worlds of the Western population.

The media's narrative construction of poverty porn is an invitation to the unexplored realms of the underprivileged and the harsh realities that constitute their struggles for survival. These are journeys into the private lives of the people who are now exposed to the public through the media lens. Such exposure strips them of their individuality and right to privacy at an unconstitutional level and these so-called "township tours" have the quality of being "social pornography" (Kirshenblatt-Gimblett 1998: 54). The pornographic aspects of exposure and voyeurism are inherent in the spectacles of poverty porn as their political principle has always been a form of attention-seeking through transgressive visuals. Film, television, and news media have a strong impact on the popularization of Dharavi, especially in shaping a prior understanding of it (Dyson 2012: 266). The sensationalizing effect created by the "Western curiosity and fascination with the slum" is evident in films like *Slumdog Millionaire* (2008) which focuses on marketing the Third World context to a wider transnational audience (Dyson 2012: 255).

Poverty Porn and Othering in Popular Culture

Visual media narratives shape reality as a simulation through the repetition of images. Whether in the form of news reporting, television programming, filmmaking, or social media engagements, visual images paint the picture of a context more effectively than words because they easily capture the attention of those who perceive it. The main function of such images is the dissemination of primary information as they link a particular region with its culture and people for the rest of the world to see. For example, a single image can represent a whole country, such as the Statue of Liberty representing the United States of America, the Eiffel Tower representing France, and the Taj Mahal representing India. Globally familiar cultural symbols and identities are easy to recognize without a description. However, other images with less global visibility need additional descriptive narratives to give meaning to them. It is because they show ambiguity in their arbitrary image–meaning relationship. Therefore, images gain validity and recognition when they are accompanied by powerful descriptive narratives. In newspapers, images have captions and a related descriptive news report that explains their significance; in live news broadcasting, a reporter gives an explicit and clear description of what happens at the moment; in cinema and other digital media, there are additional technical and performative aspects that give the narrative a totality in terms of meaning construction.

The hegemony of Western media is reflected in representations of foreign issues. The ideology of the Western perspective is often characterized by an urge to stereotype and romanticize Eastern countries and spaces outside the West as the normalized "Other" (Said 1978). The impacts of cultural imperialism, global capitalism, and Western modernity have contributed to the new world-making through certain archetypes that refuse to see things from the actual contexts in which an authentic view is possible. The many stereotypes that are sensationalized in news media reporting and broadcasting are reflected in other entertainment platforms as well, especially entertainment media forms such as popular films, reality television, comedy shows, and video games (Ross 2019). Film productions have the capacity to construct a cultural imperative that asserts a view that forces one to imagine certain places as a signifier of misery and violence (Isea 2018). Critically acclaimed films like *Gandhi* (1982), *The Constant Gardener* (2005), *Blood*

Diamond (2006), and *Slumdog Millionaire* (2008) are examples of cinema using "Third World" struggles to create "an extensive repertoire of images about the South which has considerable bearing on how Northern audiences view the South and, arguably, on how Southern elites see their own subalterns" (Sengupta 2010: 601). The portrayal of India in films produced in the West celebrates the idea of an uncivilized, pre-modern, socially backward, savage, and traditional land (Ramasubramanian 2007). Filmmakers and reporters have frequently subscribed to a Western gaze to create spectacles out of conditions like poverty (Shah 2006; Shome 1996).

For instance, the film *Slumdog Millionaire* depicts the "slum" as a representation of the Indian living conditions and the slum-dweller as a collective identity of the majority of Indians. The rags-to-riches narrative of the film presents the story of Jamal, a young Mumbai slum-dweller whose life changes when he wins a competition game show to become a "millionaire". *Slumdog Millionaire* draws a picture of an existing Indian context where poverty is one of the harrowing realities faced by the developing nation. However, the film does not just focus on this reality but overemphasizes it by "framing slums as worthless spaces that are worlds-unto-themselves" and "reinforcing orientalist stereotypes about slum-dwellers" (Sengupta 2010: 613). The vicious cycle of poverty in developing countries reflects the problem of economic development emerging as a result of unemployment, low income, and unequal wealth distribution (Marger 2007; Nurkse 1952). Mitu Sengupta (2010) notices that such a representation lacks a clear understanding of the deep social, political, and economic parameters and is only concerned about contextualizing a "culture of poverty" as a background for the Indian slum-dweller to participate in an Indian version of a British game show (*Who Wants to Be a Millionaire?*) (607). The film's motifs to romanticize the poor have been criticized as "poverty porn" as the film ultimately subscribes to the hidden notion behind the idea of poverty porn that the poor in developing countries need the help of the West to succeed (Miles 2009).

Wendy Keys and Barbara Pini state that poverty porn is "a genre that focuses on entertainment, titillation, and sensationalism, and a de-contexualising of financial deprivation, alongside an associated emphasis on individual failure and personal irresponsibility" (2014: 3). The emergence of poverty porn television has legitimized socioeconomic conditions through programming (Beresford 2016; Jensen 2014; Cooper and Paton 2021). The genre of reality television, for instance, has developed the possibility of sensationalizing suffering through new formats suitable to the changed socio-economic structure in a globalized scenario. Anna McCarthy argues that the ideology of reality television is based on neoliberal values that focus on the individual as an agent with responsibility – referring to it as "neoliberalism's theatre of suffering", reality television connects with audiences through responses that evoke a shared sense of suffering (McCarthy 2007: 34). Poverty porn identifies "suffering" as a universal phenomenon that uniformly affects human populations of all cultures and social systems. It uses this commonality to find an opportunity in the most diversified cultures such as India to create an emotional mass market for profit. In other words, poverty porn achieves its goals through the cultural homogenization of suffering.

Poverty porn facilitates the structuring of the "Other" in popular culture. Viewing the Other from a distance is what defines the Western approach to identifying, defining, and appropriating the Other as a subject of low culture and development. The identification of the Other allows the Westernizers to project their gaze onto the unique cultural, geographical, and indigenous coordinates to find the exotic quality that contradicts the Western way of life. For example, the rural population is often imagined as pre-modern savage victims in the dominant popular imaginations of the West (Pini, Mayes, and Rodriguez Castro 2017). The existence of the Oriental and Occidental differences in an unbalanced power equilibrium allows the Westerner to culturally appropriate and control the Orient. Such appropriations use media as a means to regulate the desires in popular culture to orchestrate the agenda of disseminating the 'Western knowledge of the Eastern world' as legitimate. This strategy of Westernizing the Orient starts with the construction of the Eastern stereotypical Other as an irrational, feminized, psychologically weak non-European while reiterating the European as a rational, authoritative, and masculine image (Said 1978). Since Otherness is viewed as a form of marginalization and exclusion (Warf 2010), representing the Other in popular media facilitates the parochial ideology with which a dominant system of signifiers gives meaning to a category of people and their geographies, cultural differences, beliefs, and practices. The representation of the "Slumdog" within the Hollywood text attracts the universal gaze into the image of the Other and finds the possibility of a spectacle out of it. The ironic combination of the "Slumdog" and "the millionaire" reveals the rhetoric of Othering as a form of juxtaposing two contradicting categories of identities to achieve an emotive response among those who perceive it. Mary Grace Antony (2012) argues that the film and its marketing endorsed Western interventionist rhetoric by using Orientalist tropes to represent poverty. The way the "Slumdog" represents an India that is poor, non-progressive, and filthy and the "millionaire" represents a capitalist West that is rich, productive, and successful shows how a popular cultural medium like cinema sensationalizes the poverty porn culture in favor of Western interests.

Poverty Porn and the Rhetoric of Sensationalism

Media representation, reporting, and coverage of disastrous events, natural calamities, and sociopolitical issues in non-Western countries involve a pattern of presenting gruesome images, videos, and statistics that magnify the severity of a situation to exaggerated proportions. Broadcasting different aspects of victimhood, such as the loss of life, property, and social status of individuals, through cinema, television, and documentaries is a common phenomenon observed in the media discourses focusing on South Asian countries. The mediated image of the victim is strengthened when the media intervenes in the personal space of individuals, communities, and survivors to make them subjects by framing them in front of the disasters they are a victim of. As the media projects its gaze toward a disaster and its victims through direct interviews of the victims themselves, descriptions of the bystanders, and views from authorities, a connection is made between these images and the audience. What this connection establishes is a one-dimensional view from higher power positions that do not consider understanding things from the perspective of the victims.

Tara Rose (2019) observes that news media contributes significantly to concretizing the existing power imbalances in the social structure by "systematically over-accessing people in powerful and privileged institutional positions – officials, experts, politicians – often to the detriment of alternative viewpoints" (399). Debates surrounding the issues of the developing nations rely on the rhetoric of "expert opinions" in newsroom discussions and interactions where people with conflicting interests use the tragedies of the victims to substantiate their own agendas. Corporate media that run multiple platforms for information dissemination in India are influenced by Western ideology. The impact of Western technology and culture over the world makes media discourses Western-centric and the concept of "de-Westernization" has been observed through skepticism (Murthy 2012: 198; Ranganathan 2011). The Eurocentric approach follows the Western criteria to distinguish societies (Hall 1992: 277), and media models outside the West are bound to their standard prototypes rather than being defined by regional elements. India's domestic media channels marketize the country's failures and crises in their news to highlight problems for news value. News channels create contexts in which different politicians and representatives of political ideologies come to argue about the failure or success of the system in ameliorating a problem. These debates are arranged at national and regional levels, allowing the participation of a range of people to express their opinions, accusations, and justifications to a wide audience connected through technology. Such platforms often cross the boundaries of rational discourse and become a stage for name-calling, stereotyping, and propaganda to maintain the status quo of power relations. The "poor" subject or the "victim" in poverty porn discussions is overlooked by narratives that seldom concentrate on individual problems. These narratives are part of a bigger view because they try to "expose" the authorities that control the system's political affairs. Edward Wasserman (2013) observes that:

> Nowadays, the safest and least contentious justification for covering poverty is the notion that it's a byproduct of some kind of policy failure or social break-down. The coverage, hence, fits comfortably under the umbrella of the news media as an organ of accountability, a means for calling on officialdom – chiefly public sector officialdom – to explain what went wrong, and for demanding officials tell the public what they plan to do about it. The possibility that nothing went wrong, that poverty is not aberrant but normal, that the system is oper-ating precisely as it is designed to operate, and that it reproduces poverty sys-tematically as a routine feature of a maldistribution of social product and life chances, is one that fits poorly into that worldview.
>
> *Wasserman 2013: 139*

In creating a poverty porn rhetoric, victimization is rendered as an effective strategy for framing the Other. Mirjam Vossen (2017) identified victim framing as one of the main strategies of Western media in creating narratives of poverty porn. To project the image of the dispossessed as a symbol of the social, cultural, political, and economic situation of the land, facts and reality are presented with emotion. The construction of emotional reality is essential to the ideology of poverty porn as emotions add value to suffering, and poverty porn narratives portray those who suffer as subjects who deserve to be treated with sympathy and compassion. The tactic of "aestheticizing poverty" makes us visualize the poor as a failed subject without having to pay much attention to the conditions that produce such inequality (Ibrahim 2017: 2–4). There has always been a popular viewer-ship for shocking images of poverty porn in developing countries. Many disasters and crises are identified by the "uniqueness" of these notorious images. For example, the dead child's picture from the 1984 Bhopal gas tragedy (Tiwari 2021) and Kevin Carter's Pulitzer Prize-winning photograph "the vulture and the little girl" show the severity of the context more powerfully than any other descriptive format. Media representation of some of the worst disasters that happened in India, such as the Bhopal gas tragedy, the 2004 earth-quake and tsunami in the Indian Ocean, and the 2017 Uttarakhand earthquake, showed the extremity of these events through pictures and videos of victims in agony. Pictures of dead bodies, animals, the wounded in the hospital, and homeless people, were used by international media to narrate the horrifying realities that created victims.

Changing Frames of Poverty Porn

Since suffering is universal and persistent, the demand for poverty porn is always there. It survives through emotional manipulation achieved through images of contemporary crises. In recent times, deaths related to the COVID-19 pandemic in India caused panic when pictures of human misery flooded media platforms all around the world. These images spoke stories of cemeteries full of dead bodies waiting for their turn to be buried, floating dead bodies in the Ganges, patients suffering in hospitals due to shortage of oxygen cylinders, migrant workers traveling across states on foot, helpless people trapped in Western countries, the suffering of hospital workers, the police brutality against people violating social distancing, etc. They immediately enhanced the fear already brought about by the pandemic in society. The fearmongering by media during a crisis is the immediate result of how a situation is exploited for news value. These images are used in a way to generate sympathy and invite people to subscribe to the media agents in the form of viewership, selling of newspapers, donations, and solidarity (Chatterjee 2018; Flinders 2014). The sensationalizing effect of poverty porn places only the vulnerable human subject in its popular frame while strategically avoiding the privileged and the powerful. It is significant to understand that the marginalized are always stripped of the dignity and privacy they deserve. They are sacrificed for news value when they become collective representations of an event, crisis, or social context bigger than their individual human identity.

The media's framing of disaster events and tragedies depends on the type of audience they are addressing. The bias in framing is explicit when it comes to reporting home events. For example, Kellner (2004) criticizes the corporate media in the United States for being the instruments of propaganda during and after the World Trade Center attacks. The live footage of the terrorist attack telecasted through television played a major role in elevating the nationalistic emotions of the American people to create a populist mandate for America's war on terrorism.

> The live television broadcasting brought a "you are there" drama to the September 11 spectacle. The images of the planes striking the World Trade Center, the buildings bursting into flames, individuals jumping out of the window in a desperate attempt to survive the inferno, the collapse of the towers, and subsequent chaos provided unforgettable images that viewers would not soon forget. The drama continued throughout the day with survivors being pulled from the rubble, and the poignant search for individuals still alive and attempts to deal with the attack produced resonant iconic images seared deeply into spectators' memories. Many people who witnessed the event suffered from nightmares and psychological trauma. For those who viewed it intensely, the spectacle provided a robust set of images that would continue to resonate for years to come, much as the footage of the Kennedy assassination, iconic photographs of Vietnam, the 1986 explosion of the space shuttle Challenger, or the death of Princess Diana in the 1990s provided unforgettable imagery.
>
> *Kellner 2004*

The power of mediated images affects the perception of the audience in their meaning-making process. The purpose of these images is that they sensationalize an event or a context in favor of the narrator or those who benefit from the ramifications of the narrative. The reporting of the 9/11 attacks showed the horrifying nature of the event with visuals of survivors, fire brigades, and police officials, but it was broadcasted as a means to create a sense of national disaster rather than emphasizing individual suffering. When national disasters are portrayed in the West, communities outside the mainstream are presented as subjects in a victimized position. Voorhees et al. (2007) found that when Hurricane Katrina hit the US Gulf Coast in 2005, the affected minority groups were portrayed in the media "in a passive or 'victim' role and are rarely shown in positions of expertise". Lewis (2005) criticizes the media portrayal of poor African-Americans during the disaster:

> There they were unsheltered, uninsured, unpossessed … yet still enduring and striving like all poor people anywhere. But, unlike their poor White analogs, [Blacks were] vilified, ridiculed and demonized by the national media as being almost congenitally depraved because they 'took' whatever they could to feed, warm and solace their families.
>
> *19*

Similarly, Valencio and Valencio (2018) analyze the BBC reports of the UK flood crisis during the 2015–2016 period:

> The public vision of the field of the crisis was blurred. Adopting a complex narrative approach requires that the editorial team clarify the rationality of the actors involved, uncovering the deepest meanings of their voices and practices. Each case of disaster-related reporting analyzed could be compared with the presentation of a piece of an intricate puzzle to the public, yet the public still had to fit the pieces together to see the final picture. When these pieces were fitted together, a preliminary map of the social structure and the dynamics of the crisis emerged; however, no piece of news fully explored its potential to define the variety of articulations among the actors involved.

Poverty porn is obsessed with the production of disenfranchised subjects that have no significance without the tragedies they are involved in and the miseries they carry to the forefront of society. The "poor" in the poverty rhetoric lack identity and are responsible for a collective Other through which a negative image of the community is created through homogenization and stereotypical explanations (Paterson, Coffey-Glover, and Peplow 2016). In addition to the way it devalues individual identity, one of the main disadvantages of subscribing to the media rhetoric of poverty porn is the negative way it affects the psychological realm of the masses. It encourages the viewer to have a biased point of view against certain people, and poverty porn pictures create a false sense of hope through the invocation of guilt as a natural human emotion. Dortonne (2016) observes that poverty porn makes people feel "uncomfortable, disconnected, and guilty".

In order to keep events sensationalized, media have to keep using different images and repeat the act of publishing them at regular intervals. However, the continuous dissemination of the recurring images of poverty porn reduces their sensationalism. According to Downes (2016), they ultimately lead to "compassion fatigue", a "phenomenon whereby graphic or upsetting imagery ceases to have an impact because it has been seen so many times before" (Downes 2016: 22). In a technologically networked era of media production, the poverty porn "clickbait" is effective only in creating short-term impacts because there are a countless number of platforms that constantly produce narratives, counter-narratives, opinions and reports every minute. The investigation of Feltwell et al. (2017) showed that online counter-discourses can challenge the dominant narratives of poverty porn. The competition of media platforms in an era where information outburst is the norm creates a numbing effect; a state defined by the lack of understanding of the intensity and importance of situations because of the simultaneous existence of multiple parallel narratives. The emergence of collective indifference as a social order can affect the format of media sensationalism. This demands more future research to understand poverty porn's victimized Other through different perspectives.

Conclusion

As a moralistically derogatory term, poverty porn encapsulates the anxieties and pleasures that emerge as a result of observing the suffering of others. Poverty porn can promote empathy and conscious attention to the seriousness of problems through its "ability to make precarious lives visible" (Hester 2014: 213). However, the way media use images and visuals as symbols that signify a stereotypical picture of particular regional spaces makes poverty porn a strategy for sensationalizing suffering and emotions to exploit the empathetic bias of the audience. The rhetorical strategies involved in representing poverty porn as a regional phenomenon reveal the media's tendency to visualize certain regions as backward while consciously avoiding others. The power and hegemony of the Western media ecosystem are rampant in the globalized world order where media conglomerates are the gatekeepers of information and the way they filter information creates narratives that favor a certain worldview. The practice of highlighting the miseries of the marginalized in non-Western geographical spaces masks the universality of these problems.

Poverty porn studies expose the ethical imbalance ingrained in media representations of the Western/non-Western to open up a context where discourses are not limited within the binaries created by images and rhetoric. The significance of such studies is how they de-Westernize poverty to enhance rational approaches that acknowledge the omnipresence of human misery and the varying factors that contribute to it. This ultimately means thinking outside the frames of media representation and understanding human suffering as a cyclic and universal phenomenon, not something such as an "Asian phenomenon". Visuals that depict the human condition of the East through media platforms emphasize the notion of Oriental suffering which has been created and romanticized by the West as a unique and overwhelming phenomenon. The construction of narratives and stories about the suffering of the non-Western has been done in a way to make audiences believe that these "spaces" are special and cannot be found elsewhere. The invocation of curiosity and amazement, mixed with a sympathetic emotional attitude, creates the Western observer who wants to gaze upon the suffering of others, learn about the way those who suffer survive in undesirable circumstances and present them to the whole world as objects of poverty porn. This practice has been a dominant aspect that defines Western media when they engage with situations outside the purview of their establishments. The perception of India in Western media has been through poverty porn images where the narrative of a developing Third World country with dirty slums is enforced as the authentic standard version. The image of slum-dwellers who roam through the thickly populated Dharavi suburban areas became the conceptualization of Indians in these narratives.

The problem of poverty porn in such image constructions is that they establish a fundamental distance between the observer and the observed, the Occident and the Orient, and the privileged and the underprivileged. This alienating effect is symptomatic of a dysfunctional relationship between people belonging to different social, cultural and economic categories. It produces a sense of inequality that devalues human dignity through the representation of suffering individuals on screen. Poverty porn as rhetoric and narrative depends on the gratification of the viewer, which happens as a result of their emotional contact with disturbing images. Contemporary use of poverty porn covers political crises and disaster events where the affected victims become subjects in live media reports that describe their lived experiences. Digital technologies boost the spontaneous and immediate exposure of poverty porn images to the public sphere and the way they go "viral" or "trending" shows the elevated sensationalizing effect of poverty porn in the contemporary media atmosphere. The capturing of the same images by different media and their dissemination through different platforms intensify the impact of poverty porn sensationalism. Repeated dissemination of images, visuals, and narratives that centralize the suffering of the poor undermines their subjectivity by creating an environment where suffering is desensitized. The ultimate result of Western media's use of poverty porn is the loss of sensitivity and empathy they initially tried to marketize for sensationalism.

References

Antony, M. G. (2012) '"Slum-Pups No More": Rescuing India's Slum Children', *Journal of Intercultural Communication Research*, 41(1): 17–36.
Basu, K. (2012) 'Slum Tourism: For the Poor, by the Poor', in F. Frenzel, K. Koens and M. Steinbrink (eds.), *Slum Tourism: Poverty, Power and Ethics*, Abingdon: Routledge, pp. 66–82.
Basu, M. (2010) '*Rang De Basanti*: The Solvent Brown and Other Imperial Colors', in R. B. Mehta and R. V. Pandharipande (eds.), *Bollywood and Globalization*, London: Anthem Press, pp. 93–110.
BBC (2014) 'India Mars Mission: New York Times Apologises for Cartoon', *BBC*, 6 October. Available at: www.bbc.com/news/world-asia-india-29502062 (accessed 6 October 2022).
Beresford, P. (2016) 'Presenting Welfare Reform: Poverty Porn, Telling Sad Stories, or Achieving change?' *Disability & Society*, 31(3): 421–425.
Chatterjee, N. (2018) 'Poverty Porn Sells, But It Isn't Helping the Poor', *The Print*, 29 July. Available at: https://theprint.in/opinion/poverty-porn-sells-but-it-isnt-helping-the-poor/90141/ (accessed 25 July 2022).
Cooper, V., and Paton, K. (2021) 'Accumulation by Repossession: The Political Economy of Evictions under Austerity', *Urban Geography*, 42(5): 583–602. DOI:10.1080/02723638.2019.1659695
Dortonne, N. (2016) 'The Dangers of Poverty Porn', *CNN*, 8 December. Available at: https://edit ion.cnn.com/2016/12/08/health/poverty-porn-danger-feat/index.html (accessed 28 July 2022).
Downes, L. (2016) 'The Visual Representation of Global Development Issues in a Higher Education Environment: Perception, Interpretation, and Replication', *Policy & Practice: A Development Education Review*, 23: 16–37. www.developmenteducationreview.com/sites/default/files/article-pdfs/Downes%20Focus23_0.pdf
Dyson, P. (2012) 'Slum Tourism: Representing and Interpreting "Reality" in Dharavi, Mumbai', *Tourism Geographies*, 14(2): 254–274.
Feltwell, T., Vines, J., Salt, K., Blythe, M., Kirman, B., Barnett, J., Brooker, P., and Lawson, S. (2017) 'Counter-Discourse Activism on Social Media: The Case of Challenging "Poverty Porn" Television', *Computer Supported Cooperative Work*, 26: 345–385. DOI: 10.1007/s10606-017-9275-z

Flinders, M. (2014) 'Down and out in Bloemfontein', *OUP Blog*, 14 March. Available at: https://blog.oup.com/2014/01/bloemfontein-poverty-porn-slum-tourism-2014/ (accessed 25 July 2022).

Frenzel, F. (2012). 'Beyond "Othering": The Political Roots of Slum Tourism', in F. Frenzel, K. Koens and M. Steinbrink (eds.), *Slum Tourism: Poverty, Power and Ethics*, Abingdon: Routledge, pp. 21–48.

Gilbert, A. (2007) 'The Return of the Slum: Does Language Matter?', *International Journal of Urban and Regional Research*, 31(4): 697–713.

Gilbert, A. (2009) 'Extreme Thinking about Slums and Slum Dwellers: A Critique', *SAIS Review*, 29(1): 35–48.

Hall, S. (1992) 'The West and the Rest: Discourse and Power', in S. Hall and B. Gieben (eds.), *Formations of Modernity*, London: Polity Press in Association with the Open University.

Hall, S. (1996) 'New Ethnicities', in D. Morely and K. H. Chen (eds.), *Stuart Hall: Critical Dialogue in Cultural Studies*, London: Routledge, pp. 275–331.

Hamilton, L., Tokpa, L. M. B., McCain, H., and Donovan, S. (2021) '#WhiteSaviorComplex: Confidentiality, Human Dignity, Social Media, and Social Work Study Abroad', *Journal of Social Work Education*. DOI: 10.1080/10437797.2021.1997685

Hariman, R., and Lucaites, J. L. (2016) *The Public Image: Photography and Civic Spectatorship*, Chicago: University of Chicago Press.

Hester, H. (2014) 'Weaponizing Prurience', In B. Korte and F. Regard (eds.), *Narrating Poverty and Precarity in Britain*, Berlin: De Gruyter, pp. 205–224.

Ibrahim, Y. (2017) 'The Re-Aestheticisation of Poverty: Blogging Hunger in the Age of Austerity', *Social Identities – Journal for the Study of Race, Nation and Culture*, 24(3): 364–379. http://dx.doi.org/10.1080/13504630.2017.1281114

Indian Express (2010) 'India to Complain about BBC's "Poverty Porn" Mumbai Film', *Indian Express*, 25 January. Available at: https://indianexpress.com/article/entertainment/entertainment-others/india-to-complain-about-bbcs-poverty-porn-mumbai-film/ (accessed 6 October 2022).

Isea, A. (2018) 'The Unveiling of Pelo Malo: The Naked Truth of Co-Producing Poverty-Porn', *New Cinemas: Journal of Contemporary Film* 16(2): 143–156.

Jensen, T. (2014) 'Welfare Commonsense, Poverty Porn and Doxosophy', *Sociological Research Online*, 19(3): 1–7. DOI: 10.5153/sro.3441

Kellner, D. (2004) '9/11, Spectacles of Terror, and Media Manipulation: A Critique of Jihadist and Bush Media Politics', *Critical Discourse Studies*, 1(1): 41–64.

Keys, W., and Pini, B. (2014) 'Aestheticising Rural Poverty: Representations of White Working Class Youth in the Documentary *Rich Hill*', *Studies in Documentary Film*, 12(1): 1–15, DOI: 10.1080/17503280.2017.1357108

Kirshenblatt-Gimblett, B. (1998) *Destination Culture: Tourism, Museums and Heritage*, Berkeley, CA: University of California Press.

Lewis, D. L. (2005) 'Unchanged Melody: The Negro and the Flood', *The Crisis*, 112: 6.

Marger, M. N. (2007) *Social Inequality: Patterns and Processes*, New York: McGraw-Hill.

McCarthy, A. (2007) 'Reality Television: A Neoliberal Theatre of Suffering', *Social Text*, 25(493): 17–42. DOI: 10.1215/01642472-2007-010.

Miles, A. (2009) 'Shocked by Slumdog's Poverty Porn', *The Times*, 14 January. Available at: www.thetimes.co.uk/article/shocked-by-slumdogs-poverty-porn-ld2jzkk7mjl (accessed 6 October 2022).

Murthy, C. S. H. N. (2012) 'Indian Cinema as a Model for De-Westernizing Media Studies: A Comparative Study of Indian Philosophical and Western Cultural Theories', *Asia Pacific Media Educator*, 22(2): 197–215.

Nurkse, R. (1952) 'Some International Aspects of the Problem of Economic Development', *The American Economic Review*, 42(2): 571–583.

Paterson, L., Coffey-Glover, L., and Peplow, D. (2016) 'Negotiating Stance within Discourses of Class: Reactions to Benefits Street', *Discourse and Society*, 27(2): 195–214. DOI: 10.1177/0957926515611558

Pini, B., Mayes, R., and Castro, L. R. (2017) 'Introduction: Beyond Stock Photographs – Imagining, Experiencing, and Researching Rural Education', *Discourse: Studies in the Cultural Politics of Education*, 38(3): 321–327. DOI: 10.1080/01596306.2017.1306978

Ramasubramanian, S. (2007) 'A Content Analysis of the Portrayal of India in Films Produced in the West', *Howard Journal of Communications*, 16(4): 243–265. DOI: 10.1080/10646170500326533

Ranganathan, M. (2011) 'De-Westernizing Media Education and Research in India', *The Hoot*, 24 November. Available at: http://asu.thehoot.org/story_popup/the-west-and-the-rest-part-i-5612 (accessed 19 October 2022).

Ross, T. (2019) 'Media and Stereotypes', in S. Ratuva (ed.), *The Palgrave Handbook of Ethnicity*, Singapore: Springer Nature, pp. 397–413.

Said, E. W. (1978) *Orientalism*, New York: Penguin Books.

Seaton, T. (2012) 'Wanting to Live with Common People …? The Literary Evolution of Slumming', in F. Frenzel, K. Koens and M. Steinbrink (eds.), *Slum Tourism: Poverty, Power and Ethics*, Abingdon: Routledge, pp. 49–65.

Sengupta, M. (2010) 'A Million Dollar Exit from the Anarchic Slum-World: Slumdog Millionaire's Hollow Idioms of Social Justice', *Third World Quarterly*, 31(4): 599–616. DOI: 10.1080/01436591003701117

Shah, S. P. (2006) 'Producing the Spectacle of Kamathipura: The Politics of Red Light Visibility in Mumbai', *Cultural Dynamics*, 18(3): 269–292.

Shome, R. (1996) 'Race and Popular Cinema: The Rhetorical Strategies of Whiteness in City of Joy', *Communication Quarterly*, 44(4): 502–518.

Simon, D. (2011) 'Situating Slums', *City*, 15(6): 674–685.

Stobie, C. (2020) Precarity, Poverty Porn and Vernacular Cosmopolitanism in NoViolet Bulawayo's *We Need New Names* and Meg Vandermerwe's *Zebra Crossing*', *Journal of Postcolonial Writing*, 56(4): 517–531.

Tiwari, A. (2021) '16 Heartbreaking Images from Bhopal Gas Tragedy Show Why We Will Never Forget the Darkest Hours', *India Times*, 3 December. Available at: www.indiatimes.com/news/bhopal-gas-tragedy-images-501522.html (accessed 10 August 2022).

Valencio, N., and Valencio, A. (2018) 'Media Coverage of the 'UK Flooding Crisis': A Social Panorama', *Disasters*, 42(3): 407–431.

Voorhees, C. C., Vick, J., and Perkins, D. D. (2007) ' "Came Hell and High Water": The Intersection of Hurricane Katrina, the News Media, Race, and Poverty', *Journal of Community & Applied Social Psychology*, 17(6), 415–429.

Vossen, M. (2017) *Framing Global Poverty: European Newspapers, NGOs and Citizens on Poverty in Developing Countries*, Amsterdam: Lenthe Publishers.

Warf, B. (ed.) (2010) 'Other/Otherness', in *Encyclopedia of Geography*, vol. 1, Los Angeles: Sage, pp. 2107–2108. https://dx.doi.org/10.4135/9781412939591.n853

Wasserman, E. (2013) 'Ethics of Poverty Coverage', *Journal of Mass Media Ethics*, 28(2), 138–140. DOI: 10.1080/08900523.2013.784668

Weiner, E. (2008) 'Slum Visits: Tourism or Voyeurism?', *New York Times*, 9 March. Available at: www.nytimes.com/2008/03/09/travel/09heads.html (accessed 6 October 2022).

9

RHETORIC OF PROTEST, TRADITION AND IDENTITY

Polish Songs of Freedom and Resistance

Agnieszka Kampka

Introduction

The chapter aims to discuss protest rhetoric using selected examples of songs that have become signs of resistance and struggle for freedom in Poland. The rhetoric of protest is a variety of linguistic, visual and audio messages. A song as a whole composed of melody and lyrics becomes a unit of this multimodal persuasive communication.

The persuasive function of music (with and without lyrics) appears in many dimensions of social life, from religious or state rituals and ceremonies, through films, advertisements and computer games, to the manifestation of identity, e.g. being a fan of a particular band or genre. The interest in music in rhetorical studies – evident since the 1980s – stems from the increased presence of music in social life linked to new technologies, the development of the music market and the possibilities of music dissemination (Sellnow 1999). Rhetorical research focuses on music as a form of communication (Chesebro et al. 1985), analysing mainly lyrics (e.g. Gonzalez and Makay 1983) in protest songs, and exploring connections between music and social movements and music as a social phenomenon (Matula 2000).

Rhetorical impact increases as recordings of different performances of these songs spread on the Internet, and the web becomes the space where protests are carried out, just like streets or squares. Today, a video of singing protesters, or a clip in which music accompanies photos from demonstrations, are popular rhetorical forms used by ordinary web users. Through editing, protest scenes can be inserted to illustrate well-known lyrics of resistance songs. Comments under such videos create yet another context in which the song appears. A single rhetorical action, such as singing a song in a city square, becomes a repeated message that can be transformed in many ways. The remix culture poses new challenges to rhetorical researchers and requires a focus on the delivery and negotiation of meanings of particular forms, styles and symbols. Rhetoric is a dynamic process of answering the exigencies of a particular rhetorical situation.

Therefore, rhetorical analysis should not be limited to analysing the lyrics or melody; one has to consider the context in which the song is created and performed. The way a

DOI: 10.4324/9781003195276-12

piece is received depends on the listeners' previous (not only musical) experience (Matula 2000). The melody of songs themselves and the impact of the music are not analysed in detail in this chapter, although it is a fact that energetic, catchy, and easily remembered tunes are often featured during protests. This study explores the social reception of protest songs by going beyond the lyrics and the music. The object of analysis becomes a specific performance or a set of contexts in which the song appears. The selected songs have become well-known and meaningful to members of a specific cultural community – Poles living at the turn of the twentieth and twenty-first centuries.

The analysis has two parts. First, it concerns the rhetorical situation in which the song in question first appeared – a primary, first-order rhetorical situation. The song's lyrics, the musical genre (be it a poetic ballad or a rock track) and the circumstances of the song's creation are linked to exigence and constraints, the two critical elements of any rhetorical situation. Secondly, the analysis follows the successive rhetorical situations in which the song appeared in the public sphere (and recorded in videos available on YouTube). Again, the question arises about exigence and constraints and how similar or different they later are from those of the original rhetorical situation. What makes a song recur – in its original or transformed form – in different social, political and cultural contexts is the identification mechanisms associated with it and the topoi used. They initially appear in the song's lyrics but gradually begin to emerge from subsequent significant song performances, concerts, demonstrations, or recordings for the Internet.

The two songs discussed below in the Global and Pop Culture Patterns section are examples of the universality of protest rhetoric. They show how certain songs circulate across cultures and how they are used for similar or increasingly new rhetorical purposes. *Mury* [Walls], a song that originated as a protest against a particular regime – General Franco in Spain – was adapted by Poles opposing communism, only to return to the streets years later by Belarusians fighting against Lukashenko's regime. The second song – *Bella ciao* – is known around the world as a symbol of opposition to fascism and, at the same time, as a stadium chant. While popularized by a popular TV series, it began to accompany protests against political, economic, environmental or gender inequalities.

The second section, Repetition of Topoi, discusses songs that originated in the 1980s, during the rise of the Solidarity movement and the struggle against communism, and that reappeared in the Polish public sphere during the 2015–2020 protests against the restriction of women's rights. These periods are not politically comparable with each other. However, their juxtaposition shows the persistence of specific rhetorical patterns and their changes (Molek-Kozakowska and Kampka 2021). *Ballada o Janku Wiśniewskim* [Ballad about Janek Wiśniewski] commemorates the victims of workers' strikes, while *Wstydzi się ciebie kraj* [The country is ashamed of you] is a contemporary reworking of this song. *Chcemy być sobą* [We want to be ourselves] and *Arahja* are rock songs treated as generational manifestos. They describe social divisions and have become a cry for the right to freedom.

This study confirms that the activities of the Solidarity movement before the fall of communism in 1989 are still shaping Polish contemporary culture. Protest singing continues to be a source of contentious ideas and important social behaviour in relation to forms of protest. The continuity is evident in the recent protests (2015–2020) organized in response to the Law and Justice government's decisions to tighten abortion laws. The results of the rhetorical analysis of selected songs prove the constant persuasive effectiveness of certain topoi used in similar (in terms of audience expectations – constraints) and different (in terms of circumstances – exigence) situations.

Theoretical Framework

The theoretical background to the present analysis is drawn from the concept of rhetorical situation (Biesecker 1989; Bitzer 1968; Garret and Xiao 1993; Vatz 1973), which has been repeatedly used in various studies on music and especially protest songs (Oliveri 2020). In this study, it is Mary Garret and Xiaosui Xiao's (1993) approach that is adopted. The rhetorical situation is created in a dynamic interaction of three elements: the rhetorical exigency, the constraints, and the rhetor. Garret and Xiao have shown the value of discursive traditions in analysing specific rhetorical situations (1993: 38). This approach allows a good understanding of how similar persuasive texts work in different circumstances.

This analysis focuses on two elements of the rhetorical situation: exigence and constraints. Exigency is a problem that demands a solution, "something waiting to be done" (Bitzer 1968: 6), "expressions of the situational audience's unsolved questions, concerns, anxieties, frustrations, and confusions, which need modification by discourse" (Garret and Xiao 1993: 39). According to Bitzer, constraints are all the circumstances that a rhetor must take into account to respond to an exigence. In Garret and Xiao's terms, they are also "the audience's expectations for an appropriate discourse in a given circumstance" (1993: 39).

Scott Consigny (1974) argues that topoi are the way to deal with a rhetorical situation, which helps answer these questions. A rhetorical situation is an initially undefined context that the rhetor must define and order, according to the time, place, circumstances in which they act and the targeted audience. Topoi are the tools a rhetor uses to deal with exigence, that is, to formulate a problem well and to define a situation according to some already tried ways. A topos gives structure and allows a new situation to be shown in a familiar framework. It helps the audience to accept the way the rhetor defines the situation, to consider as appropriate a given way of speaking about it (Garret and Xiao 1993: 37). Topoi are the rhetor's sphere of freedom and, at the same time, the boundaries within which he can move in order to communicate with his audience. Topoi are to some extent universal in nature and therefore form an inventive and argumentative resource that the rhetor can use. However, they must always be adapted to a given communicative community's values, myths, and prejudices; they must be commonplace for a specific audience. Otherwise, they will not fulfil their function.

Topos is one of the concepts causing many definition difficulties (Leff 2006). In this study, it will be understood in two ways: (1) as a recurring motif in a given culture, art, or literature (Abramowska 1982; Curtius 1972); and (2) as a cultural source of argumentation, based on shared knowledge and values (Leff 2006; McKeon 1973). Topoi are beliefs, images, symbols, patterns of thought and expression that can be used to construct an argument tailored to a particular place, time and audience.

The use of accurate topos is related to *kairos*, i.e. taking the right action at the right time (Gelang 2021). *Kairos* can explain why a song becomes a generational or group anthem seemingly by accident. Its message is sometimes read independently or even against the author's intentions. Matching the form and content to a particular historical moment and the audience's expectations is crucial.

The effective selection of topoi is made possible by identification mechanisms, described by Kenneth Burke (1969). Identification is a mutual relationship between sender and receiver rooted in a community of feelings, expectations, attitudes, values (Woodward 2003). This function favours constructing simplified, black and white axiological schemes and using groupthink to mobilize the audience (Massaka 2009: 404). Protest songs strengthen the sense of unity and reaffirm group members' right thinking. Less frequently, they are an attempt to present a position to outsiders, justify the movement's demands, or attract new members (Sellnow 1999: 67).

Methodology and Data Collection

The initial stage of the research procedure was the selection of material. The songs were chosen according to the researcher's knowledge as a participant in the studied culture. Three selected songs (*Mury, Chcemy być sobą* and *Arahja*) are mentioned in the ranking lists of the most important songs that various radio stations and cultural institutions created to celebrate Poland's independence in 2018. The other three (*Bella ciao, Ballada o Janku Wiśniewskim* and *Wstydzi się ciebie kraj*) were chosen for their popularity and use in pop culture. A selection criterion was also the existence of various YouTube videos related to these songs. These are recordings of various performances of the song, including protest scenes and examples of the use of the work in popular culture. The variety of contexts in which the song appeared, i.e. different types of audience (in terms of age, lifestyle, political views), and the diversity of interpretations, confirmed that the song is not linked to one type of rhetorical situation. The same questions about exigence and constraints are posed for each piece.

The next steps of the analysis are as follows: (1) examining the lyrics and the historical circumstances of its creation (identifying topoi); (2) analysing selected YouTube recordings as individual rhetorical situations (topoi, *kairos*, identification mechanisms); (3) identifying similarities and differences between these rhetorical situations, finding recurring patterns.

The main research questions will therefore be: (1) What is the exigence? What is the issue of the protest? Does the audience need self-definition or a definition of the opponent? Is the aim to commemorate victims or to mobilize for struggle? (2) What are the constraints? What symbols, characters, and images used in the text of the song will be familiar to the audience and stimulate the audience's emotions? What is the basis of the topoi used?

The protest songs discussed in the chapter grew out of cultural and national traditions. They are an expression of group identity, a call for freedom and subjectivity, and a voice of opposition and community at the same time. Protesters worldwide use music to express their anger or joy. They reach out to different traditions and transform them:

> In Botswana protesters drew on traditionally licensed 'songs of rebellion' against chiefs to mock current politicians. In Wisconsin old labour and folk songs were rewritten and performed. Carnivalesque themes in Occupy Wall Street echoed Caribbean carnivals, while in Greece rhetorical tropes were anchored in Greek traditions of oratory.
>
> *Werbner et al. 2014: 18*

The selected songs can be seen as the aural equivalents of the concept of iconic images, according to John Luis Lucaites and Robert Hariman (2001). Firstly, all participants in public culture recognize them. Secondly, they are treated as representations of important historical events. Thirdly, they evoke strong emotional responses. Fourthly, they are repeatedly reproduced and reinterpreted in various media and used in different social situations. Like iconic photographs, iconic songs reflect social knowledge and dominant ideologies, shape understandings of particular events and periods of history, and influence political identifications and behaviour (Hariman and Luicates 2001: 37). Songs that are recognizable symbols of a specific community (iconic songs) touch upon the social identity of its members. They are also an element of the discursive memory that binds the community together, i.e. shared knowledge, beliefs, value systems, moral judgements or political views (Charaudeau 2002).

Although music, in general, is a vital tool in propaganda and political communication because it allows us to understand the national spirit and cultural identity (Massaka 2009: 206), today songs have added rhetorical power that derives from multimodality, that is, the integration and interaction of different modes and media. In its own way, each of these modes serves a persuasive purpose. The music stirs emotions (pathos), the words persuade (logos), and the performer (artist or singing crowd) affirms the rightness of chosen behaviour (ethos). Songs can mobilize, show the power of a nation, state or ideology, express protest, release social pressure, and change social attitudes. Protest song videos can be a part of the protest, a form of civic activity. However, in this analysis, they are treated primarily as evidence of a song's rhetorical potential and an example of how a piece of music appears in different situations in which its meaning and interpretation change.

Global and Pop Culture Patterns

This section will discuss two examples: (1) *Mury* by Jacek Kaczmarski, and (2) *Bella ciao*. *Mury* was inspired by a Catalan song by Llach. The song became the anthem of the Solidarity movement and a symbol of the fight against the communist regime, and years later, a voice in the debate on shared values. *Bella ciao* was originally an Italian partisans' song which accompanies worldwide protests, popularized in the *La Casa de Papel* series. The Polish version appeared during the recent Polish protests against restricting women's rights.

The role of music in the time of communist opposition in Poland was significant. Rock and punk bands and cabaret, as well as sung poetry popular among students, were critical of the authorities (Głuszak 2020). Contestation music in the 1970s and 1980s in Poland, as in other socialist countries, drew on urban culture, folk and Romantic traditions (Massaka 2009). These were often high-class poetic pieces, using many motifs from European and national history, culture, and art. This style corresponds to the known and expected forms of communication (constraints). Contestation songs primarily have an integrative function, reinforcing existing views and rarely persuading people to change them. So the use of topoi and identification mechanisms is crucial.

Mury [Walls]

Mury [Walls] (lyrics: J. Kaczmarski, music: L. Llach) is a song inspired by a piece by Catalan singer Lluís Llach *L'Estaca*, a symbol of protest against Franco's dictatorship. Jacek Kaczmarski wrote the Polish text in 1978 (Adilamw 2011). However, the similarity concerns only the melody and the oppositional context. The lyrics are entirely different.

In the 1980s, the song was popular in the Polish anti-communist underground and sung during strikes. Its refrain was the signal of the underground Radio "Solidarity". Kaczmarski's song, translated into Russian and Belarusian, was sung, among others, during the anti-government protests in Belarus in 2020 and was used in the election campaign of Svitlana Tikhanouskaya (Nadya Pavyluchik 2021). Thus, we are dealing with a song used in different countries and periods, but in similar situations – during the fight against an oppressive system. This is due to the symbolism of the lyrics, the dynamic melody and the growing legend of the power of this song to help bring down the regime.

Jacek Kaczmarski was a Polish bard whose artistic achievements consisted of songs and poems of a high creative level, full of allusions and references to world literature and art. Artistic programs he performed in the 1980s (with Przemysław Gintrowski and Zbigniew Łapiński) concerned moral attitudes and ethics of resistance. They referred to biblical texts and historical events and figures. There is an array of topoi in the literary (recurring motifs) and rhetorical dimensions (references to shared experiences and beliefs for argumentative purposes).

The bard was an important figure in the socialist countries of Eastern Europe. The term "bard" originated in medieval culture. However, in the twentieth century, it came to mean a poet who usually sang his own written and composed songs to the accompaniment of a guitar. The authorial song was a phenomenon that emerged in the USSR as early as the 1940s. Poetic musical storytelling was a form of opposition to censorship, a fight against the totalitarian system (Głowania 2010). Such bards included Bulat Okudzhava and Piotr Vysotsky in the Soviet Union, Wolf Biermann in the GDR, Karel Kryl and Jaromir Nohavica in Czechoslovakia, and Tamás Cseh in Hungary. As a result, the stereotype of the bard as a rebellious voice of conscience was formed; their work was a protest against indoctrination, a call for moral behaviour. Because they worked against the official dominant culture, they often drew on folk traditions or models from rogue poetry. Most often, they sang ballads. The ballad is a genre with a long and rich tradition (Cohen 2021; Kendrick 1983; McGill 2016), taking many different forms, both literary and musical. Almost all of the examples discussed in this chapter fall into this genre.

After the social and political transformation after 1989, the song *Mury* continued to appear in the Polish public space. It became a symbol for those who identified themselves with the post-Solidarity (in opposition to the post-communist) side of the political scene. History is an essential factor in creating Polish identity (Kampka 2012). As the years passed, *Mury* appeared more and more often in anniversary contexts commemorating the Solidarity movement and the fight against communism.

Mury was read as a metaphor for the fight against the communist system. The most important character is the lonely poet-singer who gives people hope with his inspired singing: *He added strength with his song/ He sang that dawn was near [...] He sang that it was time for the wall to fall/ They sang along with him.* The refrain is a metaphorical image of the struggle for freedom: *Rip the walls' teeth-bars out/ Break the chains, break the whip/ And the walls will fall, fall, fall/ And bury the old world.*

The following stanzas tell how the people listening to the singer realized their power and took up the fight: *Until they saw how many there were/ They felt the power and the time/ And with a song that the dawn was near/ They walked through the streets of the cities/ They tore down monuments and tore up cobblestones.* People became aware of their power and ability to change situations. The energetic, lively rhythm, and the mobilization for action proved to be a more popular motif than the image of the lonely singer-poet opposing the crowd, intoxicated by the newly acquired power (*Whoever is alone – is our worst enemy!/ And the singer was alone too*). However, the song's ending is decidedly negative, a warning: *And the walls grew, grew, grew,/ The chain swayed at the feet.*

According to the last stanza, the lyrics of *Mury* can be read as a universal message about how easily victims can become oppressors. The overthrow of one system does not necessarily lead to building a better one. The text also uses the topos of the lonely poet-prophet, whose voice ceases to be heard when he begins to proclaim uncomfortable truths. However, a less bitter interpretation dominated the general perception. Poles focused on the metaphor of walls as a symbol of communism or, more broadly, of the power that society resists. This interpretation was in line with the exigence and expectations of the audience.

Thus, *Mury* is an example of a song whose significance for protests or identity building and persuasive value was based somewhat on simplifying the message itself. The exigence to which this song responds is when the audience needs reassurance about the rightness and desirability of the resistance being undertaken. The musical genre and the topoi used in the lyrics allow identification by citizens who have a sense of their own weakness in the fight against a powerful system. The need for hope and encouragement are the audience's strongest expectations.

Bella ciao

The song *Bella ciao* is a different case. This nineteenth-century folk song of Italian workers complaining about the hard work in the fields of northern Italy was modified by anti-fascist Italian partisans during World War II. Over time, this version became a famous anti-fascist anthem. The song was performed by artists worldwide, in dozens of languages. It gained new popularity due to its use in the popular TV series *La Casa de Papel*, in which it appeared as a symbol of freedom.

The song is often used in sports and political contexts. Football fans sing it to support their team or against their rivals. For example, after their opponents lost their chance to win the national competition for the fifth time, Portuguese fans of SL Benfica hummed a version in which the words "Bella ciao" were changed to "Penta Xau" [bye, bye fifth] (Luis Jorge 2018). In the political context, an ecological version of the song accompanies protests demanding political action against global warming (11.11.11 – Koepel van Internationale Solidariteit 2012). The song accompanied a movement against the far-right Brazilian presidential candidate Jair Bolsonaro ("Bella ciao" was replaced by #EleNão [not him]) (Fernando Mattos 2018).

Colombians, protesting in 2019 against the violation of the constitution, and human rights, and environmental destruction by the government of Iván Duque sang *Duque Chao* (Radio Encuentros Pedagógicos 2020). Italians sang *Bella ciao* in lockdown during the COVID-19 pandemic in 2020, and Macedonian artists produced a satirical version, *Corona ciao* (Dac and Aleksandar 2020). The persuasive potential of this song is related to the melody and the easy-to-repeat phrase "Bella ciao", often replaced by similar-sounding words.

Various artists performed the Polish translation of the song, but it was not widely known and recognizable. This situation changed with the series *La Casa de Papel*. Since 2016, there have been mass protests in Poland against the tightening of anti-abortion laws. The last wave of demonstrations in 2020 was related to the Constitutional Court ruling restricting the possibility of abortion. The majority of protesters were women and young people. The shouts, chants, and banners used many pop culture quotes and often featured vulgarisms, word games, and ironic use of stereotypes (Kampka 2023; Kiełbiewska 2018).

Feminist versions of the song *Bella ciao* have appeared before in various countries (e.g. Julia Gonzalo 2019). The Polish version (lyrics by Łaja Szkło) refers directly to the decision of the Constitutional Court, interpreted as a declaration of war on women and a desire to take over their bodies (OKO.press 2020). The refrain uses the similarity in sound between the Polish word *ciało* [body] and the Italian original *ciao*: *So if you don't want your body/ to say ciao, body, ciao, ciao, body ciao, ciao!/ Then take a banner like the other sisters/ and carry your rebellion down the street.* Opposing the system was a need of the moment (exigence), and the feminist and pop culture language code adjusted to the communication style expected by the audience (constraints).

Using hyperbolic images, the song's author calls for resistance and struggle: *Let our anger burn in thousands of throats that shout: enough victims, enough victims, away from us, faith!/ We are equal/ We are free,/ and the world will hear our song!* There are topoi of sisterhood, joint opposition, shouting as a tool of struggle against oppression. Finally, the song ends with a rejection of government and patriarchy.

Bella ciao is an example of a song whose persuasive meaning during protests is connected with adding a certain sense. The content of the Italian original does not have to mobilize overtones. It is not a call to arms but tells an individual story of a partisan ready to die for his homeland. These topoi are universal – the motif of a lonely grave, flowers blooming on a soldier's grave, and a girl being bid farewell by a soldier/partisan is typical for soldiers' songs. One of the best known Polish independence songs, *Rozkwitały pąki białych róż* [White rosebuds blossomed], is a classic example of this.

However, the symbolic meaning of *Bella ciao* goes beyond soldierly/partisan rhetoric. The song has become a symbol of the fight against an oppressive system due to various performances and pop-cultural contexts. Thus, music quotations and their meaning are growing out of intertextuality, typical of contemporary protests (Werbner et al. 2014).

We can therefore speak of global and glocal rhetoric. The same song is used in different countries and situations. Its persuasive effectiveness may depend on the message itself (as in the case of *Mury*), the context (the association of *Bella ciao* with a generalized fight against fascism), or media-mediated associations (the popularization of the song in a TV series). Local examples and symbols can become globally known through popular culture and social media. They can then be used by another local community because people will recognize in them the embodiment of their own experiences or demands. Using globally known symbols (verbal, musical, visual), local protest can become understandable to people from other countries and cultures. At the same time, the protesters themselves can see their demands in a global context.

Repetition of Topoi

This section discusses four examples of Polish songs: *Ballada o Janku Wiśniewskim* [The Ballad about Janek Wiśniewski], *Chcemy być sobą* [We want to be ourselves], *Wstydzi się ciebie kraj* [The country is ashamed of you], and *Arahja*. The first two were written during the communist era. The former commemorates a worker killed during protests; the latter talks about the desire for freedom. Both songs have been used many times in popular culture. The third one is a contemporary reworking of *Ballada o Janku Wiśniewskim*, telling the story of police behaviour during protests in defence of women's rights. The fourth is a rock song originally about the Berlin Wall but now reads as a story about social divisions. These works, related to the period of communist opposition before 1989, have acquired new meanings in contemporary Polish popular culture and during the 2020–2021 protests for women's rights. The analysis shows the persistence of symbolism and the creative reinterpretation of topoi.

Rhetoric of Protest, Tradition and Identity

In Polish pro-independence and patriotic rhetoric, the most extensive collection of symbols and imagery is associated with Romanticism. The topoi present in the Romantic poetry recurred in the work of poets of the First and Second World Wars, the democratic opposition of the 1980s, and are still resonant in nationalist rhetoric and beyond. These motifs can also be found in the song lyrics analysed here.

Ballada o Janku Wiśniewskim *[Ballad about Janek Wiśniewski]*

Ballada o Janku Wiśniewskim [The Ballad about Janek Wiśniewski] commemorates the events of December 1970, when the communist authorities pacified protests against rising food prices (Tofifest Film Festival 2012). As a result, workers were shot at in one of the cities, Gdynia, and a young boy, Zbyszek Godlewski, was killed. His friends carried his body through the city streets to the authorities' headquarters. The photo depicting this scene is one of Poland's iconic images. The title character, Janek Wiśniewski, is a symbolic figure with a popular Polish name, the personification of struggling workers and victims (several dozen people killed and over a thousand injured). After the fall of communism, the ballad's popularity led to the naming of one of the streets in Gdynia after Janek Wiśniewski. In the original rhetorical situation, exigence responds to the audience's fear and suffering and satisfies the need to mourn the dead and justify the sacrifice.

The song appeared in two important Polish films: *Człowiek z żelaza* [Man of Iron] (1981, directed by Andrzej Wajda) and *Psy* [Dogs] (1992, directed by Władysław Pasikowski). *Człowiek z żelaza* tells the story of the genesis of the Solidarity movement and shows the struggle of Polish workers against the communist system. The ballad appears there as a pathetic and emotional form of remembrance of the victims and heroes. *Psy* is a controversial film showing how degenerated employees of the former security service find themselves in the new political system. The song appears in an iconoclastic scene when the ex-security agents carry away a drunken colleague, singing this ballad. *Janek Wiśniewski fell* – the sentence referring to the death of a young worker – becomes a description of the drunken agent's unconsciousness. The ambiguity of the Polish term *padł* [fell] is used here, which can mean: he gave his life, died in battle; but also: he fell, fell over, is very tired or has just lost consciousness from drinking. Moreover, the deep irony is that the singers could have been the ones who shot the workers. These seemingly disparate uses of song paradoxically serve the same challenges of the moment. Exigence is the need to confirm clear moral divisions in the recent Polish history: heroes on the side of Solidarity and villains on the side of the communist system.

The song's lyrics are very much rooted in Gdynia's topography (which is the basis of the identification), listing the districts from which the workers came and the names of the streets through which the workers carried the body of the slain. The ballad describes the dramatic clashes, the tanks, and the wounded. The text accuses authorities of being bloodthirsty thugs: the party shoots at workers (and it should be remembered that this is the Polish United Workers' Party). The ballad calls for revenge and an assurance that the young man's sacrifice will bear fruit.

Significant topoi are: (a) the courage of the workers (*we stood bravely and threw accurately*); (b) the opposition of powerless people to the authorities' power (*against the cops, against the tanks*); (c) the merciless power strikes at the weakest (*children, older people, women fall*); (d) the brotherhood of the fighting men (*shipyard boys, avenge your comrade*); (e) the mothers' cry, sacrifice from which a better future grows (*don't cry mothers, it's not for nothing [...]/ For bread and freedom, for a new Poland/ Janek Wiśniewski fell*).

These topoi, often appearing in Polish culture and patriotic literature, are part of the discursive Romantic tradition and are therefore natural and understandable for the audience (constraints).

Wstydzi się ciebie kraj [*The country is ashamed of you*]

In 2020, the peaceful protests against the introduction under the rule of Law and Justice restriction of the right to abortion were mainly attended by women, including very young girls. The authorities countered the demonstrations in various ways, with media reports of police brutality. The band Burakura published on YouTube a song called *Wstydzi się ciebie kraj* [The country is ashamed of you], based on the *Ballad about Janek Wiśniewski* (Burakura 2021). The melody and some topoi borrowed from the historical song were a response to the moment's demands (exigence). This time the addressees were policemen. They are called "ladies' boxers"; "members of the ZOMO unit". The ZOMO are communist militia units used to pacify protests. In contemporary Polish political discourse, this term appears as an invective. It can describe: (1) association with the former political system, aspiration to authoritarianism, (2) readiness to use violence, (3) mindless submission to authority and readiness to carry out brutal orders. The sender addresses the police officers, appealing to their sense of decency: *not every order must be obeyed [...]/ apologize and take off your stained uniform*. The topoi of mother and wife are repeated. They are shown as important figures associated with moral values. This time not as despairing witnesses, but as persons judging the ethical stance of the addressees: *Does your mother already know/ that you are hitting other women today [...] do you have the courage to say: Wife, today I stood where the ZOMO stood*. The last sentence paraphrases the statement of Jarosław Kaczyński, the Law and Justice party leader. He insulted in this way his political opponents during one of the anniversaries of the fall of communism. However, many of these politicians were participants in workers' strikes, persecuted by the authorities. As in the original text, there are specific situational details in the new song. There is also the threat of punishment of the perpetrators (the policemen themselves, the government and the bishops). The uplifting ending is also similar to the original: *Don't cry, sisters, don't lose heart/ Believe in our victory in the fight/ Believe that soon the country will be more beautiful.*

This song demonstrates the continuity of topoi and, at the same time, their ability to transform and be used in a new rhetorical situation. The reference to a symbolic song from the fight against communism becomes another argument confirming the rightness of protesters' actions. At the same time, it is an unspoken comparison of the current government to the communist regime, which is a deep irony since Law and Justice identifies itself as a party that originated from the anti-communist opposition and is determined to settle accounts for the crimes of the previous system. However, this comparison resonates with the discursive expectations of the audience (constraints).

Chcemy być sobą [*We want to be ourselves*]

The rock song *Chcemy być sobą* (lyrics: Z. Hołdys) was written in 1981 (during martial law) and was considered one of the manifestos against communism (1981Perfect 2009). Censorship was in force in Poland at that time, so the lyrics do not contain any provocative content. Instead, the text can be just an expression of youthful rebellion, searching for identity. The alternating verses, *I'd like to be myself/ I'd like to be myself still/ I'd like to be myself/ I'd like to be myself finally*, in the later part turn into the plural: *we want to be ourselves*. They can be only a call for the right to be free and discover one's own identity, which is vital for the identification mechanisms with the young audience listening to the piece (constraints).

However, the situational reading of these lyrics was utterly different (*kairos*). In the 1980s, during the band's concerts, the audience changed the title phrase and the chorus's words to *We want to beat ZOMO*, taking advantage of the similarity in sound of these two phrases: *be yourself/ beat ZOMO* [być sobą/ bić ZOMO]. The song responded to the needs of a young audience living in an oppressive system. It defined the problem (exigence): you have the right to be yourself, to demand freedom. Moreover, the reworking of the song gave the audience a hint as to what they could do to achieve the goal.

In the lyrics, there is the topos of shouting as a form of self-expression and opposition (*I scream right in the frightened face!*); the metaphor of the intimidated and unified society: *on the stairs, there is a caretaker, who is afraid/ even to expose himself, he clutches a broom in his hand/ the grey nylon coat*. These are people and behaviours characteristic of everyday life in 1980s Poland: the screams of rebellious youth at rock concerts and the figure of a watchman with a broomstick in a block of flats. At the same time, these are symbols used in popular culture texts, films, cabaret and posters. Both images can be read as the universal experience of a young person feeling the burden of the existing social order and the specific experience of people living in an oppressive political system. Both can become a basis for identification.

The lyrics also contain the motif of a mad dance (*The crowd around dances a tango possessed/ Feet tired, they trample the crown/ The king of the ball delays, his eyes are mad*) which is a common topos in European culture. However, these verses also evoke Polish literary tradition. The motif of dance, in which the participants lose themselves, appears in one of the most famous Polish dramas, Stanisław Wyspiański's *Wesele* [The Wedding], a work about the dreams, dilemmas, weaknesses and actions of Polish society during the partitions of Poland and the struggle for independence. The particular dance mentioned in the song, the tango, may refer to the drama *Tango* by Sławomir Mrożek. This drama, which shows a somewhat inverted struggle between generations, is interpreted as an image of rejection of the hitherto prevailing order, a symbol of revolution, struggle against the imposed authorities, and striving for individual freedom. The meaning of these two literary allusions harmonizes with the possible interpretations of the song lyrics from a universal perspective and a concrete one, related to the Polish reality of the 1980s. The motif of the madmen's dance appeared in many films, novels and cabaret performances describing the everyday life of the time. It is worth noting that *Wesele* and *Tango* are literary works belonging to the school reading canon and, therefore, are well-known and recognizable.

The song *Chcemy być sobą* appears in the sensational film *80 milionów* [80 Million] (2011, directed by Waldemar Krzystek). The story shows the Solidarity movement just before introducing martial law and the security service's actions against oppositionists. The screenplay is based on facts. The song accompanies the final scene, depicting a symbolic clash between protesters and the police. It was also used in the promotional video, which combines contemporary rap, the original performance of the song, scenes from the film and archive materials (kinoswiat.pl 2011). Also, the title *We still (want to be ourselves)* directly refers to the historical song. In this rhetorical message, the song of the Perfect band is a symbol of the heroic past. The fight against communism is sometimes presented in a pathetic, martyrological frame. However, there are also narratives emphasizing the cleverness of the oppositionists and the energy, emotionality and sense of humour of the young people. Both the film *80 milionów* [80 Million] and the song by Perfect are closer to the latter type of persuasive story about Solidarity. In this case, the rhetorical appeal (exigence) is the need to commemorate the past in a form that will be attractive to young people (constraints), allowing them to identify with the heroes of a period that they do not know because it was the time of their grandparents or parents.

Nowadays, the song appears at concerts in its original version, functioning as an ordinary piece of music and as a "song with a past", referring to one of the rhetorical topoi about mass opposition to communism.

Arahja

Another song that Polish artists often use as a protest against divisions is the song *Arahja* by the band Kult. The song was written in 1988 and referred to the Berlin Wall. Due to censorship, however, the lyrics do not contain any direct references to Berlin.

The simple lyrics are based on juxtaposition and repetition: *my house divided by a wall/ The staircase divided by a wall/ The bathroom on the left/ The kitchen on the right [...]/ My body divided by a wall/ Ten fingers on the left side/ The other ten on the right side/ The head's equal part on each side [...]/ My street divided by a wall/ The neon lights on the right side/ The left side all dimmed/ From behind the curtain I observe both sides [...]/ The left side never wakes up/ The right side never falls asleep.*

The challenge in the original rhetorical situation was to describe the experience of a young man living in a city divided by a wall and a world divided by an iron curtain. Exigence was the translation of a geopolitical situation into ordinary everyday emotions. The audience's expectations were linked to the need to rebel against these constraints.

The rhetorical power of this song's lyrics lies in its repetitive, simple structure and imagery. The reference to the human body is compelling. The use of the words "right and left side", which in the lyrics describes the sides of the street, in later interpretations often referred to the political scene and right/left-wing views or parties. In these words, we can therefore observe a process of metaphorization of physical and cognitive experience.

In recent years, the song has appeared in the Polish public sphere in various contexts as a commentary on the socio-political situation, the intense polarization of society, the rule of the Law and Justice party, and disputes over democracy (exigence). The band *Hey* (2017) sang it with thousands of participants at the Woodstock Festival, and the singer's emotion was reproduced in many Internet recordings. This festival is regarded as somehow oppositional to the government of the Law and Justice Party. The controversial artist Michał Szpak (2021) sang it at one of the galas. An element of his stage costume – a duck, pinned to his arm – was an apparent reference to the Law and Justice Party (the duck, "kaczka" in Polish, is a symbol of Kaczyński, the leader of the party). Karolina Micuła (2017), during the actors' song contest, exposed her breasts and painted her body white and red (the colours of the Polish flag), thus "embodying" and illustrating the dispute about women's rights. A Polish discourse scholar analysed it: "'A divided Polish woman' is therefore at the same time a participant in national disputes and – in the bodily dimension – their object" (Steciąg 2019: 27). The song was also in the government gala concert during the 100th anniversary of regaining independence (Niepodległa 2020). The scenography – a video showing red and white silhouettes (a symbolic representation of national divisions) – gave the lyrics an unambiguous interpretation. The song is thus an example of a shared cultural text known and used by both sides of an argument in a strongly polarized society, even if each of them would point to different reasons for the divisions.

The metaphorical nature of the lyrics, resulting from censorship, became its rhetorical potential. However, due to the universality of the topoi (the two opposing sides), the song retains its persuasive power regardless of changes in the rhetorical situation. The audience can identify with either side. The most important thing is that the song allows them to express their experience of division and disagreement.

Conclusion

The rhetorical power of protest songs depends on the community of ideas, symbols and values shared by the protesters. The above analyses confirm the persistence of selected topoi, including new ways of actualizing them on the Internet, and the globalization of protest rhetoric mediated by popular culture.

The songs discussed confirm the validity of Vatz's (1973) argument that rhetoric does not result from a reaction to a situation (exigence). Instead, rhetoric itself could create such a situation. For the audience, a situation only appears as a perceptible, comprehensible whole when someone describes it, and language always carries valuation and potential impact. The songs analysed above appeared in a specific context and helped the audience interpret their situation. *Mury* filled oppositionists with the hope that the communist system could be overcome; singing *Bella ciao* made protesters on different sides of the world feel part of a great community of revolt against injustice. A young man singing at a festival with hundreds of others, *my house divided by a wall* or *we want to be ourselves*, confirms his interpretation's accuracy. He feels not alone because others similarly perceive reality.

The answer to the first research question relating to exigence is that the urgent issue is the desire for freedom. These songs appear in situations where the recipients feel enslaved, restricted, persecuted, and deprived of their rights. In all cases, the songs help with self-definition and contain elements that allow the audience to feel part of a community. The differences lie in the way the opponent is defined. In the songs related to the women's protests (*Bella ciao, Wstydzi się ciebie kraj*), the opponents are pointed out directly: the brutal police, the government, and the bishops who want to limit women's rights. In songs from the communist era, a somewhat undefined force symbolized by walls, bars, shackles and whips restricts freedom (*Mury, Ballada o Janku Wiśniewskim*). In *Arahja* and *Chcemy być sobą* the opponent is an indefinable system, which can be understood as a specific political regime or social norms.

The answer to the question of constraints requires the indication of song aims. The results point to three of them: to commemorate the victims, mobilize for struggle, and self-expression. The first purpose is realized, among other things, through a detailed description of the situation, topography, characters and actions (*Ballada o Janku Wiśniewskim, Wstydzi się ciebie kraj, Bella ciao*). The topoi used include: (a) a memorable song; (b) a brotherly or sisterly bond; (c) an individual who becomes a symbol and inspires action; (d) the value of sacrifice. The second objective, mobilization (*Mury, Bella ciao*), is achieved through topoi: (a) the power of collective action and (b) hope for a better future. Common to both aims is the reference to time, *kairos*, the exceptional moment that is just happening and that makes action meaningful.

The third aim is realized primarily in the two songs *Arahja* and *Chcemy być sobą*. It is related to the simplicity and repetitiveness of the text, the topos of division, oppositions and opposing values. The musical form is also significant here; these are rock songs by popular bands performed during concerts that attracted large audiences who joined the performers in shouting out the repeated verses. Shouting as a form of struggle is common for protest songs and is a topos used in all described pieces.

The results of the analysis presented here demonstrate that the persistence or recurrence of specific works in public space is highly correlated with the characteristics of the rhetorical situation. It is not about the actual political or social similarity of the different moments when people take to the streets in protest. What is essential is the exigence, that is, the issue that needs to be clarified, explained and defined at a given moment.

The analysed songs used in social conflicts confirm the validity of observations concerning the dynamics of the rhetorical situation and the interdependence between its elements (Garret et al. 1993). First, the rhetor (the song's author, the performer) comes from the audience. Jacek Kaczmarski singing *Mury* was a member of the opposition. The women singing *Arahja* were members of this divided community. The girl singing *Bella ciao* was one of the women affected by the abortion ban. Secondly, the songs were a reaction to the anxiety and disorientation of the audience; they grew out of the need to put things in order, interpret the surrounding reality, and indicate the right (possible) actions and behaviours. This need is exigence, the unresolved questions of the audience that the rhetorical message is supposed to answer. According to Garret and Xiao, the third element of the rhetorical situation, constraints, is the audience's expectation of appropriate discourse in the given circumstances. The striking workers, the protesting women, expected a call to action, a dynamic message that would allow them to mobilize and believe that their efforts made sense. The audience listening to *Ballada o Janku Wiśniewskim* or *Wstydzi się ciebie kraj* needed commemoration of the victims and a clear statement of moral principles, confirmation of the rightness of their own ethical beliefs. Young people singing *Chcemy być sobą/Chcemy bić ZOMO, Mój dom murem podzielony* or *Bella ciao* wanted to be able to shout out their emotions, frustration, anger, express their identity.

A rhetorical situation is created in the tension between audiences' needs and the possibilities of satisfying them through the ability of the rhetor to choose a form of delivery in line with the audience's expectations.

Establishing a relationship between the rhetor and the audience is possible by referring to a community of knowledge, experience or emotions (identification). The means to this end are topoi, at the same time permanent and changeable, universal and specific. Polish rhetoric, exemplified by the rhetorical situations related to songs described here, combines old historical patterns and motifs, symbols typical of post-communist countries, elements characteristic of European culture and, finally, universal images, sounds and words present in global media culture.

References

Sources: The Songs Analysed

Mury [Walls]

Adilamw (2011) Mury, www.youtube.com/watch?v=hwD6i9eOiYE (accessed 20 November 2021).
Nadya Pavlyuchik (2021) Volny Chor – Mury Wrocław Polska, www.youtube.com/watch?v=QC–qxcAhkEk (accessed 30 December 2021).

Bella ciao

11.11.11 – Koepel van Internationale Solidariteit (2012) Sing for the Climate: Do It Now – De Clip, www.youtube.com/watch?v=OVnedIW1y8E (accessed 20 December 2021).

Dac & Aleksandar (2020) Aleksandar i Dac – corona ciao (Bella Ciao COVER) ft. Brasstet Skopje, www.youtube.com/watch?v=KK8zXgRCntU (accessed 21 November 2021).

Fernando Mattos (2018) Ele Não! (Bella Ciao), www.youtube.com/watch?v=Tw0x0cZXSmY (accessed 5 May 2021).

Julia Gonzalo (2019) Bella Ciao Feminista Cáceres, www.youtube.com/watch?v=DkTPs–wQxxQ (accessed 10 June 2021).

Luís Jorge (2018) Pendta xau (Bella ciao), www.youtube.com/watch?v=U7kIZonPv10 (accessed 30 November 2021).

OKO.press (2020) Bella ciało, ciało, ciało, www.youtube.com/watch?v=HWBR17D3Ng4 (accessed 20 December 2021).

Radio Encuentros Pedagógicos (2020) Duque chao!, www.youtube.com/watch?v=rYzjnPewT2Q (accessed 4 May 2021).

Chcemy być sobą [We want to be ourselves]

1981Perfect (2009) 02. Perfect – Chcemy być sobą, słowa: Zbigniew Hołdys, www.youtube.com/watch?v=1qeMxFRD100 (accessed 30 December 2021).

KinoSwiatPL (2011) My nadal (chcemy być sobą) – Abradab feat. Grzegorz Markowski, www.youtube.com/watch?v=z9qOXLg8fb4 (accessed 10 June 2021).

Ballada o Janku Wiśniewskim [Ballad about Janek Wiśniewski]

Tofifest Film Festival (2012) Krystyna Janda – Ballada o Janku Wisniewskim (z filmu Czlowiek z zelaza, 1981), www.youtube.com/watch?v=XIPNJNc4id0 (accessed 20 December 2021).

Wstydzi się ciebie kraj [The country is ashamed of you]

Burakura (2021) "Wstydzi się ciebie kraj" – Burakura, www.youtube.com/watch?v=spbSKgSxPxA (accessed 30 December 2021).

Arahja

Hey (2017) Arahja #Woodstock2017, www.youtube.com/watch?v=8klMG6E3bow (accessed 30 June 2021).

Karolina Micuła (2017) Arahja (Koncert Finałowy #38PPA), www.youtube.com/watch?v=NAMz0bViAGc (accessed 20 June 2021).

Michał Szpak (2021) "Arahja" Gala Medal Wolności Słowa Gdańsk, www.youtube.com/watch?v=AHaN8z1Nl8c (accessed 20 December 2021).

Niepodległa (2020) Ewa Farna – Arahja / Koncert dla Niepodległej, www.youtube.com/watch?v=YSkcqObDFD4 (accessed 10 November 2021).

English-Language References

Biesecker, B. A. (1989) 'Rethinking the Rhetorical Situation from within the Thematic of Difference', *Philosophy and Rhetoric* (22)2: 110–130.

Bitzer, L. F. (1968) 'The Rhetorical Situation', *Philosophy and Rhetoric* (1)1: 1–14.

Burke, K. (1969) *A Rhetoric of Motives*, Berkeley: University of California Press.

Charaudeau, P. (2002) 'A Communicative Conception of Discourse', *Discourse Studies* 3: 301–318.

Chesebro, J. W., Foulger, D. A., Naghman, J. E., and Yannelli, A. (1985) 'Popular Music as a Mode of Communication, 1955–1982', *Critical Studies in Mass Communication* (2)2: 115–135.

Cohen, R. (2021) *Transformations of a Genre: A Literary History of the Beguiled Apprentice*, Cham: Palgrave.

Consigny, S. (1974) 'Rhetoric and Its Situations', *Philosophy and Rhetoric* (7)3: 175–186.

Garret, M. and Xiao, X. (1993) 'The Rhetorical Situation Revisited', *Rhetoric Society Quarterly* (23)2: 30–40.

Gelang, M. (2021) 'Kairos and Actio – a Rhetorical Approach to Timing', *Res Rhetorica* 8(3): 111–124. DOI: 10.29107/rr2021.3.6

Gonzalez, A. and Makay, J. J. (1983) 'Rhetorical Ascription and the Gospel According to Dylan', *Quarterly Journal of Speech* 69(1): 1–14.

Kampka, A. (2012) 'Rhetorical Value of Temporal Categories in the Construction of Political Identities', in M. Załęska (ed.), *Rhetoric and Politics: Central/Eastern European Perspectives*, Newcastle: Cambridge Scholars Publishing.

Kampka, A. (2023) 'Banners and Memes – the Rhetoric of Protests in Defence of Democracy and Women's Rights in Poland in 2015 and 2020', *Performance Research* (27)3–4: 123–132. DOI: 10.1080/13528165.2022.2155423.

Kendrick, L. (1983) 'Rhetoric and the Rise of Public Poetry: The Career of Eustache Deschamps', *Studies in Philology* (80)1: 1–13.

Leff, M. (2006) 'Up from Theory: Or I Fought the Topoi and the Topoi Won', *Rhetoric Society Quarterly* (36)2: 203–211.

Lucaites, J. L. and Hariman, R. (2001) 'Visual Rhetoric, Photojournalism and Democratic Public Culture', *Rhetoric Review* (20)1–2: 37–42.

Matula, T. (2000) 'Contextualising Musical Rhetoric: A Critical Reading of the Pixies' 'Rock Music', *Communication Studies* 51: 218–237.

McGill, M. L. (2016) 'What Is a Ballad? Reading for Genre, Format, and Medium', *Nineteenth-Century Literature* (71)2: 156–175.

McKeon, R. (1973) 'Creativity and the Commonplace', *Philosophy and Rhetoric* (6)4: 199–210.

Molek-Kozakowska, K. and Kampka, A. (2021) 'Talking Politics: The Influence of Historical and Cultural Transformations on Polish Political Rhetoric', in O. Feldman (ed.), *When Politicians Talk. The Cultural Dynamics of Public Speaking*, Singapore: Springer.

Oliveri, J. D. (2020) 'On Strike: The Rhetorical Anatomy of a Contemporary Protest Song', *Clio: WCSU History Journal* (46)1: 113–131.

Sellnow, D. D. (1999) 'Music as Persuasion: Refuting Hegemonic Masculinity in "He thinks he'll keep her"', *Women's Studies in Communication* 22: 66–84.

Vatz, R. E. (1973) 'The Myth of the Rhetorical Situation', *Philosophy and Rhetoric* (6)3: 154–161.

Werbner, P., Webb, M., and Spellman-Poots, K. (2014) 'Introduction', in P. Werbner, M. Webb and K. Spellman-Poots (eds.), *The Political Aesthetics of Global Protest: The Arab Spring and Beyond*, Edinburgh: Edinburgh University Press.

Woodward, G. C. (2003) *The Idea of Identification*, Albany: State University of New York Press.

Other-Language References

Abramowska, J. (1982) 'Topos i niektóre miejsca wspólne badań literackich' [Topos and some commonplaces in literary studies], *Pamiętnik Literacki* [Literary Memoir] (73)1–2: 3–23.

Curtius, E. R. (1972) 'Topika' [Topics], *Pamiętnik Literacki* [Literary Memoir] (63)1: 231–265.

Głowania, K. (2010), '"Poderżnijcie gardło mi, poderżnijcie żyły, tylko nie zerwijcie strun, co srebrem lśniły…": wielcy bardowie Rosji' ["Slit my throat, slit my veins, but don't break the strings that glittered with silver…": the great bards of Russia], *Pisma Humanistyczne* [The Humanities Letters] 7: 33–45.

Głuszak, K. A. (2014) *Muzyka i piosenka popularna jako narzędzia opozycji politycznej w Polsce w latach 80. XX wieku* [Music and popular song as tools of political opposition in Poland in the 1980s], PhD dissertation, University of Warsaw. Available from: www.depotuw.ceon.pl/bitstr eam/handle/item/764/ca%C5%82y%20tekst.pdf?sequence=1 (accessed 30 June 2021]

Kiełbiewska, A. (2018) 'Retoryka «czarnego marszu» na materiale haseł prezentowanych w przestrzeni publicznej' [The rhetoric of the 'black march' on the material of slogans presented in public space], *Res Rhetorica* 5(3): 2–21. DOI: 10.29107/rr2018.3.1

Massaka, I. (2009) *Muzyka jako instrument wpływu politycznego* [Music as an instrument of political influence], Łódź: Ibidem.

Steciąg, M. (2019) 'Dyskurs protestów kobiet w Polsce w latach 2016–2017: artystyczne wizualizacje, wokalizacje, werbalizacje' [The discourse of women's protests in Poland in 2016–2017: artistic visualizations, vocalizations, verbalizations], *Acta Universitatis Lodziensis. Folia Linguistica* 53: 21–31. DOI: 10.18778/0208–6077.53.02

10

A DESCRIPTIVE STUDY OF ARABIC RHETORICS

Rabeea Al-Mubarak and Ian E. J. Hill

Introduction

In the Arabic-speaking world, the discipline of rhetoric (*'ilm al-balāgha*) is held in high esteem. In one typical assessment, the ninth-century (CE) scholar ibn Qutaybah wrote, "Of all peoples, the Arabs are the most eloquent extempore orators: they have the most mellifluous tongues, they are models of clarity of expression, and they speak with the most pithy concision when required" (2017: 145). In the following century, ibn 'Abd Rabbihi would place oratory as the "central jewel" in his "unique necklace" of Arabic achievements to laud oratory's preeminence (Jones 2012: 38). Beyond oratory, however, the scope of Arabic rhetoric covers ancient, yet ongoing, traditions of poetics, logic, disputation, religious discourse, jurisprudence, textual criticism, and theory, such that multiple volumes would not suffice to cover its many permutations. And though the centralizing force of the Islamic tradition seems to project Arabic rhetoric as a theologically-centered field, the science (*'ilm*) of *balāgha* has also become de-theologized over time such that closer attention paid to each particular Arabic rhetorical form reveals both complementary and divergent rhetorical practices. The historical multiplicity of Arabic rhetorics hence presents many challenges for a concise descriptivist project, the present chapter included.

Therefore, rather than aiming to provide an exhaustive account of Arabic rhetoric, the purpose of this chapter is to describe it as a multifaceted space of theological, social, cultural, and political trends and contentions. We argue that Arabic rhetoric may be best described as a unified yet also dispersed body of rhetorical practice, criticism, and knowledge production that includes but also surpasses theological applications. Whether in examining the origins of *al-balāgha* as adjacent to Islamic theology, or in analyzing a contemporary political example through classical rhetorical concepts, we suggest that understanding the religious influence on Arabic rhetoric is necessary but not sufficient for understanding contemporary rhetorical practices. The tenth-century rhetorician and Qur'anic scholar al-Bāqillānī claimed, "the Qur'an cannot be separated from any of the rhetorical sciences nor from any type of eloquence" (1950: 54). In one sense, al-Bāqillānī was correct about the intertwining of Islam and *al-balāgha*. However, his assertion does not recognize how past and present Arabic rhetorical theories and practices also

148 DOI: 10.4324/9781003195276-13

flourished in non-religious aspects of life, and how it has developed through historical cross-cultural contacts as well as contemporary transcultural rhetorical actions.

In order to bracket the broad scope of Arabic rhetoric and foreground different aspects of its development, this chapter focuses on four key themes that address the early theological impetus of *balāgha*, but also attend to its vibrant range and transcultural reach. To do so, we first discuss the Qur'an's reputation as the peak of Arabic eloquence. Later *'aḥādīth* (reports of the sayings and actions of the prophet Muhammad) further inculcated Islamic principles of eloquence in day-to-day affairs by codifying communicative right conduct. Second, continuing with the theological impetus of Arabic rhetoric but emphasizing its critical and interpretive implementations, we consider how principles of Qur'anic exegesis formulated competing models of Islamic rhetorical criticism. Third, turning to its formalization as a body of rhetorical knowledge, we describe the main tenets of the dominant tradition of Arabic oratory, *al-balāgha*. This includes overviews of its primary sciences – *'ilm al-ma'ānī* (science of sentence types), *'ilm al-bayān* (science of tropes), and *'ilm al-badī'* (science of verbal ornamentation). To highlight these sciences' contemporary relevance, we analyze a portion of a recent statement published by alQaws – a Palestinian feminist-queer organization operating in the United States and a number of occupied Palestinian cities. Our analysis highlights cross-cultural overlaps between the science of *balāgha* and stylistic concepts found within the Western rhetorical tradition. This conceptual overlap leads to the fourth and final section, where we attend to the uptake of Aristotle's *Rhetoric* in the philosophical commentaries of al-Fārābī, ibn Sīnā (Avicenna), and ibn Rushd (Averroes), and then consider how contemporary rhetorical critics have applied Western rhetorical theories to Arabic discourses.

The Qur'an, *Aḥadīth*, and Ideal Eloquence

The prophet Muhammad looms large for *'ilm al-balāgha*. Since, historically, the Qur'an has been considered the pinnacle of Arabic eloquence, Muhammad is either its revealer and transmitter (for the faithful) or its author (for non-believers and certain sects). Whether one is faithful or one only finds aesthetic beauty in the holy book, the Qur'an's composition lends itself to oral recitation, which in turn helped propagate doctrine orally before widespread literacy and print culture reproduced the text in the now-standardized version. Qur'anic rhetoric's facilitation of recitation as an *aide-mémoire* to transmit and teach the text indicates its rhythmic and narrative allure, but at minimum Muhammad delivered perhaps the most read book in human history, which marks Muhammad as a central figure in Arabic rhetoric, and globally through the Qur'an's translation into most of the world's primary languages. In terms of the sheer scale of its influence and its motivation of action and belief, few texts can rival the Qur'an.

More directly, six *'āyāt* (Qur'anic verses) draw attention to Qur'anic rhetoric's quality by issuing challenges to its readers (and doubters of the Qur'an's divine origins) to create comparably eloquent and consequential rhetoric. For instance,

> if you doubt what We have revealed to Our servant, produce one *sūrah* [Qur'anic chapter] comparable to it. Call upon your idols to assist you, if what you say be true. But if you fail (as you are sure to fail), then guard yourselves against the Fire whose fuel is humans and stones, prepared for the unbelievers.
>
> *2014: 2.23–24*

In another example that provides a counterargument to the co-presence of the Bible and the Qur'an, which indicates to the unfaithful that both might be complementary "works of sorcery," Allah advises Muslims to say "Bring down from God a scripture that is a better guide than these and I will follow it, if what you say is true!" (28.49). These verses that issue the rhetorical challenge are known as *taḥaddī*. According to tradition – both as legend and as observable fact – nobody has met the *taḥaddī* challenge, although many have tried.

This human incapacity to meet the *taḥaddī* challenge combined with esteem for the divine led Arabic theologians and rhetoricians to concur that the Qur'an's rhetoric cannot be reproduced or imitated. This concept, known as *i'jāz al-Qur'ān*, or the Qur'an's rhetorical inimitability, facilitated a genre of Qur'anic textual interpretation that attempted to prove this inimitable quality via close readings of the text. In each instance, the early critics corroborated Allah's judgment of inimitability. Al-Khaṭṭābī asserted Qur'anic inimitability "because it has come forth with the most eloquent words compounded in the most beautiful composition containing the most valid ideas," as well as "its effect on hearts and souls," or its emotional and embodied effects (Aḥmad and Sallām 2014: 15 and 46). Al-Rummānī focused his attention on "ten elements" of "rhetorical eloquence" to identify its inimitability – the Qur'an's use of concision, simile, metaphor, sonic harmony, periodic rhyme and assonance, paronomasia, permutation (of words' roots), implication, hyperbole, and "beautiful rendition" (*al-bayān*), as well as the doctrine of *ṣarfa* which holds that Allah disallowed or prohibited Arabs from producing rhetoric comparable to the Qur'an's (53–54). Famed literary critic and Qur'anic scholar al-Jurjānī claimed that the text's inimitability derives from the combination of word choice, word meaning, and word order (*naẓm*), which is the linguistic and rhetorical rules that govern how patterns of language mesh with patterns of human psychology to produce eloquence (96; al-Jurjānī 1982). Al-Bāqillānī followed al-Jurjānī's lead by touting Qur'anic *naẓm*, and thereby rejected the concept that poetic figures (*badī'*) determine *i'jāz*, since they do not "transcend human experience" (1950: 53–56). *Al-bayān*, *al-badī'*, and *al-naẓm*, and the ways that they help delineate the Qur'an's rhetorical features, comprise some of the foundational components of *al-balāgha*, which are explicated further below. Regardless, the Qur'an's apparent inimitability and its challenge to produce comparable rhetoric also pose these same challenges to all of its translators and translations (Blankenship 2020; Lawrence 2017).

Another of Muhammad's rhetorical legacies entails his exhortations to right speech and conduct that have been passed down through the transmission of *'aḥādīth* (reports of the Prophet's words and actions transmitted via documented oral lineage and later recorded). Many *'aḥādīth* either include somewhat banal recommendations for how to speak that mirror many of the world's rhetorical traditions, or exemplify Muhammad's words as a model for appropriate conduct. The *ḥadīth* tradition is vast and includes many controversial reports whose legitimacy is a source of ongoing contestation. Nonetheless several *'aḥādīth* that report about good speech should suffice to indicate Muhammad's influence on everyday Arabic rhetoric. For example, Muhammad recommended what ancient Greeks referred to as *parrhesia*, or speaking truth to power by telling an audience what it does not want to hear. "The most excellent *jihād* is the uttering of truth in the presence of an unjust ruler," according to a *ḥadīth* compiled by Khaṭīb al-Tabrīzī (Ali 1987: 398.) Muhammad offered much advice about general decorum as it relates to rhetoric and influence, such as, "Verily, Allah does not love those who are obscene or coarse or those who yell at the top of their voices," and "No one who carries tales about others will go to Paradise," according to reports collected by al-Bukhārī (1997: 140 and 143). Muhammad indicated that one's rhetoric is a window into one's character, not just on the surface level of decorum and propriety, but as a defining attribute, such as in "If you hear someone say that people are ruined, he is himself the most ruinous" (324). The scope of the advice offered by Muhammad on decorum, public speaking, interpersonal communication, and other speech acts in thousands-upon-thousands of ʾaḥādīth transmitted, compiled, and proliferated over the centuries is, alone, a vast topic that traces the development of everyday Arabic rhetoric for non-religious contexts alongside their religious applications.

Over the centuries, as writers took up the *taḥaddī* challenge, often with rhetoric that approaches or perhaps surpasses that of the Qur'an in terms of inventiveness and extraordinary stylistic wordplay, many instances of remarkable writing emerged. Al-Harīrī's *Impostures* (*Maqāmāt*) is a notable example of Arabic rhetorical aesthetics and invention that is itself rather inimitable. *Impostures* tells 50 tales about Abu Zayd, a rogue-ish petty criminal orator who uses his eloquence to swindle audiences out of food and money, often by extemporaneously meeting near-impossible rhetorical challenges, such as an oration in which every other word is written with dots, an oration composed of lengthy palindromes (e.g. a poem that reads the same forwards and backwards), and the improvisation of linguistic riddles. Whether such rhetorical excellence meets or exceeds that of the Qur'an is, in retrospect, a moot point, but of direct concern for the author who risked possible condemnation for sacrilegiously challenging the Qur'an's inimitability. The fictional exercise "violates the laws of God," but its merits as a pedagogical tool for Arabic rhetoric trumps its impiety, according to al-Harīrī (2020: 6). The "utility" (6) of Abū Zayd as an oratorical model whose rhetoric facilitates persuasion in a wide range of circumstances with a wide range of audience types configures the central role of eloquent oratory for all societal functions. As just one example of the *maqāmāt* genre, al-Harīrī's functional secularization of inimitable *balāgha* was not new when it appeared, but it serves as a reminder that, although they grew and spread together, Islamic scholarship and *al-balāgha* gradually developed into mutually informing, yet separate, fields of study. Arabic rhetoric should not be conceived as a mere appendage to Islamic studies, its relevance not confined to a specific historical period, and its scope not limited to the concept of *balāgha*. The next section examines Qur'anic exegesis to further describe the wide scope of Arabic rhetoric and its continuous development as a site of contention and debate between different perspectives, with the following section then delving into *al-balāgha*'s traditional tripartite structure.

Qur'anic Exegesis and Rhetorical Criticism

Critical interpretation, in the form of Qur'anic exegesis, demonstrates both a pragmatic use of Arabic rhetoric and how the concept of *balāgha* pertains to more domains than the invention of oratory and the stylistic crafting of eloquence. *Tafsīr*, or the use of rhetorical, linguistic, historical, comparative, theological and other associated methods to interpret and explain meanings in the Qur'an, has had a profound influence by shaping divergent Islamic traditions and sects. A famous Qur'anic verse states, "to you We have revealed the Book to manifest the Truth about all things, a guide, a blessing, and joyful tidings for the Muslims" (2014: 16.89). Although the Qur'an asserts the universality of its revelation, the text nonetheless contains many ambiguous passages that invite or necessitate differing interpretations. With textual ambiguity, the impetus to find Qur'anic answers to all of life's conundrums, and Allah's commands to follow the rules and laws proclaimed in the Qur'an (*sharī'a*), a vast exegetical tradition developed in order to discover legitimate interpretations of ambiguous passages, to understand new situations according to differing Islamic doctrines, and to advance Islamic jurisprudence. The Egyptian al-Suyūṭī, for one, identified 80 distinct '*ulūm al-tafsīr*, or exegetical disciplines (Boullata, in Aḥmad and Sallām 2014: xi), while the Persian exegete al-Rāzī, who also wrote a treatise on *al-balāgha*, asserted that the phrase "I seek refuge in God" involves "10,000 significant areas of enquiry, more or less" (2018: 3). Rhetorical criticism, via the analytical tools of *al-balāgha* and its associated arts of argumentation and reasoning, has provided the conceptual foundations for centuries of Islamic theology and jurisprudence.

Tafsīr requires extensive rhetorical training. In short, a "qualified exegete" must "be well-acquainted with a pool of linguistic and stylistic devices that enable [them] to undertake the linguistic, rhetorical and textual analysis of the Qur'an" (Abdul-Raof 2010: 170). This discipline is therefore related to comparable rhetorical practices in both Judaic exegesis (Katzir 2018) and the Greco-Roman Christian tradition, as exemplified by St. Augustine's *On Christian Doctrine*. Not every variety of *tafsīr* explicitly depends upon rhetoric, but most approaches use one or more rhetorical elements to produce valid interpretations of the Qur'an's rampant ambiguous poetics.

At times, exegetes advocated two related disciplines, *tafsīr* and *ta'wīl*, although in early Islam the terms synonymously meant "to explain the meaning of an expression and its underlying signification" (Abdul-Raof 2010: 104). Later, *tafsīr* was distinguished from *ta'wīl*, with the former meant to refer to interpretation of the more literal *'āyāt*, and the latter referring to exegesis of allegorical or otherwise ambiguous implied meanings (El Fadl 2001: 307–308). Also, *ta'wīl* became associated with Sufi-oriented exegesis wherein the analytical revelation of hidden interpretations "was a kind of spiritual realization of the meaning of the Qur'an" (Cooper in al-Ṭabarī 1987: xxviii). In this vein, *ta'wīl* has been associated with overt attempts at unconventional, sometimes rebellious, interpretations that underscored constitutive ambiguities in Qur'anic passages, and resulted in conflicting interpretations between and across divergent Islamic schools of thought (Abdul-Raof 2010: 102–108). Regardless of theological schisms, over time, *ta'wīl*'s close conceptual resemblance to *tafsīr* and its methodologies resulted in *'ilm al-ta'wīl* often becoming subsumed by *'ilm al-tafsīr*. Both al-Rāzī's *tafsīr* and al-Ṭabarī's *ta'wīl* use rhetorical concepts to examine non-literal passages, since passages that display clear literal meanings either require little-to-no critical interpretation, or their meanings have solidified over time by scholarly consensus. Yet, as al-Rāzī (in 32 volumes) and al-Ṭabarī (in 12 volumes) proceeded from *sūrah* to *sūrah*, *'āyah* to *'āyah*, and sometimes from word to word, they also examined passages that have ready-at-hand literal interpretations in order to complete their exegetical tasks.

One such exegetical task, *ijtihād*, is the rigorous pursuit of exegetical legal interpretations for the purpose of determining *sharī'a*, a task that demonstrates the power of rhetorical criticism to help compel religious schisms, such as the one between Shi'a and Sunni Muslims. While modern state laws have adapted different forms of more or less secular governmental conventions, historically, the interpretation of ambiguous legal problems depended upon the use of rhetorical tools to explicate doctrinally acceptable *sharī'a* law from legitimate sources, namely the Qur'an and *'aḥādīth*. Suggesting that semantic squabbling shaped the split between Shi'a and Sunni doctrines runs the risk of reducing a long and complicated history in a simplistic, overly deterministic way.

Nonetheless, the rhetorical exegesis of influential interpreters sometimes contributed to the characterization of whole sects as infidels, depending on whether legal exegetes interpreted certain Qur'anic passages literally or figuratively. A key dispute over the power and legitimacy of the Shi'a Imams, for example, derived, in part, from a specific figurative interpretation of two *'āyāt* that refer to Islam's legitimate interpreters as "people who know" (2014: 16.43) and "people in authority" (2014: 4.59). Depending on exegetes' theological commitments and rhetorical stances regarding who inherited religious authority after the death of Muhammad, the authoritative and knowledgeable people in these *'āyāt* refer either to Shi'a Imams, or in Sunni interpretations of the two ambiguous references, a range of rulers, exegetes, jurists, theologians, Muslims in general, and even Christian and Jewish authorities as the monotheistic precursors to Allah's revelation to Muhammad (Stewart in al-Nu'mān 2017: 261–262). Divergent interpretations from influential Shi'a and Sunni juridical exegetes thereby exemplify the role of rhetorical analysis in justifying this split.

Sunni exegete al-Shāfi'ī rejected the concept that political power, such as that of Shi'a Imams, authorized interpretive legitimacy. Al-Shāfi'ī categorized *'āyāt*, their meanings, and their audiences as "restricted" (specific), "unrestricted" (general), or "partly restricted" in order to advocate for the use of particular rhetorical concepts to interpret legal and textual ambiguity (2015: 29–31). These critical concepts included assessing contextual clues, reasoning, inference, consensus building, appeals to authority, and analogy, as well as concepts derived from *al-balāgha*, such as analyzing passages based upon their word order or tropes. In direct refutation of al-Shāfi'ī, the Shi'a jurist al-Nu'mān denounced the rhetorically based *ijtihād* methods of reasoning, inference, analogy, inference, and appeals to consensus in order to assert that Shi'a Imams should always resolve questions of textual ambiguity. Owing to his rejection of Sunni *ijtihād*, al-Nu'mān was empowered to accuse al-Shāfi'ī and other likeminded scholars of committing heresy because they "created a new religion" with their rhetorical methodologies (2017: 50–51). By associating conventional Sunni methods of *tafsīr* with apostasy, al-Nu'mān took a stance against the role of rhetorically attuned disciplines and their power to influence the development of competing religious laws. Thus, differing theological interpretations depended upon the deployment or the rejection of forms of rhetorical criticism in order to determine the rules of rightful conduct.

More recently, feminist assessments of Islam exemplify how the practical application of rhetorical exegesis can affect everyday life, in addition to demonstrating how contemporary exegetes have transformed *tafsīr* in a way that indicates the ongoing transcultural transformation of Arabic rhetoric. Aysha A. Hidayatullah presents feminism as an "edge" of Qur'anic revelation that either confines exegetes within the limits of divine revelation or compels them to push beyond the Islamic edge of *tafsīr* into a more secular realm (2014: 19). Hidayatullah's and other recent feminist approaches to *tafsīr* deviate from focusing on individual *āyahs* as the bases of textual interpretation by focusing on the whole Qur'anic text via an intratextual comparative method. So rather than rhetorically analyzing a passage in isolation, "all verses should be read in light of the Qur'an's overall trajectory toward justice and social transformation" (87). This interpretive method challenges patriarchies by providing a "justification for the exegetes to depart from literal readings of the text that are problematic for women" (99), in addition to updating *tafsīr* with more modern social, cultural, and linguistic sensibilities (27–31). Thus, feminist exegetical redress can be viewed as a means to understand the relationship of modern-day non-religious rhetoric to *al-balāgha*'s Islamic legacy.

The Tradition of *Balāgha*

Having described the development of *'ilm al-balāgha* into a mode of rhetorical criticism irreducible to a unified and solely religious field, this section provides a general description of the principal sub-disciplines of *al-balāgha*, including *'ilm al-ma'ānī* (science of sentence types), *'ilm al-bayān* (science of tropes), and *'ilm al-badī'* (science of verbal ornamentation). For purposes of illustration, the technical description of *al-balāgha* is followed by a brief analysis of the introductory paragraph of a public statement by alQaws – a Palestinian anti-colonial, queer, feminist organization. Published as part of the "Rallying Queer Cry for Liberation" that took place in Haifa during the recent 2021 Spring Palestinian uprising, our analysis showcases the expansive nature of Arabic rhetorical practices beyond discourses in the Middle East and even into English translation. While underscoring the continued relevance of *al-balāgha* as a means of both invention and criticism, alQaws's statement also exemplifies transcultural dimensions in contemporary Arabic rhetorical forms. By broaching autochthonous concepts from *'ilm al-balāgha* along with well-known notions within Western rhetoric, our analysis foregrounds transcultural resonances across rhetorical traditions, just as it stresses the need for transnational interpretations of Arabic rhetorical forms.

Historically, Arabic rhetoric has been conceptualized as a positive and generally praiseworthy discipline, which marks an important distinction between *al-balāgha* and the Greco-Roman rhetorical tradition. Literally signifying "reaching an end" (e.g., a location, a purpose), "effectively attaining something" (such as maturity, adolescence, a life goal, or an intended meaning), or successfully relaying or transmitting something (such as an object or information), both past and present-day uses of the notion of *balāgha* in Arabic are neither denotatively nor connotatively associated with manipulation, deceit, error, and Platonic valuations of rhetoric as "cookery," "flattery," "sophistry," or "vacuity" (Rashwan 2021; Halldén 2005; Heinrichs 1998). Instead, the concept of *balāgha* is closely correlated with *faṣāḥa* – "eloquent appearance and conveyance," "clear manifestation," and "linguistic fluency" in composition, as well as "phonetic smoothness" in delivery. It is not surprising, therefore, that the three overlapping sub-disciplines of *'ilm al-balāgha* emerged as systematic studies of the different communicative means that facilitate clarity, effective communication, and semantic-stylistic congruity between utterances, speakers' intentions, the psychological states of addressees, and contextual demands.

Al-ma'ānī, literally "meanings," focuses on how different grammatical constructions and orderings of propositions' elements (order system, or *al-naẓm* in Arabic) yield different meanings, express different emotions and attitudes, and could be used to carry out divergent pragmatic functions that produce differing rhetorical effects. *Al-ma'ānī* is not mere adherence to grammatical rules. Rather, it is how distinct syntactic organizations of propositions allow speakers to perform differing rhetorical actions (interrogate, exhort, plea, order, etc.), and to address different kinds of audiences, such as those who are neutral, skeptical, or already in partial but not full agreement with the rhetor. At this level of analysis, the grammatical, the aesthetic, and the pragmatic are inextricably intertwined with rhetorical purposes and situations. Although different Arabic rhetoricians have gradually elaborated different classifications of order systems, most of the rhetorical treatises on *'ilm al-ma'ānī* include recurrent elements. These include: modes of reporting an event and informing addressees, ellipsis, succinctness, moderation, verbosity in syntactic constructions, and foregrounding and backgrounding, wherein placements of lexical items, subjects and predicates, or whole phrases in the beginnings or endings of sentences convey different intentions and emphases, just as they yield differing rhetorical effects. All of these possible alterations of word orderings of phrases and clauses reveal divergences across potential rhetorical situations and audiences' stances, just as they facilitate the evocation of different ideas, states of mind, and emotions – possibilities that have been further elaborated through *'ilm al-bayān*.

Meaning the science of "conveyance," "manifestation," "unveiling," or "clarification," *'ilm al-bayān* concerns the study of tropes. Although many tropes have been conceptualized and placed in differing positions within hierarchized classifications, simile, allegory, and metonymy have repeatedly featured as the three focal tropes in Arabic rhetorical treatises. Here, similar to *'ilm al-ma'ānī*, we encounter a systems-based approach through which rhetoricians have attempted to, first, descriptively typify and name the different constituent components of figures of speech and, second, exhaustively account for the possible combinations of these types and elements, along with the normative evaluations of the rhetorical and pragmatic affordances of each of these combinations. Uses of simile, for example, have been described as involving a likened-to, a likened, a semantic simile feature that links the former two, and a simile element through which the similitude is linguistically realized – which could be a likening particle, noun, or verb (Abdul-Raof 2006: 199–205). While always at the rhetor's disposal, different linguistic renderings and rhetorical exploitations of these components affect divergent pragmatic functions. For example, single, multiple and compound, or ellipted simile features could be used in a single phrase or multiple phrases to demonstrate dimensions of semantic similarity between a likened and a likened-to, just as differing simile elements could be used, or ellipted, to linguistically establish this similarity. Along with possibilities of syntactic reversals (i.e., foregrounding and backgrounding) between the likened and the likened-to at the phrasal level, possibilities of ellipsis, succinctness, moderation, and verbosity in tropes and other figures of speech clarify how *al-bayān* and *al-ma'ānī* are inseparable in realizing forms of eloquent speech and writing.

Finally, signifying the "inventive," "creative," "founding for the first time," "beautifying," and "elevating," *'ilm al-badī'* focuses on the stylistic means of embellishment and their effects upon immediate or potential receivers. Though similarly including classificatory taxonomies that seek to exhaustively account for all forms of embellishment, normative valuations of what rhetors should and should not do are more prominent in rhetorical treatments of *'ilm al-badī'*. Recurrent admonitions against certain embellishments include, for instance, the usage of inkhorn and foreign terms, catachresis, and violations of grammatical rules and pragmatic norms of propriety. More broadly, however, *'ilm al-badī'* divides rhetorical tools of beautification into semantic and lexical forms of embellishment. While semantic embellishment (e.g., antithesis, chiasmus, hyperbole, litotes, paronomasia, euphemism, and other rhetorical figures familiar in the Western tradition) allows for substitutions of synonymous lexical items without affecting the presence of the ornamentation, in lexical embellishment the ornamentation is intrinsic to the lexical choice, and without which the ornamentation disappears (e.g., puns, alliteration, assonance, parallelism and repetition of words as well as phrasal structures).

These three sub-disciplines are simultaneously realized in concrete rhetorical actions. For example, the opening paragraph from alQaws's statement (2021), which I (Al-Mubarak) have translated more literally with bracketed commentary that illustrates aspects of Arabic rhetoric that are either absent or backgrounded in the English version of the statement, demonstrates all three:

> Departing from [with a connotative sense of a soaring beginning] the spirit of our latest Palestinian uprising, and with all the love and rage we have, and with all the exhaustion and frustration we have, we invite you to join the demonstration 'Rallying Queer Cry for Liberation 2021'; let us [but also "so that" – an affirmative, exhortative, and justificatory rhetorical act facilitated by the Arabic prefix "li"] place our experiences and voices at the center, and let us confront violence and deferral and marginalization, and let us emphasize that ["anna" – affirmative construction] the causes of gender and sexual diversity are causes for the entire society, and that [another affirmative construction] every time is their time.

Apropos of a call for action and a statement of solidarity addressed to unify politically diverse audiences, including those potentially unaware or skeptical of the centrality of alQaws's feminist and queer cause to the Palestinian struggle, the *naẓm* in the first sentence begins by foregrounding the Palestinian cause as the unifying inspiration and exigency giving rise to the "Rallying Cry." This syntactic foregrounding is further bolstered by an element from *al-bayān*, simile (*fan al-tashbīh*): an unmarked and effective likening of the latest Palestinian uprising with a spirit – "*rūḥ*," in the singular – through which the protest is said to soaringly launch, emphasizing thereby that it is an irreducible constituent within the diverse yet unified uprising, rather than emerging from its fringes. This simile is unmarked because it is a commonplace expression, and it is effective because the likened-to (a living being), the simile feature (vitality, vibrancy, and the more-than-earthly), and the simile element (a particle such as "like" or "as") are all ellipted, rendering the simile likening more stylistically succinct, semantically powerful, and therefore pragmatically effective. Together, these elements of *al-maʿānī* and *al-bayān* that launch the statement set the emotional and argumentative framing for a number of semantically modifying and syntactically and phonetically embellished phrasal constructions (*al-badīʿ*) that immediately follow.

Specifically, having foregrounded the situational and communal spirit giving rise to the statement, the first sentence proceeds with parallel and succinct affirmations of the diverse emotions animating the Palestinian population's uprising: "with all the love and rage we have, and with all the exhaustion and frustration we have." These clauses involve phonetic consonance in three consecutive lexical items (*ḥub* [love], *ghaḍab* [rage], *taʿab* [exhaustion]) that lead to a direct invitation to women to participate in the protest. This is then followed by another set of parallel, though less succinct, affirmative and instructive exhortations ("*let us* place our experiences and voices at the center, and *let us* confront violence and deferral and marginalization, and *let us* emphasize that the causes of gender and sexual diversity are causes for the entire society") that are similarly made possible through Arabic systems of propositional arrangement, *al-maʿānī*, and embellishment, *al-badīʿ*. To buttress these pleas and exhortations, the paragraph concludes with a pithy, affirmative, alliterative, polyptotonic, and consonant expression that became a well-known slogan during the uprising: "*wa 'nna kulla 'wānin huwa 'wānuhā*," meaning "and surely every time is its time." Besides its simultaneous embellishing and mnemonic functions, the slogan, which draws upon a commonplace expression that Palestinian rappers Daboor & Shabjdeed's song "Inn Ann" popularized during the uprising, allows alQaws to render its relatively uncommon cause more common, placing it at the

center of a rhetorical stage from which it had been marginalized, both locally and globally. Indeed, as much as alQaws's statement anchors itself within a local community
to which it belongs, its transnational character and participation in multiple rhetorical
commonplaces is equally manifest in its deployment of loan translations of terms key to
the statement's action (such as "queer," "gender," and "neoliberalism"), its repeated use of
a series of Arabic terms that establish cross-national forms of solidarity (such as *'ist'mār*
[colonialism], *'ist'mār 'istītānī* [settler colonialism], *taḥarror* [liberation], *nasawyya* [fem-
inist]), and the seemingly unremarkable, but rhetorically significant publication of the
statement in similar, but not identical, English and Arabic versions that together carry
out the statement's overarching rhetorical purpose.

To elaborate, the two versions both exemplify and enact the principles of political
solidarity and alliance, where a shared liberatory purpose unifies distanced tongues
and communities without collapsing them under a singular linguistic and rhetorical
hegemonic force. The Arabic and English versions of the statement forge an alliance
across differences by being semantically, pragmatically, and through loan translations,
linguistically resonant. However, with each attending to the contextual demands of its
respective addressees, neither statement amounts to a literal one-to-one translation of
the other. For example, despite many stylistic overlaps, a number of the stylistic choices
from *'ilm al-badī* highlighted in the analysis above are absent from the English version.
Especially when viewing style not as mere ornamentation, but as a matter of emotional
and political appeal through shared linguistic, imaginative, and phonetic orientations,
stylistic overlaps and differences amount to political attunement and materialize forms
of solidarity across differences. The same could be said in certain word choices from *'ilm
al-bayān*. For instance, rather than directly naming the "Palestinian Authority" as the
English statement does, the Arabic version pragmatically only alludes to it as "*wukalā'uhū
fī al-ḍaffa al-gharbiyya*" (his – i.e., colonialism's, agents in the West Bank). As a negative reference common among those critical of the Palestinian Authority, this rhetorical
allusion empowers alQaws to speak their truth and appeal to individuals critical of this
authority, while at the same time bypassing any direct confrontation that might alienate
those sympathetic with this authority's mission.

Overall, the three sciences of *al-badī*, *al-ma'ānī*, and *al-bayān* work together to
achieve *al-balāgha*'s aims of "reaching," "transmitting," and "attaining" an end. In the
case of alQaws's "Rallying Cry," elements from all three sciences cooperatively ensure
the congruity between alQaws's message and its purpose. By seizing transnational means
of rhetorical production, such as publishing the statement in Arabic and in English, the
statement ties together, rather than homogenizes, heterogeneous traditions, audiences,
and rhetorical commonplaces. Beyond underscoring the international nature of the
Palestinian struggle for liberation and self-determination, alQaws draws attention to
cross- and trans-cultural dimensions to Arabic rhetoric that are not merely the product
of modern times, and as the following section briefly describes, stretch back to the first
few Islamic centuries.

Aristotelian and Contemporary Transcultural Rhetorical Influences

Arabic rhetoric displays many distinctive elements, such as *i'jāz*, *ṣarfa*, and *naẓm*, that
distinguish it from other rhetorical traditions, but it did not develop in a vacuum free
from contact with non-Arabic rhetorical traditions. This section aims to account for
several historical and contemporary ways that Arabic rhetorics have absorbed and

extended Western rhetorical theory, which further demonstrates the transcultural and transnational dimensions of the topic. Especially notable during the medieval period are the translation-commentaries of Aristotle's *Rhetoric* by famous Arabic philosophers al-Fārābī, ibn Sīnā (Avicenna), and ibn Rushd (Averroes) that demonstrate that the communication of ideas around the Mediterranean Sea and beyond was "an unprecedented process of cultural transmission and transformation" (Vagelpohl 2008: vii). Much later, beginning in the twentieth century and continuing today, the influx of North American and European critical theory, literary theory, discourse analysis, and sociology, among other related fields, has influenced the development of Arabic rhetoric as a domain of modern academic scholarship, and prompted negative criticisms of assessing Arabic rhetoric via European rhetorical terminologies, concepts, and theories (Rashwan 2021). Therefore, non-Arabic influences on Arabic rhetorics have transformed both rhetoric as the practice of persuasive oratorical invention via the figure of Aristotle and rhetorical criticism via the work of current Arab rhetoricians.

Throughout the medieval period the commentary tradition held a central place in Arabic scholarship as a means of translating and conveying non-Arabic content to Arabs, incorporating that content into an Arabic philosophical worldview, and adapting it for more localized purposes. As medieval Arabic philosophy developed over the centuries, Aristotle's *Rhetoric* served different purposes for the commentary writers who were both incorporating Greek influences into particular social contexts, as prescribed by the economic, educational, and political goals of those who sponsored the commentaries, and incorporating it into individual philosophical programs. Not being straightforward translations of Aristotle's treatise, the commentaries indicate points of divergence and emphasis that distinguish the Greek and Arabic rhetorical traditions. One important divergence between Aristotle in the Greco-Roman rhetorical tradition and Aristotle's influence on the Arabic rhetorical tradition is the greater focus placed by al-Fārābī and ibn Rushd on the importance of enthymemes – "the pillar of persuasion," according to the latter (Ezzaher 2015: 81). As logicians, these two authors seized upon Aristotle's dictum that persuasion occurs best via examples and enthymemes (34) to explicate the importance of the different kinds of enthymemes, their relationship to syllogisms and other argumentative structures, and their usefulness, according to al-Fārābī, "in all types of matters" (26). Thus, the commentary writers extended the domain of rhetoric and the concept of enthymemes beyond forensic, deliberative, and epideictic genres to include, most importantly for them, the domains of philosophy and, by contextual implication, theology.

The Qur'an is rife with references to debate and disputation (McAullife 1999), and famous theologian Abū Ḥāmid al-Ghazālī explicitly linked the Aristotelian emphasis on enthymemes and Qur'anic debate. In *The Just Balance*, he suggested that each of the "five scales" that comprise the "just balance" of Qur'anic disputation are five varieties of Aristotelian and Stoic syllogistic argumentation schemes that all rely on two premises and a conclusion (Gwynne 2014: 152). For al-Ghazālī, Qur'anic syllogisms demonstrate the infallible logic of Allah and assert the primacy of direct, personal engagement with the Qur'an as the path to piety, rather than either adherence to exegetical traditions and their "eternal" cultivation of theological controversies (al-Ghazālī 1978: 76) or appeals to the authority of Imams. However, constructing syllogisms from Qur'anic verses required al-Ghazālī to extract them from their respective *suwar* and then rearrange the *'āyāt* into the desired argumentative structure. In the process of rearranging *'āyāt* into syllogisms, al-Ghazālī often dropped or implied conclusions and premises, thereby rendering his examples as enthymemes. For example, he withholds both premises (disbelieving in Allah's power is erroneous and believing in it is righteous) and the conclusion (Allah's power provides humans with the natural world) from several enthymematic formulations of the argument before enunciating a complete syllogism that imbues the informal logic of three decontextualized *'āyāt* with a formal structure (42). Thus, conceptually, in a process similar to the Neo-Platonic reassessment and adoption of Plato's pagan idealism for Christian purposes, the direct application of the non-Arabic, non-Islamic Aristotelian tradition of rhetoric and argumentation reveals, in explicit fashion, core principles of Islamic faith, such as God's omnipotence (16), that divine revelation was received by humans (32), and the existence of only one God (37).

The importance of the Aristotelian commentaries for Arabic rhetoric derives from its influence on later scholarship on argumentation and rhetoric, and from empowering later importation of transcultural influences into the discipline. First, the rhetorical implications of logic were important to *tafsīr*'s frequent promotion of and reliance upon reasoning as a medieval transcultural phenomenon. Brandon Katzir has argued that the tenth-century (CE) Arab-Jewish rabbi Saadya Gaon's rhetoric combined Greco-Roman, Jewish, and Arabic rhetorical traditions that belied his Egyptian birth, Babylonian residence, and eventual appointment as head of an Iraqi rabbinical academy (2017: 161–162). Maimonides, the Jewish Arab scholar who composed a treatise on logic based upon Arabic commentaries on Aristotle, further exemplifies this transcultural adaptation of Aristotelian rhetorical and argumentative principles. Arabic rhetoric, one might assert, need not be tied solely to *al-balāgha*'s history, since it emerged from "interconnected" rather than separate regional traditions that depended on more disciplines than just oratory and rhetoric (162). In turn, "Islamized" Aristotelian rhetoric, along with Aristotle's preserved manuscripts, reentered the European intellectual sphere after Muslims lost control of the Iberian Peninsula in the late fifteenth century (Borrowman 2008). Second, the foundation provided by Aristotle's influence on Arabic rhetoric and dialectic "set the tone" for latter-day transcultural influences on Arabic rhetoric and society (Patel 2009: 233). Abdulrazzak Patel, for one, argued that foreign influence played a key role during the Arab Renaissance (late nineteenth to early twentieth centuries) with respect to the Lebanese, Christian linguist Saʿīd al-Shartūnī's oratorical manual. This foundational grounding of Aristotelian rhetoric within Arabic intellectual cultures thus set precedence for a wide-ranging importation of foreign rhetorical theory into the domain of Arabic rhetoric.

Turning to more modern foreign influences and the contemporary field of Arab rhetorical criticism, we suggest that non-Arabic approaches to Arabic rhetoric expand both the conception of Arabic rhetorics as well as non-Arabic rhetorics through transcultural contact and exchange. The re-contextualization of Aristotelian rhetoric and argumentation into classical Islamic philosophy and the science of *balāgha* was viable for medieval commentary writers, and so too is the importation of twentieth- and twenty-first-century non-Arabic rhetorical theory and criticism. The contributions of contemporary scholars like Kefaya Diab and Nicole Khoury demonstrate the fruitfulness of transcultural rhetorical criticism when analyzing contemporary Arabic rhetoric. In order to understand the activist influence of Mohammed Bouazizi's self-immolation as a form of Arabic visual rhetoric, which is credited with sparking the 2011 Tunisian revolution, Diab invokes European and North American critical theory to argue that repeated viewing of Bouazizi's immolation and injuries provoked collective "senses" of vulnerability, responsibility, and agency among Tunisians. In turn, when combined with pan-Arab cultural conceptions of collective responsibility and community loyalty (2021: 267), the act of self-immolation served as the revolutionary motive for Tunisians.

From a differing perspective on contemporary Arabic rhetoric, Nicole Khoury examines the rhetoric of *Al-Raida*, a Lebanese feminist academic journal, by using critical discourse analysis and the theories of Michel Foucault in order to assess the persuasive effects of how the global feminist movement materialized in Lebanon. Khoury found, for instance, that the "rhetorical function" of the journal shifted away from promoting imported and impractical feminist political interventions at the national and international levels amidst the Lebanese civil war. For instance, advocacy of international "development" programs to increase the employment of women shifted toward the promotion of politically attuned narratives and literature that promoted feminism at the local level (2018: 110–111).

The examples of Aristotle's influence on Arabic rhetorical invention and Diab's and Khoury's incorporation of non-Arabic rhetorical theory and methodologies into their criticism of contemporary Arabic rhetorics show the transcultural relevance of these foreign sources for understanding Arabic rhetoric, as well as how Arabic rhetoric can facilitate understanding of the foreign influences. In these ways, a transcultural approach to understanding Arabic rhetoric's simultaneous emic and etic characteristics enhances analyses of transnational events like the spread of medieval Arabic philosophy, the Arab Spring, and the worldwide transformation of feminism. Thus, an important element of understanding Arabic rhetoric involves understanding it both in isolation and as an important and foundational contributor to the world's shared rhetorical traditions.

Conclusion

Rather than portraying it as an internally coherent field (e.g., Chowdhury, 2015), this chapter's purpose was to describe Arabic rhetoric as a simultaneously unified yet dispersed body of rhetorical practices and knowledge production. We described *al-balāgha*'s early Islamic history and development, its ongoing functional use as a means of Qur'anic exegesis, the three traditional elements that define the science of *balāgha*, and, finally, we accounted for Arabic rhetorics' interaction with and further development through contact with non-Arabic sources. The lenses of unity and dispersion demonstrated the interplay between Qur'anic and non-Qur'anic rhetorics, Arabic and non-Arabic sources, and *al-balāgha* as a form of religious interpretation as well as a larger form of literary and rhetorical criticism. Just as early attempts at demonstrating the holy book's rhetorical inimitability were focal to the formation of *al-balāgha* as a theologically motivated endeavor, a closer reading of early and contemporary Arabic oratorical treatises also reveals its debt to non-religious forms (Qutbuddin, 2019). Therefore, as we suggested above, a thorough description of *al-balāgha* must account for its multiple historical lineages and its applications within heterogeneous fields of inquiry and sites of social action.

Indeed, whether in our description of the encounter between Greek rhetoric and Islamic philosophy, our brief account of al-Ḥarīrī's *Impostures*, or in our broaching of contemporary social justice activism in the Middle East, this chapter suggests grounds for future research, just as it gestures towards answering some recent calls within the field of comparative rhetoric. In particular, by closely reading alQaws's statement through classical categories from *'ilm al-balāgha*, our analysis highlights, first, the need to adopt more cross-cultural and transnational foci regarding rhetorical theory and practice in Arabic contexts (Scholz 2019: 182). Second, it underscores the need for critical, comparative approaches that show "how rhetoric enacts a process of discursive invention, intervention, and transformation … [that brings about] effective communication and [affects] new discursive alliances and new forms of inquiry and discovery" (Mao 2021: 18). And third, this chapter reiterates the need to attend to situated rhetorical practices at the intersection between de-colonial, gender, and performance studies in order to build "relationships between multiple traditions, multiple histories, [and] multiple practices" (Bratta and Powell 2016). Along with a focus on convergent and divergent tendencies that animate its history, attending to these calls allows for thicker descriptions of cross-sectional solidarities and transformations within Arabic rhetorics, those that occurred elsewhere, and their comparative re-contextualizations with other rhetorical traditions (Mao et al. 2015). As the *'ilm* that studies the available means of forming bonds and relationships, rhetoric itself might as well be approached as a primary site where transcultural bonds and relationships have been formed, and transformed.

References

Abdul-Raof, H. (2006) *Arabic Rhetoric: A Pragmatic Analysis*, New York: Routledge.
Abdul-Raof, H. (2010) *Schools of Qur'anic Exegesis: Genesis and Development*, New York: Routledge.
Abou El Fadl, K. (2001) *Speaking in God's Name: Islamic Law, Authority and Women*, Oxford: Oneworld.
Aḥmad, M. K., and Sallām, M. Z. (eds.) (2014) *Three Treatises on the I'jāz of the Qur'ān*. Translated by I. J. Boullata and T. L. DeYoung, Reading: Garnet.
al-Bāqillānī. (1950) *A Tenth-Century Document of Arabic Literary and Criticism: The Sections on Poetry of al-Bāqillānī's I'jâz al-Qur'an*. Translated and edited by G. E. VonGrunebaum, Chicago: University of Chicago Press.
al-Bukhari, M. (1997) *Imam Bukhari's Book of Muslim Morals and Manners*. Translated by Y. T. DeLorenzo. Alexandria, VA: al-Saadawi.
al-Ghazali. (1978) *The Just Balance*. Translated by D. P. Brewster. Lahore: Sh. Muhammad Ashraf.
al-Ḥarīrī. (2020) *Impostures*. Translated by M. Cooperson. New York: New York University Press.
Ali, M. M. (1987) *A Manual of Hadith*, 2nd ed., Atlantic Highlands: Curzon.
al-Jurjānī. (1982) 'Al-Jurjani's Theory of Discourse [*Dala'il I'jaz al Qur'an*]'. Translated by M. Larkin. *Alif: Journal of Comparative Poetics* 2: 76–86.
al-Nu'mān, A. (2017) *Disagreements of the Jurists: A Manual of Islamic Legal Theory*. Translated by D. J. Stewart. New York: New York University Press.
alQaws (2021) 'A Rallying Cry for Queer Liberation'. English version available at: www.alqaws.org/news/A- Rally ing- Cry- for- Queer- Lib erat ion- 2021?cate gory _ id= 0. Arabic version available at: www.alqaws.org/اخبار/الحرية-الكويرية-صرخة-2021-?category_id=0 (accessed 27 February 2022).
al-Rāzī, Fakhr al-Dīn (2018) *The Great Exegesis, al-Tafsīr al-Kabīr, Volume l: The Fātiḥa*. Translated by S. Saeed. Cambridge: The Royal AAL Al-Bayt Institute for Islamic Thought and The Islamic Texts Society.
al-Shāfi'ī, M. I. I. (2015) *The Epistle on Legal Theory: A Translation of al-Shāfi's Risālah*. Translated by J. E. Lowry. New York: New York University Press.
al-Ṭabarī, A. B. J. (1987) *The Commentary on the Qur'ān*, vol. 1. Translated by J. Cooper. New York: Oxford University Press.
Blankenship, K. Y. (2020) *The Inimitable Qur'ān: Some Problems in English Translations of the Qur'ān with Reference to Rhetorical Features*, Boston: Brill.
Borrowman, S. (2008) 'The Islamization of Rhetoric: Ibn Rushd and the Reintroduction of Aristotle into Medieval Europe', *Rhetoric Review* 27(4): 341–360.
Bratta, P. and Powell, M. (2016) 'Introduction to the Special Issue: Entering the Cultural Rhetorics Conversations', *Enculturation: A Journal of Rhetoric, Writing, and Culture*. Available at: http://enculturation.net/entering-the-cultural-rhetorics-conversations (accessed 27 February 2022).
Chowdhury, S. Z. (2015) *Introducing Arabic Rhetoric*, London: Dar Al-Nicosia Publishing House.
Diab, K. (2021) 'The Rise of the Arab Spring through a Sense of Agency', *Rhetoric Society Quarterly* 51(4): 261–275.

Ezzaher, L. E. (ed. and trans.) (2015) *Three Arabic Treatises on Aristotle's Rhetoric: The Commentaries of al-Fārābī, Avicenna, and Averroes*, Carbondale: Southern Illinois University Press.

Gwynne, R. W. (2014) *Logic, Rhetoric, and Legal Reasoning in the Qur'ān: God's Arguments*, New York: Routledge.

Halldén, P. (2005) 'What Is Arab Islamic Rhetoric? Rethinking the History of Muslim Oratory Art and Homiletics', *International Journal of Middle East Studies* 37(1): 19–38.

Heinrichs, W. (1998) 'Rhetoric and Poetics', in J. S. Meisami and P. Starkey (eds.), *Encyclopedia of Arabic Literature*, London: Routledge, pp. 651–656.

Hidayatullah, A. A. (2014) *Feminist Edges of the Qur'an*, New York: Oxford University Press.

Ibn Qutaybah. (2017) *The Excellence of the Arabs*. Translated by S. B. Savant and P. Webb. New York: New York University Press.

Jones, L. G. (2012) *The Power of Oratory in the Medieval Muslim World*, New York: Cambridge University Press.

Katzir, B. (2017) 'The Truth of Reliable Tradition: Saadya Gaon, Arabic Rhetoric, and the Challenge to Rhetorical Historiography', *Rhetorica* 35(2): 161–188.

Katzir, B. (2018) 'Paths of Virtue: Legal Rhetorics in Judaism and Islam', *Rhetoric Society Quarterly* 48(1): 28–48.

Khoury, N. (2018) '(Re)defining the First Mark of Development: Lebanese Feminist Discourse in *Al-Raida*, 1976–1985', *Al Raida* 42(2): 86–112.

The Koran (2014) Translated by N. J. Dawood. New York: Penguin.

Lawrence, B. (2017) *The* Koran *in English: A Biography*, Princeton: Princeton University Press.

Mao, L. (2021) 'Redefining Comparative Rhetoric: Essence, Facts, Events', in K. Lloyd (ed.), *The Routledge Handbook of Comparative World Rhetorics: Studies in the History, Application, and Teaching of Rhetoric Beyond Traditional Greco-Roman Contexts*, London: Routledge, pp. 15–33.

Mao, L., Wang, B., Lyon, A., Jarratt, S. C., Swearingen, C. J., Romano, S., Simonson, P., Mailloux, S., and Xing, L. (2015) 'Manifesting a Future for Comparative Rhetoric', *Rhetoric Review* 34(3): 239–274.

McAuliffe, J. D. (1999) '"Debate with Them in the Better Way": The Construction of a Qur'ānic Commonplace', in *Myths, Historical Archetypes and Symbolic Figures in Arabic Literature: Towards a New Hermeneutic Approach*. Proceedings of the International Symposium in Beirut, June 25th–June 30th, 1996. Beirut: Franz Steiner Verlag, pp. 163–188.

Patel, A. (2009) 'Nahḍah Oratory: Western Rhetoric in al-Sharṭūnī's Manual on the Art of the Orator', *Middle Eastern Literatures* 12(3): 233–269.

Qutbuddin, T. (2019) *Arabic Oration: Art and Function*, Leiden: Brill.

Rashwan, H. (2021) 'Comparative *Balāghah*: Arabic and Ancient Egyptian Literary Rhetoric through the Lens of Post-Eurocentric Poetics', in K. Lloyd (ed.), *The Routledge Handbook of Comparative World Rhetorics: Studies in the History, Application, and Teaching of Rhetoric Beyond Traditional Greco-Roman Contexts*, London: Routledge, pp. 386–403.

Scholz, J. (2019) 'Modern Arabic Rhetorical Manuals: A Transcultural Phenomenon', in L. Abu-Er-Rub, C. Brosius, S. Meurer, D. Panagiotopoulos, and S. Richter (eds.), *Engaging Transculturality: Concepts, Key Terms, Case Studies*, London: Routledge, pp. 170–184.

Vagelpohl, U. (2008) *Aristotle's Rhetoric in the East: The Syriac and Arabic Translation and Commentary Tradition*. Boston: Brill.

PART III

Descriptive Studies of Political Rhetoric

11

THE DEMOCRAT'S LINGUISTIC STANCE TOWARDS MIGRATION IN ELECTORAL CAMPAIGNS

Ethos, Logos, and *Pathos* in Barack Obama's and Joe Biden's Discourses

Teresa Fernández-Ulloa and María del Carmen López-Ruiz

Introduction

In 2021, more than 2 million migrants were stopped while attempting to enter the United States from Mexico illegally, which was more than those in 1986 or 2000. This was due to Biden's administration easing border policies and the collapse of economies in Latin America due to the pandemic (U.S. Border Patrol, n.d.). Illegal immigration has been a permanent problem in the United States, so it has become a topic to deal with in any political campaign.

In this research, we focus specifically on the different rhetorical mechanisms used in political speeches of Democrat leaders Barack Obama and Joe Biden when dealing with the topic of immigration, since, in the last couple of decades, this issue has been one of the most critical ones for citizens to examine when choosing whom to elect.

We analyze, turning to Aristotle's rhetorical instruments, how the politicians try to convince, and organize their speeches in various ways (considering the factors affecting the credibility of the speaker, or *ethos*; strategies of *logos*, or those related to the arguments; and *pathos*, or how emotions are raised), and then we compare the two politicians' resources to convey the similarities and differences. To do so, we analyze the text using Charaudeau's strategies (2005, 2006, 2009).

Thus, the main objective of this chapter is to study, with the discourse analysis tools, the rhetorical elements of speeches of the last two Democrats running for the presidency of the United States, as these elements relate to immigration policies. To carry out the study, we have compiled a corpus of eight campaign-related political speeches, four by Obama and four by Biden (2008, 2016 (Obama), 2020 (Biden)), following Bowker and

DOI: 10.4324/9781003195276-15

165

Pearson's 2002 strategies regarding designing textual corpora. There was a phase of data collection and a corpus design phase, a storage phase, and a corpus management phase. For the data collection phase, we collected a corpus of 14 speeches of both candidates. To do so, we searched Google with the help of specialized searching algorithms, which included the keywords "immigration," "immigrants," "democrats," "Biden," "Obama," "immigration policies," "political campaign," and "immigration reforms" (e.g. Obama+ political campaign+immigration policies before:2008-11-20 site:democrats.org), and we reduced the number of speeches to eight for this study. For more details, see Fernández Ulloa and López Ruiz (2022, pp. 107–109).

Once the corpus was created, we analyzed the transcriptions of the speeches to classify the language used by both Democrat candidates, Barack Obama and Joe Biden, into three patterns (drafted by Aristotle in his *Rhetoric*): *ethos*, *logos*, and *pathos*.

Obama's and Biden's Discourses Related to Immigration

Barack Obama

Barack Obama's speeches have been studied from many perspectives, not all of them linguistic, though: the power of his words in pragmatic terms (Sayegh and Nabifar 2012); the use of metaphors (Lesz 2011); persuasive language (Wang 2010); gestures, kinesics, and proxemics (Requeijo Rey 2010), etc.

During the 2012 presidential elections, Obama "decided to change his immigration policies during his campaign and adapt his speech accordingly" (López Cirugeda and Sánchez Ruiz 2013, p. 81). As these two researchers state, in two of his most representative speeches specifically addressed to a Latino audience (the one at the National Association of Latino Elected and Appointed Officials Annual Conference, 2012, and the remarks on Comprehensive Immigration Reform, 2013), he frequently appeals to justice and patriotism, and makes local references in the form of recognition. He also uses conceptual metaphors about the American dream, personification, repetition, and synesthesia.

His analogies seem to prove that he conceives the American dream as a path to citizenship. His use of such metaphors, something ubiquitous in Obama's speech, makes him base his words addressed to Latinos on the uniqueness of the United States provided by the mosaic of cultures that come together under the same identity.

Junaidi (2019) mentions that Obama seems to use pejorative words sometimes to describe immigrants, perhaps because they are so widespread in American society: "illegal immigrants," "undocumented immigrants," "undocumented population," "undocumented foreigner." He prefers the second of these, considered politically correct. Obama attempts not to include (evaluative) adjectives to describe immigrants, which indicates his attempt not to offer a negative image. Negative adjectives are used sometimes to give an idea of vulnerability.

As Junaidi (2019) points out, a characteristic of Obama's speech is that he relates immigration to national security, family/children, economy, refugees, humanitarian crisis, and education; that is, primarily related to the economy. The author also mentions that Obama sees America as a "nation of immigrants" but emphasizes the law as a basis for immigrants to achieve citizenship.

Obama always observes that North America is made up of immigrants: "We define ourselves as a nation of immigrants. That's who we are, in our bones" (2013, January 29), although he will always insist on the importance of it being legal. He often mentions it in his discourses, pointing out how the immigration system "has been broken for a very long time" (2014, November 20). In his discourse of November 21, 2014, he states that "too often, the immigration system feels fundamentally unfair," but he insists on "secure borders" and indicates that "over the past six years, illegal border-crossings have been cut by more than half."

Joe Biden

President Joe Biden took the oath of office on January 20, 2021, when the United States faced a public health and economic crisis due to the COVID-19 pandemic. Also, with Biden preparing to enter the White House, the feeling that the border was opening spread across many countries, which only aggravated a significant problem in the United States. The classic border "problem" with Mexico, and the arrival of illegal immigrants from this country, not to mention the situation of separated families, DACA children, and other long-term problems, was enlarged with the massive arrival of Haitians, Brazilians, and Venezuelans, among others, and the inability to react, or the overreaction, of the border guard.

The Biden Administration is moving to save a critical Obama-era immigration program that shields undocumented immigrants brought to the United States as children from deportation by proposing a new regulation, the latest attempt to preserve it.

According to some studies, Biden's rhetoric is full of empathy and emotion (Pedrini 2021). Ahmed and Amir (2021) have also studied his speech, stating that it includes many directive and representative acts. Analyzing the speech acts highlights the U.S. President's demanding, informative, and supportive nature. He uses direct and indirect speech acts to invite, request, command, challenge, and urge people to do what he thinks is right.

In his first speech as President, he "made a sweeping call for unity, truth and racial justice as the nation faces one of its darkest hours in the midst of a raging pandemic and bitter political division" ("Read Joe Biden's…" 2021, January 21). "Unity" is one of the main themes of the speech, which is why Biden used that word eight times. Biden cites historical figures such as St. Augustine and President Abraham Lincoln to reinforce the theme (Ahmed and Amir 2021, p. 45). He uses rhetorical figures to bring a solid impact to convey his ideas; juxtaposition, to contrast and highlight the differences between two thoughts: "We have much to do in this winter of significant dangers and possibilities"; "Together we will write an American story of hope not fear, of unity not division, of light not darkness." He also uses anaphora, as in "here we are" in the following example, to add weight to his ideas: "Here we stand in the shadow of the dome of the Capitol, completed in the midst of the Civil War when the union itself was literally hanging by a thread. However, we hold on. We prevail. Here we are… Here we are… Here we are…" (p. 45).

Objectives and Methodology

In the following section, we describe in detail the linguistic features of each one of the three rhetorical elements in the speeches that compose our corpus of work and show examples that will illustrate the strategic elements of language used by each orator. The following section aims to underline the importance of discourse analysis for a better understanding.

Analysis: Ethos, Logos, *and* Pathos

Ethos

Before providing examples in the discourses of Obama and Biden, it is necessary to remember that *ethos* is a strategy responsible for configuring the image of credibility possessed by the speaker of a speech, something very important for any politician. *Ethos* is attributed to the action of *delectare*, which, in other words, refers to the act of "appeal" or "persuade," emphasizing fundamentally the willingness of the orator to show to his/her audience that he/she is someone that can be trusted. The speaker intends to win the audience's trust, who do not want to stop listening to the speaker. The word *ethos*, on the one hand, comes from the Greek term ἦθος, *êthos*, that is, "custom," "character," "use." In this sense, it refers to the ethical and moral disposition of the speaker.

To study precisely all the features that identify the *ethos* of the two speakers presented here, we lean on the classification of characteristics of *ethos* described by Charaudeau (2006) as a reference. In this way, we start from the premise that the image of any speaker will not only be delimited by what he says but by how he says it, which will lead the audience to forge an identity of the speaker. In this sense, two types of well-differentiated identities can be distinguished: on the one hand, the *ethos* of **credibility**; on the other, the *ethos* of **identification** (Charaudeau 2005, p. 36). The first *ethos* is the one that alludes to reason to show that the speaker can legitimize his own identity, something that will be reinforced by the arguments of another of the strategies, the *logos*. On the other hand, the *ethos* of identification primarily concentrates on a type of identity of an affective and psychological nature. Through it, the speaker intends to approach a heterogeneous audience, where they might be allies, opponents, or undecided.

Each of these types of *ethos* (credibility and identification) distinguishes other subtypes of *ethos* that help specify more adequately in what sense rationality or affection concerns the speaker's image. In this sense, there are many *ethe* that the two speakers share, although they present different strategies and resources. Something prevalent, of course, in both Obama's and Biden's discourses, although more common in the latter, is the "us" vs. "they" ideologies distinction and polarization ("ingroup" and "outgroup," respectively (Van Dijk 1995, p. 150). This discursive polarization is typically characterized by reinforcing the positive qualities of "we," the ingroup, and "their" negative attributes, those of the outgroup. At the same time, the negative qualities of the ingroup and the positive ones of the outgroup are typically de-emphasized, attenuated, mitigated, or simply ignored or hidden. In this way, we get an "ideological framework" (Van Dijk 1998), which can be applied to all levels of discourse.

Among the examples, Obama says, "I will be working with others to offer an amendment to make this provision closer to what we proposed last year" (2007, May 23), and Biden, "And, like everything about this election, the threat Donald Trump poses to our national security, and to who we are as a country, is so extreme, we cannot afford to ignore it"; "His erratic policies [Trump's] and failures to uphold basic democratic principles have muddied our reputation, our place in the world, and our ability to lead it" (2019, July 11).

These statements also show considerable resources of discursive polarization, based on the opposition of identity and the *ethos* of "us" vs. "they," for which various mechanisms are used: disqualifications, appreciative adjectives, positive and negative politeness, etc.

These two types of *ethos* (both credibility and identification) are reinforced by the *ethos* of competence (by using this kind of *ethos*, the speaker wants to show that he is someone qualified as a political person, that he has acquired enough experience and training throughout his career). Now, he knows how to exercise the different functions of government. The speaker allows himself to advise the opponent to demonstrate his worth as a politician (self-praise and disqualification of the adversary might be used). Verbs in deontic modality, expressing duty, syntactic repetitions, and conditional statements are usually the techniques preferred by politicians:

> I will support amendments aimed at fixing the temporary worker program that Senator Bingaman and others have offered. And if we're going to have a new temporary worker program, those workers should have the opportunity to stay if they prove themselves capable and willing to participate in this country.
>
> *Obama 2007, May 23*

> Now I believe they have a duty to make sure their algorithms and platforms are not misused to sow division at home, or to empower the surveillance state, facilitate repression and censorship in China and elsewhere, spread hate, or spur people to violence.
>
> *Biden 2019, July 11*

Another example of *ethos* would be the *ethos* of **efficacy** or **virtue**, used whenever the speaker wants to show fidelity to his principles or appeal to the false and prejudiced principles of the Other.

> But for reform to work, we also must respond to what pulls people to America and what pushes them out of their home countries. Where we can reunite families, we should. Where we can bring in more foreign-born workers with the skills our economy needs, we should. And these goals are not mutually exclusive. We should not say that Spanish speaking or working class immigrants are only good enough to be temporary workers and cannot earn the right to be a part of the American family.
>
> *Obama 2007, May 23*

> As Vice President, I secured commitments from the leaders of El Salvador, Guatemala, and Honduras to take on the corruption, violence, and endemic poverty in their countries that are driving people to leave their homes.
>
> *Biden 2019, July 11*

The *ethos* of **performativity** helps to concretize the promises related to the welfare of the society the politician addresses. The volitional modality is frequent in these cases. Among the examples: "And at the appropriate time, I will be offering another amendment with the President [Presiding Officer Senator Menendez] to sunset the points system in the bill" (Obama 2007, May 23), and "As Vice President, I secured commitments from the leaders of El Salvador, Guatemala, and Honduras to take on the corruption, violence, and endemic poverty in their countries that are driving people to leave their homes" (Biden 2019, July 11).

The *ethos* of **commitment** alludes to the promises of the orator when focusing on the pledge of a necessary change that will only arrive upon his presidency: "And if Congress is unable to move forward in a timely fashion, I will send up a bill based on my proposal and insist that they vote on it right away" (Obama 2013, January 29); "We need to work again with Canada and Mexico as neighbors – not adversaries. And we need to focus on the root causes driving migrants to our border" (Biden 2019, July 11).

Finally, the *ethos* of **sincerity** is described as the way the orator must describe himself as a person who can be trusted, whose words have a value in the receiver because he can be trusted not only as a political leader but also as a good person: "So if we're truly committed to strengthening our middle class and providing more ladders of opportunity to those who are willing to work hard to make it into the middle class, we've got to fix the system" (Obama 2013, January 29); "We have to be honest about our friends that are falling short and forge a common agenda for action to address the greatest threats to our shared values" (Biden 2019, July 11).

Logos

Logos is a strategy of the arguments that point straight to the reason. It comes from the Greek root λόγος, *lógos*, "reason," "argument," "word," or even "thought." This principle is directly related to the doctrine of *docere*, "teach," "refer," and "convince," which is achieved using all the rational and logical arguments the speaker puts across. In this sense, the discursive importance lies fundamentally in the message conveyed by the speaker, Obama and Biden in this case: the arguments they use to defend their thesis must be well-founded, for only in this way can they persuade.

The argumentative scheme of Charaudeau (2005, 2009) has been used as a model of analysis in this study. We resort to the following **strategies**: essentialization, analogy, and singularization (Charaudeau 2009: 290); and the **actions** of problematizing, taking sides, elucidating, and proving (2009: 280).

We will provide examples from both politicians regarding strategies and actions related to *logos* in speeches related to immigration.

Strategies

The procedure of *essentialization* consists of assuming that the audience will understand some ideological words by the meanings by which a specific group understands them (the orator and his group). This is the procedure used by political parties, the press, etc., when talking about familiar topics such as feminism and immigration. Opinions may be diverted even if they refer to the same issue, yet the ideological idea in that word can be different for some people. Whereas immigration may have a negative association of ideas for some groups, it can have a positive ideological meaning for others.

> We cannot forget that democracy is the root of our society, the wellspring of our power, the source of our renewal. It strengthens and amplifies our leadership to keep us safe in the world. It's the engine of our ingenuity that drives our economic prosperity. It's the heart of who we are and how we see the world – and how the world sees us.
>
> *Biden 2019, July 11*

Analogy refers to comparing one situation to another similar situation in the past. Circumstances may not be similar though, making the statement false or not sufficiently supported (and therefore easily contradicted).

We must enact a forward-looking foreign policy for the world as we find it today – and as we anticipate it will be tomorrow.

Much has shifted in the past few years. The international landscape is more crowded, competitive and complicated. And when we look at what's different today, two key points stand out, one is that the speed and intensity of our gravest challenges means that the fates of nations are more intertwined than ever before.

Biden 2019, July 11

Finally, *singularization* refers to the action of trying to explain one concept out of the many meanings that a specific word can have so that everyone takes it during the speech the way the orator intends it to be taken: "Now, this debate deserves more than the usual politics, because for all the back and forth in Washington, as I said last night, this is about something bigger. <u>This is about who we are</u>. Who do we want to be?" (Obama 2014, November 21).

Actions

Problematizing consists of informing the receiver of the message (the audience) that two possible actions can be drafted upon a specific problem that troubles society. For instance, an orator can start his argumentation by asking the audience whether it is appropriate to intervene in a war. With this question, the audience encounters the "problem" of having to decide about the matter being conveyed by the orator. The orator will arrange then two possibilities: *No to war* statements / *Yes to war* statements, and why. The problem arises from the possibility of choosing, especially in those circumstances when the audience has not been offered a second choice before.

Last year I spoke at one of the marches in Chicago for comprehensive immigration reform. I looked out across the faces of the crowd. I saw mothers and fathers, citizens and noncitizens, people of Polish and Mexican descent, working Americans, and children. And what I know is that these are people we <u>should embrace, not fear</u>. We can and should be able to see ourselves in them.

Obama 2007, May 23

Once the orator has explained and argued which one of these two possibilities is the most convenient one, he will have *taken sides* over the matter under discussion:

to fix the system in a way that does <u>not</u> require <u>us to revisit the same problem in twenty years,</u> I continue to believe that <u>we need stronger enforcement</u> on the border and at the workplace. And that means a workable mandatory system that employers must use to verify the legality of their workers.

Obama 2007, May 23

To take sides, it will be necessary for him to explain the motives of his decision. In other words, which arguments (for and against) intervene in his opinion to take that side and not the other, and why these arguments are more important than the ones provided by those who defend the other position (*elucidating*): "and the overarching purpose of our foreign policy must be to defend and advance the security, prosperity, and democratic values of the United States" (Biden 2020, July 29).

Finally, he will be required to *prove* and validate the motives presented to the audience to underline that his point of view is effectively supported and cannot be contradicted by the audience. At this point, Charaudeau (2009, p. 280) argues that argumentative texts can only be defined as a general cognitive activity on account of the amount of linguistic and discourse resources employed by orators to convey their points of view to convince the audience. An example from Biden:

> I'm going to invest literally hundreds of billions of dollars to make housing a right, not a privilege. It's a basic right to have a roof over your head. We're going to create a hundred billion dollar affordable housing fund to build and upgrade affordable homes that exists [sic] now, build, upgrade them.
>
> *Biden 2020, July 29*

Pathos

Pathos-based rhetorical strategies are those that get the audience to "open up." We will see how Obama and Biden intend to change the behavior, feelings, intentions, or viewpoint of others by communicative means that are based on emotional aspects related to immigration. To do so, they might use fears, hatreds, prejudices, inclinations, convictions, and ideals common to their audience. Different techniques can be utilized to manipulate, for example, vivid language, personal stories of the politician or others, figurative language (metaphors, similes …), vocal variety, cadence, and repetition. They insist on the sincerity of their words and how excited they are about what they propose. The fear technique is also widely used, considered by Zheng (2000) a reinforcement strategy (together with testimony, quotes from historical and religious speeches, emotion and investment techniques, and logical fallacies). All these show that *pathos*, therefore, not only helps to legitimize arguments of the speaker's *logos*, and affects, either directly or indirectly, on his *ethos* as the hero of the story, in narrative terms, but also has an impact on the adversary's *ethos*, as the antagonist. This obvious *logos/ethos/pathos* relationship demonstrates how close the three strategies are and the effectiveness, in perlocutionary terms (Searle 1980 [1969]), they can have on the speech.

With all the previous pragmatic considerations in mind, many examples show the power of emotions and persuasion concerning *pathos* in Democrat electoral speeches related to immigration. Abstract nouns and persuasive adjectives are used to describe the situation and foster compassion:

> And I think that it is critical that as we embark on this enormous venture to update our immigration system, that it is fully reflective of the powerful tradition of immigration in this country and fully reflective of our values and our ideals.
>
> *Obama 2007, May 23*

There are prospective promises: "Our Statue of Liberty invites in the tired, the poor, the huddled masses yearning to breathe free" (Biden 2019, July 11). And also comparative language in gradation from the lesser to the most important values: "The answer to this threat is more openness – not less. More friendships, more cooperation, more alliances. More democracy" (Biden 2019, July 11). And the use of words to inspire fear: "We are facing enemies – both without and within – hoping to exploit the fissures in our society, undermine our democracy, break up our alliances, and return us to an international system where might determines right" (Biden 2019, July 11).

Discussions and Conclusion

Democrats are not afraid of showing themselves as conscious of the situation of immigrants and paying more attention to the motives of their migration than to the problems that may arise economically and internationally for the country. Therefore, emotions play a vital role in their argumentation.

Regarding Obama's persuasive electoral speeches about immigration, it can be said that his master rhetorical elements are based on justice, the glorification of the country, the pride of the origins of Americans, the history of the country, and compassion for the helpless. Our results lead us to affirm that Obama attempts to convince the public through personal details so that the targeted population can see themselves in a similar situation (basically with the idea that if he could do it, they can do it too). For example: "She [Astrid] was brought here as a little girl, and grew up believing in America and in her identity as an American, just like Malia or Sasha" (2014, November 21). His rhetoric develops the strategy of *pathos* in the same direction as *logos*. Both approaches are surrounded by his persona (*ethos*), which in Obama's case is more robust than in Biden's because it is composed not only of the political image but also of the personal one. The targeted receiver gets to the latter image thanks to the literary language used by the orator and the frequent use of personal linguistic devices such as personification, metonymy, conceptual metaphors, and the concept of identity and common sense:

> And part of what makes America exceptional is that we welcome exceptional people like Astrid. It makes us stronger. It makes us vibrant and dynamic. It makes us hopeful. We are a nation of immigrants, and that means that we're constantly being replenished with strivers who believe in the American Dream. And it gives us a tremendous advantage over other nations. It makes us entre-preneurial. It continues the promise that here in America, you can make it if you try, regardless of where you come from, regardless of the circumstances of your birth.
>
> *Obama 2014, November 21*

On the other hand, Biden exemplifies the perfect model of contraposition, because he compares the country between the two distinct rival lines of Democrats vs. Republicans, emphasizing the acts and performances of his rival, Trump, whom he sees as the opposite of what the President of the nation should be: "It was a tragedy that shot a direct line between Trump and the crusade of his policies to unleash hate and fear against the Latino community" (2020, July 29). Whereas Obama uses the personal tone so that the potential receiver gets closer to the political scenario and can see himself individually in the speech – "[...] the humanity of students like my father who came to America in search of a dream" (2007, May 23) – Biden talks more widely about the entire popula-tion and the whole of the Democratic stance and the Republican (Trump's) stance as two very differentiated schemes of government. He draws a line between the Republicans and Trump, who seems to be isolated as one individual separated from the group following Biden's pragmatic devices: "Then I worked with a Republican Congress to approve a $750 million aid package to help support those reforms" vs. "Trump announced an end to our aid – to Central America – via tweet, with no understanding of the consequences" (2019, July 11). From this cognitional context, *logos* is demonstrated using figures and numbers to show his speech's logical pieces of evidence. He underlines the differences between his government project and that of the Republicans, reflecting on the *ethos* of Trump to highlight the strength of his statements. From this point of view, one could argue that Biden's argumentation and functional *ethos* are shown over the speech as the counterperson of Trump. His logical scheme pattern is to show "what must be done," something that the receiver infers by valuing what the Other (in his speech, Trump) is not doing or has not done so far. He indicates:

> I'm going to do what the Justice Department says should be done, should be done and not politicize it. It's the most dangerous thing that's happened so far is the politicization of the Department of Justice. It's become the Department of Trump and that's wrong.
>
> *2020, September 23*

Finally, *pathos* is used through compassion, love, and emotion; and *ethos* is personified in the image of the Democratic stance, not his personal one. There are several examples of his identity in his speeches, but the major spectrum of his words is based on affirmations that he claims on behalf of the party he is representing. His language is descriptive, comparative, exemplificative, inclusive, metaphorical, effective, plain, empathic, and sometimes repetitive when his goal is to make a statement utterly clear to the potential audience:

> And I think we have to do it, but only one way to do it. We've got to show up and vote. But I believe the American people are not going to be turned off. I believe no matter what the administration does to try to make it hard to vote for everyone, not just people of color, but everyone, no matter what, I think they're going to vote.
>
> *Biden 2020, September 23*

We can observe several differences in the way the two politicians talk about immigration and the solutions that the government could offer to win the presidency. This qualitative study has come to the following conclusions regarding the Democratic persuasive language in their political campaigns:

(A) **Ethos:** With regards to the *ethos* (Charaudeau 2005), Democrats perform the *ethos* related to sincerity (through credibility), performativity (promises for the future), virtue (what must be done), competence (discourse feedback justified by facts and not only by words), and commitment (policies welcoming immigrants).

(B) **Logos:** Following Charaudeau's (2006) argumentative techniques, the defense of immigration from the Democrats' stance has to do with drafting new policies in its favor through reasons connected to economic improvement and the welfare state. Democrats tend to identify the American people with the concept of liberty since it is a nation created from thousands of waves of immigrants that had to abandon their countries of residence to flee from war or persecution ("We are a nation of immigrants, and we must respect that shared history as this debate moves forward," Obama 2007, May 23; "We have to be honest about our friends that are falling short and forge a common agenda for action to address the greatest threats to our shared values," Biden 2019, July 11). Leading on from this analogy to the past, Democrats describe Americans essentially as one nation which searches for integrity, inclusion, and freedom. In this freedom, acceptance of immigration is born (techniques of essentialization and singularization). The problem presented to the audience arises from whether the government should implicate the whole country in such matters. Democrat leaders underline the importance of taking a leading role in immigration matters, taking care of immigrants, and providing the audience with information related to economic results. They also include humanitarian reasons such as the fact that the immigrants are just like Americans in the past (leading back to the analogy mentioned above) and they must help those in need. This does not mean that they are not aware of some immigrants' dangers to the civil population. Obama indicates, "I am not saying that illegal entry should go unpunished" (Obama 2007, May 23); "[...] we'll keep focusing enforcement resources on actual threats to our security. But that means felons, not families" (Obama 2014, November 21).

(C) ***Pathos:*** Democrats prefer to get to the people's hearts to persuade them of the statement that the orator is claiming, and that is why the element of *pathos* is as much developed as the message conveyed in argumentative statements, or even more. Obama has been demonstrated to foster these resources much more than Biden. Having enumerated the number of persuasive devices used in the speeches analyzed, this study has intended to prove that the most extensive devices to spark persuasion are the following: repetition; an exaltation of common values; use of modal markers; the importance of belonging; rhetoric and literary resources such as metaphor, metonymy, and personification; the enumeration of different topics (history and culture of the nation, the picture of the good citizen, the American dream, etc.); fear; the reference to famous characters who are essential to the American population and history; the presence of God; the allusion to the origins of the country; and dramatic statements referring to the Other, amongst others.

Democrat leaders are conscious of the power of words and the sensibility that the immigration topic arouses in the population; that is why their rhetoric strategies are more focused on the potential receiver than on the main population. They use metaphor to get closer to this audience and to make the information easily understood, but also to implement the use of persuasion (*pathos*) through personal stories and other literary techniques such as comparisons (self-other) that are linked to the image of the orator (*ethos*) and the logical arguments that eventually convince the audience to vote in their favor. We can see examples of this function when they include metaphors about war, health, leadership, strength, etc. The three elements of Aristotelian rhetoric are unanimously united through the speaker selection. The results regarding the issue studied (migration) and the context are convincing and reasonable from a persuasive point of view. Democrats rely on the positive representation of the self against the negative picture of the Other, underlining the differentiation between, in terms of Van Dijk (1995), the ingroup (We) and the outgroup (the Other, him being Trump in the case of Biden: "[Trump is] Dangerously incompetent and incapable of leadership," 2019, July 11).

To sum up, we hope that this study can shed some light on the issues of immigration and other problems related to migration in the context of American elections, when the votes of the newcomers are of great significance and when words, apart from facts, have a real influence on the potential population whose lives depend on the policies of the government. The Democratic discourse on immigration provides notable examples of an *ethos* committed to immigrants, a discursive *logos* based on factual facts, and a *pathos* potentially aimed at persuasion through mechanisms of inclusion (the immigrant as a member of the group, the group being the American nation, historically built up through thousands of generations of immigrants).

References
English-Language References

Ahmed, H. R., and Amir, S. (2021). Speech Act Analysis of Joseph R. Biden, Jr.'s Inaugural Address on January 20, 2021 as the 46th President of the USA (February 6, 2021). *Electronic Research Journal of Social Sciences and Humanities*, *3*(I), 43–55. Available at https://ssrn.com/abstract=3780457

Bowker, L., and Pearson. J. (2002). *Working with Specialized Language: A Practical Guide to Using Corpora.* London: Routledge.

Fernández Ulloa, T., and López Ruiz, M. del C. (2022). Immigration in Barack Obama's and Joe Biden's Campaign Discourses: Rhetorical Analysis. *EID&A*, *22*(1), 103–124.

Junaidi, S. T. (2019). Who Are Americans? Analysis of Obama and Trump's Political Speeches on Immigration. *CELTIC: A Journal of Culture, English Language Teaching, Literature & Linguistics*, *6*(2), 73–87. Available at https://ejournal.umm.ac.id/index.php/celtic/article/view/9947/pdf

Lesz, B. (2011). *To Shape the World for the Better: An Analysis of Metaphors in the Speeches of Barack Obama.* Tromsø, Norway: University of Tromsø. Available at https://munin.uit.no/bitstream/handle/10037/3540/thesis.pdf?sequence=1&isAllowed=y

López Cirugeda, I., and Sánchez Ruiz, R. (2013). Persuasive Rhetoric in Barack Obama's Immigration Speech: Pre- and Post-Electoral Strategies. *Camino Real*, *5*(8), 81–99. Available at https://ebuah.uah.es/xmlui/bitstream/handle/10017/19993/persuasive_Cirugeda_CR_2013_N8.pdf?sequence=1&isAllowed=y

Pedrini, P. P. (2021). Joe Biden's Inauguration Speech: A Persuasive Narrative. *Global Journal of Human-Science*, *21*(4), 13–18. Available at https://globaljournals.org/GJHSS_Volume21/2-Joe-Bidens-Inauguration-Speech.pdf

President Obama's Immigration Accountability Executive Actions (n.d.). *Ballotpedia*. Available at https://ballotpedia.org/President_Obama%27s_Immigration_Accountability_Executive_Actions

Read Joe Biden's Full Inaugural Address: "End This Uncivil War" (2021, January 20). *ABC News*. https://abcnews.go.com/Politics/read-joe-bidens-full-inaugural-address-end-uncivil/story?id=75351694

Sayegh, K., and Nabifar, N. (2012). Power in Political Discourse of Barack Obama. *Journal of Basic and Applied Scientific Research*, *2*(4), 3481–3491. Available at www.textroad.com/pdf/JBASR/J.%20Basic.%20Appl.%20Sci.%20Res.,%202(4)3481-3491,%202012.pdf

U.S. Border Patrol (n.d.). U.S. Border Patrol Total Apprehensions (F.Y. 1925 – F.Y. 2020). Available at www.cbp.gov/sites/default/files/assets/documents/2021-Aug/U.S.%20Border%20Patrol%20Total%20Apprehensions%20%28FY%201925%20-%20FY%202020%29%20%28508%29.pdf

Van Dijk, T. A. (1995). Ideological Discourse Analysis. *New Courant*, *4*, 135–161. Available at www.discourses.org/OldArticles/Ideological%20discourse%20analysis.pdf

Van Dijk, T. A. (1998). *Ideology: A Multidisciplinary Approach.* London: Sage Publications.

Wang, J. (2010). A Critical Discourse Analysis of Barack Obama's Speeches. *Journal of Language, Teaching and Research*, *1*(3), 254–261. Available at www.academypublication.com/issues/past/jltr/vol01/03/12.pdf

Zheng, T. (2000). Characteristics of Australian Political Language Rhetoric: Tactics of Gaining Public Support and Shrinking Responsibility. *Journal of Intercultural Communication*, *4*. Available at www.immi.se/intercultural/nr4/zheng.htm

Other-Language References

Aristotle. (2017) [IV b. C.]. *Retórica*. Barcelona: Plutón Ediciones.
Charaudeau, P. (2005). *Le discours politique. Les masques du pouvoir*. Paris: Vuivert.
Charaudeau, P. (2006). *El discurso político*. San Pablo: Contexto.
Charaudeau, P. (2009). La argumentación persuasiva. El ejemplo del discurso político. In M. Shiro et al., *Haciendo discurso. Homenaje a Adriana Bolívar*. Caracas: Facultad de Humanidades y Educación. Universidad Central de Venezuela (pp. 277–295).
Requeijo Rey, P. (2010). El estilo de comunicar de Obama. *Cuadernos de Información y Comunicación, 15*, 263–285.
Searle, J. (1980) [1969]. *Actos de habla*. Madrid: Cátedra.

Discourses

Biden, J. (2019, July 11). Remarks as Prepared for Delivery by Vice President Joe Biden in New York City, New York. *Democracy in Action*. Available at www.democracyinaction.us/2020/biden/bidenpolicy071119foreignpolicy.html
Biden, J. (2020, July 28). Joe Biden Racial Equity Plan Speech Transcript. *Rev.* Available at www.rev.com/blog/transcripts/joe-biden-racial-equity-plan-speech-transcript-july-28
Biden, J. (2020, July 29). Joe Biden speaks with UnidosUS Action Fund Transcript. *Rev.* Available at www.rev.com/blog/transcripts/joe-biden-speaks-with-unidosus-action-fund-online-event-transcript-july-29
Biden, J. (2020, September 23). Joe Biden Racial Equity Discussion. *Rev.* Available at www.rev.com/blog/transcripts/joe-biden-racial-equity-discussion-transcript-september-23
Biden, J., and Obama, B. (2020, July 23). Joe Biden Campaign Video with Barack Obama Transcript. *Rev.* Available at www.rev.com/blog/transcripts/joe-biden-campaign-video-transcript-july-23
Obama, B. (2007, May 23). Barack Obama's Remarks at Senate Floor Speech on Comprehensive Immigration Reform. *American Rhetoric.* Available at www.americanrhetoric.com/speeches/PDFFiles/Barack%20Obama%20-%20Senate%20Floor%20Immigration%20Reform.pdf
Obama, B. (2013, January 29). President Obama's Remarks on Immigration Reform. *The New York Times.* Available at www.nytimes.com/2013/01/30/us/politics/full-transcript-of-president-obamas-remarks-on-immigration-reform.html
Obama, B. (2014, November 20). Remarks by the President in Address to the Nation on Immigration. *Obama White House Archives.* Available at https://obamawhitehouse.archives.gov/issues/immigration/immigration-action#
Obama, B. (2014, November 21). Remarks by the President on Immigration (Del Sol High School, Las Vegas, Nevada). *Obama White House Archives.* Available at https://obamawhitehouse.archives.gov/the-press-office/2014/11/21/remarks-president-immigration

12

POLITICAL RHETORIC IN JONATHAN SWIFT'S *CONDUCT OF THE ALLIES*

Boosting and Hedging as Persuasive Devices

Rosa María López-Campillo

Introduction

Persuasion, as an interactive communicative process in which an addresser aims to influence the beliefs, attitudes, and behavior of the addressee, plays a prominent part in political rhetoric. Persuasion and political discourse are, indeed, closely connected. According to Partington (2001: 116), "Politics is persuasion, and persuasion is conducted predominantly through language." The strategic choice and combination of various linguistic devices is essential to attain effective overall persuasiveness. As the overlapping of different rhetorical strategies creates a powerful interplay that ensures persuasive political communication, it is often necessary to isolate them for the sole purpose of analyzing their efficiency as communication strategies (Charteris-Black 2011: 9). A very influential political writer during the last years of the reign of Anne Stuart (1710–1714), Swift resorted to a variety of linguistic means to attain persuasion (Müllenbrock 1997). The main concern of this chapter is to explore two of the main rhetorical devices employed by Jonathan Swift: boosting and hedging. These communicative strategies were used by the author to emphasize or soften respectively the strength of the propositional information provided (Holmes 1984). By resorting to these linguistic expressions of certainty and doubt, he would manage to manipulate the political message sent to his readers at will by reducing or increasing the force of his statements. Learning how he managed to become such an effective propagandist at a time when the press was used – though not officially acknowledged – as an organ of political influence, and printed materials were used to spread ideas and shape public opinion (Barker 2000), is the main aim of this study. To this end, I will analyze both persuasive devices in *The Conduct of the Allies and of the Late Ministry, in Beginning and Carrying on the Present War* (1711), a "wonder-working pamphlet" (Foot 1984: 293) believed to have acted as a catalyzer for the termination of the War of the Spanish Succession during the government's peace campaign. As a classical eighteenth-century British author, Swift is known to have masterfully used pathos,

178

DOI: 10.4324/9781003195276-16

ethos, and logos in his political works. However, there seems to have been no attempt so far to analyze Swift's production in the light of current different sociolinguistic theories within the tradition of Critical Discourse Analysis (henceforth CDA). By applying contemporary linguistic theories to his work, such as Fairclough's social-theoretical approach to discourse within the tradition of Critical Discourse Analysis (1992) and face theory as developed by Brown and Levinson (1987), we will surely deepen our knowledge on the writer's expertise as a political polemicist and propagandist.

Prior to analyzing the different purposes for which Swift resorted to the boosting and hedging devices in *The Conduct of the Allies*, I will briefly contextualize the issue debated, introduce Jonathan Swift as a political writer, and then present the linguistic theoretical frameworks and methodology employed. A summary of the conclusions reached in addition to some final remarks will close the present research essay.

The Sociopolitical Context: Jonathan Swift as a Political Writer

In no previous stage in British history had party politics been conducted with such intensity and clarity as in the reign of Anne Stuart (1702–1714). The party conflict between Whigs and Tories, which had been emerging in England since 1660 and had led to the clash during the Exclusion Crisis, continued to develop after the Glorious Revolution, and reached a new height of intensity in the reign of Queen Anne (Harris 1993: 169). This period was to witness an upsurge of old struggles and an increasing polarization along political and religious lines both in Parliament and society in general. At the time there were two main sources of political tension: a constitutional one, centering around the powers of the Crown and the executive and the growing strength of Parliament and the people; and a religious one, which confronted Anglicans and Dissenters (Harris 1993: 53). Other sources of contention were the problem of the British Protestant Succession and the Union of England and Scotland, to which would be added a further major issue: the intervention of Britain in the War of the Spanish Succession (1702–1713). No other issue generated such heated public debate as the controversy over the termination of Queen Anne's war, except for the English Civil Wars and Interregnum. According to Müllenbrock (1997: 11), this "was the first example in England of a public debate of a great national issue with full media participation", where "aspects of foreign, military, domestic and social policy combined to form a set of complex issues of the utmost significance". Each of them might have been solved by different alternative routes. Articulating those options and deciding the most suitable ones foreseeably produced heated debate not only at Westminster but beyond parliamentary walls, attracting a wide range of writers, from Grub Street hacks to literary figures of the stature of Jonathan Swift, who would put his pen at the service of the Tory ministry.

Whigs and Tories held opposing ideological views and interests, which made political strife extremely intense as party divisions permeated society. Many of the government's decisions had a direct impact on the lives of a significant proportion of the population, with the result that people became politicized, at least to some degree. All levels of English society were caught up in the rage of party, from the gentry, to the mercantile and professional classes, right down to the mob. They often had the chance to give expression to their political feelings through petitions, demonstrations, riots and, for those with the right to vote, at the polls (Harris 1993: 202). Particularly important was the role of general elections in feeding party conflict at the time. Owing to the Triennial Act (1694), which guaranteed new Parliaments every three years, up to five general elections were held in Anne's reign, which fueled continual political confrontation because of the shifting patterns of popular allegiance. Although most could be identified either as Tories or Whigs, there was still a significant number of undecided voters who could be persuaded to join with either party if they could be convinced that a vital interest was endangered. And although only around a quarter of adult males had the right to vote at the time, contested elections often involved the unenfranchised in their turbulence and partisanship (Speck 1994: 1–3).

Equally relevant was the expiry of the Licensing Act in 1695, which meant the end of state censorship and brought the publication of an avalanche of political literature, a phenomenon that marked a shift in English print culture. Particularly relevant was the rapid emergence of new periodicals, which allowed the spread of constant and regular information on political developments, compared to books or tracts. Neither would the influence of the press be limited to the metropolitan area – it also extended at the end of this period to different provinces so that political propaganda could also have an impact and influence on the nation at large. According to Harris (1993: 20), even without a licensing Act it was still possible to regulate the press through the common law of seditious libel. However, administrations found it better to counter an opposition press with their own pro-government propaganda, a tactic which – although quite successful – inevitably increased the intensity of public political debate.

As early as the beginning of the eighteenth century, both government and opposition alike realized that public opinion had become a significant element of political life. A breakthrough occurred when experienced politicians deliberately appealed to public opinion to test the popularity of their views and justify their actions. This was the case of Robert Harley, a very influential politician who pulled the strings from the ministry and set up the government propaganda machinery, including press dissemination and an intelligence network, to fulfill his designs (Downie 1979: 69). Harley would plan the birth of different pro-government publications and periodicals such as *The Review* and *The Examiner* and hire the services of the most skillful writers available, from Grub Street scribblers to renowned authors such as Jonathan Swift, Daniel Defoe, and Arthur Maynwaring. Both political parties would "hire their services and finance the publication of numerous pamphlets, essays, newspapers and broadsides to defend their policies and remain in power, especially of those who excelled in rhetorical skill and could play the game as persuasive propagandists" (López-Campillo 2018). Harley's systematic use of propaganda shows his perceived necessity of seeking public approval, a characteristic that was to become a permanent feature in party politics from then on.

Jonathan Swift was a Whig by birth, education, and political principle, but also unwaveringly loyal to the conservative Church of England. Like other prominent political writers such as Defoe or Maynwaring, he was productive in several genres and changed party at some time in his life, which confirms a certain fluctuation in political allegiance at the time. Fortunately, Swift's everyday experiences, thoughts, and reactions were recorded in his *Journal to Stella* (1776), a series of letters posthumously published and written between his arrival in England in 1710 and 1713, which he mostly addressed to his intimate friend, Esther Johnson. This inestimable work is an excellent source to become acquainted with "the story of Swift's growing intimacy with the Tory leaders, of the success of his mission, of the increasing coolness towards older acquaintances, and of his services to the Government" (Aitken (ed.) 1901: xvii). Another inestimable source of information is his publication, *The History of the Last Four Years of the Queen* (1758), which describes the political ins and outs from 1710 up to the signing of the Peace Treaty of Utrecht. These primary sources together with some contemporary publications and secondary historiographical sources have allowed the contextualization of the debate and proper interpretation of the pamphlet analyzed.

According to the information gathered, it is manifest that a momentous period began for Swift in 1710, when the Tory ministry headed by Robert Harley and Henry St. John was replacing the late Whig government. The new administration, determined to bring hostilities with France to an end, was also assuming a more protective attitude toward the Anglican Church. After cleverly making overtures to Swift, Harley managed to recruit Swift, who quickly became the Tories' chief pamphleteer and political writer. By the end of October 1710, he had taken over *The Examiner*, a Tory journal whose straightforward aim was polarization and to which he contributed essays until 14 June 1711. Commissioned by Harley, he then began to prepare *The Conduct*, which appeared on 27 November 1711, some weeks before the motion in favor of a peace was finally approved in Parliament. The turning-point debate was initiated with the publication of this pamphlet, which sold prodigiously according to contemporary records and the author's own estimation (Jackson 2015: 143–144). It became a platform from which all genres were effectively coordinated to foster growing antagonism against the former ministry, Marlborough's circle and the allies.

Theoretical Framework, Data, and Methods

Political discourse is concerned with exercising power to control other people's beliefs, thoughts, and behavior and is, therefore, purpose-oriented, deliberately constructed with particular goals in mind (Crespo-Fernández 2018: 789–790). As a form of public communication, its primary motivation is to strategically achieve certain instrumental goals whose attainment is expected to benefit those who are behind the production of the message (Fairclough 1989). Consequently, its study must combine the description of the linguistic forms and the functions that these forms are intended to serve in the social contexts where they occur (Paltridge 2012). Whether social and political judgments or analysis of linguistic forms come first, "political discourse is made up of, and must allow for, both" (Wilson 2001: 411). As CDA is concerned with the discursive construction of social and political knowledge as well as with how power, manipulation, and ideology are asserted through language in public discourse, this is the theoretical framework into which our study is embedded (Fairclough and Wodak 1997; Fairclough 2005; Wodak 2009; Krzyzanowsi and Forchtner 2016). I will specifically draw on Fairclough's (1992, 1995) social-theoretical approach to discourse. This scholar offers a three-dimensional model of discourse, i.e., discourse as a piece of text, discourse as an instance of discursive practice, and discourse as an instance of social practice, which I find especially useful to explore how the relationship between discursive practices and the social and cultural context contributes to securing power and hegemony. These three interrelated dimensions will require a different but mutually explanatory kind of analysis (Janks 2006: 329).

From this perspective, Swift's pamphlet is conceived as a form of social and political action which performs a range of communicative functions such as legitimizing power, exerting social control, and eventually influencing the readership's behavior. Following van Dijk (2006), we assume that its study should not be limited to the structural properties of text or talk itself, but also include a systematic account of the relations between the political context and discursive structures. An account of the boosting and hedging structures and strategies in our case must necessarily be politically contextualized to find out whether "they effectively emphasize or de-emphasize political attitudes and opinions, garner support, manipulate public opinion, manufacture political consent, or legitimate political power" (van Dijk 1997: 25). It follows that a critical analysis of these persuasive linguistic devices will allow insight into the way political power and persuasion were enforced in early eighteenth-century Britain.

The present study is also embedded in Brown and Levinson's (1987) politeness theory. This theory draws heavily upon Goffman's (1955) notion of face, i.e., the positive public image we seek to establish in social interactions. To maintain harmony in interactions and portray a positive image of ourselves to others, when expressing a communicative goal, the addresser must choose the right words in order to prevent potential conflict and save face. Brown and Levinson distinguished between two coexisting and complementary dimensions of face: positive face, i.e., "the desire (in some respects) to be approved of"; and negative face, i.e., "the desire to be unimpeded in some actions". These authors suggest that when we are rude to people, or we apologize, we commit face-threatening acts directed at the person we are talking to, or directed at ourselves, respectively. In order to maintain face and avoid conflict and feelings of embarrassment, speakers resort to politeness strategies, namely bald on-record, off-record, positive politeness and negative politeness (see Brown and Levinson 1987, for a full account). From this point of view, hedging and boosting devices are tied to conventions of politeness and tact through the notion of face.

The corpus studied consists of a single pamphlet entitled *The Conduct of the Allies* produced by Jonathan Swift and published in 1712 as a piece of political propaganda elaborated to prepare the English nation for a peace that was being secretly negotiated and justify the treacherous and ignominious proceedings of the Tory ministry then in office. The choice of *The Conduct* as the source of data for the present research is not random: this pamphlet has been, and is still, regarded as one of the most influential political works in the history of British literature. It is, therefore, a piece of political discourse that deserves an in-depth linguistic analysis to determine why it was such an efficient and persuasive piece of propaganda. The study of the hedging and boosting devices employed will no doubt help to gain a clear insight into how Swift managed to move hearts and shape belief.

As for the linguistic research method employed, considering *The Conduct* as a text with a sociopolitical purpose (Fairclough 1992: 138), I start from a micro-level, relating relevant boosting and hedging linguistic patterns in Swift's pamphlet to strategic political behavior and analyzing the functions both devices perform in discourse. In other words, I have basically followed a "bottom-up" approach to analyze and interpret the use of boosting and hedging in the pamphlet. Although the type of research carried out has been basically qualitative, quantification of the linguistic means employed has also shed some light on the relative frequency of both strategies, the main linguistic devices utilized in each case, and their significance as persuasive devices. As there is a wide range of boosting and hedging resources present in the text, they were initially classified according to their linguistic nature and then contextually analyzed to determine their pragmatic functions. However, to identify most attenuation and reinforcement markers, a detailed analysis and manual classification of boosters and hedges has been conducted taking necessarily into consideration both the linguistic and the sociopolitical context for their interpretation and explanation.

It is important to say that I have not followed any taxonomy put forward by other authors, as there is not any that responds to the singular characteristics of our corpus.

There is a wide range of linguistic means that may be used as hedges or boosters, as can be seen in many studies where the taxonomies suggested do not necessarily coincide (Salager-Meyer 1995; Wilanová 2005; Fraser 1996, 2010, among others). At the same time, while there is no limit to the number of linguistic expressions that can be regarded as attenuators or emphasizers, neither are there clear-cut lists of hedging or boosting expressions possible. On the other hand, "no linguistic items are inherently hedges but can acquire this quality depending on the communicative context or the co-text" (Clemen 1997: 6). In fact, the prototypical linguistic forms for attenuation do not always carry a hedging nuance (Salager-Meyer 1994: 152). The same occurs in the case of boosters. Appropriate interpretation in any case depends on a rigorous contextual analysis. Thus, for instance, in (1) "I doubt" does not have an intentional tentative stance but rather functions as a booster or intensifier instead. Conversely, in (2), the use of the alternative conjunction "or" does not intend to express tentativeness or uncertainty but emphasizes the seemingly endless length of time necessary for British economic recovery, to level an attack against the unnecessary prolongation of the war.

(1) Another point, which I doubt those have not considered who are against any peace without Spain, is that the face of affairs in Christendom, since the emperor's death, has been very much changed.

The Conduct: 74

(2) Towards clearing ourselves of this monstrous incumbrance, some of these annuities will expire or pay off the principal in thirty, forty, or a hundred years.

The Conduct: 80

As already mentioned, this study is primarily embedded in Brown and Levinson's (1987) politeness theory, because of its relevance particularly in attenuation, and Fairclough's (1992) social-theoretical sense of discourse. Apart from this, and more specifically, I have also looked at different taxonomies of boosters and hedges carried out by such authors as Fraser, Hyland, Urbanová, and Salager-Mayer in order to have a more comprehensive understanding of the subject at hand.

Analysis: Boosting and Hedging

For political discourse to be persuasive, arguments must be presented credibly and convincingly. To attain this aim, the writer needs to take special care in the way he supports his claims, represents himself, and engages the readership. These goals can be attained through different linguistic and rhetorical features, very notably through boosting and hedging, which will be dealt with separately for the sake of clarity. It must be borne in mind though that it is quite awkward to find just hedging or boosting devices being used exclusively in academic and political discourse. As we will see in the course of the analysis, what is typically found instead is the coexistence of accentuation and attenuation markers. In fact, according to Charteris-Black (2011: 9), it is the inter-twining of a varied range of rhetorical features which creates a powerful interplay that contributes to ensure persuasive efficiency as it helps conceal the contribution of any single stratagem.

Hedges and boosters may also be used for purposes that do not have to do with attenuation or reinforcement, respectively. There are instances in the corpus where they contribute to giving either an ironical twist to an utterance, as in (3), or a sarcastic nuance, as in (4).

(3) The person who brought over the articles said in all companies (and _perhaps believed_) that it was a pity we had not demanded more, for the French were in a disposition to refuse us nothing we would ask.

The Conduct: 73

(4) By what motives or what management we are thus become the dupes and bubbles of Europe? _Surely_ it _cannot_ be owing to the stupidity arising from the coldness of our climate, since those among our allies, who have given us _most_ reason to complain are as far removed from the sun as ourselves.

The Conduct: 58

Let us now consider the different pragmatic functions boosters fulfill in our corpus.

Boosting

Boosters are used in the pamphlet for different rhetorical and pragmatic purposes. According to their relationship to discourse meaning, they may be content-oriented, speaker-oriented, or hearer-oriented strengthening devices. Content-oriented boosters allow the creation of a structurally and communicatively well-organized and coherent text. Discourse organization is in fact the most frequent function performed by boosters in our corpus. These accentuation markers, while serving the purpose of emphasizing specific items within an utterance, have primarily a textual and cohesive function. By making concrete parts of the utterance more prominent than others, the message becomes more clearly structured and therefore more accessible to addressees. Discourse-oriented emphasizers like the ones underlined in examples (5) to (10) make it easier for readers to know how information has been organized in the text and what information to concentrate on, which aids and enhances comprehension. In example (5), Swift uses ordinal adverbs "first/secondly/lastly" to enumerate and indicate the sequence in which the three reasons that make up the discourse unit will be presented. By signaling the order in which discursive units are presented by the addresser, they contribute to their coherence. At the same time, by underlining explicitly each of the claims made, the writer will better manage to draw the readers' attention to the arguments provided to criticize British participation in the war, the ministry's mistaken war policy, and the disloyal and ungrateful conduct of England's allies:

(5) This will be manifest by proving the three following points:

First, that against all manner of prudence or common reason, we engaged in this war as principals, when we ought to have acted only as auxiliaries.
Secondly, that we spent all our vigor in pursuing that part of the war which could least answer the end we proposed by beginning it (…).
Lastly, that we suffered each of our allies to break every article in those treaties and agreements by which they were bound, and to lay the burden upon us.

The Conduct: 20–21

Political Rhetoric in Jonathan Swift

These textual devices, which help the writer communicate his claims more effectively with the target audience, can perform a variety of functions within discourse. According to Hyland and Tse (2004: 169), the functions performed by these so-called "interactive resources" are the following:

(a) Transitions, which express semantic relations between main clauses, e.g.

(6) <u>Thus</u>, we became principal in a war in conjunction with two allies, whose share in the quarrel was beyond all proportion greater than ours.

The Conduct: 24

(b) Frame markers, which refer to discourse acts, sequences, or stages, e.g.

(7) <u>Let me now consider</u> in what manner our allies have observed those treaties they made with us, and the several stipulations and agreements pursuant to them.

The Conduct: 41

(c) Endophoric markers, which pertain to information in other parts of the text, e.g.

(8) In order to carry it on with great vigor, a grand alliance formed, wherein the ends proposed to be obtained are plainly and distinctly laid down <u>as I have already quoted.</u>

The Conduct: 70

(d) Evidentials, which grammatically mark a speaker's evidence or information source, e.g.

(9) <u>Everybody knows</u> that our land and malt tax amount annually to about two millions and a half.

The Conduct: 79

(e) Code glosses, which are used to elaborate on what has just been said by the writer either through reformulation or exemplification (Hyland 2007), e.g.

(10) No wonder, then, if the general cry in all such meetings be against any peace, either with Spain or without, which <u>in other words</u> is no more than this, that discontented men desire another change of ministry.

The Conduct: 79

Writers must not only present the propositional content effectively but need to explicitly manage their own performance of "self" and establish the presence of the readers in the discourse. Pronouns play a key role in the construction of "self" and "others", which is not an objective representation of facts but a version of reality that politicians construct discursively through different linguistic devices. They exploit the flexibility of pronominal reference to construct these different identities and use pronouns to show affiliation or create distance between them. Pronominal choices between "I", "you", "we", and "they" clearly indicate the perspective from which statements should be interpreted and help distinguish the writer's own identity and position from those of others. In political language, the use of pronouns is essential as they fulfill legitimizing strategic functions by granting authority to the speaker and promoting positive self-presentation (Chilton 2004: 37).

Subjectivity constitutes a major persuasive device in political discourse. The unifying semantic feature of boosters is a high degree of subjectivity. When writing or speaking, the addresser needs to express his own standpoint and evaluation in contrast to his political opponents' views. To establish the writer's stance or authorial identity, particularly useful is the use of self-mentions, most frequently rendered by employing first person "I", as well as related forms "me", "mine", "my", or "myself", as opposed to reader pronouns, used to express engagement with the addressees. By marking your views with the first person, you leave readers in no doubt of your stance while claiming credit for what you are saying (Hyland 2007). As we can see in (11), the pronoun "I" becomes a powerful means employed by the writer from the very beginning to emphasize his role and assume responsibility for the judgments or opinions voiced:

(11) I cannot sufficiently admire the industry of a sort of men, wholly out of favor with the prince and people (…) I lay it down for a maxim that no reasonable man (…) can be of the opinion for continuing the war upon the footing it now is.

The Conduct: 4

(12) For my own part, when I saw this false credit sink upon the change of the ministry, I was singular enough to conceive it a good omen.

The Conduct: 82–83

With few exceptions, such as "for my own part" in (12), the author will continually resort to the pronominal first person "I" to construct an authorial self. By emphasizing his personal stance and assuming responsibility for his statements rather than disguising his own opinion to the audience, his claims sound straightforward and therefore truthful and convincing. Assertion of his authority is strengthened using common epistemic boosting verbs accompanying first person "I" such as "know" or "say" in (13) and (14).

(13) (…) if any one should ask why our general continued so easy to the last, I know no other way probable, or indeed so charitable, to account for it, as by that unmeasurable love of wealth which his best friends allow to be his predominant passion.

The Conduct: 60

(14) I say that these very people, without giving themselves time to breathe, should again enter into a more dangerous, chargeable, and extensive war, for the same or perhaps a greater period of time, and without any apparent necessity.

The Conduct: 25

As is characteristic in political discourse, Swift will resort to first person plural pronominal forms as well, to reflect his standpoint and foster engagement with the readership, enhancing persuasion as a result. The use of "we", "our", and "us" in (15) will allow him to involve the audience in what he is saying. Through this linguistic device he will not only attribute his views to himself but to his addressees as well, to "set up an 'in-group' of like-minded people to which the [audience] is positioned as belonging, and thus to construct consensus" (Hunston 2000: 191). As can be seen below, the use of first person plural forms will slightly downplay his authoritative personal role by bringing in the reader, but the anti-war stance reflected is no less assertive:

(15) As to the war, <u>our</u> grievances are, that a greater load has been laid on <u>us</u> than was either just or necessary, or than <u>we</u> have been able to bear; that the grossest impositions have been submitted to, for the advancement of private wealth and power (...) and that the part of the war which was chiefly <u>our</u> province, which would have been most beneficial to <u>us</u> and destructive to the enemy, was wholly neglected.

The Conduct: 4

On the other hand, the writer's opponents or "others" are referred to with third person pronominal forms such as "they" or demonstrative "those" to show detachment and strategically enhance polarization between the late Whig-biased ministry and moneyed men versus the present Tory-based ministry and landed men:

(16) <u>Those</u> who, either by writing or discourse, have undertaken to defend the proceedings of the late ministry (...) have spent time in celebrating the conduct and valor of our leaders and their troops, in summing up the victories <u>they</u> have gained and the towns <u>they</u> have taken. Then <u>they</u> tell us what high articles were insisted on by our ministers and those of the confederates, and what pains both were at in persuading France to accept them.

The Conduct: 4

Very interestingly, and exceptionally, as in (17), the readership or "public" is initially referred to with pronominal forms "they", "themselves", and "their" instead of third person "we" to distance himself from his in-group when referring to the people in the nation who, unlike himself, have been deluded by the late ministry:

(17) I think it highly necessary that <u>the public</u> should be freely and impartially told what circumstances <u>they</u> are in, after what manner <u>they</u> have been treated by those whom <u>they</u> trusted so many years with the disposal of their blood and treasure, and what the consequences of this management are likely to be upon <u>themselves</u> and <u>their</u> posterity.

The Conduct: 4

This device will allow the author to stress a credible authorial identity and legitimize his purpose of "opening the eyes of the nation". He will construct a favorable image of himself, enhancing truthfulness and reliability through attitudinal adverbs and adjectives such as "freely" and "impartially".

To defend his postulates, Swift will quite frequently also resort to assurances, which are highly assertive speaker-oriented boosters used to express certainty and foster conviction (Urbanová 2000: 60). By expressing assurance, the writer intends to enhance the degree of certainty in his assertions and inspire confidence in the intended readers, although, as will be seen in the section on hedging, he will have to resort to attenuating devices to make his claims sound less absolute and save face before the audience. To firmly support his claims against the British allies and the prolongation of the war, Swift will employ a wide range of linguistic assurance boosters:

(18) It is true indeed, the danger of the Dutch by so ill a neighborhood in Flanders might affect us very much in the consequences of it.

The Conduct: 22

(19) If we do not hearken to a peace, others certainly will, and get the advantage of us there, as they have done in the war.

The Conduct: 84

(20) And as they increase their trade, it is obvious they will enlarge their strength at sea, and that ours must lessen in proportion.

The Conduct: 40

(21) It was at that time but too apparent that the inclinations of the Spaniards were on the duke's side.

The Conduct: 70

Maximizing/minimizing degree boosters are other types of speaker-oriented accentuation devices. They show the writer's attitude to a proposition by reinforcing a certain quality either positively or negatively (Kozubíková Sandová 2014: 96). These positive or negative evaluations are commonly rendered through adverbial expressions and/or superlatives:

(22) The last is what has been usually called *pro aris et focis*; where no expense or endeavour can be too great, because all we have is at stake, and consequently our utmost force to be exerted; and the dispute is soon determined either in safety or utter destruction.

The Conduct: 7

(23) In that published by the States they say very truly, that they are nearest and most exposed to the fire.

The Conduct: 14

Intensification can also be attained through emphatic linguistic devices. Emphasis may be expressed resorting to auxiliaries "do", "does", or "did", purposely used to add extra cogency to the illocutionary force of a proposition as in (24), sometimes reinforced by adding other emphasizers as in (25), or resorting to other boosting devices such as foregrounding as in (26).

(24) But the complaints made in our declaration do all, except the last, as much, or more, concern almost every prince in Europe.

The Conduct: 16

(25) The Dutch wars in the reign of king Charles II. (…) <u>did indeed</u> keep the king needy and poor by discontinuing or discontenting his parliament, when he most needed their assistance.

The Conduct: 11

(26) It is obvious (…) that whoever annually runs out, and continues the same expenses, must every year mortgage a greater quantity of land than he did before; and as the debt doubles and trebles upon him, <u>so does</u> his inability to pay it.

The Conduct: 25

Another linguistic resource contributing to stronger emphasis to the claims made by the writer is repetition. It is one of the rhetorical devices that Swift frequently relies on as a persuasive tool as it is quite an effective means of making a message memorable and believable without needing to add a logical support. This literary device, in which a word, phrase, or clause is repeated two or more times, following different possible patterns, may be used for diverse purposes. One of the most common reasons is to highlight the relevance of a message by purposely drawing the recipient's attention to particular parts of an utterance, as can be seen in (27) where the author criticizes the deceitful Whig justification to continue the wearying war based on England's opulence and supremacy through the repetition of "the + noun + of England" instead of employing the coordinated and less repetitive alternative, "the power, courage and exhaustible riches of England".

(27) When we offer to lament the heavy debts and poverty of the nation, it is pleasant to hear some men answer all that can be said by crying up <u>the power of England, the courage of England, the inexhaustible riches of England</u> (…) This is the style of men at ease, who lay heavy burdens upon others, which they would not touch with one of their fingers.

The Conduct: 88

One of the most powerful boosting devices frequently employed by Swift to give emphasis to his claims is rhetorical questions. These have the effect of a forceful statement intended to emphasize a particular point and convince an audience that the speaker has the right opinion (Halmari 2005: 116–117). Structured as either yes/no, alternative, or wh-questions, they are not designed to elicit an answer but to make a point that the addresser expects the addressee will recognize and agree with. By directly addressing the readers, this device manages to reinforce the emotive nuances of the message. These questions manage to arouse their interest, lead them to a thought which is expressed or presupposed, and get them to reflect on their own response to them. They enable the writer to indirectly convey his commitment to the specific answer and intend to convince the readership of his arguments by referring to common or presupposed knowledge shared by discourse participants, as seen in (28), where the author appeasingly denounces Austria's ingratitude and her perfidious failure to justly comply with her commitments.

(28) What returns of gratitude can we expect when we are no longer wanted? Has all that we have hitherto done for the imperial family been taken as a favour, or only received as the due of the *augustissima casa?* Will the house of Austria yield the least acre of land, the least article of strained and even

usurped prerogative, to resettle the minds of those princes in the alliance who are alarmed at the consequences of this turn of affairs occasioned by the emperor's death?

The Conduct: 76

Although rhetorical questions are not expected to be responded to, an answer may be supplied by the addresser to attain certain rhetorical effects, as seen in (29), where the response provided makes the obvious reply much more categorical to further stress the allies' disinterest in fulfilling their stipulated commitments, thus igniting the indignation of the English people:

(29) <u>But perhaps our allies will make up this deficiency on our side by great efforts on their own?</u> Quite the contrary; both the emperor and Holland failed this year in several articles and signified to us some time ago that they cannot keep up to the same proportions in the next.

The Conduct: 83–84

The forcefulness of rhetorical questions will be enhanced at times by resorting to additional boosting devices. Thus, rhetorical questions combined with parallelism and coordination can become most forceful and persuasive, as in (30), where the rhetorical question that asserts the deplorable image of England turned into the laughing-stock of Europe is preceded by seven conditional clauses where he clearly states and emphasizes the arguments that support his claim.

(30) But if all this be true; if, according to what I have affirmed, we began this war contrary to reason; if, as the other party themselves upon all occasions, acknowledge, the success we have had was more than we could reasonably expect; if, after all our success, we have not made that use of it which in reason we ought to have done (...) if all this, I say, be our case, it is a very obvious question to ask, <u>by what motives or what management we are thus become the dupes and bubbles of Europe?</u>

The Conduct: 58

Hearer-oriented boosters are quite infrequent in the corpus compared to speaker-oriented and content-oriented emphasizers. One kind of hearer-oriented booster is empathizers, which direct attention to the addressee and emphasize relevant parts of the message, allowing him to concentrate on the important part of the addresser's utterances (Urbanová 2000: 60), as in (31) and (32).

(31) <u>Give me leave to suppose</u> the continuance of the war was the thing at heart among those in power both abroad and at home, and then I can easily show the consistency of their proceedings.

The Conduct: 73

(32) <u>Compare</u> such a weak condition as this with so great an accession of strength to Austria, and then <u>determine</u> how much an emperor in such a state of affairs would either fear or need Britain.

The Conduct: 76

They explicitly address readers by selectively focusing their attention and, at the same time, include them as participants in the text (Hyland 2001: 39). They relate to the recipient's experience and knowledge of the world, to "assumed shared background information" (Holmes 1984: 353). By relying on the background knowledge of the audience, these markers explicitly refer to and build a relationship with the reader, enhancing the sense of engagement with the addressee.

Hedging

Hedges are speaker- or writer-oriented rhetorical devices purposely employed by the addresser to withhold complete commitment to a proposition and therefore communicate more precisely the degree of truthfulness or accuracy to be attributed to his assertions. The presence of hedges in political discourse is motivated by conventions of tact and politeness and, from this viewpoint, hedging can be considered an effective euphemistic strategy to maintain harmony in communicative exchange (Crespo-Fernández 2005). As claims made by writers can challenge the readers' beliefs, they tend to moderate their views to sound less categorical or dogmatic, as in (33). Thus, the introduction of the hedging expression "I presume" – which could have been suppressed altogether – softens a statement that would otherwise sound like a most forceful denunciation and an extremely emotional appeal aimed at fueling the English people's indignation against her allies.

> (33) I presume it will appear, by plain matters of fact, that no nation was ever so long or so scandalously abused, by the folly, the temerity, the corruption, the ambition of its domestic enemies; or treated with so much insolence, injustice, and ingratitude, by its foreign friends.
>
> The Conduct: 20

Let us now consider the different pragmatic functions hedges fulfill in our study.

Hedging is a useful rhetorical device that contributes to negative politeness and prevents threatening the addresser's face. Following Brown and Levinson (1987), "a face-threathening act" (or FTA) is considered as a violation of the addresser's privacy and freedom of action that may be compensated with hedges. Hedges may be considered in terms of positive and negative politeness. While positive politeness strategies strengthen the addressee's positive face, negative politeness strategies serve to mitigate the effect the utterance may produce on the recipient. Hence, "negative politeness enables the speaker to go on-record (...) but with redress, which means that the speaker makes an effort to minimize the imposition, authoritativeness or directness of his/her utterance" (Wilamová 2005: 85). Common downgraders are represented, for instance, by expressions such as "quite", "rather", "enough", "(a) little", "in part", or "nearly", among others. The downtoning hedge "hardly" in (34) minimizes the size of the imposition on the reader and serves as a form of self-protection for the writer.

> (34) Otherwise it could hardly enter into any imagination, that while we are confederates in a war with those who are to have the whole profit (...) we dare not think of any design (...) where there is the least prospect of doing good to our own country.
>
> The Conduct: 32

Assumption is one of the most common functions fulfilled by hedges. Here the addresser does not make a firm assertion in relation to the message, but rather indicates that he is not willing to take full responsibility for the claims expressed. By attenuating the degree of commitment to the claims made, the writer renders an image of humbleness and truthfulness which contributes to attaining an overall balance that makes his position and statements more convincing. According to Brown and Levinson (1987), hedges are strategies employed for politeness to minimize the face threat hidden behind every act of communication. This is often accomplished when expressing subjectivity about a claim by employing epistemic verbs that explicitly minimize the degree of commitment to the proposition, as well as different introductory phrases such as "to my/our knowledge", "it is our view", among others. Common assumption markers used in the pamphlet are "I think", "I suppose", or "I believe":

(35) I think it plainly appears, by both declarations, that England ought no more to have been a principal in this war than Prussia or any other power who came afterward into that alliance.

The Conduct: *16*

(36) The emperor, however sanguine he may now affect to appear, will I suppose be satisfied with Naples, Sicily, Milan (…) rather than engage in a long, hopeless war for the recovery of Spain.

The Conduct: *84*

(37) Lastly, those who are so violently against any peace without Spain's being restored to the house of Austria, have not, I believe, cast their eye upon a cloud gathering in the north, which we have helped to raise, and may quickly break in a storm upon our heads.

The Conduct: *92*

Another common pragmatic function is the expression of uncertainty, commonly expressed through tentative modal auxiliary verbs such as "may/might", as in (38); modal lexical verbs like "seem", as in (39); or different adjectival, adverbial, and the nominal modal phrases "likely/possibility", as in (40) and (41); which can be combined with other hedges. These hedging devices can be used to appear moderate, conciliatory, open for disagreement, reducing the imposition on the recipient and therefore enhancing rapport with the readership.

(38) The Dutch might, perhaps, have grown resty under their burden; but care was likewise taken of that, by a barrier treaty made with the States, which deserves such epithets as I care not to bestow, but may perhaps consider it, at a proper occasion, in a discourse by itself.

The Conduct: *71*

(39) But whatever might have been the reasons for this proceeding, it seems they are above the understanding of the present lord treasurer.

The Conduct: *56*

Political Rhetoric in Jonathan Swift

(40) <u>I think</u> it highly necessary that the public <u>should</u> be freely and impartially told (…) what the consequences of this management are <u>likely</u> to be upon themselves and their posterity.

The Conduct: 3–4

(41) And by this method one part of the nation is pawned to the other, with <u>hardly</u> a <u>possibility</u> left of being ever redeemed.

The Conduct: 24

Conditional clauses also constitute a common linguistic device in the pamphlet that serves the purpose of toning down the proposition, often used to express uncertainty and to mitigate offense. Common conditional markers such as "if", "provided that", or "unless", among others, can direct and shape addressees' interpretations on events while helping the addresser maintain "face" when dealing with some politically risky topics or face-threatening issues (Wilson 1990: 21), as can be seen in the example below where the negative imposition is attenuated through "supposing":

(42) <u>Supposing</u> this to be true, I do assert that, by parity of reason, we must expect one just so much worse about two years hence.

The Conduct: 87

Hedges can also be employed to express detachment. It is a particularly useful means to refer to "the others", as opposed to first person "I/we", in a polite or acceptable way. The use of "some", when associated to people, will make reference to the writer's opponents: generally, to the late ministry and the Whig moneyed as in (43), but at other times, to any of the allies, as in (44), where the writer attempts to save face and protect himself from potential conflicts.

(43) Then it is natural to inquire (…) whether a peace, without that impracticable point which <u>some people</u> do so much insist on, be really ruinous in itself, or equally so with the continuance of the war.

The Conduct: 6

(44) The motives that may engage a wise prince or state in a war I take to be one or more of these: either to check the overgrown power of <u>some</u> ambitious neighbor.

The Conduct: 7

Depersonalization is another target pursued when resorting to hedging devices. In this case, they are employed to circumvent the use of direct reference to a specific subject, creating fuzziness around who the referent of the sentence is. One of the most relevant linguistic strategies used by Swift is extraposed clause constructions, which provide the means to thematize attitudinal meanings as an explicit proposition at the beginning of the clause while concealing the source of this attitude with an impersonal subject (Herriman 2000). Extraposition is a marked construction in which new information is moved to the end of the clause or sentence where readers process it more easily while, at the same time, it grants the writer the opportunity to downplay his personal role (Rodman 1991).

A frequent grammatical structure present in the pamphlet is extraposed "it", frequently co-occurring with "to" and "that" complement clauses controlled by adjectives, as can be seen in (45) and (46), but verbal predicates are also common. This impersonal subject "it" allows writers to increase the facticity of a statement, i.e. to add the impression of the presentation of objective and impersonal knowledge, allowing the writer to remain in the background (Khamkhein 2014: 58). This linguistic strategy allows the writer to shift responsibility for an evaluation and provides writers with more evaluative options than the use of a single modal verb or lexical item (Hyland and Tse 2004: 124).

(45) <u>It is therefore necessary</u>, as well as prudent, to lend them assistances, and help them to win a strong secure frontier.

The Conduct: 9

(46) Whether this war was prudently begun or not, <u>it is plain that</u> the true spring or motive of it was the aggrandizing of a particular family.

The Conduct: 60

Hedges are also employed to express indetermination. This is typically expressed through approximators of quantity, degree, frequency, and time. Intentional fuzziness or vagueness can make statements more acceptable to the recipient, thus boosting their chance of ratification and lowering the risk of negation, as happens with common hedges like "almost":

(47) But during that whole war the sea was <u>almost</u> entirely neglected, and the greatest part of six millions annually employed to enlarge the frontier of the Dutch.

The Conduct: 13

Another frequent approximator is "about", utilized when handling figures, quantity, or time. Whereas Swift sometimes gives exact figures as an effective boosting device that helps the writer be perceived as highly convincing, although ostentatious, at others he introduces the hedge to reflect imprecision and thus convey a more truthful image, as in (48). The balance attained through the combination of these two strategies turns the addresser into a knowledgeable and reliable source:

(48) The Spanish army on the side of Catalonia is, or ought to be, <u>about</u> fifty thousand men, exclusive of Portugal. And here the war has been carried on almost entirely at our cost. For this whole army is paid by the queen, excepting only seven battalions and fourteen squadrons of Dutch and Palatines; and even fifteen hundred of these are likewise in our pay.

The Conduct: 54

Finally, it is relevant to point out that FTAs can also violate the addresser's positive face. These include acts that can harm the writer's self-image, such as apologies, self-humiliations, or confessions, as can be seen in examples (49) and (50)). Sharing intimate feelings or shortcomings creates a climate of trust, of mutual understanding, that promotes empathy, a harmonious relationship with the readership, and conviction:

(49) This was a prospect so very inviting that, <u>to confess the truth</u>, it could not be easily withstood by any who have so keen an appetite for wealth or power.

The Conduct: 59

(50) <u>I have not skill enough</u> to compute what will be left, after these necessary charges, towards annually clearing so vast a debt, but believe it must be very little.

The Conduct: 80

Conclusion

The importance of hedging and boosting as persuasive devices in political discourse is beyond doubt. As demonstrated in the course of the analysis, by modifying the force of a statement, either weakening or intensifying it respectively, Swift manages to express his attitude not only to the propositional content of the utterance but towards the listener or reader himself. The application of contemporary theories of CDA has allowed us to take a fresh look at the author and discover how skillfully he employed and combined boosters and hedges as a political propagandist to swing public opinion behind the Tories. The present study has shown that while Swift as a political writer needs to sound knowledgeable and confident to the readership, he needs to attenuate his claims to make his stance notably less dogmatic, which enhances his power of conviction. Thus, on the one hand, he resorts to boosting, to make his stance clear, add emphasis, and convince his readers of the truthfulness of his statements, allowing the creation of a structurally well-organized and coherent text. On the other, assumption, detachment, depersonalization, indetermination, and uncertainty were the most frequent pragmatic uses of hedges in our corpus. However, the underlying reason for them was most frequently to maintain courtesy. In fact, politeness seems to be an all-pervasive motivation for practically all the cases of hedging in the pamphlet, particularly negative politeness. Mitigating the effect that the utterance may produce on the addressee becomes an unquestionable target for Swift as an effective political propagandist. It is, however, the combination and judicious balance between boosters and hedges which makes his discourse most effective as far as persuasion is concerned. Indeed, these rhetorical strategies do not function in isolation but are deliberately grouped in boosting or hedging clusters which are combined with alternative hedges or boosters respectively to attain maximum power of conviction.

Discovering why and how Swift used rhetorical strategies, such as hedging or boosting, at the time to attain persuasion to shape minds and move hearts, compared to other contemporary Tory and Whig polemicists or even present-day political propagandists, is no doubt quite an interesting although somewhat neglected research topic which is in no way exhausted. Hopefully, this chapter will inspire other researchers.

References

Barker, H. (2000) *Newspapers, Politics and English Society 1695–1855*. Harlow: Pearson Education.

Brown, P. and Levinson, S. D. (1987) *Politeness. Some Universals in Language Usage*. Cambridge: Cambridge University Press.

Charteris-Black, J. (2011) *Politicians and Rhetoric. The Persuasive Power of Metaphor*. London: Palgrave.

Chilton, P. (2004) *Analyzing Political Discourse: Theory and Practice*. London: Routledge.

Clemen, G. (1997) 'The Concept of Hedging: Origins, Approaches and Definitions', in R. Markkanen and H. Schröder (eds.), *Hedging and Discourse. Approaches to the Analysis of a Pragmatic Phenomenon in Academic Texts*. Berlin: Walter de Gruyter, 235–248.

Crespo-Fernández, E. (2005) 'Euphemistic Strategies in Politeness and Face Concerns', *Pragmalingüística* 13: 77–86.

Crespo-Fernández, E. (2018) 'Euphemism as a Discursive Strategy in US and Local Politics', *Journal of Language and Politics* 6: 789–811.

Downie, J. A. (1979) *Robert Harley and the Press. Propaganda and Public Opinion in the Age of Swift and Defoe*. Cambridge: Cambridge University Press.

Fairclough, N. (1989) *Language and Power*. London: Longman.

Fairclough, N. (1992) *Discourse and Social Change*. London: Arnold.

Fairclough, N. (1995) *Critical Discourse Analysis: The Critical Study of Language*. London: Longman.

Fairclough, N. (2005) 'Critical Discourse Analysis, Organization Discourse and Organizational Change', *Organization Studies* 26: 915–935.

Fairclough, N. and Wodak, R. (1997) 'Critical Discourse Analysis', in T. A. Van Dijk (ed.), *Discourse as Social Interaction*. London: Sage.

Foot, M. (1984) *The Pen and the Sword. Jonathan Swift and the Power of the Press*. London: Collins.

Fraser, B. (1996) 'Pragmatic Markers', *Pragmatics* 6(2): 167–190.

Fraser, B. (2010) 'Pragmatic Competence: The Case of Hedging', in G. Kaltenböck, W. Mihatsch, and S. Schneider (eds.), *New Approaches to Hedging*. Bingley (UK): Emerald.

Goffman, E. (1955) On Face-Work: An Analysis of Ritual Elements in Social Interaction. *Psychiatry: Journal for the Study of Interpersonal Processes*, 18, pp. 213–231.

Halmari, H. (2005) 'In Search of Successful Political Persuasion: A Comparison of the Styles of Bill Clinton and Ronald Reagan', in H. Halmari and T. Virtanen (eds.), *Persuasion across Genres: A Linguistic Approach*. Amsterdam: John Benjamins.

Harris, T. (1993) *Politics under the Later Stuarts. Party Conflict in a Divided Society 1660–1715*. Harlow: Pearson.

Herriman, J. (2000) 'The Functions of Extraposition in English Texts', *Functions of Language* 7(2): 203–230.

Holmes, J. (1984) 'Modifying Illocutionary Force', *Journal of Pragmatics* 8: 345–365.

Hunston, S. (2000) 'Evaluation and the Planes of Discourse: Status and Value in Persuasive Texts', in S. Hunston and G. Thompson (eds.), *Evaluation in Text: Authorial Stance and the Construction of Discourse*. Oxford: Oxford University Press.

Hyland, K. (2001) 'Bringing in the Reader. Addressee Features in Academic Articles', *Written Communication* 18(4): 549–574.

Hyland, K. (2007) 'Applying a Gloss: Exemplifying and Reformulating in Academic Discourse', *Applied Linguistics* 28(2): 266–285.

Hyland, K. and Tse, P. (2004) 'Metadiscourse in Academic Writing: A Reappraisal', *Applied Linguistics* 25(2): 156–177.

Jackson, C. (2015) 'Jonathan Swift's Peace of Utrecht', in R. E. de Bruin et al. (eds.), *Performances of Peace: Utrecht 1713*. Leiden: Brill.

Janks, H. (2006) 'Critical Discourse Analysis as a Research Tool', *Discourse: Studies in the Cultural Politics of Education* 18(3): 329–342.

Kozubíková Sandová, J. (2014) *Speaker Involvement in Political Interviews*. Frankfurt: Peter Lang.

Khamphein, A. (2014) 'Linguistic Features of Evaluative Stance: Findings from Research Article Discussion', *Indonesian Journal of Applied Linguistics* 4(1): 54–69.

Krzyzanowsi, M. and Forchtner, B. (2016) 'Theories and Concepts in Critical Discourse Studies: Facing Challenges, Moving beyond Foundations', *Discourse and Society* 7(3): 253–261.

López-Campillo, R. M. (2018) 'Political Discourse in John Tutchin: Hedges as Euphemistic and Persuasive Devices', in E. Crespo-Fernández (ed.), *Taboo in Discourse. Studies on Attenuation and Offence in Communication*. Bern: Peter Lang.

Müllenbrock, H. J. (1997) *The Culture of Contention: A Rhetorical Analysis of the Public Controversy about the Ending of the War of the Spanish Succession, 1710–1713*. Munich: Fink.

Paltridge, B. (2012) *Discourse Analysis: An Introduction*. New York: Bloomsbury Publishing.

Partington, A. (2001) *Persuasion in Politics*. Bologna: Universitarie di Lettere.

Rodman, L. (1991) 'Anticipatory IT in Scientific Discourse', *Journal of Technical Writing and Communication* 21(1): 17–27.

Salager-Meyer, F. (1994) 'Hedges and Textual Communicative Function in Medical English Written Discourse', *English for Specific Purposes* 13(2): 149–170. https://doi.org/10.1016/0889-4906(94)90013-2

Salager-Meyer, F. (1995) 'I Think That Perhaps You Should: A Study of Hedges in Written Scientific Discourse', *The Journal of TESOL France* 2(2): 127–143.

Speck, W. A. (1994) *The Birth of Britain. A New Nation 1700–1710*. Oxford: Blackwell.

Swift, J. (1711) *The Conduct of the Allies and the Late Ministry, in beginning and carrying on the Present War*. London: John Morphew.

Swift, J. (1758) *The History of the Last Four Years of the Queen*, in H. Davis (ed.) (1973), *The History of the Last Four Years of the Queen with an Introduction by Harold Williams*. Oxford: Basil Blackwell.

Swift, J. (1776) *The Journal to Stella*, in G. A. Aitken (ed.) (1901). London: Methuen & Co. The Journal to Stella, by Jonathan Swift (gutenberg.org).

Urbanová, L. (2000) 'Accentuation in Authentic English Conversation', *BRNO Studies in English* 26: 57–64.

Van Dijk, T. A. (1997) 'What Is Political Discourse Analysis?', *Belgian Journal of Linguistics* 11(1): 11–52.

Van Dijk, T.A. (2006) 'Discourse and Manipulation', *Discourse and Society* 17(3): 359–383.

Wilamová, S. (2005) 'On the Function of Hedging Devices in Negatively Polite Discourse', *BRNO Studies in English* 31: 85–93.

Wilson, J. (1990) *Political Speaking: The Pragmatic Analysis of Political Language*. Oxford: Blackwell.

Wilson, J. (2001) 'Political Discourse', in D. Schiffrin, D. Tannen, and H. Hamilton (eds.), *The Handbook of Discourse Analysis*. Oxford: Blackwell.

Wodak, R. (2009) 'What CDA Is About. A Summary of Its History, Important Concepts, and Developments', in R. Wodak and M. Meyer (eds.), *Methods of Critical Discourse Analysis*, 2nd ed. London: Sage.

13

THE RHETORIC OF THE IMMIGRATION DISCOURSE OF FAR-RIGHT PARTIES IN SPAIN AND FRANCE

Isabel Negro

Introduction

Immigration has become a salient topic, as evidenced by the wide research into the European press coverage of the 2015 refugee crisis (Georgiou and Zaborowski 2017; Greussing and Boomgaarden 2017) and the media representation of refugees and asylum seekers in the Australian press (Gale 2004), and the Spanish and British press (Porto 2022; Romano and Porto 2021).

It has also become a widely debated topic in the last three decades, which partly accounts for the rise and electoral successes of many European right-wing nationalist parties across Europe such as Santiago Abascal's Vox in Spain, Marine Le Pen's Rassemblement National in France, Matteo Salvini's League in Italy, or Viktor Orbán's Fidesz in Hungary. All these parties use a populist discourse where immigration is a core issue on which they take a hard-line stand.

Immigration discourse has received much scholarly attention in recent years, the focus being on the link between immigration and populism (Mudde 2015; Moffit 2017, 2020; Stanley 2020), and on the representation of migrant groups in (i) right-wing political discourse in some countries like Austria (Wodak et al. 1997), France (Van der Valk 2003), Greece (Triandafyllidou 2000), Poland (Cap 2018) and the USA (Dematra 2017); (ii) parliamentary discourse (Van Dijk 2000, 2019); (iii) the European media (Ebert et al. 2018; Rubio-Carbonero and Zapata-Barrero 2017;[1] Rubio-Carbonero 2020).

Much research on the immigration phenomenon has been carried out following a Critical Discourse Analysis (hence CDA) approach (e.g., Wodak et al. 1997; Reisigl and Wodak 2009; Hart 2011;[2] Rubio-Carbonero 2020) and a multimodal discourse approach. These investigations examine the structures employed in immigration discourse. Rubio-Carbonero (2020) claims that political discourse on immigration is based on four structures: highlighting, diminishing, homogenizing and normalizing. Triandafyllidou (2000) postulates the ingroup/nation / outgroup-immigrants dichotomy as the basis of immigration discourse in Greece, Italy and Spain. Van Dijk (2000) advocates two

198

DOI: 10.4324/9781003195276-17

analytical categories: semantic structures and formal structures, the latter including argumentative structures and topoi (arguments).

This chapter seeks to gain an insight into the way immigration discourse is built by right-wing parties in Europe on the basis of a corpus of public discourse fragments produced by Santiago Abascal, leader of the Spanish party Vox, and Marine Le Pen, leader of the French party Rassemblement National. Vox irrupted in Spain's political landscape in 2014 and won its first parliamentary seats (11% of the vote) in the regional elections in Andalusia (southern Spain) held in December 2012. Vox has grown into the third largest party in Parliament following the Andalusian elections of December 2018. In much the same way, support for Rassemblement National has climbed from 18% in 2010 to about 24% today.

Both Vox and Rassemblement National have been derided as far-right and populist, nationalist, anti-immigrant and anti-Islam. Immigration is at the core of their agenda, and both parties have campaigned for tougher policies on immigration in order to reduce it.

Vox has used the immigration move from Africa as a springboard for their anti-illegal immigration discourse. Abascal's speeches, as shown in the corpus, focus on the negative impact of massive African immigration. Between 2015 and 2021 over 23,000 foreigners – about half of them minors and young immigrants – entered Spain illegally. Most arrived by sea on the Canary Islands or crossed the border at the north African enclaves of Ceuta and Melilla, which have the European Union's only land borders with Africa.

In contrast, in Le Pen's narrative, immigration is linked to religion and national security, since over 40% of migrants to France are Maghrebian immigrants whose allegiance to Islam collides with the national defence of the concept of secularism. As for the link between immigration and national security, it has been emphasized by Le Pen since the 2016 Islamist terrorist attacks perpetuated by children of immigrants who grew up in France. In the 2021 presidential campaign Le Pen claimed that French identity and Christian heritage are threatened by Muslim immigrants from the Maghrebian countries.

A distinctive feature of immigration in France is the marginalization of minorities. While in Spain they may just not be integrated, in France they often live in urban ghettos where violence, drugs and the unemployment rate are high. This is clearly illustrated in Abascal's and Le Pen's discourse. While Abascal puts the emphasis on the cultural clash, Le Pen highlights the link between immigration and a higher crime rate.

In order to analyse the construction of the immigration discourse of Vox and Rassemblement National, we follow an approach that integrates CDA and rhetoric. Unlike recent work combining CDA and constructivist (Morales-López 2017; Pujante 2017) or cognitive (Browse 2018) rhetoric, our research integrates the CDA analytical method within the classical rhetorical approach (Aristotle 1991), which claims that the construction of political discourse relies on three modes of argumentation, namely logos (communicating and explaining policy/rational argumentation), ethos (the speaker's credibility and reliability) and pathos (emotional appeals). While the use of logos, ethos and pathos structures has been examined in discourse research (e.g., Charteris-Black 2009; Poggi 2005)[3] and the classical rhetoric roots of CDA have been acknowledged by Wodak (2011), to the best of our knowledge the Aristotelian modes have not been integrated into CDA.

Specifically, the present chapter pursues three aims: (1) to analyse the structures and strategies employed in Abascal's and Le Pen's immigration discourse; (2) to show how

199

Analytical Framework

As earlier mentioned, our conceptual and theoretical approach is subsumed within CDA, which posits discourse as a form of social practice (see, e.g., Caldas-Coulthard and Coulthard 1996; van Dijk 1993; Fairclough 2003, 2012, 2013; Fairclough and Fairclough 2013; Fairclough and Wodak 1997). In Fairclough's (2012) terms, discourse is a category "designating particular ways of representing particular aspects of social life" (p. 453). CDA thus focuses on the social analysis of discourse (Wodak 2001; Wodak and Meyer 2015; Van Dijk 2005). This implies that CDA takes into account the most relevant contextual factors, both social and historical ones, which contribute to the production and interpretation of a given text. In this sense, CDA advocates reciprocal relationships between discourse and the situations, institutions and social contexts in which it takes place. Discourse is both socially constitutive as well as socially conditioned. It is constitutive in the sense that it "legitimates, reproduces or challenges relations of power and dominance in society" (Van Dijk 2005, p. 353). On the other hand, CDA encompasses a historical and cultural dimension, which is particularly noticeable in political discourse, one of the major CDA research areas.

CDA was further developed by Chilton (2011, pp. 775–776), who elaborated on its cognitive dimension and pinpointed the underlying values in legitimizing exclusionary attitudes towards immigration and refugees in the UK media.

As earlier mentioned, discourse is historical, i.e., it can only be understood in its historical context. The relevance of this dimension is highlighted by the discourse-historical paradigm (Wodak 2001, 2009; Wodak et al. 1997; Reisigl and Wodak 2009), whose epistemological background is provided by Critical Theory and symbolic interactionism. In line with Critical Theory, the goal of CDA is to challenge discourse that (re)produces inequality, mystification and oppression, "to demystify discourse by deciphering ideologies" (Wodak 2011, pp. 52–53). In addition, like Critical Theory, CDA emphasizes the need for an interdisciplinary approach (Chilton et al. 2010) to properly understand how language functions in constituting and transmitting knowledge and power, and in organizing social institutions. CDA is also inspired by symbolic interactionism inasmuch as it analyses the ways in which social structures are built and maintained.

Wodak and her associates implemented a method of description and analysis which focused on three aspects (Wodak and Meyer 2015): (1) main discourse topics; (2) main nomination, predication and argumentative structures; and (3) principal claims and topoi employed to justify them.

A more recent version of the model was developed to explore the discourse construction of nation and national identity in Austria and Hungary (Kovács and Wodak 2003; Wodak et al. 2009) and in the European Union (Muntigl et al. 2000; Wodak and Van Dijk 2000). The new version involves three basic categories: topics/contents, strategies and linguistic devices. The topics include the linguistic construction of a common political past, present and future, a common culture, and the national territory. These topics provide the basis for Abascal's construction of national identity.

Wodak et al. (2009) distinguish four types of macro-strategies which subsume more specific strategies:

(a) Constructive strategies are used to build and establish a national identity. They include strategies of assimilation (emphasizing intra-national sameness or identity) and strategies of dissimilation (emphasizing difference).
(b) Perpetuation and justification try to maintain, support and reproduce national identities. Perpetuation strategies serve to highlight the need to support continuity, to discursively construct an action/event as a threat to national identity. In contrast, justification strategies seek to defend controversial acts or events.
(c) Transformation strategies aim to transform the negative aspects of national identities into positive ones.
(d) Dismantling strategies serve to demolish existing national identities or elements of them. A major dismantling strategy is other-negative presentation.

It is our contention that the CDA structures and strategies are linked to the classical rhetoric modes of logos, ethos and pathos. Thus, as displayed in Table 13.2, the logos dimension of discourse relies on nomination, predication and argumentative structures, on the one hand, and constructive and dismantling strategies, on the other hand. The ethos dimension is built through the discursive characterization of Abascal and Le Pen and constructive strategies. Finally, emotional appeals and claims reflect the pathos dimension in Abascal's discourse.

Methodology

The analysis that follows is based on a small-scale corpus research. The data were gathered by means of an Internet search. The sample is made up of the public discourse on immigration produced by Abascal and Le Pen between January 2019 and September 2021. The data set consists of 22 texts belonging to various genres: speeches, interviews, public statements, and TV broadcasts. The texts were accessed online and transcribed. They are presented in Table 13.1.

It is worth noting the close relationship between Abascal's discourse and the socio-historical context in which it was produced, following the massive arrival of immigrants on the Canary Islands in 2020 and in Ceuta in 2021. In contrast, Le Pen's immigration discourse spans longer, because it is a recurring topic in French politics which Le Pen brings up in Rassemblement National's meetings, local and presidential election campaigns, and at the beginning of a parliamentary year.

We carried out a qualitative analysis of the sample. We analysed three basic categories: structures, claims and appeals. Following Wodak and Meyer (2015), we classified the structures under three groups: nomination, predication and argumentative structures. Nomination structures are involved in the discursive construction of social actors and processes. Predication structures are involved in the discursive characterization of social actors and events. Argumentative structures encompass claims of truth and rightness about immigration.

All these structures pertain to the logos, with the exception of the discursive self-characterization of Abascal and Le Pen, which pertains to the ethos. The last category, namely appeals, constitutes the pathos. Nominal and predication structures are

Table 13.1 Research corpus

Abascal's public discourse	Le Pen's public discourse
Speech in Lanzarote (5 December 2020)	Speech in Thor (19 January 2019)
Parliamentary speech (16 December 2020)	Speech in the Spinoza Foundation in Geneva (21 January 2019)
Interview (20 January 2021)	TV interview in a regional chain in Mayotte (26 March 2019)
Parliamentary speech (3 February 2020)	Public statement in Hénin-Beaumont (8 September 2019)
Interview (27 April 2021)	Speech in Fréjus (15 September 2019)
Interview (18 May 2021)	Parliamentary speech (7 October 2019)
Public statement in Ceuta (19 May 2021)	Speech (6 March 2020)
Speech in Ceuta (19 May 2021)	Radio interview (21 October 2020)
Speech in Seville (24 May 2021)	Intervention in a TV debate (11 February 2021)
Parliamentary speech (15 September 2021)	Radio interview (11 March 2021)
	Radio interview (14 September 2021)
	Speech in the RN 17th Congress in Perpignan (4 July 2021)

implemented by lexical categories (ideological anthroponyms, collectives, particular speech verbs), constructive strategies (generic we, national we, positive self-presentation), dissimilation strategies (contrast us-them), and dismantling strategies (other-negative presentation, strong negative terms, metaphor).

Corpus Analysis

This section analyses the structures and strategies deployed by Abascal and Le Pen in their discursive construction of immigration. We have grouped them into three distinct categories on the basis of the three modes of argumentation postulated in the classical rhetorical approach, namely logos, ethos and pathos, as shown in Table 13.2.

The Logos Dimension of Immigration Discourse

As we see in the table, the logos dimension is the most relevant and is implemented by a wide range of structures and strategies. Constructive strategies are employed in the discursive construction of social actors (logos) and the speakers (ethos). Dissimilation strategies aim to highlight the differences between the different actors (the in-group vs. the out-group), and dismantling strategies are used to characterize immigration and immigrants.

The analysis of the logos dimension involves the analysis of two aspects:

- The main discourse topics.
- The main nomination, predication and argumentative structures.

While Abascal's discourse focuses on controlling illegal immigration to maintain the security of borders, Le Pen's discourse focuses on cutting legal immigration of non-EU

Immigration Discourse of Far-Right Parties in Spain

Table 13.2 Structures and strategies in Abascal's and Le Pen's immigration discourse

Mode of argumentation	Structures/appeals	Abascal's strategies/claims	Le Pen's strategies
Logos	Nomination structures • Discursive construction of social actors • Discursive construction of processes	Constructive strategies (national *we*, generic *we*) Ideological anthroponyms Collectives Arguing, blaming, rebutting	Generic *we* Collectives Arguing, promising
	Predication structures • Discourse characterization of social actors • Discourse characterization of events	Dissimilation strategies (us/them) Dismantling strategies (other-negative presentation) Dismantling strategies (negative predication, metaphor)	Dismantling strategies (other-negative presentation) Dismantling strategies (negative predication, metaphor)
	Argumentative structures • Claims of truth • Claims of rightness	Loss of national identity Immigration is a social/ economic threat Cultural diversity is a threat Immigrants feel unrooted Border protection	Loss of national identity Immigration is a social/ economic threat Cultural diversity is a threat
Ethos	Discursive characterization of Abascal and Le Pen (credibility)	Constructive strategies (positive self-presentation) Commitment to the defence of national interest	Constructive strategies (positive self-presentation) Commitment to the defence of national interest
Pathos	Appeal to patriotism Empathy toward the in-group	Use of generic *we*	

citizens (Muslims) and making obtaining asylum, residency rights and French nationality harder. Le Pen associates Muslim immigration with terrorism and goes so far as to speak of a European-level Islamization. In addition, Abascal lays out his stand on immigration within the conceptual framework of national identity through the discursive construction of sameness (1) and difference (2):

(1) *Las fronteras sirven para defender nuestra prosperidad, nuestra libertad, nuestras leyes, nuestra cultura y la herencia que hemos recibido de nuestros padres.*[4]

24/05/2021

(2) *[...] importar gente que no puede adaptarse [...] porque no puede, porque han nacido, han vivido en culturas incompatibles con la nuestra, totalmente diferentes.*

24/05/2021

...re involved in the discursive construction of social actors
...important social actors who are discursively constructed in the
...by Abascal and Le Pen are national *we* and their political party.
...ally realized by the possessive *nuestros/-as* in (1, 3), is used to reinforce
...ty (a collective past and future, a common national culture, common polit-
..., common emotional attitudes manifested to the "outward groups" and similar
...ural dispositions), while generic *we* is employed to explain the political party's
...dpoint about immigration (4):

(3) *España es nuestra patria, fue la de nuestros abuelos y será la de nuestros nietos.*

24/05/2021

(4) *Nosotros no estamos contra el inmigrante.*

5/12/2020

Le Pen uses the first-person singular pronoun *je* to explain her party's immigration agenda (combined with generic *we*) and her viewpoint (5, 6):

(5) *Je supprimerai la possibilité de régulariser les clandestins.*

11/03/2020

(6) *Je m'attaque à l'idéologie islamiste.*

11/02/2011

Although the in-group is usually referred to through a toponym (*los españoles*) in Abascal's speeches, and as a community (*le peuple français*) by Le Pen, both expressions highlight national identity.

Policy-makers only play a role in Abascal's discourse. Abascal uses ideological anthroponyms to refer to the Spanish government (*el gobierno de todos los colores, la izquierda*), and metonymic toponyms to criticize the government of the Maghrebian countries (*Africa, Marruecos, Argelia*).

The discursive construction of mental processes is richer in Abascal's discourse. The pervading process in Abascal's and Le Pen's discourse is arguing. Both argue against illegal immigration and accuse the government of not fighting it (7). Abascal's discourse occasionally reflects the working of other processes: he rejects negative arguments (8), calls for the building of a wall at the borders of Ceuta and Melilla to stop the flow of immigrants (9), blames the Spanish government for migrants' deaths in the Mediterranean (10), criticizes the governments of the Maghrebian countries for migrants' massive arrival on Spanish shores (11), rebuts the accusation of racism and turns it on his political opponents while accusing them of rejecting nationals (12, 13).

(7) *L'État n'a pas le courage d'attaquer les islamistes.*

21/10/2020

(8) *No necesitamos miles de inmigrantes ilegales para pagar las pensiones. Una mentira repetida mil veces […]*

16/12/2010

(9)   *Las vallas altas hacen buenos vecinos.*

(10) *[…] ellos son los responsables de la gran tragedia que se vive en los mares.*
05/12/2020

(11) *Marruecos y Argelia, países que han abandonado a sus nacionales y se niegan a aceptarles de vuelta.*
05/12/2020

(12) *Racistas son ellos, los que están mintiendo a millones de personas que viven en África, diciéndoles que aquí está la tierra prometida.*
05/12/2020

(13) *Demuestran una clarísima endofobia, un odio a su propio pueblo.*
05/12/2020

Predication structures are involved in the discursive characterization of social actors and events. In Abascal's speeches, policy-makers are negatively depicted as 'elites' and 'oligarchies', and qualified as 'racist' (*racistas*) and 'unsupportive' (*insolidarios*). Immigrants are negatively constructed through two types of strategies of difference: dissimilation strategies and dismantling strategies. Dissimilation strategies serve to emphasize the difference between the in-group (us) and the out-group (them) by framing immigrants as others, alien to the in-group. They are only found in the discourse of Abascal. The relevance of this structure has been highlighted in research on immigration discourse (e.g., Van der Valk 2003).

The dichotomy us/them is also manifested in Abascal's and Le Pen's discourse through parallelism that contrasts social assistance benefits or health care facilities for immigrants and the lack of these for nationals. Such parallelism is realized by a complex sentence containing a relative clause postmodifying a noun phrase that denotes the benefit that immigrants have obtained (affirmative verbs *dar/accorder* 'give', *recibir* 'receive') but nationals have not (negative verbs *no llegan* 'do not receive', *negar* 'deny', *manquer* 'lack').

(14) *Llevamos décadas dando ayudas sociales que no llegan a los españoles más necesitados a quien entra ilegalmente.*
24/05/2021

(15) *Vienen en muchos casos a recibir las ayudas sociales que se niegan a los españoles.*
05/12/2020

(16) *Il faut couper toutes les aides qui, en réalité, sont accordées aux clandestins et qui coûtent une véritable petite fortune et tout cet argent manque dans les infrastructures, les investissements économiques de Mayotte.*
26/03/2019

(17) *Están utilizando los servicios sanitarios que a veces no llegan a los españoles.*
24/05/2021

...d to impress upon the audience that immigrants have a
...ifferent cultural background that make them unable to live

...igration anarchique est une menace pour leur vie quotidienne, pour leur
de vie.

07/10/2019

(19) *El problema es la cultura, que [...] es incompatible con nuestra manera de vivir.*
05/12/2020

Dismantling strategies attempt to identify enemies and criticize developments in society and policies. One dismantling strategy is negative predication. Abascal and Le Pen use derogatory terms to refer to immigrants (*enemigos* 'enemies', *minorité violente* 'violent minority', *gens nocifs* 'harmful people', *criminels barbares* 'barbaric criminals') and to describe their actions (*exactions barbares* 'barbaric exactions'). Other-negative presentation thus works as a strategy of the politics of fear (Wodak 2015):

(20) *[...] están con los enemigos de los españoles.*

15/09/2021

(21) *À supposer que ces criminels barbares agissent seulement par folie je le dis: la France n'est pas une terre d'asile psychiatrique!*
08/09/2019

(22) *[...] ces exactions barbares par de prétendus déséquilibrés souvent venus d'ailleurs.*
08/09/2019

We will now analyse the discursive characterization of events. Again, Abascal resorts to the dismantling strategy of negative predication to describe migrants' arrival on Spanish shores. Negative predication is achieved through the use of strongly negative words and metaphor. Abascal describes the inflow of immigrants as being a crisis and as a senseless event (*una locura*). Granting permission to stay in Spain is regarded as a betrayal of the Spanish people (*traición al pueblo español*), and the stay of undocumented children is seen as a kidnapping committed by the Spanish government (*secuestro de estado*). Le Pen also uses hyperbolic negative terms (*processus destructeur* 'destructive process', *folie migratoire* 'migratory madness') to describe the immigration phenomenon itself.

Negative qualification of immigration is also achieved through metaphor. The role of metaphor in politics and in the discourse of political leaders (Charteris-Black 2004, 2005, 2006, 2009, 2013; Musolff 2004; Negro 2015) has been widely investigated from the cognitive perspective. The natural disaster or natural phenomena metaphors describe immigrants' massive entry into Spain/France as an avalanche (23), a flood (24–26) or a torrent (27). All the metaphors map the feature of large amount onto the source domain, thus highlighting the detrimental effects of immigration:

(23) *[...] la avalancha migratoria ha provocado el agravamiento de la emergencia social y una grave crisis de inseguridad, además de la muerte total del turismo.*
16/12/2020

(24) *Chaque jour qui passe voit s'accélérer la submersion de nos rues, de nos villages, de nos villes, par une immigration aujourd'hui parfaitement incontrôlée.*

08/09/2019

(25) *Notre pays est soumis aux dangers indissociables de la submersion par l'immigration.*

15/09/2019

(26) *[...] flux ininterrompu qui déferle sur nos villes, sur nos bourgs et jusqu'au moindre village.*

07/10/2019

(27) *Le torrent migratoire est en train de balayer nos systèmes sociaux, fait exploser tout le système pénal, porte atteinte à l'unité de la nation.*

07/10/2019

Argumentative structures also contribute to the construction of the logos. From a CDA perspective, political discourse is regarded as primarily a form of argumentation involving practical arguments (Fairclough and Fairclough 2013: 1). The argumentative structures underlying Abascal's and Le Pen's immigration discourse construct their viewpoint on this issue and reveal their ideological position. Their speeches contain two central claims:

(1) Claims of truth regarding their views about immigration.
(2) Claims of rightness regarding action against (illegal) immigration.

Far-right discourse relies on four claims of truth concerning immigration: (1) loss of national identity; (2) immigration is a social/economic threat; (3) cultural diversity is a threat; and (4) immigrants feel unrooted.

First, Abascal and le Pen posit immigration as a threat to national identity, and as a threat to the nation:

(28) *[...] une immigration délirante qui transforme certains endroits en zones de non France, des zones où l'on se sent étranger dans son propre pays.*

19/01/2019

(29) *Aimer la France et prendre le risque de la voir disparaitre est tout de même assez contradictoire [...] L'effacement des frontières, de son identité entraîne sa disparition.*

14/09/2021

In Abascal's discourse national identity is established through assimilation strategies like the use of national *we* and the nation-is-a-house metaphor (*nuestra casa*). Abascal thus uses metaphor with different purposes: (i) as a dismantling strategy to characterize the massive arrival of immigrants in Spain; and (ii) as a constructive strategy to reinforce the national territory.

The second major claim made by Abascal and Le Pen to legitimize their position is that immigration is a social, economic and cultural threat.

Both Abascal and Le Pen highlight the link between immigration and increased insecurity (30–33), which in Le Pen's view is caused by the violent killings committed by immigrants:

(30) *Exigimos que se detenga esa inmigración ilegal, que genera incertidumbre, que genera inseguridad.*

05/12/2020

(31) *Le lien entre l'insécurité et l'immigration massive ne fait plus aucun doute pour les gens de bonne foi.*

06/03/2020

(32) *Un sentiment d'insécurité s'installe en France […] qui pourrit la vie des gens.*
19/01/2019

(33) *Insécurité physique avec ces meurtres gratuits, ces lynchages […] pour des motifs futiles.*

08/09/2019

Immigration is also a financial burden:

(34) *Je vois les effets d'une immigration clandestine qui pèse sur nos finances.*
11/03/2020

Finally, immigration is a cultural threat. Cultural diversity is believed to cause conflict and destroy the country's cultural heritage:

(35) *Nous nous opposons au principe de la société multiculturelle, qui est une société multi-conflictuelle.*

04/07/2021

(36) *Nous ne pouvons pas gaspiller cet héritage au nom d'une soumission au multiculturalisme qui a échoué partout.*

21/01/2019

(37) *Partout dans le monde, les sociétés multiculturelles sont les plus violentes, les plus criminelles.*

21/01/2019

Reference to all the negative consequences of immigration (financial ruin, destruction of national unity, insecurity) is illustrated in (38):

(38) *[…] los que asaltan nuestras fronteras nos quieren llevan a la ruina, dividir el país y sembrar el pánico en las calles.*

15/09/2021

The immigration as a threat claim accounts for the activation of the war metaphor in Abascal's discourse. The war metaphor proves to be a very useful dismantling strategy by describing the illegal incoming of immigrants as an offensive (39) or as an invasion (40, 41). In this war scenario, nationals show resistance (42). It is worth noting that the metaphor has a strong negative connotation:

(39) [...] *le berceau de notre civilisation est l'objet d'une offensive migratoire d'ampleur continentale.*

06/03/2020

(40) [...] *la invasión migratoria que azota España.*

16/12/2020

(41) *Nos encontramos ante una auténtica invasión del territorio nacional.*

19/05/2021

(42) *Aquí estamos nosotros para resistir.*

05/12/2020

Abascal and Le Pen also make a claim about the negative effects of migration for immigrants themselves, who feel unrooted:

(43) [...] *a ser arrancados de su tierra, de sus familias, de sus sociedades y de sus raíces.*

18/05/2021

(44) *Vous avez réinstauré partant des rives de la Méditerranée une nouvelle traite d'êtres humains, avec ses tragédies et ses déracinements.*

07/10/2019

Claims of rightness are made through modality, factual evidence and metaphor. Abascal uses modals of obligation to present immigration proposals such as the deportation of illegal immigrants (45) and of migrants legally entitled to be in Spain if they have committed an offence (46):

(45) *España tiene el deber y el derecho de expulsar al que está ilegalmente en nuestro suelo.*

19/05/2021

(46) [...] *debe retirar la nacionalidad a cualquiera que al haya obtenido y se dedique a delinquir.*

05/12/2020

In other speeches Abascal defends the need to control immigration and the need for border control as the way of maintaining Spanish identity and ensuring stability. In order to support the first claim, he provides factual evidence:

(47) *este año han llegado un 25% más de inmigrantes ilegales a todo el territorio nacional y un 800% más a las islas Canarias.*

16/12/2020

(48) *420.000 personnes entrent chaque année dans notre pays [...] 40.000 mineurs isolés coûtent 50.000 euros chacun par an.*

21/10/2020

To sustain his claim about tough border control, Abascal relies on the nation-is-a-house metaphor:

(49) *Tiene que llegar el mensaje de que el que entra ilegalmente en nuestra casa, en España [...] debe abandonar toda esperanza de trabajar legalmente entre nosotros.*

05/12/2020

(51) *En España no se entra dando una patada en la puerta.*

05/12/2020

The nation-is-a-house metaphor discussed earlier frames borders as a protective wall which must be defended because lack of border control endangers national unity:

(52) *Las fronteras son las paredes de nuestra patria.*

24/05/2021

(53) *Nuestra casa está protegida por unas paredes, por unas fronteras que guardan nuestra prosperidad, nuestra cultura, nuestra identidad, nuestra libertad.*

20/01/2021

(54) *El país que deja de defender sus fronteras deja de ser una patria.*

24/05/2021

The Ethos Dimension of Immigration Discourse

The ethos dimension of discourse is concerned with building up the speaker's credibility and reliability through his discursive characterization. The credibility of Abascal and Le Pen is grounded on reliability and commitment to the defence of the national interest.

Abascal's and Le Pen's reliability is built upon constructive strategies that seek to legitimate their position. Positive self-presentation is one such strategy. In order to make sure that the audience does not see Vox and Rassemblement National as racist, Abascal and Le Pen use the strategy of denial:

(55) *Nosotros no rechazamos la inmigración; nosotros no rechazamos, menos aún, a las personas, a los inmigrantes.*

24/05/2021

(56) *Nosotros no incitamos al odio y a la fobia contra el inmigrante.*

05/12/2020

(57) *A nosotros no nos importa el color de la piel de las personas.*

05/12/2020

Immigration Discourse of Far-Right Parties in Spain and France

(58) *Je n'ai pas de sentiment négatif à l'égard des étrangers. Je n'ai aucune haine des étrangers.*

11/03/2021

Abascal makes explicit claims to being "not xenophobic":

(59) *Claro que Vox tiene una posición distinta, claro que no es desde la invitación al odio ni desde la xenofobia.*

05/12/2020

Abascal's reliability is more clearly established by expressing feelings of empathy for immigrants:

(60) *[…] la solidaridad es importante y hay que mostrar compasión.*

05/12/2020

Abascal and Le Pen's credibility is also grounded on their commitment to the defence of national interest, which they claim to be their political goal (60, 61) or their driving force (62):

(61) *Nuestra misión es defender los intereses, los derechos, las libertades y la prosperidad de los españoles.*

05/12/2020

(62) *Estamos aquí para defender los intereses de los españoles.*

24/05/2021

(63) *Le seul fil conducteur qui nous guide c'est l'intérêt national, parce que ce qui nous porte c'est l'amour de la France et des Français.*

19/01/2019

The Pathos Dimension of Immigration Discourse

In order to garner support and manipulate public opinion, Abascal's discourse plays upon sentiments. Pathos is construed from appeals to patriotism.

Examples (63–65) reveal the appeal to emotional attachments to the country:

(64) *A nosotros nos mueve el amor por nuestros compatriotas, el amor a España, que es nuestra.*

24/05/2021

(65) *Vox tiene una posición distinta […]desde el amor a España y a nuestros compatriotas, que en nuestro país tiene prioridad.*

05/12/2020

(66) *Esta España que nos pertenece, a la que amamos.*

03/02/2020

A common past and future enhances the pathos element of Abascal's discourse:

(67) *Adelante en defensa de la herencia de nuestros padres. Adelante en defensa del futuro de nuestros hijos.*

05/12/2020

Discussion

As we see, Abascal and Le Pen confront similar immigration issues and their positions do not vary significantly. We can observe common patterns and divergences along the three discursive dimensions:

1. Logos

The discourse of Abascal and Le Pen is built upon the perception of immigrants as dangerous outsiders who endanger national identity and unity (topos of threat). Such threat element is consistently developed in their public discourse. (Illegal) immigration threatens the nation's security and prosperity and is associated with crime and public spending on social assistance and health care. This view is manifested through the use of dismantling strategies, particularly other-negative presentation, which prevail in Le Pen's discourse. Abascal also employs dissimilation strategies to construe difference and highlight differences between nationals and immigrants.

2. Ethos

The ethical dimension of both Abascal's and Le Pen's discourse relies on two elements: (a) positive self-characterization; (b) explicit denial of racism through the strategy of impression management. Yet the ethical element is more clearly formulated in Abascal's discourse.

3. Pathos

Only Abascal makes emotional appeals to generate political consent. His appeals are associated with national identity insofar as he claims to be exclusively moved by patriotic feelings. The pathos element is also manifested through the use of national-we, which creates solidarity, and lexis denoting empathy to the in-group, who are seen as victims.

Conclusion

This chapter has provided evidence of the close relationship between discourse and society through the analysis of the construction of immigration issues in the discourse of Abascal and Le Pen, the respective leaders of the far-right parties Vox and Rassemblement National. The analysis yields two main findings: (i) the prevalence of the Aristotelian mode of logos over ethos and pathos; and (ii) the combination of constructive and dismantling strategies in the far-right narrative about immigration and immigrants. The working of the logos dimension is manifested in the discursive construction of social actors (immigrants, policy-makers, the Spanish/French people, Abascal and Le Pen themselves) and processes (arguing, demanding, blaming), as well as the claims of truth and rightness employed by Abascal and Le Pen to justify their standpoint about (illegal) immigration. The ethos dimension reveals the construction of Abascal's and Le Pen's self-image as non-racist politicians committed to national interest, while the pathos dimension shows the emotional appeals of discourse (appeals to nationalism). Abascal and Le Pen mainly resort to dismantling strategies to back their stand, among which other-negative presentation proves to be a powerful strategy which enhances the negative effects of immigration and combines in Abascal's discourse with dissimilation strategies that highlight the contrast between the in-group and the out-group.

This research intends to contribute to future rhetorical studies by broadening the CDA analytical framework through the integration of the Aristotelian ethos and pathos dimensions, which play a central role in the legitimization of ideological positions.

Notes

1 Rubio-Carbonero and Zapata-Barrero have developed an analytical framework to study the construction of Catalan political discourse on immigration.
2 Hart's analysis of immigration discourse is based on Talmy's theory of Force Dynamics.
3 Poggi (2005) analyses the use of logos, ethos and pathos strategies in persuasive discourse through the analysis of political and advertising fragments, and dialogues in the health domain, in terms of a hierarchy of goals.
4 The translations of the original quotes are presented in the Appendix.

References

Aristotle (1991) *Rhétorique*. Paris: Editions Gallimard.
Browse, S. (2018) *Cognitive Rhetoric: The Cognitive Poetics of Political Discourse*. Amsterdam: John Benjamins.
Caldas-Coulthard, C. R. and Coulthard, M. (eds.) (1996) *Texts and Practices: Readings in Critical Discourse Analysis*. London: Routledge.
Cap, P. (2018) 'From "Cultural Unbelonging" to "Terrorist Risk": Communicating Threat in the Polish Anti-Immigration Discourse'. *Critical Discourse Studies* 15(3): 285–302.
Charteris-Black, J. (2004) *Corpus Approaches to Critical Metaphor Analysis*. Basingstoke: Palgrave Macmillan.
Charteris-Black, J. (2005) *Politicians and Rhetoric: The Persuasive Power of Metaphor*. Basingstoke: Palgrave Macmillan.
Charteris-Black, J. (2006) 'Britain as A Container: Immigration Metaphors in the 2005 Election Campaign'. *Discourse & Society* 17(5): 563–581.
Charteris-Black, J. (2009) 'Metaphor and Political Communication', in A. Musolff and J. Zinken (eds.), *Metaphor and Discourse*. Basingstoke/New York: Palgrave Macmillan.
Charteris-Black, J. (2013) *Analysing Political Speeches: Rhetoric, Discourse and Metaphor*. Basingstoke: Palgrave Macmillan.
Chilton, P. (2011) 'Still Something Missing in CDA'. *Discourse Studies* 13(6): 769–781.
Chilton, P., Tian, H. and Wodak, R. (2010) 'Reflections on Discourse and Critique in China and the West'. *Journal of Language and Politics* 9(4): 489–507.
Demata, M. (2017) '"A Great and Beautiful Wall": Donald Trump's Populist Discourse on Immigration'. *Journal of Language Aggression and Conflict* 5(2): 274–294.
Eberl, J. M., Meltzer, C. E., Heidenreich, T., Herrero, B., Theorin, N., Lind, F. and Strömbäck, J. (2018) 'The European Media Discourse on Immigration and Its Effects: A Literature Review'. *Annals of the International Communication Association* 42(3): 207–223.
Fairclough, N. (2003) *Analysing Discourse: Textual Analysis for Social Research*. London/New York: Psychology Press.

Fairclough, N. (2012) 'Critical Discourse Analysis'. *International Advances in Engineering and Technology* 7: 452–487.

Fairclough, N. (2013) *Critical Discourse Analysis: The Critical Study of Language*. London: Routledge.

Fairclough, I. and Fairclough, N. (2013) *Political Discourse Analysis: A Method for Advanced Students*. London/New York: Routledge.

Gale, P. (2004) 'The Refugee Crisis and Fear: Populist Politics and Media Discourse'. *Journal of Sociology* 40(4): 321–340.

Georgiou, M. and Zaborowski, R. (2017) *Media Coverage of the "Refugee Crisis": A Cross-European Perspective*. Strasbourg: Council of Europe.

Greussing, E. and Boomgaarden, H. G. (2017) 'Shifting the Refugee Narrative? An Automated Frame Analysis of Europe's 2015 Refugee Crisis'. *Journal of Ethnic and Migration Studies* 43(11): 1749–1774.

Hart, C. (2011) 'Force-Interactive Patterns in Immigration Discourse: A Cognitive Linguistic Approach to CDA'. *Discourse & Society* 22(3): 269–286.

Kovács, A. and Wodak, R. (eds.) (2003) *NATO, Neutrality and National Identity: The Case of Austria and Hungary*. Vienna: Böhlau.

Moffitt, B. (2017) 'Populism in Australia and New Zealand', in C.R. Kaltwasser et al. (eds.), *The Oxford Handbook of Populism*. Oxford: Oxford University Press, 121–139.

Moffitt, B. (2020) *Populism*. New York: John Wiley & Sons.

Morales-López, E. and Floyd, A. (eds.) (2017) *Developing New Identities in Social Conflicts: Constructivist Perspectives* (vol. 71). Amsterdam: John Benjamins.

Mudde, C. (2015) 'Populist Radical Right Parties in Europe Today', in J. Abromeit et al. (eds.), *Transformations of Populism in Europe and the Americas: History and Recent Trends*. London/New York: Bloomsbury, 295–307.

Muntigl, P., Weiss, G. and Wodak, R. (2000) *European Union Discourses of Un/employment. An Interdisciplinary Approach to Employment Policy-Making and Organizational Change*. Amsterdam: John Benjamins.

Musolff, A. (2004) *Metaphor and Political Discourse. Analogic Reasoning in Debates about Europe*. New York: Palgrave.

Negro, I. (2015) 'Hugo Chávez and the Building of His Self-Image through Metaphor'. *Ibérica* 29: 83–104.

Poggi, I. (2005) 'The Goals of Persuasion'. *Pragmatics & Cognition* 13(2): 297–335.

Porto, M. D. (2022) 'Water Metaphors and Evaluation of Syrian Migration: The Flow of Refugees in the Spanish Press'. *Metaphor and Symbol* 37(3): 252–267.

Pujante, D. (2017) 'The Discursive Construction of Reality in the Context of Rhetoric', in E. Morales-López and A. Floyd (eds.), *Developing New Identities in Social Conflicts: Constructivist Perspectives*. Amsterdam: John Benjamins, 41–66.

Reisigl, M. and Wodak, R. (2009) 'The Discourse-Historical Approach (DHA)'. *Methods of Critical Discourse Analysis* 2: 87–121.

Romano, M. and Porto, M. D. (2021) 'Framing CONFLICT in the Syrian Refugee Crisis: Multimodal Representations in the Spanish and British Press', in L. Filardo- Llamas, E. Morales- López and A. Floyd (eds.), *Discursive Approaches to Sociopolitical Polarization and Conflict*. London: Routledge, 153–173.

Rubio-Carbonero, G. (2020) 'Subtle Discriminatory Political Discourse on Immigration'. *Journal of Language and Politics* 19(6): 893–914.

Rubio-Carbonero, G. and Zapata-Barrero, R. (2017) 'Monitoring Discriminatory Political Discourse on Immigration: A Pilot Study in Catalonia'. *Discourse & Society* 28(2): 204–225.

Stanley, J. (2020) *How Fascism Works: The Politics of Us and Them*. New York: Random House.

Triandafyllidou, A. (2000) 'The Political Discourse on Immigration in Southern Europe: A Critical Analysis'. *Journal of Community & Applied Social Psychology* 10(5): 373–389.

Van Der Valk, I. (2003). 'Right-Wing Parliamentary Discourse on Immigration in France'. *Discourse & Society* 14(3): 309–348.

Van Dijk, T. A. (1993) 'Principles of Critical Discourse Analysis'. *Discourse and Society* 4(2): 249–283.

Van Dijk, T.A. (ed.) (1997) *Discourse Studies: A Multidisciplinary Introduction*. Vol. 2. *Discourse as Social Interaction*. London: Sage.

Van Dijk, T. A. (2000) 'On the Analysis of Parliamentary Debates on Immigration', in M. Reisigl and R. Wodak, *The Semiotics of Racism: Approaches to Critical Discourse Analysis*. Vienna: Passagen Verlag, 85–103.

Van Dijk, T. A. (2005) 'Critical Discourse Analysis', in D. Schiffrin et al. (eds.), *The Handbook of Discourse Analysis*. New Jersey: Blackwell Publishing, 349–371.

Van Dijk, T. A. (2019) 'Ideologies, Racism, Discourse: Debates on Immigration and Ethnic Issues', in J. ter Wal and M. Verkuyten (eds.), *Comparative Perspectives on Racism*. London: Routledge, 91–115.

Wodak, R. (2001) 'The Discourse-Historical Approach'. *Methods of Critical Discourse Analysis* 1: 63–94.

Wodak, R. (2009) *Discursive Construction of National Identity*. Edinburgh: Edinburgh University Press.

Wodak, R. (2011) 'Critical Linguistics and Critical Discourse Analysis'. *Discursive Pragmatics* 8: 50–70.

Wodak, R. (2015) *The Politics of Fear: What Right-Wing Populist Discourses Mean*. London: Sage.

Wodak, R. and Meyer, M. (eds.) (2015) *Methods of Critical Discourse Studies*. London: Sage.

Wodak, R. and Van Dijk, T. A. (eds.) (2000) *Racism at the Top*. Klagenfurt: Drava.

Wodak, R. et al. (1997) *The Discursive Construction of National Identity*. London: Sage.

Appendix

(1) Borders serve to defend our prosperity, our freedom, our laws, our culture and the heritage we have received from our parents.

(2) […] importing people who cannot adapt […] because they cannot, because they were born, they have lived in cultures that are incompatible with ours and totally different.

(3) Spain is our homeland, it was the homeland of our grandparents and it will be the homeland of our grandchildren.

(4) We are not against immigrants.

(5) I will remove the possibility of regularizing illegals.

(6) I will attack the Islamist ideology.

(7) The state lacks the courage to attack Islamists.

(8) We do not need thousands of illegal immigrants to pay pensions. A lie repeated a thousand times […]

(9) High fences make good neighbours.

(10) […] they are responsible for the great tragedy that is taking place in the seas.

(11) Morocco and Algeria, countries that have abandoned their nationals and refuse to take them back.

(12) It is they who are racist, who are lying to millions of people living in Africa, telling them that here is the promised land.

(13) They show a clear endophobia, a hatred of their own people.

(14) For decades, we have been giving social benefits that do not reach the most needy Spaniards to those who enter the country illegally.

(15) They often come to receive the social benefits that are denied to Spaniards.

(16) We must cut all the aid that is actually given to illegal immigrants and which costs a small fortune, and all this money is missing from Mayotte's infrastructure and economic investments.

(17) They are using health services that are not provided to Spaniards.

(18) lawless immigration is a threat to their daily lives, to their way of life.

(19) The problem is culture, which [...] is incompatible with our way of life.
(20) [...] they are with the enemies of the Spaniards.
(21) Assuming that these barbaric criminals are only acting out of madness, I say this: France is not a psychiatric asylum.
(22) [...] these barbaric exactions by so-called unbalanced people who often come from elsewhere.
(23) the migratory avalanche has led to a worsening social emergency and a serious insecurity crisis, as well as the total death of tourism.
(24) With each passing day, the flooding of our streets, our villages and our cities by immigration that is now completely uncontrolled accelerates.
(25) Our country is subject to the inseparable dangers of submersion through immigration.
(26) [...] an uninterrupted flow of immigrants that is sweeping through our cities, towns and even the smallest village.
(27) The migratory torrent is in the process of sweeping away our social systems, exploding the entire penal system and undermining the unity of the nation.
(28) [...] a delirious immigration that transforms certain places into areas of non-France, areas where you feel like a stranger in your own country.
(29) Loving France and taking the risk of seeing it disappear is quite contradictory [...] The removal of its borders, of its identity leads to its disappearance.
(30) We demand a halt to this illegal immigration, which generates uncertainty and insecurity.
(31) The link between insecurity and mass immigration is no longer in doubt for people of good faith.
(32) A feeling of insecurity is taking hold in France that is ruining people's lives.
(33) Physical insecurity with these gratuitous murders, these lynchings for futile reasons.
(34) I see the effects of illegal immigration which weighs on our finances.
(35) We oppose the principle of the multicultural society, which is a multi-conflict society.
(36) We cannot waste this heritage in the name of a submission to multiculturalism.
(37) All over the world, multicultural societies are the most violent, the most criminal.
(38) [...] those who assault our borders want to lead us to ruin, divide the country and sow panic in the streets.
(39) [...] the cradle of our civilization is the object of a migratory offensive of continental proportions.
(40) [...] the migratory invasion that is sweeping Spain.
(41) We are facing a real invasion of our national territory.
(42) We are here to resist.
(43) [...] to be uprooted from their land, from their families, from their societies and their roots.
(44) You have reinstated a new trade in human beings from the shores of the Mediterranean, with its tragedies and uprooted people.
(45) Spain has the duty and the right to expel those who are illegally on our soil.
(46) [...] must withdraw the nationality of anyone who has obtained it and has committed a crime.
(47) 25% more illegal immigrants have arrived this year in Spain and 800% more to the Canary Islands.

(48) 420,000 people enter our country every year. 40,000 unaccompanied minors cost 50,000 euros each per year.
(49) The message has to get through that anyone who enters our house, in Spain, illegally [...] must abandon all hope of working legally among us.
(50) You do not enter Spain by kicking in the door.
(51) Borders are the walls of our homeland.
(52) Our home is protected by walls, by borders that guard our prosperity, our culture, our identity, our freedom.
(53) A country that ceases to defend its borders ceases to be a homeland.
(54) We do not reject immigration; we do not reject, even less, the people, the immigrants.
(55) We do not incite hatred and phobia against immigrants.
(53) We do not care about the colour of people's skin.
(56) I have no negative feelings towards foreigners. I have no hatred of foreigners.
(57) Of course, Vox has a different position, of course it is not an invitation to hatred or xenophobia.
(58) Solidarity is important and we have to show compassion.
(59) Our mission is to defend the interests, rights, liberties and prosperity of the Spanish people.
(60) We are here to defend the interests of the Spanish people.
(61) The only guiding thread is national interest, because what carries us is the love of France and the French.
(62) We are moved by love for our compatriots, by love for Spain, which is our homeland.
(63) Vox has a different position [...] from the love for Spain and our compatriots, which in our country has priority.
(64) This Spain that belongs to us, which we love.
(65) Let us defend the heritage of our fathers. Let us defend our children's future.

14

RHETORIC OF POLISH POLITICAL DISCOURSE ON FAMILY

Ewa Bogdanowska-Jakubowska and Nika Bogdanowska

Introduction

Family has always been at the top of the Polish hierarchy of values. Family bonds constitute the basis of Polish interpersonal relations. Family functions as a point of reference and provides support of all kinds, financial included. In Poland, one of Europe's most devout Catholic countries, there exists a whole spectrum of family models (from traditional families through "patchwork" families and single-parent families to same-sex couples) but it is the traditional family that constitutes the most widely accepted model. This is a model based on the conservative vision of the gender order, resembling *the strict father* model of the family which is supported and protected by a strong father. Its morality implies a division into absolute rights and wrongs, and requires obedience to the father; it is based on authority and control (Lakoff 2002). The father represents *hegemonic masculinity* – the dominant form of masculinity, associated with marriage, power and physical strength (Connell 1987).

The type of femininity related to the Polish traditional model of family is the stereotype of *matka Polka* (the Polish mother) – "selfless, devoted to her husband and children, and having no other interests than her home" (Jakubowska 2007: 337). It epitomizes traditional, Catholic values, among which family is one of the most important. We identify the stereotype with *emphasized femininity*, which is complementary to hegemonic masculinity and is meant to satisfy the man's interests and needs (Connell 1987). Nowadays, Polish women perform different forms of femininity (e.g. *resistant femininity*, represented by women that assume the emancipated style of life (Connell 1987)), often combining professional work with family life. The stereotype of *matka Polka* is considered a relic of the past; however it is still powerful among conservative-thinking Poles (Jakubowska 2009).

The 1980s, the decade of *Solidarność* (the Polish trade union "Solidarity") and opposition to the communist regime, ended in the Round-Table Talks and the first free parliamentary election, which led to the fall of communism in Poland in 1989. The "neoliberal revolution – the dismantling of the socialist welfare state with its generous universal health care system, job security and state support for families – took place as part of the systemic transformation in the 1990s" (Graff and Korolczuk 2022: 33). This resulted in

218

DOI: 10.4324/9781003195276-18

great sociocultural changes: the opening to the West and democratization of social life were accompanied, *inter alia*, by "re-traditionalisation of gender roles" and "sentimentalisation of home and family" (Szwed and Zielińska 2017: 118). Szwed and Zielińska (2017) explain that the changes were caused by a combination of two factors: a reaction to the former communist authorities' emancipatory policy; and the growing power of the Roman Catholic Church, which played a significant role in overthrowing communism in Poland. Graff and Korolczuk (2022: 86; Graff 2009) write about "the politicization of gender and sexuality" – the conservative political and media discourse about gender was an expression of anxiety about national identity in the process of Poland's EU accession. In 1993, Poland passed a new abortion law (described as a church-state compromise), which allowed for abortion only due to fetal defects and when the pregnancy put the woman's life at risk or resulted from rape. Abortion on social grounds was no longer legal. In the 2000s, Polish liberal civil society continued to develop; gender and LGBT equality were part of democratization. Simultaneously, the promotion of the conservative values of "domesticity, motherhood and focus on childcare" went together with anti-genderism (a critique of neoliberalism and feminism) (Graff and Korolczuk 2022: 33).

Since 2015, when the right-wing populist *Prawo i Sprawiedliwość* party (PiS; Law and Justice) won the parliamentary election, the Polish political arena has become dominated by populist discourse in which conservative family values are emphasized. It presents a heteronormative worldview, which organizes society according to paternalistic principles: the traditional gender roles and the traditional model of family. The concept of Polish family propagated by PiS has been accurately represented by the Polish philosopher and feminist politician Magdalena Środa (2021; our translation): "Family is not only 'sacred', but also strongly enmeshed with myths of naturalness, eternal existence, monogamy, harmony, etc." Using the noun *myth*, Środa implies the falseness of the ideas on which the concept of family is founded. This idealized picture is contrasted with what happens or may happen in real life – domestic violence (the *topos* of comparison/difference): "And even if a family member has beaten his wife to death, no one should criticize the family, because its value is greater than that of individual rights to security, body integrity and happiness." A sequence of rhetorical questions completes Środa's picture of the PiS conceptualization of family: "What do we need the convention on preventing violence against women and children for? What do we need a critique of nepotism for? What do we need democracy for?" At the end, the exclamation *Family is sacred!* (the Polish traditionalists' credo) sounds sarcastic.

Our chapter discusses the rhetoric of the Polish right-wing populist (RWP) discourse, which aims to restore the traditional patriarchal order and impose on society the "only acceptable" model of family. We have employed the principle of triangulation, using a variety of methodological and theoretical perspectives (Cicourel 1969; Wodak et al. 2009), and analyzing different types of data, e.g. political speeches, debates, interviews, newspaper articles and posters. The texts (by members of the United Right and their supporters) have been selected with respect to: the topic – family and its members, women and children in particular; the ideology – conservative, right-wing populist; and the time of publication – 2015–2022.

The Discourse-Historical Approach

In the analysis of the rhetoric of Polish RWP discourse on family, the Discourse-Historical Approach (DHA) has been used. Developed by Ruth Wodak and her Vienna group (Wodak 2001; Wodak et al. 2009; Wodak and Reisigl 2015), the DHA, one of the most prominent approaches to Critical Discourse Studies (CDS), is interdisciplinary and combines pragmatics, "sociolinguistics and studies on narration, stylistics, rhetoric and argumentation with historical and sociological research" (Reisigl 2018: 45).

Discourse is understood as "a complex bundle of simultaneous and sequential interrelated linguistic acts, which manifest themselves within and across the social fields of action". These acts are very often texts which belong to different genres (Wodak 2001: 66). Social fields of action (e.g. the field of political action) are segments of social reality which constitute "the 'frame' of discourse". Thus a discourse may include various perspectives on social reality (Reisigl 2018). "Through discourses, social actors constitute objects of knowledge, situations and social roles as well as identities and interpersonal relations between different social groups and those who interact with them" (Wodak et al. 2009: 9).

The DHA is a problem-oriented approach in which an interpretation of discourses and texts is integrated with an analysis of four layers of context (Wodak 2001: 67): the immediate linguistic co-text; the intertextual and interdiscursive references in the text; the extralinguistic social variables and institutional frames of a specific context of situation; and the broader sociopolitical and historical contexts. The DHA involves an interest in the rhetoric of analyzed discourse, especially in persuasion (e.g. argumentation strategies, *topoi* – "'inference warrants' granting the transition from arguments to conclusion" (Kienpointner 1991: 46; Bogdanowska 2008)), tropes (e.g. metaphors and metonymies) and genre theory (e.g. concerning political speeches and debates) (Reisigl 2018).

The DHA is applied in research on, *inter alia*, identity politics, discrimination, nation-building, nationalism, national identity and social order. The DHA has been used in studies on various political discourses, RWP discourses included. Among them, there are various case studies, e.g. of argumentation in Austrian RWP discourse (Reisigl 2007b); RWP discourse in Europe (Wodak, KhosraviNik and Mral 2013; Wodak 2015, 2019a, 2021); Holocaust denial in Austria (Engel and Wodak 2013); and collective memory in Austrian RWP discourse (Wodak and Forchtner 2014).

The choice of this interdisciplinary and multi-perspectival approach allows for an adequate analysis of the rhetoric employed in the Polish RWP discourse on family.

Right-Wing Populist Rhetoric

Populism is "a phenomenon rooted in the very concept of democracy" (Pelinka 2018: 618): populists claim that they represent the "true" understanding of democracy. Populism systematically appeals to the people (*demos*), a supposedly homogeneous group or a nation inhabiting a particular geographical region (Zienkowski and Breeze 2019). Mény and Surel (2002: 3) pose the question whether populism should not be interpreted as "a pathology of democracy", or "political pathology", in which democratic rules and mechanisms are distorted. Although populist parties claim they are not anti-democratic (Rydgren 2018), the populist understanding of democracy is reduced to the rule of the majority. "Populism speaks on behalf of the majority, even if representing only a minority of the electorate" (Pelinka 2018: 623). The (national) interests of the majority matter, while the rights of minorities (e.g. social, ethnic, religious, political minorities) are neglected (Pelinka 2018).

Populist parties view society as "ultimately separated into two homogeneous and antagonistic groups, the 'pure' people versus 'the corrupt elite'" (Mudde 2004: 543).

The elites (the political class of the privileged, the so-called establishment) are "usually considered inimical to the people and the nation" (Germani 1978: 88). Populists accuse them of putting their own interests ahead of the interests of the common people (Rydgren 2018: 1–2), whom they idealize (Feldman 2019).

RWP parties are "primarily defined by the construction of common enemies" (Wodak 2013: 29). They discursively construct themselves as the "saviors", defending the people against their enemies – the others, e.g. sexual minorities, immigrants (Muslims, "terrorists"), the EU (see Wodak 2013). They reject social equality and oppose "the social integration of marginalized groups", and instrumentalize sentiments of anxiety and disenchantment (Feldman 2019: 26). Addressing the collective common ground, they continuously construct fear:

> right-wing populism does not only relate to the *form* of rhetoric but to its specific *contents*: such parties successfully construct fear and – related to the various real or imagined dangers – propose scapegoats that are blamed for threatening or actually damaging our societies, in Europe and beyond.
>
> *Wodak 2015: 1*

Right-wing populists claim to represent the homogeneous people, who are said to share ethnic and cultural identities, and past experiences, and identify with the same worldview.

Discussing right-wing populism in Europe in the second decade of the twenty-first century, Wodak (2019a: 66–67) calls the period "the post-shame era": RWP shamelessness is manifested in exclusionary rhetoric, "bad manners", anti-politics ("a specific attitude and related discourse that systematically undermine democratic institutions"), "the humiliation of other participants, defamation, lies, and ad hominem attacks". The rhetorical strategies typical of the RWP discourse are (Van Leeuwen and Wodak 1999; Engel and Wodak 2013; Wodak 2013: 27–29; Wodak 2014; Wodak 2015: 28):

* *calculated ambivalence* – conveying two contradictory messages in one utterance addressed to different audiences sharing different ideologies;
* *constructing conspiracy theories*;
* *moral evaluation* – legitimation by reference to value systems;
* *mythopoesis* – legitimation achieved by narratives (about the past or future);
* *provocation*;
* *scapegoating* – expressing irrational hostility towards the other;
* *shifting blame*;
* *victim-perpetrator reversal*.

The Rhetoric of Polish RWP Discourse on Family in the Twenty-First Century

Europe is experiencing a rise in right-wing populism (Bevelander and Wodak 2019). In Central Europe (e.g. in Hungary and Poland), the neoliberal model which was implemented during the post-communist transformation is now being replaced with illiberal democracy; the type of democracy which retains "the majoritarian trappings of democracy, while curtailing civil and political rights for opponents and minorities" (Feldman 2019: 36). Illiberalism is "a deeply gendered political transformation" which changes "the meanings of human rights, women's rights and equality in a way which privileges the rights and normative needs of families over women's rights" (Grzebalska and Pető 2018: 164). One of the major tenets of Central European illiberalism is *familiarism*, which views the traditional family as the foundation of the nation (Kemper 2016). According to Pető and Grzebalska (2016), Fidesz and PiS, the Hungarian and Polish ruling parties respectively, "use nationalist ideas about the family to attack human rights, emphasising the rights and interests of 'traditional' families over those of individuals and minorities". The concept of "family mainstreaming" has been introduced as central in their policy-making.

Illiberal, nationalist parties aim to strengthen the nation by making it ethnically homogeneous, cherish myths of the past, and postulate returning to traditional values and morals (family values, traditional gender roles) (Pelinka 2018; Rydgren 2018; Wodak 2019a). PiS is one of them, endorsing a traditional Christian fundamentalist agenda and patriarchal gender norms. Since 2015, when it won the general election and formed the United Right (the conservative governing coalition of which PiS is the leading party), it has radicalized and turned into a "full-blown right-wing populist" party "with strong inclinations toward authoritarianism" (Graff and Korolczuk 2022: 26).

The Traditional Model of Family According to the PiS Party

Since its 2015 parliamentary election success, PiS has declared the need for a pro-family and pro-natalist policy. The party promised welfare programs that were to transform the lives of low-income Poles. The welfare programs were the part of the party's program "The Good Change" which helped PiS win the election. Its flagship 500 Plus program gave parents a monthly subsidy for every child, without any income threshold. Officially, the program, presented as a nation-building, patriotic enterprise, was to solve the problem of declining birth rate. It was to improve families' standard of living and *give dignity back to them* (however, critics perceived it as an attempt to win voters). In a policy statement, Beata Szydło, the then Prime Minister, maintained that, unlike their predecessors, they would support *the badly-off part of society*, treating *the resources devoted to this cause not as expenses but as investments* in the development of the country, society and Polish families (18 November 2015; our translation). The dominant *topos* used in the program was the *topos* of burdening (if a person "is burdened by specific problems, one should act in order to diminish these burdens" (Reisigl 2014: 78)).

The need to protect Polish families and children is repeatedly said to be a priority. Politicians of PiS often employ an *argumentum ad antiquitatem* (appeal to tradition), which says "if something existed in the past or was used in the past, it must be right". The concept of marriage is traced back to Roman law. Family is depicted as *od wieków ostoja państwa polskiego* (the mainstay of the Polish state for centuries), which is now threatened (*There are groups that want to dismantle the traditional model of family*). Marriage is pictured in a biological perspective: Przemysław Czarnek, a member of Andrzej Duda's presidential campaign team and a PiS MP, argued on TVP Info, a state-owned news channel, that *there is nothing like same-sex marriages in nature* and *the basic function of the family is procreation*. In an interview for the German tabloid *Bild*, foreign minister Witold Waszczykowski (2016) said, *[w]hat moves most Poles [is] tradition, historical awareness, love of country, faith in God and normal family life between a woman and a man*. These words constitute the gist of the United Right ideology. Jarosław Kaczyński, the leader of the ruling PiS party, defined the family as:

Rhetoric of Polish Political Discourse on Family

(1)

a social cell/unit of completely fundamental significance for the continuity of generations, for passing on culture, civilization, for the stability of greater collectivities. But we see family this way: One woman, one man in a stable relation and their children. This is a family!

Kaczyński 2019; our translation

He employed here the *topos* of consequence ("something follows as a direct result of something else" (Wodak et al. 2009: 41)) and the *topos* of definition ("a person or thing designated X should carry the qualities/traits/attributes consistent with the meaning of X" (Wodak 2011: 44)). The first sentence of the excerpt is a truism, used as a rhetorical device. The conjunction *but* in the second sentence implicates contrast between the traditional model of family, approved of by PiS, and other models of family, e.g. single-parent families, same-sex marriages, etc. Family is conceptualized here in terms of the metaphor THE FAMILY IS A SIGNIFICANT CELL OF THE ORGANISM (THE SOCIETY IS AN ORGANISM).

Describing the opposition (the Civic Coalition), Kaczyński offered a defaming other-presentation, implying that the *demolition of Poland* he accused them of is triggered by an external enemy (see 2). Constructing their image, he employed the *argumentum ad populum* (appeal to the people), which is aimed to justify the masses' traditional worldview (*the imposition of sexual revolution on Poland*) (for the difference between plausible *topos* and fallacious *argumentum ad* see Reisigl 2007b), and the *topos* of danger and threat (which can be paraphrased as "if there are specific dangers and threats, one should do something against them" (Wodak 2001: 75)). According to Kaczyński, the demolition also has an effect on the traditional Polish family, which is a significant constituent of Polish identity.

(2)

They offer a compete demolition of Poland for the sake of external interests. These interests also involve the imposition of a sexual revolution on Poland, destroying family, national tradition, everything that constitutes our identity.

Kaczyński 2021; our translation

The dominant role of family in the PiS ideology is also visible in institutions they have created or declared an intent to establish, e.g. the Ministry of Family, Labour and Social Policy. The Polish Parliament is currently hearing a bill proposed by the government on the foundation of a Polish Institute of Family and Demography. It would educate Poles on the *vital role of the family in the social order* and have the power to restrict divorces in order to increase the birth rate in Poland. According to the author of the bill, establishing the institute *is a life-and-death matter for Poland* (Wróblewski 2021; our translation). The adjective *life-and-death* is used metaphorically and literally at the same time. Saying, *I do not blame any government after 1989, but I don't have any doubt that the institute is being established too late*, Wróblewski makes a disclaimer, tacitly acknowledging that he, in fact, blames previous governments for not establishing such an institution. He implies that, in contrast to those governments, the current government is ready to take action in this respect. It is a positive self-presentation of the governing party. At the end, he provides reasons for establishing the institute: *We must counteract negative demographic trends and take care of the family*. Two *topoi* are used here, the *topos* of reality ("Because reality is as it is, a specific action/decision should be performed/made" (Wodak 2015: 78)) and the *topos* of urgency (actions need to be taken very quickly because of a difficult situation (Wodak 2011)).

Other Models of Family

As has already been mentioned, the current situation of the Polish family is described in the ruling party discourse with the use of the *topos* of danger and threat. The LGBT community (a minority) is presented as an aggressor and an internal enemy, accused of attacking the traditionally thinking Poles who share Christian values (the majority). In 2019, the Ordo Iuris Institute for Legal Culture, a Polish Catholic organization known for its anti-LGBT, anti-abortion and anti-divorce activism, formulated the Charter of Family Rights (Ordo Iuris 2019), which has been ratified by some local governments. As the institute declared, the Charter was created to counteract the undermining of the rights of families and to secure the legal identity and constitutional position of marriage. In fact, it constitutes an attack on single-parent families and the LGBT community (victim-perpetrator reversal). A local government member supporting PiS, commenting on the importance of the Charter, described the situation of the family in Poland in terms of threat:

(3)
The Charter of Family Rights wouldn't be necessary, if it weren't for the aggression of the LGBT community. The resolution wouldn't be necessary, if it weren't for an assault on Christian values which have been accepted and respected in Poland for centuries. Today, the majority has been placed before the firing squad [not been given a choice] by the minority. Western countries have already been defeated in the battle and have got rid of Christian values. Poland remained alone at the defense post of Latin Europe.

Lewandowski 2020; our translation

In (3), the metonymy AN ATTACK ON THE VALUES FOR AN ATTACK ON THE GROUP and the metaphor PLACING SOMEBODY BEFORE THE FIRING SQUAD IS DEPRIVING SOMEBODY OF CHOICE are employed. Battle and confrontation terminology is used (e.g. *defend, be defeated in the battle*). The argumentation is based on the *topos* of history ("because history teaches that specific actions have specific consequences, one should perform or omit a specific action in a specific situation" (Wodak 2011: 44)) and the *topos* of singularity (Reisigl 2007a). Poland is conceptualized as the only defender of Christian values. Due to its geopolitical situation, in the past Poland was depicted as the bulwark of Christendom. The expression *być na posterunku obrony Europy łacińskiej* (be at the defense post of Latin Europe), popular among Polish right-wing politicians, may be traced back to 1683, when John III Sobieski defeated the Ottoman army at the Battle of Vienna. After that, he was called the Savior of the Western European civilization. The expression *Latin Europe* refers to Roman-derived cultures with which Western Christianity, Roman Catholicism in particular, is traditionally identified. Nowadays, however, the ruling party sees a threat to Christian values not only in the East but also in the West, epitomized by the EU.

Attacks on the LGBT community intensified during the second presidential campaign of Andrzej Duda in 2020. During one of the election rallies, the Polish president said

Rhetoric of Polish Political Discourse on Family

that the promotion of LGBT rights is a more destructive ideology than communism. The comparison of LGBT to communism constituted a moral evaluation of LGBT people. He also depersonalized and dehumanized the group, saying that *LGBT is not people, it's an ideology*. He declared that he was against gay marriages and adoption by gay couples, which he perceived as an element of *foreign ideology*. He pledged to *defend children against LGBT ideology* (the *topos* of threat) and *ban the propagation of LGBT ideology* (the *topos* of law and order – "If I or we get the power, we will provide for/guarantee law and order" (Reisigl 2014: 79)). LGBT ideology, and as a result LGBT people, are conceptualized as a threat to the social order in Poland and the Polish traditional family, and a common enemy (the metaphor LGBT IS A THREAT/AN ENEMY). PiS instrumentalizes the LGBT community as a scapegoat. Wodak (2015) calls such actions a "politics of fear". Przemysław Czarnek said during a televised debate, *Let's stop listening to these idiocies about human rights. These people are not equal to normal people.* He used the *topos* of comparison/difference (the presupposition "we are superior compared to them" (Wodak et al. 2009: 40)) and the *argumentum ad populum* ("often aiming to justify prejudiced emotions and opinions of a social group, instead of relevant arguments" (Reisigl 2007a: 382)). They are stigmatized as "others" in comparison to "us", the so-called *normals*. Talking about LGBT, Witold Waszczykowski, a former Minister of Foreign Affairs in the PiS government, also based his argumentation on the *topos* of difference (see 4). The modal verb *musieć* (must/have to) was used to distance the speaker from the proposition he did not agree with. Here, the fallacious *argumentum ad hominem* ("a verbal attack on the opponent's personality and character instead of trying to refute the opponent's arguments" (Reisigl 2007a: 382)) was used. The fact that *they do not establish families* constitutes the "undesired differentness" (see Goffman 1963).

(4)
We can understand references to human rights, as all people have to be equal. But it is common knowledge that the concept of LGBT is an ideology which demands privileges – privileges that this group does not deserve, because they do not establish families.

Waszczykowski 2020; our translation

Kaja Godek, an ultra-conservative anti-abortion campaigner and head of the Foundation *Życie i Rodzina* (Life and Family), is the face of a bill whose working title is "Stop LGBT", aimed to keep LGBT away from the public space. In an interview for *Do rzeczy*, a conservative weekly magazine that supports PiS, she provides reasons for the need to pass the bill. To achieve a contrasting effect, she uses antithesis, enumerating accusations against her opponents (see 5).

(5)
Anyone who protests against this project supports changing the image of the Holy Mother into sexual organs, attacks on churches, extreme leftists' excesses, demoralizing children in the parades and drawing them into the LGBT movement.

Godek 2021; our translation

Godek conceptualizes LGBT parades in terms of the metaphor PARADES ARE A TOOL FOR RECRUITING CHILDREN TO A PARTICULAR COMMUNITY.

Then she employs the *topos* of illustrative example (see 6), quoting the manipulations and misrepresentations of the state-owned Polish Television, which is effectively controlled by PiS. Such narratives (mythopoesis) are often used to legitimize anti-LGBT attacks.

(6)
In candid camera documentaries, presented on Public Television, teenagers get money for participating in the parades. At the same time they get integrated with the community, which is, and will be, detrimental to their development.

Godek 2021; our translation

To defame the LGBT community, Godek, apart from making false allegations, uses the negatively marked expression *homo-propaganda* (see 7). The metaphor PLOWING IS CHANGING COMPLETELY (*przeoranie rzeczywistości społecznej* – plowing of social reality) is used; this time it is change for the worse.

(7)
Homo-propaganda involves deep demoralization and the plowing of social reality to finally make a political demand for homo-marriages and homo-adoptions.

Godek 2021; our translation

Women

In the Polish ruling party's official narration, there are declarations of gender equality; ensuring equal rights for women and ending gender-based violence are promised. However, this conflicts with Christian fundamentalism, which is expressed in criticism of Western values and narratives about moral crisis and progressive forces that are undermining the nuclear family. It is visible in comments on women's traditional social roles. Speaking *ex cathedra*, Czarnek uses hypophora, which consists in asking a question and simultaneously providing an answer to it (see 8). The *topos* of consequence and fallacious hasty generalization are the basis of his argumentation. Women's social role is reduced here to giving birth (the more frequently the better), which is treated as a moral obligation. By choosing a career, they threaten their family (the metaphor THE WOMAN'S PROFESSIONAL CAREER IS A THREAT TO THE FAMILY). For Czarnek, this leads to *tragic consequences*: women give birth to fewer children than they could. However, Czarnek does not blame women for that; at least in the beginning, they appear to be innocent. He implicates other forces (e.g. education!) and denies women's right to be treated as equal. Although men's social role is not directly stated, it can be inferred that, for Czarnek, whatever they do will not be deemed detrimental to the family.

(8)
What to do to attack the family? To attack the woman, saying 'you are like a man' [...] The role of the woman is to maintain the family, irrespective of how her husband behaves [...] Go and work, drive a tractor or combine, study, make a career. First, a career, next perhaps a child.

Czarnek 2020; our translation

In a similar vein, a professor of the Catholic University of Lublin and advisor to the Minister of Science and Education talks about women in terms of their fertility, using the *topos* of consequence, hasty generalization and the *topos* of opposites (if women manifest "spiritual depravity" which is detrimental to their family, they should change their lifestyle and live in accordance with the traditional family ethos) (see 9). Women are subjected to a moral evaluation. Pride, vanity, self-centeredness and egotism are features which they are accused of showing. Women are held responsible for what happens to the family (the metaphor THE WOMAN IS A THREAT TO THE FAMILY).

(9)
If such an attitude becomes widespread, this will kill the family, shut down women's fertility. People need home to be understood not as a place, but as an ethos.

Skrzydlewski 2021; our translation

The "negative" impact of education is not explicitly stated, but implied. One solution offered is a school reform: one of the priorities of the education policy of the government is *ugruntowywanie dziewcząt do cnót niewieścich* (establishing womanly virtues in girls). These are traditional Catholic womanly virtues, such as "compliance, nurturance and empathy", related to emphasized femininity (Connell 1987: 187). The statement itself as well as the choice of (archaic) words produced a lot of controversy, and soon became subject to memes and the cause of numerous student protests across Poland.

The United Right and pro-life organizations have made attempts to limit access to abortion or even ban it completely under the pretense of protecting disabled children (employing the *topos* of savior, typical of the RWP rhetoric (Wodak 2015)). Kaczyński made their intentions clear:

(10)
we will strive to make even the cases of very difficult pregnancies, in which the child is condemned to death or heavily deformed, end with a delivery, and to cause the child to be christened, buried and have a name.

Kaczyński 2016; our translation

An abortion ban seems to be aimed not at saving children, but at ensuring their eternal salvation, in line with the teaching of the Roman Catholic Church, which in Poland collaborates with the ruling party in this and other ideological enterprises. In October 2020, the Polish Constitutional Tribunal ruled that abortion due to fetal defects is unconstitutional, rejecting the most common of the few legal grounds for pregnancy termination. This meant further restricting the abortion law which was already one of the strictest in Europe. The ruling resulted in large anti-government rallies across Poland organized by *Strajk Kobiet* (Women's Strike), a grassroots movement promoting women's rights. As a result, the implementation of the ruling was postponed. It was finally put into effect in January 2021, which led again to protests. Since the law changed, many Polish women have started traveling abroad for legal pregnancy termination. Commenting on the increase in abortion tourism, Kaczyński stated:

(11)
I know that there are advertisements in the press which every dull-witted person can understand and she can arrange for herself an abortion abroad, be it cheaper or more expensive.

Kaczyński 2021b; our translation

He used the *topos* of people ("If the people favor a specific action, they will be able to perform it" (Wodak 2015)) and implied that the abortion ban is purely ideological; it does not matter whether and how many women seek termination.

Another important problem concerning family, women and children in particular, is domestic violence. The ruling party does not deny the problem, but sees the main causes of domestic violence in the decay of family relations and traditional social values. The government wants to take Poland out of the Istanbul Convention (the Council of Europe Convention on preventing and combating violence against women and domestic violence). In March 2021, the bill called "Yes to family, no to gender", submitted by Ordo Iuris and the Christian Social Congress, and supported by the Polish episcopal conference and PiS, was sent to parliamentary committees for examination. The bill presents the Convention as promoting "gender ideology" and wants to replace it with a convention on family rights. Michał Wójcik, a deputy Minister of Justice, said: *We do not agree to a third sex, culturally and socially conditioned. What is it anyway? [...] We will not agree to an attack on the institution of the family*. His rhetorical question is intended as a challenge, showing complete disregard for LGBT people, and is used to justify their exclusion. Others even claim that the Convention does harm to women instead of protecting them. Marek Jurek sees in it a threat to children: *We do not want our children and grandchildren to be subject to social experiments*. The noun *experiment* has acquired strongly negative connotations in RWP discourse, in which it is used to refer to actions which are not approved of. Some see a solution to the problem of domestic violence in the family itself and use the metaphor GOOD FAMILY RELATIONS ARE THE BEST PROTECTION AGAINST DOMESTIC VIOLENCE. The *topos* of authority ("if one refers to somebody in a position of authority, then the action is legitimate") (Wodak 2011: 44; *authorization legitimation* in Van Leeuwen and Wodak 1999: 104) is employed to support the arguments against the Istanbul Convention, although there is no reference to any particular academic authority and the revelations presented as "research results" may be easily shown to be false. The Convention is also discredited for supposedly including lies (the Convention *refers to religion as a reason for violence against women*). The positive image of family proposed by PiS and its supporters is contrasted with the negative image of the family model propagated by the EU (*Your vision of the family is tragic and terrible*). In the parliamentary debate on the Ordo Iuris bill, Janusz Kowalski (PiS) said: *What do you need this convention for? So that the gender poison could justify your existence. So that you could beat Poland with the gender baton*. Posing a question and then answering it (hypophora), he tried to force his own answer. The negative presentation of the opposition, which is against Poland's withdrawing from the Istanbul Convention, is based here on two metaphors: GENDER IDEOLOGY IS A POISON/A BATON. Both are aimed at criminalizing the opposition.

Children

For the United Right and its supporters, the word *child* has an extended meaning – it refers to a human being from the moment of conception. Thus, biologically, the concept includes both a fetus and a young person between birth and puberty. This has legal consequences: they claim that the child is legally protected both before and after the birth. Pro-life organizations have launched an aggressive anti-abortion campaign, flooding Polish cities with billboards. The campaign differs from earlier ones, which, for example, showed pictures of aborted fetuses. This time, the posters depict a well-developed fetus inscribed in a red heart. However, this cannot be treated as a change for the better. The

Figure 14.1 The poster of the anti-abortion campaign: I am dependent [on you]. I trust you

Figure 14.2 The poster of the anti-abortion campaign: I am 11 weeks old

picture is accompanied by a caption (see Figure 14.1), which appeals to the mother-to-be's sense of moral responsibility. In some posters, there is also information concerning perinatal hospices, which are meant to serve as the only solution for women who are made to give birth to malformed and terminally ill babies, after the Constitutional Tribunal ruled that abortion due to fetal defects is unconstitutional. In another billboard poster, the photo depicting the baby's feet is accompanied by the inscription *I am 11 weeks old* (Figure 14.2). In both cases, these are manipulations aimed at making people believe that the fetus is a well-developed baby endowed with subjectivity (the sentences with first person singular verb forms). In both cases the fallacious *argumentum ad misericordiam* (appeal to pity) is employed: the authors try to evoke pity in order to persuade and silence their opponent (Walton 1997; Kienpointner 2009).

The Polish RWP discourse is against anti-discriminatory training and sexual education in schools. During the 2020 presidential campaign, President Duda called the latter neo-Bolshevism, which, according to him, sexualizes children. He used the idiomatic expression *próbuje się dzieciom wciskać ideologię* (they try to feed children an ideology [a line] – "tell them something that is not true"). The impersonal form makes it unclear who is the agent of the action. However, Duda makes it finally explicit, saying: *I do not want children to be indoctrinated at schools against their parents' will*. His words are in line with the current policy of the Ministry of Education, aimed at a radical school reform.

Conclusion

The analysis of the Polish RWP discourse reveals the ruling party's intention, not only to win the voters who already share their worldview (the family model included), but also to impose their worldview on those who think differently. One may, however, wonder whether it is an ideological revolution or just a result of their desire to control people. The "strict father" family model is the only "right" model supported by PiS. The population of Poland should not only be ethnically homogeneous, but also represent one family lifestyle approved by the Church and the party. Family is conceptualized as a stronghold under attack from the enemies from within (the LGBT community, emancipated women) and from outside (the West, the EU, identified with liberal democracy and progressive thought). As to the family members, (1) children are threatened from the moment of conception (by pro-choice movements), and they are also ideologically threatened (by schools, progressive activists, e.g. the LGBT activists); (2) the role of men (husbands and fathers) is taken for granted, rarely explicitly referred to, as their power and control is part and parcel of the "strict father" family model; (3) women (wives and mothers), although declared to be equal to men, are often conceptually reduced to human incubators, whose well-being and health do not count. Although the family is presented as having the highest value (*sacred*), it may have some flaws (e.g. domestic violence), for which the others are blamed. In the Polish RWP discourse on family, exclusionary rhetoric dominates. The most frequent rhetorical strategies employed are moral evaluation, scapegoating, shifting blame, and victim-perpetrator reversal.

References

English References

Bevelander, P. and Wodak, R. (eds.) (2019) *Europe at the Crossroads: Confronting Populist, Nationalist and Global Challenges*. Lund: Nordic Academic Press.

Cicourel, A. V. (1969) *Method and Measurement in Sociology*. New York: Free Press.

Connell, R. W. (1987) *Gender and Power: Society, the Person and Sexual Politics*. Cambridge: Polity Press.

Engel, J. and Wodak, R. (2013) '"Calculated Ambivalence" and Holocaust Denial in Austria', in Wodak, R. and Richardson, J. E. (eds.), *Analysing Fascist Discourse*. New York: Routledge, pp. 83–106.

Feldman, M. (2019) 'On Radical Right Mainstreaming in Europe and the US', in Bevelander, P. and Wodak, R. (eds.), *Europe at the Crossroads: Confronting Populist, Nationalist and Global Challenges*. Lund: Nordic Academic Press, pp. 23–48.

Germani, G. (1978) *Authoritarianism, Fascism and National Populism*. New Brunswick, NJ: Transaction Books.

Goffman, E. (1986 [1963]) *Stigma. Notes on the Management of Spoiled Identity*. New York: A Tochstone Book, Simon & Schuster Inc.

Graff, A. (2009) 'Gender, Sexuality, and Nation – Here and Now: Reflections on the Gendered and Sexualized Aspects of Contemporary Polish Nationalism', in Oleksy, E. (ed.), *Intimate Citizenships: Gender, Sexualities, Politics*. London: Routledge, pp. 133–146.

Graff, A. and Korolczuk, E. (2022) *Anti-Gender Politics in the Populist Moment*. London: Routledge.

Grzebalska, W. and Pető, A. (2018) 'The Gendered Modus Operandi of the Illiberal Transformation in Hungary and Poland', *Women's Studies International Forum*, 68, pp. 164–172.

Jakubowska, E. (2007) 'Gender and Face', in Santaemilia, J., Bou, P., Maruenda, S. and Zaragoza, G. (eds.), *International Perspectives on Gender and Language* (CD edition). Valencia: Universitat de Valencia, pp. 333–351.

Jakubowska, E. (2009) 'Metaphors of Femininity', in Wysocka, M. (ed.), *On Language Structure, Acquisition and Teaching. Studies in Honour of Janusz Arabski on the Occasion of His 70th Birthday*. Katowice: Wydawnictwo Uniwersytetu Śląskiego, pp. 143–153.

Kemper, A. (2016) *Foundation of the Nation. How Political Parties and Movements Are Radicalising Others in Favour of Conservative Family Values and Against Tolerance, Diversity, and Progressive Gender Politics in Europe*. Friedrich-Ebert-Stiftung. Available at: http://library.fes.de/pdf-files/dialog/12503.pdf (accessed 21 February 2022).

Kienpointner, M. (1991) 'Rhetoric and Argumentation: Relativism and Beyond', *Philosophy and Rhetoric*, 24(1), pp. 43–53.

Kienpointner, M. (2009) 'Plausible and Fallacious Strategies to Silence One's Opponent', in van Eemeren, F. (ed.), *Examining Argumentation in Context: Fifteen Studies on Strategic Maneuvering*. Amsterdam: Benjamins, pp. 61–75.

Lakoff, G. (2002) *Moral Politics: How Liberals and Conservatives Think*. Chicago: University of Chicago Press.

Mény, Y. and Surel, Y. (2002) 'The Constitutive Ambiguity of Populism', in Mény, Y. and Surel, Y. (eds.), *Democracies and the Populist Challenge*. London: Palgrave Macmillan, pp. 1–21.

Mudde, C. (2004) 'The Populist Zeitgeist', *Government and Opposition*, 39(4), pp. 541–563.

Ordo Iuris (2019) 'Local Government Charter of the Rights of the Family'. Available at: https://en.ordoiuris.pl/family-and-marriage/local-government-charter-rights-family (accessed 27 December 2021).

Pelinka, A. (2018) 'Identity Politics, Populism and the Far Right', in Wodak, R. and Forchtner, B. (eds.), *The Routledge Handbook of Language and Politics*. New York: Routledge, pp. 618–629.

Pető, A. and Grzebalska, W. (2016) 'How Hungary and Poland Have Silenced Women and Stifled Human Rights', *The Conversation*, 14 October. http://theconversation.com/how-hungary-and-poland-have-silenced-women-and-stifled-human-rights-66743 (accessed 20 February 2022).

Reisigl, M. (2007a) 'Discrimination in Discourse', in Kotthoff, H. and Spencer-Oatey, H. (eds.), *Handbook of Intercultural Communication*. Berlin: Mouton de Gruyter, pp. 365–394.

Reisigl, M. (2007b) 'The Dynamics of Right-Wing Populist Argumentation in Austria', in Van Eemeren, F. H., Blair, J. A., Willard, C. A. and Garssen, B. (eds.), *Proceedings of the Sixth Conference of the International Society for the Study of Argumentation*. Amsterdam: Sic Sat/International Center for the Study of Argumentation, pp. 1127–1134.

Reisigl, M. (2014) 'Argumentation Analysis and the Discourse-Historical Approach. A Methodological Framework', in Hart, Ch. and Cap, P. (eds.), *Contemporary Critical Discourse Studies*. London: Bloomsbury, pp. 67–96.

Reisigl, M. (2018) 'The Discourse-Historical Approach', in Flowerdew, J. and Richardson, J. E. (eds.), *Routledge Handbook of Critical Discourse Studies*. London: Routledge, pp. 44–59.

Rydgren, J. (2018) 'The Radical Right: An Introduction', in Rydgren, J. (ed.), *The Oxford Handbook of the Radical Right*. New York: Oxford University Press, pp. 1–13.

Szwed, A. and Zielińska, K. (2017) 'A War on Gender? The Roman Catholic Church's Discourse on Gender in Poland', in Ramet, S. P. and Borowik, I. (eds.), *Religion, Politics, and Values in Poland*. New York: Palgrave Macmillan, pp. 113–136.

Van Leeuwen, T. and Wodak, R. (1999) 'Legitimizing Immigration Control: A Discourse-Historical Analysis', *Discourse Studies*, 1(1), pp. 83–118.

Walton, D. (1997) *Appeal to Pity: Argumentum ad Misericordiam*. Albany, NY: SUNY Press.

Waszczykowski, W. (2016) In the article 'The Conspiracy Theorists Who Have Taken Over Poland', by Christian Davies, *The Guardian*, 16 February. Available at: www.theguardian.com/world/2016/feb/16/conspiracy-theorists-who-have-taken-over-poland (accessed 20 July 2021).

Wodak, R. (2001) 'The Discourse-Historical Approach', in Wodak, R. and Meyer, M. (eds.), *Methods of Critical Discourse Analysis*. London: Sage, pp. 63–94.

Wodak, R. (2011) *The Discourse of Politics in Action. Politics as Usual.* Basingstoke: Palgrave Macmillan.

Wodak, R. (2013) '"Anything Goes!" – The Haiderization of Europe', in Wodak, R., KhosraviNik, M. and Mral, B. (eds.), *Right-Wing Populism in Europe: Politics and Discourse*. London: Bloomsbury, pp. 23–38.

Wodak, R. (2014) 'The Strategy of Discursive Provocation – a Discourse-Historical Analysis of the FPÖ's Discriminatory Rhetoric', in Feldman, M. and Jackson, P. (eds.), *Doublespeak: The Rhetoric of the Far-Rights since 1945*. Stuttgart: ibidem-Verlag, pp. 101–122.

Wodak, R. (2015) *The Politics of Fear: What Right-Wing Populist Discourses Mean*. London: Sage.

Wodak, R. (2019a) 'Analysing the Micropolitics of the Populist Far Right in the "Post Shame" Era', in Bevelander, P. and Wodak, R. (eds.), *Europe at the Crossroads: Confronting Populist, Nationalist and Global Challenges*. Lund: Nordic Academic Press, pp. 63–92.

Wodak, R. (2019b) 'Entering the "Post-Shame Era": The Rise of Illiberal Democracy, Populism and Neo-Authoritarianism in EUrope', *Global Discourse*, 9(1), pp. 195–213.

Wodak, R. (2021) 'Re/nationalising EU-rope: National Identities, Right-Wing Populism, and Border- and Body-Politics', in Barkhoff, J. and Leerssen, J. (eds.), *National Stereotyping, Identity Politics, European Crises*. Leiden: Brill, pp. 95–121.

Wodak, R. and Forchtner, B. (2014) 'Embattled Vienna 1683/2010: Right-Wing Populism, Collective Memory and the Fictionalisation of Politics', *Visual Communication*, 13(2), pp. 231–255.

Wodak, R. and Reisigl, M. (2015) 'Discourse and Racism', in Tannen, D., Hamilton, H. E. and Schiffrin, D. (eds.), *The Handbook of Discourse Analysis*. Chichester: Wiley Blackwell, pp. 576–596.

Wodak, R., De Cillia, R., Reisigl, M. and Liebhart, K. (2009) *The Discursive Construction of National Identity*. Edinburgh: Edinburgh University Press.

Wodak, R., KhosraviNik, M. and Mral, B. (eds.) (2013) *Right-Wing Populism in Europe: Politics and Discourse*. London: Bloomsbury.

Zienkowski, J. and Breeze, R. (2019) 'Introduction: Imagining Populism and the People in Europe', in Zienkowski, J. and Breeze, R. (eds.), *Imagining the Peoples of Europe: Populist Discourses across the Political Spectrum*. Amsterdam: John Benjamins, pp. 1–18.

Polish References

Bogdanowska, M. (2008) 'Topika' (The topics), in Wilczek, P. (ed.), *Retoryka*. Waszawa: PWN, pp. 35–56.

Czarnek, P. (2020) In the article 'Przemysław Czarnek tak widzi rolę kobiety: ma rodzić dzieci i czekać, aż niewierny mąż się nawróci' (Przemysław Czarnek sees the woman's role in this way: She is to give birth to children and wait for the return of the unfaithful husband), by Maria Lipińska, Wiktoria Beczek, *Gazeta.pl*, 2 October, Available at: https://wiadomosci.gazeta.pl/wiadomosci/7,114883,26361580,przemyslaw-czarnek-tak-widzi-role-kobiety-ma-rodzic-dzieci.html (accessed 30 December 2021).

Godek, K. (2021) 'Godek: To głosowanie pokaże, kto w Sejmie stoi po stronie lobby LGBT' (Godek: This vote will show who in the parliament supports the LGBT lobby). Interview with Kaja Godek, *Do Rzeczy*, 29 October. https://dorzeczy.pl/opinie/218968/godek-to-glosowanie-pokaze-kto-stoi-po-stronie-lobby-lgbt.html (accessed 28 December 2021).

Kaczyński, J. (2016) In the article 'Prezes PiS: Będziemy dążyli do tego, aby aborcji było dużo mniej niż obecnie' (PiS President: We will try to radically decrease the number of abortions), *Dziennik Gazeta Prawna*, 12 October. Available at: www.gazetaprawna.pl/wiadomosci/artykuly/983726,kaczynski-o-aborcji.html (accessed 30 December 2021).

Kaczyński, J. (2019) In the article 'Wywracanie rodziny' (Overturning the family), by Konrad Kołodziejski, *Sieci*, 17 September. Available at: www.wsieciprawdy.pl/sieci-wywracanie-rodziny-pnews-4141.html (accessed 16 July 2021).

Kaczyński, J. (2021a) In the article 'Kaczyński o opozycji: Proponują kompletne zdemolowanie Polski w imię interesów zewnętrznych' (Kaczyński about the opposition: They offer complete demolition of Poland for the sake of external interests), by Rafał Wójcik, *Gazeta Wyborcza*, 26 February. Available at: https://wyborcza.pl/7,75398,26829305,kaczynski-o-opozycji-proponuja-kompletne-zdemolowanie-polski.html (accessed 16 July 2021).

Kaczyński, J. (2021b) 'Jarosław Kaczyński dla "Wprost": Każdy średnio rozgarnięty człowiek może załatwić aborcję za granicą' (Jarosław Kaczyński for "Wprost": Every dull-witted person can arrange an abortion abroad). An interview with Jarosław Kaczyński by Eliza Olczyk and Joanna Miziołek, *Wprost*, 23 May. Available at: www.wprost.pl/kraj/10449780/jaroslaw-kaczynski-dla-wprost-kazdy-moze-zalatwic-aborcje-za-granica.html (accessed 16 July 2021).

Lewandowski, K. (2020) In the article 'Samorządy bronią się przed Krucjatą Zjednoczenia Chrześcijańskich Rodzin i Ordo Iuris' (Local governments defend against the crusade of the Christian Family Union and Ordo Iuris), by Magdalena Kozioł, *Gazeta Wyborcza*, 28 August. Available at: https://wroclaw.wyborcza.pl/wroclaw/7,35771,26247117,krucjata-zjednoczenia-chrzescijanskich-rodzin-i-ordo-iuris.html (accessed 27 December 2021).

Skrzydlewski, P. (2021) In the article 'Odkryliśmy, co to są cnoty niewieście. Czarnek chce kobiety bogobojnej, która doskonale przędzie' (We have discovered what womanly virtues are. Czarnek wants a pious woman that can spin well), by Dominika Sitnicka, *OKO.press*, 21 July. Available at: https://oko.press/odkrylismy-co-to-sa-cnoty-niewiescie-czarnek-chce-kobiety-bogobojnej-ktora-doskonale-przedzie/ (accessed 27 December 2021).

Środa, M. (2021) 'Święta polska rodzina w państwie PiS' (The sacred Polish family in the PiS state), *Gazeta Wyborcza*, 30 March. Available at: https://wyborcza.pl/7,75968,26931856,swieta-polska-rodzina-w-panstwie-pis.html (accessed 15 April 2021).

Waszczykowski, W. (2020) In the article 'KE promuje LGBT. "To niebywałe i musimy bić na alarm"' (The European Commission promotes LGBT. It's unusual and we must raise the alarm), *Do Rzeczy*, 17 September. Available at: https://dorzeczy.pl/kraj/153846/ke-promuje-lgbt-to-niebyw ale-i-musimy-bic-na-alarm.html (accessed 19 July 2021).

Wróblewski, B. (2021) In the article 'Bartłomiej Wróblewski: Nie będę kandydował na rzecznika rodziny' (Bartłomiej Wróblewski: I will not run for family ombudsman), by Katarzyna Wójcik, *Rzeczpospolita*, 5 December. Available at: www.rp.pl/prawo-dla-ciebie/art19168351-bartlomiej-wroblewski-nie-bede-kandydowal-na-rzecznika-rodziny (accessed 27 December 2021).

15

MULTIMODAL NATIONALIST RHETORIC IN FINLAND

From Banal to Extreme Political Persuasion

Eemeli Hakoköngäs and Inari Sakki

Introduction

Populist nationalism has brought the nation to the forefront of public debate and mobilized the ideal of a nation as a monocultural and mono-ethnic entity (Antonsich 2021). With populist nationalism we refer to ideology that is characterized by, for example, anti-elitism, speaking for "common people" and questioning the legitimacy of those in power. However, this is only one loud version of nationalist rhetoric. In addition to direct populist nationalism, in this chapter we also focus on mundane and banal forms of everyday nationalist rhetoric that occur in news photos and everyday advertising. Although banal and direct nationalist rhetoric are different modes of communication serving different purposes, they are not separate from each other. We argue, that when talking about nations and nationalism, the different modes of rhetoric draw from the same symbolic repository of shared knowledge to appeal to and mobilize the audience.

The structure of the chapter is as follows. First, the chapter presents the general context of rhetoric research in the era of the re-emergence of nationalism in Europe and in Finland. Second, the chapter focuses on multimodal rhetoric as a field of research. Multimodality here refers to the analysis of rhetoric in all its forms, paying attention to the interplay between different semiotic modes, such as verbal, visual, and sonic action in the construction of meaning. This is followed by the sections presenting banal and extreme multimodal nationalist rhetoric in Finland. Research on news photos and advertising is selected to represent the former, while research on political campaign video and Internet memes is chosen to represent more exclusionary nationalism. Finally, in the conclusions, the different findings are merged together and discussed in the context of future development of research on multimodal nationalist rhetoric.

The Rise of (New) Nationalist Rhetoric

Nationalist rhetoric has attracted the interest of social scientists for centuries. Nationalism refers to an ideology in which individuals' and groups' loyalty, obligation and allegiance to

DOI: 10.4324/9781003195276-19

a nation are emphasized. Several specific types of nationalism can be distinguished, such as defining nation and nationality in terms of ethnicity (ethnonationalism), or shared citizenship (civic nationalism) (for the history of the concepts, see Jaskułowski 2010). Common to different types is that in nationalist rhetoric, nations are often constructed as singular and specific entities with unique characteristics, history, and dispositions that can be strategically mobilized for different purposes.

In the late twentieth century, changing global power relations, technological advances and the emergence of new global threats led some scholars to discuss the end of nationalism (e.g., Salter 1975). However, it was soon noted that nationalism was not disappearing but taking new forms (Kaldor 1993; Billig 1995). Although its final definition and novelty is a matter of dispute (Valluvan 2017), the term *new nationalism* was broadly adopted to refer to the modes of nationalism that emerged at the end of the 1990s in many Western countries.

The emergence of new nationalism is closely connected to developments in communication technology (Horsti 2015; Horsti and Saresma 2021), especially the Internet since the 1990s, and the spread of various forms of social media since the 2000s (Mihelj and Jiménez-Martínez 2021). Technology has provided low-threshold arenas and tools to engage in different kinds of nationalist rhetoric and to construct virtual communities to strengthen nationalist sentiments, identities, and mobilization (Eriksen 2007). The new nationalism and new technology have paved the way for the emergence of multimodal nationalist rhetoric. Strong evidence shows how the dynamics of the Internet and social media discussions can maintain and strengthen nationalism with altered intensity, and change the ways in which nationalism is transformed, negotiated and disseminated in new forms (Pettersson and Sakki 2017; Sakki et al. 2018). As this chapter argues, the multimodal approach on nationalist rhetoric provides sophisticated new methods for analyzing the expressions of new nationalism in the Internet era.

The examples in this chapter come from Finland, a country that constitutes a particularly interesting setting for examining multimodal nationalist rhetoric. The Nordic countries, known for their history as social democratic welfare states (Jungar and Jupskås 2014), have in the twenty-first century experienced the rise of nationalist and populist movements. Also in Finland, as a result of international migration, new nationalism leaning on anti-immigration, anti-multiculturalist and anti-Islamic messages was shown in the success of the populist Finns Party in the three national elections in the 2010s. In addition, having a relatively high Internet and social media diffusion compared to other countries (Strandberg 2013), in Finland the success of nationalist movements has largely been due to their skillful use of the opportunities of new media to claim media space and mobilize support for their agendas (Pettersson 2017; Horsti 2015).

In Finland, the break between the old and new nationalism can also be disputed, as there exists a discursive continuity in the nationalist rhetoric from the 1930s to the 2010s regarding the content of speech focusing on the threats posed by external others and internal enemies. However, the most significant change seems to have happened in the form of rhetoric: the present-day nationalist persuasion is more self-conscious and employs more sophisticated tools, such as factuality-enhancing strategies and reversed racism (Sakki, Hakoköngäs and Pettersson 2018). Multimodal features of the online environment allow for derogatory speech to be communicated in a socially acceptable way (Forchtner and Kolvraa 2017). Additionally, anonymity and the absence of the social barriers of face-to-face communication have lowered the normative threshold for expressions of hate and bitterness (Bilewicz and Soral 2020; Burke and Goodman

2012). In Finland, right-wing populist rhetoric has purposefully striven to normalize anti-immigration sentiments in the country (Nortio et al. 2021) and managed to affect everyday political discussion (Horsti 2015). These changes in the discussion culture have stretched the boundaries of what is considered acceptable in public speech, resulting in the problematization of the concept of hate speech as well as a polarization between lay people's and elites' representations of hate speakers (Sakki and Hakoköngäs 2022).

Multimodal Rhetoric: New Modes of an Old Phenomenon

The study of rhetoric, rooted in ancient Greece, is the analysis of persuasive purposes and their effects in human communication. In Aristotle's (1991) perspective on rhetoric the notions of ethos, logos, and pathos were central. Ethos refers to taking a morally trustworthy stance, and logos refers to rhetorical persuasion by providing proof in support of an argument. Pathos refers to appealing to the emotions of the audience. For centuries, the analysis of rhetoric was mainly focused on direct political communication and especially its verbal (spoken and written) forms. The rise of new rhetoric in the 1960s (e.g., Perelman 1979) directed attention to more mundane rhetoric and paved the way for a more diverse understanding of persuasion through not only text and spoken word but also photographs, videos, sonic features, and their interconnection.

It is not a coincidence that the renewal of rhetorical research took place in the same decades as information technology altered the Western media sphere. Television news brought distant events closer to people's lives and enabled advertisers and politicians to utilize new persuasive opportunities (Gregg 1977). In this sense, new methods of rhetoric in the era of the Internet can be seen as a continuation of this development (Mihelj and Jiménez-Martínez 2021).

Compared to normative rules and practical constraints of mainstream media, social media has relatively little control over the content. The low cost of communication has provided nationalist movements with possibilities for reaching new audiences on social media (Huntington 2016). However, virtual platforms have also required the rhetoric to be adapted to the customs and style of new generations (Forchtner and Kølvraa 2017). In Finland, populist right-wing movements seem to have more successfully adapted and made use of the potential provided by social media than other established actors in the political sphere (Horsti and Saresma 2021).

Despite the ever-increasing role of multimodality in everyday life, research addressing the special features of new multimodal rhetoric in the use of new nationalist persuasion remains scarce. In the present chapter we address these specific features by drawing from our own recent research (e.g., Martikainen and Sakki 2021a; Hakoköngäs and Sakki 2019; Sakki and Martikainen 2021; Hakoköngäs et al. 2020). Four empirical examples demonstrate the different modes of nationalist rhetoric. News photos and political campaign videos represent more classic objects of rhetorical analysis, while everyday goods advertisements and Internet memes represent more recent and less studied nationalist speech. These examples demonstrate how multimodality provides a means for nationalist rhetoric appealing to national stereotypes and the continuity of the nation, creating threatening outgroup stereotypes, and evoking strong emotions through ironic humor.

Multimodal rhetoric always aims at producing an effect in an audience. To be effective, it needs to be aware of the existing representations of the audience. This means that persuasion fails if the rhetoric remains meaningless in the given social and cultural context (Blair 2004; Smith 2007). To address the audience, rhetoric needs to draw from socially shared knowledge, which in the context of nationalist rhetoric is provided by master narratives of the nation. This common story – including historical myths, events, and figures and their attached meanings – serves as a symbolic repository of shared meanings to provide a common ground with the audience (Reicher and Stott 2020). To understand nationalist rhetoric in Finland, it is thus necessary to be aware of the historical context from which Finnish nationalism emerges.

Finland's geopolitical location in the North between Sweden and Russia affects the political sentiments in the country. Finland was an integral part of Sweden until 1809, after which it was annexed as an autonomous Grand Duchy of Russia. Multimodal rhetoric played a highly important role in the development of the idea of Finland as a separate nation from its historical rulers. The nationalist movement in the late nineteenth century cultivated Finnish language and music, established a national mythology, and supported fine arts depicting Finnish history and culture separate from Russia and Sweden. Finland declared independence from Russia in 1917 and maintained its sovereignty against the Soviet Union during World War II (1939–1945). After balancing between the great powers in the Cold War era, Finland joined the European Union in 1995 (for more details, see Kirby 2006).

The above-described events constitute some of the core elements of the hegemonic master narrative of Finland, which has been strengthened and disseminated, for example in history textbooks, for a century (Hakoköngäs and Sakki 2016). This narrative is nationalist in the sense that it mainly provides material for the construction of a positive and distinctive Finnish national identity, although there have also been signs of increased diversification of nationalist narratives (Sakki and Hakoköngäs 2020; Hakoköngäs and Sakki 2022). However, replacing established meanings is not easy, as deep-rooted and naturalized meanings are resistant to change (Hakoköngäs and Sakki 2016). In fact, attempts to shift shared narratives toward a more inclusive and self-reflective direction have given nationalist voices a rhetorical opportunity to present themselves as protectors of the "correct version of history" and the related values.

Contents, Forms, and Functions of Multimodal Nationalist Rhetoric in Finland

To understand the following research examples of multimodal nationalist rhetoric in Finland, it is necessary to look at the methodological approach employed in the analysis of various forms of research material. To a large extent, we drew our approach from the principles of *multimodal discourse analysis* (MDA) (Kress 2012) and *critical discursive psychology* (CDP) (Edley 2001; Wetherell 1998), which together constitute a method that could be labelled as *multimodal critical discourse analysis* (MCDA) (Kilby and Lennon 2021).

Kress (2012) defined MDA as an approach to communication in which "all modes are framed as one field, as one domain" (p. 38). In practice, the focus of MDA research is on different modalities (e.g., verbal, visual, and sonic) and how they co-construct a persuasive argument that is more than a sum of its parts. The approach has its roots in social semiotics, expecting the communication to draw from the socially shared reserve of meanings (Kress 2012). CDP, in turn, emphasizes the need to consider the social and political context in which the discourse is situated and directs the researcher to examine rhetorical maneuvers of political discourse both at the micro and macro levels (Wetherell 1998).

MCDA provides a means of examining the *contents* (what is being said), *forms* (use of discursive strategies and rhetorical resources), and *functions* (social and political consequences) of a speech combining different modes of communication (Sakki and Pettersson 2016). As Kilby and Lennon (2021 p. 3) outline, "MCDA allows for a more nuanced understanding of how different discursive components can come together to co-produce meanings." The sections below demonstrate how these three aspects of rhetoric were identified from different types of material. We employed MCDA from a social constructionist epistemological perspective, understanding the analyzed multimodal material not only as expressions of opinions and beliefs but as acts intending to shape the social reality.

National Stereotypes in Photojournalism

Our first perspective, news photos in photojournalism, represents a less studied form of banal nationalist rhetoric in Finland. We explored how the news in Finland produced images of decent and duteous Finnish people and immoral and undisciplined Swedish people – the historical outgroup for the Finns – during the first wave of the COVID-19 pandemic (see Martikainen and Sakki 2021a).

Newspapers in general provide an effective discursive space for boosting positive national identity and establishing negative outgroup identities (Billig 1995; Van Dijk 1993). Skey (2014) noted that in times of crisis, the news employs hyperbolic and exclusionary language, resulting in distinctive group boundaries between "us" and "them". Multimodality adds an extra layer to news rhetoric, reinforcing national stereotypes and a sense of national superiority.

Photojournalism employs news photos' ability to convey a persuasive message. Sometimes, images imply meanings that are difficult or inappropriate to verbalize in text. The images used in journalism are the result of several intentional or unconscious choices to present the subject matter in a certain way. Photographs especially have rhetorical power, as they appeal to emotions and emotive processing of the message. Photographs also have reality-evoking quality, and in the context of news, photographs are often regarded as objective documentation or visual proof of the issue (Joffe 2008).

We collected news stories reporting on COVID-19 in Sweden from two Finnish newspapers during the first phase of the pandemic in the spring and summer of 2020 (Martikainen and Sakki 2021a). Altogether, 183 images with related headlines and captions were analyzed. In practice, the elements of communication – images, captions, and headlines – were first analyzed separately and then as a whole to understand the relations between the elements. The convergent and divergent semantic orientations of images, captions, and headlines were identified and interpreted by employing the concepts of *co-contextualization* (elements convey congruous meanings and reinforce each other's semantic potential) and *re-contextualization* (elements communicate controversial meanings, resulting in the expansion of semantic potential) (Liu and O'Halloran 2009).

In COVID-19 news reporting, we found discourses of *morally superior Finns* and *immoral Swedes*. The latter stemmed from the national stereotype of Swedes as talkative, socializing and outgoing people (Daun, Verkasalo and Tuomivaara 2001) who could not accept restrictions on social life, even if it meant becoming infected with the virus. In Finland, this negative stereotype is rooted in the history of Finland's subordination by the Swedes (Kirby 2006). The image of social and happy Swedes was transmitted through visual images depicting people spending time on outdoor terraces and enjoying refreshments. However, the textual elements (captions, headlines), such as "The

Corona Policy of Sweden Astonishes" and "Swedish Way Would Have Caused Deaths," painted a different image. The Swedish coronavirus policy was implied to be too loose and therefore ineffective, resulting in numerous infections and deaths. The images and text *re-contextualized* each other, constituting an argument condemning Swedes' seemingly careless behavior during the COVID-19 pandemic.

The construction of a direct comparison between a morally superior "us" and immoral "them" was multimodally reinforced in other news articles. For example, *Ilta-Sanomat* released an article entitled "Images Show the Stark Difference Between Finland and Sweden" accompanied by two images representing the difference in the behavior of Finns and Swedes during COVID-19. The Finnish photo featured a couple of people on the stairs of Helsinki Cathedral (in the city center) with no one else nearby, thus complying with the call for social distancing. In contrast, the image taken in Stockholm showed a crowd queueing at an ice cream parlor, emphasizing amusement and pleasure seeking. The legend on the Finnish photo told that strict safety restrictions were quickly introduced in Finland, while the legend on the Swedish photo cited the lyrics of a famous Swedish pop song glorifying partying. The images and related captions strengthened the stereotypical image of Finns as being more conscientious than Swedes (Daun, Verkasalo and Tuomivaara 2001). Hence, photos and accompanying text communicated congruent meanings co-contextualizing each other, constituting an argument that there is a clear difference between responsible Finns and freewheeling Swedes.

Besides the use of re- and co-contextualization, photojournalism about COVID-19 in Finnish news used several other multimodal rhetorical strategies to create national stereotypes. *Flagging*, the presentation of the national flag as a symbol to gather different meanings of national identity (Billig 1995; Finell 2019), was one of the central rhetorical means used. The Finnish flag, dating back to the mid-nineteenth century, is one of the more deeply rooted symbols in the Finnish collective memory. Its colors, blue and white, are enough to activate the nationalist meaning potential (Hakoköngäs 2017).

In COVID-19 news, flags were visually used to compare Swedish and Finnish policies during the pandemic. The presentation of Finland and Sweden as competitors arises from the representation of a rivalry between a little brother (Finland) and big brother (Sweden). This stereotype also draws from the common history of the countries, as the images of the flags waving side-by-side encourages connotation of the athletic competition that has existed between the countries since the 1920s. The association between this national rivalry and COVID-19 policy was made explicit in a caption in *Ilta-Sanomat*: "Until Friday afternoon there were 94 fatalities of Corona confirmed in Sweden and 15 in Finland (...) At last, a Finland–Sweden match, in which it is very nice to lose, absolutely!" The sarcastic tone of the caption indicates that Finland is happy to lose this particular competition.

Taken together, nationalist rhetoric in news photos in photojournalism is based on the selective interplay of multimodal resources, the processes of co- and re-contextualization, and widely known historical symbols. In particular, images seemed to imply meanings that may have been difficult or inappropriate to verbalize in text and, in this way, the news enabled construction of a negative stereotype of Swedes while maintaining a positive stereotype of Finns.

Continuity of the Nation in Advertising

The second perspective demonstrates another form of banal nationalist rhetoric: advertising videos of everyday goods. This section draws from our study addressing how

Finnish dairy product advertisements reference the nation's past (Hakoköngäs and Sakki 2019). To better understand the mundane nationalist messages in advertising, we analyzed a select sample of 15 advertisement videos launched between 2010 and 2016 by the biggest dairy product company in Finland. The analysis shows that advertisements may have multiple simultaneous goals. At the surface level, they introduce novel products or make the brand better known. At the same time, advertisements may subtly repeat and construct ideas on nationalism by employing multimodal rhetoric.

In Western countries, advertising is one of the key agents in everyday life, advocating for certain products, lifestyles, and ideologies. In political advertising, video is usually the most direct format, as shown in the next section, but advertisements for everyday goods convey the nationalist rhetoric message more subtly, as reinforcing national sentiment is not their only goal. Castelló and Mihelj (2018) made a distinction between two types of nationalism in the context of consuming. *Political consumer nationalism* targets the domestic economy by encouraging the consumption of domestic products. *Symbolic consumer nationalism* reinforces nationalist sentiments in the form of consumption. These forms may also overlap each other, simultaneously mobilizing both political and symbolic consumption.

In Finland, as in many other European countries, food has become a subject of strong emotions, as the removal of trade restrictions inside of the European Union has raised concerns about the destruction of national food cultures and local food production. Recently, other issues, such as global warming and a growing interest in animal rights, have made animal-based products a subject of debate. In wealthy Western countries, food is not just used to satisfy hunger but as a way of representing various social, political, and cultural meanings (Holtzman 2006). This dimension of food loaded with meanings has given advertisers an impetus to appeal to both political and symbolic consumer nationalism in order to get their products sold.

Following Shelley's (1996) distinction between demonstrative and rhetorical argumentation, we focused on the videos representing the latter. Rhetorical argumentation refers to the multimodal interpenetration of verbal and visual arguments in communication (see also Blair 2004). After distinguishing the visual, verbal, and sonic elements constituting the narration (content) of the videos, we paid special attention to identification of the three appeals – *ethos*, *pathos*, and *logos* – and related rhetorical means such as *enthymeme* (an incomplete argument) in the videos (form). Finally, to interpret the ideological meanings (functions) of the videos, we examined the *rhetorical situation* (Kjeldsen 2007) of the first two steps of the MCDA analysis. The rhetorical situation of the above-described research material was the recent concern regarding the future of dairy production in Finland.

In the selection of videos, we were especially interested in the use of history and how the advertisers discussed the "past" in the advertisements. The videos emphasized food production as an unbroken and historical Finnish tradition. This idea of traditionality was constructed by making extensive use of visual, verbal, and sonic modes of multimodal communication. All three appeals, ethos, pathos, and logos, were present. For example, the advertisement "Young Dairy Farmers" presented daily life on a Finnish family-owned farm. Two and a half minutes long, the video, published by a Finnish dairy company, Valio, presents a documentary-like view of the life of young Finnish farmers. Tranquil scenes from farms are shown and farmers are telling why they like and appreciate their work.

The video was explicitly framed to speak about Finnishness from the beginning. The narration employed the rhetorical strategy of repetition by mentioning the "Finnish company," and "Finnish countryside" where "Finnish farmers" do "Finnish work" ("Young Dairy Farmers," 00:03–00:22). The video ends with a slogan, "With love for Finnish milk," leaving the audience in no doubt about the national context depicted.

Ethos, the sense of credibility, was appealed to via the documentary-like nature of the video. The interviews with the actors were conducted using intimate close images and text presenting the names of the interviewed farmers. These choices distanced the video from the ordinary staged advertisement and created a feeling of journalistic object-ivity (Joffe 2008). The credibility is convincing in the opening lines, which stated, "For over 100 years, Valio's milk has come from the Finnish countryside," accompanied by an image of the rural Finland landscape. The video appealed to *logos*, reasoning, by giving exact statistics, such as "Behind our milk stands Finnish expertise and around 7,400 Finnish farms (…) We employ more than 30,000 Finns in the country and in cities." The numbers also aimed to improve respect for the company as an employer, with the reference to cities indicating that the employment effect is not limited to the countryside. Half of the Finnish population live in urban areas.

The appeal to *pathos*, emotion, was a result of showing the commitment of young farmers to their work. Similar to the dairy company, this indicates a long history of dairy farming in the family. The idea of a chain of generations was verbally and visu-ally strengthened with the metaphor "stepping into the shoes of the old," which was concretized by an image of a woman putting on her shoes. The narration continued, "They have a positive attitude regarding the future," which was followed by an image of a man and two children, the successors of the tradition, in a cowshed.

In the multimodal narration of the advertisement, the use of ethos, pathos, and logos together constituted an enthymeme, a rhetorical means arguing for probable truth. The advertisement is calling on customers to participate in the honored tradition of Finnish dairy production. This call was suggested in an interviewee's statement: "Valio is defin-itely a source of pride. That we can produce high-quality Valio milk for Finns is a value in itself" ("Young Dairy Farmers," 2014). The references to values and their preservation imply the obscured claim that there is an unnamed threat to Finnish work. Smith (2007) noted that successful persuasive enthymeme takes advantage of the everyday knowledge shared by the group. In the *rhetorical situation* (Kjeldsen 2007) of the 2010s, the threat was cheap imported foreign dairy products, and the call was for consumers to support domestic production.

To summarize, nationalist rhetoric in Finnish dairy product advertisements served as both political and symbolic consumer nationalism (Castelló and Mihelj 2018). Customers were invited to buy domestically produced goods in order to support Finnish family entrepreneurs and thereby the domestic economy. Simultaneously, the rhetoric appealed to an implicit nationalist sentiment by raising the idea of the value of Finnish traditions, a chain of generations, and Finnish work. On a more general level, the emphasis on con-tinuity represented not only the continuity of dairy production but of the Finnish nation and its traditions.

Outgroup Derogation in Political Election Videos

The third perspective illustrates how exclusive nationalist rhetoric employs multimodality in political communication on social media (see Sakki and Martikainen 2021). The election campaign video of the Finnish populist party, the Finns Party, used visual and sonic features to create an idea of refugees threatening Finnish women and children and the entire country more broadly. This section provides a textbook example demonstrating why the focus on verbal narration is not enough to capture the nationalist and racist messages of current political rhetoric.

Pettersson (2017) argued that the success of the Finns Party is closely connected to their skillful use of new media, which has enabled politicians to mobilize support for their political agendas and claim media space in traditional media. The effective spread of the nationalist and anti-immigration ideology has contributed to the mainstreaming of their rhetoric among the political "elite" (Sakki and Pettersson 2018) and led to normalization of nationalist and xenophobic discourse in society (Horsti and Nikunen 2013).

To better understand the appeal of populist rhetoric on social media, we focused on one publicized video, "KETUTUS – A story of being seriously pissed off" ("V niin kuin Ketutus"), released by the Finns Party in March 2019 before the parliamentary elections in Finland. The approximately six-minute-long short film includes moving and still images, a cartoon, and animation. The general message of the video is that the political elite and journalists are corrupt and that the refugees coming to Finland are a threat. After the video launched and was disseminated, mainly via YouTube, it was accused of promoting political violence. As a result of the controversy the video provoked, it received hundreds of thousands of views on YouTube (see Sakki and Martikainen 2021).

Before conducting the analysis, we transcribed the video, scene by scene, across its verbal, visual, sonic, and action-related modes. Aligning with traditions of CDP, we were centrally concerned with examining the construction and mobilization of ingroup (Finnish citizens) and outgroup (refugees, elites) divisions in the political communication, where multimodality allowed for a more nuanced understanding of how different discursive components could come together to co-produce meanings. Our MCDA analysis focused on exploring how the different modes of video narration were deployed to *re-contextualize* the meanings of each other, which is how incongruent and controversial messages contribute to the activation of new meaning potentials (Liu and O'Halloran 2009). This re-contextualization could happen through such processes as abstraction, addition, substitution, deletion, and evaluation (Machin 2013).

The analysis showed that the overtly racist message about refugees was largely missing from the video's verbal narration, while visual and sonic resources were used to convey that message. The entire narration is framed as a transition from a good past to a horrendous future, as the leaders defraud the fatherland's culture, traditions, and values: "The country that was previously safe for women and children is history." Visual rhetoric was used to construct an image of ordinary Finns as victims and sufferers of the threat of unwanted refugees. The visual images depicted the outgroup as an overt threat. The visual narration showed (1) an innocent-looking white teenage girl being kidnapped by dark-skinned men in a van, (2) a woman and child negotiating a smoke-filled street, (3) a black silhouette holding a knife while people flee, (4) a woman lying bleeding in the street, and (5) a black man detonating explosives. This visual storyline was used to reinforce the typification and homogenization of refugees as criminals, rapists, and terrorists. The threatening visual message was accompanied by sonic means, such as the sound of explosions, breaking glass, and people screaming, conveying obviously negative connotations. The rapidly changing shots reinforced the feeling of chaos and alarm to portray the refugees as a threat.

In the video, visual and sound resources functioned as *intersemiotic additives* (Liu and O'Halloran 2009), adding new information to the verbal mode (Machin 2013). In the video, this verbal mode was a neutral narrator's voice telling "a fairy tale," which functioned to obscure the purpose and prevent accusations of racism. The same purpose was served by the different depictions of the ingroup and outgroup. The ingroup was most often depicted by live images, while the outgroup was shown in animated and cartoon-like images. In the rhetoric, the cartoon-like visualization framed the message as humor, allowing for the expression of xenophobic views (Billig 2001). Thus, the multimodal rhetoric conveyed strong imagery of the threatening "Other," although, verbally, words such as "refugee," "immigrant," and "Islam" were never spoken. This use of visual and sonic modes allowed the authors to deny accusations of racism from their political opponents and the public (Sakki et al. 2018).

To conclude, multimodal analysis of the video showed how the racist message was exposed by other features but avoided in the direct verbal means of communication. Visual images (e.g., dark-skinned, bearded men), a faster transition between scenes, and menacing sounds (e.g., screaming, breaking glass, and explosions) created a threatening representation of refugees as a "dangerous Other" (Wodak 2015). The negative stereotype called for the audience to take action against liberal immigration policies to protect the ingroup, the Finns and the Finns Party supporters.

Derogatory Humor in Internet Memes

The fourth perspective demonstrates the role of Internet memes, a specific type of multimodal rhetoric used by extremist nationalist groups in Finland in the social media era. We analyzed a total of 426 Internet memes posted by Soldiers of Odin and Finland First between 2015 and 2017 in public Facebook groups (see Hakoköngäs, Halmesvaara, and Sakki 2020). The analysis shows how humor is employed to evoke moral rage and mobilize people to take action against the decisions of the political elite.

A meme is user-generated online content that typically combines still images and text, videos, or animations that are created for distribution on social media networks (Shifman 2014). The widespread use of Internet memes for both nationalist rhetoric and harmless amusement has made them a distinguishable mode of communication with their own conventions of expression and ways of interpretation (Huntington 2016). Memes are created and shared anonymously, and their light form makes them easy to be shared on different platforms. Their anonymity together with the difficulty of monitoring their content on social media has made them an appealing tool for extremist rhetoric (Hatakka 2020). This new media has provided different movements a chance to get their agendas heard in the political sphere (Horsti 2015).

Humor has been noted to play an important role in extremist rhetoric (Billig 2001). When used as a rhetorical tool, humor can conceal derogatory messages as mere jokes (Malmqvist 2015), which results in the legitimation of racist discourse. Ironic humor on social media can be employed to convey a sense of communion and of segregation (Gal 2019). The use of humor has also been driven by extremist movements' need to redefine their identity to appeal to contemporary youth cultures (Forchtner and Kølvraa 2017).

The analyzed Finnish extremist groups used memes in their communication by posting simple still images consisting of one or more images (a graphic image or photograph) and accompanied by written text either co-contextualizing or re-contextualizing each other (Liu and O'Halloran 2009). In our MCDA analysis, we observed the interplay between the different parts, e.g., color, font, size, and layout (contents), to identify the rhetorical strategies of persuasion (forms), such as credibility-enhancing strategies and outgroup stereotyping. The goals of rhetoric (functions) were interpreted in the broader rhetorical context (Kjeldsen 2007) – the polarized discussion on asylum politics in Finland between 2015 and 2017.

The contents of the analyzed memes revolved around themes such as national history, mythology, and symbols explicitly tied to nationalist rhetoric. Across the material, quirky humor and satire were the most pervasive methods. Humor in the memes included cartoon-like images, and caricatures, exaggerated alignment of images, hyperbole, parody, pastiche, and image manipulation. The humor was targeted at Islam or Muslims, asylum seekers, and refugees as well as ideological opponents (e.g., liberals) and politicians. The memes constructed an image of the ingroup, ordinary Finns, as a benign but naïve people exploited by foreigners and greedy politicians.

For example, a meme posted by Soldiers of Odin in 2017 demonstrates how derogatory humor works as a tool of rhetoric. The meme showed two photographs with accompanying captions. Above was a black-and-white image depicting Finnish children transported to security in Sweden during World War II. This photo was captioned with "War children in 1939–1945." The children in the image looked at the viewer with serious and fearful looks. The image below was a photograph in color depicting adult men taking a selfie of themselves in a boat. The men were smiling and showing a sign of victory with extended fingers. The caption (written in quotation marks) stated: "'War children in 2015–2016.'" In the rhetorical context in which the meme was posted, the latter image was associated with the refugees coming to Finland. The discrepancy in the nonverbal behavior of the depicted people as well as the quotation marks around the caption of the latter image indicate re-contextualization, in which the differences between the two historical situations of seeking security were strikingly emphasized.

Re-contextualization invited readers to read the meme as satire, an ironic humor assuring the absurdity of comparing the present-day refugees to the war children of the past. The argument is that the figures in the old image were innocent and involuntary children seeking refuge, while those in the modern image are well-off young men. As a result, humor was associated with the emotions of a shared traumatic moment in the nation's history and anger toward people who exploit the welfare state in the present. The meme also created a stereotype of immigrants as crooks trying to take advantage of the host country.

Combining ironic humor typical to youth cultures with social media communication (Forchtner and Kølvraa 2017) is purposefully used in far-right groups' nationalist rhetoric. The memes consisted of only a few elements that nonetheless resulted in a nuanced multimodal rhetoric. Exploiting satirical humor in social media communication can be seen as adaptation of the form of rhetoric to attract new audiences and recruit like-minded supporters. The rhetorical aim of this humor is to arouse emotions, especially anger toward the outgroup, and question the credibility of those currently in power.

Conclusion

This chapter addressed multimodal nationalist rhetoric in Finland in the 2010s. By presenting examples from our previous studies, we demonstrated how different methods of multimodal communication, including news photos in photojournalism, dairy product advertisements, political election videos, and Internet memes, can be used to spread nationalist messages. In the era of new media, the analysis of both banal and direct (new) nationalist rhetoric cannot focus merely on spoken and written narration. Rather, there is a need to take into account multimodal communication to reach a more diverse understanding of the current contents, forms, and functions of persuasion.

Multimodal rhetoric employs the classic appeals of ethos, pathos, and logos (Aristotle 1991), positioning it in a long continuum of strategic persuasion. However, multimodal rhetoric also creatively employs the possibilities provided by new technologies to play with verbal, visual, and sonic modes through co-contextualization and re-contextualization (Liu and O'Halloran 2009). The requirements of nationalist rhetoric have changed and affected at least the form of rhetoric, becoming more subtle to avoid backlashes such as racist accusations (Sakki et al. 2018). In this transformation, multimodality is strategically used to avoid accusations and to present arguments that would lose their power when explicated in words.

The four illustrations of our previous studies hold an important lesson regarding the role of multimodality in nationalist discourse. Our first example about COVID-19 reporting in newspapers showed how images can be used by photojournalism to imply meanings that are difficult or inappropriate to verbalize in text. The second study on dairy commercials demonstrated how a nationalist sentiment was constructed through the co-construction of semiotic meanings raising the value of Finnish traditions, a chain of generations, and Finnish work. Third, the multimodal analysis of the populist party's electoral video allowed us to further expose the racism underlying verbal communication, and to pay attention to the power of co-construction of meanings through visual and sonic tools in the expression of racism. Fourth, the analysis of Internet memes demonstrated how simple multimodal combinations can suffice to create persuasive and mobilizing exclusionary nationalist discourse.

At the surface level, nationalist rhetoric seems to be closely connected to current day-to-day affairs, such as the struggle against the COVID-19 pandemic, imported products, and fear of refugees. However, as our examples demonstrated, a shared feature across the different forms of nationalist rhetoric is drawing from deep-rooted everyday knowledge, that is, the symbolic repository of shared knowledge and collective memories, such as historical struggles with neighboring countries (Blair 2004; Smith 2007; Kress 2012). The Internet memes and election video discussed previously employed a wide variety of symbols of Finnishness, such as historical characters, fine arts, and several references to the national epic *Kalevala* and other mythologies, that we were unable to cover in this chapter. These symbols date to the early days of the nationalist movement in Finland in the nineteenth century (Hakoköngäs et al. 2020).

While we focused exclusively on nationalist rhetoric in the Finnish context, it is worth noting that nationalist persuasion does not happen in a vacuum but is a result of various international influences (Sakki and Martikainen 2021). The symbolic repository used in extremist rhetoric is not necessarily constrained only to national grand narratives but may also employ more broadly shared cultural knowledge based on ancient myths, the Bible, and widespread visual imagery to appeal to emotions and support the construction of a social identity on the basis of a certain ideology (Martikainen and Sakki 2021b).

The rise of new nationalism and the power of its rhetoric have gone hand in hand with the development of information technology, particularly the proliferation of social media (Horsti and Saresma 2021; Mihelj and Jiménez-Martínez 2021). The spread of multimodal material in new media environments has already resulted in the collapse of customary mnemonic temporal and spatial contexts in which the meanings of semiotic resources have thus far been relatively stable (Merrill 2020). For the analysis of multimodality, this means that there is a need for more international perspectives, such as comparative approaches, to understand how the same semiotic resources are creatively and flexibly used internationally for nationalist persuasion.

Combining MDA (Kress 2012) and CDP (Edley 2001; Wetherell 1998) into MCDA (Kilby and Lennon 2021) provides a useful tool for approaching the contents, forms, and functions of nationalist rhetoric. As both approaches take seriously the social and political implications of meaning constructed through multiple discursive modalities, this combination enabled us to better identify and unpack the complexity of nationalist rhetoric as discursive, affective, and performative acts that construct social reality.

Taken together, the immediate message of nationalist rhetoric – its content – is often culture-specific and addresses day-to-day political issues. However, the forms and functions of rhetoric are not likely to be limited to a certain cultural context. Thus, we hope that the notions presented in the present chapter are not only of interest to researchers studying Finland and Finnish nationalism but would provide a starting point to employ multimodal rhetorical analysis in other contexts and in different types of materials.

References

Antonsich, M. (2021) 'Everyday Nation in Times of Rising Nationalism', *Sociology*, 54(6): 1230–1237.

Aristotle (1991) *On Rhetoric: A Theory of Civic Discourse*, Oxford: Oxford University Press.

Bilewicz, M. and Soral, W. (2020) 'Hate Speech Epidemic: The Dynamic Effects of Derogatory Language on Intergroup Relations and Political Radicalization', *Political Psychology*, 41(S1): 3–33.

Billig, M. (1995) *Banal Nationalism*, London: Sage.

Billig, M. (2001) 'Humour and Hatred: The Racist Jokes of the Klu Klux Klan', *Discourse and Society*, 12(3): 267–289.

Blair, J. A. (2004) 'The Rhetoric of Visual Arguments', in C. A. Hill and M. Helmers (eds.), *Defining Visual Rhetorics*, London: Lawrence Erlbaum Associates, pp. 41–62.

Burke, S. and Goodman, S. (2012) '"Bring back Hitler's gas chambers": Asylum Seeking, Nazis and Facebook – A Discursive Analysis', *Discourse and Society*, 23(1): 19–33.

Castelló, E. and Mihelj, S. (2018) 'Selling and Consuming the Nation: Understanding Consumer Nationalism', *Journal of Consumer Culture*, 18(4): 558–576.

Daun, Å., Verkasalo, M. and Tuomivaara, P. (2001) 'Stereotypes among Finns in Sweden: The Character of Finns versus Swedes', *Ethnologia Europaea*, 31(1): 55–62.

Edley, N. (2001) 'Analysing Masculinity: Interpretative Repertoires, Ideological Dilemmas and Subject Positions', in M. Wetherell, S. Taylor and S. J. Yates (eds.), *Discourse as Data: A Guide for Analysis*, London: Sage, pp. 189–228.

Eriksen, T. H. (2007) 'Nationalism and the Internet', *Nations and Nationalism*, 13(1): 1–17.

Finell, E. (2019) 'National Identity, Collective Events, and Meaning: A Qualitative Study of Adolescents' Autobiographical Narratives of Flag Ceremonies in Finland', *Political Psychology*, 40(1): 21–36.

Forchtner, B. and Kølvraa, C. (2017) 'Extreme Right Images of Radical Authenticity: Multimodal Aesthetics of History, Nature, and Gender Roles in Social Media', *European Journal of Cultural and Political Sociology*, 4(3): 252–281.

Gal, N. (2019) 'Ironic Humor on Social Media as Participatory Boundary Work', *New Media and Society*, 21(3): 729–749.

Gregg, R. B. (1977) 'The Rhetoric of Political Newscasting', *Communication Studies*, 28(4): 221–237.

Hakoköngäs, E. (2017) 'Visual Collective Memory: A Social Representations Approach', PhD dissertation, University of Helsinki.

Hakoköngäs, E., Halmesvaara, O., and Sakki, I. (2020) 'Persuasion through Bitter Humor: Multimodal Discourse Analysis of Rhetoric in Internet Memes of Two Far-Right Groups in Finland', *Social Media + Society*, 6(2).

Hakoköngäs, E. and Sakki, I. (2016) 'Visualized Collective Memories: Social Representations of History in Images Found in Finnish History Textbooks', *Journal of Community and Applied Social Psychology*, 26(6): 496–517.

Hakoköngäs, E. and Sakki, I. (2019) 'The Past as a Means of Persuasion: Visual Political Rhetoric in Finnish Dairy Product Advertising', *Journal of Social and Political Psychology*, 7(1): 507–524

Hakoköngäs, E. and Sakki, I. (2022) 'Mutable and Multilevel Schematic Templates: Narratives of Collaboration between Finland and Nazi-Germany in Finnish History Textbooks', in I. Brescó de Luna and F. van Alphen (eds.), *Reproducing, Rethinking, Resisting National Narratives. A Sociocultural Approach to Schematic Narrative Templates in Times of Nationalism*, Charlotte, NC: Information Age Publishers, pp. 195–215.

Hameleers, M., Powell, T. E., Van Der Meer, T. G., and Bos, L. (2020) 'A Picture Paints a Thousand Lies? The Effects and Mechanisms of Multimodal Disinformation and Rebuttals Disseminated via Social Media', *Political Communication*, 37(2): 281–301.

Hatakka, N. (2020) 'Expose, Debunk, Ridicule, Resist! Networked Civic Monitoring of Populist Radical Right Online Action in Finland. Information', *Communication and Society*, 23(9): 1311–1326.

Holtzman, J. D. (2006) 'Food and Memory', *Annual Review of Anthropology*, 35: 361–378.

Horsti, K. (2015) 'Techno-Cultural Opportunities: The Anti-Immigration Movement in the Finnish Mediascape', *Patterns of Prejudice*, 49(4): 343–366.

Horsti, K. and Nikunen, K. (2013) 'The Ethics of Hospitality in Changing Journalism: The Response to the Rise of the Anti-Immigrant Movement in Finnish Media Publicity', *European Journal of Cultural Studies*, 16(4): 489–504.

Horsti, K. and Saresma, T. (2021) 'The Role of Social Media in the Rise of Right-Wing Populism in Finland', in H. Tumber and S. Waisbord (eds.), *The Routledge Companion to Media Disinformation and Populism*, London: Routledge, pp. 376–385.

Huntington, H. E. (2016) 'Pepper Spray Cop and the American Dream: Using Synecdoche and Metaphor to Unlock Internet Memes' Visual Political Rhetoric', *Communication Studies*, 67(1): 77–93.

Jaskułowski, K. (2010) 'Western (Civic) versus Eastern (Ethnic) Nationalism. The Origins and Critique of the Dichotomy', *Polish Sociological Review*, 171(3): 289–303.

Joffe, H. (2008) 'The Power of Visual Material: Persuasion, Emotion and Identification', *Diogenes*, 55(1): 84–93.

Jungar, A. C. and Jupskås, A. R. (2014) 'Populist Radical Right Parties in the Nordic Region: A New and Distinct Party Family?', *Scandinavian Political Studies*, 37(3): 215–238.

Kaldor, M. (1993) 'The New Nationalism in Europe', *Peace Review*, 5(2): 247–258.

Kilby, L. and Lennon, H. (2021) 'When Words Are Not Enough: Combined Textual and Visual Multimodal Analysis as a Critical Discursive Psychology Undertaking', *Methods in Psychology*, 5.

Kirby, D. (2006) *A Concise History of Finland*, Cambridge: Cambridge University Press.

Kjeldsen, J. E. (2007) 'Visual Argumentation in Scandinavian Political Advertising: A Cognitive, Contextual, and Reception Oriented Approach', *Argumentation and Advocacy*, 43(3–4): 124–132.

Kress, G. (2012) 'Multimodal Discourse Analysis', in J. P. Gee and M. Handford (eds.), *The Routledge Handbook of Discourse Analysis*, London: Routledge, pp. 35–50.

Liu, Y. and O'Halloran, K. (2009) 'Intersemiotic Texture: Analyzing Cohesive Devices between Language and Images', *Social Semiotics*, 19(4): 367–388.

Machin, D. (2013) 'Introduction: What Is Multimodal Critical Discourse Studies?', *Critical Discourse Studies*, 10(4): 347–355.

Malmqvist, K. (2015) 'Satire, Racist Humour and the Power of (Un)Laughter: On the Restrained Nature of Swedish Online Racist Discourse Targeting EU-Migrants Begging for Money', *Discourse and Society*, 26(6): 733–753.

Martikainen, J. and Sakki, I. (2021a) 'Boosting Nationalism through COVID-19 Images: Multimodal Construction of the Failure of the "Dear Enemy" with COVID-19 in the National Press', *Discourse and Communication*, 15(4), 388–414.

Martikainen, J. and Sakki, I. (2021b) 'Myths, the Bible, and Romanticism as Ingredients of Political Narratives in the Finns Party Election Video', *Discourse, Context and Media*, 39.

Merrill, S. (2020) 'Following the Woman with the Handbag: Mnemonic Context Collapse and the Anti-Fascist Activist Appropriation of an Iconic Historical Photograph', in S. Merrill,

E. Keightley, and P. Daphi (eds.), *Social Movements, Cultural Memory and Digital Media: Mobilising Mediated Remembrance*, London: Springer, pp. 111–139.

Mihelj, S. and Jiménez-Martínez, C. (2021) 'Digital Nationalism: Understanding the Role of Digital Media in the Rise of "New" Nationalism', *Nations and Nationalism*, 27(2): 331–346.

Nortio, E., Niska, M., Renvik, T. A. and Jasinskaja-Lahti, I. (2021) '"The Nightmare of Multiculturalism": Interpreting and Deploying Anti-Immigration Rhetoric in Social Media', *New Media and Society*, 23(3): 438–456.

Perelman, C. (1979) 'The New Rhetoric: A Theory of Practical Reasoning', in C. Perelman (ed.), *The New Rhetoric and the Humanities*, London: Springer, pp. 1–42.

Pettersson, K. (2017) 'Save the Nation! A Social Psychological Study of Political Blogs as a Medium for Nationalist Communication and Persuasion', PhD dissertation, University of Helsinki.

Reicher, S. and Stott, C. (2020) 'On Order and Disorder during the COVID-19 Pandemic', *British Journal of Social Psychology*, 59(3): 694–702.

Sakki, I. and Hakoköngäs, E. (2020) 'Celebrating Nationhood: Negotiating Nationhood and History in Finland's Centenary Celebrations', *Nations and Nationalism*, 26(4): 864–882.

Sakki, I. and Hakoköngäs, E. (2022) 'Dialogical Construction of Hate Speech in Established Media and Online Discussions', in K. Pettersson and E. Nortio (eds.), *The Far-Right Discourse of Multiculturalism in Everyday Talk: Reproduction and Contestation in the Nordic Region*, London: Palgrave Macmillan, pp. 85–111.

Sakki, I., Hakoköngäs, E., and Pettersson, K. (2018) 'Past and Present Nationalist Political Rhetoric in Finland: Changes and Continuities', *Journal of Language and Social Psychology*, 37(2): 160–180.

Sakki, I. and Martikainen, J. (2021) 'Mobilizing Collective Hatred through Humour: Affective–Discursive Production and Reception of Populist Rhetoric', *British Journal of Social Psychology*, 60(2): 610–634.

Sakki, I. and Pettersson, K. (2018) 'Managing Stake and Accountability in Prime Ministers' Accounts of the "Refugee Crisis": A Longitudinal Analysis', *Journal of Community and Applied Social Psychology*, 28(6): 406–429.

Salter, L. M. (1975) 'The End of Nationalism: A Call for a Declaration of Interdependence', *International Lawyer*, 9(1): 143–152.

Shelley, C. (1996) 'Rhetorical and Demonstrative Modes of Visual Argument: Looking at Images of Human Evolution', *Argumentation and Advocacy*, 33(2): 53–68.

Shifman, L. (2014) *Memes in Digital Culture*, Cambridge, MA: MIT Press.

Skey, M. (2014) 'The Mediation of Nationhood: Communicating the World as a World of Nations', *Communication Theory*, 24(1): 1–20.

Smith, V. J. (2007) 'Aristotle's Classical Enthymeme and the Visual Argumentation of the Twenty-First Century', *Argumentation and Advocacy*, 43(3–4): 114–123.

Strandberg, K. (2013) 'A Social Media Revolution or Just a Case of History Repeating Itself? The Use of Social Media in the 2011 Finnish Parliamentary Elections', *New Media and Society*, 15(8): 1329–1347.

Valluvan, S. (2017) 'Defining and Challenging the New Nationalism', *Juncture*, 23(4): 232–239.

Van Dijk, T. A. (1993) *Elite Discourse and Racism*, London: Sage.

Wetherell, M. (1998) 'Positioning and Interpretative Repertoires: Conversation Analysis and Post-Structuralism in Dialogue', *Discourse and Society*, 9(3): 387–412.

Wodak, R. (2015) *The Politics of Fear: What Right-Wing Populist Discourses Mean*, London: Sage.

16

BETWEEN ADVERSARINESS AND COMPROMISE

A Rhetorical Analysis of Greek Political Discourse in Times of Crisis

Assimakis Tseronis and Dimitris Serafis

Introduction

In Greek antiquity, rhetoric was inextricably related to politics, not only in the narrow sense of politics as deliberation about a future course of action but also in the broader sense as active engagement and participation in all public proceedings of the polis (Harris 2017). In modern times, rhetoric has been associated with embellishment and manipulation, and as such it has been connected mainly to appearances and demagogy (Martin 2013). This is a rather unfortunate development that does not do justice to the analytical and explanatory potential of rhetorical categories for the study of argumentative communication in general and political discourse in particular.

Greek scholars who study rhetoric are mainly affiliated to university departments in classics, ancient philosophy, and pedagogy. In academic literature but also in journalism and texts produced by users in social media, references to rhetorical strategies and rhetorical figures abound. Nevertheless, there are not many attempts to use rhetorical categories in a systematic way for the study of communication in general or political communication in particular. Moreover, when rhetorical concepts are indeed used for conducting analyses of discursive or social phenomena, these are most of the time borrowed from the classical Aristotelian tradition, and hardly ever updated with modern developments to the study of rhetoric and argumentation.

In this chapter, we apply two concepts from classical rhetoric, namely topoi and endoxa as they have been revised within two modern approaches to argumentation theory, to the analysis of two fragments of parliamentary speeches. In doing this, we agree with Amossy (2017: 262–263) who writes that "Political discourse is meant not only to persuade by rationally justifying a choice, but also to reinforce existing values and shared opinions, so that citizens can be mobilized, in times of crisis to defend these values." At the same time, we acknowledge that political discourse in general and parliamentary discourse in particular are characterized by both adversariness and compromise (see Ilie 2017). In the approach we take, we assume that political discourse

DOI: 10.4324/9781003195276-20

This chapter has been made available under a Creative Commons Attribution-No Derivatives 4.0 license.

249

ideally seeks to balance the manipulatory and deceitful dimension of politics with the deliberative and rational one. The combination of concepts from classical rhetoric and modern argumentation theory helps to explain how this tension is managed.

In parliamentary debates, adversariness is expected, but compromise is also necessary since the parties and the MPs do not only need to follow certain institutional rules but also to accept certain starting points. Especially at a time of crisis for the whole nation, one would expect the MPs and party leaders to be ready to put aside certain antagonisms and focus on the shared attempt to deal with the problem. For the purposes of illustration of the analytical and explanatory relevance of these categories, as they have been revised in the two models of argumentation we adopt, we analyse the speeches of the government and opposition leaders during the 2010 parliamentary debate on the signing of the first memorandum of understanding between Greece and the "troika" of the European Commission, the European Central Bank and the International Monetary Fund. In the analysis we show how each speaker balances between adversariness and compromise in the discussion of this crucial bill that was the beginning of a change in the financial and political status quo in both Greece and Europe, and how they manage to address the multiple audiences and their own political agendas under the constraints of the institutional setting and the expectations set by the external audience (national and European).

The Study of Rhetoric in Contemporary Greek Humanities and Social Sciences Scholarship

The academic study of rhetoric among Greek scholars in modern times remains to a large extent in the hands of classicists, philosophers and pedagogues. As a result, one finds more studies about the ancient Greek texts rather than studies that make use of the rhetorical theory developed in these texts in order to analyse contemporary communication.

Besides numerous publications of translations from Ancient to Modern Greek of the original works by the sophists, Aristotle and the Attic orators, Greek classicists have published a number of studies focusing on rhetoric and the Athenian democracy (Alexiou 2020), rhetoric and persuasion in different genres and institutional settings (Papaioannou et al. 2020), as well as on more specific topics such as the performance dimension of oratory (Serafim 2017) and rhetoric and emotions (Spatharas 2019). Rhetoric in Byzantium has not received enough attention yet, with the exception of a monograph by Papaioannou (2013).

Scholars from philosophy departments in Greece have published studies that focus on the intricate relationships between classical rhetoric and ancient philosophy (see Balla 1997 on Plato and rhetoric, and Protopapas-Marneli 2005 on Stoics and rhetoric). Bassakos (1999) has proposed a re-assessment of rhetorical concepts, such as stasis, as tools for the critical study of modern political philosophy (see also the studies collected in the volume by Kindi et al. 2019).

While rhetoric is present in the Greek school curriculum in both a direct way (through the study of classical orators in original or translated versions) and an indirect way (through the teaching of writing and composition), it is in the last decades that scholarly research about the teaching of rhetoric has been conducted (see Egglezou 2014a, 2014b for primary school, and Papadopoulou and Pangourelia 2018 as well as Sachinidou 2015 for Lyceum). Moreover, in the last two decades several associations for the promotion of the teaching of the rhetorical skills of public speaking and debating have been founded, and debate tournaments have been organized at local and national level among teams from high schools and universities.

A quick look at scholarly work published in the Greek language shows that the study of rhetoric is influenced almost exclusively by the classical Aristotelian categories. With very few exceptions, Greek scholars seem to ignore or overlook the developments of modern rhetorical theory in the twenty-first century and the connections between rhetoric and argumentation (see Aune 2008 and Kock 2022 for an overview of the most important authors from the US and Europe). At the same time, there is no systematic study of the connections between rhetoric and linguistics, except maybe in the work of Nakas (2005) who has studied extensively the language patterns that characterize known rhetorical figures in a variety of spoken and written genres. Scholars working in text linguistics and discourse analysis refer occasionally to some of the most well-known categories of rhetoric, such as the three persuasive means or the rhetorical canons and figures, but they do not make any systematic use of these categories, or of elaborations proposed within contemporary rhetorical scholarship, as a method for analysis. In the next section, we introduce two of these contemporary extensions of rhetorical concepts which can prove useful for the study of political and parliamentary discourse in particular.

Revisiting and Expanding Classical Rhetorical Categories: Endoxa and Topoi

When studying contemporary Greek political discourse, researchers in humanities and social sciences draw from a combination of theoretical approaches ranging from text linguistics to (critical) discourse analysis and sociology or political theories, without however making a systematic use of categories from classical rhetorical studies or of categories developed in modern approaches to rhetoric and argumentation (see, for example, the studies in Hatzidaki and Goutsos 2017). Rhetoric is either treated too broadly as "rhetorical strategies" without any further specification, or too narrowly as the search for rhetorical figures in political speeches. On the other hand, in the international literature on political discourse and deliberation, a rhetorical turn is attested (see Finlayson 2007; Martin 2013; Hatzisavvidou and Martin 2021). As Martin (2013: 88) explains, political rhetorical analysis "involves employing rhetorical categories to explore how political actors make interventions to control or 'appropriate' particular situations". At the same time, discourse scholars such as Wodak (2009) and Fairclough and Fairclough (2012) incorporate insights from classical rhetoric and modern argumentation studies into the frameworks that they propose for the study of political discourse in particular (see Amossy 2017 for a brief overview, and Tseronis 2013 for a review).

Two concepts from classical rhetoric that have been elaborated and incorporated in contemporary approaches to discourse and argumentation studies and which are particularly relevant for the study of political discourse are topoi and endoxa (Rubinelli 2009). Endoxon (plural: endoxa) is defined by Aristotle in the book of Topics (A1, 100b 21–23) as "generally accepted opinions [...] which commend themselves to all or to the majority or to the wise that is, to all of the wise or to the majority or to the most famous and distinguished of them". As such, endoxa characterize dialectical arguments, that is arguments whose premises are not merely true or false but are somehow connected to what a particular audience knows. Arguments based on endoxa have higher chances of persuading an audience since they adapt to the values, beliefs, and norms of that audience. Topos (plural: topoi) in Aristotle was used in two senses: (a) as inferential principles, from which arguments can be drawn, and (b) as possible themes of the discussion, what Rigotti and Greco (2019: 21) describe, respectively, as the "topoi from" and the "topoi around". While originally topoi described a system for the invention stage in the process of arguing, in modern approaches (see Perelman and Olbrechts-Tyteca 1969) topoi have been employed as an analytic tool.

Within discourse studies, the Discourse Historical Approach (DHA) (see Reisigl and Wodak 2016) can be regarded as the first framework that has consistently employed concepts from rhetoric, specifically, the Aristotelian concept of topos to identify argumentation strategies that permeate concrete instances of public communication. For the study of right-wing populist discourse in Austria, for example, DHA identifies a series of topoi, including the topos of people, of anger, of liberty, and of law and order. Working within the DHA, Boukala (2016) proposed to include the Aristotelian concept of endoxon in order to describe the dominantly accepted values and knowledge in a specific socio-cultural context. In that respect, topoi should be seen as (re)activating endoxa during the development of a dialectical syllogism. According to the author, the interplay of topoi and endoxa can better encapsulate content-logical (topoi) and contextual (endoxa) premises which govern the syllogisms that pave the way to a(n) (often implicitly) defended standpoint.

Within argumentation studies, it is the pragma-dialectical model of argumentation (van Eemeren 2010) and the Argumentum Model of Topics (Rigotti and Greco 2019) that have drawn insights from rhetoric in order to provide a contextualized and situated account for the analysis and evaluation of argumentation (see also Kock 2022). Pragma-Dialectics, developed by van Eemeren and Grootendorst (2004), is an encompassing theoretical framework combining philosophical and pragmatic insights in order to account for both the descriptive and the normative dimensions in the study of argumentative communication. Van Eemeren and Houtlosser (1999, 2002) have extended the pragma-dialectical theory with rhetorical insights, by introducing the concept of strategic manoeuvring.

In the strategic manoeuvring approach (van Eemeren 2010), the analyst assumes that argumentative discourse is the result of a strategic design that seeks to strike a balance between the dimension of reasonableness and the dimension of effectiveness. More specifically, the argumentative moves identified in the discourse are assumed to be the result of choices made regarding the content (topical potential), the ways of adapting to audience demand, and the selection of suitable presentational devices. As van Eemeren (2010) explains, the three aspects of strategic manoeuvring relate to major categories from classical rhetoric, namely the systems of topoi, the discussion of audience and endoxa, as well as the system of choices concerning the canon of elocutio. Selection from the topical potential concerns the material for the arguments at the argumentation stage and for the other argumentative moves in the other stages of a critical discussion, and thereby relates to the sense of topoi as both inferential principles and possible themes of discussion. Adaptation to audience demand requires the speaker or author to secure communion with the views and preferences of the targeted audience, by appealing to the different types of audience and their respective views and preferences. Selection from presentational devices refers to the communicative means that are used in presenting the various argumentative moves.

The Argumentum Model of Topics (AMT) developed by Rigotti and colleagues (see Rigotti and Greco 2019) complements the strategic manoeuvring approach in a productive way. The AMT acknowledges the heuristic and warranting function of topoi and incorporates them in a systematic way in order to account for the inference processes involved in argumentative discourse. It claims that inferences are part of argumentation schemes, namely "the structures that connect the premises to the standpoint or conclusion in a piece of real argumentation" (Rigotti and Greco 2019: 208). To reconstruct the passage that connects standpoint and argument(s), the proponents of the AMT distinguish between two components, the procedural-inferential component and the material-contextual component. These two interrelating components are based on two core concepts of the rhetorical (Aristotelian) tradition, namely topos/topoi (locus/loci in the Latin tradition) and endoxon/endoxa. If taken together, these components encapsulate the (onto-)logical (see loci) and the contextual (see endoxa) premises that the speaker or author must take into consideration in order to effectively draw an inference in different socio-cultural circumstances.

More specifically, the "procedural-inferential component" consists of (a) the locus "as the source from which arguments are taken" (Rigotti and Greco 2019: 210), and (b) the maxim, which realizes the inferential principle(s) that stem(s) from each locus (Rigotti and Greco 2019: 209). For example, the statement "if the cause is present, the effect will be present" (Rigotti and Greco 2019: 208) would be an appropriate maxim related to the so-called "locus from final cause" that falls under the means-end type of argumentation. On the other side, the "material-contextual component" includes (a) the endoxon, which is defined as "a general premise that is accepted by the relevant public [...] in a specific argumentative situation" (Rigotti and Greco 2019: 214), and (b) the datum, which is a "premise of a factual nature" (Rigotti and Greco 2019: 215). The maxim–datum interplay makes these two components converge to a first conclusion/minor premise, creating a quasi-Y structure that points to the final conclusion, that is, the defended standpoint (see Rigotti and Greco 2019: 208–216 for an overview).

The concept of strategic manoeuvring helps the analyst to explain how the text under analysis has come to be produced, that is, as a result of choices that the speaker or writer made regarding the three aspects of topical potential, audience adaptation and presentation. Such an explanation is of importance for the reconstruction of argumentation and eventually for its evaluation. At the same time, the AMT distinguishes the elements that play a role in the inference process that underlies the justification of the claims made in argumentative communication. As such, the model helps to connect the argumentative claims both with the context in which they have been put forward (by identifying the endoxon that relates to the claim) and with the logical bridge necessary for warranting their argumentative function (by identifying the locus that makes the passage to the claim). While the AMT provides the deeper inference structure of an argument, the strategic manoeuvring approach seeks to connect the production of the argument to the situational context. As van Eemeren (2010: 108, n. 36) observes, the distinction of the endoxon component in the AMT links the topical potential aspect of strategic manoeuvring with the audience demand.

Political Rhetoric and Parliamentary Debates

Politics has been connected with speech (λόγος) since antiquity, while rhetoric as the art of finding the available means of persuasion in any given situation has been used and abused by political agents ever since. It is this connection with speech, both as language and as reasoning, that has drawn discourse analysis scholars into the study of the various genres of political communication (see studies collected in volumes edited by Cap and Okulska 2013; Chilton and Schäffner 2002; Fetzer 2013; and Wodak and Forchtner 2017, among others), and has made political theorists pay attention to the use of language in political communication (Finlayson 2007; Martin 2013). As Cap and Okulska (2013) and Fetzer (2013) observe, political communication in its broadest sense occurs in three different domains: (a) highly institutionalized settings such as the parliament, involving politicians, political parties, governments and ministers (what Fetzer refers to as "politics from above"); (b) highly diversified settings where citizens, non-governmental social institutions and other public or private initiatives express their political views (what Fetzer refers to as "politics from below"); and (c) the media where political discourse from either of the two other domains is represented and commented upon. Among the genres of political communication that have received most attention (in both international and Greek scholarship), one finds political speeches, election posters, policy papers, (parliamentary) debates, press conferences, and political interviews.

Parliamentary discourse belongs to the highly institutionalized discourses of political communication and consists of a number of sub-genres which mainly fall under the deliberative genre of rhetoric (see Ilie 2017). It is during parliamentary debates that ministers and MPs as well as party leaders deliver speeches and interact with the ultimate goal of collectively reaching decisions regarding legislation and policies. As Ilie (2010: 13) notes, "Parliamentary interaction exhibits a permanent competition for power and leadership roles, but also for fame and popularity as concrete manifestations of MPs' public image." Depending on the type of parliament and the institutional and cultural specificities, parliamentary debates in some countries can be characterized by more adversarial and confrontational behaviour than others (see Georgalidou et al. 2019 for a study about aggressive behaviour in the Greek parliament).

Tsakona (2009: 87–88), who describes the Greek parliamentary system as a highly competitive one, observes that

> the main interest of Greek politicians is not to provide political and legal arguments on the issues discussed; rather, they address a wider audience using a familiar (i.e. everyday and conversational) mode in order to attract the attention of the public and persuade them that their policies are right, that their criticisms are justified, and that they have something better to propose than their opponents.

Because the ultimate goal of parliamentary debates remains collective decision-making regarding national policy, one would expect this to be reached on the basis of exchange of arguments and the assessment of their quality. Even if on the surface MPs may use creative language and humour, as Tsakona observes, it should still be possible to identify what the rhetorical and argumentative function of such a presentational choice can be (see previous section about strategic manoeuvring). Tsangaraki (2022), who studied argumentation in the Greek parliament with a focus on the sub-genre of the speeches of the prime minister and the leader of the opposition during plenary debates, identifies repetitions, digressions, *ad hominem* attacks and attacks about inconsistency as typically occurring strategies employed by the speakers in order to achieve their goals while observing the institutional and generic constraints of the rhetorical situation (see also Zarefsky 2008).

Sample Analysis: The Debate on Greece's First Bailout Program

In this section, we analyse two fragments from the speeches that prime minister George A. Papandreou and the opposition leader Antonis Samaras gave during the plenary parliamentary debate on May 6, 2010 concerning the measures proposed by the government for the implementation of the European Financial Stability Facility (see Appendix). We first provide a short description of the political context. In the analysis, we focus on the arguments that can be reconstructed from what is said by the two speakers, by combining the insights about strategic manoeuvring and the argumentative inference process that we presented above.

Following a series of meetings with EU officials concerning the financial stability of Greece, and only seven months after the parliamentary elections of 2009, prime minister Papandreou, leader of the Panhellenic Socialist Movement (PASOK), announced Greece's immediate recourse to the European Financial Stability Facility in April 2010. As a result, Greece entered an almost ten-year turbulent period during which continuous austerity bailout programs were implemented by the successive cabinets, under the strict supervision of the so-called "troika" of the International Monetary Fund (IMF), the European Commission and the European Central Bank (ECB). From 2009 until 2015, Greece witnessed the rise and fall of several governments and a thorough rearticulation of its political and party system. The established socialist party (PASOK) ended up being totally marginalized and the former marginal radical left SYRIZA started leading the Greek opposition, before leading a coalition government (2015–2019) with the nationalist ANEL party (see Serafis et al. 2022 and references therein, for an overview). At the same time, the Greek far right gained momentum when the openly neo-Nazi party, Golden Dawn, entered the Greek parliament in 2012.

Papandreou's predicament in this debate was that his party had been elected (in October 2009) on a political platform which was promising extension of social benefits against the right-wing New Democracy (ND) party led by Kostas Karamanlis, while under the current situation he had to persuade PASOK's electorate, the MPs of the party and the Greek people about the adoption of austerity fiscal reforms, and extensive privatizations. Samaras, on the other hand, who had been elected president of the ND party after Karamanlis' defeat, had to repair the negative image that the party inherited from his predecessor while at the same time he had to manage the expectations that other EU conservative governments had of the role his party could play in the crisis. Samaras was not denying the necessity and the very core of fiscal reforms, but he was fiercely opposing tax increases and salary/pension cuts. He was proposing, instead, a (re-)negotiation of the "troika's" bailout terms through a program of extensive privatizations that could enable Greece to avoid a shocking decrease in living conditions.

Because of the institutionalized activity of the parliamentary debate in general and the specific circumstances of this particular debate, the audience addressed by both politicians is assumed to be heterogeneous, consisting of individuals or groups who have either different opinions or different starting points, what van Eemeren (2010: 110) refers to as a multiple and mixed audience. The audience addressed consists of the two politicians' own party members, the members of the other parties attending this discussion, the Greek people watching the discussion, but also the politicians and citizens of other EU member states and of countries outside the EU. In his speech, Papandreou frames the discussion about the voting of the bill as a dilemma ("Either we vote and implement the Agreement, or we condemn Greece to bankruptcy"). He creates a generalized feeling of blame, stressing the responsibilities of the previous ND government but also of every other political party, indirectly including his own. On the other hand, Samaras frames the discussion as concerning a decision about subordination of the country to foreign supervision institutions ("Today we are called to discuss the literal subjugation of the country under foreign control mechanisms"). He elaborates on an alternative proposal concerning the ways that the country may decrease the deficit, namely by privatizations. On various occasions throughout the speech, Samaras warns or even threatens about actions his party may take regarding the protection of the so-called red lines. The two fragments (see Appendix) that we selected to analyse below present in a rather condensed form the main arguments of the two speakers.

Papandreou's argument for voting for the specific bill can be summarized as follows:

1. The main opposition party should vote in favour of the bill
1.1 The parliaments of EU member states are voting in favour of providing financial support to Greece
1.2 The opposition party bears the main responsibility for the current financial state

In the fragment under analysis (and throughout most of his speech), Papandreou refrains from formulating a standpoint that explicitly states the goal as "voting for the bill". Instead, he makes the presentational choice to connect the act of voting with the act of taking responsibility, and thereby to appeal to the audience's sense of duty as well as to the endoxon stating that the government is the responsible guardian of the society. When it comes to choices from the topical potential, his first reason in support of the standpoint is based on a comparison between what the parliaments of the other EU countries have done and what the vote of the Greek parliament should be. The underlying reasoning that connects this with the standpoint would be a "locus from analogy", explicated in terms of the maxim: if A similar to B does C, then B should do C too (see Rigotti and Greco 2019: 261). By choosing this argument, Papandreou seeks to present the actions of the foreign parliaments as solidarity towards the Greek people, therefore connecting his argumentation to an appeal to the EU institutions while simultaneously emphasizing a pro-EU/IMF profile. At the same time, such a topos seeks to appeal to the indebtedness that the Greek people and the Greek parliament should feel since it would be ungrateful of them to reject the offer of help by the foreign governments.

In the second argument, Papandreou chooses to attack the opposition by pointing to the responsibility that it bears for the current financial state. With this, he refers back to an extensive part of his speech where he enumerates actions of the previous government that increased the country's debt. He thereby presents the ND party as the main accountable political force for the financial turbulence that his government needs to fix as a responsible guardian of Greek society. The scheme that links this argument with the main standpoint is based on a "locus from definition", which takes the form of the maxim: if X is predicated on a definition, then X is predicated on the defined term as well (see Rigotti and Greco 2019: 302). As such the opposition is defined as irresponsible, contrary to the dominant values of the guardian of the society, and is expected to vote for the bill if they want to restore their image. Papandreou makes an interesting choice regarding the presentation of his second argument, formulating it not as an assertion but as a slogan-like elliptical statement that follows a conditional: "if you do not assume your responsibilities, the conclusion will be simple: you have been irresponsible as Government and irresponsible as Opposition. You defected as Government and you are defecting as Opposition." In choosing this formulation, he appeals to the memory and the emotions of the voters of his party and of those citizens who did not vote for the ND party in the last elections, being disappointed with the numerous scandals concerning mismanagement and police oppression by the previous government.

The choice to confront the opposition with the request to assume responsibility for the ND party's previous mismanagement of the country's finances is a risky one, when considering Papandreou's main goal, which is to have the other parties vote for the bill. On the one hand, it increases the adversariness which goes counter to the spirit of consensus that the members of the parliament would be expected to show at a time like this. On the other hand, it is probably the only argument he can use, given that historically both parties are to blame for the current state, as they have been alternating in power since the restoration of democracy in 1974. Since he cannot openly and one-sidedly blame his own party (even though he does that in an indirect way when he states in an earlier part of his speech: "Yes, we were all to blame, some of us less, and some of us more, all those who governed Greece"), he chooses to appear critical towards the opposition. This is a choice that may eventually appeal to a large part of the Greek public that has been disappointed by the previous government under the ND party. At the same time, Papandreou chooses to present the endorsement of the support by the foreign governments as "help" of the EU member states towards the Greek people and to pass over the fact that Greece's bailout was minimizing the financial threat for these foreign governments too.

Samaras' argument for voting against the specific bill can be summarized as follows:

1.   The opposition party will not vote the bill
1.1 The measures proposed in this bill will put the country into recession
1.2 These measures do not provide any hope
1.3 The government does not need the support of the opposition for the bill to pass
1.4 The opposition party does not want to become an accomplice to the destructive consequences of these measures

Samaras chooses to present the opposition's main argument for voting against the bill in a clear and unequivocal way, by stating that the proposed measures will lead the country to further recession. This appears as a conclusion to the first part of his speech in which he elaborates on his party's alternative plans for dealing with the sovereign debt crisis. Here, as in other parts, Samaras makes the topical choice to emphasize the financial consequences of the proposed measures for the country's economy, something which constitutes a clear argument from negative consequences that contrasts with the rather vague formulations that Papandreou used when discussing the consequences of the measures for the Greek citizens. The argument connects with the standpoint through the "locus from termination and setting up" which is realized in terms of the maxim: if X is bad, X must be avoided (see Rigotti and Greco 2019: 263).

Samaras proceeds with the rebuttal of Papandreou's comparison between the attitude of the foreign parliaments regarding the support towards Greece and the Greek opposition's reluctance to vote for the bill. This is a rather delicate move for him since he needs to appeal both to the expectations of the EU partners and to those of his own party members. On the one hand, Samaras was expected to confirm his commitment to the decision taken by the parliament, since the EU partners required reassurances about the payment of the debt, while, on the other hand, he had to appear firm about his party's decision to vote against the bill. He seeks to balance these two goals by using a dissociation between the "help" that the foreign parliaments offer and the "concrete measures" that the Greek parliament is asked to vote. His second argument connects with the standpoint through the "locus from ontological implications" which is realized through the maxim: if X is/is not compliant with dominantly accepted implications, X must/must not be followed (see Rigotti and Greco 2019: 254). Given the situation and the pro-EU orientation of his party, Samaras, just like Papandreou, chooses to present this as "help" and to background the fact that this is a decision that the governments of the EU member states had to take in order to secure their own exposure to the risks of the debt crisis. To that effect, he even makes an explicit promise when he states that "The foreign parliaments know that what they will offer, they will get back." The second argument appears at first sight to be a repetition of the first and main argument, concerning the consequences of the measures. But this time, the argument is not presented in factual terms but rather in emotional terms with reference to the concept of hope and the use of the metaphor of the patient and the drug. In doing this, Samaras appeals to the concerns of the Greek citizens who are described as the patients who risk dying from the proposed measures. By emphasizing that it is the government that takes the decision about the dosage of the drug and that the EU partners are only responsible for the recommendation of the drug, Samaras seeks to keep the delicate balance between his internal and external audience.

The last two arguments emphasize the adversary character of the discussion. By stating that the bill will pass even without the opposition's positive vote, which is true since the government had the majority of seats in the parliament, Samaras seeks to point out Papandreou's inconsistent behaviour of criticizing the opposition so vehemently while asking them for support. This argument connects to the main standpoint through the "locus from final-instrumental cause", which is realized through the maxim: if X is/is not a means to achieve a goal, then X should/should not be employed (see Rigotti and Greco 2019: 258). By making this topical choice, Samaras seeks to argue also towards the international creditors that his involvement in the vote is not necessary for the ultimate implementation of the proposed reforms. Through his last argument Samaras emphasizes that he (and his party) do not want to be associated with the negative consequences that this agreement will have for the Greek people, and uses the word "accomplice". By making such a topical and presentational choice, Samaras clearly appeals to the expectations of his own party members and party supporters, thereby risking appearing to prioritize the party's own interests in coming to power again over the country's need for a political consensus at a time of economic crisis. Similar to the second argument by Papandreou, this, too, is an argument based on the "locus from definition", whereby Samaras seeks to portray his party as being in accordance with their presupposed role (see endoxon) to protect the citizens from the negative consequences of the proposed measures, the difference being that the two leaders have opposite views about what the negative consequences entail.

Compared to Papandreou who makes the topical choice to emphasize responsibility and duty, Samaras stresses the concept of hope, both in the passage under study and in other parts of his speech. In this fragment as well as in the rest of his speech, he is interested in establishing the image of his party as one that offers an alternative solution to the problem while remaining a partner that the other EU member states can trust. He thus seeks to appeal to the expectations of multiple audiences both within his own party and the party's voters as well as within the EU. On the one hand, as leader of the ND party, he was struggling to control a heterogeneous parliamentary group that consisted of MPs who favoured certain measures of the proposed agreement and MPs who supported an anti-PASOK, anti-austerity position. On the other hand, his party's steady commitment to Greece's EU/Eurozone membership did not permit him to fiercely oppose the bailout program (as, for example, the left-wing parties, SYRIZA and the Communist party KKE, did during this parliamentary debate).

What Future for Contemporary Greek Rhetorical Studies?

In this chapter, we made use of the classical rhetorical concepts of topoi and endoxa as these have been revised within two contemporary models of argumentation theory, namely Pragma-Dialectics and the Argumentum Model of Topics, in order to show how politicians balance between adversariness and compromise given the constraints of the situation and the multiple audiences that they address. The goal was to update Greek scholarship on contemporary rhetorical studies and to show the analytical and explanatory potential of these concepts as a complement to the customary focus on the use of rhetorical figures and of the three means of persuasion in political communication. In our sample analysis of the parliamentary speeches by prime minister Papandreou and the leader of the opposition Samaras during the debate about the first bailout program, we focused on the micro-level with the aim to account for the rhetorical strategies that go beyond the choice of words, and to acknowledge both the rational and emotional dimensions of political discourse, addressed by the content-logical (see loci) and contextual (see endoxa) lines of reasoning.

Compared to linguistic analysis, frame or content analysis of political speeches, the reconstruction of the arguments produced by politicians allows one to study the reasoning and inference processes, and to uncover the connections between what is said and what is meant. Focusing on the arguments exchanged in political communication makes it possible to assess their quality and their contribution to political action by explaining how they are grounded in beliefs, values or knowledge shared between the speaker and the audience. The proposed analysis could be expanded by carrying out a systematic evaluation of the argumentation produced by the two speakers both in terms of the cogency of their arguments and in terms of their rhetorical efficiency. Moreover, the study of political communication remains incomplete if one does not pay attention to the non-verbal aspects of politicians' performance (see studies in Poggi et al. 2013) or to the use of images in printed and online political communication (see Seizov 2014; Serafis et al. 2020; Tseronis 2017; Veneti et al. 2019).

Rhetorical studies of Greek political discourse could benefit from enriching their analytical toolkit not only with concepts such as topoi and endoxa but also with the list of specific types of arguments, such as the so-called practical or pragmatic arguments, or specific types of rhetorical strategies such as apologia and dissociation. Identifying specific types of arguments, instead of generally talking about the arguments used in discourse, and specifying the rhetorical strategies that speakers or authors of texts exploit, can contribute to a nuanced analysis and evaluation of political discourse. The way forward is to open up to interdisciplinarity and make the most of the synergies between classical studies of rhetoric and modern approaches to argumentation studies, as well as approaches to discourse and multimodal analysis.

Acknowledgements

We are grateful to the COST Action CA17132 'European Network for Argumentation and Public Policy Analysis' (www.publicpolicyargument.eu) for enabling us to meet and work on the ideas presented in this chapter.

References

English References

Alexiou, E. (2020) *Greek Rhetoric of the 4th Century BC: The Elixir of Democracy and Individuality*, Berlin: Walter de Gruyter.

Amossy, R. (2017) 'Understanding Political Issues through Argumentation Analysis', in R. Wodak and B. Forchtner (eds.), *The Routledge Handbook of Language and Politics*, London: Routledge, 262–275.

Aristotle. (1960) *Topics*, trans. E. S. Forster (Loeb Classical Library), Cambridge, MA: Harvard University Press.

Aune, J. A. (2008) 'Coping with Modernity: Strategies of 20th-Century Rhetorical Theory', in A. Lunsford, K. Wilson, and R. Eberly (eds.), *The SAGE Handbook of Rhetorical Studies*, London: Sage, 85–109.

Boukala, S. (2016) 'Rethinking Topos in the Discourse Historical Approach: Endoxon Seeking and Argumentation in Greek Media Discourses on "Islamist Terrorism"', *Discourse Studies* 18(3): 249–268.

Cap, P. and Okulska, U. (eds.) (2013) *Analyzing Genres in Political Communication: Theory and Practice*, Amsterdam: John Benjamins.

Chilton, P. and Schäffner, C. (eds.) (2002) *Politics as Text and Talk: Analytic Approaches to Political Discourse*, Amsterdam: John Benjamins.

Egglezou, F. (2014b) 'Argumentative Literacy and Rhetorical Citizenship: The Case of Genetically Modified Food in the Institutional Setting of a Greek Primary School', in Ch. Kock and L. Villadsen (eds.), *Contemporary Rhetorical Citizenship*, Amsterdam: Leiden University Press, 183–204.

Fairclough, I. and Fairclough, N. (2012) *Political Discourse Analysis: A Method for Advanced Students*, London: Routledge.

Fetzer, A. (ed.) (2013) *Pragmatics of Political Discourse: Explorations across Cultures*, Amsterdam: John Benjamins.

Finlayson, A. (2007) 'From Beliefs to Arguments: Interpretive Methodology and Rhetorical Political Analysis', *The British Journal of Politics & International Relations*, 9(4): 545–563.

Georgalidou, M., Frantzi, K., and Giakoumakis, G. (2019) 'Addressing Adversaries in the Greek Parliament: A Corpus-Based Approach', in M. Chondrogianni, S. Courtenage, G. Horrocks, A. Arvaniti, and I. Tsimpli (eds.), *Proceedings of the 13th International Conference on Greek Linguistics*, 106–116.

Harris, E. M. (2017) 'Rhetoric and Politics', in M. J. MacDonald (ed.), *The Oxford Handbook of Rhetorical Studies*, Oxford: Oxford University Press, 53–62.

Hatzidaki, O. and Goutsos, D. (eds.) (2017) *Greece in Crisis: Combining Critical Discourse and Corpus Linguistics Perspectives*, Amsterdam: John Benjamins.

Hatzisavvidou, S. and Martin, J. (2021) 'Introduction to the Special Issue: Rhetorical Approaches to Contemporary Political Studies', *Politics* 42(2): 149–155.

Ilie, C. (ed.) (2010) *European Parliaments under Scrutiny: Discourse Strategies and Interaction Practices*, Amsterdam: John Benjamins.

Ilie, C. (2017) 'Parliamentary Debates', in R. Wodak and B. Forchtner (eds.), *The Routledge Handbook of Language and Politics*, London: Routledge, 309–325.

Kock, Ch. (2022) 'The Reception of Ancient Rhetoric in Modern Argumentation Theory and Pedagogy', in S. Papaioannou, A. Serafim, and M. Edwards (eds.), *Brill's Companion to the Reception of Ancient Rhetoric*, Leiden: Brill, 489–513.

Martin, J. (2013) *Politics and Rhetoric: A Critical Introduction*, London: Routledge.

Papaioannou, S. (2013) *Michael Psellos: Rhetoric and Authorship in Byzantium*, Cambridge: Cambridge University Press.

Papaioannou, S., Serafim, A., and Demetriou, K. (eds.) (2020) *The Ancient Art of Persuasion across Genres and Topics*, Leiden: Brill.

Perelman, Ch. and Olbrechts-Tyteca, L. (1969) *The New Rhetoric. A Treatise on Argumentation*, Notre Dame: University of Notre Dame Press.

Poggi, I., D'Errico, F., Vincze, L., and Vinciarelli, A. (eds.) (2013) *Multimodal Communication in Political Speech. Shaping Minds and Social Action. International Workshop, Political Speech 2010 Rome, Italy*, November 10–12, 2010, Berlin: Springer.

Reisigl, M. and Wodak, R. (2016) 'The Discourse-Historical Approach (DHA)', in R. Wodak and M. Meyer (eds.), *Methods of Critical Discourse Studies*, 3rd ed., London: Sage, 23–61.

Rigotti, E. and Greco, S. (2019) *Inference in Argumentation: A Topics-Based Approach to Argument Schemes*, Cham: Springer.

Rubinelli, S. (2009) *Ars Topica: The Classical Technique of Constructing Arguments from Aristotle to Cicero*, Berlin: Springer.

Sachinidou, P. (2015) 'Argumentative Strategies in Adolescents' School Writing', in F. H. van Eemeren and B. Garssen (eds.), *Scrutinizing Argumentation in Practice*, Amsterdam: John Benjamins, 151–174.

Seizov, O. (2014) *Political Communication Online: Structures, Functions, and Challenges*, London: Routledge.

Serafim, A. (2017) *Attic Oratory and Performance*, London: Routledge.

Serafis, D., Greco, S., Pollaroli, C., and Jermini-Martinez Soria, C. (2020) 'Towards an Integrated Argumentative Approach to Multimodal Critical Discourse Analysis: Evidence from the Portrayal of Refugees and Immigrants in Greek Newspapers', *Critical Discourse Studies* 17(5): 545–565.

Serafis, D., Kitis, E. D., and Assimakopoulos, S. (2022) 'Sailing to Ithaka: The Transmutation of Greek Left-Populism in Discourses about the European Union', *Journal of Language and Politics* 21(2): 344–369.

Spatharas, D. (2019) *Emotions, Persuasion, and Public Discourse in Classical Athens*, Berlin: De Gruyter.

Tsakona, V. (2009) 'Linguistic Creativity, Secondary Orality, and Political Discourse: The Modern Greek Myth of the "Eloquent Orator"', *Journal of Modern Greek Studies* 27: 81–106.

Tseronis, A. (2013) 'Review of I. Fairclough and N. Fairclough, Political Discourse Analysis. A Method for Advanced Students', *Journal of Argumentation in Context* 2(2): 269–278.

Tseronis, A. (2017) 'Analysing Multimodal Argumentation within the Pragma-Dialectical Framework', in F. H. van Eemeren and W. Peng (eds.), *Contextualizing Pragma-Dialectics*, Amsterdam: John Benjamins, 335–359.

van Eemeren, F. H. (2010) *Strategic Maneuvering in Argumentative Discourse: Extending the Pragma-Dialectical Theory*, Amsterdam: John Benjamins.

van Eemeren, F. H. and Grootendorst, R. (2004) *A Systematic Theory of Argumentation: The Pragma-Dialectical Approach*, Cambridge: Cambridge University Press.

van Eemeren, F. H. and Houtlosser, P. (1999) 'Strategic Manoeuvring in Argumentative Discourse', *Discourse Studies* 1: 479–497.

van Eemeren, F. H. and Houtlosser, P. (2002) 'Strategic Maneuvering: Maintaining a Delicate Balance', in F. H. van Eemeren and P. Houtlosser (eds.), *Dialectic and Rhetoric: The Warp and Woof of Argumentation Analysis*, Dordrecht: Kluwer, 131–159.

Veneti, A., Jackson, D., and Lilleker, D. G. (2019) *Visual Political Communication*, Cham: Palgrave Macmillan.

Wodak, R. (2009) *The Discourse of Politics in Action: Politics as Usual*, Dordrecht: Springer.

Wodak, R. and Forchtner, B. (eds.) *The Routledge Handbook of Language and Politics*, London: Routledge.

Zarefsky, D. (2008) 'Strategic Maneuvering in Political Argumentation', *Argumentation* 22(3): 317–330.

Greek References

Balla, Ch. [Μπάλλα Χ.] (1997) *Πλατωνική Πειθώ. Από τη Ρητορική στην Πολιτική* [*Platonic Persuasion. From Rhetoric to Politics*], Αθήνα: Πόλις [Athens: Polis].

Bassakos, P. [Μπασάκος Π.] (1999) *Επιχείρημα και Κρίση* [*Argument and Crisis*], Αθήνα: Νήσος [Athens: Nesos].

Egglezou, F. [Εγγλέζου Φ.] (2014a) *Η Διδασκαλία της Επιχειρηματολογίας στην Πρωτοβάθμια Εκπαίδευση. Από τον Προφορικό στον Γραπτό Λόγο: Θεωρία και Πράξη* [*The Teaching of Argumentation at Primary Education. From Oral to Written Discourse: Theory and Practice*], Αθήνα: Εκδόσεις Γρηγόρη [Athens: Ekdoseis Gregore].

Kindi, V., Balla, Ch. and Faraklas, G. (eds.) [Κιντή Β., Μπάλλα Χ., Φαράκλας Γ. (επιμ)] (2019) *Τόποι: Αντίδωρα στον Παντελή Μπασάκο* [*Topoi: Gifts for Pantelis Bassakos*], Ρέθυμνο: Πανεπιστημιακές Εκδόσεις [Rethymno: Panepistimiakes Ekdoseis].

Nakas, Th. [Νάκας Θ.] (2005) *Σχήματα (Μορφο)λεξικής και Φραστικής επανάληψης (α΄ τόμος)* [*Patterns of (Morpho)lexical and Phrastic Repetition*, vol. 1], Αθήνα: Πατάκης [Athens: Patakis].

Papadopoulou, M. and Pangourelia, E. [Παπαδοπούλου Μ. και Παγκουρέλια Ε.] (2018) 'Η Ρητορική στην εκπαιδευτική πράξη: η επιχειρηματολογία στην ελληνική διαχρονία της', στο Κ. Ντίνας (επιμ.) *Figura in Praesentia – Μελέτες αφιερωμένες στον καθηγητή Θανάση Νάκα* ['Rhetoric in educational practice: Argumentation in Greek diachrony', in K. Dinas (ed.), *Figura in Praesentia – Studies Dedicated to Professor Thanasis Nakas*], Αθήνα: Πατάκης [Athens: Patakis], 388–404.

Protopapas-Marneli, M. [Πρωτοπαπά-Μαρνέλη Μ.] (2005) *Ρητορική, η Επιστήμη των Στωικών* [*Rhetoric, the Science of Stoics*], Αθήνα: Σμίλη [Athens: Smile].

Tsangaraki, E. [Τσαγκαράκη Ε.] (2022) *Ελληνικός Κοινοβουλευτικός Λόγος*, Διδ. Διατριβή Εθνικό και Καποδιστριακό Πανεπιστήμιο Αθηνών, τομέας Γλωσσολογίας [*Greek Parliamentary Discourse*, Doctoral dissertation defended at the National and Kapodistrian University of Athens, section of Linguistics]. http://dx.doi.org/10.12681/eadd/51264

Appendix

Fragment from Papandreou's speech in the Greek parliament on May 6, 2010 (Greek text copied from the official document of the Minutes, followed by translation in English provided by the authors of the chapter)

Σήμερα, καλώ και πάλι την Αξιωματική Αντιπολίτευση: Τολμήστε να αναλάβετε για μια φορά την ευθύνη για τις πράξεις σας. Τολμήστε την υπέρβαση, τουλάχιστον ως ανάληψη ευθύνης για τα πεπραγμένα. Τολμήστε να στηρίξετε μια προσπάθεια, για τη σωτηρία της χώρας. Τολμήστε για δυο λόγους: Τα κοινοβούλια των άλλων χωρών αποφασίζουν, οι λαοί των άλλων κρατών-μελών αποφασίζουν να στηρίξουν την Ελλάδα. Αποφασίζουν να δώσουν δάνεια στην Ελλάδα. Αποφασίζουν ενωμένα να δώσουν μια μάχη για τη σωτηρία της χώρας μας. Εμείς, απέναντι σε αυτούς, τι λέμε; Δεν δείχνουμε ότι υπάρχει η ενότητα των πολιτικών δυνάμεων, τουλάχιστον από αυτούς που είχαν και ιδιαίτερη ευθύνη, κύριε Σαμαρά. Και αυτό είναι ένας δεύτερος λόγος. Διότι αν δεν αναλάβετε τις ευθύνες σας, το συμπέρασμα θα είναι απλό: Ανεύθυνοι ως Κυβέρνηση, ανεύθυνοι και ως Αντιπολίτευση. Λιποτακτήσατε ως Κυβέρνηση, λιποτακτείτε και ως Αντιπολίτευση. (Χειροκροτήματα από την πτέρυγα του ΠΑΣΟΚ)

Today, I call once again on the Opposition: dare for once to take responsibility for your actions. Dare to go the extra mile, at least as a way of assuming responsibility for what has been done. Dare to support an effort to save the country. Dare for two reasons: The parliaments of the other countries are deciding, the people of the other member states are deciding to support Greece. They are taking the decision to give loans to Greece. They are deciding unitedly to fight for the salvation of our country. What do we say to them? We are not showing them that there is unity of the political forces, at least of those who had a certain responsibility, Mr. Samaras. And that's the second reason [why you need to vote for the bill]. Because if you do not assume your responsibilities, the conclusion will be simple: you have been irresponsible as government and irresponsible as

Greek Political Discourse in Times of Crisis

opposition. You defected as government and you are defecting as opposition. (Applause from the PASOK party members)

Fragment from Samaras' speech in the Greek parliament on May 6, 2010 (Greek text copied from the official document of the Minutes, followed by translation in English provided by the authors of the chapter)

Με τα μέτρα που προτείνετε σήμερα, μας βάζετε πιο βαθιά στο φαύλο κύκλο της ύφεσης και γι' αυτό δεν πρόκειται να ψηφίσουμε το νομοσχέδιό σας. (Χειροκροτήματα από την πτέρυγα της Νέας Δημοκρατίας)

Θα πω κάποια ρητορικά ερωτήματα. Μας λέτε: «όταν η Ελλάδα ζητά από τα άλλα ευρωπαϊκά κοινοβούλια να ψηφίσουν τη χρηματοδότηση, πώς εσείς την καταψηφίζετε;». Απαντώ. Τα άλλα κοινοβούλια ψηφίζουν βοήθεια προς την Ελλάδα, εμείς ψηφίζουμε για συγκεκριμένα μέτρα. Τα ξένα κοινοβούλια ξέρουν ότι αυτά που θα δώσουν, θα τα πάρουν, εμείς ξέρουμε ότι αυτά που θα πάρουμε θα τα υποστούμε αλλά, πέραν από τη χρηματοδότηση θέλουμε και την ελπίδα. Γι' αυτόν το λόγο συνεχώς είμαστε εδώ, για να προσφέρουμε λύσεις ελπίδας, άλλο μίγμα οικονομικής πολιτικής. Και αυτό είναι πολύ διαφορετικό, γιατί τα άλλα κοινοβούλια ψηφίζουν να δοθεί στην Ελλάδα ένα φάρμακο, δεν ψηφίζουν τη δοσολογία του φαρμάκου. Εσείς εδώ προτείνετε ένα φάρμακο σε δοσολογία που κινδυνεύει να σκοτώσει τον ασθενή και αυτό εμείς σας το επισημαίνουμε και δεν μπορούμε να το δεχτούμε. Και εν πάση περιπτώσει, δεν καταλαβαίνω ποιο είναι το πρόβλημα. Αν εσείς πιστεύετε στα μέτρα που προτείνετε σήμερα, τι σας νοιάζει η δική μας άρνηση; Έτσι κι αλλιώς, αυτό το νομοσχέδιο «περνάει» - κάτι που είπατε εδώ πέρα με περισσή κομπορρημοσύνη- χωρίς τη δική μας βοήθεια. Δεν μας έχετε ανάγκη εμάς. Αν πάλι δεν πιστεύετε στα μέτρα που προτείνετε σήμερα, τότε δεν ψάχνετε για στήριξη, αλλά για συνενόχους στην καταστροφή και εμείς συνένοχοί σας δεν πρόκειται να γίνουμε! (Χειροκροτήματα από την πτέρυγα της Νέας Δημοκρατίας)

With the measures you are proposing today, you are putting us deeper into the vicious cycle of recession and that is why we are not going to vote for your bill. (Applause from the New Democracy party members)

I will raise some rhetorical questions. You tell us: "while Greece asks the other European parliaments to vote for its funding, how do you vote against it?" I answer: The other parliaments are voting to aid Greece, we are voting on specific measures. The foreign parliaments know that what they will offer, they will get back, we know that what we will receive will be with a cost but, in addition to the funding, we also want hope. That is why we are constantly here to offer solutions of hope, another mixture of economic policy. And this is where the difference lies, because the other parliaments are voting about giving Greece a medicine, they are not voting for the exact dosage of the drug. You are proposing here a drug at a dosage that risks killing the patient and we are pointing this out to you and we cannot accept it. And in any case, I do not understand what the problem is. If you believe in the measures you are proposing today, what do you care about our refusal? In any case, this bill "will pass" – something you stated here bragging – without our help. You don't need us. If, on the other hand, you do not believe in the measures you are proposing today, then you are not looking for support, but for accomplices to the disaster, and we will not become your accomplices! (Applause from the New Democracy party members)

PART IV

Rhetorical Analysis of Academic and Professional Texts

17

THE FAILING ESSAY

Broadening the "Composition" of Critical Pedagogy in the Age of Digital Literacy

Bradley A. Hammer

Introduction

Nearly 40 years ago, Stephen North charged writing program administrators to "produce better writers, not better writing" (1984, p. 438) and thereby redefine the central role of writing instruction. North first helped us imagine that the rhetorical processes of writing, with their ability to extend and complicate student thinking, were more important than our traditional understandings of "quality". In his seminal essay, North laid the groundwork for decentralizing the material products of composition – leaving them subjugate to the processes of critical engagement. This essay will extend North's understanding of the rhetorical processes of writing in the evolving age of e-literacy, situated in the growing irrelevancy of traditional essay-bound text and unimodal formulations of first-year composition. This essay will further set the scene for a new and disciplinary way to teach first-year writing courses while examining the evolving multimodal genre of "e-composition". This text will further analyze the changing spaces of composition and the evolving formulations of multimodal discourse to extend our traditional understandings of literacy as it demarcates the need to redefine the very structures and purposes of the traditional academic essay. Simply, the academic and web-based spaces for composition are changing rapidly and radically. And, as yet, there is no regularized theory-based pedagogy designed specifically for these evolving spaces of composition to clearly demarcate the rhetorical limits of what it means to "compose" multimodal academic texts.

Renaming the Spaces of Composition

North sought to challenge the rhetorical essentiality of the written page and thereby engage students critically in the processes of composing for cognitive, not purely sentence-level skills. Consequently, he posited a simple, yet important rhetorical dichotomy that drew developmental distinctions between writers (composers) and writing (texts).

With his deemphasizing of texts, North offered the field a recalibration of writing instruction. In this work, he articulated that "writers" and "writing" improve divergently and with an asynchrony of goals. Thereby, North created a charge for later

DOI: 10.4324/9781003195276-22

Compositionists to uncover the causal links between writing process and the development of critical thought.

With the ubiquity of the Internet, the very spaces, modes of production and contexts for composition have shifted. Through the burgeoning rhetorics of multimodality, everything we knew about writing is changing. Our understanding of writerly genre and rhetorical literacy has expanded and continues to develop daily. From wikis to podcasts, today's texts have become richly multimodal as academics *and* students alike compose in virtual spaces. What used to be the static and unchanging page has been replaced by temporally non-fixed compositions. These productions provide virtual spaces for voice and provoke reader response. Understanding these new rhetorical contexts is essential for the critical pedagogue. That is, where it was once difficult to publish, now, anyone and everyone has a space for dissemination. These developments raise a multitude of questions about both rhetoric and composition and how we teach both literacy and skills while promoting critical thought. As such, compositionists, like never before, are teaching in a uniquely transformational moment, an occasion that obliges us to look to the future of scholarly communication and redefine the very rhetorical "composition" of academic discourse in the first-year course.

Caught up in the Essay Rut

As the spaces, modes of production, contexts for dissemination, and digital products of writing change radically, the traditional first-year writing course, steeped in critical literacy, must develop rhetorical habits of mind for students who will invariably engage in the emerging forms of e-literacy. Unlike the multimodal contexts of modern composition, the static traditional academic essay's purposes, products and processes fail to offer a richly dialogic, audience-focused, and multimodal construct of today's academic writing. Further, the essay in its traditional rhetorical forms fails to engage students in the multiple forms of critical web-literacy that are essential to the modern student, writer and consumer of online content. That is, e-based contexts for composing have not altered the fundamental rhetorical principles of literacy. Yet, instructors are now seeking a pedagogy that embraces a new rhetoric that can address the shifting and variant modes of today's writerly production.

Technology and the web have produced a world of writerly exchange that challenges the relevancy of the temporally fixed and audience-disconnected rhetorical forms of composition within the traditional formulations of the college essay. As such, the traditional "college paper" has become outmoded, not merely in the ways that populist writing is now disseminated but also in the ways academics themselves produce and publish knowledge. Text-based exchange is merely one rhetorical formulation of a larger multimodal discourse for today's academic and social response. It's not by coincidence that academics have led the charge to engage the latest writerly technologies like blogging while extending our own academic voices into online and multimodal spaces. A modern genre like podcasting can extend a critical instructor's vision of the "engaged" writer with its ability to extend not only the temporal and rhetorically static nature of the otherwise isolated argument but rather to situate scholarly and intertextual composition within a community of active and critical web-based responders.

Typified in the retooling of our own core literature (see: CCC Online which seeks to "shape the direction of rhetoric and composition research and pedagogy in the 21st century" through an e-Journal that publishes "multimedia texts"), academics are seeking broader, more responsive and multimodal contexts for dissemination. Consequently, in a moment of "regularize[ation]" (WPA Outcomes Statement) for the first-year writing course, compositionists must match the intellectual goals they have for writers with a genre for e-composition. In so doing, instructors can produce both scholarly forms of new web-based literacy as well as richer opportunities for student inquiry, audience, and asynchronous peer-response. Of greater concern is the emergence of these new writerly spaces without a developed rhetoric, steeped in critical literacy for students to approach, craft, respond to or disseminate their productions. Developing an academic discourse to surround this new literacy is our field's central responsibility in these shifting times.

Writing Technology and Its Rhetorical Aims

Charged with the work of critical literacy, first-year writing instructors were among the first in the academy to embrace technology. Many of us forget how "radical" the technological shift of the 1980s seemed, as our students moved away from hand-written and/or typed texts, and, for the first time, used computers to "process" words. Arguably, one of the earliest (pre-Internet) uses of the desktop computer was as "word processor", allowing writers to more easily edit and revise texts, freeing them concomitantly from the foils and frustrations of spelling and grammar. Consequently, computers became tools for student writers to produce more richly rhetorical, longer, cleaner and more readily editable texts. As such, our rhetorical deconstruction of the vision of technology, situated as an "aid" to the composing process, both informed and perhaps stymied its earliest uses. In the earliest years of writing with computers, few classrooms made richly rhetorical and non-instrumentalist use of technology. However, today's students, well versed in the emerging forms of e-literacy, are bored with the conventional, temporally fixed, and no longer ubiquitous modes of writerly exchange offered by traditional text. These same students seek genres of relevancy for the many rhetorical forms of writing they already engage. In truth, our core disciplinary goal of the last 25 years (i.e., to get students to engage *daily* in more writerly activities) has been actualized through the multiple forums of emerging technology. Put simply, students, without the prompting of a writing course, now compose volumes of text daily – wholly unlike any other period in academic history.

These students are not merely texting, e-mailing, and posting memes. Rather, they are engaged in the forms of response writing that, with a developed set of rhetorical skills in modern critical literacy, will prove richly academic. We see these rhetorical forms every day, as students both compose and respond to multimodal genres, craft their rhetorical deconstructions of our courses on ratemyprofesor.com, or engage in asynchronous, web-based debate on the very topics and issues they find germane. In so doing, they are voluntarily engaging in discourse communities, responding to the work of others and entering into an intertextual exchange with a real audience. What is essential to note with these modern, self-directed compositions is twofold:

1. Students are freely and enthusiastically engaging in the rhetorical processes of composition as never before.
2. Our current theory and pedagogy has yet to fully engage these emerging forms of e-composition/e-literacy in complex, critical and rhetorically defined ways.

It's not that blogging is inherently an inferior or less "academic" genre, rather, we as compositionists have yet to fully develop the pedagogical and rhetorical vocabulary to engage students academically with multimodal composition. And, while many instructors and students engage daily in these richer forms of e-composition, our classrooms (as well as our rhetorical theory) still lack a developed, and consistent pedagogy to merge the latest e-genre with our long-standing and academic goals for critical literacy.

Consequently, the promise of technology to engage students critically/analytically with these new forms of literacy predisposes our work toward a revisionist, perhaps heretically new construction of "academic writing". As we seek these new spaces, modes, and rhetorics for academic composition, we must question what instructional value is retained within our traditional forms of writing. We must not only question the relevancy of the traditional essay in first-year composition, but further, begin to question the very rhetorical delineations of today's "literate student". Put simply, we must bring into question how, and in what complex ways, the traditional academic essay "fails" to engage our students in the evolving and essential forms of modern literacy.

As technology alters how our students write, instructors are forced to respond by extending the very definitions and forms of academic writing. As we produce new pedagogical schema, steeped in the multimodal forms of composition, we are forced to produce not merely new processes and spaces for composing, but also a new rhetoric. Arguably, the pedagogical richness of our field's burgeoning theory would be better served through the production of new, richly academic, and multimodal formulations of composition. Whether wed to a traditional skills-centric agenda or to the larger theory-based goals of cultural literacy, the first-year course must move beyond the old forms of composition that, with the passing of each new day, decline in both real-world use and pedagogical relevance.

New Media

Each new semester brings students (we've all seen their faces and attitudes about being stuck in "freshman comp") who ask themselves "why write" in schooled contexts, for more than just a grade. Yet, these same students, outside of schooled contexts, are writing with both interest and self-motivation in web-based genres that not only hold their attention but are now clearly part of the public discourse.

Compositionists must begin to ask if there are ways to engage students more complexly with writing processes that are academic, self-directed, and rhetorically rich? Who amongst us is unaware that our students ask themselves, the night before the paper is due, "why write" beyond the grade? Both acknowledging and accepting the consequences of this reality dictates taking a close and deconstructionist look at the rhetorical limitations of traditional text-based genres. To say that our students are merely "lazy" or "bored" fails to address the reality that our students write daily (and robustly) within myriad forms of e-composition. In effect, they are rhetorically sophisticated in complex ways that remain outside our teaching. Technology provides the spaces, media, and genre for these modernist compositions. And, as we seek to name a uniquely disciplinary genre that supports the type of critical engagement with written discourse we have long sought in our critical literature, we must embrace how technology has altered the very understanding of what it means to compose.

E-composition is not merely the production of electronic versions of traditional texts. Rather, this form of composition complicates and extends the rhetorical elements of "writing", to include rich asynchronous compositions with multimodal, non-temporal, and "composite" productions of student analyses and critical reflection. Unlike the traditional essay that centralizes "argument", web-based genres can also centralize the processes of publication, development of voice, and the other rhetorical cornerstones of our historic "best practices".

The Changing Definition of "Academic" Writing

For compositionists, the gap between skills and critical literacy cannot be bridged in an ethos of service to traditional academic genres. In this age of "standards" and accountability, the push toward skills will always win. And, as post-secondary institutions pressure writing program administrators to foreground and regularize students' rhetorical skills, we need to reimagine how, and for whom, we are asking students to compose. Consequently, those expressivist goals most central to our literature are subsumed by departmental/institutional objectives situated in rhetorically non-sophisticated definitions of proficiency. Concomitantly, in non-school contexts, our students are developing writerly expertise and rhetorical skills in electronic discourse modes that radically alter how information is disseminated. We now teach in an age where our students, through the technologies of the web, write daily in genres that are outside the traditional academic discourses on "rhetorical knowledge". By all accounts, this profusion of composed correspondence, analysis, reflection, argumentation, and peer-centered response fulfills the field's central and widely cited pedagogical promise – to engage students daily in the practices of self-directed, responsive, problem-posing, analytical, intertextual and "real" writing.

Like my students, many instructors see a distinct rhetorical difference between school and "informal" e-writing. To be sure, some vocal critics argue convincingly that a real disjuncture exists between "fad" genres like blogging and traditionally "academic" forms of research-based analytical discourse. To this argument I would agree – not because blogging is inherently less academic than the traditional thesis-driven essay but rather because our rhetorical theory and pedagogy has yet to define the critical methods for teaching e-composition while promoting students' interest, research, analysis, theory-building and critical thought.

In an age of multimodal composition, where newly defined rhetorical forms of composition displace traditional customs and practices, the traditional essay no longer supports a discourse of cultural relevancy, literacy, or student interest. As such, compositionists are now considering how, and in what ways, the traditional essay retains relevance within the academy.

Where Is the "Academic" in Multimodal Composition?

If first-year writing students abandoned the rhetorical limitations of the traditional thesis-driven essay, would their compositions still be considered fundamentally academic? Moreover, would our courses remain defined disciplinarily as "writing", "rhetoric", "composition" or "communication literacy"? My question is really threefold:

1. Is the traditional college essay inherently more academic and rhetorically rich than e-genres?
2. Does the crafting of traditional, thesis-driven argumentative essays in our courses stifle or engender a richly nuanced, unbiased, and critically interrogative voice in student writers as they engage in the rhetorical processes we value (research, analysis, revision, problem-posing, collaborative discovery, peer-to-peer response, etc.)?

3. What, if any, genre could replace the traditional essay in the first-year course to more adequately and richly arouse our disciplinary, expressivist, critical thinking, rhetorical, and literacy goals for first-year students?

Technology contexts have produced a distinctly opportunistic moment, a backdrop for the re-interpretation of traditional rhetorical forms of academic composition for the first-year course. To be sure, many writing courses engage in (and many teacher-researchers have advocated for) a pedagogy focused on extending the rhetorical forms of writing in the first-year classroom.

Over the past 35 years, rhetoricians have re-formulated the schema of academic writing, beyond the text, as a process of intellectual discovery and critical learning. During this period, teacher scholars attempted to define the relationship between the process of writing and the rhetorical process of critical learning. In this thread of inquiry, it became clear that writerly goals were moving away from the centrality of texts, their structures, grammar, and style, to include the cognitive and intellectual effects that writing process could exert on first-year students. This work re-contextualized the question, "why write", by making students' own intellectual development and the deepened awareness of their rhetorical situation, not the arguments within their texts, the core answer. And, while the National Council of Teachers of English, the Conference on College Composition and Communication, the Council of Writing Program Administrators, and even many universities are today on board with this larger value, the actual rhetorical structures of evaluation within many writing programs, and the textbooks that gird their pedagogy, are nonetheless situated in a skills-based role. Consequently, a real and pronounced disjuncture exists between rhetorical theory and the day-to-day practices in the first-year classroom.

Invention in First-Year Writing

The field of Rhet/Comp has seen many lives and evolved over many reconstructions. With the development of new models for freshman writing, we have moved well beyond the central binary debates: "product versus process", "grammar versus meaning", and "skills versus critical thinking". However, in the confines of the classroom, students' rhetorical knowledge is commonly supplanted by an institutionally defined charge for "skills". Yet, this agenda and pedagogical charge is not wholly our own. This charge, situated in a model of sentence-level "error and correctness", was long ago dismissed by the field at large, yet remains forcefully present in the structures, funding, and pedagogy of today's rhet/comp programs. At stake is the very disciplinary nature of rhetorical instruction. Yet, as instructors of first-year writing, we have failed to define (and therefore cannot teach) the rhetorical formations, processes, and genre that would demarcate our own disciplinary legitimacy and, as such, live subjugate to the instructional needs of the institution, as we struggle to insert disciplinary goals within a genre of writing that is both waning in relevancy and essentially not our own.

Beyond the "Service" Essay

For now, the traditional argumentative or "service" essay exists as the regularized and ubiquitous form of academic discourse. Concomitantly, this genre serves as the universal rhetorical mode of linguistic response within the time-honored history of college writing. Arguably, the pervasive use, continued preservation, and pedagogical value of the traditional thesis-driven essay pivots on its ability to afford students opportunities to respond to the work of others, thereby fostering a scholarly dialogue between readers and writers. A rhetorical understanding of the value of this structured form of linguistic interchange is perceived to set the groundwork for a distinctly "academic" form of writing. Consequently, this formulation of writing is valued as a dialogic where student writers respond to the voices and positions of others. Put simply, technology does more than merely afford students new ways to compose old forms. Rather, technology itself becomes the new cultural/social/academic space for students' rhetorical analyses – to posit *and* deconstruct arguments. The Internet, as it cultivates myriad formations of web-based community, provides rich spaces for students to deconstruct rhetorically the work and compositions of others.

Building Online Writerly Communities

Within the traditional college essay, instructors oftentimes work to connect students rhetorically to the writer/reader dialogic. This form of teaching pushes students to step into and interrogate a larger history and community of thought on a given topic through their composing processes. This sense of community building, through the processes of composition, supports Harris' (1989, p. 11) claim of how students are "drawn" to "the idea of community" being "central to our work" – what Bizzell (1982, p. 191) popularized as initiating students into an "academic discourse community". However, when our practices fail to engage students in the electronic discourse communities that they now engage daily, we offer them limited rhetorical modes for writing and idea-exchange that fail to address the relevant forms of today's writerly communities.

Before compositionists fully embrace or dismiss the traditional essay, we need to understand what, if any, role it serves in educing, for students, an academic formation of critical literacy. While the central claim or thesis within the essay suggests the existence of an implied and oppositional audience, the typical college essay, in fact, exists without real audience in a monologist vacuum (punctuated within the teacher/student hierarchical relationship). In this pyramid structure of learning, there exists a real antagonist in the text (i.e., the grader) but no adequate opportunities to create real dialogue within the reader/writer divide. Simply, as Freire (1973, p. 78) contends, "dialogue cannot take place between antagonists". Consequently, as students anticipate "what the teacher wants", no real teacher/student dialogue can ensue.

While peer-revision and other process pedagogies attempt to subvert the punitive authority of the student/teacher dichotomous relationship, the structures of grading more forcefully situate the teacher as the central and perhaps only relevant audience. Even with progressive pedagogies that include peer-to-peer response, students intuit rightly that the instructor serves as the central audience. This rhetorical formulation diminishes the dialogic potential of the students' compositions and situates the essay as no more than a mechanism for evaluation. Within this formulation of academic writing, critical response between students and teachers takes place in the margins of the text and tends to assert an authoritative (non-dialogic and "non-community-based") discourse on quality – where opportunities for student learning are defined, not by the positions and questions held by real readers but rather within the isolating confines of the traditional classroom where responses are centralized inside of the individual instructor's beliefs regarding "good writing". Conversely, real opportunities for dialogic writing must include legitimate web-spaces for students to extend the borders of audience, whereby they are forced, as budding rhetorical scholars, to defend the intellectual limits of their own texts. And, it is only in these web-based spaces that students can extend the isolating boundaries of the traditional classroom and publish as real writers as they seek out and defend against real audiences. Evidenced by the massive presence of self-directed online student writing, the web, through its ability to promote real authorship, delimits for students a meaningful answer to the central question of "why write".

It is a rare student who will willingly "take chances" and "try-on" complex rhetorical moves, unique writerly voices, unconventional views, and alterative/unpopular analyses in their school-based writings. Query your first-year writers and invariably you will find students unvested in their own texts and focused not on complex, rhetorical, and nuanced analytic work but on producing safe and formulaic papers.

Simply, the spaces, modes, processes, and media of composition are changing. At stake is understanding the pedagogical implications of that shift and the real instructional value that the web can provide with first-year writers who seek a deeper rhetorical understanding of modern literacy through engagement with real audiences.

That the essay has changed with the altering face of the academy is not in question. Rather, at stake is understanding the pedagogical implications of that shift and the real instructional and rhetorical value of thesis-driven argumentation with first-year writers who seek, through a deeper understanding of e-literacy, to engage with real audiences.

Caught-up in the Essay Rut

Beginning in the earliest grades, students learn to write traditional thesis-driven essays. In this rhetorical structure, budding scholars take on complex issues as they conduct (typically without real audience) lit-review style "research" and declare (what the teacher hopes) is an unbiased rhetorical "stance". Yet, as these same students "enter the college curriculum", they bring "default forms" of "thinking and writing" (Dombek et al. 2004, p. IX) that either support their positional/biased logic or the students' grade-centric perceptions of "what the teacher wants". And, for these students (who otherwise engage daily and willingly in dynamic forms of web-based discourse), the traditional essay form actually reinforces the rhetorical and linguistic artificiality of the college essay, through the absence of real audience. These analyses present the disjuncture between traditional forms of academic writing and student engagement with assignments. As such, the methods of scholars in rhet/comp need altered goals, spaces, and linguistic formulations of first-year writing to complicate, through the development of a new genre ("e-composition"), the very processes that engage students more complexly. Through these changes, instructors may engage students with real analysis, problem-posing inquiry, reflection, engagement, theory building, research, revision, collaborative discovery, peer-to-peer response, writerly community, and student publication.

In this spirit, as I visit my colleagues and graduate students who teach writing, I frequently see hard-working, sincere, and earnest teachers who are stifled by the intellectual confines inherent to a genre that necessitates more disputative (for/against, pro/con) reasoning than dialogic exchange. While many theorists and teacher/scholars have done good work in defining ways for first-year classrooms to make this genre work, the task is inevitably an onerous one for instructors charged with addressing a skills-based deficiency.

Consequently, the first-year classroom is a critical time to extend our definitions of composition as we break the cycle of students' oftentimes positional and thereby unsophisticated reasoning.

The Rhetorical "Character" of Academic Writing

For compositionists, what makes writing process "academic" (i.e., rhetorically rich) is its ability to afford students opportunities for self-examination, problem-posing inquiry, analytical dialogue between readers and writers, and critical interrogation of biased and assertive logic. And, with the spirit of these goals, first-year writing programs work to bridge the divide that separates a local institution's need for skills, with a national charge for writing as critical inquiry. Unfortunately, the products of that inquiry typically centralize thesis-driven argumentation and, therefore, claim-making as the starting point for the students' actual writings. As such, the "strong and direct thesis", followed in the essay by its support, remains central to university discourse modes. In this form of inquiry, the investigator (i.e., the student author) sets out to assert a particular causal link between two defined variables. As an example of a typical thesis from one of my first-year students, Susan writes, "Slavery, as a major economic engine of the early 19th century, both codified and perpetuated the harmful racial attitudes that oppressed African Americans, well past emancipation." Within this thesis, Susan asserts her belief about the production of modern-day racism. With her claim, she is positioning her belief within a body and history of academic literature. Consequently, in support of a claim, a writer may unintentionally use the papers' citations to establish a close ideological stance within the text. With her attempt at an "unbiased" thesis, Susan is not merely claim-making toward some larger truth, but rather, setting up, in the rhetorical traditions of the academy, a structure, format, and process for the "academic" validation of her positional belief. Consequently, her central claim, which suggests a causal link between *slavery* and the development of *racial attitudes*, is not merely represented on the page as her positional "belief", but rather, as the paper unfolds, part of a larger history of academic thought on the topic. As such, the student fancies herself an unbiased "scholar" (reinforced by the positional/argumentative citations that gird her own logic/ analyses) as her strategy for "alignment" with prior scholars actually undermines real opportunities to challenge positionality. Consequently, the academic thesis not only suppresses her opportunities for real engagement with oppositional belief but further provides her with a feigned and uncritical neutrality, where the processes of her academic writing (i.e., research, reflection, theory building, etc.) help her to merely situate her positionality and assertive beliefs as she superficially removes the "I" from her text. Yet, for the first-year writer, whose fundamental goal is not merely the production of an argumentative text, real opportunities exist to engage in a distinctly academic and non-positional form of inquiry. As such, the student who substitutes a thesis claim for critical inquiry and discovery, can engage richly in a uniquely "academic" rhetorical process where her voice is defined beyond her position and situated outside the discrete claims of those arguments that have come before. Only in this way can she come to offer richly new and original insight into the theory and claims that fix her evolving reasoning. In this fashion, before she learns to assert and support her own positional claims, she engages in a form of rhetorical deconstruction that asks her to richly problem-pose and critique those positions that have come before. Thereby, the writer bypasses ideological alignment to uncover bias and subjectivity in the literature as a "scholar". In this fashion, the student is no longer voiced *by* the literature but rather is re-situated in the role of critic. And, through the processes of e-composition outlined within this chapter, today's ethnologies can afford students rich opportunities to engage in this form of critical and non-positional dialogue as they establish real academic voice in non-temporally and non-spatially-fixed modes of composition. Put simply, the rhetorical construction of the traditional thesis-driven essay actually stifles intellectual curiosity and concomitantly promotes what I will term "positionality".

I Don't Need Technology / My Assignments have ALWAYS Worked

It is important to note that technology is not rhetorically neutral. That is, if we choose to ignore technology and its effects on the intellectual relevancy of our assignments (as we wed ourselves to the old rhetorical forms of composition), we must be aware that our students are still free to employ their own knowledge of diverse technologies in ways that alter radically how they engage with the very tasks we assign them. As a simple example, it takes little time for a student, charged with the construction of a traditional essay, to find (without leaving her dorm room) and word-search (without reading a single page of text) a deluge of refereed/academic journals to either construct or support her essay. In altering the very academic/rhetorical value of our assignments, Microsoft Word includes an "autosummarize" tool that allows students to create pseudo "original" text that they can "re-compose" from web-based content with a single click of the mouse. These "texts" can then be handed in as "unique" compositions. In fact, Microsoft boasts that their "autosummarize" tool "works best on well-structured documents, such as reports, articles, and scientific papers" (http://office.microsoft.com/en-us/word-help/automatically-summarize-a-document-HA010255206.aspx). Sadly, these are the very types of compositions that traditional first-year courses engage. And, by using MS Word Autosummarize to identify the key points in a document, students no longer need to actually read assignments to respond effectively to the work of others. This is but one example of how technology alters radically the ways in which students engage with traditional assignments. As such, our failure to embrace technology affirms a tacit acknowledgment and perhaps endorsement of the types of practices that instructors may consider cheating, yet which students might consider merely available. In fact, I've oftentimes considered if a student spent three seconds to autosummarize my own writing into an "original" response or "analytical" essay, would I even be able to assess it as my own work? And, as I attempt this very exercise in the confines of my own office, I realize that with today's technology a student could easily produce a seemingly "original" essay, with very little revision, that outwardly addresses a thoughtful analysis of any academic work they find on GoogleScholar. With this reality, can we honestly advocate for a status quo in the first-year writing classroom? Moreover, are newer technologies adequately addressing these concerns or merely extending them? As such, consider how much of your own effort is wasted, as you read student essays, worrying about the originality and authorship of your students' writing. Technology has radically altered the pedagogical value of our traditional assignments. Do your students make any appreciable use of the library in their research? Do they read texts in their entirety when online versions provide searchable indices? With these realities, no one is surprised that our assignments encourage plagiarism. Writing becomes a battle between universities that spend millions of dollars on "internet bot software" to catch plagiarizers, and the disengaged students that feign interest in, and meaning from, outmoded approaches to instruction. In candid conversations with many of my students, they tell me about the ways in which they use technology to nullify not merely the burden of our assignments but, worse, to make irrelevant both our instructional goals for the processes of writing as well as its intellectual and rhetorical value.

The traditional forms of writing do not merely bore students; they encourage disengagement because they fail (as students embrace technology) to necessitate deep and rich engagement. Simply, technology, even in its current infancy, affords students real opportunities to subvert the intellectual value of our assignments. However, more importantly, in understanding the declining relevancy of our work, our students now enter our classes with more developed and complex understandings of today's forms of writing than our classes, steeped in antiquity, can ever address. And, without a pedagogy steeped in a genre that supports key rhetorical goals, our assignments will be relegated to a role of diminishing relevance, locked in a position of service and gatekeeping.

Positionality, Oppositional Antagonism, and the Traditional Essay Form

While our students often know more about the evolving multimodal genres and web-based reformulations of today's writing than their instructors, they tend to lack a critical lens into developing those writings in academic and rhetorically sophisticated ways. That is, while many of my students blog (and know much more about blogging than I do), their blogs tend to engage less in argument, analysis, critical reflection, and intertextual support than I would deem traditionally and richly "academic". Consequently, illuminating how technology is more than just a "fad", or simply a word-processing medium to more easily produce traditional essays, is a fundamental goal of this project. For many, discussions about technology merely conjure advances in the mechanical processes of writing – i.e, computers are merely tools for word processing, allowing students to be freed from sentence-level minutiae. At stake is not merely the simplifying potential and mechanical value of technology. Rather, instructors of composition are focused on how technology can radically alter the ways in which readers and writers engage in deliberative, collaborative, and asynchronous inquiry. As such, this chapter seeks to recognize the complex rhetorical ways in which the traditional academic essay "fails" students in the university classroom.

Traditional academic writing that asks students to make and support claims forces them into a binary position that denies real opportunities for ongoing dialogue between writers and readers. In this linguistic formulation of writing, there is no room for the complexity of reasoning, intellectual nuance, growth, or discovery. This is the very antithesis of compositionists' rhetorical aims for first-year writing. And, as students position their arguments along binaries, their texts characterize the writer's oftentimes polemic stance, asserted through the essay's central claim. This "positionality", I argue, stifles real inquiry because – to the extent that the student essay supports, not challenges (or deviates from) its central claim – there exists the absence of critical reflection. And as any writing student can attest, the thesis-driven essay as a rhetorical exercise cannot have weak, indirect, or conflicting support for the central claim. And, with the direct and assertive claim, the essay becomes driven by a distinctly positional, if not polemic logic where reasonable exceptions to the claim must be either dismissed or ignored. Consequently, the rhetorical structures of "good" academic writing mandate an absence of ambiguity and non-linear certainty. This way, instructors often read absolutist arguments in our students' grade-centric texts, where complex topics take on pro/con and right/wrong analyses. The linear argument, characteristic of the traditional essay form, is fundamentally constructed as an audience-absent dialogue, confined to the student/teacher dichotomous and hierarchical relationship. Moreover, within this static and temporally fixed form, there is no room for real response, the evolution of thinking, or non-linear support for a claim. Rather, our students understand well the evaluatory contexts of the teacher/student dichotomous relationship within which they compose. Whereas blogging, as one example, resists a static/fixed conception of argument, affording the composer opportunities to "take back" claims as their writing/thinking, in dialogue with real readers, evolves in asynchronous ways. Only with the advent of these newer forms of community-based writing can instructors begin to see how the traditional contexts of claim-making are actually quite non-academic as they support a temporally fixed stance on certainty. Put simply, the essay, through the positionality demarcated by the fixed thesis, creates a binary-driven argument, where belief is situated either with or against the text. As such, sentences are strung together, structured not as an intellectual journey of discovery but rather to support those claims already established with unwavering certainty. And, with this reductive method of debate, the essay, as a rhetorical form, necessitates a writer's defense of position, not inquiry – thereby failing, through its non-exploratory assertions of certainty/truth, to allow for "writers and readers to relate to each other" (Hassett 1995, p. 471). As such, regularizing this form of disputative and unreasoned discourse is antithetical to the larger goals of critical thought.

A Pedagogy of Positionality

The pedagogical significance of student positionality is defined by a distinct stifling of real dialogue and shared exploration between readers and writers. Through the positional stance of the temporally fixed argument, students are encouraged in the assertion of ideology – fostering a binary debate that promotes both enmity with readers and a polarizing of logic – traits that are generally antithetical to the intellectual inquiry sought after by instructors of writing. Regarding the development of critical thought, the thesis-driven essay is, quite simply, *failing* our students. In fact, the very self-effacing moments of internal discovery (what Flowers and Hayes (1980, p. 21) refer to as the writer's "creative process") that instructors seek in their students are muted by the necessitation for positional defense. Thereby, the antagonism forwarded by the asserting of the author's claim "crystallizes relations between readers and writers" (Green et al. 1995, p. 383) in ways that create conflict rather than community or discovery. Consequently, the ubiquitous and regularized processes of traditional academic genres serve to foster discord, rather than dialogue.

A History of Challenging the Traditional Essay

Like Hassett (1995) suggests academic writing should necessitate a "perspective focused on decreasing antagonism". Consequently, this chapter argues that "dissention" is "inherent" not only in a "democratic society" but in the contexts of the classroom (Totten 1992, p. 17). Thus, instructors must employ a pedagogy that encourages students to become "questioner[s]" (Spellmeyer 1989, p. 262) who write in "pursuit of understanding" not claim-making. These rhetorical moves are what Emig names "powerful learning strategies" (Emig and Villanueva 1977, p. 122).

Building toward a Genre of Disciplinarity

Central to compositionist literature and practice is the belief that there exists a causal link between the processes of writing and the development of critical, nuanced, and non-static thought. This tradition, beyond mere service, is the larger *disciplinary* goal of writing instruction. Toward this understanding, Emig was amongst the earliest to define the causal link between writing and learning where the development of "higher cognitive functions" (Emig and Villanueva 1977, p. 122) is related to language development. As well, Odell (1980) writes about "helping" to define this relationship between the "process of writing and the process of learning" (p. 42). Even Montaigne, oftentimes quoted as the progenitor of the "distinct" (Spellmeyer 1989, p. 262) essay genre and father of a type of methodological "humanism" (Screech and Fumaroli 2000, p. xii) that challenged the binary logic of religious dogmatism, might argue against the "conventional" nature of today's thesis-driven essay to "obscure" the "complexity" of "coherence" (Spellmeyer 1989, p. 262). Understanding the processes by which students come to this sense of academic coherency (i.e., critical literacy) underscores the central themes in our core literature. Simply, a thesis-driven discourse within academic writing is an "insistence" on "one right answer or position" and "encourages mindlessness" (Totten 1992, p. 39) over reflection, dialogue, and critical interrogation of oppositional belief. Resisting this form of writing, Flower and Hayes (1980) taught us that writing should be a process of "discovery" (p. 21) where students create meaning – a process antithetical to the answer-driven assertion implied by and embedded within the thesis. By using discovery, not assertion, as the basis for writing, students can make or use their compositions to challenge a discourse that focuses on "correct answers as opposed to reflecting upon important problems for which there are no right answers" (Sykes 1995, p. 71).

Expressivism and a Coming to Voice

As resistance to traditional models of writing instruction, early versions of "expressivism" (Mlynarczyk 2004, p. 4) birthed a process-oriented and non-informationist pedagogy to engender student voice and engage writers beyond the five-paragraph essay. In this vein, compositionists like David Bartholomae, when asked, "what I believe in", answered that professional academies should not have the "authority" to "order or organize work in composition". Rather, Bartholomae argued that individual compositionists should be able to do "work that one could believe in" (Bartholomae 1989, p. 38). This critique of the field set the scene for individual compositionists to step forward and re-invent, not merely the genre of academic writing, but further re-invent the very contexts for why we ask students to write. This chapter recognizes this goal as it seeks to support individual compositionists who argue in local institutions about the changing role and current relevancy of their labor. And, as technology and its multimodal genre ongoingly shift and become reinvented within the public discourse, local compositionists will have to ongoingly reinvent the genre of college composition as they keep in mind the larger intellectual goals that our discipline has long sought.

In a similar challenge, Hillocks (2002) also asks instructors to confront the very "character of teaching" and to begin to "think deeply and critically about the problems and issues facing a society of increasing diversity" (p. 3). Irrespective of this focus, the field still lacks a disciplinarity genre and will remain silenced within an academy that views the ubiquitous first-year writing course as both utilitarian and informationist. Consequently, this chapter will set forth a new genre for first-year writing that positions Composition in a unique disciplinarity stance, beyond mere "service" – offering a new rhetorical model for learning that affords students the type of richly intellectual exploration (over argumentation) that our earliest theorist's work sought to define.

Theory versus Practice: Naming the Disjuncture

Every day that the pedagogy of writing instructors is wed to the traditional essay form, there will continue to be a very real disjuncture between Composition theory and the institutional goals of service. This disjuncture dictates a first-year pedagogy steeped in instrumentality – a schism between theory and practice that Connors (1995) suggests can be understood historically as "two ways of thinking about freshman comp" – either instruction in "thinking and in expression" but also a pedagogy of instrumentality that calls for "drill[s]" (p. 10). In fact, Behrens (1980) suggested that we as compositionists separate ourselves into "two main camps" – "liberal-humanists" (forged by the progressivist ideology of our theory) and "utilitarian-pragmatists" (p. 561) (a pedagogy fixed by the constraints of being situated as a service-oriented practice within departments of English). But, Behrens presents a false dichotomy. That is, his binary of pragmatism negates the very disciplinarity that e-composition now makes possible. Consequently, instead of seeking and promoting what Langer and Applebee call "a clear understanding of the kinds of learning that writing can foster", there is little hope that service-oriented methodologies for the teaching of writing can promote an "integrating" of students' "new information with previous knowledge and experience" (1987, p. 10) – a skill essential for altering the very complexity of their reasoning skills.

Bridging the Gap

Almost 40 years ago, Patricia Bizzell, in her review of the field, declared, "Composition studies has become established as an academic discipline" (1982, p. 191). Yet, faced by the same concerns over the discipline's service role, she questioned, "just how much progress has been made" when the field offers little more than instruction on how to "teach students how to write for their other college courses" (ibid.). Perhaps Bizzell was too quick to declare disciplinarity. That is, while disciplinarity did exist in 1982 (within our literature), the *practice* of Composition was, and still is, situated outside of a uniquely Compositionist genre. Consequently, service to the core curriculum, then and now, dictates the disciplinary limits of our work.

For compositionists, teaching with instrumentalist goals serves as a contradiction to the rhetorical aims of the course. Our work has been appropriated, coopted, and separated from our disciplinary ambitions. As Rhetoric scholars, we need to serve as better advocates for our disciplinary borders by defining a clearer pedagogy with explicit professional boundaries within the academy. Without a distinctly Compositionist genre to actualize our theory, the academy's desire for a service pedagogy will remain unassailable. Our professional organizations, primary journals, and key theory have (for almost three decades) rallied against the academy's uses of our labor. In response, Compositionists have made the complex and important arguments against instrumentality that relate writing to higher-order thinking. However, the academy remains, like our predominantly contingent and "quasi-faculty" positions, unmoved. From a distinctly instructional and thereby non-disciplinary position, Composition inhabits the physical, professional, and psychological spaces of non-belonging. As such, our field could not fully develop the "theoretical premises and pedagogical techniques" necessary to challenge instrumentalists' dictates. Consequently, our key theorists often produce, within their textbooks, pedagogy that actually "reaffirm[ed] the traditional academic discourse values" (ibid.).

As the service of our labor remains instrumentalized, it asserts the centrality and rhetorical purposes of those writing conventions of disciplines that are not ours. Consequently, distinctly Compositionist goals will remain subordinate in the classroom and secondary to the institutional needs defined by our service. However, with the development of a distinct genre, steeped in the historic goals of our literature, Compositionists can argue with disciplinary authority for both institutional autonomy and pedagogical relevance. As such, we must reframe the rhetoric by which we argue for a more invited and institutionalized place of belonging within the academy. Without disciplinarity, we have no assailable rhetorical defense against the institutional constraints that seek our labor to support goals that are not our own.

Why a Genre of "E-Composition"?

As the definitions of cultural and academic literacy change, Compositionists are uniquely positioned to take-on the discourse of technology and e-composition within our courses. The time for boldness is upon us. Simply, the discourse that surrounds the teaching of Composition has, for many years, been a treatise on literacy. In short, the rhetorical elements of literacy are ever-shifting toward the multimodal structures of e-composition. Furthermore, if Compositionists create both pedagogy and theory to drive the academic contexts for these structures, our labor can gain new relevancy within disciplinary borders.

Do Traditional "Skills" Matter?

This text is in no way arguing that skills are irrelevant in the teaching of academic writing. Rather, in a very real way, students enter the academy ill-prepared to engage in the type of writing essential for critical engagement with ideas, texts, and discourse. However, it is time to ask ourselves if there are both pedagogical and institutional ways to separate a genuine need for skills from the disciplinary goals of Composition.

So, at hand, are really two distinct issues:

1. Can we turn to Compositionist literature and theory to define the relevance of a distinctly disciplinary course in e-composition, wholly divorced from a pedagogy steeped in traditional skills?
2. Can that literature (and the published goals established by our key professional organizations) provide a rich backdrop to develop clearly disciplinary forms of teaching within e-composition?

To suggest that students need skills that require instructional "service" is, without question, true. However, it does not follow automatically that Compositionists (certainly those instructors trained outside of Basic Writing pedagogy) are best equipped to do this work. Certainly, as a sub-discipline, "basic writing", with its vital theorists, professional journals, pedagogy, and disciplinary goals, can better address this work. While "basic writing" does fall under the "Compositionist" heading, the necessitation for "skills" forces all Compositionists to engage in a formulation of basic instruction that is not their own. Consequently, I am not arguing within this text to eliminate the service course and replace it with a disciplinary course in comp theory. Rather, I am arguing that the university begin to see the essentiality of addressing students' written deficiencies as two distinct areas (i.e., service and literacy).

The scope of this text is not to indict the traditional college essay beyond its relevancy within the first-year course. That larger indictment is for each discipline to define uniquely, within the changing scope and rhetorical forms of academic dialogue and publication. Consequently, I argue that the first-year classroom, as an intellectual starting point in understanding the processes of inquiry within the arts and sciences, is neither the time nor place for the type of positional argumentation inherent to the traditional college essay. Without this understanding, we negate the urgency to develop the emerging forms of e-composition (e.g., blogging) already taking form. As such, our students produce mechanically sound yet intellectually vacant writings. These texts are often devoid of complex reasoning and outside of the multimodal forms of writer/reader dialogue that real academics now engage. With this understanding, the first-year classroom necessitates the teaching of critical literacy as much as skills; therefore this chapter will conclude by recommending two discrete areas for further inquiry.

1. The defining of a new genre(s) for first-year writing that engages multimodal composing to develop students' critical literacy skills.
2. The development of a nationally accredited first-year writing course (certified through both the National Council of Teachers of English and the Conference on College Composition and Communication) that utilizes this new multimodal genre.

References

Bartholomae, David, Freshman English, Composition, and CCCC, *College Composition and Communication*, Vol. 40, No. 1 (Feb., 1989), p. 38.

Behrens, Laurence, Meditations, Reminiscences, Polemics: Composition Readers and the Service Course, *College English*, Vol. 41, No. 5 (Jan., 1980), p. 561.

Bizzell, Patricia, Review: College Composition: *Initiation into the Academic Discourse* Community, *Curriculum Inquiry*, Vol. 12, No. 2 (Summer, 1982), p. 191.

Brubacher, John, and Rudy, Willis, *Higher Education in Transition: A History of American Colleges and Universities*, Transaction Publishers, New Brunswick, 1997, p. 5.

Connors, Robert, The New Abolitionism: Toward a Historical Background. Essay included in: *Reconceiving Writing, Rethinking Writing Instruction*, edited by Joseph Petraglia, Lawrence Erlbaum Associates, 1995, p. 10.

"Council of Writing Program Administrators", *WPA Outcomes Statement for First-Year Composition*, http://wpacouncil.org/positions/outcomes.html/, 11 July 2012.

Dombek, Kristin, Herndon, Scott, and Bartholomae, David, *Critical Passages: Teaching the Transition to College Composition*, Teachers College Press, New York, 2004, p. IX.

Emig, Janet and Villanueva, Victor. Writing as a Mode of Learning, *College Composition and Communication*, Vol. 28, No. 2 (1977), pp. 122–128.

Flower, Linda and Hayes, John, The Cognition of Discovery: Defining a Rhetorical Problem, *College Composition and Communication*, Vol. 31, No. 1 (Feb., 1980), p. 21.

Freire, Paulo, By Learning They Can Teach, *Convergence*, Vol. 6, No. 1 (1973), p. 78.

Greene, Stuart, and Ackerman, John, Expanding the Constructivist Metaphor: A Rhetorical Perspective on Literacy Research and Practice, *Review of Educational Research*, Vol. 65, No. 4 (Winter, 1995), p. 383.

Harris, Joseph, The Idea of Community in the Study of Writing, *College Composition and Communication*, Vol. 40, No. 1 (Feb., 1989), p. 11.

Hassett, Michael, Increasing Response-ability through Mortification: A Burkean Perspective on Teaching Writing, *A Journal of Composition Theory*, Vol. 15, No. 3 (1995), pp. 471–488.

Hillocks, George, *The Testing Trap: How State Writing Assessments Control Learning*, Teachers College Press, New York, 2002, p. 3.

Langer, Judith, and Applebee, Arthur, *How Writing Shapes Thinking: A Study of Teaching and Learning*, NCTE, Urbana, 1987, p. 10.

Mlynarczyk, Rebecca, Personal and Academic Writing: Revisiting the Debate, *Journal of Basic Writing*, Vol. 25, No. 1, 2006, p. 4.

North, Stephen, The Idea of A Writing Center, *College English*, Vol. 46, No. 5 (September 1984).

Odell, Lee, *College Composition and Communication*, Vol. 31, No. 1 (Feb., 1980), p. 42.

Screech, Michael Andrew, and Fumaroli, Marc, *Montaigne & Melancholy: The Wisdom of the Essays*, Rowman & Littlefield, 2000.

Spellmeyer, Kurt, A Common Ground: The Essay in the Academy, *College English*, Vol. 51, No. 3 (March 1989), p. 262.

Sykes, Charles, *Dumbing Down Our Kids: Why America's Children Feel Good about Themselves But Can't Read, Write, or Add*, St. Martin's Press, New York, 1995, p. 71.

Totten, Samuel, *Educating for the Development of Social Consciousness and Social Responsibility, Social Issues in the English Classroom*, ed. C. Mark Hulbert and Samuel Totten, National Council of Teachers of English, Urbana, IL, 1992, p. 17.

18

DIVERSE VOICES?

A Rhetorical Analysis of First-Year Composition Textbooks and Open Education Resources

Mary F. McGinnis

Introduction

Researching textbooks is important because these resources send messages of valuation to our students. That is, the ideas and people discussed in textbooks show students that those ideas and people are worthy of being talked about. Previous research has found that issues of difference are often left out of first-year composition (FYC) textbooks. In a previous study, I found that articles on issues of marginalization – race, class, sex, gender, disability, sexuality, religion, language, or immigrant status – were absent from 53% of the textbook corpus I studied (McGinnis 2018). The purpose of this study is to update the research on FYC textbooks to see what has changed and to compare occurrence of diversity in FYC textbooks to occurrence of diversity in open educational resources (OERs) available for FYC courses.

Composition Studies' Calls for Diversity

Marginalization and FYC textbooks has been a concern for the field of composition studies for a while. *(Re)Visioning Composition Textbooks: Conflicts of Culture, Ideology, and Pedagogy* (edited by Xin Liu Gale and Fredric G. Gale), published in 1999, contains articles that focus on wide-ranging topics, from rhetorics to readers, from culture to publishing. One article in particular, by Yameng Liu, titled "Self, Other, In-Between: Cross-Cultural Composition Readers and the Reconstruction of Cultural Identities," addresses the problem of textbooks and incorporation of difference. She explains that "composition textbooks with an inter- or cross-cultural theme" often "gloss over" issues related to "deep-seated theoretical difficulties concerning identity and difference, self and other, knowing and knowledge, representing and representation, appearance and reality, truth and falsehood, comparison and contrast, and East and West" (Liu 1999: 71). Further, she wants readers to be aware of the use of terms like "misrepresentation" and "stereotype" because users of inter-/cross-cultural readers often put those terms in a binary with "reality" or "facts" at the "expense of [a] commitment to an antifoundational conception of culture or discourse" (Liu 1999: 71). Instructors "tend to forget that what

284

DOI: 10.4324/9781003195276-23

[they] call 'stereotypes' are more often *factually* based rather than unsupported by any credible data or observations" (Liu 1999: 72; her emphasis). She encourages composition instructors who teach with inter- or cross-cultural readers to think about and use the "co-existence of two or more independent 'authorizing agencies'" and use the space those two agencies create to open up "brave, new, hybridized, and heteroglot in *between* different signifying systems" (Liu 1999: 90; her emphasis). This practice opens up new rhetorical understandings of marginalized groups – students would see both the "authorizing agency" they occupy and the "authorizing agency" where course readings on marginalization reside.

Another article that adds to the call for diversity in FYC textbooks was published in 2009 by Martha Marinara, Jonathan Alexander, William P. Banks, and Samantha Blackmon, called "Cruising Composition Texts: Negotiating Sexual Difference in First-Year Readers." This text draws attention to the absence of sexuality in textbooks. The field of rhetoric and composition has taken a "social turn," and it "has steadily taken seriously calls not only to be inclusive multiculturally but also to examine critically discourses of sexism, racism, and classism that marginalize students, their experiences, and their literacies" (Marinara et al. 2009: 269). This turn has destigmatized discussion of lesbian, gay, bisexual, and transgender (LGBT) issues in the FYC classroom, too; however, Marinara et al. recognize that the "large-scale, empirical research necessary even to know what is and is not going on in the majority of college writing classrooms" needs to occur (Marinara et al. 2009: 270). To begin answering questions about how "LGBT people/issues/concerns" are treated in FYC, they reviewed a selection of FYC readers from Pearson Longman, Bedford/St. Martin's Press, Houghton Mifflin, and Prentice Hall to analyze them for LGBT issues and authors. They found that of the "290 readers examined, only 73 texts included readings with identifiable queer content. This means that in over two-thirds of the texts [they] examined, LGBT people and perspectives were noticeably absent" (Marinara et al. 2009: 276). Their research has allowed me to frame my own research and anticipate how sexuality alongside other issues of difference is treated by FYC textbooks.

Marginalized Voices in Textbooks

Bias in textbook publishing has been a concern for many years; for instance, Gwyneth Britton and Margaret Lumpkin, in their 1977 article, examine the changes that occurred after the introduction of publishers' guidelines for public school textbooks. They recap publishing house "guides" from the early to mid-1970s that "identified the problems [of bias in textbooks] and acknowledged the importance of basic equalitarian values" (Britton and Lumpkin 1977: 40–42). After comparing the pre-guideline textbooks (1958–1970) to post-guideline textbooks (1974–1976), the authors found small shifts – after publisher guidelines were set forth, stories with male main characters increased by 1%; female main characters increased by 2%; ethnic minority male representation increased by 3%; and ethnic minority female representation increased by 2% (Britton and Lumpkin 1977: 43–44). However, they found that career role "imbalance" persisted – "males of all races were shown in 249 different career roles … and females were depicted in 49 different career roles," while "ethnic minority males were assigned to only 34 different career roles and females to 14" (Britton and Lumpkin 1977: 44). Thus, while publishers may have positive intentions when it comes to incorporating articles that contain marginalized voices, Britton and Lumpkin's research showed that representation of marginalized people is slow in coming to the public school textbook publishing industry.

Problematic or absent treatment of marginalized voices in textbooks is not limited to primary school or FYC textbooks. For example, in 1990, Susan Feiner and Bruce Roberts analyzed the treatment of race and gender in economic textbooks, asserting that the "most widely used" economics textbooks have "a long tradition of blindness toward questions concerning the economic status of minorities and women," although their study showed that improvements had been made (Feiner and Roberts 1990: 159). However, publishers, by neglecting to include texts that engage issues of marginalized people, do, in fact, serve an audience that is too narrow – an audience that is, ostensibly, white, cismale, heterosexual, middle-class, able-bodied, American, monolingual, and English-speaking. As Sandra Jamieson asserts in "Composition Readers and the Construction of Identity," articles included in FYC textbooks often have an imagined audience of white, male readers (Jamieson 1997: 168). Robert Perrin notes that readings by women and minorities are included in FYC readers more often than in the past because publishers have "followed the lead of scholar-teachers in those areas," changing as the market changes (Perrin 1988: 73). It is the responsibility of scholar-teachers to direct publishing companies' practices, using purchasing power to force them to change with the field they publish textbooks for.

Because purchasing and using textbooks that support our values, as rhetoricians and teachers of writing, is our responsibility, Eliot Rendleman urges us to examine "the possible unintended effects" of FYC textbooks as we use them to teach "students how to write and think critically" (Rendleman 2011: 11). He explains that we must become "hyperconscious of race, class, gender, and *valuation*" (Rendleman 2011: 11; emphasis mine). When Rendleman invokes valuation, he refers to the implicit ideas about the "worth of objects and people and the process of assigning that worth" that appear in FYC texts (Rendleman 2011: 5). He explains that one way that valuation occurs is through "celebration, denigration, or disregard" (Rendleman 2011: 5) of minority issues or experiences. Thus, when marginalized voices are ignored by or left out of FYC textbooks, they are given a reduced value, devalued. Through this exclusion, students learn that marginalized groups and the problems marginalized people face are not worth talking about.

In addition, scholars argue that textbooks, even when they try to include marginalized groups, often posit marginalized groups in problematic, tokenizing, non-intersectional ways. Again, as scholars suggest, we must be cognizant of messages of valuation sent by articles included in FYC textbooks and what students learn implicitly and explicitly from these articles (Rendleman 2011; Jamieson 1997; Marinara et al. 2009; Martin 2008). For example, Marinara et al. found that LGBT issues, when they aren't excluded, are often "ghettoized" in controversial topics sections that reinforce dichotomies (i.e. for/against gay marriage debates that don't leave room for nuanced critique of marriage as an institution), and represent largely one kind of experience (gay, white, male) (Marinara et al. 2009: 277–278). Sandra Jamieson points out that articles giving attention to the issues that people of color and women face often reinforce "victim" narratives and "fail to empower" minority students (Jamieson 1997: 153, 152). Disability scholar Deb Martin explains that disability is often excluded from textbooks, and when it is included, despite good intentions, textbooks often portray disability in "simplified, essentialized, and/or dichotomized" ways (Martin 2008: 75, 77). In addition, disability studies scholars have criticized textbooks for applying an "add-and-stir" mentality to the inclusion of disability in FYC textbooks (Martin 2008; Ervelles 2009; Browning 2014). Ella Browning explains that the "add-and-stir" method is signified by the inclusion of a single text by a single author to represent disability (Browning 2014: 97). "Add-and-stir" is used with other types of marginalization, too, although the idea arose in disability studies. As a result, minority groups are presented one-dimensionally, as their marginalized status, and not as fully realized human beings.

Another issue that arises in FYC courses that incorporate marginalized voices is what Jonathan Alexander and Jacqueline Rhodes call "a *flattening effect* and a *flattening of affect*" (Alexander and Rhodes 2014: 431; emphasis theirs). Specifically focusing on queer issues in FYC courses, they define a "flattening effect" as a tendency to over-look differences in favor of identification through commonalities that is produced in response to people who are from marginalized groups (Alexander and Rhodes 2014: 439–440). Flattening narratives often play into a "liberal narrative of awareness" that leads to "clichéd, linear and reductive" thought (DeGenaro as cited in Alexander and Rhodes 2014: 437). A flattening effect recognizes the humanity of marginalized groups without really understanding or exploring how marginal status affects people's lives because it is ignored in favor of commonalities (Alexander and Rhodes 2014: 440–442). A "flattening affect" comes into play when texts refuse to engage with the issues surrounding marginalized people's experiences – Alexander and Rhodes cite Marinara et al.'s declaration that queerness is left out of the discussion because an author doesn't specifically invoke a queer identity in the essay being read and/or focus on queerness in the essay (Alexander and Rhodes 2014: 442). The flattening effect and the add-and-stir method are both examples of problematic strategies to incorporate marginalized voices into FYC textbooks. These two tactics illustrate that it is necessary to be thoughtful and intersectional when adding readings by and about marginalized people into textbooks because both tactics tokenize the experiences of marginalized people, trivializing and downplaying their lives and experiences. Instead, by employing intersectional readings that involve more than one form of marginalized status (i.e. articles by disabled people of color or queer women), textbooks can provide readers the opportunity to see how different forms of marginalization work in concert to affect individuals' lives and experiences.

This study adds to the field of rhetoric and composition because research on FYC textbooks needs to be updated, Open Education Resources should be discussed, and the field's treatment of marginalized groups and their diverse voices should be re-viewed and reexamined. Many of the studies that examine marginalized voices in FYC textbooks are old. For example, the Marinara et al. corpus study in 2009 – published almost 15 years ago – is one of the most recent corpus studies of minority sexuality and its represen-tation in FYC texts. Sandra Jamieson's "Composition Readers and the Construction of Identity" is 25 years old. Gale and Gale's *(Re)Visioning Composition Textbooks* is over 20 years old. Deb Martin's corpus study on disability is 15 years old, published in 2008. Thus, the research on marginalized voices in FYC textbooks needs to be updated. In addition, this study combines and expands upon previous scholarship – focusing on many types of marginalized status (most articles focus on one or two types of margin-alization – often race and gender). Including the newly popularized open educational resources in this analysis is important, as many colleges and universities are relying on them as free resources to make higher education more equitable and accessible. The goal of this research is to gain a more all-encompassing picture of how marginal groups are represented singly and intersectionally alongside other types of marginalization in FYC course materials.

Methodology

To accomplish this research, I've selected a sample of 12 texts: eight first-year composition textbooks (four rhetorics with readings and four readers) and four open educational resources for composition I courses that contain readings.

The eight first-year composition textbooks (see Table 18.1) came from the top four publishers, Cengage, Macmillan, Norton, and Pearson. Previous research found that the textbooks with the highest number of articles that discussed marginalized groups from each publisher were *Rereading America* 10th ed. (Macmillan), *The Seagull Reader: Essays* 3rd ed. (Norton), *The Longman Reader* 11th ed. (Pearson), and *Readings for Writers* 15th ed. (Cengage) (McGinnis 2018). Previous research also showed that the textbooks that had the lowest number of readings that engage issues of marginalization were *The Composition of Everyday Life* 5th ed. (Cengage), *Current Issues and Enduring Questions* 11th ed. (Macmillan), *The Norton Field Guide to Writing with Readings* 4th ed. (Norton), and *Strategies for Successful Writing* 11th ed. (Pearson) (McGinnis 2018). As a result, I have chosen to analyze these eight textbooks – four of these textbooks are readers, and four are rhetorics with readings. This corpus of hardcopy textbooks have been in publication for at least 11 years, they have at least four editions, and began publication as early as 1974.

To select the open educational resources (OERs) for this corpus, I did some internet searching. Many OERs were rhetorics without readings. Of the few that did contain readings, for this corpus, I chose Lumen Learning's *English Composition 1: Rhetorical*

Table 18.1 Corpus information

Title	Years in publication	First edition	Current edition	Number of editions	Publisher
Rereading America	24	1992	2016	10 editions	Macmillan
The Seagull Reader: Essays	21	2000	2021	4 editions	Norton
The Longman Reader	29	1987	2016	11 editions	Pearson
Readings for Writers	41	1974	2016	15 editions	Cengage
*The Composition of Everyday Life**	14	2003	2017	5 editions	Cengage
*Current Issues and Enduring Questions**	25	1995	2020	12 editions	Macmillan
*The Norton Field Guide to Writing with Readings**	11	2005	2016	4 editions	Norton
*Strategies for Successful Writing**	31	1986	2017	11 editions	Pearson
English Composition I	1	2014	2014	1 edition	Lumen
Bad Ideas About Writing	1	2017	2017	1 edition	West Virginia University
Writing Spaces	11	2010	2022	4 editions	Parlor Press, WAC Clearinghouse
88 Open Essays – A Reader for Students of Composition & Rhetoric	1	2019	2019	1 edition	LibreTexts Project

*rhetoric with readings

Methods-Based; Cheryl E. Ball and Drew M. Loewe's *Bad Ideas About Writing*; Sarah Wangler and Tina Ulrich's *88 Open Essays – A Reader for Students of Composition & Rhetoric* (found on Libretexts), and *Writing Spaces: Readings on Writing* Volume 4, edited by Dana Lynn Driscoll, Megan Heise, Mary K. Stewart, and Matthew Vetter. Most of these OERs have one edition, with the exception of *Writing Spaces*, which has four editions, spanning 2010–2022.

Coding Scheme

To code readings, I read and examined each article or image to determine whether or not it substantively addressed marginalization by discussing issues of race, class, gender/sex, disability, sexuality, religion, language, or immigrant status. This analysis included images (e.g. *Rereading America* includes "Visual Portfolio" sections of visuals for students to "read" and *Strategies for Successful Writing* contained an excerpt from the graphic novel *Persepolis*) because there were cases of students being asked to interpret meaning from them; example assignments written by students; and works by professional authors. This left me with an initial corpus of 759 articles – 188 came from OERs, 262 came from readers, and 309 came from rhetorics with readings.

While coding the readings, my focus was topic and subject matter, not identity of the author. Many readings were presented without introductions or author biographies, so students may not know if an author is a member of a marginalized group unless the reading explicitly focuses on the author's identity and group membership. Articles that discussed multiple types of marginalization (e.g. disability and class) were coded with multiple codes to emphasize intersectionality. This practice helped identify readings that avoided oversimplifying marginalization and tokenizing individuals' experiences. It is well documented that systems of privilege and oppression work in concert to shape a person's experiences (Crenshaw 2015; Hill-Collins 2000; hooks 1984), and many people experience issues of marginalization in more than one way.

Articles were coded according to discussion of issues (see Table 18.2) – simply mentioning one of the marginalized categories listed wasn't sufficient for the article to be coded with the category. There needed to be some substantive discussion of the category within the article. For example, I excluded Daniel Gilbert's "Does Fatherhood Make You Happy?" from sex/gender coding because although the article discussed fatherhood it did not have substantive discussion of gender roles; I deemed that this mere mention of fatherhood wasn't sufficient for the article to be categorized as "sex/gender," since the gender role of fathers wasn't actually the main point of the piece. In contrast, Judy Brady's "I Want a Wife" was labeled with the "sex/gender" code because the piece explicitly outlined the gender role expectations of wives. In the coding scheme, gender and sex have been conflated. While sex refers to biology and physicality and gender refers to masculinity, femininity, and gender presentation, in this research sex was rarely used without gender and vice versa. In addition, I included transgender issues in this code.

To define disability in the coding scheme, the Americans with Disabilities Act (ADA) set the standard for what was codified as disability. The ADA website uses the following definition for disability: "(i) A physical or mental impairment that substantially limits one or more of the major life activities of such individual; (ii) A record of such an impairment; or (iii) Being regarded as having such an impairment as described in paragraph (f) of this section" (Department of Justice: §35.108a). Thus, in this research, disability is coded similarly – any discussion of any physical or mental difference that inhibits an

Table 18.2 Coding scheme

Category	Code	Criteria
Race	R	Discussion of race or skin color, racial politics, white privilege, or racial stereotypes.
Class	C	Discussion of poverty, social class, economic benefits, or government assistance.
Gender/Sex	G/S	Discussion of biological sex, sex category, maleness, femaleness, masculinity, femininity, gender identity, gender presentation, sex roles, sex stereotypes, transgender issues.
Disability	D	Discussion of disability, any physical or mental difference that inhibits an individual or an individual's body to function in a way that limits daily life was coded as a disability.
Sexuality	S	Discussion of sexuality (including heterosexuality); lesbian, gay, bisexual, or queer issues; pornography; heteronormativity; marriage or relationship issues; kink; or sexual acts.
Religion	R	Discussion of religion, spirituality, or religious beliefs and the lack thereof.
Language	L	Discussion of language diversity, ESL, multilingualism, or ELL issues.
Immigrant Status	I	Discussion of immigration, refugee status, or asylum issues.
None	N	Discussion of something other than the issues listed above.

individual or an individual's body to function in a way that limits daily life earned the disability code. This category included topics like blindness, ADHD, amputation, stuttering, cancer, addiction, and HIV. Coding was completed by listing all articles in a text and adding codes to a spreadsheet.

Findings

Overall Statistics

Analysis of the 759 articles shows that 401 articles (52.8%) did not discuss issues of race, class, sex, gender, disability, sexuality, religion, language, or immigrant status. These articles generated 931 codes, which I'll discuss more in depth below. The coding showed that in this corpus,

- 18% of articles addressed race
- 8% addressed class
- 12% addressed sex/gender
- 3% addressed disability
- 5% addressed sexuality
- 4% addressed religion
- 3% addressed language
- 4% addressed immigration (see Figure 18.1)

As I coded texts, articles that addressed multiple kinds of marginalization received a code for each kind of marginalization included – some articles had two or more codes.

Rhetorical Analysis of Composition Textbooks

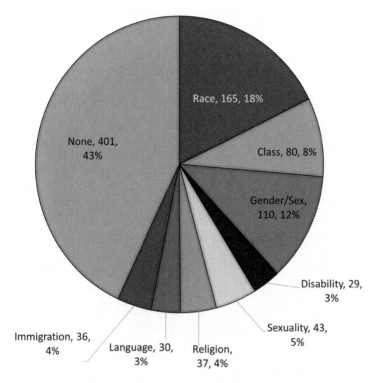

Figure 18.1 Coding breakdown (n=931)

This is how the 759 articles generated 931 codes. Thus, "none" (articles that did not discuss issues of difference) represented 43% of *codes* and comprised 52.8% of *articles*. These findings show that calls for further inclusion of marginalized voices in FYC course readings are valid, with less than half of the corpus articles (358/759, 47.2%) analyzed showing engagement with issues of marginalization.

Further, when analyzing the types of marginalization discussed in each text (see Figure 18.2), readers were responsible for 47% of the 530 codes that addressed marginalization, with 32% from rhetorics with readings, and 21% of codes coming from OERs. When reviewing total texts' codes and the number of articles per text, we see that readers have 251 marginalization codes from the 262 articles (95.8%); rhetorics with readings have 171 marginalization codes in the 309 articles (55.3%); and OERs have 108 marginalization codes in the 188 articles (57.4%). These statistics are a little surprising because, while readers are responsible for 47% of codes, the number of articles included in these texts comprise only 30% of the corpus. On the other hand, rhetorics yield 32% of codes but contain the largest number of articles (43%) in the corpus. OERs generate 21% of codes and comprise 26% of the corpus.

Thus, readers in this corpus are shown to have a much higher chance of including articles that employ issues of marginalization.

Readers, Rhetorics, OERs, and Marginalization

When comparing the different forms of marginalization coded and the types of texts in the corpus, readers contain the largest percentage of codes for race, gender/sex, class,

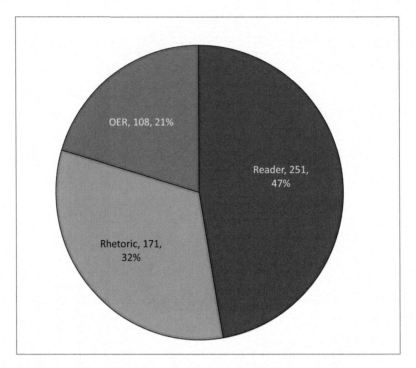

Figure 18.2 Number of codes per text type (n=530)

sexuality, religion, and immigration, making up 51% or more of the codes in each category (see Figure 18.3). Rhetorics contained the largest percentage of codes for the disability category, and OERs contained the largest percentage of codes for the language category.

Intersectionality and Multiple Marginalizations

On a bright note, this research shows that there are a number of intersectional articles in the corpus where we see more than one type of marginalization being discussed alongside others. Because each textbook has a different number of articles, percentages will be used. As mentioned above, the corpus comprised 759 articles and generated 931 codes; not every article in the corpus incorporated marginalization and some articles had multiple codes because they examined more than one type of marginalization. The corpus contained 138 articles (18.1% of the corpus) that included multiple types of marginalization – these articles earned anywhere from two to six codes. Figure 18.4 shows in bold the number of articles that contained multiple marginalizations per text. There were no articles that engaged all eight types of marginalization studied.

When comparing the total number of articles that explore marginalization and the number of articles that take an intersectional approach (again, see Figure 18.4), discussing more than one type of marginalization, it is clear that some texts do a better job of incorporating marginalized experiences than others. For example, the text *Rereading America* contains only 51 articles, but most articles (86%) address an issue of marginalization and almost half (41%) incorporate multiple marginalizations, while several other textbooks

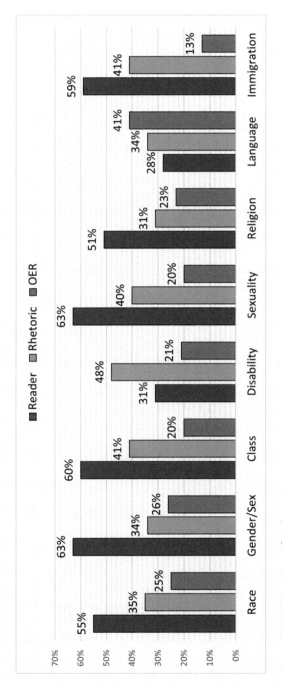

Figure 18.3 Percentage of codes per type

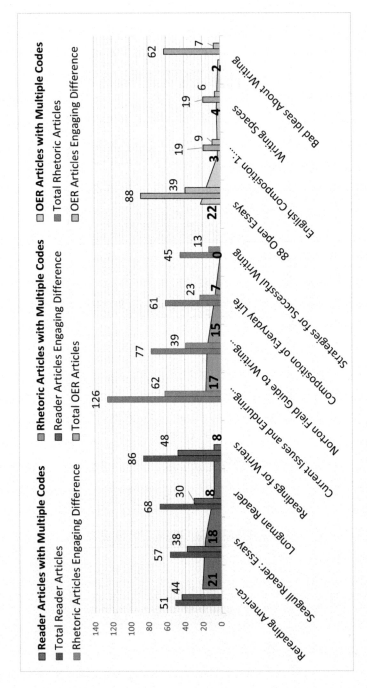

Figure 18.4 Difference and multiple marginalizations per text

Rhetorical Analysis of Composition Textbooks

Table 18.3 Percentages of readings addressing difference and with multiple codes

Title	Readings addressing difference	Readings with multiple codes
Rereading America	86%	41%
Seagull Reader: Essays	66%	32%
Longman Reader	44%	12%
Readings for Writers	56%	9%
Current Issues and Enduring Questions	49%	13%
Norton Field Guide to Writing with Readings	51%	19%
Composition of Everyday Life	38%	11%
Strategies for Successful Writing	29%	0%
88 Open Essays	44%	25%
English Composition 1: Rhetorical Methods-Based	47%	16%
Writing Spaces	32%	21%
Bad Ideas About Writing	11%	3%

incorporate far fewer articles that address issues of marginalization. Figure 18.4 shows the total number of articles per textbook, the number of articles per textbook that incorporate marginalization, and the total number of articles that engage more than one type of marginalization. This chart emphasizes that a textbook containing a large number of readings doesn't guarantee that students using the textbook will be exposed to issues of marginalization. For example, Table 18.3 shows that *Rereading America*, with its 51 articles, has 86% of them engaging issues of marginalization while 41% of the total articles discuss more than one type of marginalization. In contrast, *Current Events and Enduring Questions* contains the largest number of articles (126), yet 49% of its articles incorporate marginalization and 13% of the book's total articles engage more than one type of marginalization. In addition, when reviewing Table 18.3, there is evidence that some textbooks may be oversimplifying the experiences of marginalized people or even tokenizing marginalized groups by not incorporating articles that view marginalization in an intersectional way. An example of this would be *The Longman Reader*, and its depiction of disability – it includes two articles on the topic. In the professional article included in the text, Cherokee Paul McDonald's "View from the Bridge," the speaker interacts with a blind child who is fishing; and the student article on disability, "Party with a Purpose" by Erica Zwieg, explains how Ryan White's struggle with HIV/AIDS inspired a dance marathon movement. Both of these articles are written from the point of view of an able-bodied person, and they present disability in a one-dimensional way that emphasizes how the lives of disabled people may be used to inspire those without disabilities, what Stella Young calls "inspiration porn."

Representation of Race in the Corpus

The race code was the largest category present in the overall data analysis at 18% of the total codes recorded. This is a small increase from previous research that showed race in FYC readings 16% of the time (McGinnis 2018). Upon examining the way racial issues appear in the corpus, the data (see Figure 18.5) show that readers incorporate race 30%

Mary F. McGinnis

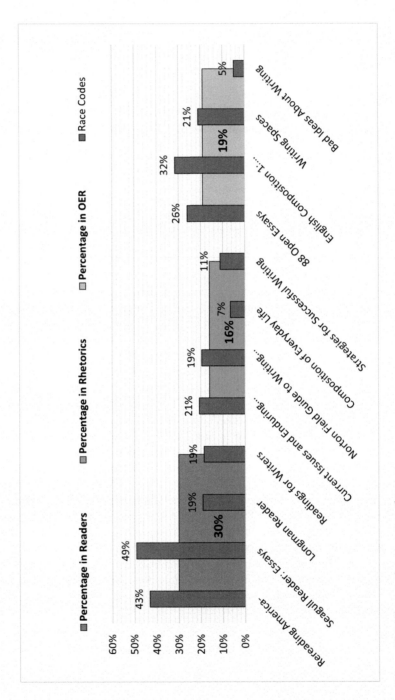

Figure 18.5 Race codes per text and text type

of the time, while rhetorics (16%) and OERs (19%) incorporate race less, by almost half and two-thirds respectively. Readers and OER texts made up the top four FYC textbooks that included race, while one OER and rhetorics with readings made up the bottom four.

The Seagull Reader: Essays was the text that addressed racial issues the most, with 49% of its readings incorporating race, while Bad Ideas About Writing addressed racial issues the least, with only 5% of readings engaging racial issues. Previous research (McGinnis 2018) showed that 36.8% of articles in The Seagull Reader: Essays addressed race, so the new edition shows a marked increase of 12.2%. The textbook with the second highest number of codes on race, Rereading America, also showed an increase from prior research (McGinnis 2018) – going from 40% to 43%.

Examples of articles that are coded race include Stephanie Coontz's "What We Really Miss About the 1950s," Jessie Daniels's "Twitter and White Supremacy, A Love Story," Jamaica Kincaid's "Girl," Malcolm X's "The Ballot or the Bullet," Abraham Lincoln's "First Inaugural Address," Frederick Douglass's "Learning to Read," Martin Luther King's "Letter from the Birmingham Jail," and Ta-Nehisi Coates's "The Case for Reparations."

Representation of Gender/Sex in the Corpus

Gender/sex was the second largest overall category coded, representing 12% of codes. This was a decrease from previous research that showed gender/sex discussed 16% of the time (McGinnis 2018). The data (see Figure 18.6) show that readers include discussion of gender/sex 21% of the time. Rhetorics with readings incorporate gender/sex 12% of the time, and OERs incorporate gender/sex the least at 9.6% of the time.

The textbook with the largest focus on gender/sex in this corpus was Rereading America with 37% of its readings addressing gender/sex issues. This was an increase from prior research where Rereading America contained gender/sex-focused articles 33.3% of the time (McGinnis 2018). The texts with the lowest percentage of readings on gender/sex came from the OER corpus, Writing Spaces and Bad Ideas About Writing. This is not surprising, as these texts focus mostly on writing.

Examples of texts from this category are Jamaica Kincaid's "Girl," Judith Ortiz Cofer's "The Myth of a Latin Woman: I Just Met a Girl Named Maria," Allan G. Johnson's excerpt from The Gender Knot: "Patriarchy," Amy Tan's "Mother Tongue," Amy Ellis Nutt's excerpt from Becoming Nicole: The Transformation of an American Family, Ruth Padawer's "Sisterhood Is Complicated," Amani Al-Khatahtbeh's excerpt from Muslim Girl, Matt de la Peña's "Sometimes the 'Tough Teen' Is Quietly Writing Stories," Michael Kimmel's "A War Against Boys?," Hillary Rodham Clinton's "Remarks to the United Nations Fourth World Conference on Women Plenary Session," and Leila Ahmed's "Reinventing the Veil."

Representation of Class in the Corpus

Class was the third largest category, coded at 8% of the corpus. This statistic is consistent with previous research, which also showed class as a topic of discussion in FYC textbooks 8% of the time (McGinnis 2018). The data show (see Figure 18.7) that readers engage class the most at 16% of the corpus, while OERs engage class almost half as much at 9%. Rhetorics with readings engage class the least at 7%.

The textbook that engaged class the most was Rereading America, which contained class issues in 29% of its readings. This was up from 24.4% found in previous research

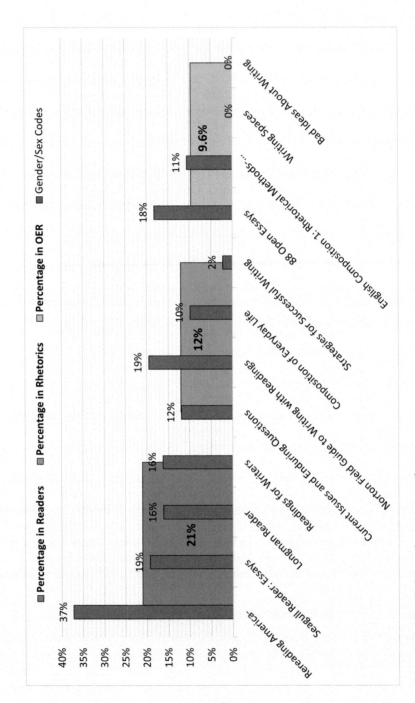

Figure 18.6 Gender/sex codes per text and text type

Rhetorical Analysis of Composition Textbooks

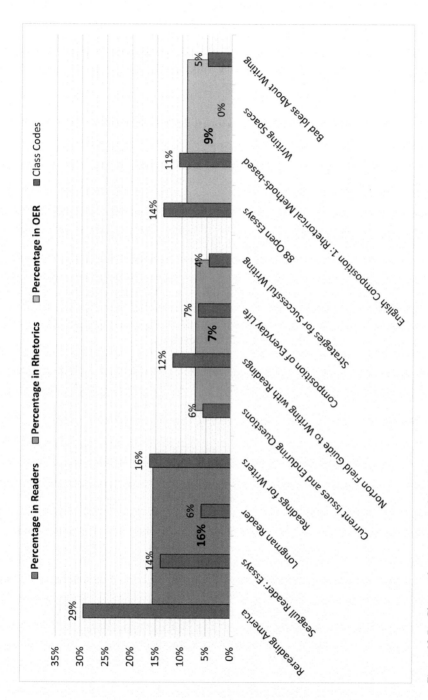

Figure 18.7 Class codes per text and text type

(McGinnis 2018). The textbook that engaged class issues the least was the OER *Writing Spaces* with zero readings engaging class issues.

Examples of articles from this category are Mike Rose's "Blue-Collar Brilliance," Judith Ortiz Cofer's "A Partial Remembrance of a Puerto Rican Childhood," Anjali Pattanayak's "There is One Correct Way of Writing and Speaking," Natalie Standiford's "The Tenacity of Hope," James Hamblin's "Living Simply in a Dumpster," and Henry David Thoreau's "Civil Disobedience."

Representation of Sexuality in the Corpus

Sexuality is the first of the lesser-represented codes in the corpus at 5%; however, this was a 1% increase from the 4% reported in previous research (McGinnis 2018). This code was most prevalent in readers (see Figure 18.8), showing up 8% of the time, and least represented in the OERs, showing up 4% of the time. Rhetorics with readings included discussion of sexuality issues 5% of the time. This finding could use further consideration, too, to determine how often heterosexual issues are discussed versus other types of sexuality issues, like LGBQ issues, celibacy, kink, etc.

The textbook that included readings on sexuality the most was *Rereading America* with 16% of its readings addressing sexuality. This statistic almost doubled from previous research, which recorded *Rereading America* incorporating sexuality issues 8.9% of the time (McGinnis 2018). The textbooks that included sexuality the least were OERs: Lumen's *English Composition I: Rhetorical Methods-Based* and *Bad Ideas About Writing* – neither included readings that speak of sexuality.

Examples of articles coded sexuality are Maxine Hong Kingston's "No Name Woman," Jamaica Kincaid's "Girl," Judith Ortiz Cofer's "The Myth of a Latin Woman: I Just Met a Girl Named Maria," Michael Pollan's "Why 'Natural' Doesn't Mean Anything Anymore," Kathleen Norris's "Celibate Passion," and Mimi Schippers's excerpt from *Beyond Monogamy: Polyamory and the Future of Polyqueer Sexualities.*

Representation of Immigration in the Corpus

Immigration was one of the more under-included forms of marginalization in this research, appearing 4% of the time; however, compared to previous research, the appearance of immigration issues has more than doubled, from 2% (McGinnis 2018). Again, readers included immigration issues most often at 7.3% of the time (see Figure 18.9), while OERs included these issues the least at 2.1% of the time. Rhetorics with readings addressed immigration issues 4.2% of the time.

The text that addressed immigrant issues the most, at 11% of its readings, was the OER *English Composition I: Rhetorical Methods-Based* from Lumen Learning. This was followed by *Rereading America* at 8%, which was an increase from previous research that recorded immigration issues occurring only 2.2% of the time (McGinnis 2018). The texts that incorporated immigration issues the least were the rhetoric with readings *Strategies for Successful Writing* and the OER *Bad Ideas About Writing*, both of which included zero readings that attend to immigration issues.

Examples of articles that discuss immigrant status are Marcelo M. Suárez-Orozco and Carola Suárez-Orozco's "How Immigrants Become 'Other'," José Orduña's "Passport to the New West," Noel Ignatiev's "Introduction to How the Irish Became White," and Sonia Sotomayor's "A Latina Judge's Voice."

Rhetorical Analysis of Composition Textbooks

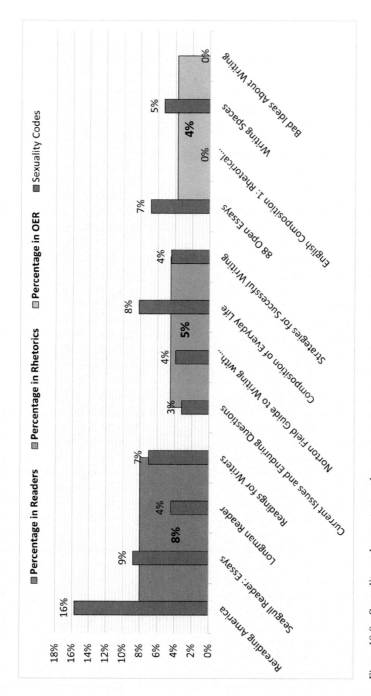

Figure 18.8 Sexuality codes per text and text type

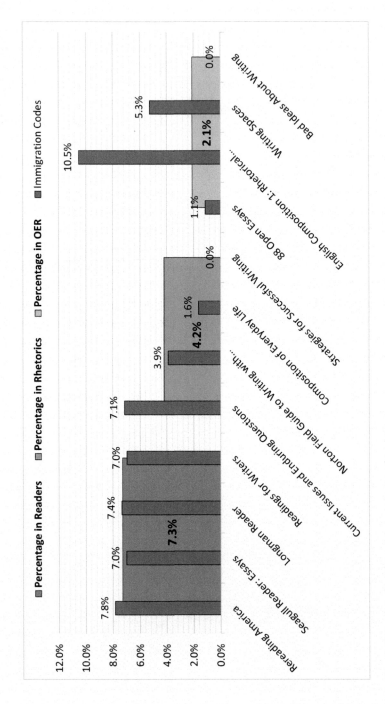

Figure 18.9 Immigration codes per text and text type

Representation of Religion in the Corpus

This corpus incorporated religious issues 4% of the time – this statistic was the same as in previous research (McGinnis 2018). Readers incorporated religion the most at 6.9% of the time (see Figure 18.10). This finding needs further exploration to determine whether or not the reader corpus's discussion of religion operates as an effort to reinforce the dominant Christian ideologies in the United States or as an effort to incorporate non-mainstream religion into the FYC curriculum to increase understanding of their practices. Rhetorics with readings discuss religion the least at 3.6%, and OERs incorporate religion 4.3% of the time.

The text that discusses religion the most is *The Seagull Reader: Essays*, with 12.3% of its readings – this statistic was the same as found in previous research (McGinnis 2018). The texts that discuss religion the least are the OERs *English Composition I: Rhetorical Methods-Based* and *Bad Ideas About Writing*, and the rhetoric with readings *Strategies for Successful Writing*, all of which had zero readings that discussed religion.

Examples of articles that engaged religion are Edward O. Wilson's "Letter to a Southern Baptist Minister," Martin Luther King Jr.'s "Letter from Birmingham Jail," Malala Yousafzai's "Who Is Malala?," Leila Ahmed's "Reinventing the Veil," and Sojourner Truth's "Ain't I A Woman?"

Representation of Language in the Corpus

Language codes showed up in the corpus 3% of the time – this is 1% lower than found in previous research (McGinnis 2018). This could be due to the smaller sample size; however, the addition of OERs, which largely focused on language (and writing) more than any other type of text (6% – see Figure 18.11), should have prevented this category from having lowered representation, so the cause of this difference is unclear and would need further research. Both readers and rhetorics with readings included language difference in 3% of their corpus.

The texts that incorporated the largest focus on language difference were both OERs – Lumen's *English Composition I: Rhetorical Methods-Based* at 16% and *Writing Spaces* at 11% of readings. The texts with the lowest integration of language difference were readers, *Rereading America* and *Readings for Writers*, and rhetorics with readings, *Current Issues and Enduring Questions* and *The Composition of Everyday Life*, all with 2% of their readings addressing language difference. Compared to previous research, *Rereading America*'s engagement with language difference stayed about the same; however, *Readings for Writers* and *Current Issues and Enduring Questions* both increased their language difference representation from 0 to 2%, while *The Composition of Everyday Life* decreased by 1.3% (McGinnis 2018).

Examples of articles that focused on language were Amy Tan's "Mother Tongue," Dan Wilkins's "Why We No Longer Use the 'H' Word," José Orduña's "Passport to the New West," Steven Alvarez's "Official American English Is Best," and Sara P. Alvarez, Amy J. Wan, and Eunjeong Lee's "Workin' Languages: Who We Are Matters in Our Writing."

Representation of Disability in the Corpus

Disability codes appeared in the corpus the fewest number of times with 3% (29 readings) – this statistic is the same as found in previous research (McGinnis 2018). This

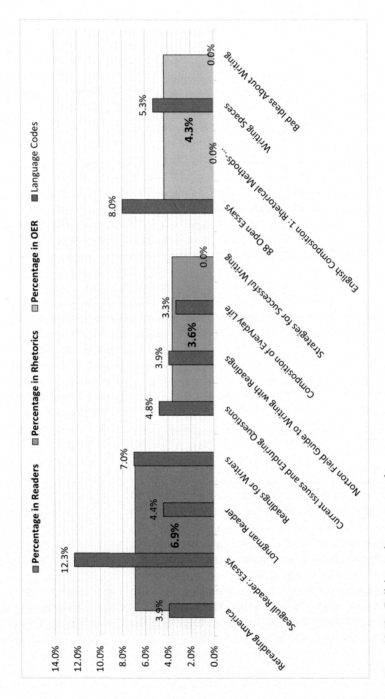

Figure 18.10 Religion codes per text and text type

Rhetorical Analysis of Composition Textbooks

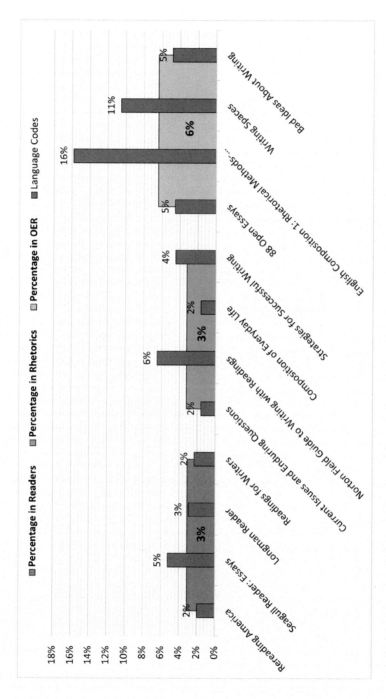

Figure 18.11 Language codes per text and text type

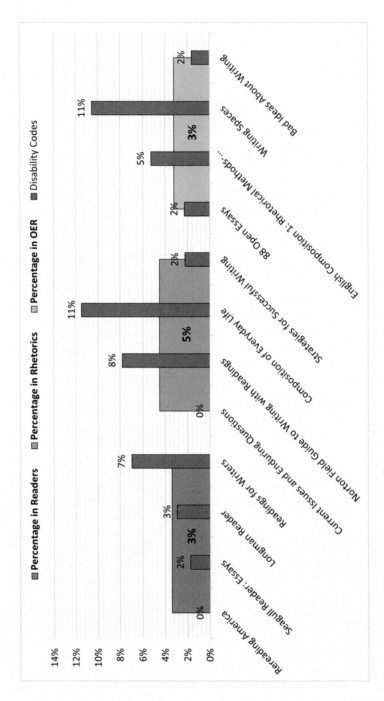

Figure 18.12 Disability codes per text and text type

was the only category where rhetorics with readings contained a larger percentage of codes than the other types of texts, with 5% of their articles addressing disability issues (see Figure 18.12). Readers and OERs both include disability codes 3% of the time.

The texts that incorporated disability issues the most were *The Composition of Everyday Life* and *Writing Spaces*; both texts included disability in 11% of their readings. For *The Composition of Everyday Life*, this is an increase from 6.7% (McGinnis 2018). The texts that included disability the least were the readers *Rereading America* and *Current Issues and Enduring Questions*, both with zero readings that involve disability. This is a decrease by 2.2% for *Rereading America* based on previous research (McGinnis 2018). Examples of articles from the disability category are Rachel Donegan's "The Rhetorical Possibilities of Accessibility," Johnna S. Keller's "The Politics of Stairs," Natalie Standiford's "The Tenacity of Hope," Adrienne Green's "The Boldness of Roxane Gay's *Hunger*," and Nancy Mairs's "Disability."

Discussion

Overall, this study has illuminated that while OERs are useful because they cut down on student costs and increase accessibility, they do not accomplish all of the goals that composition studies sets out for itself – namely, the OERs of this corpus do a nice job when it comes to analyzing language and writing, but they lag far behind other resources available when a composition instructor wants to bring issues of marginalized groups into the curriculum. As rhetoricians and teachers of writing, we need to prepare students for democratic citizenship, so they will be ready and able to engage in the important debates of our time, which often revolve around issues of marginalization.

Based on this research, it is apparent that work still needs to be done to increase the representation of marginalized groups and experiences in FYC textbooks. This research showed that the inclusion of readings on race, sexuality, and immigration has increased. These representations are important. For example, the images depicted in these textbooks can potentially counteract the new stereotypes of people of color that Bradley Greenberg and Jeffrey Brand identify as appearing more frequently in the news – "e.g. Black suspects are less human, more dangerous, and less trustworthy than White suspects; Blacks as athletes and entertainers run amok; Blacks are victims of big-city police oppression" (Greenberg and Brand 1994: 10). These small increases in representation of race, sexuality, and immigration could be a result of the #BlackLivesMatter movement and heightened attention to the violence and police brutality people of color face, the increasing politicization and visibility of the LGBTQ community, and the recent concerns about Central American refugees fleeing violence in their home countries.

This research also shows that while focus on class, disability, and religion has stayed steady, the readings on gender/sex and language in this corpus are fewer than expected.

Conclusion

Change is coming, but it is coming very slowly. While this corpus shows that 47.2% of the articles incorporate at least one of the types of marginalization studied, more than half (52.8%) do not. FYC textbook and OER editors could be doing a better job of bringing opportunities to engage with race, class, gender/sex, sexuality, immigration, religion, language, and disability into the FYC classroom. When textbooks exclude (purposefully or not) marginalized voices, they teach that only certain voices and experiences – voices and experiences that fall into the dominant hegemony by being white, middle-class, cisgender, heterosexual, non-immigrant, Christian, English-speaking, and/or able-bodied – are worth listening to and reading about. Marginalized students deserve to see themselves and their experiences represented in their FYC course readings. In addition, it is crucial for students who are members of dominant groups to learn about the experiences of marginalized people, so they can learn about those unlike themselves and develop a sense of empathy for people who are not like them.

As I have analyzed this corpus, I have identified other issues that should be analyzed in future research – for example, the findings on sexuality or religion could be unpacked through further in-depth analysis and a second round of coding to identify what specific sexuality issues or religious issues are being discussed and in what context. For example, are the readings emphasizing a dominant religion? Or are readings linking certain religions with specific stereotypes?

Finally, Sandra Jamieson has an interesting point when she explains that her analysis shows "essays by women and people of color are *about* women and people of color, often placing these identities in competition," often explaining what it is like to live as a woman or person of color, which shows that authors' imagined audiences are often assumed to be white and male (Jamieson 1997: 164; her emphasis). In juxtaposition with this, Jamieson adds that essays by white men focus on other, more academic topics, illuminating that "the content of the models considered 'particularly appropriate' for white male writers is clearly different from that presented as 'appropriate' for people of color and women" (Jamieson 1997: 165). It would be a good idea to take on this type of analysis and focus on author identity alongside article topic. This would enable researchers to see how writings by members of marginalized groups compare to writings by members of dominant groups, testing whether or not Jamieson's assertions are still true, and to learn how other types of marginalization may affect an author's topic or imagined audience.

References

Alexander, J. and Rhodes, J. (2014) 'Flatten Effects: Composition's Multicultural Imperative and the Problem of Narrative Coherence,' *College Composition and Communication* 65(3): 430–454.

Bridwell-Bowles, L. (1995) 'Discourse and Diversity: Experimental Writing within the Academy,' in L. Wetherbee Phelps and J. Emig (eds.), *Feminine Principles and Women's Experience in American Composition and Rhetoric*, Pittsburgh: University of Pittsburgh Press.

Britton, G. and Lumpkin, M. (1977) 'For Sale: Subliminal Bias in Textbooks,' *Reading Teacher* 31(1): 40–45.

Browning, E. (2014) 'Disability Studies in the Composition Classroom,' *Composition Studies* 42(2): 96–116.

Crenshaw, K. (1989) 'Demarginalizing the Intersection of Race and Sex: A Black Feminist Critique of Antidiscrimination Doctrine, Feminist Theory, and Antiracist Politics,' *The University of Chicago Legal Forum* 8: 136–167.

Davis, V. (2006) 'Our Excellence: Where Do We Grow from Here?' in D. Roen (ed.), *Views from the Center: The CCCC Chairs' Addresses 1977–2005*, Boston: Bedford/St. Martin's Press.

Department of Justice. 'The Americans with Disabilities Act of 1990 and revised ADA regulations implementing Title II and Title III,' *ADA.gov.* www.ada.gov/2010_regs.htm.

Ervelles, N. (2009) 'Rewriting Critical Pedagogy from the Periphery: Materiality, Disability, and the Politics of Schooling,' in S. Gabel (ed.), *Disability Studies in Education: Readings in Theory & Method*, New York: Peter Lang.

Feiner, S. and Roberts, B. (1990) 'Hidden by the Invisible Hand: Neoclassical Economic Theory and the Textbook Treatment of Race and Gender,' *Gender and Society* 4(2): 159–181.

Gale, Xin Liu and Gale, Fredric G. (eds.) (1999) *(Re) Visioning Composition Textbooks: Conflicts of Culture, Ideology, and Pedagogy*, New York: State University of New York Press.

Greenberg, B. and Brand, J. (1994) 'Minorities and the Mass Media: 1970s to 1990s,' in J. Bryant and D. Zillmann (eds.), *Media Effects: Advances in Theory and Research*, Mahwah, NJ: Lawrence Erlbaum Associates, Inc.

Hill-Collins, P. (2000) *Black Feminist Thought*, Philadelphia: Routledge.

hooks, b. (2015) *Feminist Theory: From Margin to Center*, Philadelphia: Routledge.

Jamieson, S. (1997) 'Composition Readers and the Construction of Identity,' in Severino, Guerra, and Butler (eds.), *Writing in Multicultural Settings*, New York: MLA.

Liu, Y. (1999) 'Self, Other, In-Between: Cross-Cultural Composition Readers and the Reconstruction of Cultural Identities,' in X. Gale and F. Gale (eds.), *(Re) Visioning Composition Textbooks: Conflicts of Culture, Ideology, and Pedagogy*, New York: State University of New York Press.

Marinara, M., Alexander, J., Banks, W., and Blackmon, S. (2009) 'Cruising Composition Texts: Negotiating Sexual Difference in First-Year Readers,' *College Composition and Communication* 61(2): 269–296.

Martin, D. (2008) 'Add Disability and Stir: The New Ingredient in Composition Textbooks,' in *Disability and the Teaching of Writing*, Boston: Bedford/St. Martin's Press.

McGinnis, M. (2018) *Dealing with Difference: A Rhetorical Analysis of First-Year Composition Textbooks*, Ball State University, *Proquest Dissertation and Theses*.

Moneyhun, C. (1996) 'Marginalized/Marginalization,' in P. Heilker and P. Vandenberg (eds.), *Keywords in Composition Studies*, Portsmouth: Boynton/Cook.

Perrin, R. (1988) 'Textbook Writers and Textbook Publishers: One Writer's View of the Teaching Canon,' *Journal of Teaching Writing* 7(1): 67–74.

Powell, M. (2012) 'Stories Take Place: A Performance in One Act,' *CCC* 64(2): 383–406.

Purnell, R. (2006) 'Using Language to Unlock the Limits,' in D. Roen (ed.), *Views from the Center: The CCCC Chairs' Addresses 1977–2005*, Boston: Bedford/St. Martin's Press.

Rendleman, E. (2011) 'Balancing Act: Student Valuation and Cultural Studies Composition Textbooks,' *Composition Forum* 24. http://compositonforum.com/issue/24/balancing-act-textbooks.php.

Royster, J. J. (2006) 'When the First Voice You Hear Is Not Your Own,' in D. Roen (ed.), *Views from the Center: The CCCC Chairs' Addresses 1977–2005*, Boston: Bedford/St. Martin's Press.

Young, I. (2004) 'Five Faces of Oppression,' in L. Heldke and P. O'Connor (eds.), *Oppression, Privilege, and Resistance*, New York: McGraw Hill.

19
DEMONSTRATING AND DEBATING CLIMATE CHANGE

The Function of Rhetoric from Science to the Public

Ferenc Jankó and Priszcilla Hafenscher

Introduction

Since climate influences our culture, it is not surprising that climate change has also become a part of the human world after decades of scientific, public, and political discourses from the second half of the twentieth century (Hulme 2016, 2021). Climate change has improved scientific knowledge, but it has also become a veritable cultural and social construct by integrating into our communications – into thinking, talking, discussing, writing, and imagining. Hence, it has also incorporated itself into language through new words and expressions such as climate crisis, climate emergency, climate strike, climate anxiety, climate refugees, global heating, climate hysteria, carbon market, carbon footprint, carbon diet, and many others (Koteyko 2015). Various "word of the year" assessments have reflected this development.

Climate change thus forms a major part of environmental communication that relays complex information from various scientific disciplines to the public. On the one hand, we use this kind of communication to convince and motivate people toward climate action. On the other hand, we also utilize it to persuade and debate with people holding opposing views. Hence, studying several aspects of climate change communication is an intriguing pursuit (Nerlich et al. 2010; Pearce et al. 2015). Climate change discourses and narratives have become important issues in the expanding field of climate change communication, in which rhetorical aspects have also been highlighted. Non-experts in rhetoric have conducted some rhetorical studies on climate change. These sorts of studies have melded with the general discursive or linguistic approaches. For that reason, this chapter presents rhetorical studies of climate change in dialogue with research on discourses and narration. It seeks to understand how we talk and write about climate change, how climate change discursively forms our perceived world, how we argue, and how we debate climate change using oral and written language ranging from scientific texts to public "climate talks".

310

DOI: 10.4324/9781003195276-24

Linguistic Research on Climate Change

Rhetoric, narrative, and discourse are interconnected concepts that reflect the plasticity created by linguistic and cultural activity. According to Dryzek (1997/2013), climate change fits within different discourses like *survivalism* (i.e., climate catastrophe), *denial of limits* (i.e., climate scepticism), or *environmental problem solving* (e.g. mainstream climate policy). Detection of climate change discourses became a vibrant research topic at the turn of the millennium, particularly following the Third Assessment Report of the Intergovernmental Panel on Climate Change (IPCC TAR) in 2001, as the topic increasingly penetrated public discourse. Evolving research focused on the various ways society encounters the emerging global mega-problem at the level of coping. These ways range from alarmism to denial and from techno-optimism action to the small steps toward possible change (Ernaut and Segnit 2006, 2007; Risbey 2008). Many researchers concentrated on the language of catastrophe and fear. This research direction flourished particularly after Al Gore's Nobel prize-winning documentary, *An Inconvenient Truth* (Johnson 2009; Morales 2017). The question of fear appeal remains an unresolved issue and is in continuous dispute; some consider it counterproductive, while others deem it necessary (Hulme 2008; O'Neill; Cole 2009; Tannenbaum et al. 2015; Chapman et al. 2017; Bouman et al. 2020; Kundzwicz et al. 2020; Lamb et al. 2020).

Discourses are thus the highest level at which we can study how people understand and represent what is happening, moreover, how people create a discursive reality embedded into the context of linguistic production and interpretation (Fløttum and Gjerstad 2017). Or, to be more nuanced, discourses are formed by those in power who can make their voices heard, be it politicians, media workers, celebrities, or scientists, who often represent the "elite" on a given case or issue. People in such positions can also be referred to as epistemic workers or communities (Castree 2014). Narratives somehow fit into the larger frame of discourses, but *frames* are also crucial to narratives because they guide the viewing and interpretation of a given case or event. Frames also arrange the participants and provide a possible way of "reading" the story. Frames have a strategic role in storytelling, in which narrative tone and style play parts. Narrative analysis is commonplace in media research, where the practice of journalists and other media communicators is studied (Wozniak et al. 2015; Fløttum and Gjerstad 2017).

While narrative or discourse analyses usually address complex text corpora in a longer time frame, a single person or a single text can be the subject of rhetorical analysis, as exemplified by Greta Thunberg's speeches (Evensen 2019; Vavilov 2019; Houdek and Phillips 2020; Michael 2021). However, academic research frequently confuses the notions of discourse, narrative and rhetoric (Hartmann 2010; Supran and Oreskes 2021) because these all refer to how we use *language* regarding climate change (Fløttum 2017; Fløttum and Gjerstad 2017).

The public meaning of rhetoric was misunderstood amidst the climate change debates. The recent focus on rhetoric and climate science was thus not always a purely academic question (Walsh 2017). Offline and online public discussions contrast the two concepts, i.e., rhetoric and science, and present them as opposites by treating rhetoric as either a non-scientific encounter of significant issues that promotes propaganda over fact-based arguments, or a form of demagoguery. Rhetoric is, admittedly, about persuasion, but it is not only applied by climate change sceptics. Rhetoric is inherently also a part of science (Gross 2006). Moreover, a traditional and – to some extent expected – form of rhetoric does permeate our talks and scientific texts. Nevertheless, employing the same old rhetorical flourishes and commonplace phrases could also indicate a source of ironic self-criticism (Graham 1957). In the case of climate science, the role of rhetoric is much more obvious because of the need to combine facts with values to communicate uncertainty (e.g. climate change model predictions) and a call to engagement for and action on climate change (Walsh 2015, 2017). The related literature includes a remarkable attempt to grasp the rhetorical aspects of climate change communication. Yet in terms of rhetoric, this body of research focused mostly on sceptics, which provided some basis to confuse rhetoric and scepticism.

To address the linguistic and rhetorical aspects of climate denialism, some researchers returned to the roots of science studies and classical rhetorical traditions. The academic trends of science studies were initially concerned with the criticism of mainstream scientific discourse (Latour 2004; Ceccarelli 2011). For example, Besel (2011) applied the Latourian tradition of science and technology studies to examine the rhetorical climate debate and used the actor-network theory to enhance understanding of the role of rhetoric during these controversies. Addressing the climate change controversy, similarly, Jankó et al. (2014) also departed from the seminal science studies works of Latour (1987) and Gross (2006) by combining the science studies approach with the elements of basic Aristotelian rhetoric, applying the three genres of scientific speech: forensic, epideictic and deliberative. Addressing visual rhetoric of climate change, Walsh (2015) used Isocrates' aspects of rhetoric. These included: (1) employed strategies or heuristics achieving new forms of knowledge, (2) internal logical structure, (3) *kairos*, i.e., the temporal moment applicable for the rhetorical act, (4) audience of communication, (5) appeals to emotions, values, authorities, and sources of evidence, (6) style and presentation, (7) political effects on communities, and (8) positive or negative effects on democratic deliberation. Walsh also supplemented these classical aspects with semiotic and critical analysis of visual rhetoric. Bloomfield and Tillery (2019) focused on rhetorical strategies and rhetorical *topoi* of climate change sceptics, which is similar to Ceccarelli (2011), who involved all the antecedents of the Greek rhetorical tradition to reinforce her "supportive orientation" toward mainstream science. These examples – some detailed below – show the potential to employ rhetorical analysis to construct wiser, more considerate, and more useful climate change discourses – an insight Walsh (2017) underscored in his focus review of rhetoric in climate change debates. Here, Walsh (2017) also applied the classical rhetorical traditions and outlined a dualistic range of *sophistic* (with the emphasis on emotions and persuasion) and *rational* rhetoric (with balanced stress on logic and rationality) to contrast the discourses of mainstream climate change science and climate change sceptics.

Beyond scepticism, scientific attention on rhetoric has only recently focused on youth climate change movements, e.g. on Greta Thunberg's speeches and rhetoric. Evensen (2019) argued that the rhetoric of the #FridaysForFuture movement places too much emphasis on science as the necessary basis of our actions. According to Evensen, the movement should acknowledge the limits of science and equally rest on social scientists, philosophers and ethicists. Furthermore, it should emphasize social inequity problems. In her analysis, Michael (2021) focused on the persuasive role of rhetoric in youth climate movement messages, specifically those of Greta Thunberg, by referring back to the basic concepts of *logos* (logical argument), *ethos* (speaker credibility) and *pathos* (emotional argument) within classical rhetoric. She argued that Thunberg's use of rhetoric successfully combines ecocriticism with eco-activism.

Linguistic perspectives also point to the direction of words and metaphors, indicating that even small elements of language serve as building blocks in our argumentation and persuasion communications, i.e., in accommodating science (Nerlich et al. 2010). Forgách and Pléh (2022) have recently argued that proper metaphors must describe the enormity of climate change and imply human responsibility but must also stress opportunities to intervene and solve the problem without confusing interpretations and creating a mood of despair. Some examples of these sorts of metaphors include hothouse instead of greenhouse, climate breakdown or climate catastrophe, climate destruction instead of climate change, or global overheating instead of global warming. This approach is comparable to Cohen's (2010) earlier suggestion concerning the lessons of using warfare metaphors during World War II.

Research on Climate Change Science Debates

The historical roots of present anthropogenic climate change debates were also studied from the viewpoint of linguistic research (Hamblyn 2009; Liverman 2009; Sörlin 2009). Hamblyn (2009) argued that recent discourses echoed many real or perceived phrases, metaphors, and quotations from climate change icons like Arrhenius, Callendar, Keeling, or Hansen. With the appearance of climate change sceptics at the turn of the millennium, it became evident that scientific rhetoric would assume a central role. Communication scholars responded by increasing their study of scientific rhetoric. The first focus of this chapter is to review the related research. The language employed in speeches and texts in debates ranging from the "Chapter 8" controversy to "Climategate" can distinguish mainstream climate science from the climate sceptic community. Both above-mentioned debates were about scientific arguments for publicity and various background occurrences, how a climate change argument about human responsibility is worded, how background email consultations frame published scientific results and their readings (Edwards and Schneider 2001; Ryghaug and Skjølsvold 2010; Grundmann 2013).

'Climategate" – the scandal involving over a thousand partly sensitive emails hacked from a university server – was a part of the so-called "hockey stick controversy'. This controversy broke at the end of the 1990s when paleoclimate researcher Michael Mann and colleagues published their first temperature reconstructions for earlier centuries. These reconstructions were later extended to cover a span of a thousand years. Mann's study and subsequent follow-up studies became the canon of paleoclimate research and became signposts to the central argument of the IPCC, which claims unprecedented warming from the 1990s to the present, with human activity playing a major role in this temperature shift. It is not coincidental that the issue fell into the crosshairs of climate sceptic investigations. The controversy unfolded in the media, but several scientific publications also contributed to the dispute.

Unsurprisingly, the controversy drew the interest of science studies practitioners. Among the first was Besel (2011), who analysed the two Committee on Energy and Commerce hearings in 2006; the hearings investigated the debate on Mann et al.'s initial study from 1998 by summoning numerous scientists. Besel interpreted these events as "trials of rhetorical strength" where not only the scientific material was important, but also the rhetorical positioning surrounding it. Furthermore, Besel demonstrated that the controversy served as an example of how climate scientists and sceptics mobilized competing actor-networks to rhetorically defend or attack the important mainstream research signposts. Namely, Besel showed how climate change sceptics organized a network of denial with the same rhetorical features to attack Mann and how global warming believers defended Mann et al.'s study as a crucial node in its network. "By rhetorically invoking other nodes in the network to support the single node that was attacked, global warming believers were able to use the weight of the entire network as a potent inventional resource" (Besel 2011: 132). This study also demonstrated that actor-network theory offers a deeper insight into scientific controversies where authors, texts, contexts and rhetoric could be analysed in their complexity.

Another example is Ceccarelli (2011), who, in "manufactured controversies" such as global warming, focused on the rhetorical strategies and tools contrarians use to delay and hinder policy action. By criticizing the balancing norm in American media and institutional practice, Ceccarelli outlined how climate sceptic politicians and various experts manufactured controversy and employed the uncertainty of scientific results as a tool.

Based on a scientometric comparison, Jankó et al. (2014) focused on the rhetorical practices of mainstream and contrarian scientists using the assessment of the IPCC Working Group I on the Physical Science Basis and an opposing, partisan climate change sceptic report published by the Heartland Institute, which is a conservative think tank. Using similarly cited references, Jankó et al. revealed the varying rhetorical styles of the opposing report editors and authors, i.e., reviewers. Jankó et al. started with Latour's (1987) seminal work, *Science in Action*, which offers an approach to literature analysis, and with Gross's guidance on Aristotelian rhetoric that "a report is forensic because it reconstructs past science in a way most likely to support its claims; it is deliberative because it intends to direct future research; it is epideictic because it is a celebration of appropriate methods" (Gross, 2006: 25). Hence, Jankó et al. demonstrated that forensic language was the dominant rhetoric in the mainstream IPCC report as it generally contained overall statements with grouped citations, in many cases with comments (or as Latour says: *modalities*). Conversely, the contrarian report used epideictic rhetoric by explaining the work of the cited scientists in detail and celebrating the scientists by highlighting their field research and their efforts during the observations, which played on the implicit opposition of climate modellers and field scientists. However, Jankó et al. argued that both reviewing methods aim at credibility. The narrated verbatim quotations with conclusions in the sceptic report render the text more believable, whereas the IPCC report editors synthesized the literature using grouped citations. This technique places the reviewers in the foreground with the text, thereby increasing their credibility.

Through deeper rhetorical investigation, Jankó et al. (2014) identified two cases. The "battle of key references" refers to a situation when "key authors" and their papers are referenced in both assessments, and they line up for a predetermined battle: the IPCC report used the key references of the sceptical report to demonstrate uncertainties, while the contrarian report criticized the results or methods of the IPCC's key authors using their key authors. The vocabulary of the report authors was quite similar. When citing a friendly author, they apply the verbs "find", "indicate", "report", "show", "conclude", but use the verbs "claims", "contends" and "challenges" to present counter-opinions when citing opposing authors. Clauses starting with *however*, *although* or *nevertheless* were crucial on both sides. These words were applied to diminish the main sentence with a negative modality or dissolve uncertainty. These involved cases in which two reports offered disparate interpretations of a study result or when two studies obtained two disparate facts from the same reference.

Summing up, the above-mentioned study showed how authors mobilize other authors in the form of citations and references and use these as rhetorical tools to back their arguments or to criticize and demolish opposing findings. We could detect that citations do indeed form actor-networks, just as Besel (2011) had suggested. Medimorec and

Pennycook (2015) endorsed and supplemented the study results via a text analyser that proved that IPCC editors applied language that was far more cautious and conservative.

Concerning climate change science, article abstracts have come into focus in connection with the so-called "consensus debates", the second focus of this chapter. Departing from the study of Oreskes (2004), climate change consensus debates heated up after the publication of Cook et al. (2013), when consensus figures, i.e., what proportion of scientists support the anthropogenic course of global warming, became key tools in climate change communication to the public. Without detailing the controversy of whether consensus messaging is a useful tool in persuading uninformed or unengaged people (Pearce et al. 2017; Russil 2018), the simple abstract rating method of Cook et al. shed light on the abstract writing habits of researchers. Cook et al. categorized more than 10,000 article abstracts according to the position authors took regarding anthropogenic global warming. The study established three basic categories: (1) abstracts that explicitly or implicitly endorse anthropogenic climate change by stating or implying that humans are causing global warming or that refer to anthropogenic climate change as a known fact, (2) no position abstracts, and (3) abstracts that explicitly or implicitly reject the anthropogenic origins of climate change. A large proportion (66%) of the "no position" abstracts concentrated on how authors rhetorically relate to the paradigmatic idea of anthropogenic global warming. Based on quantitative textual analysis, Jankó et al. (2020) argued that most pro-consensus or pure scientists (Fahnestock 1986; Hyland 2006; Pielke 2007) indicated no need or intention to refer to the human origin of climate change. The abstract rating is, thus, rather about rhetoric. Hence, "no position" abstracts and the related articles left more room for rhetorical manoeuvring in the hands of those who review and reinterpret the abstracts and related articles.

Science Goes to the Media

A 1986 German *Spiegel* cover depicting Cologne Cathedral flooded by the sea serves as a symbol of climate change, both as a media topic and as a phenomenon with powerful visual potential. Today, climate change communication is increasingly present in the online space, where blogs became the initial explicit discussion and debate forums before the rise of social media platforms, which frequently serve as little more than "echo chambers" that repeatedly rearrange our communication from scientific to public discourses. This development led to the *democratization* of knowledge-making and access (but also to *fragmentation*, seeing the newest trends in anti-scientific movements). It also opened up the possibility of the *contextual model* in public understanding of science with interaction and dialogues. However, science communication has remained anchored in the *deficit model* of promoting one-way communication to educate and inform the public. Moreover, these trends also accelerated the linguistic progress of the formation and diffusion of new word compositions regarding climate change (Koteyko 2015; Pearce et al. 2015). The colourful and rapidly changing media landscape provided climate communication with broad and expanding research attention where the importance of visual imagery (here, as rhetoric) is also notable. Hence, we briefly review these areas below.

News Media

Scientific discourses would not reach the public without the media, which places the burden of responsibility on the news media. Balance as a journalistic norm in climate change controversy is a crucial issue (Moser 2010). Consequently, news media strongly affects public perception by filtering and determining the quality and quantity of information reaching the public (Boykoff and Rajan 2007). It can also stimulate or hinder engagement and policy responses (Russil 2008).

Beyond the debates, rhetoric and framing of the news and the linked visuals should be chosen based on scientific knowledge regarding environmental psychology, risks, and climate communication rather than on uninformative clickbait aspects. However, scientific literature is ambiguous in many aspects of effective communication. News story narratives and frames can address climate change causes, impacts and solutions/actions and awaken various emotions. Whether these emotions help to engage people and motivate them to individual actions or whether they hinder action through apathy or calm optimism is a matter of debate (Rebich 2011; Chadwick 2015; Feldman and Hart 2016). Research on the interaction of text and visuals in the news has also brought various results. For example, images that echo the story may produce greater salience and memorability; in other cases, they appear to have a limited effect on emotions (Geise 2015; Feldman and Hart 2016). What is crucial, independent of visuals and textual framing, is the selecting of key story aspects and making these more salient to the detriment of the others (Entman 1993), which has a profound influence on public judgement and opinion about the "climate story". Frames focus on scientific uncertainties and the cost of mitigation policy that turn people against climate action, especially during and after an economic crisis (Morton et al. 2011; Boykoff and Boykoff 2007). In contrast, emphasizing long-term economic gains of mitigation and the threats of inaction, even in the present, leads to support. However, people tend to underestimate the dangers as long as the risks are framed as geographically distant issues that remain abstract and do not appear to affect daily life (Rabinovich and Morton 2012).

Social Media Platforms

Explicit debates around anthropogenic climate change and the key questions highlighted by the sceptics remained limited in traditional scientific forums. Hence, internet platforms, such as science blogs – which experts in the field often maintain – assumed the role of "extended peer communities", i.e., direct access to firsthand scientific information and interpretations. Some of these platforms provided a virtual unfolding of science-in-the-making. Together with climate blogs representing the mainstream views (RealClimate) or directly criticizing the denial views (ScepticalScience, DeSmogBlog), the number of climate sceptic or critical blogs also grew rapidly. Some garnered global reach (Watts Up With That, Bishop Hill, Climate Etc., Climate Audit, JoNova etc.), especially after Climategate, which marked their peak (Nerlich 2010; Sharman 2014). Both groups of blogs are similarly active with the same working mechanism of posting mainly scientific article reviews complete with comment sections.

Nerlich (2010) identified particular religious metaphors as "effective framing devices" circulating in the sceptical blogosphere. These metaphors depicted mainstream science as a religion replete with believers, dogmas, prophets, zealots, etc. Moving beyond Climategate, researchers explored how the opposing blogs contributed to the polarization of online public discourses (Elgesen et al. 2015; van Eck et al. 2019).

While framed news stories are mediated in one manner exclusively – from the journalists to the audience – social media, including the previously mentioned blogs, provides a broad platform in which to react, comment, share and debate issues. A novelty is the arena where mixed-attitude communities of sceptics and activists exist and share views; however, these debates are often exhausted in the employment of negative remark exchanges rather than the employment of sophisticated argumentation (Williams et al. 2015). As previously noted, polarization has also increased. Like-minded people have significantly more conversations with each other, which entails fewer mixed communities than like-minded communities (Williams et al. 2015). This fact hinders argumentation, confirmation and refutation, making climate change rhetoric unilateral. Practically, social media provides "echo chambers" or "information bubbles" to climate change deniers in which the community validates and reinforces climate denier views and keeps original sources of scientific information well hidden (Matthews 2015; Walter et al. 2018; Boomfield and Tillery 2019).

Despite the rise of sceptics, new media forms possess advantages in climate change discourses. Issues in which people can share their opinions and experiences tend to become more personalized and concrete, which proved hard to achieve through news media (Anderson 2017). As Walsh (2015) pointed out, instead of conventional rhetoric of climate communication, this topic needs to be involved in people's daily lives, values and decisions. This personalized and concrete "social media rhetoric" could include a "friend's" online travelogue of the melting glaciers posted on Facebook, or even a dialogue about the increasingly common weather anomalies in everyday life. One comment may be enough to associate weather events with climate change; thus, the entire group of participants in the conversation are likely to believe in climate change and perceive the increased risk (Borick and Rabe 2014; Leiserowitz et al. 2013).

In addition to "friends", social media also brims with influencers, who reach their followers easily and instantly via pictures, videos, podcasts or textual posts. Social media influencers profoundly affect attitudes, behaviour and decisions (Casaló et al. 2020), which they reach with many rhetorical tactics, like attention-attracting, claiming expertise, meaningfulness and mood affecting (Zhou et al. 2021; Okuah et al. 2019). Thus, influencers play a new, third party role in climate communication. Good examples are green women influencers who effectively promote sustainable, zero-waste lifestyles, thereby helping people tackle climate change at the individual level (Yıldırım 2021). This is the rhetoric of "hero-story", where the green heroes save the world with ordinary actions, implying that anyone can be a hero.

Visual Rhetoric of Climate Change

Visuals like pictures and diagrams can also serve as persuasive rhetorical tools and assume an impressive role in climate communication. Images hold a specific point of view and provide reasons for holding the view, just as textual arguments do (Walsh 2015). Even a complex argument becomes easily comprehensible to laypeople via imagery (Hannigan 2006), which facilitates climate communication. Images may be independent or connected to a text, in which case the image should mirror the rhetoric. Namely, figures in scientific articles show objective information that avoids emotional evocation; however, graphs about climate change-induced rainforest loss or rising mortality rates may stir sadness, anger or anxiety in people just as the famous "hockey stick" inspired many debates and scandals. Images with a wider cultural meaning provoke stronger emotional responses and facilitate lines of identification with visual subjects (Smith and Joffe 2009). It is easier to identify personally with a "climate refugee" who lost everything to a bushfire than it is to identify personally with a graph depicting rising temperatures. Moreover, if people adopt the perspective that these events are near rather than far – that climate change could bring similar catastrophes to their doorstep – they might become more motivated to take action. Although imagery is a key tool in shaping people's conceptualization of climate change (Leiserowitz 2006), imagery reflecting climate change disasters in distant places can instil a false sense of security that such events could not happen closer to home (Moser 2010; Spence et al. 2012). The challenging role of visual rhetoric is bridging this psychological distancing from climate change and its consequences.

Visual rhetoric, especially photographic imagery, can connotatively argue the need for action from different perspectives. The first one is "climate change causes", which include pictures of fossil fuel plants and deforestation. These images tend to lay the blame for climate change on people. This approach rarely moves people to action, as people blame others rather than themselves (Hamilton and Kasser 2009). This form of visual rhetoric fails to address many other psychological barriers, such as limited cognition, ideologies, social norms and perceived risk (Gifford et al. 2011). The second starting point of arguing climate change with visuals is "solution", which includes things like solar panels. The "solution" approach is also a double-edged sword because it presents climate change as easily solvable. On one hand, it gives people hope, but on the other hand, it also reduces the significance of the issue (O'Neill and Nicholson-Cole 2009; O'Neill et al. 2013; Metag et al. 2016). Its efficacy is controversial in the literature. On the one hand, Carlson et al. (2020) found that solution visuals grab attention better than negative imagery. On the other hand, Chapman et al. (2016) noted that among the three types of rhetoric, "impact" visuals grab the most attention and provide the greatest motivation for people to alter personal behaviour and support climate change policy.

However, the third and the most common approach, which shows the "climate change impact", also exhibits a debatable effect on emotions and motivation. This category includes CO_2 level graphs, maps depicting average temperature change in the recent decades, and suffused iconic pictures like underweight polar bears and melting ice sheets. These catastrophic, fear-inducing and dramatic visuals emphasize the reality of climate change as a real problem. They also create a sense of urgency by calling for immediate action in the face of dire consequences that destroy wildlife and humanity. This approach can be categorized as a form of persuasive reasoning because it grabs attention and emphasizes the importance of combating climate change. However, it also tends to overwhelm people and triggers hopelessness rather than positive motivation, which often leads to psychological and geographical distancing (O'Neill 2013; O'Neill et al. 2013; O'Neill and Nicholson-Cole 2009).

According to some studies, many of the image types that climate change advocates, journalists and non-governmental organizations regard as effective visuals usually fall short of expectations in communication. For instance, "climate clichés" are not only often overused, but the sadness and empathy the clichés attempt to evoke seem forced (Hulme 2009). Furthermore, people often associate images of droughts and deforestation with social issues like third world poverty rather than with climate change (Chapman et al. 2016). Instead, the most convincing images are of individuals or people who are not politicians or environmental activists (Nicholson-Cole 2005; Braasch 2013; Chapman et al. 2016). Moreover, images are more engaging if direct eye contact between the image subject and the viewer is established (Banse 2013; Chapman et al. 2016). The other decisive factor that determines the effectiveness of a visual is "localization", through which local or national problems are more relatable than melting glaciers or destroyed rainforests in distant places (Nicholson-Cole 2005). Distance visuals tempt people to believe that climate change is a remote problem from which they can remain detached and from which they will suffer no consequences (Manzo 2010). However, other studies have yielded contrasting results (O'Neill and Hulme 2009) or mixed findings (McDonald et al. 2015; Chapman et al. 2016). Depicting climate change as a global problem that affects different localities in various ways remains the duty of scientists and photographers alike.

Conclusion

Climate change is a powerful concept that is fundamentally reshaping all aspects of our physical and cultural world, from economy to politics and from science to arts. Our language follows these trends. Environmental communication, particularly climate change communication, deserves our attention. This chapter provided an overview of the research terrain of climate change discourses, narratives and rhetoric that mirrored the central questions in climate change communication concerning our language. It also addressed how we can create different worlds of understanding discursively or linguistically. We demonstrated that related research examined the deepest elements of rhetoric concerning the controversy between mainstream and opposing groups. The review of the media landscape further nuanced and coloured this reality. Rhetoric is an important tool for communicating engagement and action in climate change debates and beyond; however, the most effective or ineffective means of communication are still under debate. When examining communication, we may see the merits, opportunities, and difficulties present in the field. We must also note that communication alone cannot provide a universal cure for managing, let alone solving, climate change.

References

Adger, W. N., Benjaminsen, T. A., Brown, K., and Svarstad, H., 2001. Advancing a Political Ecology of Global Environmental Discourses. *Development and Change* 32, 681–715.

Anderson, A. A., 2017. Effects of Social Media Use on Climate Change Opinion, Knowledge, and Behavior. In *Oxford Research Encyclopedia of Climate Science*. https://doi.org/10.1093/acrefore/9780190228620.013.369

Banse, L., 2013. Seeing Is Believing – A Guide to Visual Storytelling Best Practices. Resource Media. Available online: www.resource-media.org/wp-content/uploads/2013/04/Visual-storytelling-guide.pdf (accessed 26.01.2022).

Besel, R. D., 2011. Opening the "Black Box" of Climate Change Science: Actor-Network Theory and Rhetorical Practice in Scientific Controversies. *Southern Communication Journal* 76 (2), 120–136. https://doi.org/10.1080/10417941003642403

Bloomfield, E. F. and Tillery, D., 2019. The Circulation of Climate Change Denial Online: Rhetorical and Networking Strategies on Facebook. *Environmental Communication* 13, 23–34. https://doi.org/10.1080/17524032.2018.1527378

Borick, C. P. and Rabe, B. G., 2014. Weather or Not? Examining the Impact of Meteorological Conditions on Public Opinion Regarding Global Warming. *Weather, Climate, and Society* 6 (3), 413–424. doi: 10.1175/WCAS- D-13-00042.1.

Bouman, T., Verschoor, M., Albers, C., Böhm, G., Fisher, S. D., Poortinga, W., Whitmarsh, L., and Steg, L., 2020. When Worry about Climate Change Leads to Climate Action: How Values, Worry and Personal Responsibility Relate to Various Climate Actions. *Global Environmental Change* 62, 102061 https://doi.org/10.1016/j.gloenvcha.2020.102061

Boykoff, M. T. and Boykoff, J. M., 2007. Climate Change and Journalistic Norms: A Case-Study of US Mass-Media Coverage. *Geoforum* 38, 1190–1204. doi: 10.1016/j.geoforum.2007.01.008

Boykoff, M. T. and Rajan, S. R., 2007. Signals and Noise. Mass-Media Coverage of Climate Change in the USA and the UK. *EMBO Reports* 8, 207–211. doi: 10.1038/sj.embor.7400924

Braasch, G., 2013. Climate Change: Is Seeing Believing? *Bulletin of the Atomic Scientists* 69 (6), 33–41. doi: 10.1177/0096340213508628

Carlson, J. M., Kaull, H., Steinhauser, M., Zigarac, A., and Cammarata, J., 2020. Paying Attention to Climate Change: Positive Images of Climate Change Solutions Capture Attention. *Journal of Environmental Psychology* 71, 101477. doi: 10.1016/j.jenvp.2020.101477

Casaló, L. V., Flavián, C., and Ibáñez-Sánchez, S., 2020. Influencers on Instagram: Antecedents and Consequences of Opinion Leadership. *Journal of Business Research* 117, 510–519. doi: 10.1016/j.jbusres.2018.07.005

Castree, N., 2014. *Making Sense of Nature. Representation, Politics and Democracy.* New York: Routledge.

Ceccarelli, L., 2011. Manufactured Scientific Controversy: Science, Rhetoric, and Public Debate. *Rhetoric and Public Affairs* 14 (2), 195–228.

Chadwick, A. E., 2015. Toward a Theory of Persuasive Hope: Effects of Cognitive Appraisals, Hope Appeals, and Hope in the Context of Climate Change. *Health Communication* 30 (6), 598–611. doi: 10.1080/10410236.2014.916777

Chapman, D. A., Corner, A., Webster, R., and Markowitz, E. M., 2016. Climate Visuals: A Mixed Methods Investigation of Public Perceptions of Climate Images in Three Countries. *Global Environmental Change* 41, 172–182. doi: 10.1016/j.gloenvcha.2016.10.003

Chapman, D. A., Lickel B., and Markowitz, E. M., 2017. Reassessing Emotion in Climate Change Communication. *Nature Climate Change* 7, 850–852. https://doi.org/10.1038/s41558-017-0021-9

Cohen, M. J., 2010. Is the UK Preparing for 'War'? Military Metaphors, Personal Carbon Allowances, and Consumption Rationing in Historical Perspective. *Climate Change*. doi:10.1007/s10584-009-9785-x

Cook, J., Nuccitelli, D., Green, S. A., Richardson, M., Winkler, B., Painting, R., Way, R., Jacobs, P. and Skuce, A., 2013. Quantifying the Consensus on Anthropogenic Global Warming in the Scientific Literature. *Environmental Research Letters* 8, 024024. doi:10.1088/1748-9326/8/2/024024

Dryzek, J., 2013 [1997]. *The Politics of the Earth: Environmental Discourses*, 3rd ed. Oxford: Oxford University Press.

Edwards, P. N. and Schneider, S. H., 2001. Self-Governance and Peer Review in Science-for-Policy: The Case of the IPCC Second Assessment Report. In C. A. Miller and P. N. Edwards (eds.), *Changing the Atmosphere: Expert Knowledge and Environmental Governance.* Cambridge, MA and London: MIT Press, 219–246.

Elgesem, D., Steskal, L., and Diakopoulos, N., 2015. Structure and Content of the Discourse on Climate Change in the Blogosphere: The Big Picture. *Environmental Communication* 9, 169–188. doi: 10.1080/17524032.2014.983536

Entman, R. M., 1993. Framing: Toward Clarification of a Fractured Paradigm. *Journal of Communication* 43, 51–58. doi: 10.1111/j.1460-2466.1993.tb01304.x

Ereaut, G. and Segnit, N., 2006. *Warm Words: How Are We Telling the Climate Story and Can We Tell It Better?* London: Institute for Public Policy Research.

Ereaut, G. and Segnit, N., 2007. *Warm Words II: How the Climate Story Is Evolving and the Lessons We Can Learn for Encouraging Public Action.* London: Institute for Public Policy Research.

Evensen, D., 2019. The Rhetorical Limitations of the #FridaysForFuture Movement. *Nature Climate Change* 9, 428–433. https://doi.org/10.1038/s41558-019-0481-1

Fahnestock, J., 1986. Accomodating Science: The Rhetorical Life of Scientific Facts. *Written Communication* 3 (3), 275e296. https://doi.org/10.1177/0741088386003003001

Feldman, L. and Hart, P. S., 2016. Using Political Efficacy Messages to Increase Climate Activism: The Mediating Role of Emotions. *Science Communication* 38 (1), 99–127. doi: 10.1177/1075547015617941

Feldman, L. and Hart, P. S., 2018. Is There Any Hope? How Climate Change News Imagery and Text Influence Audience Emotions and Support for Climate Mitigation Policies. *Risk Analysis* 38 (3), 585–602. doi: 10.1111/risa.12868

Fløttum, K., 2017. Language and Climate Change. In K. Fløøttum (ed.), *The Role of Language in the Climate Change Debate.* New York and London: Routledge, 1–10.

Fløttum, K. and Gjerstad, Ø., 2017. Narratives in Climate Change Discourse. *WIREs Climate Change* 8, e429. doi: 10.1002/wcc.429

Forgács, B. and Pléh, Cs., 2022. The Fluffy Metaphors of Climate Science. In S. Wuppuluri and A. C. Grayling (eds.), *Metaphors and Analogies in Sciences and Humanities*, Synthese Library, vol. 453. Cham: Springer, 447–477. https://doi.org/10.1007/978-3-030-90688-7_22

Geise, S. and Baden, C., 2015. Putting the Image Back into the Frame: Modeling the Linkage between Visual Communication and Frameprocessing Theory. *Communication Theory* 25 (1), 46–69. doi: 10.1111/comt.12048

Gifford, R., Kormos, C., and McIntyre, A., 2011. Behavioral Dimensions of Climate Change: Drivers, Responses, Barriers, and Interventions. *WIREs Climate Change* 2, 801–827. doi: 10.1002/wcc.143

Graham Jr., C. D., 1957. A Dictionary of Useful Research Phrases. *Metal Progress* 71 (5), 71.

Gross, A. G., 2006. *Starring the Text. The Place of Rhetoric in Science Studies.* Carbondale: Southern Illinois University Press.

Grundmann, R., 2013. "Climategate" and the Scientific Ethos. *Science, Technology & Human Values* 38 (1), 67–93.

Hamblyn, R., 2009. The Whistleblower and the Canary: Rhetorical Constructions of Climate Change. *Journal of Historical Geography* 35, 223–236.

Hamilton, C. and Kasser, T., 2009. Psychological Adaptation to the Threats and Stresses of a Four-Degree World. A paper for "Four Degrees and Beyond" conference, Oxford University, 28–30 September 2009 www.eci.ox.ac.uk/events/4degrees/ppt/poster-hamilton.pdf (accessed 26.01.2022).

Hannigan, J., 2006. *Environmental Sociology. A Social Constructionist Perspective.* 2nd ed. New York: Routledge.

Hartmann, B., 2010. Rethinking Climate Refugees and Climate Conflict: Rhetoric, Reality and the Politics of Policy Discourse. *Journal of International Development* 22, 233–246. doi: 10.1002/jid.1676

Houdek, M. and Phillips, K. R., 2020. Rhetoric and the Temporal Turn: Race, Gender, Temporalities. *Women's Studies in Communication* 43 (4), 369–383. doi: 10.1080/07491409.2020.1824501

Hulme, M., 2008. The Conquering of Climate: Discourses of Fear and Their Dissolution. *The Geographical Journal* 174 (1), 5–16. https://doi.org/10.1111/j.1475-4959.2008.00266.x

Hulme, M., 2009. *Why We Disagree about Climate Change. Understanding Controversy, Inaction and Opportunity.* New York: Cambridge University Press.

Hulme, M., 2016. *Weathered. Cultures of Climate.* London: King's College London.

Hulme, M., 2021. *Climate Change.* New York and London: Routledge.

Hyland, K., 2006. Disciplinary Differences: Language Variation in Academic Discourses. In K. Hyland and M. Bondi (eds.), *Academic Discourse across Disciplines*. Frankfurt: Peter Lang, 17–45.

Jankó, F., Drüszler, Á., Gálos, B., Móricz, N., Papp-Vancsó, J., Pieczka, I., Pongrácz, R., Rasztovits, E., Soósné Dezső, Zs., and Szabó, O., 2020. Recalculating Climate Change Consensus: The Question of Position and Rhetoric. *Journal of Cleaner Production* 254, 120127. https://doi.org/10.1016/j.jclepro.2020.120127

Jankó, F., Móricz, N., and Papp-Vancsó, J., 2014. Reviewing the Climate Change Reviewers: Exploring Controversy through Report References and Citations. *Geoforum* 56, 17–34. http://dx.doi.org/10.1016/j.geoforum.2014.06.004

Johnson, L., 2009. (Environmental) Rhetorics of Tempered Apocalypticism in An Invonvenient Truth. *Rhetoric Review* 28 (1), 29–46. doi: 10.1080/07350190802540708

Koteyko, N., 2015. Corpus-Assisted Analysis of Internet-Based Discourses: From Patterns to Rhetoric. In J. Ridolfo and W. Hart-Davidson (eds.), *Rhetoric and Digital Humanities*. Chicago: University of Chicago Press. https://doi.org/10.7208/9780226176727-014

Kundzwicz, Z. W., Matczak, P., Otto, I. M., and Otto, P. E., 2020. From "Atmosfear" to Climate Action. *Environmental Science and Policy*, 105, 75–83. https://doi.org/10.1016/j.envsci.2019.12.012

Lamb, W., Mattioli, G., Levi, S., Roberts, J., Capstick, S., Creutzig, F., Minx, J. C., Müller-Hansen, F., Culhane, T., and Steinberger, J. K., 2020. Discourses of Climate Delay. *Global Sustainability* 3, E17. doi:10.1017/sus.2020.13

Latour, B., 1987. *Science in Action. How to Follow Scientists and Engineers through Society.* Cambridge, MA: Harvard University Press.

Latour, B., 2004. Why Has Critique Run out of Steam? From Matters of Fact to Matters of Concern. Crital Inquiry 30, 225–248.

Leiserowitz, A., 2006. Climate Change Risk Perception and Policy Preferences: The Role of Affect, Imagery and Values. *Climatic Change* 77, 45–72. https://doi.org/10.1007/s10584-006-9059-9

Leiserowitz, A., Maibach, E., Roser-Renouf, C., Feinberg, G., and Howe, P., 2013. *Extreme Weather and Climate Change in the American Mind*, April 2013. New Haven, CT: Yale Project on Climate Change Communication. Available at SSRN: https://ssrn.com/abstract=2292599 or http://dx.doi.org/10.2139/ssrn.2292599

Liverman, D. M., 2009. Conventions of Climate Change: Constructions of Danger and the Dispossession of the Atmosphere. *Journal of Historical Geography* 35, 279–296.

Manzo, K., 2010. Beyond Polar Bears? Re-Envisioning Climate Change. *Meteorological Applications* 17, 196–208. https://doi.org/10.1002/met.193

Matthews, P., 2015. Why Are People Skeptical about Climate Change? Some Insights from Blog Comments. *Environmental Communication* 9 (2), 153–168. doi: 10.1080/17524032.2014.999694

McDonald, R. I., Chai, H. Y., and Newell, B. R., 2015. Personal Experience and the "Psychological Distance" of Climate Change: An Integrative Review. *Journal of Environmental Psychology* 44, 109–118. doi: 10.1016/j.jenvp.2015.10.003

Medimorec, S. and Pennycook, G. 2015. The Language of Denial: Text Analysis Reveals Differences in Language Use between Climate Change Proponents and Skeptics. *Climatic Change* 133, 597–605. doi: 10.1007/s10584-015-1475-2

Metag, J., Schäfer, M. S., Füchslin, T., Barsuhn, T., and Königslöw, K. K., 2016. Perceptions of Climate Change Imagery: Evoked Salience and Self-Efficacy in Germany, Switzerland, and Austria. *Science Communication* 38 (2), 197–227. https://doi.org/10.1177/1075547016635181

Michael, M., 2021. When Ecocriticism and Rhetoric Meet: An Analysis of Greta Thunberg's No One Is Too Small to Make a Difference. *Research Journal of English Language and Literature* 9 (1), 33–35.

Morales, A. W., 2017. *The Rhetoric of Scientific Authority: A Rhetorical Examination of An Inconvenient Truth*. Graduate Theses and Dissertations. http://scholarcommons.usf.edu/etd/6910

Morton, T. A., Rabinovich, A., Marshall, D., and Bretschneider, P., 2011. The Future That May (or May Not) Come: How Framing Changes Responses to Uncertainty in Climate Change Communications. *Global Environmental Change* 21, 103–109. doi: 10.1016/j.gloenvcha.2010.09.013

Moser, S. C., 2010. Communicating Climate Change: History, Challenges, Process and Future Directions. *WIREs Climate Change* 1, 31–53. doi: 10.1002/wcc.011

Nerlich, B., 2010. 'Climategate': Paradoxical Metaphors and Political Paralysis. *Environmental Values* 19 (4), 419–442. doi: 10.2307/25764266

Nerlich, B., Koteyko, N., and Brown, B., 2010. Theory and Language of Climate Change Communication. *WIREs Climate Change* 1, 97–110. doi: 10.1002/wcc.002

Nicholson-Cole, S., 2005. Representing Climate Change Futures: A Critique on the Use of Images for Visual Communication. *Computers, Environment and Urban Systems* 29, 255–273.

Okuah, O., Scholtz, B. M., and Snow, B., 2019. A Grounded Theory Analysis of the Techniques Used by Social Media Influencers and Their Potential for Influencing the Public Regarding Environmental Awareness. In *Proceedings of the South African Institute of Computer Scientists and Information Technologists* 36, 1–10. https://doi.org/10.1145/3351108.3351145

O'Neill, S., 2013. Image Matters: Climate Change Imagery in US, UK and Australian Newspapers. *Geoforum* 49, 10–19. https://doi.org/10.1016/j.geoforum.2013.04.030

O'Neill, S. and Nicholson-Cole, S., 2009. "Fear Won't Do It": Promoting Positive Engagement with Climate Change through Visual and Iconic Representations. *Science Communication* 30 (3), 355–379. doi: 10.1177/1075547008329201

O'Neill, S., Boykoff, M., Day, S., and Niemeyer, S., 2013. On the Use of Imagery for Climate Change Engagement. *Global Environmental Change* 23, 413–421. https://doi.org/10.1016/j.gloenvcha.2012.11.006

Oreskes, N. 2004. Beyond the Ivory Tower: The Scientific Consensus on Climate Change. *Science* 306, 1686. doi: 10.1126/science.1103618

Pearce, W., Brown, B., Nerlich, B., and Koteyko, N. 2015. Communicating Climate Change: Conduits, Content, and Consensus. *WIREs Climate Change* 6, 613–626. doi:10.1002/wcc.366.

Pearce, W., Grundmann, R., Hulme, M., Raman, S., Kershaw, E. H., and Tsouvalis, J., 2017. Beyond Counting Climate Consensus. *Environmental Communication* 11 (6), 723–730. https://doi.org/10.1080/17524032.2017.1333965.

Pielke Jr., R. A., 2007. *The Honest Broker*. Cambridge: Cambridge University Press.

Rabinovich, A. and Morton, T. A., 2012. Unquestioned Answers or Unanswered Questions: Beliefs about Science Guide Responses to Uncertainty in Climate Change Risk Communication. *Risk Analysis* 32, 992–1002. doi: 10.1111/j.1539-6924.2012.01771.x

Rebich, H. S., 2011. *Thematic and Affective Content in Textual and Visual Communication about Climate Change: Historical Overview of Mass Media Sources and Empirical Investigation of Emotional Responses* [Dissertation]. Santa Barbara, CA: University of California.

Risbey, J. S., 2008. The New Climate Discourse: Alarmist or Alarming? *Global Environmental Change* 18, 26–37. doi:10.1016/j.gloenvcha.2007.06.003

Russill, C., 2008. Tipping Point Forewarnings in Climate Change Communication: Some Implications of an Emerging Trend. *Environmental Communication* 2, 133–153. doi: 10.1080/17524030802141711

Russill, C., 2018. The "Danger" of Consensus Messaging: Or, Why to Shift from Skeptic-First to Migration-First Approaches. *Frontiers in Communication* 3 (37). https://doi.org/10.3389/fcomm.2018.00037

Ryghaug, M. and Skjølsvold, T. M., 2010. The Global Warming of Climate Science: Climategate and the Construction of Scientific Facts. *International Studies in the Philosophy of Science* 24 (3), 287–307. doi: 10.1080/02698595.2010.522411

Sharman, A., 2014. Mapping the Climate Sceptical Blogosphere. *Global Environmental Change*, 26, 159–170. doi: 10.1016/j.gloenvcha.2014.03.003

Smith, N.W. and Joffe, H., 2009. Climate Change in the British Press: The Role of the Visual. *Journal of Risk Research* 12, 647–663. https://doi.org/10.1080/13669870802586512

Sörlin, S., 2009. Narratives and Counter-Narratives of Climate Change: North Atlantic Glaciology and Meteorology, c.1930–1955. *Journal of Historical Geography* 35, 237–255.

Spence, A., Poortinga, W., and Pidgeon, N., 2012. The Psychological Distance of Climate Change. *Risk Analysis* 32, 957–972. https://doi.org/https://doi.org/10.1111/j.1539-6924.2011.01695.x

Supran, G. and Oreskes, N., 2021. Rhetoric and Frame Analysis of ExxonMobil's Climate Change Communications. *One Earth* 4, 696–719. https://doi.org/10.1016/j.oneear.2021.04.014

Tannenbaum, M. B., Hepler, J., Zimmerman, R. S., Saul, L., Jacobs, S., Wilson, K., and Albarracín, D., 2015. Appealing to Fear: A Meta-Analysis of Fear Appeal Effectiveness and Theories. *Psychological Bulletin* 141 (6), 1178–1204.

Van der Linden, S., Maibach, E., and Leiserowitz, A., 2015. Improving Public Engagement with Climate Change: Five "Best Practice" Insights from Psychological Science. *Perspectives on Psychological Science* 10 (6), 758–763. doi: 10.1177/1745691615598516

van Eck, C. W., Mulder, B. C., and Dewulf, A., 2019. "The truth is not in the middle": Journalistic Norms of Climate Change Bloggers. *Global Environmental Change* 59, 101989. https://doi.org/10.1016/j.gloenvcha.2019.101989

Vavilov, E.-M., 2019. *Lessons about Activism from a Swedish High School Student: A Rhetorical Analysis of Greta Thunberg's Public Speeches on Climate Change*. Master thesis. Jönköping University School of Education and Communication.

Walsh, L., 2015. The Visual Rhetoric of Climate Change. *WIREs Climate Change* 6, 361–368. doi: 10.1002/wcc.342

Walsh, L., 2017. Understanding the Rhetoric of Climate Science Debates. *WIREs Climate Change* 8, e452. doi: 10.1002/wcc.452

Walter, S., Brüggemann, M., and Engesser, S., 2018. Echo Chambers of Denial: Explaining User Comments on Climate Change. *Environmental Communication* 12 (2), 204–217. doi:10.1080/17524032.2017.1394893

Williams, H. T. P., McMurray, J. R., Kurz, T., and Hugo Lambert, F., 2015. Network Analysis Reveals Open Forums and Echo Chambers in Social Media Discussions of Climate Change. *Global Environmental Change* 32, 126–138. doi: 10.1016/j.gloenvcha.2015.03.006

Wozniak, A., Lück, J., and Wessler, H., 2015. Frames, Stories, and Images: The Advantages of a Multimodal Approach in Comparative Media Content Research on Climate Change. *Environmental Communication* 9, 469–490.

Yıldırım, S., 2021. Do Green Women Influencers Spur Sustainable Consumption Patterns? Descriptive Evidences from Social Media Influencers. *Ecofeminism and Climate Change* 2 (4), 198–210. https://doi.org/10.1108/EFCC-02-2021-0003

Zhou, S., Barnes, L., McCormick, H., and Blazquez Cano, M., 2021. Social Media Influencers' Narrative Strategies to Create eWOM: A Theoretical Contribution. *International Journal of Information Management* 59, 102293. doi: 10.1016/j.ijinfomgt.2020.102293

20

A DESCRIPTIVE STUDY OF RHETORIC IN SOUTH KOREAN BUSINESS TEXTS

CEOs' Quality Management Rhetoric and Audience Responses

Mansup Heo

Introduction

In countries with a large economy, governments cannot cover all areas of people's lives, and private companies share their role in the country's growth and expansion of social safety nets. Even in the post-globalization era, the more companies there are that fill a significant portion of tax revenues and increase jobs, the more stable society will be (Park 2021). In companies, decision-making authority and responsibility are concentrated on the head of the company. CEOs' public statements (e.g., Steve Jobs' presentation for the iPhone launch in 2007) sometimes change the landscape of their company and industry and profoundly impact on society (Gallo 2010, p. 15). On the other hand, CEOs' remarks can also stifle innovation, put their company at risk, and create anti-business sentiment (Jung & Choi 2021, p. 85). That is why the CEOs' public remarks are critical.

Moreover, their remarks tend to be designed to convince their workers, customers (the public), and the media, so they almost invariably contain some rhetorical elements. Rhetoric refers to the use of means by a speaker to persuade an audience (Aristotle 1954). This chapter explores how the business texts presented by South Korean CEOs are rhetorically structured and perceived by the public, focusing on quality management discourse.

The top 10 South Korean business groups by total assets include *Samsung* (home appliances, mobile phones, and semiconductors), *Hyundai Motor* (automobiles), *SK* (semiconductors and mobile communications), *LG* (home appliances and second cells), *POSCO* (steel), *NH* (finance), *Hanwha* (military industry), *Lotte* (hotels and department stores), *GS* (construction), and *Hyundai Heavy Industries* (shipbuilding) (Abe 2021). The rhetoric that CEOs of these companies have commonly used is "Total Quality Management (TQM)" (Ha & Yoon 2019; Yoo 2010). As seen in some books and booklets (Escobar 2015; ISO 2015), TQM is sometimes abbreviated as QM (Quality Management).

DOI: 10.4324/9781003195276-25

TQM or QM refers to management that enhances the overall quality of corporate activities to realize customer satisfaction and strengthen market competitiveness. QM can be divided into four subcategories: quality planning, quality assurance, quality control, and quality improvement (Rose 2005). The ISO (International Organization for Standardization), which has spread the quality management standard called "ISO 9000 series" globally, defines quality management as a management approach that benefits all organization members and society in general (Lee & Cho 2006). In this respect, quality management has become a universal goal pursued by many of today's companies. CEOs commonly use rhetoric to make their employees and the public understand quality management and to elicit cooperation from them.

Quality management is known to be realized by entrepreneurship, which challenges new technologies, constantly innovates, and puts great faith in customer satisfaction (Dudek-Burlikowska 2015, p. 229). An empirical study showed a heavy impact of entrepreneurship on TQM implementation in some Egyptian companies (Soliman 2019, p. 179). However, it was also highlighted that, in the neoliberal system, entrepreneurs have been contributing to job instability and labor market flexibility under the guise of quality management and efficiency (Kim 2012). Quality management is also considered a standard fit for neoliberalism (Gibbon & Henriksen 2012). As long as such positive and negative viewpoints exist, CEOs' rhetoric on quality management may be perceived as a controversial issue rather than a universal axiom among members of South Korean society.

Business administration has been positively dealing with quality management to improve efficiency (Ha & Yoon 2019). However, rhetoric can approach quality management regarding persuasion and communication from a different perspective. Even if a CEO presents a quality management-related message in good faith, the audience may interpret it negatively without following the speaker's intentions. Since quality management is a common and popular business text that aims to persuade employees and the public, it is urgent to explore its rhetorical structure and audience responses.

Quality Management Rhetoric and Entrepreneurship

The quality first principle of *Samsung* founder Lee Byung-cheol (1910–1987) and *LG* founder Koo In-hoe (1907–1969) was evaluated in South Korea as "the entrepreneurial spirit that led the industrial revolution in this country" (Lee 2015, p. 203). Through continuous innovation and quality improvement, the two companies, which used to make low- and mid-priced products with a high defect rate in the 1970s, have become top players in the home appliance industry, with a 47% share of the global TV market in 2021.

Samsung Electronics Vice Chairman Lee Jae-yong, grandson of Lee Byung-cheol, emphasized the "super gap," another expression of quality management, through public speeches such as "to lead the 4th industrial revolution and prepare for future semiconductor demand, we must maintain the technological super-gap" (2018, August 6)[1] and "Let's create a super-gap in the system semiconductor sector as well" (2020, February 20).[2] The "super-gap" aims to be No. 1, significantly different from second place in terms of quality and efficiency.

Samsung's quality priority is assumed to have been shared with other large and mid-sized companies in South Korea (Park 2015). For instance, Chung Mong-koo, honorary chairman of *Hyundai Motor Group*, developed the group with assets of $28.1 billion in

2000 into the world's fifth-largest auto group with $193.6 billion in 2019, while using the slogans of "quality management" and "field management."[3]

TQM messages delivered by Korean businesspeople are accompanied by entrepreneurship and focus on customer satisfaction, product superiority and safety, market share, defect prevention, creativity, professional technologies, continuous improvement, profitability, and participation of members (Becker & Glascoff 2014; Lee & Cho 2006). Entrepreneurship that values innovation, competition, risk-taking, creativity, rationality, and technology was reported to improve firm performance by enhancing the quality of products and services (Sandberg & Hofer 1987; Wiklund & Shepherd 2005).

From the perspective of rhetoric that deals with the persuasive nature of the content, quality management is a "solution and persuasive theme" that CEOs present to their corporate members and social community, facing a "rhetorical situation" such as economic crisis and intensifying international competition. A rhetorical situation is a specific condition where a person in a responsible position should express his/her opinion and make a rhetorical choice (Bitzer 1968). Such rhetorical choice is to choose an argument and practice that seem appropriate to the situation and put this argument and method in a spoken or written form. As proposed by Bitzer (1968, p. 2), "The presence of rhetorical discourse obviously indicates the presence of a rhetorical situation." A leader's rhetorical discourse is a product of a rhetorical situation. The situation is an antecedent of the leader's agenda, and the leader is believed to actively interpret the situation and attempt a fitting response (Light 1991).

To the audiences who carefully watch and evaluate what the leader says, the leader's theme should appear as a rational decision and intuitive insight to cope with the situation. If business rhetoric is an argument out of context or a tautology, it would not be accepted by employees, the media, and the public. The quality management rhetoric of top management in South Korean companies has been usually regarded as a pragmatic argument relevant to their respective rhetorical situation (Lee & Cho 2006).

Confucian Values

The quality management rhetoric in South Korea appears to have pursued a compromise between commercial goals and social responsibility. In general, the rhetoric includes both commercial and ethical aspects. According to several scholars, Korean entrepreneurs' quality management rhetoric combines capitalist business ethics and Confucian ideas, fitting the Korean cultural environment (Jang 2021).

The quality management discourses proposed by the CEOs of large Korean companies are very similar to those of entrepreneurs in Hong Kong, Japan, and Singapore (Chen 1979). South Korean companies generally graft the ethical concepts of benevolence (*rén*), righteousness (*yi*), propriety (*lǐ*), wisdom (*zhi*), and sincerity (*xin*) of Confucianism onto their management (Park 2007).

Since Confucian traditions still influence the Korean people's language and lifestyle, the convergence between Western business practices and Confucian culture is effortlessly accepted by Korean businesspeople (Gong 2002; Heo & Park 2016; Jensen 1987). As noted by Xing (2015), a Chinese scholar, "South Korea continues to preserve Confucian culture, and most of its citizens still approve of Confucian ethics and morality." Some Koreans agree with Kahn's (1966) argument that Confucian capitalism can ameliorate the contradictions of Western capitalism.

In the relationship between Confucian virtues and quality management, managers with benevolence (*rén*, 仁) love their employees and treat them generously as part of a larger community. Benevolence enables smooth communication between employers and workers in quality management processes (Lee 2015, p. 210). Righteousness (*yi*, 义) is for business leaders to fairly evaluate the performance of their employees by the standards of quality management so that the employees can have a clear understanding of what they should and should not do (Kim 2016). Propriety (*lǐ*, 禮) is the state where benevolence is reflected in practical actions. Management should value employees and protect their self-esteem regardless of their position. Entrepreneurs are expected to be loyal to consumers, society, and the country and respect the interests of these three sectors. Wisdom (*zhi*, 知) is to educate employees so that they acquire sufficient knowledge and skills to achieve the goals of quality management (Park 2007, p. 65). Both Confucianism and quality management theory underscore the importance of education. Regarding sincerity (*xin*, 信), Confucius said that, without it, a person is like a wagon without a yoke (equivalent to a car without a steering wheel today). In the process and consequent stages of quality management, management must not lose the trust of the employees and consumers (Kim 2016).

The quality management rhetoric of South Korean CEOs has added these Confucian virtues to the essence of their entrepreneurship, promising lifelong employment, continuing education, and technology patriotism (Lee 2015, p. 212).

Korean-Style Neoliberalism

From a progressive point of view, the quality management rhetoric in South Korea is sometimes interpreted as a byproduct of Korean-style neoliberalism. Quality management has been argued to be fundamentally capitalist-biased in that it prioritizes superiority in market competition. The main characteristics of neoliberalism are globalization of capital and labor market flexibility (Springer 2016).

The Korean-style neoliberalism especially emphasizes the growth of the country rather than the allocation of resources, with the addition of South Korea's geopolitical purpose of preserving the country from threats from North Korea and its neighboring powers. To strengthen national power, it intensively nurtures companies with international competitiveness to increase GNP and allows for an easy readjustment of the surplus labor force (Kim 2018).

As a result, 62 business groups in the form of chaebols (South Korean conglomerates controlled by a family) account for 58% of the nation's assets. The proportion of non-regular South Korean workers is twice that of the OECD's (Organization for Economic Cooperation and Development) average. These facts are the basis for Korean-style neoliberalism (Shin & Kim 2021).

Critics noted that the quality management rhetoric of chaebols, such as *Samsung*, *LG*, and *Hyundai Motor*, implies wage control and restructuring of the workers who fall behind the competition (Kim 2012). As in the case of Wal-Mart, quality management is highly likely to conflict with the interests of the working class, as it tries to secure high quality and price competitiveness by suppressing costs such as wages and maximizing labor efficiency (Park 2001).

It has been argued that high-wage benefits are concentrated on a small number of CEOs and elite white-collar workers, while many workers are pushed to the margins by automation and the like. Some claim that the quality management rhetoric of CEOs of large Korean companies is insufficient to dispel these concerns (Kim 2012; Park 2015). Warzecha (2017) argued that the main concepts of quality management, including zero defects, are nothing more than modern myths, and QM hardly becomes a standardized procedure due to its complexity.

Audience Response to Business Texts

CEOs' remarks, press releases, stock market announcements, and advertisements are used in corporate management. Since all these forms of content aim to persuade employees, the public, and the media, the persuasive effect on the audience is very important.

The audience's response to business content can be divided into supportive arguments (e.g., 'I think this content will be helpful to me') and counterarguments (e.g., 'some of this content seems to be disagreeable') (Carlet & Cardozo 1970; Schlinger 1979). Audience responses also include their perceptions of the charm (e.g., refinement), credibility (e.g., dependability), and expertise (e.g., experience) of the orator (Ku & Jang 2022; Zaichkowsky 1985).

In the case of an entrepreneur's rhetoric on a controversial issue, such as quality management, the audiences can perceive the rhetoric positively or negatively depending on whether they choose a conservative or progressive viewpoint (Graham, Haidt, & Nosek 2009; Jost, Glaser, Sully, & Kruglanski 2003). Compared to progressive listeners, South Korean conservative audiences are known to prioritize efficiency and growth and be more tolerant of labor market flexibility (Yun & Rhee 2011). However, few studies have investigated audience reactions to the CEO's public rhetoric.

Research Methods

The literature on the quality management rhetoric used by South Korean CEOs, entrepreneurship, Confucian values, Korean-style neoliberalism, and the audience's responses was reviewed. Based on the theoretical discussions, the following three research questions on the quality management remarks of the late *Samsung Electronics* CEO (and *Samsung Group* Chairman) Lee Kun-hee (1941–2020) and the responses of South Korean college students were formulated.

RQ 1: How do the *Samsung* CEO's remarks constitute quality management rhetoric?

RQ 2: Do the audience's ideological tendencies and perceptions of the CEO's charm, credibility, and expertise influence their support or refutation of the CEO's quality management rhetoric?

RQ 3: Do the audience support or refute the CEO's quality management rhetoric based on entrepreneurship, Confucian values, and neoliberalism?

By its total assets, *Samsung Electronics* is the largest company in South Korea, and its CEO Lee Kun-hee was the son of *Samsung* founder Lee Byung-cheol. Lee Kun-hee was called the second founder of *Samsung* by encouraging *Samsung Electronics* to start a semiconductor business, increasing the company's sales 40-fold and making *Samsung* the fifth most valuable brand globally (Samsung Newsroom 2021).

On October 25, 2020, when Lee Kun-hee passed away, a news video[4] from *YTN*, a South Korean cable TV channel, and a news article[5] from *Yonhap*, a South Korean news agency, introduced 19 remarks made by Lee that were widely reported in the media over

20 years. For RQ 1, these remarks were analyzed qualitatively by the rhetorical framework of the persuasive theme, rhetorical situation, and practical means based on the literature review.

Regarding RQ 2, after showing the above *YTN* news video (length: 2 minutes and 24 seconds) to 308 students in a liberal arts class at a four-year university in Seoul, a survey was conducted on these students from December 2021 to February 2022. The survey results were analyzed with the SPSS 26.0 program, and an independent sample T-test, reliability analysis, correlation analysis, and multiple regression analysis were run.

Following the literature (Graham, Haidt, & Nosek 2009; Jost, Glaser, Sulloy, & Kruglanski 2003; Yun & Rhee 2011), conservative/progressive tendencies of the audience were measured with the following factors: "Conservatism (or progressivism) is suitable for solving social problems" (5-point scale, 1 = not at all, 5 = very much).

Based on previous studies (e.g., Zaichkowsky 1985), the source's "charm" perceived by the audience included the factors of "refined," "appealing," "dignified," and "looking good." "Credibility" consisted of "reliable," "fair," "credible," "truthful," and "trying to deceive" (inverse question).

Factors of "expertise" were "appears to be experienced," "professional," "knowledgeable," "qualified," and "skillful." Factors related to the audience's "supportive arguments" about the source's quality management rhetoric were as follows: "I think this content will be helpful to me"; "This content reinforces an affinity for the source"; "I believe this content suits my situation"; "I want to inform other people about this content"; "I want to get more information about this content." Factors related to the audience's "counterarguments" were as follows: "Some of this content seems to be disagreeable"; "This content is offensive"; "This content seems stupid"; "This content insults my level of knowledge"; "This content ignores me"; "This content is unrealistic and unnatural" (Carlet & Cardozo 1970; Schlinger 1979). These 24 factors were measured on a 5-point scale, respectively.

According to the reliability analysis results of these variables of the audience responses, the Cronbach alpha values were .761 for charm, .762 for credibility, .842 for expertise, .843 for supportive arguments, and .863 for counterarguments, respectively. All values were consistently above .6.

Regarding RQ 3, the students wrote their reasons for supporting or refuting Lee's remarks in the same survey, and these descriptions were qualitatively analyzed. These results complemented the results of RQ 1 and RQ 2 and showed the audience's perceptions of entrepreneurship, Confucian values, and neoliberalism in detail with abundant examples. These responses, in which the students specifically expressed their thoughts, reflect the public's honest feelings about the CEO's rhetoric on quality management.

Quality Management Rhetoric in the *Samsung* CEO's Remarks

As a result of the analysis of RQ 1, almost all of Lee's 19 public remarks introduced in the *YTN* news video and the *Yonhap* article consisted of rhetorical content directly related to quality management. Table 20.1 summarizes a rhetorical structure of quality management where the *Samsung* CEO offers a persuasive theme (quality management for a super-class enterprise) and practical measures (innovation and performance-based promotion system) while coping with a rhetorical situation (an economic crisis).

Regarding persuasive themes, Lee's public remarks, as shown in the examples below, repeatedly present the purpose of quality management while stating "quality" as the

Rhetoric in South Korean Business Texts

Table 20.1 Samsung CEO Lee Kun-hee's quality management rhetoric

Components	Key words	Typical examples of Lee's remarks
Persuasive themes	Quality	"Throw away quantity and go for quality."
	Super-class	"We'll grow Samsung into a super-class enterprise."
Rhetorical situations	Economic crisis	"In ten years, most businesses and products that represent Samsung will disappear."
		"With China chasing and Japan taking the lead, South Korea is sandwiched between the two."
Practical means	Innovation	"Change everything except your wife and children."
	Performance-based promotion	"I boldly suppress workers with bad performance."

keyword. The emphasis is on the quality of mobile phones, zero defects, discarding quantity, pursuing quality, design competitiveness, breaking through technical limits, and transitioning from low-quality mass production to high-quality and high-profit. Specifically, Lee's rhetoric of reducing the defective rate of mobile phones is firmly imprinted on the employees by the event that hundreds of thousands of finished mobile phones are burned in the factory yard following his instructions.

Pay attention to the quality of cellphones. Aren't you afraid of customers?
Anycall mobile phone burning event at the Gumi plant in South Korea in 1995

Since I became the CEO five years ago, I have been saying, 'NO defective products, no defective products, throw away quantity and go for the quality.' Still, the reality is that we are oriented towards quantity, quantity, and quantity.
1993 Frankfurt Conference, Germany

If we can't win consumers with a design in 0.6 seconds, we can't sell a product. In the 21st century, design competitiveness will become the battlefield.
2005 Milan Design Strategy Conference, Italy

To take the lead in change, we must break through the limits of the market and technology.
2014 New Year's Address

Lee's quality management rhetoric extends to *Samsung*'s specialized quality management rhetoric, super-class. The term super-class elevates quality management to the level of the manufacturing process to reduce defective products, with the ultimate and ambitious goal of becoming the world's best company in the semiconductor, home appliance, and mobile phone fields.

We'll grow *Samsung* into a super-class enterprise globally through forward-looking and challenging management, such as developing new technologies.
1987 inaugural address

Samsung may be able to get to the 1.5 class at best. However, first-class is, in my words, the term 'absolutely' is rarely used, absolutely impossible, if we do not change to quality management now.

1993 Frankfurt Conference, Germany

Lee's super-class rhetoric aims at the extreme supremacy of quality through the term super. *Samsung*'s quality management is characterized by the symbolic rhetoric of super-class in Lee Kun-hee's era, and super-gap in his son Lee Jae-yong's era. Subsequently, Lee Kun-hee's remarks secure the legitimacy of quality management by explaining a rhetorical situation in which *Samsung* has no choice but to engage in quality management. This situation signals an economic crisis that *Samsung* and South Korea face due to the intense international competition.

This is a real crisis. Global leading companies are collapsing. No one knows when or how *Samsung* will be like this. In 10 years, most businesses and products that represent *Samsung* will disappear. We have to start over. No time to hesitate.

Comments on the media after business recovery in 2010

It is different from the past ten years, so I think the ten years of the 21st century will come very quickly. Let's be a little more mindful of our responsibilities. I'm nervous too. Employees must also pay attention and do their best.

2010 'Proud Samsung Award' ceremony

With China chasing and Japan taking the lead, South Korea is sandwiched between the two. If we do not overcome this, we will inevitably suffer a lot. That's where the Korean Peninsula is.

Comments on the media in 2007

"Innovation" is proposed as a practical way to overcome the crisis and achieve quality management and top-notch quality. Innovation is expressed in catchy and popular language, such as "To say the least, I'm not joking, change everything except your wife and children" (1993 Frankfurt Conference, Germany). As a super-class methodology, innovation continued to be mentioned. Lee's quality management rhetoric is intrinsically intertwined with entrepreneurship that emphasizes change, challenge, sacrifice, and autonomy.

We must increase our competitiveness through bone-shearing innovation.

1998 New Year's Address

We need to rearm with a sense of crisis rather than being conceited. We need to complete creative management that is not afraid of failure and is alive with the challenge, innovation, and autonomy.

Supper for the 20th anniversary of the declaration of
new management in 2013

Underlining the crisis to justify quality management, Lee unifies *Samsung* and South Korea as a single group with a shared destiny. These remarks can be an attitude to fulfill corporate social responsibility. However, Lee also has a viewpoint derived from

Korean-style neoliberalism that the growth and risks of large companies are identical to those of the state, and the large enterprises lead the state.

> Samsung has already gone beyond a company for individuals or families to become a national company.
>
> *1989 New Year's Address*

It is not easy to compare companies and countries on the same basis. However, Lee contrasted *Samsung* with South Korea in terms of quality, arguing that the former is at a better level than the latter, as shown below. He applied the class rhetoric to South Korea to demand quality improvement in this country's political and governmental arenas. The quality management rhetoric goes beyond the company to the country.

> South Korean politics is at the 4th level, bureaucrats and administrative organizations are at the 3rd level, and corporations are at the 2nd level.
>
> *Meeting with the South Korean press in Beijing, China, in 1995*

> (Question: If you give a grade to the South Korean government's economic policies?) That's a tricky question. I don't think the grade is an F, but it is not satisfactory.
>
> *Interview with a South Korean medium in 2011*

> If not only *Samsung* but the whole of South Korea do not come to their senses, they will face great chaos in 5 to 6 years.
>
> *Interview with a South Korean medium in 2007*

A "performance-based promotion system" is presented as another practical way to achieve quality management and super-class.

> *Samsung* and my HR policy is performance-based promotion. I promote workers who do good jobs so they can do better while boldly suppressing workers with bad performance. This principle remains unchanged.
>
> *Interview with a South Korean medium in 2011*

The HR policy that pursues quality management and super-class leads to a nuanced view that treats several highly productive workers as "geniuses" and degrades some workers as "free-riders who do not get kicked out."

> 200 to 300 years ago, 100,000 to 200,000 people fed monarchs and royalty, but in the 21st century, one outstanding genius feeds 100,000 to 200,000 employees.
>
> *Workshop for developing human resources in 2002*

> I help those who want to run and those who want to walk fast do like that. I leave those who don't want to walk alone. Even non-walking employees are guaranteed food, clothing, and shelter. They are not kicked out. But they must not trip over the legs of their running colleagues.
>
> *1993 Frankfurt Conference, Germany*

In conclusion, regarding RQ 1, the *Samsung* CEO's public remarks appear to have a distinct rhetorical structure consisting of persuasive themes of quality management, rhetorical situations, and practical means.

The Audience's Reactions to the Rhetoric

Regarding RQ 2, according to the descriptive statistics presented in Table 20.2, among the 308 South Korean college students who responded to the survey, 55.8% were male, and 44.2% were female. Their rating of the factor "Progressivism seems to be suitable for solving social problems" was 3.26 on average (1 = not at all, 5 = very much), while the mean of the factor "Conservatism seems to be suitable for solving social problems" was 2.73.

After watching *Samsung* CEO Lee Kun-hee's quality management rhetoric video, the surveyed college students rated Lee's charm with an average of 3.43 out of 5, his credibility with an average of 4.14, and his expertise with an average of 4.40. The average level of the audience's supportive argument for Lee's quality management rhetoric was 3.52,

Table 20.2 Descriptive statistics about the audience's perceptions

Variables	Average	SD	Skewness	Kurtosis
Progressives	3.26	.829	-.793	1.957
Conservatives	2.73	.715	.240	1.758
Source's charm	3.43	.711	-.655	.944
Source's credibility	4.14	.528	-.050	-.522
Source's expertise	4.40	.500	-.397	-.743
Supportive argument	3.52	.857	-.343	-.147
Counterargument	1.97	.690	-.704	.345

(Male = 172, Female = 136)

Table 20.3 T-test on the audience's gender and perceptions

Variables		Average	t	df	p
Progressives	Male	3.24	-.510	293.714	.611
	Female	3.29			
Conservatives	Male	2.74	.306	306	.760
	Female	2.71			
Source's charm	Male	3.42	-.465	306	.642
	Female	3.45			
Source's credibility	Male	4.12	-.558	306	.577
	Female	4.16			
Source's expertise	Male	4.37	-1.328	302.886	.185
	Female	4.44			
Supportive argument	Male	3.50	-.547	306	.585
	Female	3.55			
Counterargument	Male	1.95	-.359	306	.720
	Female	1.98			

* $p<.05$, ** $p<.01$, *** $p<.001$

Rhetoric in South Korean Business Texts

Table 20.4 Correlation analysis between the audience's perceptions

Pearson correlation coefficient

	1.	2.	3.	4.	5.	6.	7.
1. Progressives	1						
2. Conservatives	-.495***	1					
3. Source's charm	-.155**	.274***	1				
4. Source's credibility	.004	.017	.355***	1			
5. Source's expertise	-.110	.150**	.367***	.320***	1		
6. Supportive argument	-.109	.278***	.554***	.266***	.341***	1	
7. Counterargument	.070	-.244***	-.613***	-.328***	-.452***	-.591***	1

* $p < .05$, ** $p < .01$, *** $p < .001$

while the average level of the counterargument for the rhetoric was 1.97. As confirmed by the results of an independent sample T-test, due to the audience's gender, their perceptions (progressive and conservative tendencies, feelings of Lee's charm, credibility, expertise, and support and refutation of Lee's rhetoric) did not change on average (see Table 20.3). The gender of the participants did not significantly affect their perceptions of the CEO's quality management rhetoric.

As shown in Table 20.2, all variables had normality without exceeding skewness 3.0 and kurtosis 10.0, so correlation analysis and regression analysis between variables were possible.

Table 20.4 shows the results of the correlation analysis on the audience's progressive tendencies, conservative tendencies, Lee's charm, credibility, expertise, audience's support for Lee's quality management rhetoric, and objections to the rhetoric.

The audience's conservative tendency positively correlated with the audience's support for Lee's quality management rhetoric ($r = .278$, $p = .000$) and negatively correlated with opposition to the rhetoric ($r = -.244$, $p = .000$). The audience's conservative tendency showed a positive correlation with their perceptions of Lee's charm ($r = .274$, $p = .000$) and expertise ($r = .150$, $p = .009$). Accordingly, the more conservative the audience was, the more distinctly they supported Lee's quality management rhetoric, suppressed objections to the rhetoric, and perceived Lee's charm and expertise. In contrast, the audience's progressive tendency did not correlate with support and objection to Lee's quality management rhetoric and negatively correlated with Lee's charm ($r = -.155$, $p = .006$). These results imply that the progressive audience did not significantly support or oppose Lee's quality management rhetoric and perceived Lee as less attractive.

The highest correlation coefficient was -.613 ($p = .000$), which appeared between Lee's charm and the objection to Lee's rhetoric. This result indicates that the more the audience perceived Lee as attractive, the less objection they showed. There was also a high positive correlation between Lee's charm and support for Lee's rhetoric ($r = .554$, $p = .000$). In addition, Lee's expertise showed a positive correlation ($r = .341$, $p = .000$) with support for Lee's rhetoric and a negative correlation with objections ($r = -.452$, $p = .000$). Similarly, Lee's credibility showed a positive correlation with backing for the rhetoric ($r = .266$, $p = .000$) and a negative correlation with objections ($r = -.328$, $p = .000$).

Mansup Heo

Table 20.5 Multiple regression analysis of the audience's perceptions

Dependent variables	Independent variables	Std. error	β	T	Sig.	Vif
Supportive argument (Model 1)	(Constant)	.506		-.974	.331	
	Progressives	.055	.055	1.026	.306	1.329
	Conservatives	.066	.161	2.920	.004**	1.408
	Source's charm	.065	.446	8.318	.000***	1.334
	Source's credibility	.083	.060	1.172	.242	1.216
	Source's expertise	.088	.141	2.738	.007**	1.223
	$R = .591, R^2 = .350$, Adjusted $R^2 = .339$, $F = 32.475$, $p = .000$, Durbin-Watson = 2.151					
Counterargument (Model 2)	(Constant)	.374		16.142	.000	
	Progressives	.041	-.090	-1.839	.067	1.329
	Conservatives	.049	-.120	-2.383	.018*	1.408
	Source's charm	.048	-.477	-9.691	.000***	1.334
	Source's credibility	.061	-.078	-1.670	.096	1.216
	Source's expertise	.065	-.244	-5.185	.000***	1.223
	$R = .672, R^2 = .452$, Adjusted $R^2 = .443$, $F = 49.793$, $p = .000$, Durbin-Watson = 1.803					

The results of multiple regression analysis identified factors affecting audience support and objections (dependent variables) to Lee's quality management rhetoric. As confirmed by the results in Model 1 of Table 20.5, the more conservative the viewers were and the more distinctly they perceived Lee's charm and expertise, the more the viewers supported Lee's quality management rhetoric.

The relationship between the audience's conservative tendencies and their support for Lee's rhetoric showed that the t-value was 2.920, the ß value was .161, and the significance was .000. Hence, the conservative tendency positively affected the support for the quality management rhetoric. Lee's charm (t = 8.818, β = .446, sig. = .000) and expertise (t = 2.783, β = .141, sig. = .007) also had a positive effect on the audience's support for the rhetoric.

This regression model had an F value of 32.475 at p = .000 and an adjusted R^2 of .339, showing 33.9% of explanatory power. Durbin-Watson (2.151) is close to 2 and not close to 0 or 4, so there was no correlation between the residuals. All VIFs were below 10, so there was no problem with multicollinearity between independent variables.

As a result of another multiple regression analysis, the more conservative the viewers were and the more distinctly they perceived Lee's charm and expertise, the more they suppressed objections to Lee's quality management rhetoric (see Model 2 of Table 20.5). Conservative tendency negatively affected the objections to the rhetoric because the t-value was -2.383, the β value was -.120, and the significance was .018 for the objection. Lee's charm (t- = -9.691, β =. -.477, sig. = .000) and expertise (t- = -5.185, β =. -.244, sig. = .000) also showed a negative correlation with the increase in objections to the rhetoric.

This model had an explanatory power of 44.3% with $p = .000$, an F-value of 49.793, and an adjusted R^2 of .443. Durbin-Watson was 1.803, and there was no correlation between the residuals. All VIFs were below 10, so there was no problem with multicollinearity between independent variables.

Perceptions of Entrepreneurship, Neoliberalism, and Confucian Values

Regarding RQ 3, the narrative responses of 308 Korean college students who watched Lee's quality management rhetoric video were qualitatively analyzed. The results showed that the audience perceived entrepreneurship when supporting the quality management rhetoric, while they evoked neoliberalism when opposing the rhetoric. Confucian values also influenced their support and opposition to the rhetoric.

The audience supporting Lee's quality management rhetoric sympathized with the values of entrepreneurship: innovation, competition, future, challenge, creation, rationality, autonomy, and technological progress (see the examples below).

Lee's remarks are a kind of truth bomb. It makes me think about how I should change myself.

Student A

Lee says that workers must constantly compete with each other while aiming for a super-class. Competition is the most significant driving force that helps companies and individuals grow.

Student B

CEO Lee Kun-hee's remark, 'Change everything,' was a preparation stage for the digital world. Like the metaverse, the rhetoric aims for a future realized by cutting-edge science and technology.

Student C

In particular, many viewers combined the entrepreneurial spirit of the CEO and *Samsung's* revenue surge and favorably accepted the quality management rhetoric. Interestingly, the viewers responded well to the positive outcomes of entrepreneurship and quality management. This result implies that the quality management rhetoric appeals to the public much better through "success (performance)-story (entrepreneurship)."

Samsung Electronics recently recorded a 41.7% share in the global DRAM market and 33.7% in the NAND market. CEO Lee's entrepreneurial spirit played a major role in establishing *Samsung* as a world-class company regarding the quality of semiconductors and electronic products and South Korea as a rising player in the global economy.

Student D

The rhetoric, 'Change everything except your wife and children,' was a fresh shock that brought a spring breeze to our economy. CEO Lee's challenging attitude became the foundation for the success.

Student E

Lee Kun-hee increased *Samsung*'s sales dozens of times, and *Samsung Electronics* became one of the largest brands. Proper management that uses science and technology and puts quality first has made *Samsung* a top-notch company.

Student F

Chairman Lee burned hundreds of thousands of his company's cellphones and asked the employees to pay attention to quality. Through innovation, his quality management created many decent jobs and contributed to national economic growth.

Student G

The audience who refuted Lee's quality management rhetoric raised issues based on Korean-style neoliberalism, such as hyper-competition, lack of communication, alienation of workers, and a structure in which profits are concentrated on chaebols. However, they did not directly criticize quality management and entrepreneurship itself.

CEO Lee Kun-hee's remarks about super-class and fourth-class were uncomfortable. Even things that are not first-class have their value. Pro-gamer Hong Jin-ho said, 'If you get a lot of second places, people come to remember you.'

Student H

The *Samsung* CEO seeks to be super-class and says no one remembers second place, but the tenth place is also worthwhile. Regardless of the outcome, the process of doing your best is essential.

Student I

Samsung's quality-first and super-class practices entailed the sacrifice of labor rights, such as union-free management. It doesn't fit with the ESG-oriented era.

Student J

The chaebol owner's remarks about forcing quality and innovation are offensive to some people. The words 'Change everything except your wife and children' is charismatic, but on the other hand, it sounds too direct and coercive.

Student K

Many progressive viewers tended to negatively evaluate the *Samsung* CEO's quality management rhetoric as a whole, questioning only several expressions. They seemed to think that these expressions, such as "I boldly suppress workers with bad performance," "A genius feeds 100,000 employees," and "Must not trip over the legs of the running colleagues," disparage ordinary workers.

Some of Lee's remarks focus only on results. Rather than boldly suppressing people with lousy performances, we should complement each other.

Student L

I understand that Lee promotes people who do good jobs, but I can't agree that he suppresses people who do not perform well. Entrepreneurs need to give opportunities to the less proficient and those who fail and move forward with them.

Student M

As Lee said, can one genius feed 100,000 people? More than a thousand people participated in developing the South Korean space launch vehicle. In the new age of technology, collaboration is more important than the abilities of a few geniuses.

Student N

Lee's strategy of going to the super-class by improving quality through innovation led by a few geniuses has some good aspects. However, in the achievements of these geniuses, many unknown efforts are melted.

Student O

Lee's words, 'Must not trip over the legs of the running colleagues,' sound like a subtly disregarding an average worker with average performance. Chaebols have forced people into brutal and tough competition to rank them.

Student P

Confucian scriptures were textbooks for public schools in Korea until about a century ago. However, today's South Korean students, except for some college majors, do not study the subject of Confucianism at all. Almost all survey respondents were unaware of Confucian concepts such as benevolence (*rén*), righteousness (*yi*), propriety (*lǐ*), wisdom (*zhi*), and sincerity (*xin*), so they rarely used these concepts in their narrative answers. However, some of the audience's reactions to Lee's quality management rhetoric can be interpreted as strongly related to Confucian values.

Lifetime employment is an important benefit that South Korean CEOs have generously given to their employees, but Lee seldom mentions it. In fact, in large Korean companies, including *Samsung*, this traditional form of employment is gradually disappearing.

Student Q

The lifetime employment system, derived from the Confucian concept of benevolence, has been widespread in patriarchal collectivist cultures of East Asia. As a father takes care of his children, South Korean CEOs have taken responsibility for the lives of their employees through this system. Accordingly, South Korean workers could live in the middle class with full-time, stable work without risk of dismissal until 60 years of age. Student Q's disappointed response suggests that Lee's management rhetoric treats this Confucian value as insignificant.

CEO Lee's quality management requires his employees to follow the standards to improve the quality of their products. He said he evaluates the employees' performances fairly by these standards. However, Lee was once convicted of illegally passing over the right of management to his son. Lee seems to have violated the standards of South Korean society, and this wrongdoing damaged *Samsung*'s image.

Student R

The Confucian value of righteousness (*yi*) is similar to justice and fairness to uphold moral and beneficial standards for a community. It considers that every community member must abide by their respective ethical and professional duties. Student R's response stresses that this principle should apply to CEOs without exception. As argued by the concept of Confucian righteousness, the quality management rhetoric of CEOs inevitably asks them to observe the standards for justice and fairness.

> Lee's comment, 'Pay attention to the quality of cellphones. Aren't you afraid of customers?' shows that he attaches great importance to working with sincerity and getting trust from customers. In his logic, quality is trust and the most critical value of a company.
>
> *Student S*

In Student S's response, trust is closely related to the Confucian concept of sincerity (*xin*). Regarding the words of Confucius, "A person without sincerity is like a wagon without a yoke," no one trusts a person without sincerity, so the person has a fatal flaw. In Lee's words, "Aren't you afraid of customers?" the fear is focused on a potential loss of trust. Lee's quality management rhetoric contains the value of trust and sincerity (*xin*), and the audience also shares this value.

As for RQ 3, the audience's perceptions of the *Samsung* CEO's quality management rhetoric converge on discussions of entrepreneurship, Korean-style neoliberalism, and Confucian values.

Conclusions

This chapter reviewed the rhetoric of business texts in South Korea, with a particular focus on the quality management messages commonly used by corporate CEOs and audience responses. To this end, news articles on the remarks of Lee Kun-hee, the second founder of *Samsung Electronics*, were analyzed. The results showed a rhetorical structure of quality management where the CEO offers a persuasive theme (quality management for a super-class company) and practical measures (innovation and performance-based promotion system) while coping with a rhetorical situation (an economic crisis).

The results of a multiple regression analysis of the responses of 308 South Korean college students who watched a video of Lee's remarks indicated that the more conservative the viewers were and the more they perceived the CEO's charm and expertise, the more distinctly they supported the CEO's quality management rhetoric. The audience's support for the quality management rhetoric was 1.8 times higher than the objections.

Quality management rhetoric is recognized as containing discourses on entrepreneurship. Most viewers responded favorably to the entrepreneurship in the CEO's quality management rhetoric, sympathizing with the importance of challenge, change, competition, creation, innovation, rationality, autonomy, and technological progress. Furthermore, several elements of the Korean CEO's quality management rhetoric seemingly connoted Confucian virtues such as benevolence (*rén*), righteousness (*yi*), propriety (*lǐ*), wisdom (*zhi*), and sincerity (*xin*), and the Korean audience also accepted these values naturally. Quality management rhetoric sometimes faced public opposition. Many progressive viewers perceived the rhetoric as part of neoliberalism that can marginalize average workers with average performance while favoring a minimal number of highly productive white-collar workers.

The theoretical implications of this chapter can be summarized in the rhetorical approach to the three aspects: (1) South Korean CEOs' quality management remarks as a business text, (2) the audience's responses, and (3) the discourses of entrepreneurship, neoliberalism, and Confucian values.

First, in this chapter, I selected CEOs' public remarks and analyzed them in terms of rhetoric and persuasion. The rhetorical approach to business texts helps to expand the scope of rhetorical research to the business domain and introduces a rhetorical perspective to business administration. Regarding rhetoric dealing with the persuasive nature of the content, the *Samsung* CEO's quality management remarks were grasped by the rhetorical framework of the persuasive theme, rhetorical situation, and practical means, which can be applied to further analysis of other CEOs' public content. Since entrepreneurs worldwide have taken it very seriously to promote quality management strategies to workers, consumers, and the media, text analysis based on rhetoric and persuasion can also be helpful in quality management research.

People in various countries daily use *Samsung* brand cellphones and home appliances, and *Samsung*'s semiconductors work in most electronic devices on the planet. Accordingly, although *Samsung* is headquartered in South Korea, it is familiar to almost everyone worldwide. This chapter provides a valuable opportunity to deeply understand the positive-negative aspects of the publicly unknown management rhetoric of the Asian culture-based global company. As can be seen from the fact that *Samsung Electronics* has been publishing "super-class" and "super-gap" slogans over the past several decades, the quality management rhetoric reviewed in this chapter has been a linguistic and managerial strategy traditionally shared by *Samsung*'s leaders.

While entrepreneurs' public remarks are usually aimed at public persuasion, the effectiveness of such business rhetoric in practice has been very rarely tested. This chapter measured the audience's candid reactions to the rhetoric quantitatively and qualitatively. The findings suggest that most viewers support rather than refute the quality management rhetoric. Therefore, it can be concluded that the quality management rhetoric exerts a certain amount of persuasive effect on the masses.

Factors that increase public support for the quality management rhetoric and reduce objections, such as the audience's conservative tendency and perceptions of the orator's charm and expertise, were also proposed. Among these factors, charm and expertise are included in ethos, one of Aristotle's three persuasive means: ethos, pathos, and logos. It can be said that the ethos retrieved from the virtues of the orator reinforces the persuasiveness of the quality management rhetoric. Although CEOs cannot influence the ideological orientation of their audience, the results of this chapter inform the CEOs that the progressive audience can negatively receive their quality management rhetoric. Then, the orators can pay close attention to the choice of vocabulary, and it can reduce the chance of mistakes and failures in persuading the audience.

Furthermore, this chapter shows the conflicting discourses of entrepreneurship, Confucian values, and neoliberalism perceived in the South Korean CEOs' quality management rhetoric. Twenty examples of the audience's narrative responses illustrate the positive and negative emotions that the masses may feel about the rhetoric.

Many viewers took the view, "I agree with the CEO's claims because his company shows outstanding performance in sales and revenue through entrepreneurship," which suggests that the quality management rhetoric needs success (performance)-story (entrepreneurship) to appeal to the public. The South Korean audience expects the CEO's quality management rhetoric to reflect the Confucian virtues familiar to them. For instance, some of them become disappointed when lifetime employment, derived from the Confucian concept of benevolence, is neglected in the Korean CEOs' management rhetoric. The *Samsung* CEO's quality management rhetoric regards *Samsung* and South Korea as a single group with a shared destiny. Hence, the two face the same rhetorical situation and use the same solution. The CEO naturally asks both *Samsung* and the South Korean government to improve quality control capabilities. The Korean audience tends to support the CEO's rhetoric because *Samsung*'s quality management contributes to national interests such as economic growth. The Korean-style neoliberalism, which places particular importance on national development to survive severe threats from neighboring countries, including North Korea, deeply permeates the CEO's quality management rhetoric and the audience's understanding of it.

The results also confirmed that many South Korean progressive viewers experience antipathy towards the CEO's entire quality management rhetoric due to only a few expressions, such as "I boldly suppress workers with bad performance." This reaction reflects the anxiety that most workers may feel marginalized by a few executives and elite white-collars leading quality management. The South Korean progressives linked *Samsung*'s quality management rhetoric to chaebol-led neoliberalism that promotes hyper-competition ("a brutal and tough competition") and social polarization ("One genius who feeds 200,000 people"). These responses imply that the public is oriented toward an open interpretation of quality management. From an applied perspective, this chapter demonstrates that it is necessary to strengthen collaboration with ordinary people in the quality management rhetoric because quality management cannot be realized only with the company's slogan and requires persuasion for many employees and the public.

Notes

1 www.hankookilbo.com/News/Read/201808061720040046
2 www.getnews.co.kr/news/articleView.html?idxno=187855
3 www.koreaittimes.com/news/articleView.html?idxno=104608
4 www.ytn.co.kr/_ln/0102_202010252214140303
5 www.yna.co.kr/view/AKR20201025020500003

References

Abe, M. (2021) 'The Relationship between Japanese and Korean Steel Industries'. *Korean Journal of Japanese Studies* 13(1): 84–111.
Aristotle. (1954) *The Rhetoric* (W. R. Roberts, Trs.). New York: Random House.
Becker, C. M. & Glascoff, M. A. (2014) 'Process Measures: A Leadership Tool for Management'. *The TQM Journal.* 26(1): 50–62.
Bitzer, L. F. (1968) 'The Rhetorical Situation'. *Philosophy and Rhetoric.* 1(1): 1–14.
Carlet, J. W. & Cardozo, R. W. (1970) 'White Response to Integrated Advertising'. *Journal of Advertising Research* 10: 35–39.
Chen, E. (1979) *Hyper Growth in Asian Economics: A Comparative Study of Hong Kong, Japan, Korea, Singapore, and Taiwan.* New York: Macmillan.
Dudek-Burlikowska, M. (2015) 'The Concept of Total Quality Management and the Contemporary Entrepreneurship in Practice'. *Journal of Achievements in Materials and Manufacturing Engineering* 73(2): 229–236.
Escobar, S. (2015) *Principles of Quality Management.* New York: Clanrye International.
Gallo, C. (2010) *The Presentation Secrets of Steve Jobs: How to Be Insanely Great in Front of Any Audience.* New York: McGraw Hill.

Gong, Y. (2002) 'Rhetoric, Debate and Its Epistemological Basis'. *Korean Journal of Communication and Information* 19: 37–63.

Graham, J., Haidt, J., & Nosek, B. A. (2009) 'Liberals and Conservatives Rely on Different Stages of Moral Foundations'. *Journal of Personality and Social Psychology* 96(5): 1029–1046.

Ha, S. & Yoon, B. (2019) 'Effect of Quality Management Activities on the Performance–Mediation Effect of Innovation Culture Moderated by Organizational Mindfulness Support'. *Journal of Korean Society for Quality Management* 47(4): 667–685.

Heo, M. & Park, J. (2016) 'Presidential Rhetoric of South Korea and the United States: The Case of Lee and Obama'. *Asian Journal of Communication* 26(4): 301–318.

ISO (2015) *Quality Management Principles*. Geneva: International Organization for Standardization.

Jang, Y. (2018) 'Confucian Management Ideology and Entrepreneurship in Korea'. *Journal of the New Korean Philosophical Association* 92(2): 223–239.

Jensen, J. V. (1987) 'Teaching East Asians Rhetoric'. *Rhetorical Society Quarterly* 17: 135–151.

Jost, J. T., Glaser, J., Sulloy, F., & Kruglanski, A. W. (2003) 'Political Conservatism as Motivated Social Cognition'. *Psychological Bulletin* 129(3): 339–375.

Jung, K. & Choi, S. (2021) 'The Effects of CEO Innovation-Oriented and Hindrance Messages on Film Innovation and Performance: Using Content Analysis Approach'. *Korean Journal of Human Resources Development* 24(1): 85–113.

Kahn, H. (1966) *The Alternative World Futures Approach*. New York: Hudson Institute.

Kim, D. (2018) 'Anti-Communist Liberalism as an Origin of the Korean-Style Neo-Liberalism – Continuity of Anti-Communist and Developmental State to Neo-Liberalism'. *Economy and Society* 118: 240–276.

Kim. S. (2016, November 29) 'Five Confucian Virtues for Business Management: Benevolence, Righteousness, Propriety, Wisdom, and Sincerity'. E-Today. www.etoday.co.kr/news/view/142 0016 (accessed 21 January 2022).

Ku, S. & Jang, S. (2022) 'A Study of the Influence of CEO Image on Brand Value –Focused on the Legal Process of Samsung CEO and Change of Corporate Value'. *The Journal of the Korea Contents Association* 22(2): 237–254.

Kim, Y. (2012) *Korean Chaebol and the Developing Country: Rapid Growth, Dictatorship, and the Formation of a Ruling Class*. Seoul: Hanul Academy.

Lee, H. (2015) 'Korean Entrepreneurship of the Industrial Age (1960–70) and Confucianism'. *The Review of Business History* 30(1): 203–226.

Lee, Y. & Cho, Y. (2006) *TQM and Six Sigma: Quality Management for Small Business*. Seoul: Hongreung.

Light, P. C. (1991) *The President's Agenda: Domestic Policy Choice from Kennedy to Reagan*. Baltimore: Johns Hopkins University Press.

Park, C. (2021) 'Korea's Exportist Growth Regime in the Post-Globalization Era: Implications for the Welfare Regime'. *Society and Theory* 39: 265–324.

Park, C. K. (2001) 'The Neoliberal Economic Policy and the Change of the Workers' Quality of Life in Korea'. *Korean Journal of Sociology* 35(6): 79–106.

Park, J. (2007) *The Analects of Confucius and Quality Management*. Seoul: Ewha Women's University Press.

Park, S. (2015) 'Analysis on the Cohabitation of Developmentalism and Neoliberalism in Korea'. *Journal of Asia-Pacific Studies* 22(4): 5–40.

Rose, K. (2005) *Project Quality Management: Why, What, and How*. Plantation. FL: J. Ross.

Samsung Newsroom (2021) '*Samsung Electronics* Solidifies Its Brand Value with Top-Five Ranking in *Interbrand's Best Global Brands 2021*'. Samsung Newsroom. https://news. samsung.com/ global/sam sung-electronics-solidifies-its-brand-value-with-top-five-ranking-in-interbrands-best-global-brands-2021 (accessed 21 January 2022).

Sandberg, W. & Hoper, C. (1987) 'Improving New Performance: The Role of Strategy, Industry Structure and the Entrepreneur'. *Journal of Business Venturing* 2: 5–28.

Schlinger, M. J. (1979) 'A Profile of Responses to Commercials'. *Journal of Advertising Research* 19: 37–48.

Shin, Y. & Kim, T. (2021) 'A Comparative Study on the Determinants of Wage in South Korea: Focused on PIAAC Data'. *Korea Social Policy Review* 28(4): 71–96.

Soliman, A. F. (2019) 'A Proposed Model for the Effect of Entrepreneurship on Total Quality Management Implementation: An Applied Study on Dairy and Juice Manufacturing Companies in Egypt'. *International Journal of Six Sigma and Competitive Advantage* 11(2–3): 179–203.

Springer, S., Birch, K., & MacLeavy, J. (2016) *The Handbook of Neoliberalism.* New York: Routledge.

Warzecha, B. (2017) *The Problem with Quality Management: Process Orientation, Controllability and Zero-Defect Processes as Modern Myths.* Walsrode: Verlag für Planung und Organisation.

Wiklund, J. & Shepherd, D. (2005) 'Entrepreneurial Orientational and Small Business Performance: A Configurational Approach'. *Journal of Business Venturing* 20(1): 71–91.

Xing, L. (2015, January 19) 'The Humanistic Link between China and Korea: Confucian Culture'. Institute of International Studies, Fudan University. https://iis.fudan.edu.cn/en/87/78/c16642a165752/page. htm (accessed 21 January 2022).

Yoo, H. (2010) 'A Study on the Efficiency Evaluation of Total Quality Management Activities in Korean Companies'. *Total Quality Management & Business Excellence* 14(1): 119–128.

Yun, S. & Rhee, M. (2011) 'A Reconstruction of Ideology Measurement in S. Korea'. *Korean Journal of Legislative Studies* 17(3): 63–80.

Zaichkowsky, J. L. (1985) 'Measuring the Involvement Construct'. *Journal of Consumer Research* 12: 341–352.

21

DISCURSIVE STRATEGIES OF PERSUASION IN THE FILM REVIEW GENRE

The Case of the Reviewer's Ethos

Dominika Topa-Bryniarska

Introduction

As modern communication grows ever more media-centric, real and powerful changes in the written form of today's public communicative processes and information transfer at the beginning of the twenty-first century have permitted us to capture the important influence of media discourse on our everyday life.

In our study's discursive, pragmatic and rhetorical perspectives, we believe it is necessary to undertake a genre analysis that can reveal its specificity in relation to the context taken in a broad sense. As we are mainly interested in the journalistic film review, this context is the one in which the discourse is used to express judgement functions. The film review is currently one of the most widely read journalistic genres, addressing a large and diverse audience in today's consumer society (see Miller 2012, p. 131; Corrigan 2015, pp. 15, 18; Gemser et al. 2007; Zheltukhina et al. 2020, p. 2). The film review genre is the type of film analysis with which most of us are chiefly familiar because it appears in almost every newspaper, and now, on the Internet, too.

The film review genre has been studied to date in many ways. On the one hand, film reviews have been analysed to probe into their conventional rhetorical structure (Bordwell 1989) or to assess their influence and prediction effects on film demand (e.g., Eliashberg and Shugan 1997). On the other hand, the genre has been examined to see how it differs from professional film criticism (O'Regan and Walmsley-Evans 2015) and online consumer (non-expert) critics (de Jong and Burgers 2013). In addition, as Bieler et al. (2007, p. 76) suggest, the genre has become relatively popular in computational linguistics, which mostly aims to classify "an entire review as either positive or negative".

Since less attention has been given to the issue of how film journalists tend to persuade their audience (see Baud 2003; Silva et al. 2018; Onursal 2006; Taboada 2011), we aim to fill this gap by focusing on the persuasive dimension of the film review. We refer here to the act of persuasion rooted in Perelman's approach (Perelman and Olbrechts-Tyteca 1971),

DOI: 10.4324/9781003195276-26

345

where the notion of *discourse analysis* is embedded both in the framework of functional linguistics of media discourse (Shamaksudova 2020) and in that of rhetorical argumentation (Amossy 2015). Within this framework, we intend to focus, through a qualitative approach, on the reviewer's ethos, which can be integrated, in our opinion, with the major aim of a persuasive and rhetorical discourse: to act on the recipient in order to create a general disposition to an action (Danblon 2005, p. 176). Aristotle (2007, p. 39) recognizes a special role of ethos in communication, as it is "almost the most authoritative form of persuasion". In this context, the purpose of our study is twofold: to investigate the persuasive construction of the journalist's ethos in the film review genre and to see how this Aristotelian ethotic appeal is exploited to influence the audience's opinion. The first step in that investigation is to discuss the concept of *film review* seen as a contextually based persuasive discourse in light of its rhetorical dimension (Mateus 2021, p. 5) and discursive strategies of persuasion (DSPs). Next, the corpus used in the study is described to demonstrate with French, francophone, and Polish empirical examples the scope and characteristics of the ethotic appeal analysed in our chapter. Finally, the study highlights how the persuasive construction of the reviewer's ethos manifests itself by borrowing some traces of expert, filmic, phatic, and appraisive discourse.

The Film Review Genre as a Contextually Based Persuasive Discourse and the Corpus

The contextual environment of film reviews already suggests a journalistic genre: it is written by specialists (film journalists) and published in newspapers or Internet platform sections. Therefore, it is an autodeictic (self-referential) genre, originating from the field of opinion (Todiraşcu 2019) and articulated around the "pole-commentary" (fr. "pôle-commentaire") (Adam 1997, p. 9). Film reviews – like other opinion journalism genres – give very specific judgements in the form of recommendations, which are the basis of their act of persuasion. This act manifests itself through various discursive strategies involving the deliberate intention to influence. Notably, the audience for this genre is seeking to be persuaded. People read film reviews in order to make decisions about which movies they should watch. "Normally, a review aims at the broadest possible audience, the general public with no special knowledge of film. Accordingly, its function is to introduce unknown films and to recommend or not recommend them" (Corrigan 2015, p. 24). As Gemser et al. (2007, p. 44) claim, "film reviews can actively influence consumers in their selection process" but also "forecast whether a movie will become a success or not". In this sense, film reviews appear in contemporary cultural activity as distinctly persuasive discourses, capable of affecting the recipient who is vulnerable to the seductive power of their DSPs, which intend to rally the audience to the presented point of view. The impact of film reviews is thus twofold: they assess the value of a film for audiences, which influences their decision-making process, and pre-shape opinions about a film. We will discuss this feature further in the following sections.

The Film Review as a Cultural Activity

Given the persuasive communicative techniques that the film review encompasses, it can be regarded as a genre assigned to a socio-cultural activity representing an integral part of the modern information space, which functions as a media discourse on another discourse; it is subordinated to the temporal criterion and refers to an independent audio-visual object originating in contemporary culture – the film. The film review genre is thus similar to reviews of various types and modes of art, such as literature, music, and theatre. Therefore, one of the significant features of the genre is its dependent and interdiscursive character. According to Baud (2003), film reviews are a sub-genre of reviews that are part of the broader media discourse. In other words, film reviews belong to a less specific genre, namely that of *an article of cultural criticism* that informs readers about current cultural events while also delivering a point of view (Rieffel 2006, pp. 55–56). In turn, a cultural criticism article belongs to a dominant type of discourse – the journalistic discourse.

When functioning as part of the cultural and media universe, the film review makes films known to a broader audience by providing basic information and explaining how the story develops without recounting key moments or revealing the ending (so-called "spoilers"). Regarding the formal characteristics of the genre, Bieler et al. (2007, p. 75) argue that a typical review contains a conventionalized constellation of linearly ordered details (the film's title, year of release, director, screenwriter, copyright notice, and cast). The functional characteristics are closely linked with the communicative goal of the reviewer, who intends to present the film's contents to the recipient and offer a personal evaluation. The review should thus explain whether or not the film is worth viewing (see also Baud 2003). Consequently, the film review genre functions as a communicative category that discursively displays itself as a space for the circulation of meanings and evaluation and as a "prescriber" of consumer goods, i.e., films to be seen or avoided. Thus, reviewers may popularize films as mass cultural phenomena by causing them to become more familiar or even admired by many people in case of favourable reviews.

Discourse Participants

Since the film review genre represents a kind of socio-cultural practice, its pragmatic criteria need to be identified. More specifically, it is necessary to determine the status of the participants involved (for a given audience, by a particular sender), which strongly determines the functioning of this genre (see Miller 2012). The film review genre is predefined by a sort of agreement or "a media communication contract" that allows participants to identify themselves, discover the purpose and constraints of the communication, and act in which they participate (Charaudeau 2004, p. 164). Media genres are places where the credibility of the contract that binds journalism to the public space is played out (Ringoot and Utard 2009, p. 16). Through this contract, the discourse participants can recognize their respective roles. The media communication contract, therefore, functions as an operational constraint for producing and interpreting the film review as a genre. The senders-journalists (reviewers-critics), aware of the conditions of the genre, are within their ethos, i.e., "within their rights to persuade, justify and defend an idea or an action" (our translation) (Charaudeau 2009, p. 3). These "rights to persuade" legitimize the reviewers' discursive role as advisors and guides to the cinema and explain the large quantity of verbs in the film review genre (see table 6 in Todiraşcu 2019). Although their status does not usually allow reviewers – who possess skills in the field of film analysis – to put themselves in a symmetrical position with respect to the audience, they sometimes pretend to do so in the framework of "feigned dialogism" (fr. "dialogisme feint") (Adam and Bonhomme 1997, p. 37). Accordingly, the film review journalist tends to establish an empathetic and evaluative communication that can "move" directly from the sender's saying to the recipient's believing (Bonhomme 2018). Since it is the evaluation element associated with the recipient's ethos that we consider essential in the film review (Taboada 2011, p. 11), we are justified in focusing on the persuasive mechanisms related to the justified assessment techniques of this genre.

Justified Assessment

The purpose of the film review genre is a critical and explanatory judgement about current works and cultural phenomena in the context of subjective and evaluative analysis. Therefore, the film review is expected not only to talk about a specific film but also to draw attention to it in such a way as to guide and inspire the audience in their cinematic choices (Baud 2003), providing what we expect to be *a justified assessment*. This possibility of (re)interpreting reality, connected with the suggestive expression of value judgements that is typical of the justified assessment procedure, constitutes the primary concern of every film journalist to persuade the audience to adopt the advocated idea. Moreover, being a kind of discourse where the journalist wants to be an expert and advisor for the audience, film reviews encompass explanation, analysis, and interpretation, which form the basis of the justified assessment mechanism's *expression of a judgement* and *meliorative/depreciative analysis* (Prédal 1996, p. 22). Leggett (2005, p. 5) claims that "the movie review is clearly one of the least complex forms of description and evaluation".

As with other pragmatically and rhetorically oriented genres, the film review genre can be regarded as a set of contextually-based (situationally-based) constraints due to its justified assessment device. Since Miller (1984, p. 151) observes that the social and rhetorical context defines a genre as "typified actions based in recurrent situations", we would situate the film review among the discourses related to social activities with pre-established purposes: "on this basis, a distinction can be made between four types of genres depending on the degree of variation and/or originality that is permitted within the genre" (Maingueneau 2017, p. 3). According to Maingueneau's classification, genres are categorized from "Type 1 genres" to "Type 4 genres", namely from those that are not subject to variation and follow strictly pre-established formulas and schemes, like telephone directories or birth certificates, to those that require the invention of new schemes and function as an individualized verbal product, such as advertising, fantasy or entertainment programs on television. Using this scheme, we can classify film reviews, travel guides, and television news among Maingueneau's "Type 2 genres". These generally obey a genre scheme but can also "tolerate distortions and give speakers the possibility of using an original scenography: a travel guide, for example, may be presented as a friendly conversation, a novel and so on" (Maingueneau 2017, p. 3). However, although these innovations are not supposed to modify the frames imposed by the genre pattern or question them, the author of a film review, though limited by genre constraints, is nevertheless free in the choice of forms of expression, such as anecdotes, digressions, and irony, which are sometimes reminiscent of the feuilleton style, devoted to light criticism.

Since the film review belongs to the universe of opinion journalism genres, its act of persuasion, integrated with the concept of *justified assessment*, aims to elicit compliance. Substantially, persuasion is a cognitive process triggered or implemented by messages that can affect the behaviours of individuals and their worldviews (Borchers 2013). According to Bülow-Møller (2005, p. 28), each persuasive discourse has the role of creating a kind of "shared territory" that favours "common visions and solutions". Thus, the study of the film review genre leads to identifying linguistic means effectively influencing the collective imaginary and the feelings and beliefs of the audience. This framework permits us to consider the ethotic appeal related to the rhetorical construction of public speaking or oratory. In Aristotle's view, ethos is discursive: the character [ethos] of the speaker is a cause of persuasion when the speech is so uttered as to make him worthy of being believed (see also Liao 2021). In the following sections, we will focus on the construction of ethos and its discursive representation in the film review based on the assumption of its essential role in persuasion as recognized by Aristotle's rhetoric (see also Baumlin and Scisco 2018). Accordingly, the film review genre influences the recipients' decision-making processes and pre-shapes their opinions about the evaluated movie. Therefore, reviewers must engage the audience in different compelling ways to be rhetorically effective, which involves carefully crafting arguments so that the desired outcome, audience agreement with the presented opinion, is achieved. Such a look at the ethotic appeal, whereby journalists use a certain axiological system to rally their audience to the preferred viewpoint, illustrates the importance of persuasive strategies of quickly and effectively "catching" the recipient's attention. This is how the DSPs underlying the reviewer's ethos take shape. The persuasive construction of the ethotic appeal is thus regarded as one of the Type 2 genre patterns introduced by Maingueneau's classification (2017) (see Table 21.1). We will now describe the corpus selected for our study.

The Corpus

For the purposes of our study, we have selected a corpus of 80 film reviews (the corpus sources can be found at the end of this chapter). From a methodological point of view, the starting point of our analysis is to bring together favourable and unfavourable journalistic reviews of two different film genres (comedy and drama). The next step in our analysis is to examine the collected texts regarding the persuasive construction of the ethotic appeal. Therefore, the reviewer's ethos is considered a media persuasion-based mechanism that aims to foster particular views and concepts. Since we focus on the persuasive construction of ethos as one of the film review's core patterns, the corpus based on two film genres – comedy and drama – that are very dissimilar in content and expressive techniques, seemed more compelling to us to conduct a well-founded analysis. We hope that such a corpus will allow us to gain insight into the research problem more profoundly than, for example, a study based on only one or two similar film genres.

We aim to study journalistic film reviews written by professional film journalists, intending to provide evaluation and be helpful to a heterogeneous audience (movie fans, amateur viewers, and cinephiles). Thus, given its target audience, the film review genre analysed in our chapter is clearly different from academic film criticism, which targets a specialized audience, such as film studies graduates or other film experts. Furthermore, journalistic film reviews differ from scholarly film articles in that they aim to include personal and subjective reactions to and evaluations of a film rather than to interpret it during phases of "deconstruction" and "reconstruction" of the film's formal techniques and thematic content (Golio-Lété and Vanoye 2020).

The films discussed in the chapter were released in the last 11 years. The selected reviews concern two well-known French comedies, i.e., *C'est la vie!* (fr. *Le sens de la fête*) (2017) and *Serial (Bad) Weddings* (2014) (fr. *Qu'est-ce qu'on a fait au Bon Dieu?*), and three dramas that won significant awards at renowned film festivals: *Joker* (2019, USA), *Parasite* (2019, South Korea), and *Corpus Christi* (2019, Poland). Since all these productions have gained international renown and have been highly publicized, they have

Table 21.1 Four different genre types according to Maingueneau's classification (2017: 3)

Type 1 genres	Type 2 genres	Type 3 genres	Type 4 genres
These genres are not subject to variation or only to very little variation; their speakers follow strictly pre-established formulas and schemes: telephone directories, birth certificates, etc. In fact, we cannot really identify "authors" for such texts.	In this kind of genre, the roles played by their participants are set a priori. The speakers enter a pre-established scheme that, generally, they do not modify. These genres best correspond to the definition of "discourse genre" as a socially and historically constrained communication device: television news, business correspondence, travel guides, interviews, etc. However, some of these genres may tolerate distortions and give speakers the possibility of using an original formula. A travel guide, for example, may be presented as a friendly conversation, a romantic novel, etc.	These genres require the invention of the original formula: advertising, folk songs, entertainment programs on television, etc. If you know that a text is an advertisement for a car, it is not sufficient to know by means of which original script or scheme it is presented. However, such innovations are not supposed to modify the frames imposed by the genre.	This kind of genre is the most difficult to define because the logic of such genres urges people to perpetual innovation. Therefore, instead of following strict genre patterns, authors self-categorize their own verbal production, such as "essay", "story", "meditation", etc.

enjoyed good visibility within the cinema's popular cultural and public space, and many reviews have been written about them. The corpus for our study comes from the mainstream Internet platforms for films and general information and the websites of French, francophone and Polish newspapers and film magazines. The corpus includes French, francophone and Polish reviews because French and Polish are our working and research languages, so the choice of such a corpus seemed natural to us for carrying out a valid analysis. We also believe that such a bilingual corpus will allow us to conduct a more complex analysis of the ethotic appeal that we consider to be the Type 2 genre pattern in the film review. The collected reviews are homogeneous thematically (famous films on social themes) and discursively (the journalistic opinion genre practised by professionals – film journalists). However, the corpus is heterogeneous regarding its readership because it refers to two groups of potential recipients. Among the target groups with different inherent socio-cultural characteristics, there are cinephiles (those searching for cultural news and thus seeking a specialist's opinion) and spontaneous viewers (readers and Internet users) simply looking for movies to watch.

The corpus of our study consists of 80 texts, and it is the total number of journalistic reviews written for the selected films. A corpus of only 80 documents is, of course, a small one with which to examine the persuasive construction of the reviewer's ethos thoroughly. Still, we hope to provide a sufficient preliminary analysis of the ethotic appeal in the film review genre to mark the beginning of this sort of study and support further corpus research.

Method: The DSPs in the Construction of the Reviewer's Ethos

Persuasion is a complex act that produces certain psychological effects for the recipient. To rally the audience to the presented point of view, the reviewer aims to make the recipients think that what is discussed is correct and well-founded in order to recommend or discommend a particular film. Therefore, it is possible to discern two functions of the DSPs underlying the reviewer's ethos in the film review genre: motivating people to agree with the journalist's opinion (orienting behaviour) and encouraging them to act (mobilization). These two functions also refer to the major aim of rhetorical discourse, which allows for the incorporation into the film review genre of the "illocutionary tone" of advising for or advising against (Bonhomme 2015).

The film review – like other opinion journalism genres – gives very specific judgements and evaluative analysis in the form of critical remarks, which are the basis of the persuasive act of the genre. This allows for the application of rhetorical analysis, as has been argued by Bordwell (1989, p. 35): "[I] shall treat critical rhetoric as an instrument for rendering the conclusions of critical reasoning attractive to the interpreter's audience". At the core of rhetorical analysis are the three modes of persuasion employed throughout the history of rhetoric: *logos*, *ethos*, and *pathos*. Logos is usually translated as the rational appeal, and it covers arguments in the form of enthymemes, examples, statistics, quotes from authorities, etc. Ethos is the ethotic appeal, which is based on the perceived character of the speaker. Aristotle claims that when someone appears honest, well-disposed and commonsensical, their message is more likely to be listened to. Finally, pathos is the emotional appeal that covers any attempt to trigger an emotional response in the reader or listener.

The ethotic appeal can be traced in the reviewer's attempts to present a credible, interesting or sympathetic persona. In order to be rhetorically effective (and eventually persuasive), the reviewer must engage the audience in a variety of compelling ways, which involves carefully crafting arguments so that the desired outcome, that is, audience agreement with the presented opinion, is achieved. The logical appeal can be found in arguments about the film's form and content. The emotional appeal lies in the incitement of the readers' feelings through an evocative description of scenes from the film. In this respect, the film review can be seen as a persuasive macro-act that discursively displays itself in two ways. Since a film review is a genre that is occasionally meliorative or depreciative, its persuasive macro-act corresponds both to an axiological space for the circulation of meanings and values (constative macro-act) and to an advisory space for "prescribing" films to be seen or avoided (directive macro-act). The Aristotelian concept of the rhetorical situation, in which it is essential to discover credible measures to persuade the audience, can thus be correlated, among other factors, with the construction of one of the film review's constraints – the reviewer's ethos that we focus on in this chapter.

For a review to be effective, it definitely takes using the correct language and style. Therefore, as Zheltukhina et al. (2020, p. 13) concluded, reviewers primarily choose nouns and adjectives as well as comparisons, metaphors, and varied expressive structures. Other rhetorical tools include a form of mock dialogue between the reviewer and the audience, questions, and direct recipient appeals. Such DSPs constitute the critical elements of the film review formula in Type 2 genres because they are oriented towards forming the recipient's opinion. Those techniques are exercised through the ethos the reviewers adopt in the discourse and through the image they create of the audience, which help intensify the participation of the communicating partners in the discourse (Bonhomme 2014, p. 166). Hence, the DSPs can also rely on the phatic function, which pragmatically corresponds to the desire to maintain contact between the interlocutors (illocutionary scope of *arousing interest by highlighting the film's qualities and faults*) as well as to reinforce this contact (perlocutionary scope of *touching, amusing, making people think*). On the cognitive level, the phatic function serves to actualize a socio-discursive community between the reviewer and the recipient (shared values, representations, knowledge) in order to co-produce the meaning, which characterizes contemporary persuasive discourse: "Persuasion is, ultimately, the co-production of meaning" (Baldi 2020, p. 338).

The persuasive "co-production of meaning" is supposed to be used to build a specific relationship to the described phenomena in order to direct the review's reception. This procedure aims to strengthen the audience's acceptance of the proposed opinion and recommend (or discourage them from watching) a particular film, which revolves around the three Aristotelian elements of ethos. Aristotle (2007, p. 112) points to these as "three reasons why speakers themselves are persuasive". In this sense, ethos is a composite of the three following elements: moral virtue (gr. *aretê*), goodwill towards the audience (gr. *eunoia*), and practical wisdom or competence (gr. *phronêsis*). On the other hand, if the speaker displayed none of them, the audience would doubt that the speaker could give good advice. If the speaker displayed only two ethos components, e.g., was only wise and virtuous, the audience could doubt whether that speaker's intentions were good (see Rapp 2010). Thus, all three elements need to be present, though perhaps in differing degrees, in the character representation of the rhetor, and all of them contribute to perceptions of the rhetor's credibility. In addition, the three ethos elements are responsible for a recipient's favourable or unfavourable disposition toward a speaker. For this reason, the reviewer needs to appear as a credible speaker who embodies character traits that the audience values. In other words, film journalists must persuade the audience that they are trustworthy, so their recipients will accept the presented arguments.

A reviewer's practical wisdom (expertise) is based on their experiences in a subject they advise on. By establishing their general aptitude and ability, they engage with the audience and build trust. The audience treats the reviewer as virtuous when they believe or know that the reviewer does not lie and tells the truth. When reviewers show goodwill, they try to appear friendly to others and seek to find an alignment or common ground between them and their audience. In the general sense, ethos comes down to trust. It should be stressed that the speaker must accomplish this trust by *what* is said. Aristotle does not insist on the possession of a good disposition. Still, he emphasizes that one must project good character (appearance), so ethos must be situated in the speech rather than in some prior reputation of the speaker (ethos is discursive) (see Rapp 2010). Hence, the reviewer tries to build a credible discursive ethos to be persuasively effective.

The discursive configuration of the reviewer's ethos is by no means homogeneous, which can be explained by the dynamic and evolving nature of modern journalistic discourse. In the construction of ethos, the reviewer borrows traces of various discourses – expert, filmic, phatic, and axiological – and exploits them for persuasion, which is associated with the dominant discourse of the journalistic opinion genres. These discursive traces are only separable for the purpose of our analysis, as they are deeply intertwined. As a result, the reviewer's ethos in the film review genre is distinguished by a particular discursive configuration (transition) that manifests itself through the activity of criticizing (commenting and interpreting), which is essential to it. We will highlight different discursive traces underlying this activity that have been integrated into the film review in order to reveal to the audience a particular ethos that the journalist wants them to see and that is projected in the genre itself through the DSPs (see also Oswald 2020).

An Ethos Based on Phronêsis ("Practical Wisdom") and Aretê ("Virtue"): The Case of Expert and Filmic Discourse

In this kind of ethos, it is a question of adopting the posture of an expert (*phronêsis*) and a credible and truthful advisor (*aretê*) in order to play the role of authority towards the audience (expert and filmic discourse).

Expert Discourse

The reviewers occupy a superordinate position as far as they are supposed to critically judge the described film, which should persuade the recipients of the journalist's competence and legitimize this expert position in the review (*argumentum ad auctoritatem*). The ethos based on expert discourse serves to express attitudes and judgements towards the information presented in film reviews. Based on the texts of the corpus, we can discern such a committed expert ethos through the following procedures:

(a) The "I" of the reviewer expressed by the first person singular as well as marked by verbs of opinion and recommendation: "I (do not) invite" (pl. "Zapraszam"), "I (do not) recommend" (fr. "Je recommande", pl. "Polecam"), "I (do not) believe" (pl. "Wierzę"), "I (do not) think" (fr. "Je pense", pl. "Myślę")
(b) Deontic modality structures: "must", "need", "should", "(it is) necessary" (fr. "il faut que", "devoir", pl. "trzeba", "należy", "musieć", "jest konieczne")
(c) Modalizing expressions, particularly in the form of adverbs: "surely" (pl. "z pewnością"), "undoubtedly" (fr. "indubitablement", pl. "niewątpliwie"), unquestionably (fr. "incontestablement"), "assuredly" (fr. "assurément", pl. "z pewnością")

When implementing the traces of expert discourse, the indicated structures play a significant role in activating DSPs by constructing a favourable discursive ethos. The DSPs help to express the author's positive or negative opinion regarding some aspects of the film under review, as illustrated by the above-presented examples. A superordinate posture as a film specialist can be constructed in discourse more or less distanced to gain a specific impression about the evaluated film. First-person statements, verbs of opinion and recommendation, and modalizing expressions are less distanced means that explicitly announce a judgement or commentary, revealing the presence of reviewers who argue and commit themselves as experts. The journalists then hope that the audience will agree with their opinion and follow the advice. Such a process of integration is also perceptible in the use of deontic modality, one of the more distanced procedures, which – like other elements of expert discourse – contributes to making the reviewers' words more dynamic.

Moreover, deontic modality, anchored in reality, gives the discourse the appearance and tone of an indisputable generality, as it takes precedence over volition or eventuality when exerting influence. In addition, it appeals to the recipients' sensitivity by affecting their sense of duty and responsibility. In other words, we tend to assume that anything based on reality must be more "sure, objective, and rational".

In their activity of criticizing, reviewers can produce and attribute to themselves an ethos that conforms to the one hoped for by the audience and imposed by the media communication contract, namely the ethos of credible and competent professionals. Therefore, while pointing out the positive or negative elements of the described film, the journalists demonstrate their competence and virtue as a trustworthy advisor (*phronêsis* and *aretê*), by providing useful information to develop the audience's knowledge, and by being helpful, truthful, and honest with the audience (*eunoia*). The reviewer acts as a competent advisor and expert who can enhance the recipient's understanding of things by providing them with customized tools and explanations to help them understand the film being evaluated. Since the primary purpose of the film review genre is to give a justified assessment in order to aid recipients in forming their cinematic choices, reviewers evaluate the overall quality of films and decide whether and why they should be recommended or not.

Filmic Discourse

The ethos of expert and advisor (*phronêsis*) is also marked by the vocabulary belonging to the film domain. However, this lexicon is not built of strictly specialized terms, understood only by a professional readership. The target audience of the collected film reviews is broad and diverse, which is confirmed by the media carriers of the texts: Internet websites for films and general information sites, as well as newspapers and film magazines. In this case, it is more a question of adopting a credible guide-advisor posture (*aretê*): the reviewer assumes the task of advising the audience on the value of a film by describing its content and analysing its strengths and weaknesses in order to give the recipients specific tools that will help them to understand the film better. Accordingly, film reviews are dominated by film-based lexis, which helps to point out important aspects on which the journalist wants to elaborate, such as specific film genres and the characteristics of people and institutions involved in filmmaking. Among the main determinants of filmic discourse, the following means may be distinguished:

(a) Names of film genres: "drama" (fr. "drame", pl. "dramat"), "family drama" (fr. "drame familial", pl. "dramat rodzinny"), "social comedy" (fr. "comédie sociale"), "black comedy" (fr. "comédie noire"), "slapstick comedy" (pl. "komedia slapstickowa"), "bloody thriller" (fr. "thriller sanglant", pl. "krwawy thriller"), "thriller" (fr. "thriller", pl. "thriller")

(b) Terms that refer either to the process of creating a film or to its characteristics: "director of photography" (fr. "directeur de la photographie", pl. "operator filmowy"), "screenplay", "script" (fr. "scénario", pl. "scenariusz"), "static images and colour variations" (fr. "images statiques et variations de couleurs"), "costumes" (fr. "costumes", pl. "kostiumy"), "viewing angle" (fr. "angle de vue"), "wide angle lenses" (fr. "objectifs grand angle"), "long shots" (pl. "długie ujęcia"), "direction" (fr. "mise en scène", pl. "reżyseria"), "turning points" (fr. "tournants")

Discursive Strategies of Persuasion in the Film Review Genre

(c) Cultural references and allusions to other films, directors, actors, or film festivals, usually for comparative purposes: "Mostra de Venise", "Oscar", "Europa Cinemas Label", "Festival de Cannes Awards".

The activity of criticizing, based on filmic discourse, acquires an analytical dimension since the reviewer tries to "verbalize" an immaterial cinematographic work by eliciting aesthetic structures, such as acting and the scenographic, visual, and sonic aspects of the film. The analysis revealed that film reviews are marked by the frequent mention of film-related jargon, which is one of the most typical patterns of the film review genre.

Thus, reviewers can stage – as in expert discourse – the DSPs based on their practical wisdom and competence (*phronêsis*). The activation of such an ethos becomes even more visible when journalists proceed to compare the criticized film with other cinematic and/or cultural works in the form of *argumentum a comparatione* and *argumentum ab exemplo* (see, e.g., Zarefsky 2019: 108–109). As a result, the journalists' interpretations are legitimized by various cultural pre-constructs circulating within the discursive community they are addressing. These pre-constructs, in turn, favour the establishment of a cultural identification conducive to persuasive effectiveness while also shedding light on the elements deemed relevant by the reviewer.

The use of filmic discourse thus aims to attract the attention of potential recipients-viewers, who deduce the good or bad quality of the film. This process of capturing the recipient's attention, which has the perlocutionary effect of shaping and consolidating the reception of the persuasive message among the audience – while increasing the prestige of the speaker (*aretē*) – is also part of the persuasive enterprise underlying the construction of a favourable ethos in discourse.

An Ethos Based on Eunoia *("Goodwill"): The Case of Phatic and Appraisive Discourse*

While creating their ethos, the reviewers aim to appear either as experts and advisors or as common viewers, equal to the recipients (*eunoia*). When adopting the ethos of common viewers, the journalists strive to get closer to their audience by referring to their own cinema experiences. In this situation, the recipients will be able to identify with the reviewers and adhere to their points of view. Therefore, the recipient agrees to "act" as the target group (audience-readers) who will be encouraged to watch or discouraged from watching the evaluated film. For this reason, the recipients acknowledge the fact that they will be subject to the reviewer's persuasive intent, as this is the primary purpose of the film review genre.

Phatic Discourse

In phatic discourse, the reviewers do not hesitate to solicit the audience directly, or at least to make them believe that they are cooperating discursively. Procedures borrowed from this kind of discourse are as follows:

(a) Explicit directive acts as well as direct interpellation of the recipient by the use of the collective personal pronoun "you": "rush" (fr. "précipitez-vous"), "take pleasure" (pl. "zróbcie sobie przyjemność"), "go and see" (pl. "wybierzcie się"), "you will never forget" (fr. "Vous n'oublierez jamais"), "inside you" (fr. "en vous"), "you know" (pl. "znacie")

(b) Sentences expressing suggestion and those that appear to be injunctive, containing the first person plural imperative, the inclusive personal pronouns "we" and "us", and generic quantifiers such as "everyone", "all", referring to the general public: "let's say" (fr. "disons"), "let's remember" (pl. "zapamiętajmy"), "we smile" (pl. "uśmiechamy się"), "we know" (fr. "on connaît"), "for everyone" (fr. "à chacun"), "each of us" (pl. "każdy z nas"), "we are all parasites" (pl. "wszyscy jesteśmy pasożytami"), "speak to everyone" (fr. "parler à tout le monde")

In the context of phatic discourse, the activity of criticizing aims to establish some common ground between the senders and recipients. "Common ground" means the sum of the participants' mutual or joint knowledge, beliefs, and suppositions. This shared basis is discursively actualized through the procedures of mimicking interactivity (*feigned dialogism*), which should foster the co-production of the discourse meaning. In this case, DSPs are articulated around the phatic function. The illocutionary scope of the discourse then consists of the stimulation of contact, while the discursive perlocutionary scope aims to reinforce this contact (see Bonhomme 2014: 166). Thus, in order to establish and strengthen interlocutory relationships conducive to persuasion (friendship, credibility) (*eunoia* and *aretê*), reviewers use collective and inclusive pronouns "we", "us", and "you", and the generic quantifiers "everyone" and "all", which – functioning as more convincing conduits for an argument than the single voice of a journalist – allow them to give credibility to their ethos as members of a wider community. The reviewers thus speak for themselves – as viewers and commentators of the film being evaluated – while also trying to involve the recipients in the expression of this judgement surreptitiously.

As for the directive act, it can be in itself an argument that encourages or discourages the audience from going to the cinema since it is based on formulas with a clear imperative illocutionary force: the directive verbs aim at impelling the recipient toward a concrete action or goal. They also stimulate dialogue and "insert" the recipients into the discourse to orient the film's evaluation along the desired interpretative lines.

In the preceding context, the involvement of phatic discourse in the activity of criticizing must achieve two complementary goals: on the one hand, to generate the feeling of proximity anchored in the phatic function, which mimics the ethos of a viewer and a friend engaged in communication, and on the other hand, to capture the attention of the largest number of recipients by the use of the *ad populum* arguments.

Appraisive Discourse

The reviewer uses appraisive means to make the film review more concise and engaging. These attributive structures specifying various characteristics of the entities mentioned in the analysed film reviews are one of the most typical patterns of the film review and constitute, next to the film-related lexicon, the genre's core element. The use of appraisive discourse also allows reviewers to function as truthful commentators (*aretê*) to justify and defend an idea or opinion, which legitimizes their discursive role resulting from the communication contract. Reviewers thus pose as an evaluative source (like in phatic discourse) as viewer-commentators who aim to stimulate the audience's reaction by using axiological and suggestive phrases. This reader-catching function, by which the sender seeks alignment or common ground with the recipient (*eunoia*), is all the more important in the film review genre as its media carrier conditions it. To have a chance of being read, the review must be noticed and arouse interest, which applies in particular to texts published in generalist sources such as those in our corpus (press and Internet), where the attention of the potential readership risks being dispersed by too many informational "stimuli". Among the appraisive discourse markers activating the viewer-commentator ethos, three groups of means may be discerned:

(a) Valuing and devaluing structures: "incredible" (fr. "incroyable"), "essential" (fr. "incontournable"), "stunning" (fr. "sidérant"), "a rare emotional palette" (fr. "un panel émotionnel rare"), "amazing" (pl. "zdumiewający"), "revolutionary" (fr. "révolutionnaire"), "disappoints" (pl. "rozczarowuje"), "dramatic shortcomings" (pl. "dramaturgiczne niedociągnięcia"), "uncomfortable" (fr. "inconfortable"), "success" (pl. "sukces")
(b) Tropes such as comparisons and metaphors: "like a punch" (fr. "comme un coup de poing"), "like no other" (fr. "semblables à aucun autre"), "a spiritual desert" (fr. "un désert spirituel"), "high-flying Asian cinema" (pl. "wysokich lotów kino azjatyckie"), "the heart of the entire film" (pl. "serce całej produkcji"), "deepened in a similar way" (pl. "podobnie pogłębiony")
(c) Interrogative acts followed by reviewers' immediate answers: "Success guaranteed? This is not always the case" (fr. "Succès assuré? Ce n'est pas toujours le cas"), "Is it possible that Todd Phillips made an outstanding film? Oh yes!" (pl. "Czy to możliwe, że Todd Phillips zrobił film wybitny? Oj, tak!"), "One of the film's strengths? The mix of genres" (fr. "L'une des forces du film? Le mélange des genres")

The DSPs activating traces of appraisive discourse are characterized by a strong interpretive investment on the part of reviewers who relate their own experiences as viewers and commentators (*eunoia* and *aretê*). The actualization of such an ethos brings a persuasive suggestiveness to the presentation of a film, making it more captivating and vivid due to affective subjectivity marked by tropes and valuing or devaluing structures. These appraisive discourse markers are twofold: on the one hand, they give an impression of univocity and intelligibility in the film's description by presenting its characteristics in a way that is "closer" to the recipients. On the other hand, they strengthen the persuasive effect of the viewer-commentator ethos to exercise an input on the audience's minds and generate more interest. This process can capture the recipient's attention by transforming the film review genre into an axiological discourse referring to various connotations, values, and emotions (positive or negative respectively), by which reviewers endeavour to project their enthusiasm or disappointment onto the audience-viewer. It is not surprising that appraisive structures are the most popular in the research corpus since one of the main aims of any review is to evaluate the film. Evaluation descriptors, mainly adjectives and nouns, constitute a relatively frequent category which comprises terms that, despite being universal, give an idea of the lexical specificity of the analysed film reviews.

The use of rhetorical questions, in which the reviewers themselves provide the answer, suggests possible explanations or comments and goes together with persuasion. This type of interrogative act allows the journalists to anticipate the audience's propensity to identify with the presented opinion.

In persuasive communication referring to the traces of appraisive discourse, the ethotic appeal, values, and aroused emotions serve to consolidate the evoked arguments and their credibility. Using such DSPs helps avoid the recipients' critical view of the reviewers' intentions and the content of their discourse. The activity of criticizing performed in this way makes it possible to obtain a discourse dynamization effect to persuade the recipients of the correctness of the reviewers' opinions. Such persuasive effects can also be observed in the three other discourse types underlying the reviewer's ethos.

The persuasive construction of the reviewer's ethos entails a selective, specific interpretation of the described reality, and it is also one of the most effective methods of attracting and keeping the recipient's attention. In addition, by implementing some traces of expert, filmic, phatic, and appraisive discourse, journalists can appropriately reinforce and dynamize the film review's content to make it easier to remember. Accordingly, introducing those four discourse types constitutes a convenient persuasive procedure from the reviewers' perspective because – even if they are not physically present – they can project their feelings and reactions on the recipients. Therefore, the use of such DSPs can make the recipients accept the intended assessment of a particular film.

Conclusion

We can observe from the obtained data that the film review – like other journalistic opinion genres – emphasizes the sender's engagement and subjective stance in communication. As a result, reviewers typically express their opinion by describing the evaluated film with a marked presence of various DSPs. These strategies allow journalists to be perceived as actively participating in the communication. In addition, they also help mobilize the recipients, introducing them into a subjective discourse universe that is activated by modalizing and appraisal structures, such as tropes, cultural references, rhetorical questions, directive acts, and verbs of recommendation. Our findings show that contrary to a "classic" demonstrative argumentation from logos (see Zarefsky 2019, p. 34), the described "impression-type" argumentation supports the process of constructing the ethotic appeal in the film review genre. It is also a very effective technique for creating the reviewer's ethos as a committed, credible advisor and guide to choosing a good film. This kind of discursive position is actualized by introducing some traces of expert, filmic, phatic, and appraisive discourse, all integrated into the dominant journalistic discourse of the film review genre.

The analysis revealed a marked presence of lexis and structures representing filmic discourse. The use of filmic vocabulary is a necessary feature of expertise in the domain of films, and representation of judgement also correlates with such expertise (one seeks out experts to hear their judgements). The importance of domain-specific vocabulary for the analysed reviews' variety is enhanced by the recurrent reference to several aspects that make up the cinematic universe, particularly film types and (sub-)genres as well as people and institutions involved in film production, but also characters, scenes, roles, plot, etc. This densely woven web of filmic discourse is linked together by discourse-organizing structures (expert discourse) that facilitate the logical development of argumentation. In addition, film reviewers establish a discursive dialogue with the readers (phatic discourse), as part of which they promote their own comments – positive and negative. However, this expression of the cinematic experience is counteracted by a wide lexical range of assessments and evaluations (appraisive discourse). So, it should be stressed that the analytic categories we have identified in this chapter, i.e., traces of various discourse types, are mutually reinforcing to establish a persuasive reviewer's ethos. This kind of ethos construction constitutes one of the film review's inherent Type 2 genre patterns. Accordingly, the formulation of a valuing or devaluing judgement is achieved through a double ethos (expert and simple viewer) that reviewers try to adopt and through which they appeal to their audience, aiming to help diverse viewers decide whether to watch the film or not.

On the one hand, the journalists occupy a dominant position in that they are supposed to evaluate a particular film positively or negatively. The reviewers thus see themselves as experts (*phronêsis*) and credible advisors (*aretê*) who can guide the recipients in their cinematic choices. By placing themselves in this expert position, confirmed discursively by the use of the first person singular, deontic modality, verbs of opinion and recommendation, modalizing expressions, and vocabulary stemming from the film domain, the reviewers show that they possess knowledge that they want to share with the audience (expert and filmic discourse). On the other hand, the relationship between the senders and the recipients can also be egalitarian (*eunoia*) (phatic and appraisive discourse), which may correspond to the symmetrical communication model that contemporary media discourse seems to favour. In such a relationship, the recipients are invited to co-produce the discourse meaning through the use of directive acts as well as structures expressing suggestion, appraisal structures (valuing or devaluing), and tropes. Therefore, when describing selected features of a film, journalists intend to persuade the audience of their assessment by means of an axiological community of thoughts with a clearly marked justified assessment procedure. As a result, reviewers try to "shift" their enthusiasm or disappointment onto the audience. This procedure aims to achieve persuasive suggestiveness when describing the film so that the recipient gets the impression that the reviewer engages in the interaction by building not only common assessments and values but also trust and identification, thus legitimizing the double ethos that has been created.

The double ethos of the reviewer as a specialist and viewer-commentator must put the recipients in the position of having to assign a set of specificities, positive or negative, to the evaluated film, which should encourage or discourage them from going to watch it. This is how the Type 2 genre pattern of film reviews takes shape, with the reviewer describing the film by giving the recipients reference points to help them form an opinion. For this reason, film reviews only inform as far as they persuade. The more explicitly present the recipient in a review, the more evident the genre's persuasive intention becomes. Thus, the reviewer is keen on having the audience identify with the point of view presented (phatic and appraisive discourse) in order to increase and intensify its impact on the audience (expert and filmic discourse).

Such a look at the persuasive structure of the film review, whereby journalists can share a particular axiological system to form the cinematic choices of their audience, emphasizes the technique of "catching" the recipient's attention due to a deliberately chosen ethos. Thus, the DSPs in the film review are supported by an effective double ethos that helps instil a particular viewpoint in the audience. There are no cultural differences in this respect, i.e., in the analysed corpus, Polish reviews were no less marked by the persuasive construction of the reviewer's ethos (expert and viewer) than were their French and francophone counterparts. However, this observation requires further verification on a more extensive and diverse body of data, such as other contrastive studies of the journalistic film review genre.

Given the corpus for this study, it seems that the orientation towards the phatic discourse is perhaps the only set of traces that is not inevitable in film reviews. Still, we focus on the film review genre from general media carriers, such as newspapers and popular websites, of which the phatic discourse is quite characteristic. The implementation of expert, filmic and appraisive discourse is, on the contrary, inevitable and undeniably influences the construction of the reviewer's ethos. Such discursive configuration existing within the film review genre makes the reviewer's ethos more persuasively effective and allows us to gain insight into some persuasive practices of contemporary media genre analysis.

Note

This research activity is co-financed by the funds granted under the Research Excellence Initiative of the University of Silesia in Katowice (Poland).

References

English-Language References

Aristotle, 2007. *On Rhetoric. A Theory of Civic Discourse*, 2nd ed., G. A. Kennedy (trans.). New York: Oxford University Press.

Baldi, B., 2020. Persuasion We Live By: Symbols, Metaphors and Linguistic Strategies. *Quaderni di Linguistica e Studi Orientali*, 6, 337–382. Available from: doi:10.13128/qulso-2421-7220-9706 (accessed 19 November 2021).

Baumlin, J. S., and Scisco, P. L., 2018. Ethos and Its Constitutive Role in Organizational Rhetoric, in O. Ihlen and R. L. Heath (eds.), *The Handbook of Organizational Rhetoric and Communication*. Hoboken: Wiley, 201–214.

Bieler, H., Dipper, S., and Stede, M., 2007. Identifying Formal and Functional Zones in Film Reviews, in H. Bunt, S. Keizer, and T. Paek (eds.), *Proceedings of the 8th SIGdial Workshop on Discourse and Dialogue*. East Stroudsburg: Association for Computational Linguistics, 75–78.

Borchers, T. A., 2013. *Persuasion in the Media Age*. Long Grove: Waveland Press.

Bordwell, D., 1989. *Making Meaning. Inference and Rhetoric in the Interpretation of Cinema*. Cambridge, MA and London: Harvard University Press.

Bülow-Møller A. M., 2005. Persuasion in Business Negotiations, in H. Halmari and T. Virtanen (eds.), *Persuasion Across Genres: A Linguistic Approach*. Amsterdam: John Benjamins, 27–58.

Corrigan, T., 2015. *A Short Guide to Writing about Film*, 9th ed., London: Pearson.

de Jong, K. E., and Burgers, Ch., 2013. Do Consumer Critics Write Differently from Professional Critics? A Genre Analysis of Online Film Reviews. *Discourse, Context and Media*, 2, 75–83. Available from: https://doi.org/10.1016/j.dcm.2013.03.001 (accessed 20 May 2022).

Eliashberg, J., and Shugan, S. M., 1997. Film Critics: Influencers or Predictors? *Journal of Marketing*, 61 (2), 68–78. Available from: https://doi.org/10.1177/002224299706100205 (accessed 21 May 2022).

Gemser, G., Van Oostrum, M., and Leenders, M. A. A. M., 2007. The Impact of Film Reviews on the Box Office Performance of Art House versus Mainstream Motion Pictures. *Journal of Cultural Economics*, 31, 43–63. Available from: https://link.springer.com/article/10.1007/s10824-006-9025-4 (accessed 20 June 2022).

Graff, R., and Winn, W., 2006. Presencing 'Communion' in Chaim Perelman's New Rhetoric. *Philosophy and Rhetoric*, 39 (1), 45–71.

Grafton, A., Most, W. A., and Settis, S., 2013. *The Classical Tradition*. Cambridge, MA: Harvard University Press.

Leggett, B. J., 2005. Convergence and Divergence in the Movie Review: Bonnie and Clyde. *Film Criticism*, 30 (2), 1–23.

Liao, Y., 2021. The Legitimacy Crisis of Arguments from Expert Opinion: Can't We Trust Experts? *Argumentation*, 35 (2), 265–286.

Macagno, F., and Walton, D. T., 2014. *Emotive Language in Argumentation*. New York: Cambridge University Press.

Maingueneau, D., 2017. The Heterogeneity of Discourse: Expanding the Field of Discourse Analysis. *Palgrave Communications*, 3, 1–8. Available from: doi.org/10.1057/palcomms.2017.58 (accessed 11 November 2021).

Mateus, S., 2021. When Homo Rhetoricus Meets the Media: The Field and Scope of Media Rhetoric, in S. Mateus (ed.), *Media Rhetoric: How Advertising and Digital Media Influence Us*. Newcastle upon Tyne: Cambridge Scholars Publishing, 1–28.

Miller, C. R., 1984. Genre as Social Action. *Quarterly Journal of Speech*, 70, 151–176.

Miller, C. R., 2012. New Genres, Now and Then, in S. Hulan, M. Mc Arthur, and R. A. Harris (eds.), *Literature, Rhetoric and Values.* Newcastle upon Tyne: Cambridge Scholars Publishing, 127–149.

O'Regan, T., and Walmsley-Evans, H., 2015. Towards a History of Australian Film Criticism. *Screening the Past*, 39. Available from: www.screeningthepast.com/issue-39-first-release/towa rds-a-history-of-australian-film-criticism (accessed 8 May 2021).

Perelman, Ch., and Olbrechts-Tyteca, L., 1971. *The New Rhetoric: A Treatise on Argumentation*, J. Wilkinson and P. Weaver (trans.). Notre Dame, IN: University of Notre Dame Press.

Rapp, C., 2010. Aristotle's rhetoric. *The Stanford Encyclopedia of Philosophy.* Available from: stan-ford.library.sydney.edu.au/archives/win2011/entries/aristotle-rhetoric (accessed 20 May 2022).

Shamaksudova, S. K., 2020. Media Linguistics: A Comprehensive Approach to Media Training. *The American Journal of Social Science and Education Innovations*, 2 (10): 427–433. Available from: doi: doi.org/10.37547/tajssei/Volume02Issue10-69 (accessed 13 October 2021).

Taboada, M., 2011. Stages in an Online Review Genre. *Text and Talk*, 31 (2), 247–269. Available from: doi: doi.org/10.1515/text.2011.011 (accessed 22 October 2021).

Zarefsky, D., 2019. *The Practice of Argumentation. Effective Reasoning in Communication.* Cambridge and New York: Cambridge University Press.

Zheltukhina, M. R., Slyshkin, G. G., Gumovskaya, G. N., Baranova, E. A., Sklyarova, N. G., Vorkina, K. S., and Donskova, L. A., 2020. Verbal Features of Film Reviews in the Modern American Media Discourse. *Online Journal of Communication and Media Technologies*, 10 (3), 1–16.

Other-Language References

Adam, J.-M., 1997. Unités rédactionnelles et genres discursifs: cadre général pour une approche de la presse écrite. *Pratiques*, 94, 3–18.

Adam, J.-M., and Bonhomme, M., 1997. *L'argumentation publicitaire. Rhétorique de l'éloge et de la persuasion.* Paris: Nathan.

Amossy, R. 2015. Quelle vocation empirique pour l'argumentation dans le discours. *Argumentation et Analyse du Discours*, 15. Available from: doi: https://doi: 10.4000/aad.2059 (accessed 11 October 2021).

Baud, D., 2003. Analyse de genre: la critique de cinéma dans la presse quotidienne britannique. *ASp. La revue du Geras*, 39–40. Available from: doi: https://doi: 10.4000/asp.1282 (accessed 12 October 2021).

Bonhomme, M., 2014. *Pragmatique des figures du discours.* Paris: Honoré Champion.

Bonhomme, M., 2015. L'interaction entre figuralité et registres discursifs. *Pratiques*, 165–166. Available from: doi: https://doi.org/10.4000/pratiques.2391 (accessed 14 October 2021).

Bonhomme, M., 2018. Modalités et stratégies rhétoriques de l'éloge dans le discours publicitaire. *Exercices de rhétorique*, 11. Available from: doi: https://doi.org/10.4000/rhetorique.681 (accessed 15 October 2021).

Charaudeau, P., 2004. Comment le langage se noue à l'action dans un modèle socio-communicationnel du discours. De l'action au pouvoir. *Cahiers de Linguistique Française*, 26, 151–175.

Charaudeau, P., 2009. Le discours de manipulation entre persuasion et influence sociale. Available from: www.patrick-charaudeau.com/Le-discours-de-manipulation-entre.html (accessed 20 November 2021).

Danblon, E., 2005. *La fonction persuasive.* Paris: Armand Colin.

Golio-Lété, A., and Vanoye, F., 2020. *Précis d'analyse filmique*, 5th ed. Paris: Armand Colin.

Grize, J.-B., 1996. *Logique naturelle et communication.* Paris: PUF.

Onursal, A. İ., 2006. Critique de film comme genre de discours. *Dilbilim Dergisi*, 15, 263–273.

Oswald, S., 2020. Pragmatique cognitive, argumentation et perlocution. *Argumentation et Analyse du Discours*, 25. Available from: doi: https://doi.org/10.4000/aad.4793 (accessed 20 October 2021).

Prédal, R., 1996. Les lieux de la critique. *Cinémas: La critique cinématographique*, 6 (2–3), 11–28.

Rieffel, R., 2006. L'évolution du positionnement intellectuel de la critique culturelle. *Quaderni*, 60, 55–64.

Ringoot, R., and Utard, J.-M., 2009. Le genre: une catégorisation peu catégorique, in R. Ringoot and J.-M. Utard (eds.), *Les genres journalistiques, savoirs et savoir-faire*. Paris: l'Harmattan, 11–22.

Silva, F., Leal, A., Purificação, S., Ferreira, I., and Oliveira, F., 2018. Crítica cinematográfica: análise linguístico-textual, in J. Veloso, J. Guimarães, S. Purificação, and R. Sousa-Silva (eds.), *A linguistic em diálogo: volume comemorativo dos 40 anos do Centro de Linguística da Universidade do Porto*. Porto: Universidade do Porto: Centro de Linguística, 431–458.

Todirașcu, A., 2019. Genre et classification automatique en TAL: le cas de genres journalistiques. *Linx*, 78. Available from: doi: https://doi.org/10.4000/linx.3183 (accessed 20 November 2021).

Corpus Sources

French and Francophone Sources

Newspapers and Magazines

Fiches du Cinéma
France-Soir
GQ Magazine
La Croix
La Libre Belgique
La Presse
La Voix du Nord
Le Devoir
Le Figaro
Le Journal du Dimanche
Le Journal du Montréal
Le Nouvel Observateur
Le Parisien
Le Point
Le Quotidien du Cinéma
Les Échos
Le Soleil
Le Suricate Magazine
L'Express
Libération
Marianne
Moustique
Ouest-France
Paris Match
Première
So Film
SudOuest
Télérama
20 Minutes

Internet Sources

www.abusdecine.com
www.archebdo.ch
www.avoir-alire.com
www.bande-apart.fr
www.bullesdeculture.com
www.cinecure.be
www.cinefilic.com
www.cineman.ch
www.cinemateaser.com

Discursive Strategies of Persuasion in the Film Review Genre

www.cineuropa.org
www.cinoche.com
www.courte-focale.com
www.criticat.com
www.critique-film.fr
www.culturopoing.com
www.ecranlarge.com
www.francetvinfo.fr
www.journaldugeek.com
www.kinoculturemontreal.com
www.lemagducine.fr
www.l'infotoutcourt.com
www.mediafilm.ca
www.mondocine.net
www.voir.ca

Polish Sources

Newspapers and Magazines

Gazeta Wyborcza
Polityka
Polska Times
Telemagazyn
Tygodnik Powszechny
Wprost

Internet Sources

www.antyweb.pl
www.anywhere.pl
ww.cobejrzec.pl
www.culture.pl
www.film.dziennik.pl
www.dwutygodnik.com
www.esensja.pl
www.falakina.pl
www.filmawka.pl
www.film.org.pl
www.filmozercy.com
www.filmweb.pl
www.film.wp.pl
www.gloskultury.pl
www.interia.pl
www.krytykapolityczna.pl
ww.kulturacja.pl
www.kulturadostepna.pl
www.kulturaliberalna.pl
www.kulturanacodzien.pl
www.kulturalnemedia.pl
www.kulturatka.pl
www.kultura.onet.pl
www.moviesroom.pl
www.naekranie.pl
www.noizz.pl
www.okiemfilmoholika.pl

www.pelnasala.pl
www.popkulturysci.pl
www.spidersweb.pl
www.whatnext.pl
www.wpolityce.pl
www.wtonacjikultury.pl

PART V

The Visual and Affective Domains of Descriptive Rhetorical Analysis

22

VISUAL RHETORIC OF OTHERNESS IN NEWSPAPER PHOTOGRAPHS OF THE EUROPEAN REFUGEE CRISIS

Jari Martikainen

Introduction

The European refugee crisis has gained vast media exposure during the past decade, and numerous studies have explored how the media frames the public debate on the crisis and influences people's perceptions of and attitudes toward refugees (De Coninck 2020; Jarmillo-Dent and Pérez-Rodriguez 2021; Maurer et al. 2021; Triandafylliou 2018). Even though the studies of media content have traditionally focused on texts, the importance of images as a means of communication has been increasingly recognized (Batziou 2011). Previous studies have also focused on exploring how media images frame refugees as "Others" by constructing a divide between "us" (Europeans) and "them" (refugees) (Chouliaraki and Stolic 2017; Martikainen and Sakki 2021).

The opposition between refugees and European nations is constructed through diverse means in media. On the one hand, refugees are depicted as a menace threatening the political and economic well-being and civic security of European nations (Chouliaraki and Stolic 2017; Holzberg et al. 2018; Šarić 2019). This type of news coverage frequently associates refugees with criminals (Banks 2012; Drüeke et al. 2021; Holzberg et al. 2018) or welfare abusers (Banks 2012; Yap et al. 2011) harming and exploiting European social benefits. On the other hand, refugees are depicted as vulnerable victims suffering from inhumane conditions in their countries of origin and along immigration routes (Chouliaraki and Stolic 2017; Giubilaro 2020; Šarić 2019). Whereas the first depiction frames refugees as active evil-doers causing harm to Europeans, the second depiction frames them as passive victims at the mercy of European nations (Chouliaraki and Stolic 2017; Mannik 2012; Vezovnik 2017). Even though these two kinds of depictions substantially differ from each other, both frames create an asymmetrical relationship between the "deviant" refugees and "normal" Europeans (Banks 2012; Batziou 2011).

This chapter focuses on newspaper images related to the European refugee crisis and discusses the visual strategies that frame refugees as deviant in terms of the visual rhetoric of Otherness. In contrast to previous studies, this chapter approaches photographs

DOI: 10.4324/9781003195276-28

367

of refugee crises from the perspective of visual rhetoric and elucidates how rhetorical strategies are employed to construct the understanding of refugees as Others. That being said, there are also news photographs that serve to humanize refugees and engender empathy toward them. Think, for example, of the iconic image of Alan Kurdi, a Syrian boy who drowned during his refugee journey. Think of the current news images depicting Ukrainian refugees as fellow Europeans (in-group). It seems that these images work to dissolve Otherness by eliciting empathy. Nevertheless, a host of prior studies have demonstrated how the majority of news images in the European media position refugees in the realm of Otherness (e.g., Banks 2012; Drüeke et al. 2021; Holzberg et al. 2018).

Similar to other forms of visual communication, news photographs contain rhetorical and argumentative potential (Kjeldsen 2017). Even though news photographs are expected to accurately represent the events reported on, "there is widespread agreement that a photograph is never an innocent producer of pure truth, and that a photographer necessarily takes a certain perspective when capturing events" (Kjeldsen 2017: 52). Batziou (2011: 31) similarly argues that "photographs are capable of transmitting ideologically charged messages in subtle ways and influencing the reception and interpretation of news, regardless of the accompanying text." Because photographs appear to depict reality, the subtle ways news images frame refugees as Others often remain unnoticed by the audience, making photographs a powerful means of transmitting (hidden) ideologically charged messages about refugees (Amores et al. 2019; Batziou 2011). Therefore, there is a need for studies elucidating the means of visual rhetoric employed in media photographs that construct the image of refugees as Others and can encourage discrimination.

This chapter focuses on newspaper images related to the European refugee crisis. It discusses the visual strategies that frame refugees as deviant in terms of the visual rhetoric of Otherness. The chapter is structured as follows. First, it discusses the notion of Otherness in relation to the refugee crisis and elaborates on visual rhetoric as a field of study. Thereafter, the chapter presents Othering visual strategies in news images with a focus on persons, objects, environments, and means of visual expression. Finally, the chapter presents justifications for the importance of studying and increasing awareness of visual rhetoric in news images of refugees.

Otherness

The concept of Otherness, which is frequently used in studies of media coverage of refugee crises, is based on the stereotypical understanding of refugees as deviant strangers (Martikainen and Sakki 2021). Batziou (2011: 41) argues that "the practice of framing immigrants as 'others' not only reflects the dominant ideology towards them in the receiving societies, it further confirms, fixes and consequently eternalizes their perception as outsiders." This way of representation marginalizes refugees and places them in the realm of Otherness (Jarmillo-Dent and Pérez-Rodriguez 2021; Vezovnik 2017).

Stereotypical portrayals of refugees have a communicative power because they are based on, address, and strengthen the understanding of refugees as deviant and dangerous that already exists in European societies (Batziou 2011; Glâveanu et al. 2018). For this reason, even the most subtle and covert forms of prejudiced communication suffice to address and activate these stereotypical understandings (Konstantopoulou et al. 2022). Visually communicated stereotypes may function even more effectively than verbally communicated prejudices because images strongly appeal to emotions (Johnson 2011). Due to the lifelike and naturalistic illusion of photographs, news photographs may legitimize the stereotypical understanding, "making it seem as indisputable truth and functioning as 'evidence'" (Batziou 2011: 43).

The aforementioned tendency to use negative stereotypes when depicting refugees may be understood as an Othering strategy with two functions. On the one hand, it makes Europeans look better and superior compared to inferior refugees (Batziou 2011; Konstantopoulou et al. 2022). On the other hand, it homogenizes the out-group, whereby refugees are not treated as individuals but as a deviant entity, which emphasizes the difference between us and them (Batziou 2011; Câtálin-George 2014). According to Jarmillo-Dent and Pérez-Rodriguez (2021: 122), visually and verbally constructed Otherness is "a means of exerting power over the group of people that is perceived as inferior." These framings influence the way people perceive refugee crises and refugees (Batziou 2011). Therefore, it is important to understand that Otherness is constructed and not an inborn quality of a person or a group of people (Câtálin-George 2014).

The conception of Otherness in Western media is constructed based on an ethnocentric approach in terms of oppositions between European/Western and non-European/non-Western nations and cultures (Chouliaraki and Stolic 2017). The division between superior Europeans and inferior refugees who are dependent on their generosity as well as the depiction of refugees either as victims or as evil-doers echo problematic colonial attitudes (Bleiker et al. 2013; Boucher 2019). As Chouliaraki and Stolic (2017: 1164) put it, "media visualities are informed by a deep-seated orientalism that continues to reproduce historical tropes of colonial imagery in contemporary portrayals of mobile populations." By elaborating the visual rhetoric of news images related to the refugee crisis, this chapter seeks to develop an understanding of how Othering communication is constructed visually.

Visual Rhetoric

This chapter draws on Sonja Foss's (2005) conception of visual rhetoric and complements it with a sociosemiotic approach. This combination makes it possible to focus on both the visual construction of an image and its socially and culturally preferred readings. According to Foss (2005: 143), "visual rhetoric is the actual image rhetors generate when they use visual symbols for the purpose of communicating." Hence, Foss's (2005) conception of visual rhetoric emphasizes the visual construction of the image, in which the image maker aims to communicate specific meanings to an audience through a deliberate selection of certain means of visual expression. This kind of performative approach to visual rhetoric understands images as visual arguments that gain their meanings from and are studied in relation to their contexts (Kjeldsen 2017; Olson et al. 2008). Hence, when interpreting the meaning of the images, the study of visual rhetoric goes beyond the immediate image itself to constructing its meaning in relation to the social, political, and cultural context (Foss 2005; Lefsrud et al. 2015; Patton 2020). The visual rhetor's intention may not only be to communicate certain meanings but also to persuade people to adopt a certain view on the topic of the image (Olson et al. 2008). Consequently, in addition to the visual-communicative quality of the images themselves, the ways in which images are used to create meaning and influence people's thoughts and actions in a specific context can be identified as the scope of visual rhetoric research (ibid.).

Rhetoric and (social) semiotics are closely related. They are linked to the central concept of classical rhetoric known as *dispositio* (disposition) in terms of studying how the arrangement of visual elements in an image (including gesture, posture, and proximity) constructs its meaning (van Leeuwen 2017). The sociosemiotic approach to visual rhetoric emphasizes the importance of understanding elements of visual expression as carriers of specific, culturally, and socially shared meanings (Kress and van Leeuwen 2006; van Leeuwen 2017). From this perspective, making an image is not a mere visual act but simultaneously a social act. In other words, the image maker does not operate with mere visual elements but rather with socially meaningful visual elements. This kind of "socio-visual" vocabulary enables not only visual communication at large but also the use of images for certain social and political functions (Martikainen 2019).

The interpretation of meanings communicated through images, in turn, is "a critical analytical tool" that provides a "rhetorical perspective on visual imagery" (Foss 2005: 145). Examining not only the forms and contents of images but also their functions in terms of constructing and influencing social views and relations (Danesi 2017; Kress and van Leeuwen, 2006; Martikainen 2019), visual rhetoric provides a tool for critically discussing news images of refugee crises as a means of rhetorizing Otherness.

Visual Rhetoric of Otherness in Newspaper Photographs of Refugees

In the analysis of visual rhetoric, attention is given to elements presented and suggested in the image (Foss 2005). Presented elements include the subject matter (persons, objects, and environments depicted) and the means of visual expression used in depicting them (color, composition, and viewing angle). Suggested elements refer to the meanings constructed based on the visually presented elements (Foss 2005; Martikainen 2019).

In the following, examples of the visual rhetoric of Otherness in news images of refugees are given both in terms of the subject matter and means of visual expression. Even though these elements are intertwined in the image and contribute to each other's meanings (Danesi 2017), I choose to present some common means of visual expression separately to elucidate both the constructed nature of photographs and the potential of visual means of expression to construct a rhetorical stance on the images of refugees.

The meanings of certain subject matters and ways of depicting refugees are elaborated based on the literature on news images of refugees. Referring to ample literature when elaborating the meanings associated with the images, I show that there is a relatively widely shared understanding of the visual rhetoric employed in images of refugees in Western cultures. Regarding the three essential momentums of the visual rhetoric of images – form, content, and function (Martikainen 2019) – this section mainly concentrates on the first two. Function is discussed in the concluding comments.

Depictions of People

This section elaborates some of the most common ways of depicting refugees in news photographs. In addition, attention is given to authority figures (police, military, border patrols) and celebrities included in images of refugees.

Crowds of Refugees

A number of studies have brought up the fact that refugees are frequently depicted as a mass of people (Chouliaraki and Stolic 2017; Martikainen and Sakki 2021; Šarić 2019; Vezovnik and Šarić 2020). In this type of imagery, refugees are depicted as a faceless herd, with little attention given to their individual features, backgrounds, or destinations.

These images construct an understanding of refugees as a homogeneous group, implying that refugees form a distinct social type that is different from us (Bleiker et al. 2013; Lenette and Miskovic 2018; Memou 2019). Massification as a visual rhetorical strategy of Othering depersonalizes refugees and strips them of their distinct, complex identities (Banks 2012; Vezovnik and Šarić 2020; Wilmott 2017).

Massification as a visual rhetorical strategy underlines the (huge) number of refugees, which has been found to contribute to the perception of refugees as a danger to security and state sovereignty (Drüeke et al. 2021; Lenette and Miskovic 2018). These images often feature a long-distance shot that reinforces the perception of the magnitude of the refugees and makes them appear as a group of distant strangers, exceeding the boundaries of the photograph (Kress and van Leeuwen 2006). Verbal expressions such as "flow," "flood," "wave," and "current" have been used to articulate the magnitude of refugees (Drüeke et al. 2021). As an Othering visual rhetorical strategy, massification constructs the understanding of refugees as an out-group that is disturbing and even threatening the well-being of the in-group (Europeans) (Banks 2012). By communicating threat, these images construct an understanding of Europeans as victims of the refugee crisis, reinforcing the opposition between refugees and Europeans (see Vezovnik 2017).

The notion of Otherness is often further emphasized by the fact that in these massified depictions, refugees do not normally make visual contact with the viewer but often turn their backs toward the viewer so that their faces cannot be seen (Martikainen and Sakki 2021). Hence, the refugees are not depicted as individuals but as an anonymous mass of people (Kress and van Leeuwen 2006). The absence of any visual interpersonal tie between the depicted refugees and the viewer indicates their mutual detachment and makes refugees objects of the viewers' Eurocentric gaze (Kress and van Leeuwen 2006; Memou 2019).

Images of Smaller Groups of Refugees and Individuals

The visual rhetorical strategies used in photographs depicting refugee men are often different from those depicting refugee women and children. For this reason, I first elucidate the strategies used in depicting male refugees and thereafter elaborate on the strategies used in depicting female refugees and children.

Several studies have shown how most news images of refugees depict men either in refugee camps or reception centers. Frequently, they are depicted as doing nothing but spending – or killing – time (Martikainen and Sakki 2021). This kind of detachment from everyday activities makes refugee men look unproductive and lazy, which has prompted accusations of them being fake refugees exploiting the European welfare system (Banks 2012; Yap et al. 2011). This type of imagery constructs for refugee men a deviant nature that Others them from the norm of hardworking (European) men who support and take care of their families.

Another depiction of male refugees is formed by images related to them committing crimes or residing in the host country illegally. In these images, the faces of the men are often blurred/obscured, or only some part of the body (e.g., feet) is shown. Even though the reason for this obfuscation may be to protect the identity of the person, this depiction may generate an understanding that all male refugees are criminals. This visualized anonymity communicates threat and supports the stereotype of male refugees as criminals (Banks 2012; Holzberg et al. 2018; Martikainen and Sakki 2021).

Whereas images of refugee men are frequently associated with notions of crime and bogus or fake refugees, images of families – especially mothers and children – are understood as depicting genuine refugees (Chouliaraki and Stolic 2017). These images have been interpreted as a rhetorical means of showing suffering and communicating the need for help and support. Several studies have concluded that the function of these images is to generate feelings of empathy in the viewer (Chouliaraki and Stolic 2017; Johnson 2011; Lenette and Cleland 2016; Memou 2019; Šarić 2019). Images of mothers and children often include only a couple of people with recognizable facial features, which contributes to the understanding of individual suffering (Šarić 2019; Wilmott 2017). In addition, children are often depicted in closeups looking straight at the viewer, which constructs an emotional connection between the individualized refugees and the viewer (Kress and van Leeuwen 2006), making their plea for help more personal (Bleiker et al. 2013). However, images of suffering children may contribute to infantilizing refugees by depicting them as helpless and deprived of agency, which can be understood as an Othering visual strategy (Chouliaraki and Stolic 2017; Martikainen and Sakki 2021; Šarić 2019).

In several images, refugees have an untidy physical appearance and wear shabby outdoor clothing. On the one hand, this corresponds to the normalized expectation of refugees as vulnerable victims. On the other hand, these images may contribute to prejudiced perceptions of refugees as dirty and diseased (Chouliaraki and Stolic 2017). The untidy physical appearance of refugees differs from the normal and tidy physical appearance of (European) people in news images. However, neat and tidy-looking refugees – especially men – who wear branded clothes and use smart phones are also perceived as deviant since they differ from the normal expectation of shabby-looking refugees. Neat and fashionable-looking male refugees are easily categorized as bogus refugees who do not deserve to gain asylum (Banks 2012; Yalouri 2019). Hence, news images not only construct refugees' Otherness in relation to European nations but also contribute to Othering processes among the refugees themselves in terms of dividing them into genuine refugees deserving protection and bogus refugees not deserving protection.

Authorities and Celebrities in Images of Refugees

Authorities, such as border patrol, police, and helping professionals, are often depicted in images of refugees (Drüeke et al. 2021; Wilmott 2017). Because people generally only interact with these authorities in exceptional situations where the course of normal life is disturbed (Batziou 2011), their presence alienates refugees from normal life and signals an emergency. This strongly communicates the threat posed by refugees as deviant and criminal (Banks 2012; Drüeke et al. 2021; Wilmott 2017). The suggestion of alleged criminality is a powerful strategy of Othering (Batziou 2011; Vezovnik 2017). The impression of alienation from normal life and the status of the out-group are further reinforced by the fact that refugees are seldom depicted with or among locals (Wilmott 2017).

Refugees are also depicted with celebrities as part of their charity and fundraising campaigns and humanitarian work (Becker 2013; Campanioni 2021). The purpose of this kind of celebrity advocacy is often perceived in two ways. On the one hand, celebrities harness their popularity and fame to appeal to people to help refugees. On the other hand, these images may function as means of promoting celebrities' own viewpoints, careers, and public image (Becker 2013). These images featuring celebrities as saviors of refugees serve the needs of the celebrities themselves rather than the refugees, with the latter acting as display items emphasizing the warm-heartedness and generosity of the former (Campanioni 2021; Chouliaraki 2012). Campanioni (2021: 29) regards such images as promoting "global power relations that legitimate certain inequalities and injustices while obscuring others." This positioning is problematic because such charity campaigns "reproduce the issue one is fighting against" (Campanioni 2021: 29), in this case, inequality between refugees and non-refugees. Chouliaraki (2012: 1) referred to celebrity advocacy in the refugee issue as a "theater of pity" that encourages "a narcissistic disposition of voyeuristic altruism rather than commitment to the humanitarian cause." In this viewpoint, celebrity advocacy can be understood not only as a charitable gesture toward refugees but also as a means of constructing the position of refugees as Others.

Depictions of Environments and Objects

News photographs of refugees typically feature certain kinds of environments, such as borders, refugee camps, and reception centers. In addition, certain kinds of objects are repeatedly included in the images of refugees, such as border signs, fences, razor wire, vehicles (trains, buses, and boats), tents, and trash (Šarić 2019). These typical environments and objects and their associated meanings are discussed in the following paragraphs.

Borders and Refugee Camps

A host of news images depict refugees approaching the borders between European nations or gathering near borders. According to Drüeke et al. (2021), protection of borders is emphasized in media images of the refugee crisis. Typically, borders are marked with the symbols of European nations (e.g., flags or emblems of the European Union), indicating that refugees are about to enter a European territory. The inclusion of national symbols in the images underlines the refugees' status as strangers who are not native citizens of the nation state. As places of inclusion and exclusion, inside and outside, borders position refugees in the realm of Otherness (Jarmillo-Dent and Pérez-Rodriguez 2021; Memou 2019). The impression of Otherness is further emphasized through the border patrols and barriers erected to prevent refugees' free entry into the country. According to de Genova (2013), the composition of refugees, borders, and patrols in images implies illegality and threat.

News images often depict refugees in refugee camps. The shabby shelters erected for the refugees communicate the temporary nature of these shanty towns. The feeling of temporariness detaches refugees from their past (and home countries) while simultaneously denying them any glimpse of the future (destination countries). These "dehistorizing" (Mannik 2012) visual representations position refugees as in between, depriving them of past and future.

Imagery of refugees gathered near borders or in refugee camps often includes trash and waste. According to Vezovnik and Šarić (2020), waste and trash are associated with primitive cultures, constructing the sense of refugees as Others who do not belong to European or Western civilization (see also Šarić 2019; Vezovnik 2017). Waste also contributes to the division between us (clean and civilized Europeans) and them (dirty and uncivilized refugees) (Vezovnik and Šarić 2020). In addition, waste may be generalized as representing chaos, which threatens the European order and can "even become a symbol for migrants as disturbing, polluting and dirty elements unwanted in an (ethnically) clean environment" (Vezovnik and Šarić 2020: 179).

Border Walls and Razor Wire

In several newspaper images, refugee camps are surrounded by some kind of fence or barrier (often made of razor wire) to prevent the refugees from leaving the camps. Fences and barriers function as concrete Othering devices because they prevent refugees' free movement and separate them from Europeans. For this reason, refugee camps may become associated with prisons, with these fences not only separating refugees but also protecting us from them (Drüeke et al. 2021). Ample prior studies on refugee crises have analyzed border walls and fences as establishers of Otherness (Jarmillo-Dent and Pérez-Rodriguez 2021; Martikainen and Sakki 2021; Vezovnik and Šarić 2020). According to Vezovnik and Šarić (2020: 180), razor wire symbolizes "fortress Europe and its securitization policy during the refugee situation." Whereas razor wire may be associated with security and safety to some viewers, for others, it may connote aggression, pain, violence, oppression, militarization, and war (Martikainen and Sakki 2021; Smala 2003; Vezovnik and Šarić 2020). Through these connotative meanings, razor wire may add to the understanding of refugees as a threat and serve as a means of separating dangerous refugees from peace-loving Europeans.

Boats, Trains, and Buses

A plethora of studies have discussed media images of refugees in transit via trains, buses, and boats (e.g., Bleiker et al. 2013; Vezovnik and Šarić 2020), indicating their transitory status (Šarić 2019). According to Dominguez et al. (2014), boats have become a symbol of refugees in the European refugee crisis due to these recurrent media images. Refugee boats filled with unknown people are used to communicate invasion and cause fear among viewers (Bleiker et al. 2013; Falk 2010). In addition to the large number of faceless refugees in boats, their depiction from a distance and casual composition of the images may contribute to the perception of refugees as intimidating (Bleiker et al. 2013; Kress and van Leeuwen, 2006; Lenette and Miscokovic 2018). Furthermore, Mannik (2012: 254) argues that refugees arriving by boat are regarded as "the least deserving and the most threatening (...) because they have deviated from appropriate channels of entry." In many cases, the mere image of a train or a boat may infer refugees and their deviance. These transportation vehicles have been repeated in news photography to the extent that they may metonymically stand for refugees' journeys (Vezovnik and Šarić 2020). Hence, these images – in which no refugees are visible – can serve as a means of Othering them (Martikainen and Sakki 2021; Vezovnik and Šarić 2020).

Means of Visual Expression

The visual rhetoric of images relates not only to people, objects, and environments but also to the means of visual expression (e.g., framing, viewing angle, proximity, color, and direction of movement) that construct a stance on the subjects depicted in the images (Danesi 2017; Foss 2005; Kress and van Leeuwen 2006; Martikainen 2019). Visual expression is comprised of culturally preferred meanings, and by invoking these meanings, image makers can direct viewers' attention to certain aspects of the image and influence their perception of the image (Kress and van Leeuwen 2006). Next, I discuss matters related to gaze, viewing angle, and proximity (frame), which typically act together to contribute to a certain perception of refugees (Šarić 2019).

Refugees as Objects of Western Gaze

In a typical media photograph of refugees, the photographer is invisible; the photo is not normally taken amongst the refugees but from a distance, communicating that the photographer is not a part of the group of refugees but an external witness detached from them (Drüeke et al. 2021; Wimott 2017). This point of view constructs the viewers' perspective on the image; similar to the photographer, the viewer becomes an invisible voyeur observing the refugees from a distance (Memou 2019). This setting alone constructs Othering boundaries and asymmetrical power relations between us (audience of Western media) and them (refugees), in which Western media audiences become superior active subjects viewing refugees, while refugees are positioned as inferior passive objects (Lenette and Miskovic 2018; Wilmott 2017).

The aforementioned meaning communicated through the photographic setting is further confirmed by the fact that the majority of the photographs published in Western media are taken by professional photojournalists working for Western media companies and not by the refugees themselves (Memou 2019). The photos constitute and construct the Western gaze and perception on refugees (Memou 2019; Vezovnik and Šarić 2020) and tell more about the European/Western gaze than the refugees' experiences (Memou 2019). Hence, by publishing these photos, Western media not only disseminate images of refugees as Others but also construct Western spectatorship in relation to refugees as Others (ibid.).

High Viewing Angle

The use of (vertical) viewing angle is related to the expression of power in Western images. While a low angle expresses the power of the depicted person, a high angle expresses the power of the viewer (and powerlessness of the depicted person) (Kress and van Leeuwen 2006). A high angle is often employed in images depicting large crowds of refugees and images of vulnerable women and children. In depictions of large crowds, this high angle (bird's-eye view) may invoke control and surveillance. Due to the high angle and long-distance shot, the refugees appear small in size, reinforcing the authority, power, and control of Europeans over the masses of refugees (Vezovnik and Šarić 2020). In images of vulnerable and begging women and children, the high angle may also be understood as constructing asymmetrical power relations and emphasizing the helplessness of refugees, highlighting their position as victims (Martikainen and Sakki 2021). Because a high viewing angle communicates an asymmetrical power relationship that positions refugees as inferior to the viewers, it can be understood as an Othering visual strategy (ibid.).

Long Shots and Closeups

In sociosemiotics, different types of framing are associated with different kinds of social distance. A closeup represents an intimate distance, a medium shot represents a greater social distance, and a long shot represents an impersonal distance (Kress and van Leeuwen 2006; van Leeuwen 2008). Photographs depicting crowds of refugees tend to use long-shot images (Drüeke et al. 2021; Zhang and Hellmueller 2017). Long shots prevent the viewer from seeing the refugees' individual (facial) characteristics, presenting them as strangers (Batziou 2011), and distance further highlights refugees' Otherness (Drüeke et al. 2021; Šarić 2019; Wilmott 2017).

News images showing individuals or small groups of refugees frequently employ medium shots and closeups that reduce the distance between refugees and the viewer (Chouliaraki and Stolic 2017; Lenette and Cleland 2016; Memou 2019). Closeup images are especially common when depicting suffering mothers and children because they have "the potential to offer a more humanized representation of refugees" (Chouliaraki and Stolic 2017: 1168). By allowing the viewer to recognize facial expressions and the emotions communicated by them, closeups make it possible for the viewer to identify with the refugees' agony (Batziou 2011). However, despite the humanizing potential, closeups portraying refugees as victims construct an asymmetrical power relation between the inferior refugees and superior viewer (Šarić 2019; Zhang and Hellmueller 2017). In this sense, the visually rhetorical power imbalance can be understood as a means of Othering refugees.

Conclusion

This chapter examines visual rhetorical strategies that construct an understanding of refugees as Others in newspaper photographs of the European refugee crisis. This study shows that the visual rhetoric of Otherness is constructed in terms of people, objects, and environments depicted in images as well as means of visual expression.

The images of crowds of refugees at European borders represented them as a faceless collectivity about to invade European territories. This kind of visual massification functions as an Othering visual rhetorical strategy because it represents refugees as an entity deprived of distinct personalities (Chouliaraki and Stolic 2017; Martikainen and Sakki 2021; Šarić 2019; Vezovnik and Šarić 2020). In addition, this imagery portrays refugees as a threat to European nations, whereby Otherness is constructed in terms of a divide between threatening refugees and Europeans in need of protection (Martikainen and Sakki 2021). The meanings of threat are strengthened by border patrols and other authorities included in the photographs. The division between refugees and Europeans is further emphasized by news photographs in which refugees at refugee camps are separated by fences and barriers from local people, which make them appear imprisoned (see also Jarmillo-Dent and Pérez-Rodriguez 2021; Vezovnik and Šarić 2020).

This study also identifies several Othering rhetorical strategies that make refugees appear deviant from Europeans. The news photographs depicting refugee men as lazy and "killing" time in reception centers contradict the understanding of hardworking European men as supporters of their families (Banks 2012; Yap et al. 2011). Simultaneously, this imagery questions male refugees' need for asylum in terms of making them appear as social benefit abusers (Martikainen and Sakki 2021). A further Othering rhetorical strategy toward refugee men is provided by news images that associate them with crimes. In these images, the authorities' presence, as well as the blurred/obscured faces of the refugee men, may – despite the legal and ethical necessity of protecting their iden-tity – have furthered the understanding of refugee men as dangerous (Banks 2012). News photographs depicting refugees crowding onto trains, buses, and boats function as Othering visualizations, because they underline refugees' transitory status (Dominguez et al. 2014; Vezovnik and Šarić 2020) and contradict the image of European people living peacefully in their homes.

Moreover, this research shows how certain means of visual expression, such as dir-ection of gaze, viewing angle, and proximity, are used to communicate the Otherness of refugees. Photographers tend to shoot refugees from a distance, not from among them, which makes the refugees appear as distant outsiders (Memou 2019). In addition, newspaper photographs often employ a high viewing angle, which communicates an air of surveillance, placing refugees under European control (Vezovnik and Šarić 2020). A high viewing angle is also employed in images of refugee mothers and children, which communicates their helplessness. Distance, control, and helplessness communicated by long shots and high viewing angles Otherize refugees in terms of making them appear inferior and deprived of agency (Martikainen and Sakki 2021).

The visual rhetorical strategies identified in this study may influence the way people perceive refugees and relate to refugee crises. Research has shown that news photographs influence people's thoughts of, attitudes about, and behavior toward refugees (Amores et al. 2019; Martikainen and Sakki 2021; Wilmott 2017). According to Bleiker et al. (2013: 198), the influence of images is based on their power to "delineate what can and cannot be seen and thus influence what is and is not discussed publicly." The visual rhetoric of threat, control, and securitization may contribute to legitimizing tightened asylum regulations and anti-immigration measures (Batziou 2011; Wilmott 2017), xenophobia, discrimination, and feelings of fear regarding refugees (Bleiker et al. 2013; Glâveanu et al. 2018, Johnson 2011). Through their influence on public attitudes and political decision-making, media images may also affect the lives of refugees in many ways, for instance, in terms of complicating social interaction with local people and integration into the host society. In addition, the negative imagery circulated in the media and prejudiced public perceptions may be internalized by refugees themselves as a negative self-image (Glâveanu et al. 2018).

As this chapter shows, news images tend to repeat certain ways of depicting refugees, such as certain events in the refugee journey, environments, objects, and modes of visual expression. Batziou (2011) argues that the visual choices made by photojournalists often may not be conscious, but rather, they might unconsciously cite the visual vocabulary commonly used in Western media images of refugees. By repeatedly publishing similar types of images, the way they portray refugees may become naturalized and – unquestionably – taken for granted (Martikainen 2019).

Due to the one-sided media imagery of refugees in Western media, there is a pressing need to diversify the media imagery of refugees beyond the repeated stereotypes and oppositions. As Glâveanu et al. (2018) suggest, media channels should make more space for refugees' own voices by publishing photos taken by refugees themselves. This is also the wish that I would like to emphasize with the chapter at hand.

References

Amores, J. J., Calderón, C. A. & Stanek, M. (2019) 'Visual Frames of Migrants and Refugees in the Main Western European Media'. *Economics and Sociology* 12(3): 147–161.

Banks, J. (2012) 'Unmasking Deviance: The Visual Construction of Asylum Seekers and Refugees in English National Newspapers'. *Critical Criminology* 20(3): 293–310.

Batziou, A. (2011) 'Framing "Otherness" in Press Photographs: The Case of Immigrants in Greece and Spain'. *Journal of Media Practice* 12(1): 41–60.

Becker, A. M. (2013) 'Star Power? Advocacy, Receptivity, and Viewpoints on Celebrity Involvement in Issue Politics'. *Atlantic Journal of Communication* 21(1): 1–16.

Bleiker, R., Campbell, D., Hutchison, E. & Nicholson, X. (2013) 'The Visual Dehumanization of Refugees'. *Australian Journal of Political Science* 48(4): 398–416.

Boucher, D. (2019) 'Reclaiming History: Dehumanization and the Failure of Decolonization'. *International Journal of Social Economics* 46(11): 1250–1262.

Campanioni, C. (2021) 'The Right to a Dignified Image: The Fashioning and Effacement of the Refugee within the Celebrity System'. *Journal of Cinema and Media Studies* 61(1): 27–50.

Câtâlin-George, F. (2014) 'Stereotypes and Prejudice in the Perception of the "Other"'. *Procedia – Social and Behavioral Sciences* 149: 321–326.

Chouliaraki, L. (2012) 'The Theatricality of Humanitarianism: A Critique of Celebrity Advocacy'. *Communication and Critical/Cultural Studies* 9(1): 1–21.

Chouliaraki, L. & Stolic, T. (2017) 'Rethinking Media Responsibility in the Refugee "Crises": A Visual Typology of European News'. *Media, Culture & Society* 39(8): 1162–1177.

Danesi, M. (2017) *Visual Rhetoric and Semiotic. Oxford Research Encyclopedia of Communication.* Oxford: Oxford University Press.

De Coninck, D. (2020) 'Migrant Categorizations and European Public Opinion: Diverging Attitudes towards Immigrants and Refugees'. *Journal of Ethnic and Migration Studies* 46(9): 1667–1686.

De Genova, N. (2013) 'Spectacles of Migrant "Illegality": The Scene of Exclusion, the Obscene of Inclusion'. *Ethnic and Racial Studies* 36(7): 1180–1198.

Dominguez, M., Pineda, F. & Mateu, A. (2014) 'Life in a Nutshell: Evolution of a Migratory Metaphor in Spanish Cartoons'. *Media, Culture & Society* 36(6): 810–825.

Drüeke, R., Klaus, E. & Moser, A. (2021) 'Spaces of Identity in the Context of Media Images and Artistic Representations of Refugees and Migration in Austria'. *European Journal of Cultural Studies* 24(1): 160–183.

Falk, F. (2010) 'Invasion, Infection, Invisibility: An Iconology of Illegalized Immigration', in C. Bischoff, F. Falk & S. Kafehsy (eds.), *Images of Illegalized Immigration: Towards a Critical Iconology of Politics.* New Brunswick: Transaction Publishers.

Foss, S. K. (2005) 'Theory of Visual Rhetoric', in K. Smith, S. Moriarty, G. Barbatsis & K. Kenney (eds.), *Handbook of Visual Communication: Theory, Methods, and Media.* New York: Routledge.

Giubilaro, C. (2020) 'Regarding the Shipwreck of Others: For a Critical Visual Topography of Mediterranean Migration'. *Cultural Geographies* 27(3): 351–366.

Glâveanu, V.-P., De Saint-Laurent, C. & Literat, I. (2018) 'Making Sense of Refugees Online: Perspective Taking, Political Imagination, and Internet Memes'. *American Behavioral Scientist* 62(4): 440–457.

Holzberg, B., Kolbe, K. & Zaborowski, R. (2018) 'Figures of Crisis: The Delineation of (Un) Deserving Refugees in the German Media'. *Sociology* 52(3): 534–550.

Jarmillo-Dent, D. & Pérez-Rodriguez, M. A. (2021) '#MigrantCaravan: The Border Wall and the Establishment of Otherness on Instagram'. *New Media & Society* 23(1): 121–141.

Johnson, H. L. (2011) 'Click to Donate: Visual Images, Constructing Victims and Imagining the Female Refugee'. *Third World Quarterly* 32(6): 1015–1037.

Kjeldsen, J. E. (2017) 'The Rhetorical and Argumentative Potentials of Press Photography', in A. Tseronis and C. Forceville (eds.), *Multimodal Argumentation and Rhetoric in Media Genres.* Amsterdam: John Benjamins.

Konstantopoulou, V.-I., Didymiotis, O. & Kouzelis, G. (2022) 'Covert Prejudice and Discourses of Otherness during the Refugee Crisis: A Case Study of the Greek Islands' Press'. *Journal of Social and Political Psychology* 10(1): 173–190.

Kress, G. & van Leeuwen, T. (2006) *Reading Images: The Grammar of Visual Design.* London: Routledge.

Lefsrud, L., Graves, H. & Phillips, N. (2015) 'Analyzing Visual Rhetoric in Organization Research', in K. D. Elsbach & R. M. Kramer (eds.), *Handbook of Innovative Qualitative Research Methods: Pathways to Cool Ideas and Interesting Papers.* New York: Routledge.

Lenette, C. & Cleland, S. (2016) 'Changing Faces: Visual Representations of Asylum Seekers in Times of Crisis'. *Creative Approaches to Research* 9(1): 68–83.

Lenette, C. & Miskovic, N. (2018) '"Some Viewers May Find the Following Images Disturbing": Visual Representations of Refugee Deaths at Border Crossings'. *Crime Media Culture* 14(1): 111–120.

Mannik, L. (2012) 'Public and Private Photographs of Refugees: The Problem of Representation'. *Visual Studies* 27(3): 262–276.

Martikainen, J. (2019) 'Social Representations of Teachership Based on Cover Images of Finnish Teacher Magazine: A Visual Rhetoric Approach'. *Journal of Social and Political Psychology* 7(2): 890–912.

Martikainen, J. & Sakki, I. (2021) 'Visual (De)Humanization: Construction of Otherness in Newspaper Photographs of the Refugee Crisis'. *Ethnic and Racial Studies* 44(16): 236–266.

Maurer, M., Hassler, J., Kruschinski, S. & Jost, P. (2021) 'Looking Over the Channel: The Balance of Media Coverage about the "Refugee Crisis" in Germany and the UK'. *Communications* (online first), 1–22.

Media Audit Finland (2019) *LT ja JT tarkastustilasto 2019 (Statistics of Distribution 2019)*. https://mediaauditfinland.fi/wp-content/uploads/2020/08/LT-tilasto-2019.pdf (accessed April 2, 2022).

Memou, A. (2019) 'Spectacular Images of the "Refugee Crisis"'. *Photographies* 12(1): 81–97.

Olson, L. C., Finnegan, C. A. & Hope, D. S. (2008) 'Visual Rhetoric in Communication: Continuing Questions and Contemporary Issues', in L. C. Olson, C. A. Finnegan & D. S. Hope (eds.), *Visual Rhetoric: A Reader in Communication and American Culture*. Los Angeles: Sage.

Patton, T. O. (2020) 'Visual Rhetoric. Theory, Method, and Application in the Modern World', in S. Josephson, J. D. Kelly & K. Smith (eds.), *Handbook of Visual Communication. Theory, Methods and Media*. New York: Routledge.

Šarić, L. (2019) 'Visual Presentation of Refugees during the "Refugee Crisis" of 2015–2016 on the Online Portal of the Croatian Public Broadcaster'. *International Journal of Communication* 13: 991–1015.

Smala, S. (2003) 'Globalised Symbols of War and Peace'. *Social Alternatives* 22(2): 37–42.

Triandafyllidou, A. (2018) 'A "Refugee Crisis" Unfolding: "Real" Events and Their Interpretation in Media and Political Debates'. *Journal of Immigrant & Refugee Studies* 16(1–2): 198–216.

Van Leeuwen, T. (2008) *Discourse and Practice*. New York: Oxford University Press.

Van Leeuwen, T. (2017) 'Rhetoric and Semiotics', in M. J. MacDonald (ed.), *The Oxford Handbook of Rhetorical Studies*. Oxford: Oxford University Press.

Vezovnik, A. (2017) 'The Case of the "Refugee Crisis" in Slovenske Novice'. *Dve Domovini – Two Homelands* 45: 121–135.

Vezovnik, A. & Šarić, L. (2020) 'Subjectless Images: Visualization of Migrants in Croatian and Slovenian Public Broadcasters' Online News'. *Social Semiotics* 30(2): 168–190.

Wilmott, A. C. (2017) 'The Politics of Photography: Visual Depictions of Syrian Refugees in U.K. Online Media'. *Visual Communication Quarterly* 24(2): 67–82.

Yalouri, E. (2019) '"Difficult" Representations: Visual Art Engaging with the Refugee Crisis'. *Visual Studies* 34(3): 223–238.

Yap, S. Y., Byrne, A. & Davidson, S. (2011) 'From Refugee to Good Citizen: A Discourse Analysis of Volunteering'. *Journal of Refugee Studies* 24(1): 157–170.

Zhang, X. & Hellmueller, L. (2017) 'Visual Framing of the European Refugee Crisis in Der Spiegel and CNN International: Global Journalism in News Photographs'. *The International Communication Gazette* 79(5): 483–510.

23

VISUAL REPRESENTATION OF FOOD IN ITALIAN CINEMA

Fatma Nazlı Köksal and Ümit İnatçı

Introduction

Within the realms of cinematography, images of objects, persons, or landscapes maintain dimensions of meaning. Via the procedures applied by cinematography, all such images can be loaded with cultural codes. Such procedures include camera position and angle, the position of objects or people within the frame, the use of light, colour processing or colouring, and sound. In the construction of meaning, cinematography utilizes representative codes and conventions, shared by the filmmakers and the audience, enabling the audience to actively construct meaning by referring to the codes that structure mythical meanings within the social world in which the film plays out (Bignell 2002).

In numerous movies throughout cinematic history, food scenes have been evaluated upon multiple levels, including the level of supporting actors, as well as the level of leading roles. Cinematography has constructed the relationship between poverty, wealth, nutrition, and social status, the conditions of living together, the semiotic fiction of lust and desire in eating habits, and dinner table themes. The settings where themes of luxury and poverty, comedy and tragedy, and scenes of ritual and associations with food were staged coexisted with themes of human nature. Based on philosopher Ludwig Feuerbach's claim: "*We are what we eat*", it is possible to understand how cinematography has been able to establish connections between cinema's cuisine and ways of behaviour.

In cinema, the function of food, and the semantic systems in relation to food, maintain meanings beyond the palate and visual pleasure. Eating in cinematography is not only considered an aesthetic tool but also utilized as a social practice, in assisting the audience to communicate with something different, familiarization, and the establishment of connections with a world different from their own, via the indication of a strong symbolic message that implies every meaning of the movie simultaneously (Bower 2004; Balthrope 2004). In this regard, food may be considered as a thematic motive, guiding the language of cinema, since it maintains the power of carrying different and various meanings (meta-narrative) and its own sub-discourse. Bower approaches the symbolic imagery of food-related practices as a powerful semiotic system, creating meaning via filmic narration, enabling filmmakers to communicate important aspects of the characters' emotions and their personal and cultural identities, in addition to ethnic, religious, sexual, and philosophical aspects of narratives, across all film genres (Bower 2004). Moreover, producers employ social, cultural, and visual codes, and myths, of foodstuff and related practices, as a significant feature of filmic storytelling, utilizing food as a material object and food-related practices as performances, to establish a strong semiotic system. The representation of foodstuff or related practices within a film or film scene, whether major or minor, assists the producers in conveying key details of important elements, such as the characters, the plot, the setting, and so on (Bower 2004; Boswell 1993). In cinema, representational codes and conventions shared by the film producers and viewers are used; and as a result, viewers deliberately create meanings by using codes that shape mythic meanings in the social setting where film viewing occurs (Bignell 2002).

Expanding on this subject, it can be said that food has always been a star of the Italian cinema; representing hunger and recounted in conviviality. Focused on the historic art of displaying the lives of unique individuals, Italian cinema also focused on the culture of not only the country's gastronomy, where, more than anywhere else, cuisine expresses affection, taste, desires, opulence, and poverty, but also the difficult years and those that were easier. Such images recounted the genuine Italy of the past, but also the food culture, which hastily distorted customs and traditions, accelerating the emergence of the fake food agro-industry kitchen, at the expense of the real one. Food, gastronomy, and culinary art coexist perfectly with the "seventh art", managing to evoke very suggestive and charming atmospheres, while simultaneously being one of the subjects of choice, due to its strong symbolic value and the intimate ability to create scenes and compositions of undisputed beauty. In its representation in cinema, the symbols and rituals associated with food cannot be missing. Even the satirical representations of some aspects of Italianity expressed through the relationship with food, as in the way in which it is consumed, must be present.

This present study focuses on film scenes in Italian cinema in relation to food and food-related practices as a powerful semiotic system, and researches the representation of foodstuff within the social and cultural context. The study concentrates on two films, *Amarcord* (1973) by Federico Fellini and *La Cena* (1998) by Ettore Scola, examining the connotative aspects of foodstuff in terms of cultural symbolism. Furthermore, the communicative function of food in terms of cinematic language will be evaluated from the visual rhetorical perspective. Thus, this study aims to bring an alternative perspective, in relation to food in the cultural and social life context, to the field of representation of food, in light of semiotic and visual rhetoric.

Food in Cinema

Cinema, referred to as the 'seventh art' by Canevacci and Coutinho (1984), is deemed a sort of mythology of modern societies. The visual power of the cinema plays a crucial role in the reflection of the social representation of food rituals, which are part of social structures. The meaning systems established through food in movies constitute a cultural sign system that the audience can perceive. Within the history of cinematography, multifarious examples can be located when looking at the use of food as an indicator. For example, within a scene of one of the Lumiere Brothers' very first films, accepted as the building blocks of cinema, there was a baby feeding scene. Another example is the metaphorical use of meat in Sergei Eisenstein's *Battleship Potemkin*, another film with an important position in the history of cinema. The persistently consumed maggot-ridden meat in Eisenstein's film confronts the audience as the cause of the rebellion, and thus, metaphorically, represents a past that needs to be eradicated. In this sense, the symbolic meanings of food referred to in movies are much stronger than the tangible nature of food. In this line of thinking, it can be posed that the aforementioned symbolic meanings can also affect the socio-cultural structure of the audience. This is due to the fact that there is a connection between film and communal living. Cinematography is an art which represents communal living both in form and in content and is the location in which representations of the relevant era take shape within the cinematic narrative style, with the narration of the content also being shaped in the same way. For this reason, a multi-dimensional approach including the period of the movie is required for the analysis of the food scenes and the role of the food in the movies (Kanık 2018).

Beyond the feast, food arouses the semiological senses according to the meaning systems it maintains, making offerings to the palate and the eye in the cinema. Food and food-related practices, which Barthes (1997) refers to as the *"veritable grammar of food"*, are said to constitute a metaphorical "language". Barthes puts forth his argument relating to food culture via the following questions: *"Where and how is the grammar of food and culinary practices created as a language, and in what social and cultural contexts are the meanings attributed to them produced, restructured, circulated, reinforced, or the structure deconstructed?"*; *"Where do rank food and food-related practices in the cinema stand in this process?"* At this point, within cinematography, food becomes a representational language, used as a tool that is based on meaning codes, assisting in the transferral of the message and appearing in an aesthetic form. For example, discussing the role of food within movies, Anne L. Bower states how emotions such as rebellion, anger, and love are conveyed to the audience through food, and stipulates that in this way, the director can create perceptual pleasures through representational narration. As elaborated by Counihan:

> Food is a product and mirror of the organization of society on both the broadest and most intimate levels. It is connected to many kinds of behavior and is endlessly meaningful. Food is a prism that absorbs and reflects a host of cultural phenomena.
>
> *1999: 6*

There has always been a strong link, especially within Italian cinema, between storytelling and the table, between what you taste with your eyes and what you imagine you can taste with your palate. Then there is the other side of the story: the one that cinema has entrusted to lighter films, in which the kitchen, or even just a simple homemade menu, marked a moment or a passage to be reread with the attention of the small story about the daily life of the country. This is an undoubtedly interesting bond that has effectively become part of Italian culture, and is a curious source of tastes, disgusts, eating and social habits, rituals and traditions, of the country. Italy has always been firmly linked to the world of food.

From decade to decade and film to film, more than the table in story books, the table that appeared on-screen marked the profound and constant change of gastronomic traditions, as well as the customs and history of the country. Opulent and snobbish, or aristocratic and sumptuous, everyday or convivial, imbued with sensuality or despair, suffering or joy, Italian cinema has written a story with the images: from the hunger of war to the distracted opulence of today. Taste in cinema is the taste of good food but also of the conviviality typical of Italian everyday life. If there is a secret that brings together images and stories with the enjoyment of putting their ideas on the table, it takes the form of the great love of not only the film viewers of the many generations, but also the writers, directors, and actors who presented and shared the taste of cooking through the screen.

At this stage, it is important that the dimension of the cinematic representation of food, and the relationship between cinema, audience, and identification, should be understood. The identification that the audience constitutes with the cinematic narrative is a special relationship that is strengthened by narrative, form, and content techniques. Here, the narrative established with food will enhance the degree of identification, especially within the framework of daily life. Emotions such as hunger, satiety, liking, or pleasure, can find their counterparts among the audience as identification. Moreover, emotional response from the audience, the process of meaning, and empathy, can be realized via the constructed metaphor of food. The fact that food in movies represents differences such as ethnic identity, culture, and ideology, also strengthens the aforementioned effect. Therefore, when reading literature in relation to food in the cinema, the rhetoric of representation themes, which are also indicators, comes up.

Rhetoric, which deals with the image's ability to transmit impressive and persuasive messages, has a function that influences and manages perception. Visual rhetoric, in which visual images with a harmony are utilized, composes the communication process through a symbolic representation. Visual images are changed, combined, arranged, or transformed, and become the indicators used for the emergence of artistic deviation that characterizes rhetorical figures (Durgee 2003; Brummett 1991). The relationship established between the signifier and the signified in an indicator, and is the process of meaning at the same time. When we see, hear, or somehow perceive a signifier, its signified, that is, its meaning, is formed in our minds. The concept in our minds is not the same as objects in the real world. At this point, the indicator should be interpreted in a two-stage format. According to Guiraud,

> Signification is a formation that connects an object, an entity, a concept, to an indicator that can regenerate an event in our minds: a cloud is an indicator of rain; raised eyebrows to indicate surprise, barking of a dog indicates anger, the word "horse" indicates an animal. So, the indicator is a stimulus … The effect of the stimulus on the organism animates the memory image of another stimulus in a momentary; the cloud evokes rain; the word evokes the image of the object or entity.
>
> *Guiraud 1975*

Umberto Eco, on the other hand, indicates that establishing a relationship with and making sense of a product is based on the culture to which that product belongs. In this regard, products carry meanings and thoughts that are related to the political, religious, social, traditional, art, and climate of the culture within which they are located, and it is related to the sign itself, as well as how it is reproduced and given meaning. Eco tackles the connection between rhetoric and semiotics as stylistic coding and defines this relationship as semiotic-oriented rhetoric (Eco 1976). At this point, the consolidation of meaning caused by both the indicators and the interaction between the indicators necessitates a semiotic approach, as well as a rhetorical reading.

Methodological Approach

Visual rhetoric encapsulates the critical analysis of visual products such as paintings, films, advertisements, and posters, via the means of semiotics and rhetorical analysis techniques. A comprehensive visual rhetoric theory will include insights from a variety of perspectives and methodologies, including cultural, psychological, and textual studies (Hill 2004). When an image can communicate a message without the help of a detailed verbal key, its meaning is socially determined. Meaning is related to the relationship of visual forms. The effectiveness of a rhetorical design's methodology is dependent upon the use of symbols and models that are familiar and vivid for a particular audience (Ehses and Lupton 1988).

Within the rhetorical discipline, visual rhetoric has two meanings. These are a perspective on visual objects/products, and visual data. In the first, visual rhetoric is a product created by individuals in which visual symbols are used for communication. In the second, it is a perspective that focuses on symbolic processes, and thus the communication is achieved through images (Foss 2004). According to Foss, two components should be considered in the definition of visual rhetoric: presented elements and suggested elements. The naming of important physical properties of the image is the description of the presented elements. At this stage, elements related to the mass or size of the image, such as the form, shape, material from which it is made, are defined. Then the concept, idea, theme, and the presented elements of images from which the audience is likely to draw conclusions, should be defined. Analysis of both the presented and suggested elements allows an understanding of the specific communicative elements of the image, and as a result, it becomes possible for the audience to develop a meaningful image.

In this study, film scenes related to food, which constitute a content of meaning based on visual representation, will be examined through the relationship between presented and suggested elements put forward by Sonja Foss. The visual structure and meaning process through which the selected scenes are conveyed will be revealed in the relationship of the image, situation, and action. The sample of the study consists of the films of two very important Italian directors, who skilfully expressed all the problems of twentieth-century Italian society. One is Federico Fellini's *Amarcord* (1973) and the other is Ettore Scola's *La Cena* (1998). These two particular films were chosen due to the fact that the culture of gastronomy, the way of eating, and interpreting social relations, has both anthropological and cultural significance for Italian society.

Analysis of Eating Scenes from Films

Amarcord *by Federico Fellini*

Amarcord, which means "I remember", which is a joint production of Italy and France, directed by Federico Fellini, is among the most important films in the history of cinema. The movie, written by Italian director Fellini with Tonino Guerra, reflects Fellini's time in the town of Rimini, where he spent his childhood years in the 1930s. In the movie, which tells from a metaphorical point of view how fascism, which arose in the 1930s, is reflected in everyday life, education, faith, politics, and sexuality, people with compressed lives and dreams are exaggeratedly caricatured. The movie, which depicts the impacts of Italian fascism, uses symbolic and humorous language to show how fascism affects individuals on a daily basis. *Amarcord*, which is considered Fellini's masterpiece, is conveyed through the eyes of a child in adolescence, the effects of Italian fascism, Fellini's unique style, and other indicators.

One of the most important features of *Amarcord*, which Umberto Eco describes as "the reconstruction and invention of memory", is that the story is not built around

Fellini. Although Fellini was influenced by the world he lived in as a child, he does not directly point to his childhood in the film. Another striking feature of *Amarcord* is that it is political. Fellini, who generally stays away from political issues in his films, criticizes the fascist policies of his childhood in the film with a humorous language. In *Amarcord*, Fellini goes back to the ideological roots of fascism and reveals it for that pathology that has always been present in Italy, that maturation block that places him in search of authoritarian guidance. The result is the merciless portrait of a small petty Italy, dazzled by the myth of the super virile man who, however, has enormous complexes in sexual matters. His attributes diminish under the images of the pope, of Mussolini, of the king. Fellini ridicules the fascists and reveals them in their intellectual paucity and emotional dryness.

During the lunch scene in the film, Fellini builds a link between sexual appetite and the appetite to eat, by drawing attention to the behavioural differences of the figures of the family members. Within this scene, which takes place in the kitchen, the father, who is the master of the house, sits at the head of the table. All the family members are seated around the table for dinner. This scene, where there are three generations (grandfather, father, and children) at the table, observes each of the characters defending their individual positions, in accordance with their socio-cultural tendencies. The mother, however, refuses to sit at the table and also refuses to eat. The kitchen details are also appropriate for the time period's spatial and chronological setting. According to the presented and suggested elements in the scene, we can see the reactions of a patriarch father, a matriarch mother, and children, both young children and adolescents, differing accordingly, against the autocracy present as the shadow of fascism. The three generations are in conflict, each defending and questioning their individual position in accordance with the new socio-cultural trends. The father, who is in charge of the household, is seated at the head of the table. He has the desire to deal with the other members of the family and assert his authority, but he is also troubled by what is going on around him. He argues with and opposes his wife and children, and everyone has their own personal problems. There is no harmony, and none of the characters in the scene are understanding of each other. The problems derive from the differences of points of view and the needs of each in daily life. There is the presence of a joyful child who is not aware of the problems of daily life, different from his adolescent brother due to his growing sexuality, the erotic memories of an old man, and the wife who refuses to sit at the table and eat, as a punishment for her husband's autocratic attitude. Despite everything, all the members of the family are around the table to eat lunch, not so much out of necessity but out of a feudal duty. The dialogues revolve around a misunderstanding addressing the feudal relation of the society itself.

In another scene, again around the table, eating well is a sign of social status, and having lunch with both first and second courses at that time was already considered the height of well-being. In another scene set around the dinner table, we observe the family members seated around it again. On this occasion, rather than the people, we see that it is the foods on the table that are the presented elements in the scene: boiled white goose meat, soup made with boiled broth, risotto instead of bread, and red wine. We can take from this that good nutrition is upheld since the dishes on the table are generally boiled and have low salt content. All the ingredients of the lunch are cooked in white (cotto in bianco). The wine accompanying the lunch instead is red, with the father proclaiming after a sip that: "it's a good wine". The first course consisted of goose broth soup with dry pasta, however the grandfather warned his grandson not to have the soup, because his stomach would swell and there would be no room for the rest. It was a light meal for lunch; however, attention is paid to the use of salt. As suggested elements, there is a great behavioural contrast between the lightness of the meal and the aggressiveness of the conversations between the family members. There is a lot of care for eating well but not for humble and respectful relationships. The idea of eating well, staying healthy, and enjoying life, that is a deep-rooted notion stemming from the Roman era, does not coincide with the modern morals and values that were emerging during those years, where new ways of life were already in circulation due to American cinema. This displays a deteriorating dichotomy of a society which is unable to take the right path for socio-cultural renewal.

The grandfather and grandson are present in another scene centered around the table. This scene centers on the conversation between the grandfather, who is teaching his grandson about the foods that are good for sex, and the child, who is eating. He also instructs his grandson to eat his lunch at 11 p.m. and his dinner at 4 p.m. during this conversation, reiterating that this will ensure that blood circulation is harmonious with the body and that in this way a person can be completely healthy. Following this, there are pathetic dialogues between the mother and father that demonstrate the parents' conflicting matriarchal and patriarchal behaviors. In this lunch scenario, there are two different representations of the woman: one is that of a distraught mother, and the other is that of a woman who piques men's libido.

All generational and socio-cultural conflicts are served perfectly at the table for the mental digestion of the spectator. Therefore, what is happening around the table between the eating and the lively discussions of family problems is nothing more than a moral confrontation through a gastronomic circumstance. The patriarchal behaviour of the father is absorbed by the neurotic attitude of the matriarch mother who wants to defend her child not for maternal defence, but as a figure who does not want to submit to the authority of her husband. The mother and wife in one, like the figure representing the unity of the family, destroys her representation as a loving mother by refusing to eat what she cooked with her own hands, and threatening her husband that she would commit suicide. The light taste of boiled meat and broth soup contradicts the heaviness of the irritating conflict between generations and roles in the family. Therefore, semiotic suggestions that are created through a totally Fellinian hermetic metaphor are never done so by coincidence.

At the end of the film, another traditional lunch scene (the farewell lunch for the bride) appears as presented elements. In this particular scene, we see another traditional food scene. This scene of a wedding dinner features dialogues full of fun and joy, while dishes made with few ingredients (bread and wine) stand out. Here the bride and groom and a few guests are sitting at the table and the other guests are standing behind them, and it is understood that, due to their uniforms, the groom and a few guests are soldiers. It is a marriage that is pleasant and joyful, but this time it is like a dinner made with sub-par ingredients – just wine and bread – and it is unclear if the bride (Gradisca) is happy or not. Gradisca is the sophisticated middle-class woman who dreams of finding a husband like those in American films, but ends up marrying an obedient military member of the regime. Perhaps the director offers the audience a final rather satirical image of a betrayal that is the beginning of an era full of perplexity and uncertainty.

It is clear that social and cultural practices are encoded in a complex way judging from the semantically provided evidence. The dining room looks like a stage where all the attitudes reflect a micro world of everything that happens politically outside the home. On this linguistic level, another code is envisaged which is aesthetic. Aristotelian aesthetics as a theory of reflection aims to represent what generally happens everywhere through a single event.

La Cena *by Ettore Scola*

In the film *La Cena* (*The Dinner*), Ettore Scola tells relatively complicated and bitter events of a human multitude belonging to the middle class who find themselves at the restaurant "Arturo al Portico". In the film, through the tables of a Roman trattoria, the director narrates the heterogeneity of a society and its salient aspects. It is almost an episodic collage, through which it brings together different sociological aspects that coincide with one another in their moral and ethical problematics. The purpose of bringing together all these fragments of sometimes comic and sometimes dramatic dialogues is to create a sociological laboratory where an inner panorama of people trying to create a world made of their oppressed desires is reflected.

Located within the restaurant are various stories, dialogues, and the adventures of both the customers and the staff that take place in the restaurant and the kitchen, where the inconveniences, lives, and stories emerge. The restaurant is a location that is populated with differing characters, each with their own personal problems. Typically, some customers sit alone, while some sit in groups. Everyone chooses their favourite flavours from the menu. A Japanese family asks for ketchup; the waiter disapproves (because spaghetti is never seasoned with ketchup), but serves it regardless, as the customer is always right. The Italian Master of Literature asks for rice, remembering that it is the most consumed food, and wondering why Italians obsessively consume so much macaroni. Inside the kitchen, the chef gets angry and grumbles when sufficient care is not applied when cooking the meat, as the correct times and practices in cooking must be applied for each different taste. The film director uses a cine camera between the kitchen and the interior of the restaurant, coming and going between the customers and the chefs. In between the cooking practices, the composing of tastes, and the dialogues between the customers, intertwining and reflecting each other like insidious languages of a crumbled alter ego, true things are said through unspoken elements. Secret encounters of forbidden loves, amorous encounters, almost exhibitionist, but beneath it all, the presence of a sexual appetite that recalibrates human relationships in a reciprocity entirely concentrated on a subconsciousness, disturbed by the social norms linked to certain roles in a catholic puritan society. We see the diners seated at the tables in this restaurant-set scene, as well as the waiting staff serving them. Here, the restaurant serves as a setting for conversations and personal narratives between customers and staff.

At one table, there is a couple conversing, while the male watches and attracts the attention of a mature woman; the woman gets up and goes to the bathroom with the certainty that the young male will follow her, but he unexpectedly suffers a feminist attack; with the mature woman giving him a good ethical lesson. The male was very sure that the mature woman would easily allow herself to be used as a sexual conquest. Thus, the falsity of a relationship that seemed so innocent becomes evident. While within the restaurant there is a conversation about a scene from a film that narrates the crucifixion of Jesus Christ, it is intertwined with another conversation between other people about working life and worker exploitation. At this point another male enters the scene and sits with two people. They start talking about a job for him. He is a young man who believes himself to be free to choose what seems right for him. He refuses to do a job that would not meet his needs, but in reality, he is an individual who is defending his laziness. Right at this moment of reasoning, he is offered a dish with boiled artichokes, fried zucchini, and fried brain. Here, a symbolic parenthesis is inserted; artichokes with the meaning of health, fried zucchini as a weakness of personality, and the fried brain as a vain intelligence that does not reason.

The camera turns again to the table of the philosophy professor and his pupil, who were flirting as lovers. The young woman sitting at the table solemnly listens with the same seriousness as the professor with a pipe in his mouth. Only red wine can be seen at the table where the young woman leaves without eating. The young woman becomes serious and asks for a declared relationship that is no longer secret, asking if he was willing to divorce his wife; the philosophy teacher becomes aggressive and rejects this suggestion with a lot of philosophy. The heart of the young woman breaks with great disappointment; and she leaves the restaurant without having dinner. The literature teacher, the figure who is always attentive to what is spoken and what happens within the restaurant, has a conversation with the beautiful owner of the restaurant. She is a woman loved and admired, she too has secrets to keep, and she too has a lover always kept in the shadows. The literature teacher of a certain age, half poet and half wise man, makes her feel that he is aware of everything that happens inside the restaurant, including in relation to what concerns her life and feelings. She is perplexed but continues to listen to him. He speaks like an actor reciting a poem, saying:

> Food and drink symbolize the same human condition; a Greek poet said two thousand years ago. Eating a meal at a table of strangers or friends has something to do with the heart instead of the stomach; on the other hand, conviviality comes with others, and for this reason you are doing the most beautiful job in the world.

Obviously these phrases underline the most significant part of this film, as they are all structured in a gastronomic environment.

In this way, the conversations jump from one discourse to another, but all the arguments come together and complete each other as part of the intrinsic rhetoric, through which the truth becomes revealed in all aspects. At each table, a different episode is projected with the frame of a different social subject. The levels of conflict, as well as the layers of different emotions, advance according to the stages of the dinner; appetizer, first course, second course, and dessert at the end. It isn't missed that there are wines of different colours and tastes. In every meal, the accent of the conversation is different. In each step the growing temperament of the arguments is felt. All social and cultural ingredients, ethical or unethical, complement each other with the food ingredients. The tasting of every food as an Epicurean pleasure and the tasting of different conversations and behaviours as life choices build a visual, textual rhetoric, that is very representative also from the kinaesthetic point of view.

Whoever cooks, serves, or eats, they are all carried out with scepticism or with conviction, and these behavioural characters are always human beings with their defects and advantages. The choice to eat and the choice of sharing or comparing opinions around a table is a socio-cultural rite, through which the malignant but also benevolent curiosity of individuals is manifested. In this film by Ettore Scola, where the base scene is a sacred place of gastronomy, all different aspects of life – politics, ethics, spirituality, the third age crisis, masculinity, femininity, lies and innocence, lack of self-esteem and false identity, a social appetite that lacks sincerity, tainted relationships, seeking truth, etc. – are represented as a microcosm of Italian society. Dinner is like the last scene of the day, where we come to terms with daily life before going to rest; despite everything, what we eat as the last food is a gift of life. Dinner, like a theatrical stage, ends with playing cards; as a mental digestive – a game should be seen as a serious activity you need to engage in, says the literature teacher, giving his final lecture.

Conclusion

Visual rhetoric, which treats and highlights images as a form of expression of cultural and contextual meaning, rather than purely aesthetic thought, is also revealing of an attitude of thought. The creation of narrative language through visual symbols in cinema is essentially a process influenced by context. Therefore, in cinema, which is accepted as a reflection of communal representation, the function of food appears as a rhetorical form and the narrative of the content is shaped accordingly. The narrative of the movie and the visualization of this narrative, the meaning attributed to cultural identity, class, race, and ethnicity, create a sign system that can be easily understood by the audience. Therefore, the visual language created with food takes the form of an important message carrier. The analysis of food in cinematic language, and the follow-up of codes, indicators, and metaphors, in these movies, make the production, sharing, and exchange of social, cultural, economic, and political meanings understandable. While the culture and communal structure of the individual is transferred to the cinema via food in movies, the food provides a richness of representation with strong meanings in the transfer of the social, political, and economic structure of which it is a part. Within the movies discussed in this study, indicators and metaphors with relation to food can be considered as details that construct the meaning that the movie aims to establish. As such, the food scenes were analysed and the narrative fiction of the movies was discussed in the social context, according to the meanings maintained by these details. As a result, the food scenes presented in the movies are powerful carriers of codes, carrying sociological meanings, as opposed to their biological nutrition contributions to daily life. The approach, which was particularly focused upon communal class relations within the selected movies, offers a rich perspective in terms of the function of food and the meanings it produces. For this reason, the fact that food is treated as a communicative representation within the language of cinema, brings a different perspective that reveals the semiotic language attributed to food within social and cultural life.

References

Amarcord. DVD. (2006). Directed by Federico Fellini. New York: Criterion Collection.

Balthrope, R. (2004). "Food as Representative of Ethnicity and Culture in George Tillman Jr.'s Soul Food, María Ripoll's Tortilla Soup, and Tim Reid's Once upon a Time When We Were Colored." In A. L. Bower, eds., *Reel Food: Essays on Food and Film*. New York and London: Routledge, pp. 101–113.

Barthes, R. (1997). "Toward a Psychosociology of Contemporary Food Consumption." In C. Counihan & P. van Esterik, eds., *Food and Culture: A Reader*. New York and London: Routledge, pp. 20–27.

Bignell, J. (2002). *Media Semiotics, an Introduction.* Manchester: Manchester University Press.

Boswell, P. A. (1993). "Hungry in the Land of Plenty: Food in Hollywood Films." In P. Loukides & L. K. Fuller, eds., *Beyond the Stars III: The Material World in American Popular Film*. Bowling Green, OH: Bowling Green State University Popular Press, pp. 7–23.

Bower, A. L. (2004). "Watching Food: The Production of Food, Film, and Values." In A. L. Bower, eds., *Food: Essays on Food and Film*. New York and London: Routledge, pp. 1–13.

Brummett, B. (1991). *Contemporary Apocalyptic Rhetoric*. New York: Praeger Publishers Inc.

Canevacci, M. & Coutinho, C. N. (1984). *Antropologia Do Cinema: Do Mito À Indústria Cultural*. Sao Paulo: Brasiliense.

La Cena *(1998). Directed by Ettore Scola.*

Counihan, C. M. (1999). "Food, Culture, and Gender." In *The Anthropology of Food and Body: Gender, Meaning, and Power*. New York and London: Routledge, pp. 6–24.

Durgee, J. (2003). "Visual Rhetoric in New Product Design." *Advances in Consumer Research* 30: 367–372.

Eco, U. (1976). *A Theory of Semiotics*. Bloomington: Indiana University Press.

Ehses, H. & Lupton, E. (1988). "Rhetorical Handbook: An Illustrated Manual for Graphic Designers." *Design Papers* 5: 1–39.

Foss, K. S. (2004). "Visual Rhetoric." In K. Smith, S. Moriarty, G. Barbatsis, & K. Kenney (eds.), *Theory of Visual Rhetoric Handbook of Visual Communication. Theory, Method and Media*. New York and London: Routledge, pp. 141–153.

Guiraud, P. (1975). *Semiology*. London: Routledge.

Hill, C. A. (2004). "The Psychology of Rhetorical Images." In A. Hill Charles & M. Helmers (eds), *Defining Visual Rhetorics*. NewYork and London: Lawrence Erlbaum Associates, pp. 25–40.

Kanık, İ. (2018). *Gastrosinema*. İstanbul: Alfa Yayınları.

24

THE ETHOS-PATHOS CONTINUUM IN THE PORTUGUESE "OBRIGADO" ADVERTISING CAMPAIGN

Samuel Mateus

Introduction

The COVID-19 pandemic declared by the World Health Organization in March 2020 resulted in widespread confinement throughout the world. The number of deaths in the United States has reached a total of 1.14 million at the time of writing (www.worldomet ers.info/coronavirus/country/us/). At the beginning of 2021, 191 countries registered new virus mutations and 99,864,391 cases of COVID-19 (Pompeu et al. 2021). COVID-19 represented a shock to the lives of citizens and consumers. The economic impact of global lockdowns has been unmatched, with estimates of COVID-19 costing the world economy anywhere between $5.8 and $8.8 trillion (Dennis 2020). The Gross Domestic Product (GDP) of several countries across the globe decreased by double digits; the GDP of the United States decreased 48% and 32.9% in the first two quarters of 2020; the United Kingdom's economy shrank 20.4% in the second quarter; Australia went into recession after 30 years of uninterrupted growth; and Japan's GDP fell by 27.8%, which was the biggest decline since World War II (Dennis 2020).

The pandemic also had repercussions in the area of communication in terms of advertising investment. While the US advertising market increased to $646 billion in 2019, losses in 2020 in this market alone were estimated to reach $26 billion (Vorhaus 2020), and recovery will be difficult and slow. According to the COVID-19 Marketing Report: Statistics and Ad Spend, 34% of the companies surveyed had completely cancelled their advertising campaigns and 89% had decided to revise their budget, with 69% of brands indicating they decreased their budget in 2020. Also according to the same report, only 14% of marketing campaigns in the UK remained unchanged, as originally planned. On average, advertising spending decreased by 9% in Europe, with Germany and France registering a decrease in investment of 7% and 12% respectively. The same was true in the US, with *The New York Times* reporting a 15% drop in advertising revenue in the first quarter.

DOI: 10.4324/9781003195276-30

While political institutions and governments subsidized in the concerted effort to "win a war" (the rhetorical metaphor used in almost all countries) against coronavirus, brands become more important as a symbolic anchor (Mateus 2022). They occupied a place previously dominated by public institutions by adopting a vigorous advertising effort that did not promote their products and services, but was directed to health professionals and the general public. Advertising discourse put into question the already tense relationship between individual and collective pretensions, as well as the link between public (world health) and private (each individual has the right to control their own body and to choose to be, or not to be, vaccinated) claims.

On the other hand, the pandemic context has accentuated the opportunity for brands to advertise their values and commit to social responsibility campaigns, while showing concern for human dimension issues (e.g. citizens' fatigue with the curfew, the exhaustion of health professionals, loneliness, or the risk of contagion of family members). The sensitivity shown during the SARS-COV-2 pandemic proves that brands cared about their consumers and were socially committed by promoting contagion prevention behaviours and good public health practices. These advertising messages bring with them the possibility of brand loyalty by responding to the proactive and responsible role that millennials demand from companies in the pandemic context.

Ads such as Ford's "Built to Lend a Hand" and Walgreens' "Ask a Pharmacist" contributed to establish brands as pivotal agents of a solution, and as organizations available to help citizens get through the ordeal. They did that by invoking their century-old commitment to their customers, while explaining and educating how people could safely take advantage of online health services and drug delivery. For its part, McDonald's-Philippines assured its customers, through a video of CEO Kenneth Yang, that it would not hesitate to close the restaurants as a way to show the company's determination to protect the health of its customers, as well as employees and suppliers.

One thing that these ads have in common – and that they share with the generality of the commercials created and broadcast during the pandemic – is the extreme emotionalism associated with their messages. For example, Facebook's "We're never lost if we can find each other" video, constructed in an emotional tone (rhetorical pathos), presents the various facets of human emotion from a motivational perspective, including many domestic scenes and family interactions. A study based on Unruly's EMO Index measured the emotional intensity of dozens of advertisements and compared them to the national average for each country. It concluded that the Google-Japan "Arigatōgozaimasu" (Thank you) ad campaign, broadcast during the first months of the SARS-COV-2 pandemic, had three times more emotionality than the average Japanese commercial. In seventh place comes Google's North American "Thanks Healthcare" campaign, in thirteenth place the "Thank you" campaign from Coles in Australia, and in twentieth place, the German Deutsche Bank's "Danke für Ihre Unterstützung" campaign, with an emotional intensity 48% higher than the country's average.

Although feelings such as pride and gratitude are rare in advertising in non-pandemic periods, the spread of the coronavirus and the intensified effort made by medical staff made them very common during the COVID-19 pandemic. As shown by Unruly's EMO Index, the campaigns that had the most popularity were those that had a higher emotionality index and those that tended to focus on thanking communities, volunteers, citizens, and especially health professionals. These ads attested the positive attitudes (We are together; We are here for you) while suggesting behaviours to adopt (stay at home; wash your hands; do not kiss or hug people).

The most successful ads, in the first few months of the pandemic, tended to minimize the focus on their products in favour of an emotional tone on those who, every day, work and risk their lives to keep others safe and sound. According to the research that led to Unruly's EMO Index, ads that instructed consumers to relate to the brand and its products were not only less emotionally compelling, but they were associated with lower purchase intention scores. In contrast, the most successful ads were not only intensely emotional – based on confidence and optimism – but also evoked feelings of inspiration and devotion, which were shown to correlate with a better perception of their image (and brand favourability) among their viewers. Another research study concluded that "authentic advertising messages might increase positive attitudes toward brands and products, especially in times of crisis, such as the COVID-19 pandemic, when consumers sense a substantial threat. Thus, this study provides empirical evidence of the efficacy of the authenticity appeals of products" (Park et al. 2022).

This chapter examines advertising, adopting a rhetorical perspective. It is argued that Portuguese advertising in times of COVID-19 constituted its ethos from the pathetic charge (pathos) of its ads in the hybridization between ethos and pathos (Mateus 2021). From a convenience sample based on the Unilever Portugal campaign "Obrigado" (Thank you), I demonstrate how the affectivity arising from the feeling of gratitude is transmuted into the creation of a corporate self-image (and associated brands like Skip, Dove or Olá) inscribed in a re-evaluation of its ethos.

I begin with a brief discussion of rhetorical ethos in advertising. Then, I explain the concept of pathetic ethos. Finally, I briefly examine Unilever's "Thank You" campaign in Portugal using the MELCA model of rhetorical analysis (Mateus 2018: 189–207) in order to demonstrate the existence of what will be called a pathetic ethos or an Ethos-Pathos continuum.

Rhetorical Ethos in Advertising

There are two ways to consider the rhetorical ethos.

In the Roman tradition – in authors such as Quintilian or Cicero – the ethos of the speaker is related to the reputation that precedes him, and to the creation of fame or value that outweighs his words. The ethos is, thus, an extra-discursive and pre-constituted element that pre-exists the moment of the lecture to the audience. In the Greek tradition, in turn – that of authors such as Aristotle – ethos is the image that the speaker constructs for himself at the moment of the address that does not necessarily correspond exactly to his identity. The character (ethos) consists of an attempted creation that resembles a persona, a prototype of personality that is presented as real and is the object of permanent construction through discursive acts. While in the Greek tradition, the character or credibility of the speaker (ethos) is associated with the attributes that he enacts before the audience, in the Roman tradition, ethos consists of a previous discursive image created by the speaker (Maingueneau 2008: 14).

This distinction is critical. It may seem insignificant, yet it is crucial to understand today's advertising. The first determinant aspect to understand the ethos of advertising is the building of an extra-discursive character based on an intra-discursive reality. In other words, the character or credibility of today's brands is created moment by moment in their advertising exercise (intra-discursive elements) aiming to constitute themselves as reputable and authoritative (extra-discursive elements). This is, and even more so in advertising, a dynamic representation that is constructed by the speaker and negotiated by the audience at the moment the advertisement "speaks" or refers. By describing the world or products/services, advertising is simultaneously saying something about the speaker (the advertised brand, for instance). The enunciation may not be about the brand itself, but ultimately it creates and enunciates an ethos. For example, when Rolex portrays a world-class surf champion and creates a legend about conquering the ocean, these attributes related to conquest, triumph and success become also a discursive construction about the character of the brand. Rolex is not just saying the surf champion is an adventurer; it is also positioning itself as an adventurer and successful brand.

In *Rhetoric*, Aristotle (1998, 1378 a) placed prudence (phronesis), virtue (aretè) and benevolence (eunoia) as the basic qualities of ethos. They constitute a set of guidelines for discursive behaviour that extends into the character traits of the speaker. This is far beyond the instantaneous rhetorical performance which, to some extent, reinforces the interpretation that the enunciation is not about the speaker, and yet it enunciates his ethos. Since the discourse (the enunciation) is not about prudence, virtue, or benevolence, the way it is done denounces these virtues and betrays the character of the speaker. Perhaps, this is why Maingueneau (2008: 14) writes that "ethos does not act in the foreground, but in a lateral manner". This is exactly what happens in "Obrigado" campaigns where the gratitude demonstrated betrays (and exposes) the ethos of these brands. By showing gratitude they established themselves as virtuous brands. Let us not forget that ethos is the precursor of the relationships between two entities – be it a speaker and an audience, or a brand and its potential customers. It is a shaper of human activities that influences them. It assumes the catalytic role that sets the tone for the speaker and aligns what she enunciates with what she makes herself represent.

Ethos emerges not only in what is thematized (said) but in what is not thematized (what is alluded to, something unspoken but that is shown or invoked). The thematized ethos resides in the uttering of the thank you, but it extends into the unthematized ethos, that is, in what the uttering of the thank you corroborates about the image and identity of the speaker/brand. Saying thank you is thus not just a duty fulfilled, but becomes an opportunity to build the character of the speaker/brand the moment he voluntarily decides to acknowledge the recognition, in a kind of representation of society itself. It is this taking of a stand as a spokesperson that constitutes the speaker/brand as a social agent and, at the same time, as an agent endowed with character.

The second determinant aspect to understand the pandemic advertising ethos is to appreciate that the image constituted by the speaker is about commonness. The persuasive (rhetorical) effect of advertising happens to the extent that the speaker/brand conveys, in his (verbal and nonverbal) speech, the idea that he is one among many, equal among peers.

This detail is especially relevant in the case of the "Obrigado" campaigns during the SARS-COV-2 pandemic in Portugal in which the fabricated ethos makes one see that the brand is made of common people, similar to the very individuals who constitute the audience. Part of the virtue associated with this ethos comes from the ability of the speaker/brand to make itself equal, and the individuals in the audience to recognize their own ethos in them. To this extent, brands are grateful, not because they distinguish themselves from citizens, but because they constitute themselves as a moral personality equivalent to that of citizens. Just as they are grateful for society's efforts to prevent the spread of the virus, so brands are grateful. In this gesture, they adopt an image analogous to those they intend to convince. The creation of ethos works, in this context, because it advocates a pre-existing ethos in society for which the speakers/brands make themselves spokespersons.

The third key aspect of these "Obrigado" ads concerns the "embodiment" of values, making them visible, and updating them in a new enunciation. Advertising often relies on stereotypes that circulate in society. In the case of Portuguese advertising during the pandemic, it assumes the prevalent gesture of publicly recognizing the effort in fighting COVID-19. Brands amplify social gratitude around health professionals by becoming the enunciator of a public "Obrigado" (Thank you). One realizes advertising ethos or public image the moment it is based on the appropriation of this social appreciation. In this way, ethos is reinforcing the public feeling of gratitude, while consolidating the creation and development of the brand's own ethos anchored in thankfulness to health professionals (and related professions such as law enforcement officers, medical auxiliaries, firefighters, etc.). Just to recapitulate, this gratefulness ethos is based on three aspects: an extra-discursive character that emanates from discursive activity; the constitution of a common feeling that positions brands as "institutional citizens" equal to common citizens; and the recognition of a social and moral value attributed to public servants during the pandemic.

This tripartite formation is what distinguishes discursive enactment of Unilever's extra-discursive ethos as a socially responsible brand. In other words, the discursive enunciation of these advertisements embodies a collective feeling. The speaker/brand capitalizes on this shared sentiment by adopting it as a mark of its character. "Obrigado" is the typical enunciation of admiration and gratitude: it is an ethical elevation (a grandiloquent gesture) and simultaneously an ethical achievement (a creation of the ethos of the speaker/brand).

Let's dig deeper into the functioning of this special type of ethos, one that is strongly affiliated with the artistic rhetorical proof of pathos.

Pathetic Ethos

The rhetoric of pandemic advertising is based on the construction of a brand's credibility (ethos) according to emotional premises (pathos) designating what I call a hybrid concept: a pathetic ethos or an Ethos-Pathos continuum.

If one acknowledges that ethos invokes habits, customs or moral precepts, it is no less correct also to assume that it equally involves emotional precepts (invoking pathos). According to Aristotle, one is convinced not so much by the truth, but by motives that provoke effects of truth. The search for the benevolence of the audience, as the matrix of ethos, is concomitant with the arousal of passion (pathos). The Greek philosopher says that the speaker leads the audience to feel a passion "because the judgments rendered vary according to whether we experience grief or joy, friendship or hatred" (Aristotle 1998: 1738 a). If, in order to convince, the speaker creates his image from the arousal of emotions (as if he were tangling the strings of the emotional dispositions of the audience), this means that the ethos of the speaker can be built around the way his speech brings out and influences the emotions of the audience. As Maingueneau (2008: 16) states, ethos is elaborated "by means of a complex perception, mobilizing the affectivity of the interpreter, who draws his information from the linguistic material and the environment". While ethos is built through discursive appeals to benevolence, it also takes on some pathetic dimensions.

This consists in an overlapping between the two artistic proofs: ethos and pathos. And although in the rhetorical orthodoxy – since Aristotle – these proofs, despite being interdependent, are autonomous and unconnected, the discursive evolution registered with advertising recommends that we bring them closer together. In fact, one of the main features of advertising discourse is its emotional dimension. What Wharton (2013: 4) calls "rhetoric of affections" reiterates the idea that the appeal to emotions is central for advertising to induce consumption, but also satisfaction, pleasure, comfort, happiness, or social status. Mateus (2018a) draws attention to the importance of considering an affective rhetoric in advertising. Hence, affects may be rhetorically deployed, and rhetoric is, indeed, inseparable from the social construction of meaning. Affective rhetoric may be understood as "the use of affective means of persuasion to induce cooperation in beings that, by nature, respond not just to symbols but to the emotions they trigger" (Mateus 2018). Affective rhetoric is, thus, an inherent dimension of all rhetorical activity and a rhetorical analysis should include the ways affects (passions, moods, feelings or sentiments) are summoned to induce certain patterns of thinking and behaviour.

If it is true one instructs by arguments (logos), if one is moved by emotions (pathos), and if one insinuates character by the conduct of the speaker (ethos), one also understands that the very insinuation of character (ethos) comes not only from the rationality of what he says (logos) but, equally, from the emotiveness summoned by the way he speaks and how he acts (pathos). This a very important idea, because, in rhetorical orthodoxy, and in the Greek tradition, such an overlay of artistic proof merited suspicion. The mere reference to a pathetic ethos, a self-image built on emotional dispositions, would be outrageous and despicable. After all, this would imply that the hierarchy between the intelligible and the sensible, reason and emotion, mind and body, character and passion, would be destroyed. Traditional rhetorical theory is very much based on dichotomies inherited from Cartesianism. Even Locke despised rhetoric because its emotions would perturb the rationality of the argumentation.

However, one of the corollaries of the mediatization of rhetoric (when the media are introduced in the communicative exercise of persuasion) has to do, precisely, with the intermingling of rhetorical genres, but also the mixing of artistic proofs. The analysis of contemporary advertising based, on the one hand, on the rigid frame of an untouched ethos, pure or immaculate, and, on the other hand, on a spurious pathos, is hopelessly doomed to fail. A wide and solid body of research (Lerner & Rivkin-Fish 2021) has brought to light the ubiquitous presence of emotionality in contemporary culture and the term "emotionalization" has been used to refer to the legitimization and intensification of emotional discourse in the collective sphere of life (Ahmed 2014).

As I will develop next, the "Obrigado" campaigns that occurred during the COVID-19 pandemic, in Portugal, can be better understood by the blending of artistic proofs, and in particular, by the creation of a public image of the speaker/brand based on emotional dispositions. There are already some papers on the power of emotions to claim something about the world. For instance, Diez-Arroyo (2021) explores the emotional rhetoric of British tea websites to endorse cultural and patriotic claims. These are examples of social identity, collective memory, and the feeling of belonging or pride in one's country. And one would not fully understand the rhetorical effect of these ads if one did not consider the creation and sustaining of an ethos of a pathetic nature. In other words, an Ethos-Pathos continuum.

This production of the pathetic ethos is a socio-discursive, verbal and nonverbal realization that involves what is said, but also how it is said and how it is acted upon. Ethos is always a socially prescribed and evaluated behaviour and emerges from a specific communicative situation in which speaker and audience take part. This means moving away from the pathetic ethos of grandiloquence – of good speech (*bene dicendi*) as Quintilian said – widening its scope to all kinds of gestures, behaviours and conduct of the speaker. From this point of view, pandemic advertising sees its ethos created not so much at the moment of saying "Obrigado" (Thank you) but at the moment when the socially inscribed meaning of that (emotive) behaviour is recognized by the interpretive community (brand and audience including customers, suppliers, and consumers in general).

In what follows, I proceed to a more focused rhetorical analysis of Unilever's Portuguese "Obrigado" campaign in order to particularly exemplify the rhetorical constitution of the Ethos-Pathos continuum.

Rhetorical Analysis

The MELCA model of rhetorical analysis (Mateus 2018: 189–207) examines any text (written or audiovisual) from the following premises: Motivation, Exposition, Reader (Audience), Constraints, and Author. Although each of these elements helps to reinforce an Ethos-Pathos continuum, it is the Exposition that is most important since it corresponds to the ad layout.

The Motivation of a rhetorical text concerns the motive that created the need to prove something about the world. It is not way too distant from Bitzer's Exigence. "In every rhetorical situation," said Bitzer, "there will be at least one controlling exigence which functions as the organizing principle: it specifies the audience to be addressed and the change to be affected" (Bitzer 1968). The exigence consubstantiates in the event or occurrence that prompts rhetorical discourse; according to Bitzer, the exigence is that which begins the "cycle" of rhetorical discourse about a particular issue. What prompted the need to advertise public gratitude was the exceptional pandemic that introduced several curfews around the world and that demanded from public servants an extraordinary resilience. Unilever's national campaign can, thus, be described by the intention of the speaker/brand Unilever to take a proactive attitude and address Portuguese people to thank them for their efforts during the especially sensitive periods of the pandemic (in March 2020, the first containment period had just been declared). All successful rhetoric (whether verbal or visual) is a response to an exigence, a real reason to send a message (Bitzer 1968). Here the exigence was the ambiguous times of curfew and COVID-19. Society needed a wake-up call and the "Obrigado" campaign certainly helped to acknowledge the extraordinary effort of public servants and other professional classes that could not stop during the pandemic.

When it comes to advertising, one must also not forget that conveying an altruistic and humble message does not mean that it ceases to be persuasive. The persuasive effect of these ads comes exactly from the Ethos-Pathos continuum and the way the image of the speaker/brand is built around the affectivity associated with the gratitude present in the big "Obrigado". The motivation can be synthetically stated as the use of exceptional times (the COVID-19 pandemic) to help build the ethos of Unilever as a multi-brand company socially responsible and concerned with public health and well-being (this is the affective side) of its consumers – and the Portuguese in general. This involves *kairos*, or timeliness, the use of the right time and occasion. Unilever took the chance, not just to be grateful, but to build a public persona of benevolence through that very same appreciation. Failing to establish a strong kairotic appeal may lead to the audience losing interest or becoming hostile. That certainly was not the case here. In contrast, Unilever showed appropriate timing and that is precisely a central rhetorical aspect of the "Obrigado" message. They responded to the general public feeling and built their image around it.

The Reader or Audience (A in the MELCA acronym) is constituted by Portuguese citizens and, especially, Unilever's consumers who will be more sensitive to this message. This is, therefore, a very extensive mediatized audience, potentially the 11 million inhabitants of Portugal. Due to the message's audience range, small variations were made for more specific audiences (like public employees, medical staff, or the sales force). The message is simple: "Obrigado". And this has to do precisely with the universal character of the Audience. One must also make clear that the universal character of the Audience stands in contrast to the addressees of the message. In effect, the brands of Unilever are thanking particular professional classes. But the persuasive intent of this message is related with the universal audience of Unilever's consumers and Portuguese citizens. These ads are incredible examples of advertising rhetoric to clearly separate the addressees and the audience of the persuasive communication.

The Constraints relate to the vicissitudes of advertising creation during the SARS-COV-2 pandemic that forced the advertising industry to work from home, which, in turn, limited advertising production. Because the usual means of production were not available, this campaign is very simple: "Obrigado" highlighted in a short sentence; a set of brands represented by Unilever Portugal in the white strip below (Dove, Cif, Olá, Skip, etc.), and an image on a simple coloured background. The ad differentiates itself more because of its content than its simple, basic form.

Besides, because these are Mupis ('Street Furniture as an Information Point'), the message had to be necessarily short to facilitate its apprehension in fast-paced urban life. Due to the curfew, the Mupis were seen by a smaller number of people compared to the pre-pandemic period, which certainly contributed to limit the reach of the rhetorical message. Maybe this detail explains why so many Mupis were placed all over Lisbon and Porto, where chances of reaching a wider audience are greater.

As for the Author, the multiple authorship of the speaker/brand should be noted. The advertisement represents Unilever Portugal (and its various brands), and therefore it is the speaker/brand. However, the existence of an advertising agency (and its various employees) that intervened in the creation and design of this message cannot – as always – be overlooked. The rhetorical authorship is shared between a speaker/brand and a speaker/agency that speaks on behalf of Unilever Portugal. It was quite unusual, a company taking the role of publicly recognizing the severity of the pandemic and the effort of all Portuguese people to overcome it. In doing so, Unilever not only broke with the perception around the role of brands as having market and sales concerns only, it also humanized Unilever by becoming a subject of enunciation. The authorship of the ad grants its authority in the sense of creating credibility, an ethos, not the other way around: Unilever is not showing here its authority in order to justify this public attitude of being grateful. It builds its authority as a responsible brand and the way it does so is through a disseminated authorship. It is also relevant to underscore that authorship may be understood as embodying the voice of all Portuguese citizens who benefited from the tremendous effort made by these professionals. So, there are multiple layers of meaning around the Author element of the MELCA method of rhetorical analysis.

In the Exposition lies the very ethical and pathetic force of the ad. At the visual level of the ad's text, we find three symbols to represent the generalized and specialized audience: the Portuguese national flag; the bus traffic sign (public transport) alluding to public employees; and the table full of graphics in an allusion to the sales force and its focus on the volumes of goods and services transacted. The chromatic spectrum does not seem to be significant, having as its only concern to provide contrast and facilitate good reading. The brands represented by Unilever Portugal are highlighted as a visual element separate from the rest of the ad, as suggested by the white stripe.

The word "Obrigado" is stressed by the font size, visually conveying that this is the objective and essential idea of the ads. At the verbal and content level, the fundamental idea is to emphasize that the behaviour of some (the civil servants, the sales forces, some Portuguese) helps save everyone. The verbal text reads: "Thank you public servants who walk the streets for everyone" or "Thank you Portuguese who stay at home for everyone". There is not exactly argumentation since the ads assume the purpose of praising the Portuguese population. In doing so they provoke a positive disposition to accept the ethos of the speaker/brand. The lexicon is very small and simple, reinforcing a unity of ideas: to simply thank the responsible behaviour in the field of public health and the effort of the Portuguese (the sales force and the civil servants here as a synecdoche of all workers).

What is, rhetorically, more crucial in the Exposition is the connotation of thankfulness and what it means to be thankful in the pandemic context. First of all, giving thanks is a gesture of empathy (if we prefer, of sympathy – sin-pathos). But it is also a gesture of character enhancement: the one who gives thanks shows himself morally superior to the one who does not. The acknowledgement of the effort is, here, highly ethical and, at the same time, pathetic. The sympathetic gesture (sin-pathos) is a character-building gesture of the speaker/brand and, simultaneously, of an affective nature shaping the audience's dispositions around the positive image of Unilever Portugal.

Furthermore, the uncertain times, coupled with the increase in deaths, the closure of companies, and the beginning of thousands of layoffs, have left the population especially vulnerable to the COVID-19 pandemic. This vulnerability may be also interpreted as an emotional vulnerability, as shown by the successive demonstrations – in Portugal and around the world – in support of health professionals and the drawing of the rainbow and its slogan: "Everything will be alright".

The need to repeat this mantra across the world, but specially in Europe, lies in the need of people to feel psychological reassurance in an extreme uncertain time. So, "Everything will be alright" became the most visible part of uneasiness, fear of the future, and sadness caused by all the pain. These emotions were publicly exposed, and they all point to a vulnerability that is also explored in the "Obrigado". This acknowledgement of the effort of some for the benefit of all is especially relevant and rhetorically more significant in the context of the proliferation of contagion and professional burnout of doctors, nurses and auxiliary staff as hospitals became crowded (a fact most visible from September 2020 until April 2021).

While I advocate an imbrication of ethos and pathos in the "Obrigado" ad campaigns, I am not arguing for a rhetoric of pathos like Barroso does (Barroso 2019: 148):

> The rhetoric of pathos is a strategical appeal to emotion, namely: a) pity (developing an argumentum ad misericordiam or appeal to pity); b) fear (using an argumentum ad metum or appeal to fear to provoke concerns or anxious feelings about some consequence); c) flattery or adulation (to show praise and appeal to self-conviction and self-presumptuousness of consumers if they use the product or brand advertised); d) joy and enthusiasm (whether real or illusory

happiness, people feel satisfaction and fulfillment); advertisements are typically happy-ending messages and, therefore, they correspond to the expectations (needs and problems) of consumers and present an easy and simple solution to them; e) wishful thinking.

I am taking an affective-discursive approach (Breeze 2019) and bringing affective rhetoric to the forefront of advertising.

In sum, in a world already fraught with emotionality (the loss of jobs, the number of sick people, children locked up at home without school, etc.), the "Obrigado" advertising campaigns capitalized on emotionality and used emotional dispositions to create a socially responsible image (ethos). The "Obrigado" is not merely an innocent gesture of thanks. It is a thank you that simultaneously contributes to building a positive, altruistic self-image. Perhaps this is the reason that large numbers of "Obrigado" advertising campaigns throughout the world are characterized by high levels of emotionality index.

Conclusion

This chapter adopted a rhetorical framework to understand the effectiveness of the "Obrigado" advertising campaigns that appeared during the COVID-19 pandemic, and that registered a higher-than-average pre-pandemic emotionality index. It tried to deconstruct the persuasive, rhetorical appeal of being grateful. One possible way to explain these kinds of advertising is to understand it as a special way to build ethos in a time of extreme public emotionality. I pointed out that thanking is an affective precursor that triggers emotional dispositions that will capitalize on the economic and social difficulties that citizens were experiencing across the country. Also, it was argued that it was precisely this emotional incidence (contained in the "Obrigado") that allowed the speaker/brand to build its peculiar ethos.

The enunciation of appreciation may be seen as a step in the development of a socially accountable ethos, which is not thematized but only alluded to (unthematized). In essence, it is argued, gratitude (as presumed and implied in expressing gratitude) finds its rhetorical force to the extent that it produces the ethos of the speaker/brand from emotional marks that are found in the verbal act of thanking itself, but also in the general atmosphere of consternation around the virus and COVID-19. These different campaigns were illustrated by the case of Unilever Portugal in which I intended to demonstrate the creation of the speaker/brand ethos in emotional terms which was called pathetic ethos.

In the examples examined, the Ethos-Pathos continuum was based on the collective sentiment of respect and appreciation of all the professionals who helped to deal with the pandemic and ensure that people had medical assistance in the context of a generalized curfew. I tried to highlight how "Obrigado" ad campaigns were constructed under an ethos (a responsible brand) that is deeply based on a sentiment of gratitude (pathos).

The possibility of referring to an Ethos-Pathos continuum helps to explain Unilever's own decision to issue a public thank you. Here is advertising that does not advertise or promote anything, that does not dissertate on the advantages and benefits of its products. For this reason, it becomes difficult to justify this advertising campaign in strictly functional and rational terms (logos). After all, a "thank you" is not intended to increase sales; it is not intended to build customer loyalty; it does not follow a conventional marketing strategy. And yet, the speaker/brand derives great benefit from it (or it would not invest large sums of money in the advertising campaign). The "Obrigado" (thank you) campaign does not seem to fulfil a rational purpose.

It fulfils, instead, an emotional-ethical purpose. To assume only the ethos would result in an incomplete panorama of the rhetorical functioning of the campaign. In this case, we should scrutinize ethos and pathos as fundamental artistic proofs of the rhetorical value of this pandemic advertising. There is no actual, formal argumentation but an ethical foundation of the brand taking advantage of the emotional predispositions already existing in the pandemic-ridden society. The production of an image or persona (ethos) is mostly due to the emotional aspects linked to gratitude and public recognition.

The Ethos-Pathos continuum is not exclusive to the "thank you" advertising campaign, but this is certainly an appropriate example epitomizing the power of emotions, not only to convince, but to convince through the credible image of the speaker/brand.

For the time being, no one can say whether this move towards advertising solidarity and public recognition is just an extemporaneous reflection of a special event such as the pandemic, or if this demonstrates a structural transformation in advertising rhetoric. But of one thing one can be pretty sure: rhetorical persuasion in advertising is not straightforward. It can be made of successive layers of meaning. Being publicly grateful may be just one more way for companies to better establish their ethos. In the "Obrigado" campaign, the ethos may be better understood in relation to the exploration of affectivity and the social construction of affects.

References

Ahmed, S. (2014). *The Cultural Politics of Emotion*, 2nd ed. London: Routledge.

Aristóteles (1998). *Retórica*. Lisboa: INCM.

Barroso, P. (2019). "Rhetoric of Affections: Advertising, Seduction and Truth." *Media & Jornalismo*, 19(34), 143–154. https://doi.org/10.14195/2183-5462_34_10

Bitzer, Lloyd F. (1968). "The Rhetorical Situation." *Philosophy and Rhetoric*, 1(1): 1–14.

Breeze, R. (2019). "Emotion in Politics: Affective-Discursive Practices in UKIP and Labour." *Discourse & Society*, 30(1): 24–43.

Dennis, M. J. (2020). "The Impact of COVID-19 on the World Economy and Higher Education." *Enrollment Management Report*, 24(9): 3–3. doi: 10.1002/emt.30720

Díez-Arroyo, M. (2021). "Emotional Rhetoric in Tea Advertising." *ATLANTIS Journal of the Spanish Association of Anglo-American Studies*, 43(1) (June 2021): 199–220, e-issn 1989-6840. doi: http://doi.org/10.28914/Atlantis-2021-43.1.11

Lerner, L. & M. Rivkin-Fish (2021). "On Emotionalisation of Public Domains." *Emotions and Society*, 3(1): 1–11. https://doi.org/10.1332/263169021X16149420145743

Maingueneau, D. (2008). "A propósito do ethos." In A. Motta & L. Salgado (Org.), *Ethos discursivo*. São Paulo: Contexto.

Mateus, S. (2018). *Introdução à Retórica no séc. XXI*. Covilhã: Livros Labcom.

Mateus, S. (2018a). "Affective Persuasion – What Is It and Why It Matters." In C. Clark & L. Zhang (eds), *Affect, Emotion, and Rhetorical Persuasion in Mass Communication*. London: Routledge, pp. 69–80.

Mateus, S. (2021). "Acerca da associação entre Ethos e Pathos na Retórica da Publicidade." Atas do XI Congresso SOPCOM – Comunicação, Turismo e Cultura, pp. 655–665.

Mateus, S. (2022). "Social Media Advertising during the First COVID-19 Curfew." In A. Dominguez & G. Daimiel (coord.). *Estrategias de comunicación publicitaria en redes sociales: diseño, gestion e impacto*. Madrid: McGraw-Hill, pp. 361–372.

Park, J., Kim, J., Lee, D. C., Kim, S. S., Voyer, B., Kim, C., Sung, B., Gonzalez-Jimenez, H., Fastoso, F., Choi, Y. K., & Yoon, S. (2022). "The Impact of COVID-19 on Consumer Evaluation of Authentic Advertising Messages." *Psychology and Marketing*, 39: 76–89. https://doi.org/10.1002/mar.21574PARKET AL.|89

Pompeu, B., Perez, C., & Trindade, E. (2021) "Observatório da Pandemia: a publicidade e as marcas no contexto da COVID-19." *Comunicação Pública* [Online], 16(30). doi: https://doi.org/10.4000/cp.12763

Vorhaus, M. (2020). "COVID-19 Represents the Biggest Challenge to Media Advertising Expenditures Ever." Forbes.com, April 2020. www.forbes.com/sites/mikevorhaus/2020/04/27/covid-19-represents-the-biggest-challenge-to-media-advertising-expenditures-ever/?sh=47ea08007398

Wharton, C. (2013). *Advertising as Culture*. Chicago: University of Chicago Press.

WHO. (2020). WHO Coronavirus Disease (COVID-19) Dashboard. https://Covid-1919. who.int/ (accessed January 28, 2021).

25
EMOTIONAL RATIONALITY AS AN INDICATOR OF RHETORIC DISCOURSE IN POLISH AGRICULTURAL TEXTS

Maria Joanna Gondek and Paweł Nowak

Introduction

The focus of our reflections will be Polish texts which concern agriculture and rural life. In Polish discourse conducted both in the past and at present, the persuasive significance of agricultural texts is evident. On the one hand, it is conditioned by a material factor which concerns the geographical location of the Polish lands and the characteristic natural conditions resulting from it. This material factor is reflected by the etymology of the name "Poland" [Polska] which is derived from the name of land understood as a "field" [pole] that is a natural area for agricultural cultivation. Likewise, the association of the name "Poland" with the Slav people called "Polanie" indicates people who inhabited field areas and farmed them. A. Brückner in his *Słownik etymologiczny języka polskiego* [An Etymological Dictionary of Polish] writes that the adjective "polski" [Polish] used to mean "field", i.e. growing in a field, and hence it was semantically associated with what is natural or wild (Brückner 1989: 429). Today, this natural environment present in the name of Poland is significantly decreasing and undergoing rapid changes connected with economic development and urbanization. However, the historical and current presence of natural areas in the Polish territory involving woods, farmlands, mountains, coastal areas and lake surroundings is not the only factor which elucidates the significance of texts concerning agriculture. The other factor which is not of a material but of a mental nature appears to be more significant. The mental factor is formed as part of a conscious relationship of people living in these areas and taking advantage of the resources of their natural environment. This consciously formed relationship is visible in the Polish culture whose essential factor is literature and writings on agriculture. They include the poetry and prose of those Polish authors from the sixteenth century to the present who evidently use the theme of agriculture for the literary presentation of the characters' life

DOI: 10.4324/9781003195276-31

403

attitudes. Among them are: Władysław Reymont (novel *Chłopi* [The Peasants]), Henryk Sienkiewicz (novel *Rodzina Połanieckich* [Children of the Soil]), Bolesław Prus (novel *Placówka* [The Outpost]), Maria Rodziewiczówna (novel *Lato leśnych ludzi* [The Summer of the Forest People]). We argue that they create a persuasive discourse on agriculture, showing what the culture-creating relation of people to the natural environment consists in. Our studies of literary texts for which the topic of agriculture is crucial apply a method of analysis based on rhetorical categories belonging to *inventio* and *elocutio*. We use a broad understanding of agricultural discourse, which includes texts on agriculture that have persuasive or inducing features. In agricultural discourse we also include literary texts on agriculture, because in Poland, due to the lack of independence, there was no possibility of a free exchange of views. For a long time only literary fiction accomplished the tasks characteristic of discourse. In this chapter we ask how rhetorical devices shaped agricultural discourse? Did they set any characteristic features of this discourse? In an attempt to answer these questions we will look into the persuasive potential of the topos in Polish agricultural discourse and against this background we will try to diagnose its specific features.

Persuasive Potential of Topos in Polish Agricultural Discourse

Undoubtedly, topos is important from the standpoint of constructing a rhetorical message. We assume that topoi encompass the potential for the diagnosis of creating persuasiveness of Polish texts on agriculture. The fundamental significance of topoi in rhetoric results from the fact that they are conceived of as main points of reference which serve to build persuasion. The consequence of difficulty defining topos is the fact that it is primarily characterized in terms of function. Nicolaus the Sophist, using a metaphor, indicated that from a topos, as if from some place or land, we set out and arrange the relevant content (Kennedy 2003: 148). Heuristic functions of topos are discerned in rhetoric following Aristotle. He noted that topoi serve discovering appropriate premises for persuading man (Aristotle 1926: 1396 b 20–22; Grimaldi 1972: 115–135). Thus, he treated topoi as the basis for creating rhetorical reasoning, crucial from the point of view of persuasion, which he called an enthymeme (Jackson and Jacobs 1980). From the structural point of view, enthymematic reasoning corresponds to logical reasoning, apart from the fact that it leaves out obvious premises. From the formal point of view, it is distinguished by a probable status of premises and the conclusions reached on their basis. A rhetorical nature of the enthymeme consists in the fact that according to its Greek name (Gr. *en thimo* – in mind) it affects a person's mind in a complementary manner. It does not concern only the sphere of the intellect. Both a person's thoughts and feelings function in the mind in a way that is specific to the psyche. This is why enthymemes, growing out of found topoi, activate a person cognitively, volitionally and emotionally. In this context, topoi constitute the central axis for building persuasion of *logos*, *ethos* and *pathos* type. These are the three not mutually exclusive but complementary manners of accomplishing rhetorical persuasion. The reason for distinguishing them are the three spheres of human mental activity. The logos persuasion involves the human intellect, the ethos persuasion the volitive sphere, while pathos relates to feelings. Therefore, it is characteristic of rhetorical persuasion that it stimulates not only the intellect. It also affects human imagination which leads to feelings. In addition, persuasion is addressed in the volitive sphere, building a person's motivation to act.

The premises derived from topoi provide the basis for conclusions in the form of a belief adopted by the auditor. Since rhetorical persuasion affects the mind in a complementary manner, the beliefs it forms in the auditor's may contain rational and emotional elements.

We hold that agricultural discourse utilizes several topoi performing the above-mentioned functions. One of the main divisions of topoi functioning in rhetoric stresses the fact that they refer to persons or to things (Quintilian 1971: V, 10, 20). It is noted that it is not possible to form beliefs without reference to people or to things. In agricultural discourse topoi play a typical function of points which serve to derive premises for persuasion. The number of premises derived from topoi is inventively unlimited; the heuristic scope of their search is defined by the subject reality of the topos (Goodnight 1982). Hence, they need to be analysed with the view to discovering the sources of shaping argumentation associated with agriculture. Based on the review of Polish literature in which the topic of agricultural life is crucial, we observe that the topoi relating to people in agricultural discourse involve, first of all, the topos of the family (*genus*) and of the fortune possessed (*fortuna*). Among the topoi relating to things in agricultural discourse one needs to distinguish primarily the topos of place (Lat. *locus*), represented by land.

The topos of the family occupies an exceptional place in agricultural discourse. The family was frequently treated in those writings as the most fundamental, natural, human community which secures human development in various aspects. This is why the family topos may have carried a number of distinctly positive persuasion connotations in agricultural discourse. The family perceived as a natural form of human life, fulfilling the tasks of giving birth to and bringing up children, is inventively associated with writings accepting the significance of mutual love, thoughtfulness, security and care. Thereby, using the topos of the family has the potential for attaining the objective of *captatio benevolentiae* which consists in invoking the benevolence of the auditor. Poland used to be a typically agricultural country, therefore a family living in the country was portrayed as one in which children develop biologically and mentally as well as prepare for independent life in the future. Thus, the family has a persuasive impact as a community shaped against the background of generational tradition. In this context, one emphasizes the family's essential rights in the personal-social and property-economic orders. In terms of persuasion, these premises lead one to derive the desire to belong and to identify with the family community.

An important element of deriving persuasion in agricultural discourse was the multi-generational family. Such a family is depicted in Władysław Reymont's 1924 Nobel Prize-winning novel *Chłopi* [The Peasants]. The multi-generational family is an old, rural family, the Borynas, living in the village of Lipce. The family is headed by Maciej Boryna, a farmer who enjoys great authority in his family and in the entire village. He makes decisions on all the most difficult family matters. His internal conflict with his son Antek is immediately extinguished and becomes irrelevant in the face of external danger. The strength of the multi-generational Boryna family lies in the deep family unity and mutual solidarity of its members. The novel *Chłopi* [The Peasants] is the best-known Polish agricultural novel whose message is shaped around the topos of family. Family life in the countryside is portrayed during the four seasons and the work that goes with them. The good of the family is also presented as an important rationale for the decisions made, beliefs upheld, and judgements made by individual characters.

Portraying a community of family experience of childhood, adolescence, maturity and ageing was oriented persuasively towards a unique life experience unavailable outside the multi-generational family. Agricultural discourse presented multi-generational families and families consisting of parents and children as communities caring for the daily needs of their constituents. Such care involves material life and concerns securing food, protection from cold and help with diseases and setbacks. There are references to the experience of sharing a family table and going through the joys and concerns of life by parents, children, grandparents and relatives. At the same time, the family is portrayed as a community which struggles with various conditions and difficulties in carrying out such a task. The agricultural family deriving their material and economic security from the farmed land is particularly dependent on natural factors like weather, natural disasters, human, animal and plant diseases, which are variable and unpredictable over a longer period of time. It accomplishes its tasks in a social setting that varies over time and involves periods of peace, wars and various political transformations.

Agricultural discourse portrays family as a community carrying out not only material and economic tasks but also improving its members' welfare at a spiritual level. The use of the topos of the family having such characteristics is found in the agricultural novel *Rodzina Połanieckich* [Children of the Soil] by Henryk Sienkiewicz. This novel aptly reflects the social discussions that were taking place in Poland on the importance of rural life to the fulfilment of human life. In his novel *Rodzina Połanieckich* [Children of the Soil], Henryk Sienkiewicz depicts the transformation of the spiritual attitude of the main character Połaniecki. His marriage to Marynia and family life lead Połaniecki to discover that deep down he wants to act guided by religious motivation and feelings. Under the influence of his family, Płoszowski became capable of rejecting scepticism, which only "shakes the surface of his thoughts, just a wind roughens the surface of water; the depth of which is still calm" (Sienkiewicz 1898: 258). This is why employing the family topos is often bound up with deriving premises from its members' religiosity and morality. This makes it possible to show the sphere of motives shaping the life decisions of the people who make up a family community. Family in Polish agricultural discourse does not have the character of an abstract factor, but it is portrayed in the context of shaping a specific way of human life. The employment of the topos of the family is persuasively oriented towards showing that it is in the family that there is an increase of good, which has the character of a jointly developed common good, from which everyone can benefit (Krąpiec 2004: 24–51). Such good not only does not decrease the development of individual family members but provides the basis for it. Thereby, family is shown as a place preparing for disinterested love oriented towards another person. Therefore, the topos of the family is rarely associated with deriving attitudes of selfishness and struggle against the background of antagonistic interests in life. Positive associations are often derived from the religious and moral potential that guides the family in its choices. They are presented against the background of joint participation in experiencing various life events. On a spiritual level, family togetherness in relation to these events is reflected by shared ideals of life and mutual experience of celebrations of a religious and customary nature.

Agricultural discourse encompasses a belief that performing material and spiritual tasks of the family is not possible without securing adequate material resources. Among the personal topoi mentioned by authors there is a topos concerning a person's wealth and success in life (*fortuna*) (Quintilian 1971: V, 10, 26; Saiz Noeda 2003: 95–110). It is a source concerning the derivation of rhetorical argumentation regarding the quality of a person's life. The topos of *fortuna* shows the way of deriving persuasion concerning

Rhetoric Discourse in Polish Agricultural Texts

people in Polish agricultural discourse. On the ground of rhetoric, it is believed that evocation of a person's character traits provides a rationale for developing persuasions. One of the factors that influence a person's character and conduct is the possession of something material for one's own. People who own a lot of property have some characteristics by which they stand out from others. It is noted that a rich man can undergo inner transformation affected by the wealth owned and behave differently to a poor one (Aristotle 1926: 1390b 35–1391a 4). Ownership of goods is relatively frequently bound up with increasing the self-assurance of somebody who has real resources to accomplish their aims. In some cases, wealthy people may become impudent and haughty due to the fact that numerous people solicit their acquaintance and support. Thereby, the wealth possessed may lead to the desire to rule over others and to hold power. Based on this, rhetors point out that the personal topos of wealth reveals a possible characterological difference in the behaviour of the poor and the rich. The situation is similar for those randomly experiencing life in a large family and single ones, as well as those who are positively fulfilled in their life endeavours and those experiencing failures. These situations affect the quality of people's life and have the potential for changing their moral attitude. It needs to be noted that the topos of wealth functions in an analogous fashion in agricultural discourse.

The specific nature of the topos of wealth in agricultural discourse results from the nature of factors building wealth of a person living in a farming family. The dominant statement is: "But land is a real obligation, as well as real wealth" (Sienkiewicz 1898: 678). In this case it concerns primarily the wealth possessed by a person. Wealth is portrayed as a farm which consists of land which a family owns and lives off. Since Poland used to be a typically agricultural country, it was essential, first of all, to own property in the form of land. A family house is built on the land. It is a cottage or a manor house, which is the main place of residence, and outbuildings. The land possessed may involve fields, meadows, woods, orchards, gardens or lakes. The land owned has an exceptional persuasive status. It is an immovable and durable good, and, at the same time, it is characterized by a specific potentiality. Land provides the possibility for a myriad of activities with regard to growing various plants, breeding animals, building houses. Owning land opens up a real prospect of acquiring many other goods. At the same time, economic goods acquired thanks to land have the form of a means for obtaining other goods. These, in turn, enable not only material survival but also fulfilment of needs at a spiritual level. Today, the land owned functions persuasively as a constituent of wealth desired by a part of the community. Land provides the possibility of recreation and close contact with nature whose resources are rapidly shrinking affected by urbanization processes. Its ownership becomes a marker of belonging to a part of the community that has the means to pursue a better way of life. One's own land ensures not only the possibility of safe and effective relaxation after work. It is also portrayed as a real and the most stable material good. It ensures the family privacy and appropriate conditions for bringing up children. It is persuasively bound up with the possibility of ensuring the family space for pursuing various interests of household members and an active way of life. The most often invoked motifs become the family spending time outdoors with friends, recreationally tending plants in the garden and orchard, establishing small organic crops of vegetables and herbs for the sake of the family's health, owning pets, or observing and contemplating the life of nature. In this case, it is important to note, following Curtius, that a long-accepted topos can effectively rejuvenate (Curtius 2013: 104–105).

Land conceived of as a place (*locus*) is used in Polish agricultural discourse as the main topos referring to things. Land is treated as a place of common residence and daily life of a family engaged in agriculture. The land lived on is persuasively portrayed as a factor that binds the family community together and shapes the cultural identification of those who live there. Fields, mountains, rivers or woods covering land function as symbols of building the identity of family members. The connection of the land to the family is conveyed by the names used, "mother land" and "paternal land". They contain a reference to deep maternal and paternal relationships connecting children with their mother and father. Deprivation or loss, due to various factors, of the land of cohabitation is used persuasively as an element threatening family identity. It is compared to pulling a tree from its roots and is called "uprooting". Such a process is portrayed as causing spiritual confusion of individual family members. A specific place inhabited by a family is treated persuasively as a factor of creating family and national identity (Krąpiec 2004: 24). Such motifs are introduced by Bolesław Prus in his novel *Placówka* [The Outpost]. This is an important novel that takes as its focal point the assertion in Polish agricultural discourse that to agree to sell land is to agree to a lack of freedom. Józef Ślimak, a peasant, is so attached to his fatherland that despite great pressure and a series of misfortunes that befall him, he does not even allow for the possibility of selling it: "Now you want me to sell everything. If you want me to leave, carry me out into the churchyard (...) I know everything here by heart. I have moved every clod of earth with my own hands; now you say: sell and go elsewhere" (*Selected Polish Tales* 1921: 161). His uncompromising attitude is motivated by great love for the land he owns and by the promise he made to his wife before her death, that he would never get rid of the land. With his decision not to sell the land, Józef Ślimak successfully defended the village against German colonizers. Land has a potential for organizing human life and giving a common way and style of life to those living in a particular part of it. The inhabited part of land called homeland or a country, together with elements of natural landscape belonging to it (mountains, rivers, sea, lakes), become a persuasive point of departure for invoking persuasive *pathos* themes in agricultural discourse. Among the topoi referring to persons, Polish agricultural discourse was consolidated around the topos of family and possessions. The family referred to in agricultural discourse had the characteristics of a family living in the countryside. It was traditional, religious, multi-generational, and cared about its property in the form of land ownership. In this context, the role of the basic topos referring to things was played by the land as the main living place of the farming family.

Specific Nature of Persuasion in Polish Agricultural Discourse

Land ownership shaping the manner of family life in the countryside surrounded by animals and plants built the *ethos* of landowners in Polish agricultural discourse. Because from 1795 to 1918 Poland was under the partition of Russia, Austria and Germany (Prussia), the Polish gentry was distinguished by its concern for national independence. Due to the power of the partitioners, it was impossible to fight for freedom directly. That is why the landed gentry considered the defence of the land they owned and the development of Polish culture in family life as the main way of fighting and national duty. In rhetorical tradition, employing *ethos* introduces the factor of character as a set of human traits that are the result of choices made in the area of moral conduct. *Ethos* in the field of rhetoric functions in an action context because of the implemented manner of persuasion, whose aim is to make the presented content credible (Baumlin 1994: xi–xxxi; Baumlin 2006: 278–292). In the Polish literature on agriculture, we see texts in which the key to building persuasion is the credibility associated with people's actions. The credibility of persuasion is built in relation to the traits of the person formulating a message by presenting acceptance or rejection of specific moral attitudes and choices. Practically, it is accomplished with reference to the examples of various people's decisions and conduct involved in a persuasive message. The *ethos* of landed gentry functions in an analogous way in agricultural discourse. Until the mid-nineteenth century, the term "landowners" meant all inhabitants of rural areas, but from the mid-nineteenth century it was reserved for people belonging to the nobility (Gloger 1985: 495–496). The Polish landowners were a group of owners of large landed estates in the form of manors. They were called heirs, which emphasized the fact of their coming from the nobility and inheriting significant family property from their ancestors. In relation to moral attitudes persuasion using the *ethos* of the landed gentry introduced the motif of a properly managed farm, securing in a righteous manner the means to accomplish the ideal of a well led life. This required that the landed gentry demonstrate moral prudence, various agricultural skills, and diligence. At the same time, there functioned a persuasively important theme of maintaining and propagating Polish culture. This concerned religion, upbringing and teaching, as well as Polish traditions and customs. In the area of material culture, positive associations were derived from the idea of *autarky* as self-sufficiency in securing the necessary means of subsistence. Because of the political conditions that functioned historically in Poland, the *ethos* of the landed gentry introduced the affirmation of material independence and national freedom and sovereignty. From the topos of landed gentry one ambivalently derived consequences of behaviour destructive to the individual and the community, negating the need to maintain Polish culture. Generally, the motif of land connected with a manor house standing on it and surrounded by trees protecting it from the winds was a symbol of the gentry's affirmation of a way of life rooted in Polish culture. A belief was held in Polish agricultural society that the landed gentry was supposed to accomplish such tasks. The manor symbolized the defence of freedom and the cultural strengthening of the family and state community.

The topoi employed and the moral motifs introduced provided the basis for focusing on the form of *pathos* persuasion in agricultural discourse. This persuasion consisted in stimulating different, sometimes opposite kinds of feelings (e.g. love or hate, joy or sadness, hope or despair) for land and the people connected with it. In agricultural discourse, on the one hand, *pathos* was grounded in using imagination. This imagination is shaped on the basis of a sensual contact with the world of nature. The life circumstances associated with agricultural work and life close to nature create special conditions for building rich imaginations. Individual animals, plants as well as orchards, gardens, meadows, rivers, woods, fields seen in the sunshine and in moonlight, during various seasons of the year provide a myriad of sensory experiences. Rhetoric's basic manner of evoking imagery is accumulated in the ἐνάργεια factor which is understood as expressive visualization. Expressive visualization is grounded in the fact of previous formation of imagery based on sensual cognition acquired by means of sight, hearing, touch and taste. Visualization consists in making present linguistically the depicted things as if one were directly next to them and actually saw them (Quintilian 1971: VI, 2, 29). *Pathos* in agricultural discourse is not effected solely in the emotional *delectare* function, but it supports the motivational *movere* function encouraging one to take concrete action. This mode of communication dominates the novel *Chłopi* [The Peasants] by Władysław

Reymont. It is developed in many other novels on agriculture. An example of the harmonious interaction of these persuasive forms is the message presented in the novel *Lato leśnych ludzi* [The Summer of the Forest People] by Maria Rodziewiczówna. This novel played an important role in shaping the discourse on rural life. Its main topic is hard agricultural work which takes place in constant contact with nature. Nature from early spring to late autumn is depicted in the novel in terms of presenting beauty that attracts and stimulates people. The admiration for the beauty of nature is not accomplished only in contemplation, but motivates to the arduous work of farming, whose activities are designated according to the seasons: "Ten prosperous haystacks stood in the clearings, the fruit of their labour and toil. June was coming to an end, a month of sunny triumph and majesty, a splendour of colors, growth and fragrance" (Rodziewiczówna 1997: 148). Rhetorical persuasion reveals possibilities of employing imagination in a complementary manner, combining the cognitive and aspirational spheres (O'Gorman 2005: 34). In agricultural discourse, they are an element of shaping peasant realism based on working with nature. Land, which can potentially provide an infinite amount of goods, is at the same time very concrete and demanding. Animals and plants require constant care irrespective of the weather and the farmer's well-being. Results of farming work are not completely predictable and depend on a set of really functioning and variable factors. The detailed and illustrative message derived from the topos of family, property and land has the potential to evoke strong feelings motivating for action. This leads to creating messages characterized by a unique feature of emotional rationality. Rationality in agricultural discourse is based on a realistic reading of the difficult conditions associated with agricultural work and contact with the land and the consequences of its loss. Such rationality can be found in the novel *Chłopi* [The Peasants] by Reymont in the symbolic scene of Maciej Boryna sowing a field. Sowing the field draws attention to the potential contained in nature for the continual rebirth of life. The dying Boryna does not surrender involuntarily to the horror of agony, but goes out to the field and wants to experience his death consciously during the life-giving and hopeful work of sowing, which peasants do every spring:

> Later, and near the close of the night, he worked more slowly, stopped oftener, forgot to gather the earth for his seed, and sowed empty-handed: as though he were now sowing his very being in those fields of his father – all the days he had lived, all that life he had received, and was now giving back (a sacred harvest) to the Everlasting Lord.
>
> *Reymont 1925: 328*

Thus, it derives its persuasive motifs from the truth of agriculture and nature and from reading social conditions. Emotionality is, in turn, based on persuasive stimulation to aspire for what is cognized as good, beautiful and edifying for a person in farming life and in contact with nature, as well as turning back on what is destructive. Against this background, feelings of desire and love or loathing and resentment arise, reinforcing the motives of land-bound people. This emotionality is not of a dreamy or sentimental nature. Burke believes that imagination in rhetorical messages is not meant to shape belief in the reality of fiction, but to serve to intensify what is real (Burke 1969: 79). Emotionality in agricultural discourse is conditioned by the rational factors of real contact with the land that the farmer cultivates and the community that secures or violates his right to own it and his freedom of action.

The Rational Emotionality of the Rhetorical Image of Agriculture and the Countryside in Polish Literature

All these ways of describing and presenting agriculture in Polish communication and rhetoric are described as emotional rationality, which is most clearly visible in the elocution of various texts and communications about agriculture or with agriculture as a mode of rhetorical text organization. Traditional literary texts dedicated to agriculture and the countryside, from the sixteenth century to the second half of the twentieth century, also create the basis for contemporary agricultural discourse.[1] The ingredients of this discourse are: elocution full of solemnity, reverence and harmony (e.g. "Pieśń świętojańska o Sobótce"/"Song of the Midsummer Sabbath" by Jan Kochanowski (1586) and "Żywot człowieka poczciwego"/"Existence of a Good Man" by Mikołaj Rej (1568)), and the hero of the discourse. Authors of the aforementioned texts were in fact heroes of the discourse, as texts on agriculture were created at the time by landowners/ noblemen. These authors-heroes celebrated the topos of the Good Lord in poetry and prose. The Good Lord is a landowner who goes around his domain with care and appreciates both the daily toil of peasants and their overseers and the beauty, abundance and fertility of the countryside and its produce. It is these activities connected with agriculture, or in fact with the supervision of work on the land on one's estate, coupled with other experiences, that make a man become good-natured, "characterized by a gentle disposition, sincerity, and kindness' (wsjp.pl [Contemporary Polish Dictionary]). The term 'a good-natured person' was for many centuries used as praise, an expression of appreciation and respect for the person one was talking or writing about. In the twenty-first century this phrase sounds somewhat anachronic and it appears less frequently in interpersonal communication.

Of course, in the Polish monarchical system, agriculture was associated less with the land and work on it, and more with the manor, estate, garden or park, e.g. "Sofiówka" by Stanisław Trembecki (1806), "Puławy" by Julian Ursyn Niemcewicz (1804) or "Ziemiaństwo polskie"/"Polish Gentry" by Kajetan Koźmian (1839). In addition to further realizations of the topos of the Good Lord/Husbandman ("Polish Gentry"), they show the characteristic sentimentalist and classicist presentation of land, farmland, gardens and parks in a high, solemn, pathetic style as wonders of nature and places of captivating beauty. It is not a place of work, it is a place of delight, of emotion, of romance/ love and of rest, e.g. "Still in Sofijowka he may marvel/ And he will confess, if sincerity is in his mouth:/ 'What those in parts are famous, this one possesses together!'/ Weighing the immensity of the work and the numerous ornaments./ They will later say: 'It was a monarchical work!'" (our translation) (from "Sofiówka" by Stanisław Trembecki (1806)).

Contact with the land and agriculture also shapes the character and it is a place where the highest values are stored – this, in turn, is the content of Polish texts about agriculture in Romanticism, Positivism, and Modernism (Young Poland). Examples of these include ballads filled with moral teachings, uttered by characters from the people ("Daughter, – the old man says to her –/ There is no crime without punishment./ But if sincere repentance,/ The Lord God listens to criminals" – Adam Mickiewicz, "Lilije" (1822)), as well as modernist poems or dramas ("Since a peasant has something of a Piast/ something of those Piast kings – a lot! … and a great, great deal of a Piast;/ peasant is power and that's that" – Stanisław Wyspiański, "Wesele" (1901) (own translation).

Twentieth- and twenty-first-century novels, dramas, and poems present a dual, ambivalent view of the countryside and agriculture – full of admiration for everyday toil and appreciation for naturalistic and biological morality and ethics vs. mockery of villagers and contempt for their intellectual limitations, primitivism, and vegetative existence.

However, the contemporary rhetorical image of agriculture and rural areas, as well as people and activities related to them, is no longer the effect of literature or journalism of the last hundreds of years and decades, but the result of cultural and social changes that took place in Poland after World War II, and especially in the last half-century. Thanks to them or against their essence, the emotional elocution of texts on agriculture is a continuation of lofty and pathetic ways of interpreting the world of land and countryside or, in our opinion, much more interesting, the use of concepts and words connected with agriculture, land and countryside as the basis of tropes and rhetorical figures employed in texts on other subjects and in public and colloquial utterances. Linguistic constructions and rhetorical figures are then the means of axiologization of the reality interpreted in these messages, and they can both enhance the value of the world presented in the text, and, what is more and more frequent in the urbanized, postindustrial and communicative reality, depreciate people and phenomena connected with agriculture appearing in the texts, or ridicule other areas of modern man's life by analogies with agriculture and the countryside.

The Varied Rhetorical Image of Agriculture and Rural Areas in Contemporary Polish – between Literalness and Metaphor

The rhetorical construct of agriculture and the figures/tropes related to it in Polish culture at the turn of the twentieth and twenty-first century will be reconstructed on the basis of Polish language corpora, especially the National Corpus of Polish Language (nkjp.pl) which includes various texts that span the last 30 years – for this reason, this language corpus makes it possible to successfully verify textual realizations of agricultural discourse. As for other sources, we also draw from contemporary general dictionaries of the Polish language – Uniwersalny słownik języka polskiego (sjp. pwn.pl) [Universal Polish Dictionary] and Współczesny słownik języka polskiego (wsjp.pl) [Contemporary Polish Dictionary] where the most frequent contexts and uses of Polish agricultural discourse appear (vocabulary, expressions). The presence of these expressions and vocabulary confirms their central position in this discourse. We also apply selected excerpts from texts available on the Internet, concerning various areas of human life and making use of various linguistic and rhetorical mechanisms and genre patterns. These excerpts allow for the reconstruction of agricultural discourse in contemporary Polish language; they are so obvious and frequent in Polish language that we are not going to refer to specific sources, definitions or quotes as they are always cropping up in the aforementioned corpora and dictionaries as well as easy to find on popular Polish websites. Therefore we will not refer to the source of the definition or quotation each time, as they always come from the collections and dictionaries listed.

In our analyses, in addition to the aforemenetioned rhetorical methodology, we will also refer to the structuralist concept of semantic fields, created by German scholars, among others Jost Trier (Trier 1931) and Leo Weisgerber (Weisgerber 1933). According to this theory, the lexical units of any natural language form semantic fields, i.e. ordered and hierarchical sets of lexemes, connected with each other by various semantic relations. Ryszard Tokarski holds that by a lexical-semantic field we understand a group of words that are linked by a common meaning, between which there exist specific semantic relations, which are to result in a compact and hierarchical system. The thus conceived field constitutes an element of the overall lexical-semantic system.

Tokarski 1984: 11

Thus a common feature of all theories of semantic fields is the conviction that the meaning of a word determines the other lexical units in the field and therefore analysing isolated words, without presenting a connection with the others, does not make any sense. Relations between words make it possible to recreate an abstract concept grid existing in a language, invariable and different for each nation, superimposed on reality by the language system. Thus, the analysis of semantic fields may elucidate the peculiarities and forms of linguistic thinking of the world of language users or present a specific interpretation of reality by one author of a corpus of texts (in the case of literary texts and other types of linguistic creation). Lexical fields are a linguistic mantle that overlaps with conceptual fields (Tokarski 2006: 35–46). Therefore, we shall endeavour to determine semantic fields which involve words connected with agriculture and the countryside and then we shall investigate their rhetoric potential which is revealed in semantic and pragmatic relationships within specific fields and among the fields. Many of these terms both in the language system and in textual usage are characterized by ambiguity (polysemy), which is achieved by one of the most obvious rhetorical stylistic devices – metaphor. Beginning from the last decades of the twentieth century (Lakoff and Johnson 1980; Lakoff 1987), metaphor has become a perfect means of emotionalization and axiologization of argumentation in discussion, in speech, in conveying information and opinions, and in other communication-rhetoric actions (as metaphor is one of the four rhetoric tropes). Many metaphoric constructions utilized by any sender of any message are interpreted by hearers in an unambiguous way since the similarity between the themes of metaphor and the concepts evoked by them is natural, obvious and typical for them. This is because it stems from the traditions, culture, experiences and observations that every natural language user has. One of these cultural and everyday experiences is a direct or indirect contact with agriculture, the countryside and the contexts associated with them, and among these contexts also with another very important linguistic means for argumentation and emotionalization – idioms. Working on the land, people's and animals' behaviour and customs as well as other aspects of country life have become one of the most important (apart from literature and history) sources of idioms in the Polish language, e.g. *Nie zasypiaj gruszek w popiele* (equivalent of: *Make hay while the sun shines*) or *Wyskoczyć jak filip z konopi* (equivalent of: *To put one's foot in one's mouth*) (Pajdzińska 1993). Hence, we will also endeavour to assess the rational emotionality attached to the most popular contemporary collocations and paroemias based on cultivation, breeding and everyday life in the countryside.

The first of these semantic fields is formed by verbs, nouns and adjectives/adjectival participles related to agricultural work. At the centre of this field are the verbs *plough* and *sow*, and the nouns *ploughing* and *sowing*, which are related semantically and grammatically to them.

The word *plough* in its basic meaning signifies "to loosen the soil with a plough, to prepare it for sowing or planting crops" and is combined in the following constructions: *a peasant, farmer ploughs*; *to plough a field, stubble field, fallow land, land*; *to plough with a plough, horse, tractor, ox; to plough and harrow, to plough and sow.* The lexical connotations (cultural-experiential associations) emphasize that the activity of ploughing is very hard (*plough – hard, laborious work*) and difficult, and this leads to metaphorization and phraseologization of the term and the connections formed by it. *Orać jak wół [to plough like an ox]* (equivalent of: work like a slave), noted as a secondary meaning in WSJP (the Great Polish Dictionary), means "colloquially, to work hard". In the same sense, the verb is used when describing someone's life and it is said *orał całe życie [he worked hard all his life]*; *orał w swojej firmie od świtu do nocy [he worked hard in his business from dawn to dusk]* or *it seemed to him he would be able to orać w szkole [work hard] like that at school even until retirement, but his first heart attack at the age of 50 robbed him of his illusions.*

In the third meaning, the verb to plough means "to use someone for hard work" and is combined with *someone*, e.g. *orał swoimi podwładnymi [he made his staff work their guts off] not paying attention to their health and needs.* And finally, in the fourth meaning, *to plough* means "to make furrows on some surface by moving something over it" – nowadays most often in the perfective form – *przeorać* or *rozorać coś* or *komuś coś to plough* or *rip up* something or someone, e.g. *przeorać mu samochód* (to "damage the paint or bodywork of his car") or *rozorać sobie twarz [to rip up one's face]* (to "cut one's face deeply with something or against something on a larger surface"). In some contexts, *przeorać samochód* (to search a car) can also make use of a two-level metaphorization, since *orać (to plough)* here means neither to loosen the ground nor to make furrows on something, only "to search something thoroughly, methodically, in great detail, sometimes violently".

Apart from these perfect forms of the verb there is also the term *zaorać [plough]*, which, apart from completing the process of loosening the soil, metaphorically also means: a. to liquidate something, e.g. a shipyard, a factory; b. "col. to tire by prolonged work or physical exertion", e.g. a worker, an athlete; c. "col. to publicly do or say something to someone that compromises that person, e.g. a politician, an interlocutor". Thus, each time it is emphasized that a violent, agonizing process has come to an irrevocable end. Due to these connotative semantic features, the word *to plough* is also a vulgar term for having sexual intercourse, e.g. *zaorać panienkę [have sex with a girl]*.

The use of the entire semantic bundle of the word *orać [to plough]* and its derivative words in rhetorical communication indicates a very blunt, often colloquial confirmation of the author's beliefs and emphasizes the hardship and finality of the actions taken. It is not an equal, positive and inclusive communication. Rather, it serves to antagonize and build a barrier between the speaker/author and the story character or audience.

It is also unusual in the field of names of agricultural activities that the very important and positive activity of *siew [sowing]* and the verb *siać [to sow]* also refer to negative phenomena. While the first meaning of the word *siać [to sow]* "to place seeds in the ground so that plants grow out of them" and the typical collocations – *to sow buckwheat, barley, clover, corn, carrots, mint, seed, oats, millet, wheat, sunflower, grass, vegetables, grain, rye; to sow in autumn, in spring; to sow in April, in May; to sow by machine, by hand; to sow and plough, to sow and plant, to sow and harvest, to sow and reap* – are descriptive-positive, the emotional, axiological and communicative metaphorical-retrospective potential of this word for agricultural activity is already definitely negative. A person saying or doing something can *sow unrest, anarchy, chaos, ferment, horror, fear, hatred, disbelief, discord, panic, rumours, panic, terror, propaganda, racism, havoc, death, doubt, confusion, disorder, scorn, evil, destruction in others [zasiać niepokój, anarchię, chaos, ferment, grozę, lęk, nienawiść, niewiarę, niezgodę, panikę, pogłoski, popłoch, postrach, propagandę, rasizm, spustoszenie, śmierć, wątpliwości, zamęt, zamieszanie, zgorszenie, zło, zniszczenie*], i.e. "cause negative phenomena or spread something that causes them". In addition, they will *sow in the heads, in the hearts, in the minds; in the people, in the society, in the environment; in the country, in the neighborhood* [*siać w głowach, w sercach, w umysłach; w ludziach, w społeczeństwie, w środowisku; w kraju, w okolicy*], i.e. affect rhetorically not by appealing to the needs and aspirations but to the fears of most people (McQuail 2021: 446–474). Other metaphorical meanings, e.g. "to shoot in series" (*to shoot with a machine gun* [*siać z karabinu maszynowego*]) or "to scatter, splash something around" (*to scatter water droplets all over the room* [*rozsiewać krople wody po całym pokoju*]), do not change much in this assessment of rhetorical potential.

On the other hand, the word *ziarno* [*seed*], which is the basis of sowing, already has a completely different rhetorical value. It very often gives the utterance a positive, inclusive and equal character, because besides the basic meanings, "seeds of grain intended primarily for eating or sowing" and "the edible seed of certain crops", it is used in a connotative meaning – cultural and textual – "lit. a small intensity of mental or emotional states, qualities or properties". On the basis of this meaning of *seed*, one can construct a coherent and complete picture of any emotions, qualities or properties such as *the seed of love sprouts, grows, and it sprouted true love* [*ziarno miłości kiełkuje, rośnie, wyrosła z niego prawdziwa miłość*] or *The seed of wisdom that his teachers planted in him* [*Ziarno mądrości, które zasiali w nim jego nauczyciele*] *hit fertile ground and grew into a solid tree that resulted in many innovative projects.*

This field of agricultural work also includes other verbs, nouns, and adjectives/adjectival participles, such as harrow, chaff, scarify, rake, dig, plant, pick; dig, harvest, haymaking, crops, raise, manure; ploughed, dug, sowed, picked, grazed, harvested, which confirm and perpetuate the value and emotion contained in the agricultural activities expressed by the words described earlier that form the centre of this field.

Another semantic field important for the rhetorical value of communication about agriculture and the countryside in Polish culture is the field of names of male and female villagers and farm workers. This time, at the centre of the field there are three pairs of terms: quite neutral *farmer/farmwoman* [*rolnik/rolniczka*], very emotional *peasant/countrywoman (peasant woman)* [*chłop/baba (chłopka)*] (as they serve to negatively evaluate everyone who is rude, primitive and/or aggressive, regardless of their providence), and positively valuing *husbandman/goodwife* [*gospodarz/gospodyni*] (very close is also the *villager/rural woman* [*wieśniak/wieśniaczka*]). A *farmer* [rolnik], whose hypernym is the word *peasant* [*gospodarz*], meaning "a person running a farm" or "a specialist in agriculture", has no metaphorical or rhetorical meanings or emotional-valuational components established in the Polish language. Of course, contextually it can express derision, mockery, or disrespect, yet the number of constructions in which such a procedure occurs is really negligible. Certainly several dozen times less than in the case of *peasant* and *peasant woman* [*chłop* and *baba*]. The noun *peasant* [*chłop*] in its basic meaning of "col. a person living in the countryside and running a farm" also has few emotional-valuational elements, but its stylistic colloquialism causes it to mean also "col. an adult man" and "col. a man with whom someone is emotionally attached and forms a permanent couple". Both of these meanings came from the connotation of the term *peasant* as a farmer, because it is associated in Polish culture with "power, simplicity, uncomplicated personality". The colloquial meanings of the word are humorous, somewhat ironic, emotional descriptions of men. It is from here that we also derive *peasant reason* [*chłopski rozum*], the "ability of thinking with common sense, resulting from life experience and intuition, and not from possessed knowledge", the *peasant philosopher* [*chłopski filozof*], that is, "using peasant reason", as well as *peasant ancestry, peasant origins, peasant roots* and *the peasant thing/ matter*, "the thing that men do and which is not meant for women", characteristic of very many Poles.

While *peasant* [*chłop*] has a humorous and only slightly ironic character in the rhetorical actions of the speaker (this may also result from the patriarchal nature of the Polish linguistic worldview and language itself (cf. Bartmiński 2009), the rhetorical, emotional-axiological value of the noun *peasant woman* [*baba*] is sometimes humorous and slightly ironic, but as a rule it is very depreciative and aggressive.

The basic meaning of *peasant woman* [*baba*] is "col. a woman to whom the speaker has a disrespectful attitude", but it is also "col. someone's wife or lover" and "col. a woman from the village", as well as six other meanings with different semantic motivations. In the case of agriculture and the countryside, *peasant woman* is the negation of *peasant*, because the world of the countryside in Polish culture is not matriarchal, and hence "woman coming from the countryside" is evaluated negatively (see Bartmiński 2009), because it is a *country peasant woman* [*wiejska baba*] (a deliberate tautology, reinforcing the prejudice contained in the very term *peasant woman*), whose rhetorical value in Polish phraseology is defined both by proverbs: *where the devil cannot go, he sends a woman* [*gdzie diabeł nie może, tam babę pośle*]; *that's that problem out of the way* [*baba z wozu koniom lżej*] (literally: a woman out of the cart, the horses draw more lightly), as well as by fixed word combinations: *woman's logic* [*babska logika*] "lack of logic", *woman's curiosity* [*babska ciekawość*]; *woman's talk* [*babskie gadanie*]; *woman's clothes* [*babskie ciuchy*], *fancies* [*fanaberie*], *mood swings* [*humory*], *chit-chat* [*pogaduszki*], *conversations* [*rozmowy*], *affairs* [*sprawy*]; and *like a woman* [*po babsku*] (in a way characteristic of women, but with disrespect). *Baba* [*girl, as in the expression "don't be such a girl"*] is also "contemptuously: a man of little manliness, cowardly, timid and of a weak character", and *ktoś zachował się jak baba* [*someone behaved like a woman*] is one of the greatest insults to a man brought up in the twentieth century in a traditional axiological system. *Jesteś babą* [*you are a sissy*] is as negatively evaluative as *jesteś chamem* [*you are a boor*]. *Cham* [*boor*] means "contemptuously: a formerly used term for a person belonging to a lower social class", and in Poland used especially about villagers, peasants. Today, it is primarily a term meaning: "pejoratively: a man behaving rudely and boorishly, violating established conventions of behaviour and rules of coexistence with other people", and thus very similar to a prototypical form among the many words developed in the semantic field of names for villagers and farm workers – *wieśniak* [*villager*]. This name means "col. pejorat. a primitive man who does not know how to behave", although formerly this was how the villager/farmer was described. The same emotional-axiological features are present in the word *wieśniaczka* [*rural woman*], or actually *wieśniara*, because it also means "col. pejorat. a primitive woman who does not know how to behave", although previously it was simply a term for a woman living in a village.

In the field of names of male and female villagers and farm workers, there are many other words with varying rhetorical potential: *ploughman, reaper, haymaker, combine-harvester operator, carpenter, blacksmith*. Globalization and popular culture have led to the emergence in Polish communication of the expression the *Grim Reaper*, which often replaces the Old Polish *kostucha*, or *death*. In turn, the Catholic religion has perpetuated in the Polish language the positive emotionalization and valuing of the word *carpenter*, which after all was St. Joseph's profession, and a very typical paraphrase for Jesus is also a *carpenter's son*. The *blacksmith* was also a word of great importance for the European cultural circle and its rhetorical potential can be seen to this day in the saying *Każdy jest kowalem swego losu* [*Everyone is the blacksmith of their fate*], and also in the whole conceptual structure of blacksmithing (among other things, *wykuwać w trudach czyjś charakter* [*forge someone's character in hardship*], *kuźnia talentów* [*talents forge*], *odkuć się po latach* [*roar back after years*], *skuć lodem* [*to be ice-bound*]), which allows one to present many areas of human activity in categories of this craft.

The latter examples included a place name, a building in the countryside (*kuźnia* [*forge*]), and this kind of term forms the third rhetorically important semantic field connected with agriculture in Polish – the names of places and buildings. At the centre of this field are, of course, the names of human habitations – *cottage* [*chata*] and *peasant cottage* [*chałupa*], and around them there are the names of other farm buildings of the rural habitat – *cowshed, barn, pigsty,* and *henhouse. Cottage* [*chata*] and *peasant cottage* [*chałupa*] are still metaphorically/metonymically and emotionally used to denote any house or flat, for it is "col. the place where one lives at any given time" – *wracam na chatę* [*I go back to my place*], *idę do chałupy* [*I'm going to my crib*]. Whereas the word *chałupniczo* (*produkować coś chałupniczo* [*to do outwork*]) means "at home; in a small amount; on a small scale", which also links *peasant cottage* with any place of residence and confirms the near-meaningfulness of *cottage* and *peasant cottage* [*chata* and *chałupa*] with *house* and *flat*.

Among outbuildings, *barn* and *pigsty* [*obora* and *chlew*] have very popular emotional-negative rhetorical properties. A *barn* today is not only "a room or building where cattle raised on a farm are kept", but also "a disorder" (*zrobić komuś oborę*) and "to ridicule someone" (*robić komuś oborę*). The word which is used in a similar way in contemporary Polish is *pigsty* [*chlew*], which, besides the obvious meaning of "a farm building for raising pigs", is very often employed in the meaning of "col. a very dirty and neglected room" (*someone made a pigsty* [*ktoś zrobił chlew*]; *someone lives in a pigsty* [*ktoś ma chlew w domu*]).

In turn, *stodoła* [*barn*] appears in metaphorical meanings mainly in collocations: *drunk as a lord* [*pijany jak stodoła*] "very intoxicated", *barn of a house* [*wielki jak stodoła*] "huge, of great dimensions", and sometimes *foolish as a calf* [*pusty jak stodoła*] ("foolish"), because a *barn*, apart from the basic meaning of "a large farm building intended for storing hay, straw and grain", in connotative meaning evokes, above all, "size" and "being empty during the period preceding the new harvest/spring break".

One can distinguish many more such semantic fields in communication about agriculture and the countryside, e.g. the field of crop names (*grain, rye, oats, potatoes, onions, hay, pears,* etc.), the field of farm place names (*garden, yard, orchard, fallow land,* etc.), the field of farm tool names (*plough, harrow, pitchfork, axe, scythe, sickle, sower, sieve,* etc.), the field of plant names, the field of season and weather names, and many, many others.

Conclusion

We have focused our attention on rhetorical tropes and ways of contemporary use of linguistic units derived from texts about agriculture, rather than on the texts themselves, for several cultural and communicative reasons.

We focused our attention on rhetorical topoi and tropes and ways of traditional and modern use of linguistic texts and units derived from publications on agriculture. From our analysis we conclude that persuasion in Polish agricultural texts is based on several topoi related to persons or things and presents a specific form of conveying emotions. Traditionally, the person topos in agricultural discourse focuses mainly on property (*fortuna*) and family (*genus*). The topos of real estate is founded on the ownership of the land (fields, meadows, forests, orchards and lakes). Land ownership shaped the life of people in the countryside among plants and animals, and built the ethos of landowners. The ethos developed around the issue of good land use, which gives the family freedom, economic independence, security and development. On the other hand, land, with its particular characteristics of potential and endurance, is the main topos of the things that make up agricultural discourse. These topoi are the basis for building the persuasion of pathos, which includes various, sometimes opposing emotions towards the earth and people associated with it. Pathos is not only the use of imagination built on a sensual contact with the world of nature. It also supports the creation of peasant realism, based on working with nature, as well as (in our view) contributing to emotional rationality. However, the description of Polish agricultural discourse must include the non-linguistic context as well. This context consists of several elements.

First, in the Polish reality of the twenty-first century, agriculture has become, as a result of social, political and economic transformations, a much less important sphere of activity for Poles than in previous years. Because of EU regulations, mechanization of agriculture, narrow specialization, and preference for large farms, neither important journalistic texts, nor crucial political speeches, nor the most important literary texts often deal with the everyday life of the countryside and agriculture.

Second, at the turn of the twentieth and twenty-first centuries, a gap appeared between the city and the countryside in terms of the economic and social situation and access to culture and technology (especially the Internet). Hence, the metaphors and collocations that had existed for years, showing the countryside in an unfavourable light, became even more profound and brought back to public communication terms in which references to the countryside or work on the land are depreciating and negative. These are mostly colloquial words and expressions, but they build up and consolidate in the consciousness of Polish language users an image of the countryside to which one has a less and less positive and elevated attitude. The last few years have weakened this division, but only due to the inclusive and neutral language postulated by the EU which has reduced the number and frequency of use of these pejorative and ridiculing words and constructions in texts on a variety of topics, but this has not led to the neutralization or revaluation of agriculture and rural life in Polish public language.

Third, according to the data of the Polish Central Statistical Office, in 2020, 60% of Poles lived in cities and 40% lived in villages. However, only 7% of Poles are involved in agriculture because the remaining 33% of rural residents either work in the city and have small crops and livestock for themselves or, far more frequently, have recently moved to the countryside, making it a suburb of the city where they have lived for years and continue to work. These statistics represent one of the cultural reasons for the change in contemporary emotional and rational agricultural discourse in Poland.

It is for these rhetorical and contextual reasons mentioned here in this Conclusion that the discourse on agriculture in Poland has become a rhetorical discourse of agriculture that the discourses about other kinds of everyday work and activities of Poles employ in an emotional, valuing, and effective way.

Although our study is not complete, in our opinion it indicates the most important directions for further research on rhetoric and language of Polish texts on agriculture and Polish agricultural discourse.

Note

1 In this chapter, we define "discourse" as a piece of text in a context (Dobrzyńska 1990).

References
English-Language References

Aristotle (1960–1961) *Ars Rhetorica, Opera ex recensione*. I. Bekkeri, ed. 2. O. Gigon. Berolini.

Baumlin, J. S. (1994) "Introduction: Positioning Ethos in Historical and Contemporary Theory". In *Ethos: New Essays in Rhetorical and Critical Theory*. Edited by J. S. Baumlin and T. F. Baumlin. Dallas: Southern Methodist University Press, XI–XXXI.

Baumlin J. S. (2006) "Ethos". In *Encyclopedia of Rhetoric*. Edited by T. O. Sloane. New York: Oxford University Press, 263–277.

Burke, K. (1969) *A Rhetoric of Motives*. Berkeley: University of California Press.

Curtius, E. R. (2013) *European Literature and the Latin Middle Ages*. Princeton: Princeton University Press.

Goodnight, G. T. (1982) "The Personal, Technical and Public Spheres of Argument. A Speculative Inquiry into the Art of Public Deliberation". *Journal of the American Forensic Association* 18: 214–227.

Grimaldi, W. M. A. (1972) *Studies in the Philosophy of Aristotle's Rhetoric*. Wiesbaden: Franz Steiner Verlag.

Jackos, J. S. and Scott, J. (1980) "Structure of Conversational Argument. Pragmatic Bases for the Enthymeme". *Quarterly Journal of Speech* 66: 251–265.

Lakoff, G. (1987) *Women, Fire, and Dangerous Things: What Categories Reveal About the Mind*. Chicago: University of Chicago Press.

Lakoff, G. and Johnson, M. (1980). *Metaphors We Live By*. Chicago: University of Chicago Press.

Noeda, B. S. (2003) "Proof, Arguments, Places. Argumentation and Rhetorical Theory in the Institutio Oratoria, Book V". In *Quintilian and the Law. The Art of Persuasion in Law and Politics*. Edited by O. Tellegan-Couperus. Leuven: Leuven University Press.

O'Gorman, N. (2005) "Aristotle's 'Phantasia' in the 'Rhetoric': 'Lexis', Appearance, and the Epideictic Function of Discourse". *Philosophy and Rhetoric* 38/1: 16–40.

Quintilianus, M. F. (1971) *Institutio oratoria libri XII*, vols. 1–2. Edited by L. Rademacher. Lipsiae: Edition Leipzig.

Reymont, L. (1925) *The Peasants. Spring*. Translated from the original Polish by M. H. Dziewicki. New York: Alfred A. Knopf Publisher.

Selected Polish Tales (1921). Translated by E. C. M. Benecke, M. Busch, and H. Milford. London: Oxford University Press.

Sienkiewicz, H. (1898) *Children of the Soil*. Authorized and unabridged translation from the Polish by J. Curtin. Boston: Little, Brown and Company.

"The Preliminary Exercises of Nicolaus the Sophist" (2003) In *Progymnasmata. Greek Textbooks of Prose Composition and Rhetoric*. Translated with introductions and notes by G. A. Kennedy. Boston: Leiden.

Other-Language References

Bartmiński, J. (2009) *Językowe podstawy obrazu świata*. Lublin: Wydawnictwo UMCS.

Brückner, A. (1989) *Słownik etymologiczny języka polskiego*. Warszawa: Wiedza Powszechna.

Dobrzyńska, T. (1990) *Tekst w kontekście*. Wrocław: Ossolineum.

Emrich, B. (1977) "Topika i topoi". *Pamiętnik Literacki* 68/1: 235–263.

Gloger, Z. (1985) *Encyklopedia staropolska ilustrowana*. Warszawa: Wiedza Powszechna.

Krąpiec, M. A. (2004) *Rozważania o narodzie*. Lublin: Wydawnictwo Fundacja Servire Veritati Instytut Edukacji Narodowej.

McQuail, D. (2021) *Teoria komunikowania masowego*. Warszawa: Wydawnictwo Naukowe PWN.

Pajdzińska, A. (1993) *Frazeologizmy jako tworzywo współczesnej poezji*. Lublin: Wydawnictwo UMCS.

Rodziewiczówna, M. (1997) *Lato leśnych ludzi*. Warszawa: Wydawnictwo Prószyński i S-ka.

Tokarski, R. (1984) *Struktura pola znaczeniowego*. Warszawa: Państwowe Wydawnictwo Naukowe.
Tokarski, R. (2006) "Pola znaczeniowe i ramy interpretacyjne – dwa spojrzenia na język". *Ling Varia* 1: 35–46.
Trier, J. (1931) *Der deutsche Wortschatz im Sinnbezirk des Verstandes*. Bonn: Ph.D. diss.
Weisgerber, L. (1933) *Die Stellung der Sprache im Aufbau der Gesamtkultur*. Heidelberg: C. Winter.

26

RHETORIC IN TRAVEL WRITING

A Tool to Enhance Verisimilitude and Persuade Readers

David Taranco

Introduction: Travel, Travel Writing, and Rhetoric

Wandering has been closely tied to humankind since the hunter-gatherer cultures of the Palaeolithic. Agriculture, sedentary lifestyle, and other behavioural changes made it unnecessary to travel in search of water, food, and shelter. However, this did not bring roaming to an end. Resource-based nomadism was gradually replaced by a form of travelling that satisfied very different needs: warring expeditions, territorial conquests, commercial exchanges, personal enrichment, acquisition of knowledge, and so on. Over time, once writing developed well enough to become a record-keeping and communication tool, travel and, hence, travel writing came to be an effective method to disseminate ideas and convey morality.

Since the first travelogues of ancient times, every traveller-writer has been confronted by the need of being both plausible and convincing. Persuasiveness, thus, has always been a key element in the process of shaping an ethical and epistemological perspective upon readers and gaining their cognitive submission. However, not only do travellers vie for verisimilitude, but they also aim at reducing the distance with the reader so that the latter feels that he or she is journeying along with the author and having the same exploits, which also enhances plausibility and trustworthiness. As readers do not usually have the means to verify the authenticity of traveller-writers' descriptions and experiences, rhetoric – when used effectively – has a strong psychological effect upon the audience and, therefore, contributes to banishing any doubt concerning factualness and intensifying the travelling experience.

In this process, figures of speech are the tools that, using Heidegger's terminology, spring up ready-to-hand to the benefit of traveller-writers. That is to say, authors make use of rhetorical devices to achieve their persuasive goals in travel accounts without being too much concerned with the manipulation scheme that lies behind the procedure, or without even being conscious of it whatsoever. As a result of that cogent and alluring force, readers end up yielding to rhetoric and fall in a passive and receptive state, since

DOI: 10.4324/9781003195276-32

ordinary people, as Rollings aptly argues, do not 'wield and stand guard against linguistic techniques of rule'.[1]

That said, what I attempt to do in this chapter is to show how rhetoric is used by writers to escape scrutiny over verisimilitude and to shape the realm of experience in their travel accounts. This approach will afford us the opportunity to look at some specific figures of speech that are utilized in travelogues not only by virtue of their aesthetic value but also because of their persuasive effect. I have two primary goals: first, I want to identify several rhetorical devices commonly used by traveller-writers; second, I intend to show how different authors make use of them in their accounts. I would like to stress that the guiding premise of this study is that rhetoric is one of the greatest assets in the hands of writers to embellish or uglify descriptions in pursuit of an impressive persuasive harmony. But before going into detail, let us take a brief look at the origin of travel writing and how scholarship has dealt with it in past decades.

A Brief Historical Overview of Travel Writing

We may speculate that travel writing arose near the very beginning of written language. Some scholars have traced its origins back to the *Story of Wenamun*, a text written in Egypt around 1000 BCE; yet it is difficult to ascertain that this is indeed a journey report.[2] Thus, let us date back the first travelogues in times of ancient Greece and its periegeses. This was a sort of descriptive travel account that included a geographical survey, a cultural inventory (monuments and works of art), and a compilation of myths and legends. Since those early travelogues, this narrative form has evolved in accord with prevailing social and political standards: Greek and Roman ethnographic and historical records such as Herodotus' *Histories* (c. 430 BCE), Xenophon's *Anabasis* (c. 370 BCE), Julius Caesar's *Commentaries on the Gallic War* (c. 58–46 BCE) and Tacitus' *Germania* (c. 98 CE) were followed by moralizing and doctrinal accounts of pilgrimages in Christian and Muslim domains from the late Roman period to the Middle Ages, chronicles of the Crusades and early adventure accounts up to *The Travels of Marco Polo* (c. 1300), a book that marked a turning point for travel writing. In the wake of its publication, legions of venturers, explorers and fortune hunters embarked on dubious enterprises in distant lands yet unknown to Europeans and, in many a case, set about writing of their experiences. Some of those pioneer voyagers may have been moved by Petrarch's call to end the *frigida incuriositas*, that is, the intellectual indifference that ruled the Middle Ages to a great extent.[3] Others were simply impelled by pecuniary necessity or personal vanity. Columbus probably had a foot in both camps. His travels to the New World opened the way for brand-new chronicles, taxonomical accounts of lands and peoples, and geographical surveys. This travel writing produced abundant knowledge to satisfy the desire for power and wealth, and, at the same time, to entertain the European reader who longed for exoticism. The Age of Exploration, apart from bringing fruitful discoveries and harmful exploitation, increased the demand for travel accounts. People were encouraged to journey around the world to obtain empirical knowledge and education, as Francis Bacon put it in his essay *Of Travel* (1625). This yearning for wisdom was eventually challenged – and sometimes overshadowed – by a more spontaneous and individual attitude put forward by Romanticism where subjectivity was no longer a fault to be despised. As Cardinal states, the Romantic traveller could become the director and scriptwriter of the travel scenario since the accumulation of factual experience was not the only goal when travelling.[4] Soon after, tourism began to flourish and, hence, a modern configuration of travel writing that merged teaching, delighting, and moving, that is, Cicero's *docere, delectare* and *movere*, consolidated at the turn of the nineteenth century. This narrative form has continued to develop ever since around those three pillars that were already seen, to a greater or lesser extent, in the early periegeses of ancient Greece, and now constitutes a valuable source of information for historians.

The Historiographic Value of Travelogues: The (Re)Discovery

Travel writing, however, was for a long time neglected and regarded as a minor literary genre – if at all considered as such – and has only been (re)discovered in recent decades as a result of an always growing interest in cultural history and postcolonial hermeneutics. Peter Burke argues in *Varieties of Cultural History* (1997) that travel narrative might be among the most eloquent sources for the study of human societies, but, at the same time, he acknowledges that some texts are not spontaneous and objective descriptions of new experiences, so we must be on guard when determining their historiographic value.[5] I agree with Burke's admonition inasmuch as since the onset of this autonomous category of literary composition – I do consider travel writing to be an independent literary genre with its own specific characteristics – countless travelogues have undeniably been used in a bigoted and self-interested way to present foreign regions as spaces whose anthropological and cultural framework stands apart or even clashes with the traveller-writer's and the reader's shared beliefs, customs, and values. Consequently, once and again many scholars and historians dealing with travel writing have turned their attention to this partial and distorting characterization of distant lands. Mary B. Campbell's *The Witness and the Other World: Exotic European Travel Writing, 400–1600* (1988) surveys works that expound the history of encounter and empire; yet, she seems to bypass the use of rhetoric for persuasion in favour of an insightful analysis of travel narrative from a postcolonial perspective. Similarly, Mary Louise Pratt's *Imperial Eyes: Travel Writing and Transculturation* (1992) is an impressive study that shows how travel writing has been used as an ideological device to encourage and justify expansionist enterprises. It is true, as Said pointed out, that travel writing has often been exploited for the benefit of the traveller's culture.[6] Therefore, rhetorical devices such as inversion and comparison have been customary since they allow the traveller to pinpoint the travellee's anomalous dissemblance and alterity. Nowadays there is a growing awareness of how rhetorical comparison can contribute to creating hierarchical binaries, shaping frames of reference not necessarily objective or universal, and categorizing peoples. As a result, recent scholarship has been addressing the need to transform comparison and comparative rhetoric in order to be able to review predominant narratives of power by defamiliarizing the self and recontextualizing the way of presenting the other.[7] However, I believe that there is a lack of scholarship about how figures of speech are used to turn travel accounts into a cogent representation of reality despite the sometimes-biased knowledge they transmit. Talented authors succeed in driving readers along the way through subtle rhetorical devices so that they do not ever question the truth of the words conveyed and, likewise, never envision a different framework. This is extremely important because should the traveller-writer fail to win the reader over, both the text's iniquitous aspirations and its unforeseen consequences will be sterile.

Alburquerque-García is one among the scholars that have taken up the study of figures of speech in travelogues, but he has limited his survey to the use of rhetorical devices as intensifiers of meaning, introductory clauses to digressions, tools for comparison and detailed representation of reality.[8] For their part, Rollings and Sell, to name but two, have focused, respectively, on ethics and truth. What I attempt to do is to concentrate on the persuasive power of rhetoric to enhance credibility. In the following pages, I will identify six often overlooked rhetorical devices – *anacoenosis, anakephalaiosis*, definition, dialogism, *exergasia*, and foreignization – and I will show some examples that illustrate their use as persuasive tools in travelogues. It is not my intention to survey an extensive corpus of works; rather, I have selected some qualitative examples from authors who have visited Japan since the end of the seclusion period known as *sakoku* and my sample comprises books in three languages – English, French and Spanish.[9] Some of them can be considered major representative works of travel writing on Japan such as Isabella Bird's *Unbeaten Tracks in Japan* (1880), a book in which the British traveller describes her journey through Japan in 1878, a decade after the Meiji Restoration of 1868, providing us with an extraordinary picture of ordinary life in the country. Even more commercially successful than Bird's anthropological account was Pierre Loti's novelized journal *Madame Chrysanthemum* (1887). This work was widely read and translated from the original French into several languages; it also gave rise to other similar stories, and it was an indirect source of inspiration for Puccini's opera *Madama Butterfly* (1904). Loti's bestseller is regarded as a fundamental book embodying Japan's image as an exotic land in the late nineteenth and early twentieth century. Following in the steps of the French naval officer and other travellers to Japan, Vicente Blasco Ibáñez's *La vuelta al mundo de un novelista*, published in three volumes between 1924 and 1925, is one of the modern cornerstones of travel writing among Spanish-language writers, and it was soon translated into English as *A Novelist's Tour of the World* (1926). The chapters devoted to Japan were very favourably received and have seen many an edition as an independent book up to the present time. In this study, I also examine excerpts from Paul Theroux's *Ghost Train to the Eastern Star* (2008). The American author has sold millions of copies of his travelogues and is regarded as one of the key figures of travel writing in the past decades. The remaining three books that I have chosen may be less widely known, but they do provide us with plenty of examples where figures of speech are used in travel writing to persuade the readership. They are, in chronological order, Spanish author José María Gironella's *El Japón y su duende* (1964), Japan-based British writer Alan Booth's *The Roads to Sata: A 2000-Mile Walk Through Japan* (1985), and French writer and critic Dominique Noguez's *Je n'ai rien vu à Kyoto: Notes japonaises (1983–1996)* (1997).

Figures of Speech in Travelogues

Figures of speech are generally defined as any manipulation of language for persuasive, expressive or aesthetic purposes. When we come to analyse travelogues, we must bear in mind that, unlike other literary genres, travel writing is not safeguarded by a fictional agreement, which means that readers are not willing to *a priori* suspend disbelief and enter positively into the world created by the author.[10] This implies that one of the main objectives of travellers is to convey a description of reality that can be regarded as plausible and convincing, thereby the persuasive power of rhetoric – rather than its expressive or aesthetic purposes – is what must be most valued by writers who want to turn their travelogues into solid and reliable accounts.

Rhetoric, thence, constitutes a useful tool to achieve the foremost goal of travel writing. However, what my readings of a large corpus of travelogues reveal, as I have already suggested in the introduction, is that figures of speech do not only help assert

Rhetoric in Travel Writing

the authenticity of the experiences documented by the traveller-writer but also operate as a sort of hinge appliance between author and reader as they help to articulate two axes that, in principle (or in the beginning), seem to be detached and independent: the text and the act of reading. In this way, they become a key cohesive element. Drawing on Iser, we can say that readers accumulate experiences throughout the reading process, but I would like to stress that those experiences can only be validated insofar as readers can perceive themselves inside the journey and not guided from the outside.[11]

Once the rhetorical framework has effectively induced mental representations within the reader's cognitive understanding, fictitious elements, preconceived ideas, and wrong statements might be passed down to large audiences without any consistent hermeneutical inquiry or critical scrutiny. When this happens, the truth is merely imposed. We may say that travellers are supposed to remain vigilant throughout the journey to properly react to the encounter with the other. However, unbiased response is always at risk since it requires a conscious decision to undertake a bold separation from the self in order to engage in an earnest hermeneutical process. But writers do not always have the ability or the willingness to do so; rather, they tend to favour commonplaces and familiar representations of alterity. Epistemological aspirations are thus set aside, and the emphasis is placed on shared codes of understanding that leave both author and reader at ease. Figures of speech, once again, prove to be a valuable ally to gain recognition and escape scrutiny.

Rhetorical devices, therefore, play different roles in travelogues, although they are subject to the same ultimate end – persuasiveness. To summarize what has been said so far, we may conclude that figures of speech perform three major tasks in travelogues:

1. Enhance verisimilitude and, therefore, persuade the reader of the faithfulness of the traveller's descriptions.
2. Shorten the distance between the text/author and the act of reading/reader and, thereby, provide cohesion.
3. Reinforce writers' discursive authority and, in doing so, conceal their cognitive deficiencies and/or lack of hermeneutic ability.

Anacoenosis *(Communication)*

This figure of speech consists in posing a question to the audience or making an appeal to readers' cognitive background. I find that its scope in travelogues goes far beyond that of a rhetorical question. In certain scenarios, traveller-writers may share with readers doubts and concerns; in yet other cases, they may just evoke common knowledge and recollections. Whatever the case may be, this procedure succeeds in shortening the distance between the text and the act of reading in a way such that readers can feel partakers of the journey. As a result, verisimilitude is enhanced, and writers receive a yet greater endorsement.

If we examine the oldest book in my corpus for this study – Isabella Bird's *Unbeaten Tracks in Japan* (1880) – we soon witness how the author tries to get her audience involved in the account from the first pages by evoking the *jinrikisha* (rickshaw), a two-wheeled vehicle pulled by one man that was used in Japan at the time and was widely known in Europe as it was regularly reproduced through illustrations in newspapers and magazines. Bird calls upon the addressee of her first letter to share that common knowledge:

Outside were about fifty of the now well-known jinrikishas, and the air was full of a buzz produced by the rapid reiteration of this uncouth word by fifty tongues. This conveyance, *as you know*, is a feature of Japan, growing in importance every day.[12]

It comes as no surprise that some 40 years later Vicente Blasco Ibáñez, who draws largely from his predecessors since intertextuality is paramount in travel writing, brings into play the same vehicle to arouse a sympathetic response in the reader in the first chapter of his Japanese tour: 'We go about through the town in *koruma*. *The reader undoubtedly knows* what this conveyance is; a man-drawn, one-seated, high-wheeled vehicle.'[13]

Both Bird and Blasco Ibáñez resort to *kuruma* or *koruma* time and again all the way to the end of their narrations. By doing so, they keep alive this first interpolation and, hence, make sure that readers are following them through the journey from start to finish. At the same time, they manage to foreignize the text, another rhetorical device in travelogues, as shall be discussed later.

In *Ghost Train to the Eastern Star* (2008), Paul Theroux shows his willingness to involve readers into the trip by addressing them in the very first line of the book. 'You think of travellers as bold, but our guilty secret is that travel is one of the laziest ways on earth of passing the time', he begins saying, and then he proceeds to explain what travel and travel writing mean to him.[14] He opens his heart to the audience, and I cannot imagine a better way to invite his readers to follow him through the journey he is about to undertake. How could we later throw suspicion upon his anecdotes, his observations, and his descriptions? Then, once he has arrived in Japan, he again calls upon the audience to partake in each other's (common) fears because Tokyo seems to be 'more a machine than a city', and symbolizes 'an intimidating version of the future, not yours or mine, but our children's'. He even raises a question that readers are supposed to answer by drawing on deep-rooted ideas that they certainly share with the author: 'Was there any countryside left in Japan?'[15]

In both instances, as was the case with Bird's and Blasco Ibáñez's travelogues, the text and the act of reading, which in the beginning (or in theory) were two independent realities, converge as *anacoenosis* and other figures of speech come into play and the travel account moves forward. Author and readers, thus, lie in the same discursive plane and, as a result, authorial descriptions and experiences, whatever reality they may represent, gain in credibility.

Anakephalaiosis *(Recapitulation)*

This is a Greek word the use of which is basically limited to Christian theology to explain that Jesus is the Father's ultimate statement. In travelogues, it is relatively frequent to come across a sort of recapitulation or summing up of the journey. In the last pages of their travel accounts, writers are inclined to look back and provide the readership with a set of important points or highlights of the trip, and I am using the word here with that meaning.

In his book *El cuerpo humano: Teoría actual* (1989), Laín Entralgo stresses the need humans have to make a comprehensive roundup of their existences when they are in the final stage of their lives. According to the Spanish physician and philosopher, *anakephalaiosis* is a way to systematically acknowledge and classify all the assumptions and beliefs (true or not fully accurate) about any particular subject.[16]

Rhetoric in Travel Writing

It seems to me that travels, given their closed itinerary, with an unequivocal beginning and end, prompt writers to undertake a process of recapitulation before bringing down the curtain.

In *The Roads to Sata: A 2000-Mile Walk Through Japan* (1985), Alan Booth gives us an innovative and refreshing end to his recount by closing up his long trek across rural Japan with his interview by a Japanese reporter. His answers serve as a tidy and straightforward summary of his book. Here is an excerpt:

> "How long has it taken?"
> "A hundred and twenty-eight days."
> [...]
> "Did you ever feel like giving up?"
> "Once, early on, when I thought I might not be up to it, and once in Hiroshima when I began to wonder what the point was."
> "Can you say now what the point was?"
> "No."
> [...]
> "Why did you decide to do it in the first place?"
> "Because I'd lived in Japan for a quarter of my life and still didn't know whether I was wasting my time. I hoped that by taking four months off to do nothing and scrutinize the country I might come to grips with the business of living here, and get a clearer picture, for better or worse."
> [...]
> "Do you think you've learned much during the last four months?"
> "Yes, I think I've learned a bit about Japan and a lot about myself."
> The reporter closed his notebook and we shook hands and said good-bye.[17]

Throughout this interview, in a couple of pages, Booth calls attention to what he probably believes to be the focal point of his travel, that is, rather than his unexpected encounters and witty remarks, an inward-looking spiritual trip while physically enduring the actual trek through mountain roads and muddy tracks. Readers are expected to reflect on it and draw their own conclusions.

Blasco Ibáñez undertakes a very different approach. Stirred by a strong spirit of justice and peace and always prone to engage in forebodings, he seizes the opportunity to bring up in the final chapter of his account what has been a cause of distress throughout his trip – Japan's military rearmament and the expansionist aspirations of its leaders. Thus, he reiterates his fears when he says that,

> As we sail away from the Empire of the Rising Sun, I try to set a definitive opinion of it. It is not a firm and homogeneous view. In fact, I feel more forcibly than ever how dual and contradictory is the spirit of Japan [...] It remains for the future to show whether the Japanese are simply imitators or whether, after completing the cycle of imitation, they can make some original contribution to the world's progress.
>
> The future of Japan is even more enigmatic than that of other nations. One cannot divine at present whether Japan will continue to move forward, accepting progress with its ruthless destruction of the old order, or whether it will grow frightened as its rapidly multiplying workingmen begin to make the same

demands as the workingmen of the white races. In the latter case there is nothing to do but to shut the gates of Japan as in the time of the Shoguns [...] The great powers show no little severity in dealing with Japan, which continues silently to nurse its dream of dominating the greater part of Asia.[18]

Blasco Ibáñez's choice of 'firm', 'homogeneous', 'dual' and 'contradictory' to describe Japan in this recapitulatory statement does not occur by chance as he has been using those same adjectives in other parts of the account from the very beginning. With these words, the writer manages to project the reader's memory back to previous descriptions of customs, landscapes, and people where he has gradually sown his notion of a bipolar Japan, a nation caught between tradition and modernity.

If Laín Entralgo's definition of *anakephalaiosis* is extrapolated to travel writing, it can be argued that authors reaffirm themselves as the main character in the travelogue by reiterating what best matches their existence within the narrative. In that way, they ensure that the trip stands as an untransferable reality that only the participant (and persuaded) reader can share. Blasco Ibáñez ends his travelogue with a premonition that unfortunately would become true some years later: 'Who knows? When Magellan gave the name Pacific to the larger of the two world oceans, he perhaps, all unconsciously, hit upon the most cruelly ironic name of all history...'[19] This epilogue sums up the fear Blasco Ibáñez has shared with his readers all along the trip and shows his strong antimilitarism. Thus, recapitulation becomes a rhetorical device to bring to the fore the I-traveller and reaffirm his discursive authority.

We see different approaches in Bird, Booth and Blasco Ibáñez since every traveller has a unique set of perspectives and the world, as Dominique Noguez reminds us, is 'unforeseeable, intangible, indescribable, impossible to memorise'. The French writer, not surprisingly, rounds up his Japanese diaries with the following entry:

> I am definitely an absent-minded traveller. But, in the end, that's the way it is for everyone. Even the most diligent travellers only see part of it [...] I haven't seen anything at Kyoto, and neither 'Kyoto' nor Japan exist at all in full.[20]

I think Noguez hits the nail on the head with this brilliant recapitulation of a series of trips to Japan. It is obvious that every traveller-writer privileges a particular vision and see things with a subjective lens. In one of his aphoristic observations Walter Benjamin explains how a

> very confusing part of town, a warren of streets I had avoided for years, all of a sudden became clear to me when one day somebody I loved went to live there. It was as if a searchlight installed in her window now carved the district up with its beams.[21]

Travellers, similarly, tend to see what they want to see and follow their sensibilities and preconceptions to write and produce knowledge that, later, is passed down to the reader. Authority lies in the writers' ability to persuade the audience that what they have brightened with their searchlights is both sheer reality and the essence of their journeys. Hence, *anakephalaiosis* is an effective rhetorical device to remind the reader of the most significant elements of the trip and, thereby, achieve the ultimate persuasive goal.

Definition

This rhetorical device may seem easy to explain as a statement that describes the essential nature of something. However, I would like to add two further notions – persuasion and visual representation. It must be recalled that traveller-writers need to convince their readers that what they are telling them is true, so they always try to offer clear and vivid definitions. This is especially the case when they come across objects and concepts unknown to the readership and difficult to grasp. It is then that they resort to this figure of speech, the way I construe its use in travelogues.

With Japan being the geographical scope of this study, the best way to illustrate this rhetorical strategy is by looking at some distinctive Japanese features. So, first, let us focus our attention on the vehicle mentioned above – the jinrikisha. This is how it was defined by Bird:

> The *kuruma*, or jinrikisha, consists of a light perambulator body, an adjustible hood of oiled paper, a velvet or cloth lining and cushion, a well for parcels under the seat, two high slim wheels, and a pair of shafts connected by a bar at the ends. The body is usually lacquered and decorated according to its owner's taste. Some show little except polished brass, others are altogether inlaid with shells known as Venus's ear, and others are gaudily painted with contorted dragons, or groups of peonies, hydrangeas, chrysanthemums, and mythical personages. They cost from £2 upwards. The shafts rest on the ground at a steep incline as you get in – it must require much practice to enable one to mount with ease or dignity – the runner lifts them up, gets into them, gives the body a good tilt backwards, and goes off at a smart trot. They are drawn by one, two or three men, according to the speed desired by the occupants.[22]

This ekphrastic description sparks upon the reader a visual representation of the vehicle. It is an image that surely must linger till the end of the account; hence, whenever Bird uses hereafter the word *kuruma*, the reader must recall the mental conception he or she has made. If we look at Blasco Ibáñez's account, we see that he provides his audience with a similar definition of *kuruma*, a word that he regularly uses throughout the text.

Pierre Loti, one of the visitors who contributed most to Japan's biased representation in the West at the turn of the nineteenth century, describes in his novelized journal *Madame Chrysanthemum* (1887) the men who pull the jinrikisha, and calls them *djins*:

> No sooner had I landed, than there bounded towards me about a dozen strange beings, of what description it was almost impossible to make out through the blinding showers – a species of human hedge-hog, each dragging some large black thing; they came screaming around me and stopped my progress. One of them opened and held over my head an enormous closely-ribbed umbrella, decorated on its transparent surface with paintings of storks; and they all smiled at me in an engaging manner, with an air of expectation.
>
> I had been forewarned: these were only the *djins* who were touting for the honour of my preference; nevertheless, I was startled at this sudden attack, this Japanese welcome on a first visit to land (the *djins* or *djin-richisans*, are the runners who drag little carts, and are paid for conveying people to and fro, being hired by the hour or the distance, as cabs are with us).

Their legs were naked; to-day they were very wet, and their heads were hidden under large shady conical hats. By way of water-proofs they wore nothing less than mats of straw, with all the ends of the straws turned outwards bristling like porcupines; they seemed clothed in a thatched roof. They went on smiling, awaiting my choice.[23]

It is interesting to note that Loti, unlike Bird and Blasco Ibáñez, who seem to be more interested in the vehicle, pays greater attention to those who draw it. The French writer simply uses the word *voiture* (cart, in the English translation), but he mentions *djin* more than 30 times in his book. Furthermore, he sometimes adds qualifying terms such as 'steam-engine of a man', 'swift-footed', 'vociferating', 'panting', 'quick-footed', 'breathless', 'muscular', and 'speedy', which have a reinforcing effect on the runners' portrayal first given to readers. As a result, both the definition and the reiteration of the word *djin* exert a strong persuasive power.

In the 1980s, both jinrikishas and runners have become little more than a tourist attraction in Japan, and Booth, as we have seen before, does not even use any vehicle, since he is walking from beginning to end. In his journey, rather than transportation, he prioritizes sleeping accommodation. For that reason, it is no surprise that he gives us some definitions of the Japanese hostelries he is staying in. His are rather concise explanations, but good enough to enable him to use the vernacular word for the rest of the travelogue. He renders *minshuku* as 'lodging house' and *ryokan* as 'Japanese-style inn' the first time they come up in the account, and thereafter, taking for granted that readers will understand, he goes on to say things like 'the owner of the *minshuku* gave me a small cotton handkerchief with a map of Hokkaido on it', or 'I had booked myself into a *ryokan* where the downstairs dining room was decorated with photographs of steam locomotives.'[24] Although it is difficult to apprehend the difference between *minshuku* and *ryokan* for those who have not been to Japan, the words 'house' and 'inn', as well as the rest of the information provided, help to make the distinction. By sprinkling the text with Japanese terms associated with lodgings, Booth infuses into his readers the idea that travelling is real and, hence, so must be the knowledge and the experiences he is sharing.

In sum, we see that definition, used as a rhetorical device and enhanced by repetition, shortens the distance between the act of reading and the travelled space as the reader conceives the new entity as a three-dimensional body every time the alien word appears in the text. It is indeed a cognitive achievement that fosters verisimilitude and intensifies the degree of satisfaction in reading.

Dialogism

Mikhail Bakhtin introduced the concept of dialogism and heteroglossia in his book *Problems of Dostoevsky's Poetics* (1929) to show how the Russian writer succeeded in creating within his novels a polyphonic framework formed by several consciousnesses. According to Bakhtin, this plurality of voices rules out the possibility of obtaining a direct and univocal understanding of any situation. Readers, therefore, do not have an objective point of support, which means that they are compelled to interact with the text. Thus, polyphony requires them to make a choice based on their previous ideological positions or induced by their reflections on the reading. In travel writing, the encounter with other cultures often imposes upon readers the need to either approve or reject customs and practices of different nature. In this process, dialogism could definitely help in the process of confronting travellers' judgements with those of the travellee. The latter, then, would have the opportunity to call the former into question. Drawing on Bakhtin's reading of Dostoevsky, this polyphony would enable the representation of someone else's view, 'preserving its full capacity to signify as an idea, while at the same time also preserving a distance, neither confirming the idea nor merging it with its own expressed ideology'.[25] Now, from my perspective, we rarely see this happening in travelogues since, as a rule, traveller-writers aim at representing reality (or, rather, their subjectively perceived reality) as an unequivocal entity. That is to say that questioning the validity of their understanding or bringing it to examination together with someone else's reality would subsequently undermine the looked-for veracity. What my readings of travel accounts reveal is that authors do exactly the opposite, that is, they use dialogism to strengthen discursive persuasion in their travelogues.

In Blasco Ibáñez's journal, we find a few polyphonic acts whose nature corresponds to what Bakhtin calls a single and unified mass of ideology.[26] On a visit to Kamakura, the Spanish writer stops to contemplate the Great Buddha, and tells us that, 'there is a real beauty about this great image, and the calm features never fail to communicate something of their smiling serenity to the observer'.[27] He then proceeds to give voice to Gautama: 'Live in peace, poor human slaves of Pain, of Old Age, and of Death', it seems to say. 'Love one another! Above all, do not add to the world's too numerous sorrows by declaring that it cannot exist without that fatal divinity man in his vainglory has created, and proclaimed eternal – War!'[28]

We must ask ourselves for what purpose Blasco Ibáñez has summoned Buddha. We may affirm that the first half of Gautama's speech could be one of his teachings, while the second half seems to correspond to the writer's pacifist plea amid Japan's militarization. This is a subject that has been repeatedly brought up by the author throughout the text. Therefore, we can easily conclude that Buddha's extradiegetic utterance helps reinforce the writer's authoritative voice. Gautama and Blasco Ibáñez stand in the same ideological plane, which accentuates the pacifist message and strengthens its epistemological value. As Bakhtin puts it, the author is the only one who gets things right and no other opinion is well-grounded.

Fellow countryman José María Gironella, in his travelogue *El Japón y su duende* (1964), wants to convey the long-standing idea that Japan is a country full of contradictions and governed by insoluble antinomies. The writer tries hard to find binary oppositions from his first glance at Tokyo. However, his arguments are weak, and he sometimes sounds self-contradictory. Thus, not sure if he has succeeded in persuading the audience, he eventually brings in Chinese philosopher Lin Yutang to tell the readers that 'Orientals often search for disparities.'[29] In this way, the guest becomes a powerful accomplice whose words seem hardly refutable despite having been said in a different environment. But how should we know? Readers will probably accept the argument without a word of complaint and move on to the next chapter.

Theroux takes a bolder approach in *Ghost Train to the Eastern Star* by inserting a real conversation he had with Haruki Murakami while visiting Tokyo. The American novelist paves the way for the Japanese literary icon to criticize materialism and, in a veiled way, Japan. 'Material things are all that matter', says Murakami. 'The idea that it's wrong to harm others has gradually disappeared.'[30] Had those remarks been made by Theroux, their impact would have been much weaker. By having the Japanese writer criticize his own country, the author wins the reader over and drives away suspicions. He, therefore, has managed to sell his idea.

Dialogism, as illustrated in these examples, provides traveller-writers with a rhetorical tool to increase their credibility and validate their claims. Extradiegetic voices merge with that of the author to create a monologic framework that dominates the narration and shapes the understanding.

Exergasia *(Repetition)*

This figure of speech has come to be defined as the repetition of the same idea using different words and changing the tone to emphasize importance or facilitate understanding. In ancient Greece, however, it was a training by which students improved a text by means of a more solid and incisive defence of the same thesis, which was very useful for future legal pleas, political speeches, or literary criticism in public life. If we confine ourselves to travelogues, I believe that writers make use of this rhetorical device in a different way. Besides restating the point with other words to deliver it in a clear and convincing manner, they tend to wield repetition to exploit otherness and, by doing so, conceal epistemological failures and unwillingness to engage in an honest hermeneutical quest. When this happens, needless to say, mindless and ideologized travellers move away from the Greeks' rhetorical goal and end up turning this figure of speech into a mere tool for subjective and sometimes biased persuasion. In this way, repetition does not improve the text; quite the contrary, it impoverishes it by reinforcing twisted realities that the audience, very often, takes for absolute values. This stems from the fact that readers, as previously stated, do not usually stand guard against literary tricks and, consequently, fall prey to rhetorical persuasion.

If you read Noguez's diaries all in one go, you might have the strong impression that Japan is one of the noisiest countries in the world. According to the French writer, Japanese towns relentlessly produce unwanted and disturbing sounds. Annoying noises can pop up anywhere to make travellers feel uneasy. Noguez does not miss the opportunity to draw attention to noisy episodes: he finds 'speakers everywhere' (16) and 'husky noises coming out from speakers in every big avenue in Tokyo' (25); he hears 'continuous rumble' around buildings (51), and traffic lights have a 'horrible and nagging synthetic music' (72). The writer even confesses that he must come back to the same topic again and again because 'a day in Japan is taken over by noises, chirpings, and other squeaks' (77). Even inside his apartment 'there's not a single moment of silence' (90). In a brief preface to his book, Noguez tells us that, in Japan, he will behave the way he does in France and, therefore, he will write down things that 'make me sick' and things that 'delight me'. Judging by his remarks, he definitely does, particularly as far as noise is concerned. Now, this persistent and even wearisome repetition prevents him from digging deeper into city life and provides readers with a fragmentary and one-sided portrayal of urban Japan. Drawing on Halbwachs, I would suggest that Noguez carries with him his French spatial framework to Japan and searches for familiar daily life in his new surroundings to attain a state of mental tranquillity and stability.[31] He feels protected by common features and refuses to move into different arrangements; thus, otherness is presented as a threat. The same thing is true of Gironella's view of Tokyo. For him, the capital is 'chaotic and irrational' (19), 'the anti-Washington' (24), 'ugly' and 'monstrous' (31).[32] The Spanish writer does not mince his words and says that it is just the way he had been told before he came. It is obvious that, in each case, these constant remarks operate as arguments conceived to bring readers (and authors themselves) to desired conclusions. Interestingly, both writers set off – they even partly admit it – with a bunch of pre-set ideas they do not bother to contest. Instead of increasing their knowledge by challenging themselves and their prejudices, they impose a cognitive scheme easy to digest through repetition. Exergasiac acts create a series of markers that readers can certainly identify throughout the text so as not to lose track and follow the author all the way to the end.

Before this chaotic and noisy portrayal of urban Japan spread across the West in the post-World War II era, Japanese cities were seen as miniature and charming spaces under the spell of Japanism. Loti was one of the first Western visitors to use words such as 'toy', 'doll', 'doll-like', 'diminutive', and 'tiny' to describe women, hands and feet, eyes, houses, sandals, kettles, boxes and so on. Blasco Ibáñez, who drew from the French writer's books to build his own account, uses time and again those terms to further visualize that small-scale Japan. Even before getting off the boat, the Spanish novelist stands on the deck and tells us that 'houses are like toys' and 'the scene appears to have been arranged as a setting for dolls' (83), and he adds that Japanese have 'miniature gardens', and girls are 'fragile as dolls' and sing in 'thin little voices in the doorways of their toy-houses' (86). Blasco Ibáñez has not stepped ashore yet, but he has already begun to unfold the map where some of the things that he is supposed to discover during his stay in Japan have been drafted in advance.

If we move into the twenty-first century, we find that Japan is neither cute nor ugly anymore; rather, it has become a murky looking glass to foresee our future. At least Theroux puts a lot of effort into conveying that message throughout his travelogue. These are his first words when he arrives at the Japanese capital from China: 'The grey sprawl of Tokyo was an intimidating version of the future, not yours and mine, but our children's' (392). With this statement, he smooths the path straight away to make his point. The impact of his words is yet greater due to his calling upon readers through *anacoenosis*, as explained before. Then the American writer reveals that, 'having just arrived in Japan, I felt I had travelled into the future, to a finished version of all the cities I'd passed through on this trip', and he adds that 'even long ago, Japan seemed to me the future'; finally, he ventures to proclaim that 'for better or worse, a Nipponized future is the likeliest solution' (393). It is clear from the beginning that Theroux wants to raise issues such as the menace of 'soulless' and 'intimidating' urban spaces because, as he warns us, 'American big cities would evolve to become the same sort of metropolis' (393).

These examples show that travelogues are a palimpsest where travellers can rekindle their predecessors' experiences and readers can recognize previous travel accounts – regardless of their accuracy and ethical sincerity – but they also constitute a sort of log in which to collect what Paul Fry calls 'the voice of social togetherness', that is, in the case of Noguez, Gironella, Blasco Ibáñez, and Theroux, a set of preconceived ideas prevailing within a determined society for each historical time.[33] In this way, one of the best assets to achieve that goal is rhetorical repetition. However, as I have attempted to tease out, this figure of speech can be a double-edged sword as it might blur readers' sight and contribute to the perpetuation of misconceptions and prejudices.

Foreignization

This rhetorical device should not be mistaken for the unnecessary use of loanwords. As I see it, in travelogues it can be defined as the recurrent presence within the text of foreign terms that are difficult to translate. Such is the case of *kuruma*, which has been analysed earlier. This means that foreignization entails a preliminary thorough definition of the word, which, as the example of Bird has shown, often has a strong ekphrastic nature to facilitate visualization and understanding.

Foreignization, as a rhetorical device, can be related to two techniques derived from the field of translation studies: (a) foreignization, and (b) exoticization. The first one is a translation method first formulated in 1813 by the German theologian and philosopher Friedrich Schleiermacher, and further developed by Lawrence Venuti in the 1990s. It consists in trying to preserve the cultural and linguistic features of the foreign text, which requires readers to move to the author's environment. Spanish philosopher Ortega y Gasset, in a 1937 essay on translation, upholds this procedure because 'it is only when we force the reader from his linguistic habits and oblige him to move within those of the author that there is actually translation'.[34] By means of this technique, instead of domesticating the text to minimize foreignness, the cultural values of the source text are kept unharmed. As for exoticization, it takes place when foreign terms are included in the target language in pursuit of a distinct touch, whether exotic or charming; however, this is a procedure that may work against the translation by caricaturing the original culture and causing a ridiculous effect in the translated text.[35]

In travel writing, from my perspective, foreignization plays a different role. Whereas this strategy may put pressure on readers of translated books, since they will have to go through new cultural and linguistic codes, in travelogues there will be no such constraints; on the contrary, the use of foreign terms will intensify the sense of transmigration and, hence, readers will feel themselves partakers in the trip. I believe the continuous use of foreign words such as *kuruma* in Bird's and Blasco Ibáñez's accounts has a powerful persuasive effect; those terms are like a sort of tollbooth where readers have to slow the pace of reading, or even stop, so that they can decodify the word by evoking previous landmarks in the journey and remembering the original definition. Every time this process takes place, the feeling of travelling is enhanced. Thus, foreign terms prevent nonparticipatory reading and remind readers that they are experiencing a real trip along with the author. In this way, they are enticed to leave their static and familiar spatial framework to transmigrate to the travellee's space. As a result, traveller-writers achieve a yet greater degree of verisimilitude and succeed in shortening the distance between the text and the act of reading.

Since I have already analysed *kuruma* when I explored the use of *anacoenosis* (see the first figure of speech in this study), I will scrutinize now the rhetorical value of *fusuma* and *shōji* in Bird's account. When she starts her journey, the British explorer feels that first and foremost she must explain the difference between a teahouse (*chaya*) and a Japanese inn (*yadoya*):

> A teahouse or *chaya* is a house at which you can obtain tea and other refreshments, rooms to eat them in, and attendance. That which to some extent answers to an hotel is a *yadoya*, which provides sleeping accommodation and food as required.
>
> *37*

Then she proceeds to give a further meticulous description in the next three pages. She mentions several Japanese terms, but I want to draw attention to *fusuma* and *shōji* since they will be appearing again and again throughout the text. *Fusuma* are defined by Bird as 'sliding paper panels' that can be moved along 'grooves in the floor and in the ceiling' in order to partition rooms (38); *shōji* are explained as 'sliding windows, with translucent

Rhetoric in Travel Writing

paper for windowpanes' (40). These two room dividers are precious to Bird as they provide her with some privacy – but not always, based on her comical remarks – in the Japanese inns, one of the major issues during the trip, for she was the first woman to journey to northern Japan and one of the first Westerners to visit those areas. She uses these two words repeatedly in her descriptions, as we can see in the following examples: 'the *shōji* were full of holes, and often at each hole I saw a human eye' (45), 'late at night my precarious *shōji* were accidentally thrown down, revealing a scene of great hilarity' (46), 'when I drew aside the *shōji* I was disconcerted by the painful sight which presented itself' (94), '*fusuma* of wrinkled blue paper splashed with gold turned this "gallery" into two rooms; but there was no privacy, for the crowds climbed upon the roofs at the back' (131), 'my room was entirely *fusuma* and *shōji*, and people were peeping in the whole time' (144), 'on looking up, [I] saw opposite to me about 40 men, women, and children (Ito says 100), all staring at me, with the light upon their faces. They had silently removed three of the *shōji* next the passage!' (153). It is clear that Bird is not trying to foreignize the text, for the structure remains within the English domain, neither is she attempting to exoticize it – she does get close to that when she uses French words and Latinisms. Rather, I maintain that the explorer's use of the Japanese terms brings inner cohesion by reminding readers of the nature of the trip and, furthermore, helps visualize the scene in a more vivid way. Thus, the persuasive effect is stronger and, consequently, the story gains in plausibility.

Now let us peep into Noguez's observations about the foreigners he crosses paths with during his journeys in Japan. It might be odd that he fixes such a piercing regard on fellow Westerners and calls them by the Japanese pejorative word for 'foreigner' (*gaijin*). However, if my definition of foreignization in travel writing is correct, he seems to have a good reason for that. First, let us examine a few examples. At the start of his account, he tries to explain what it is like to be a foreigner in Japan: 'The invisible *gaijin* (the foreigner): they [Japanese] do the best they can to pretend they haven't seen him (being impolite to look at someone), but they have already caught a good sight of him' (16). A few pages later, he does not use the word 'gaijin', but he goes into further details: 'The foreigners (again). Suddenly, I see them among the crowds like big sick animals' (49). Little by little, Noguez draws a somehow dreadful portrayal of foreigners in Japan, and what is more interesting, he seems to share the disgust towards them. The word 'gaijin' begins to operate with all its negative connotations: 'Last night I saw a *gaijin* girl – probably an American – letting herself fall prey to two young guys' (79), he writes, suggesting she is an easy girl, and then he calls a Canadian 'gaijin' who apparently asserted falsely that he did not understand French: 'At Immigration, the *gaijin* pretended he didn't understand my question when I asked him Parlez-vous français?' (85). In Japan, Noguez warns us, 'the *gaijin* is known to be an AIDS carrier' (128); and when he comes across a pornographic movie in his hotel, he tells us that the actors are *gaijin* whose only concern is their own lust (145). Noguez seems to be annoyed by those nameless foreigners who cannot be ascribed to any particular business or occupation. They do not fit into the Japanese realm he is looking for. However, he does not feel the same repulsion towards diplomats and professionals, who, thereby, are never called 'gaijin'. The view implicitly expressed by that term is, I would say, a reductive and biased view. Now, why does Noguez use the word 'gaijin' in such a deliberate way? We could assume that, far from taking sides with the Japanese, he could be turning that expression into a sort of synecdoche for Japan's ethnocentrism in order to criticize it in a veiled way. Yet, I would suggest that the French writer does align himself with the Japanese when he looks down on foreign visitors whom he even calls 'bumpkins' because they happen to wear jeans and sneakers (147). Noguez plays the role of the intellectual traveller, and his book targets a highbrow readership. The word 'gaijin', thus, fulfils its role as a derogatory label and its use has a persuasive effect upon the reader who willingly approves Noguez's view.

Foreignization, as these examples show, helps traveller-writers to integrate readers into their personal accounts and to intensify the travelling experience. As with the rest of the figures of speech that I have analysed in this research, this rhetorical device has a powerful persuasive effect upon the audience.

Conclusion

When dealing with the rhetoric of travel writing, scholarship over the past decades has focused almost exclusively on the claim that literary strategies are ideologically contaminated, create hierarchical binaries, shape frames of reference not necessarily universal, and help perpetuate ethnocentric supremacies. I do not reject this claim, but I maintain that those practices can only bear fruit in so far as traveller-writers have previously succeeded in convincing readers of the true nature of their travelogues. Thus, there is a need, in my opinion, for a thorough analysis of how figures of speech are used as persuasive devices when portraying distant lands. And that is what I have attempted to do in this study.

By identifying and examining six often overlooked figures of speech, I have shown how the intelligent use of rhetoric can help traveller-writers to win the reader over. The examples here allow us to state the claim that authors make use of a utilitarian approach to the art of persuasion in order to make things convincing and to enhance the travel effect by involving the reader in an engaging act of reading. Thus, when used effectively, the rhetorical devices here tend to trigger a process of compliant acknowledgement and to overcome doubts. Consequently, authors' discursive truth reveals itself through rhetoric without thoughtful scrutiny. Success does not depend on truth; rather, it is founded on verisimilitude, which is determined by traveller-writers' ability to convince the audience.

After examining in detail how figures of speech are used for persuasion, we can now reaffirm with more confidence that authors rely on a series of rhetorical devices to achieve their first and foremost goal in travel writing, that is, to bridge the gap with the readership and to make sure that their arguments, whether true or not, are likely and reliable. Therefore, I consider that winning the reader's acceptance by means of rhetorical strategies is a *sine qua non* for other enterprises, such as those extensively described by scholarship up to the present time – perpetuating prejudices, creating hierarchical binaries, and justifying domination.

Notes

1 This is part of Rollings' warning against persuasive instrumentalism and ethical choices made by writers when encountering the other. See Rolling 2020, 2.

2 See Neil Rennie, *Far-Fetched Facts: The Literature of Travel and the Idea of the South Seas* (Oxford: Clarendon Press, 1995). Despite Rennie's argument, recent scholarship suggests that the *Story of Wenamun* is a work of historical fiction and not a travel report.

3 See *The Ascent of Mont Ventoux* in Petrarch's *Epistolae familiares*. The humanist poet helped pave the way for the avowal of travel as a source of joy and a means to gain knowledge.

4 Roger Cardinal, "Romantic Travel", in *Rewriting the Self: Histories from the Renaissance to the Present*, edited by Roy Porter (London and New York: Routledge, 1997), 136.

Rhetoric in Travel Writing

5 Burke says that we must learn how to use travelogues since some of them only reflect prejudices and opinions formed by conversations or reading before travelling. See Peter Burke, *Varieties of Cultural History* (Cambridge: Polity Press, 1997), 94.

6 Edward Said, *Orientalism* (New York: Vintage Books, 1979), 190.

7 See LuMing Mao, "Doing Comparative Rhetoric Responsibly", *Rhetoric Society Quarterly*, vol. 41, no. 1 (2011): 64–69; LuMing Mao, "Redefining Comparative Rhetoric: Essence, Facts, Events", in *The Routledge Handbook of Comparative World Rhetorics*, edited by Keith Lloyd (London and New York: Routledge, 2021), 15–33; Abraham Romney, "A Comparative Cultural Rhetoric Approach to Indigenous Rhetorics in the Americas", in *The Routledge Handbook of Comparative World Rhetorics*, edited by Keith Lloyd (London and New York: Routledge, 2021), 277–286.

8 See, among other articles, "Los 'libros de viajes' como género literario", in *Diez estudios sobre literatura de viajes*, edited by Manuel Lucena and Juan Pimentel (Madrid: CSIC, 2006).

9 The *sakoku* (鎖国) was a seclusion policy dictated by the Tokugawa shogunate (1603–1868) to restrain relations and trade with foreign countries. It was established by a series of edicts in the first half of the seventeenth century. It extended from 1639 to 1854, the year in which the Japan-US Treaty of Peace and Amity was signed.

10 Whereas 'suspension of disbelief' is a statement coined by Coleridge, it was Umberto Eco who first used the expression 'fictional agreement'. In his book *Six Walks in the Fictional Woods* (1994), Eco wrote that readers know that what is being narrated is an imaginary story, but they must not believe that the writer is lying. 'We accept the fictional agreement and we *pretend* that what is narrated has really taken place (…) When we enter the fictional wood we are certainly supposed to sign a fictional agreement with the author, and we are ready to accept, say, that wolves speak' (1994: 74, 77).

11 In *The Act of Reading,* Iser says that, 'as we read, we react to what we ourselves have produced, and it is this mode of reaction that, in fact, enables us to experience the text as an actual event. We do not grasp it like an empirical object; nor do we comprehend it like a predicative fact; it owes its presence in our minds to our own reactions, and it is these that make us animate the meaning of the text as a reality.' See Wolfgang Iser, *The Act of Reading* (Baltimore: Johns Hopkins University Press, 1978), 128–129.

12 Isabella L. Bird, *Unbeaten Tracks in Japan* (Rutland and Tokyo: Charles E. Tuttle Company, 1973), 4 (italics added).

13 Vicente Blasco Ibáñez, *A Novelist's Tour of the World* (New York: E. P. Dutton & Company, 1926), 87–88 (italics added for 'The reader undoubtedly knows'). I have slightly modified the translation of Leo Ongley and Arthur Livingston. They add the explanatory apposition '*jinrikishas* or *rickshaws* as the American and English call them', whereas Blasco Ibáñez used a term close to the original Japanese word (*kuruma*). Bird, as well, once she has explained what a *kuruma* looks like, makes use of this word for the rest of the account. 'I continue hereafter to use the Japanese word *kuruma* instead of the Chinese word *jin-ri-ki-sha*', says the author in a footnote (5).

14 Paul Theroux, *Ghost Train to the Eastern Star* (London: Penguin Books, 2009), 1.

15 Ibid., 392.

16 Pedro Laín Entralgo, *El cuerpo humano: Teoría actual* (Madrid: Espasa-Calpe, 1987), 25.

17 Alan Booth, *The Roads to Sata: A 2000-Mile Walk Through Japan* (New York, Tokyo and London: Kodansha International, 1997), 280–281.

18 Ibid., 159–160. I have slightly modified the original English translation, as the first sentence had been omitted.

19 Ibid., 161. The original word in Spanish is 'pacífico', whose English equivalent, as far as frequency of use is concerned, would be 'peaceful'.

20 Dominique Noguez, *Je n'ai rien vu à Kyoto* (Monaco: Éditions du Rocher, 1997), 220–221 (my translation).

21 Walter Benjamin, *One-Way Street and Other Writings* (London: Penguin Modern Classics, 2009), 74.

22 Ibid., 5–6.

23 Pierre Loti, *Madame Chrysanthemum* (London: KPI, 1985), 26–28. The English translation preserves the word *djin*, originally used by Loti in French.

24 Ibid., 5–10.

25 Mikhail Bakhtin, *Problems of Dostoevsky's Poetics* (Minneapolis: University of Minnesota Press, 1984), 85.
26 Bakhtin (ibid., 84) says that, 'All confirmed ideas are merged in the unity of the author's seeing and representing consciousness; the unconfirmed ideas are distributed among the heroes, no longer as signifying ideas, but rather as socially typical or individually characteristic manifestations of thought. The one who knows, understands, and sees is in the first instance the author himself. He alone is an ideologist. The author's ideas are marked with the stamp of his individuality. Thus, the author combines in his person a direct and fully competent ideological power to mean with individuality, in such a way that they do not weaken one another.'
27 Ibid., 97.
28 Ibid., 100.
29 José María Gironella, *El Japón y su duende* (Barcelona: Editorial Planeta, 1964), 29 (my translation). Lin Yutang (1895–1976) became a best-selling author in the West after moving to the United States in the 1930s. His works were soon translated into several languages, including Spanish, and he was widely known when Gironella wrote his book.
30 Theroux, *Ghost Train to the Eastern Star*, 407.
31 See Maurice Halbwachs, *The Collective Memory* (New York: Harper & Row, 1980).
32 My translations.
33 See Paul Fry, *Theory of Literature* (New Haven and London: Yale University Press, 2012), 256.
34 José Ortega y Gasset, "The Misery and the Splendor of Translation", in *The Translation Studies Reader* (London and New York: Routledge, 2000), 60.
35 See especially Lawrence Venuti, *The Translator's Invisibility: A History of Translation* (London: Routledge, 2008).

References

Alburquerque-García, Luis. "Los 'libros de viajes' como género literario." In *Diez estudios sobre literatura de viajes*, edited by Manuel Lucena and Juan Pimentel. Madrid: CSIC, 2006, 67–87.
Arapoglou, Eleftheria, Fodor, Mónika, and Nyman Jopi (eds.). *Mobile Narratives. Travel, Migration, and Transculturation*. London and New York: Routledge, 2014.
Bakhtin, Mikhail. *Problems of Dostoevsky's Poetics* (trans. Caryl Emerson). Minneapolis: University of Minnesota Press, 1984.
Benjamin, Walter. *One-Way Street and Other Writings* (trans. J. A. Underwood). London: Penguin Modern Classics, 2009.
Bird, Isabella L. *Unbeaten Tracks in Japan*. Rutland and Tokyo: Charles E. Tuttle Company, 1973.
Blasco Ibáñez, Vicente. *A Novelist's Tour of the World* (trans. Leo Ongley and Arthur Livingston). New York: E. P. Dutton & Company, 1926.
Blaton, Casey. *Travel Writing: The Self and the World*. New York and London: Routledge, 2002.
Booth, Alan. *The Roads to Sata: A 2000-Mile Walk Through Japan*. New York, Tokyo and London: Kodansha International, 1997.
Burke, Peter. *Varieties of Cultural History*. Cambridge: Polity Press, 1997.
Campbell, Mary B. *The Witness and the Other World: Exotic European Travel Writing, 400–1600*. Ithaca: Cornell University Press, 1988.
Cardinal, Roger. "Romantic Travel." In *Rewriting the Self: Histories from the Renaissance to the Present*, edited by Roy Porter. London and New York: Routledge, 1997, 135–155.
Carpenter, Roland H. *History of Rhetoric: Style, Narrative, and Persuasion*. Columbia: University of South Carolina Press, 1995.
Eco, Umberto. *Six Walks in the Fictional Woods*. Cambridge, MA: Harvard University Press, 1994.
Fry, Paul H. *Theory of Literature*. New Haven and London: Yale University Press, 2012.
Gironella, José María. *El Japón y su duende*. Barcelona: Editorial Planeta, 1964.
Guillaume, Xavier. "Travelogues of Difference: IR Theory and Travel Literature." *Alternatives: Global, Local, Political* 36, no. 2 (2011): 136–154
Halbwachs, Maurice. *The Collective Memory* (trans. Francis J. Ditter and Vida Yazdi Ditter). New York: Harper & Row, 1980.

Iser, Wolfgang. *The Act of Reading: A Theory of Aesthetic Response*. Baltimore: Johns Hopkins University Press, 1978.

Lloyd, Keith (ed.). *The Routledge Handbook of Comparative World Rhetorics: Studies in the History, Application, and Teaching of Rhetoric Beyond Traditional Greco-Roman Contexts*. London and New York: Routledge, 2021.

Loti, Pierre. *Madame Chrysanthemum* (trans. Laura Ensor). London: KPI, 1985.

LuMing, Mao. "Redefining Comparative Rhetoric: Essence, Facts, and Events." In *The Routledge Handbook of Comparative World Rhetorics*, edited by Keith Lloyd. London and New York: Routledge, 2021, 15–33.

Noguez, Dominque. *Je n'ai rien vu à Kyoto: Notes japonaises (1983–1996)*. Monaco: Éditions du Rocher, 1997.

Ortega y Gasset, José. "The Misery and the Splendor of Translation" (trans. Elizabeth Gamble Miller). In *The Translation Studies Reader*, edited by Lawrence Venuti. London and New York: Routledge, 2000, 49–63.

Pratt, Mary Louise. *Imperial Eyes: Travel Writing and Transculturation*. London and New York: Routledge, 1992.

Rennie, Neil. *Far-Fetched Facts: The Literature of Travel and the Idea of the South Seas*. Oxford: Clarendon Press, 1995.

Rollins, Brooke. *The Ethics of Persuasion: Derrida's Rhetorical Legacies*. Columbus: Ohio State University Press, 2020.

Romney, Abraham. "A Comparative Cultural Rhetoric Approach to Indigenous Rhetorics in the Americas." In *The Routledge Handbook of Comparative World Rhetorics*, edited by Keith Lloyd. London and New York: Routledge, 2021, 277–286.

Said, Edward W. *Orientalism*. New York: Vintage Books, 1979.

Spur, David. *The Rhetoric of the Empire: Colonial Discourse in Journalism, Travel Writing and Imperial Administration*. Durham, NC and London: Duke University Press, 1993.

Theroux, Paul. *Ghost Train to the Eastern Star*. London: Penguin Books, 2009.

Venuti, Lawrence. *The Translator's Invisibility: A History of Translation*. London: Routledge, 2008.

Youngs, Tim and Forsdick, Charles (eds.). *Travel Writing: Critical Concepts in Literary and Cultural Studies (Vol. IV Approaches to Travel)*. London and New York: Routledge, 2012.

27

ETHOS, PATHOS, AND LOGOS IN CULTURE

An Analysis and Visualization of the Rhetorical Structure of Narrative in Japanese

Tetsuta Komatsubara

Introduction

Ethos, pathos, and logos are the three modes of persuasion (Corbett and Connors 1999: 31–84) in Aristotelian rhetoric, and a number of studies have attempted to apply these three concepts to describe various types of discourse in contemporary settings, such as political discourse (Mshvenieradze 2013), business reports (Higgins and Walker 2012), and informal requests in classrooms (Ting 2018). While the effectiveness of these concepts from antiquity has been repeatedly shown in the contemporary context as well, previous studies have scarcely focused on how culture affects rhetorical organization. Through a case of narrative in Japanese, this chapter explores the analytical framework to capture cultural differences in selecting and arranging ethos, pathos, and logos in discourse.

Another purpose of this chapter is to pursue a method for the visualization of rhetorical structure consisting of ethos, pathos, and logos. The issue of how to visually represent the results of data analysis (e.g., graphs, charts, maps, diagrams) has been broadly discussed in the field of visual rhetoric (Kostelnick 1996, 2007; Hill 2004) or visualization rhetoric (Hullman and Diakopoulos 2011). However, somewhat ironically, little research has paid attention to the visual rhetoric of rhetorical analysis itself. Verbal descriptions of rhetorical discourse tend to be long and complicated, and visualizing the "gist" of the rhetorical structure can make the analysis more vivid (cf. Hill 2004: 30–33). We aim to illustrate that visualization can be especially helpful in presenting the results of an analysis whose readers mostly do not know the target language and its cultural background, such as Japanese.

Taking a narrative in Japanese as an example, we discuss the cultural bases of the rhetorical organization through ethos, pathos, and logos. Narrative is the telling of a story by someone to someone on some occasion for some purpose (Phelan 1996: 8) and can be regarded as a kind of rhetorical discourse structured by elements such as the teller, the story, the situation, the audience, and the purpose. In our case, the material is an excerpt from a Japanese TV program in which the teller aims to entertain the audience by telling a realistic story. The analysis and visualization of its rhetorical organization will indicate that, while the narrative of entertainment is primarily oriented to pathos (i.e., fun and excitement of the audience), those emotional consequences are connected with ethos and logos, and that cultural knowledge enables these three factors to shape effective language use in narrative.

Framework of Analysis

Aristotle emphasized in his *Rhetoric* three factors to which the orator must pay attention: ethos, pathos, and logos. Ethos is the character the speaker wishes to present, pathos is the mood or tone of the speech that appeals to the passions or the will of the audience, and logos is the argument the speaker is advancing (Demirdögen 2010). Once the ideas to be presented are discovered, there remains the problem of selecting, marshalling, organizing, and figuring them (Corbett and Connors 1999: 20–21).

This section reviews descriptive notions to capture the rhetorical organization of discourse in terms of ethos, pathos, and logos, which consist of communicative factors related to the dimensions of rhetoric. We also outline a method of diagramming rhetorical organization of discourse to visualize how the factors interact and structure the whole discourse. Since narrative is a form of discourse in a broad sense, the conceptual framework proposed in this section will be beneficial in the analysis of narrative as rhetoric, as shown in the case study in the next section.

Ethos

Ethos stems from the character of the speaker, especially as that character is evinced in the speech itself. Connors (1979: 285) concisely defines *ethos* as "the way in which the rhetor [=speaker] is perceived by the audience." According to Amossy (2000), there are two types of ethos: preliminary ethos and discourse ethos. *Preliminary ethos* is what the audience already knows about the speaker. The audience judges from their knowledge, or "ideology" (Baumlin 2001: 263), that the speaker ought to be a certain character, such as the belief that a criminal ought to be cruel or that a professor should be wise. *Discourse ethos* is an impression of the speaker created in the specific situation, and it involves how "to project a favorable self-image and to shape arguments in ways that accommodate differing audiences and occasions" (Baumlin 2001: 263) in discourse. In this respect, discourse ethos is the speaker's character as it emerges in language.

Cultures can have different criteria in evaluating ethos (Campbell 1998; St.Amant 2013, 2019). Since people in different cultures presuppose different knowledge in a certain genre of discourse, evaluation of preliminary and discourse ethos reflects cultural beliefs, values, and historical practices in the culture. This kind of cultural system provides the audience with norms to evaluate the speaker's character, which St.Amant (2019) called *ethos prototype*. Ethos prototype is defined as "the mental model we use to assess if a text [or a speech] is credible and worthy of our consideration or action" (ibid.: 467). If a speech of a particular genre does not match the ethos prototype, we see it as lacking ethos. To describe the ethos prototypes underlying the evaluation of ethos, we use the two dimensions that Demirdögen (2010) pointed out as basic dimensions of effective communication: (i) credibility based on expertise and trustworthiness, and (ii) likeability based on attractiveness and similarity.

Ethos Based on Credibility

Credibility is established if the speaker manages to create "the impression that he or she was a person of intelligence, benevolence, and probity" (Corbett and Connors 1999: 19), as Aristotle recognized, and as is the case even now in a broad context. Linguistic appeal to expertise is a typical way to draw the audience's attention to "qualifications, judgement, experience, and first-hand knowledge" (Higgins and Walker 2012: 198), which contribute to the credibility of the speaker.

Ethos Based on Likeability

Highlighting only the speaker's superiority, such as her expertise, good reputation, and authority, can diminish the speaker's likeability because the audience might interpret it as underlining its inferiority to the speaker. Effectiveness of ethos based on credibility may be canceled if the audience perceives the speaker as an unpleasant person. For example, aristocrats or politicians have high social status, but their preliminary ethos is often negatively evaluated by the audience. In such a case, the speaker tries to appeal to discourse ethos based on likeability by focusing on the similarities of situations, opinions, and backgrounds between the audience and the speaker.

Pathos

Pathos refers to the audience's feelings and relies for persuasive effect on triggering audience emotions such as happiness, sadness, satisfaction, pity, or fear (Aho 1985; Higgins and Walker 2012). Briefly, *pathos* is defined as "an appeal based on passion or emotion" (Green 2001: 555). The emotional appeal plays a vital part in the persuasive process because intellectual conviction is often not enough to move people's will to act (Corbett and Connors 1999: 84).

How can the speaker make the audience experience desirable emotions? The speaker cannot command the audience to feel emotions, and it is perilous for the speaker to announce to the audience that she is going to play on their emotions (Corbett and Connors 1999: 78). Therefore, the speaker must conjure up an image or situation that will make people experience the emotions the speaker wants to arouse in them (ibid.: 84). There are two strategies to arouse such emotions: (i) presenting imagery related to a certain emotion, and (ii) triggering the audience's sympathy by describing a scene in which people are inclined to experience a certain emotion.

Pathos through Imagery

We cannot arouse an emotion, either in ourselves or in others, by thinking about it. We arouse emotion by contemplating an object that stirs the emotion (Corbett and Connors 1999: 78). Thus, if the speaker seeks to arouse the pity of the audience, for example, she should provide imagery of an object that invokes pity, such as a terribly injured person or a hungry child. Imagery is an image produced in the mind by language (Yu 1996: 343), which can vary depending on culture, and can sometimes include photographic and artistic images (Higgins and Walker 2012: 198). To associate the subject with images is an effective way to arouse emotions (Hill 2004: 35–38), whether those images are visual and direct, such as sensations, or cognitive and indirect, such as memory or imagination (Green 2001: 555).

Imagery also involves imagistic language including metaphor and other figures of speech (Yu 1996: 343) such as simile, allegory, personification, and onomatopoeia. A typical example of figurative imagery is a metaphorical image of a concrete entity (e.g., person, animal) used for conceptualization of an abstract entity (e.g., theory, society), which elicits emotional responses from the audience by presenting imagery arousing a certain emotion.

Pathos through Sympathy

Another rhetorical strategy to arouse emotion is to evoke sympathy in the audience by describing a scene. A passionate (or even dispassionate; see Corbett and Connors 1999: 78–79) description aimed at the audience's sympathy is a way to intensify pathos by making the audience understand the emotion. Sympathy is understanding a person's emotion without necessarily feeling it, and one important aspect of the concept of sympathy is "the increased sensitivity to the emotions of the other person" (Wispé 1986: 318). For example, the speaker can rouse the anger of the audience based on their sympathy by describing a scene that will make the audience angry, such as a scene in which someone disparages and despises a man in regard to the things that he holds most dear. Scenes that make a person angry vary depending on the culture, so such emotion-provoking descriptions reflect how to appeal to pathos in the culture.

Logos

In exercising logos, the speaker appeals to the audience's reason. Wells (2001: 456), while admitting it has never been a simple term, defines *logos* as the verbal structure of arguments and their power to persuade. In logic, *argument* refers to any group of propositions (i.e., statements that something is the case or something is not) of which one, the *conclusion*, is claimed to be supported by the others, the *premises* (Copi et al. 2019: 5). In constructing an argument, an *inference* is drawn: The conclusion is inferred from the premises of the argument.

There are two very different ways in which a conclusion may be supported by its premises, and thus there are two classes of arguments: the deductive and the inductive. A *deductive argument* is "one whose conclusion is claimed to follow from its premises with absolute necessity" (ibid.: 26) (e.g., [Premise 1] *No man can attain perfect happiness in this life*; [Premise 2] *John is a man; therefore,* [Conclusion] *John cannot attain perfect happiness in this life*). In contrast, an *inductive argument* is "one whose conclusion is claimed to follow from its premises only with probability" (ibid.) (e.g., [Premise] *Every green apple that I bit into had a sour taste.* [Conclusion] *All green apples must be sour*).

In rhetoric, "whenever men in speaking effect persuasion [...] they do so either with examples or enthymemes" (Aristotle, *Rhetoric*, 1356b), where (i) the *enthymeme* is the equivalent of the deductive argument in logic, and (ii) the *example* the equivalent of the inductive argument. These two classes of rhetorical arguments are the sources of appeals to logos.

Logos Using Common Knowledge

An enthymeme is an argument that has one or more premises, or possibly a conclusion, not explicitly stated in the text (or speech) (Walton 2001: 93). Nonexplicit premises in an enthymeme often express generally known facts (Razuvayevskaya and Teufel 2017: 113). For example, in the argument "*All reptiles are cold-blooded animals. Therefore, lizards are cold-blooded*," the premise "*Lizards are reptiles*" is not stated explicitly, as it is a widely known fact. The explicit statement of such facts, or common knowledge, would sound both trivial and also unnatural to the audience (ibid.: 116). An enthymeme enables the speaker to omit propositions accepted by the audience and shorten the process of inference to appeal to logos.

Not only facts but the audience's ideology (Kirk 2016) and cultural knowledge can fill in the nonexplicit premises or conclusion, insofar as they are common to the speaker and the audience. For example, the enthymeme "*No country in Europe will accept this law, let alone Germany*" is valid if the audience accepts the premise "*Germany is much less likely to accept a particular law than the rest of Europe*" (Razuvayevskaya and Teufel 2017: 120). Enthymemes based on belief function as shortcuts for the speaker by utilizing prior knowledge to avoid substantive demands of evidence.

Logos Using Example

An example is an argument that connects particular cases to a general rule (Lyons 2001: 278). In examples, there are more leaps from known, observed facts, over an area of unknown, unobserved cases, to a generalization than there are in inductive arguments in logic. Typically in rhetoric, only one or two cogent examples are offered to support the generalization (e.g., *Cities have to do work together and they do work together. Organizations like C40 have been working together in climate change, for example*), for the speaker cannot risk boring their audience with an exhaustive catalogue of supporting evidence (Corbett and Connors 1999: 61). To appeal to logos by examples, the speaker normally cites well-known facts or common experiences in the culture the audience belongs to. In this respect, examples in rhetoric mirror how familiar a fact would be to the speaker and the audience in the culture.

Visualizing Rhetorical Organization

The structures of discourse in everyday life are more tangled and less precise than those given as isolated illustrations in textbooks of rhetoric. Premises of arguments may be numerous, in topsy-turvy order, and formulated awkwardly. Meanings of utterances may originate in cultural and social knowledge and values, sometimes tinged with emotional experiences. To sort out the connections of utterances and evaluate the rhetorical organization of discourse, we need certain analytical techniques.

A useful technique for the analysis of rhetorical organization is to visualize the structure of discourse with diagrams. Researchers in the field of visual rhetoric have found that visuals enhance persuasiveness (Kostelnick 1996; Hill 2004) through various stylistic functions such as engendering interest, setting the tone, establishing credibility, creating emphasis, and connotating usability (Kostelnick 1996: 26–28). However, to my knowledge, visual rhetoric to represent rhetoric itself has never been seriously pursued in the field of rhetorical studies.

Thus, this chapter attempts to develop a method to visually capture rhetorical organization by expanding the diagramming method introduced in a famous textbook of logic by Copi et al. (2019), who described a way of systematic visualization of the structure of deductive arguments (ibid.: 37–52). For example, Figure 27.1f is Copi and his colleagues'

Rhetorical Structure of Narrative in Japanese

schematic representation of a deductive argument, as follows: (1) General Motors makes money (when it does) on new cars and on the financing of loans; (2) car dealers, by contrast, make most of their money on servicing old cars and selling used ones; (3) so car dealers can thrive even when the automaker languishes (James Surowieki, "Dealer's Choice," *The New Yorker*, September 4, 2006; cited in Copi et al. 2019: 38). The visual representation of Figure 27.1f gives us an intuitive understanding of this argument in which the combination of the facts (1) and (2) supports the conclusion (3).

Figure 27.1 summarizes the notation in this chapter. To visualize arguments, we first number all the propositions it contains, in the order in which they appear, circling each number (Figure 27.1a). Dotted circles (Figure 27.1b) indicate implicit propositions (i.e., propositions that are not explicitly described in discourse), and circles in bold lines (Figure 27.1c) show propositions described in discourse more than once. Using arrows between the circled numbers, we can then construct a diagram that shows the relations of premises and conclusions without having to restate them. A solid arrow (Figure 27.1d) stands for a deductive inference by an enthymeme, and a dotted arrow (Figure 27.1e) for an inductive inference by an example. To convey the process of inference on a two-dimensional page, we adopt this convention: A conclusion always appears in the space below the premises that give it support; coordinate premises are put on the same horizontal level and bracketed (Figure 27.1f). In this way, the structure of the arguments is displayed visually in iconic form. In addition, a doubly circled number (Figure 27.1g) and a circled number surrounded by a square (Figure 27.1h) are characterized by ethos and by pathos, respectively, and these notations capture the fact that a proposition may be related to ethos and pathos as well as logos.

To illustrate the above notations, let us take two fragments of discourse: (a) "*Of course, he does not know about differential equations because he is a lawyer*" (Razuvayevskaya and Teufel 2017: 116); (b) "*For instance, he does not know about differential equations, and he is a lawyer.*" The structures of arguments in the fragments (a) and (b) contain the same propositions presented in the same order, as shown by their numbering as follows, where a bracketed sentence indicates that it is implicit in discourse:

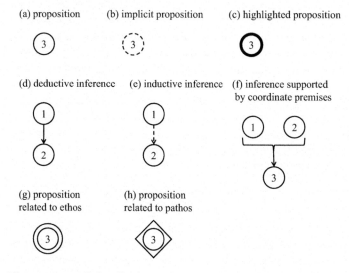

Figure 27.1 The notations of visualization

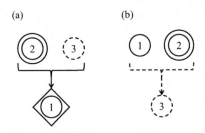

Figure 27.2 Examples of visualization

(1) He does not know about differential equations.
(2) He is a lawyer.
(3) (All lawyers do not know about differential equations.)

Figure 27.2a visualizes the rhetorical organization of the case of the fragment (a). As indicated by *because*, (1) is the deductive conclusion of an enthymeme, supported by the premise (2). (3) is an implicit coordinate premise that relates the premise (2) to the conclusion (1). (2) introduces preliminary ethos about the occupation of lawyer and describes an aspect of the character *he* is expected to have. The conclusion (1) describes how *he* lacks knowledge about mathematics and implies the speaker takes a contemptuous stance toward that person, which may appeal to pathos through sympathy. Figure 27.2b visualizes the rhetorical organization of (b). As indicated by *for instance*, (1) is shown as a premise of an example, and (2) is also a premise because it is coordinated with (1). Compared to the case of (a), the lack of knowledge about mathematics seems more neutral regarding the emotional implications. While we can inductively draw the conclusion (3) from the premises, it remains implicit in this case.

A Case Study

A teller arranges utterances to make a narrative that is effective as a whole, so analysts must consider the entirety of the relevant context to describe each utterance in relation to the rhetorical organization of the narrative. It may be difficult to follow a long transcript in a language other than English. However, since this chapter aims to explore a descriptive framework for the analysis of rhetoric in world languages, we ventured to cite a Japanese narrative that covers several pages as material for our case study, assuming that the method of visualization outlined in the previous section would help the reader to understand the structure of the rhetorical organization. Through a detailed description of the narrative, we analyze what linguistic strategies are used for rhetorical purposes, how ethos, pathos, and logos interact and integrate, and what sociocultural backgrounds underlie the three rhetorical factors.

Material

The material for this study is an excerpt from a Japanese TV program entitled *Hitoshi Matsumoto no Suberanai Hanashi* "Hitoshi Matsumoto doesn't spoil the story," in which each of the participants tells a realistic story to entertain the audience. We focused on a narrative by the Japanese comedian Daiki Hyodo, broadcasted on January 23, 2021.

The transcript below is the latter two-thirds of his four-minute talk, in which Hyodo, the teller, told a story about playing with his daughter using a drone during the state of emergency for the COVID-19 pandemic. Chihara, Tanaka, Matsumoto and the other participants were the audience responding to the talk.

Each line consists of a transcription of the Japanese and its translation. To describe the details of the narrative, such as the speed and stress of the speech and the reactions of the audience, we followed the standard glossary of transcript symbols by Jefferson (2004) (see Transcription Symbols). Phrases in bold face are the foci of analysis in the following section. Bracketed ellipses ([...]) in the transcript show omitted lines not directly relevant to the analysis here. Bracketed phrases ([xxx]) in translation indicate that the original utterance has no direct equivalent to the phrase provided. We added linguistic glosses in places where necessary to show the lexical and grammatical features of Japanese utterances, following the Leipzig Glossing Rules (Comrie et al. 2015) except for the notations using hyphens and equal signs, which would interfere with the transcription notation.

Analysis

The story, which features the teller's daughter and a drone, has been regarded as independent from the preceding part of the talk. Following Aristotle's division of a speech (Aristotle, *Rhetoric*, 1414b), the story can be divided into four parts: the introduction, the statement of the thesis, the proof of the thesis, and the conclusion.

- Introduction (lines 1–45): The daughter handles the drone poorly.
- Statement (lines 46–82): The daughter cannot land the drone on his head.
- Proof (lines 83–106): The daughter can land the drone on his head.
- Conclusion (lines 107–121): The daughter is strange.

Each of these four parts plays a rhetorical role in the whole story: The introduction provides background information and constructs suitable images of the cast; the statement focuses on the thesis in the narrative; the proof examines the thesis; the conclusion summarizes the story and reaches the punchline.

Introduction

---

001 Hyodo: maa >sore gurai< **kawa tteru nsu yo, shita no ko wa,** yaru koto nasu koto.
'Well, the younger daughter always behaves strangely like that.'

002 de, kyonen ni naru nsu ka ne,
'And it's already last year,'

003 **minna   i=suteihoomu to   iu   ka.**
everyone i=stay-home   QUOT   say   Q
'everyone [had to] stay home.'

004 **kinkyu jitai sengen ga (.) ((moving both his hands forward)) na tta toki ni,**
'During [the period when] the state of emergency [was declared],'

005 ma=**ie ni zutto oru nsu yo, kodomo ra** gakko yasumi ya kara.
'the children had stayed home all the time because they had no school.'

The excerpt started with a comment summarizing the preceding part of the talk, in which Hyodo, the father, told a story about the strangeness of his daughter, an elementary school student. These two persons are depicted as the speakers in the narrative, and their utterances are mostly reported by direct speech with quotation marks. (1) is the proposition described by line 1, which underlines an emotional stance, that is, a sense of strangeness of his daughter.

(1) The daughter is strange.

Lines 2–4 explain the situation about the state of emergency due to the COVID-19 pandemic and express the enthymeme in which conclusion (2) is inferred from the explicit premise (3) and the implicit premise (4). The word *suteihoomu* "stay-home" was a kind of slogan at that time in Japan and serves here to remind the audience of the situation. Based on this contextual priming, the predicate "*was declared*" is omitted and indicated by a metaphorical gesture instead in line 4.

(2) People had to stay home last year.
(3) The state of emergency was declared last year.
(4) (People had to stay home during the period under the state of emergency.)

Line 5 highlights a common problem during the pandemic that children had to play at home. Premise (6) is common, so the deductive conclusion (7) is easily drawn from premise (5), which is mentioned explicitly in the story and also inferred from (2) enthymematically.

(5) His children had to stay home last year.
(6) (If children have to stay home, they play at home.)
(7) (His children play at home.)

016 Hyodo:	dandan dandan yaru koto nakuna tte ki ta na tte na tta toki ni
	'When [the children and I were] getting bored little by little'
017	<u>doroon</u> ga a tta nsu yo.
	'[We] found a drone [on an online shopping site].'
018 Guest:	ho:
	'Oh.'
019 Hyodo:	chicchai ((gesturing the size of the drone)) mou >homma< 4,000 en kuraino
	'[It] is small and costs just 4,000 yen.'
	[...]
022 Hyodo:	<u>kore tobu n ka na</u> ((leaning his head)) omo te, i kkai↑ **ka tta** nsu yo ne?
	'[I] wondered if this really flies and bought it.'
	[...]
025 Hyodo:	Hommani, sugoku,
	'[It was] really [great]'
026	4,000 en demo, [konai seino ee neya, te iu gurai=
	'[and I was surprised at] the high quality even though it cost only 4,000 yen.'
027 Tanaka:	[((nodding))

Rhetorical Structure of Narrative in Japanese

028 Hyodo:	**=wa:: ((gesturing the horizontal move of the drone)) tte**		**iku shi,**
	waaa		QUOT go and
	'[it] goes like this and'		
030	nan ya ttara chotto oshi tara		
	'if [I] push [the buttons of the controller], then'		
031	**kurin ((rotating his palm))**	**tte** **mawa ttari**	[shite.
	kurin	QUOT rotate or.anything	do
	'[it] rotates like this.'		
032 Matsumoto:			[he:
			'Oh.'

In lines 16–22, the teller shifts the focus to a drone he bought to keep his children from being bored in this situation. However, it was not his children but the father himself who was interested in the drone and started to fly it, as described in lines 25–32. With the iconic expression of onomatopoeias such as *waaa* and *kurin* and the gestures of the drone's moves, (9) is repeatedly illustrated to inductively draw the implicit conclusion (10). This example indicates an aspect of the father's character: He is excited about the drone like a child and has very good skills at handling it.

(8) The father bought a drone.
(9) The father flew the drone in various ways.
(10) (The father handles the drone well.)

034 Hyodo:	hona=shita no ko ga ba:: ((gesturing the daughter approached)) tte kite,
	'Then my younger daughter rushed [to me] and'
035	ya-**yara** **shite** **hoshii** ((touching his hands to his chest)) ˚tte itte˚
	ya-do CAUS want QUOT say
	'said "let me do [that]"'
036	hode =ma, ya ttara eeyan. ((gesturing passing the controller to her))
	so well, do COND ok
	'so "you can do [it], fine"'
037	de=wa: tte yaru kedo, **yappari heta na nsu yo.**
	'and [she tried to] do, but she was poor [at handling the drone], as you might expect.'
038 Guest:	ho:
	'Oh'
039 Hyodo:	ya=ma=sono=**rajikon nanka sawa tta koto mo** [nai kara.
	'Well, because she had never touched a radio-controlled toy.'
040 Chihara:	[hai hai hai
	'Yeah, yeah, yeah.'
	[...]
045 Hyodo:	**wa::** **te ((gesturing a belly laugh))** **=sore mite warote te,**
	wa:: QUOT it see laugh and,
	'I was watching it laughing like this.'

Then, in lines 34–36, his daughter comes to him and says, "Let me play with the drone." It explicitly mentions conclusion (11) enthymematically led by the triple premises of (7),

(8), and (12). So far, the teller has told the story mostly in direct speech with the quotative marker *tte*, as in line 35, but he omits the quotative in line 36 and might be signaling the shift to a narrative style, as shown in features like free indirect speech.

(11) The daughter plays with the drone.
(12) (If there is a drone, his children play with it.)

Lines 37–40 express the enthymeme in which conclusion (13) is inferred from premises (14) and (15). (14) might be a culture-specific premise: Radio-controlled toys were very popular among boys in the father's generation in Japan but are much less popular these days, and it is common for children, especially girls, to have never played with them. (13) contrasts with (10) and describes an aspect of his daughter's personality.

(13) The daughter handles the drone poorly.
(14) The daughter had never played with a radio-controlled toy.
(15) (If someone has never played with a drone, she handles a drone poorly.)

In line 45, the father laughs at his daughter, indicating that his skill in handling the drone is much greater than his daughter's. In other words, premises (16) and (17) enthymematically draw conclusion (18), which is also inferred from premises (10) and (13). The conclusion, inherited from the implicit premise (17), can elicit sympathy for his sense of superiority toward his daughter.

(16) The father laughed at his daughter.
(17) (If someone laughs at another person, then that person believes that he is superior to the other person.)
(18) (The father believes that he is superior to his daughter in the skill of drone handling.)

Figure 27.3 visualizes the rhetorical organization of the introduction. A series of enthymemes on the topic of the drone reach conclusion (13), and it contrasts with (10) inferred from the highlighted premise (9). (18) is the pathos-oriented conclusion and gives the background of the following part of the story.

Statement

046	nori de, **sono doroon o, papa no koko ((pointing to his head)) ni no shi tara,**
	'On the spur of the moment, I said "if [you can] land the drone here,"'
047	**nanka sukina n ko taru** wa (.) tte [iu ta nsu ne. geemu tekini.
	'"[I will] buy you anything [you] want." Like a kind of game.'
048 Chihara:	[ho:::
	'Oh.'
049 Hyodo:	honnara, **manga ga hoshi** tte ii dashite, noseru (.) tte itte,
	'Then [she] said "[I] want a comic book," and said "[I] will land [it there]."'

Lines 46 and 47 describe the rule of *geeme* "game" of (19), which gives coherence to the rest of the story. It was *nori* "on the spur of the moment", and there is no necessary reason for the father to propose such a game. Therefore, it seems that he did so just to

Rhetorical Structure of Narrative in Japanese

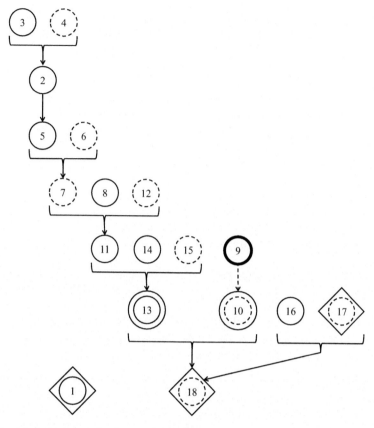

Figure 27.3 Rhetorical organization of the introduction

entertain his daughter. The implicit conclusion (21) drawn from premises (19) and (20) described in lines 46–49 is the motivation for the daughter's practice.

(19) If the daughter lands the drone on the father's head, then he buys her anything she wants.
(20) The daughter wants a comic book.
(21) (If the daughter lands the drone on the father's head, then he buys her the comic book.)

050	**renshu shi makuru** [nsu yo. ((gesturing handling the drone))
	'[and she] practiced and practiced [flying the drone].'
051 Guest:	[hh
	[...]
060 Hyodo:	**ie ju buwa:: ((gesturing the horizontal move of the drone)) tte tobashi tari**
	'[She now] flies [the drone] like this throughout the house, and'
061	**kore yabai na sorosoro tte natte**=
	'[I] thought that this is bad [and she will do it] soon.'

062	=honnin no naka de, **nose reru** (.) tte na tta	[nsu yo ne=mou gijutsu tekini.
	'In her heart, [she] thought "[I] can land it [there]" considering her skill.'	
063 Chihara:		[ho:
		'Oh.'

Lines 50–60 describe how hard the daughter practiced flying the drone and how well she improved her skill. Despite premise (13), the negative evaluation of her skill of drone handling, premises (22) and (23) yield conclusion (25), which is also inductively inferred from (24). In line 51, a guest laughed at the daughter's hard practice, indicating that the audience felt it funny that a child practiced something so hard to win a prize.

(22) The daughter practices very hard.
(23) (If one practices very hard, one handles the drone well.)
(24) The daughter flies the drone throughout the house.
(25) (The daughter handles the drone well.)

As a matter of skill, premise (26) is true, and conclusion (27) is drawn from premises (25) and (26). Therefore, (21) and (27) seem to entail conclusion (28).

(26) (If she handles the drone well, then she can land the drone on someone's head.)
(27) The daughter can land the drone on the father's head.
(28) (The father buys her the comic book.)

064 Hyodo:	nera ttekita jiki ga a tta nsu	[yo.		
	'There was a period when [she] aimed [at landing it there].'			
065 Chihara:		[ho:		
		'Yeah.'		
066 Hyodo:	nde, demo ne, <u>oto</u> de bareru nsu yo.			
	'Well, but [the approach of the drone will be] noticed because of the sound.'			
067	**funi::: ((imitating the flying sound))**	**tte**	**kikoeru**	**kara**
	funiii	QUOT	hear	because
	'Because [it] sounds like this'			
068	doroon ga chikayotte ki [tara.			
	'if the drone approaches'			
069 Guest:		[hhh		
070 Chihara:	haihai			
	'Yeah, yeah.'			
071 Hyodo:	**funi:: ((imitating the flying sound))**	**tte**	**kikoeru**	**kara=**
	funiii	QUOT	hear	because
	'Because it sounds like this'			
072	**=kita (.) ((looking back)) >tte omo tte mi tara<**			
	'[I] think "it comes" and look back, and'			
073	**doroon ga kou ((gesturing the drone approaches)) sema tte kuru nsu yo ne?**			
	'the drone is approaching like this.'			
074 Chihara:	hai			
	'Yes.'			
075 Hyodo:	>honde mou< omae >akan akan akan< ((waving both his hands))			
	'And so, "You, no, no, no,"'			

077	konnan **zettai nose rare hen** °to°, **muri** ya omae.
	'"will never land it like this," [I said], "it's impossible for you [to do it]."'
	[...]
082 Hyodo:	**zettai nose rare hende**, tte iute te.
	'I said, "you will never land it."'

However, the father refutes (27) by mentioning the sound of the flying drone in lines 66–73. Unlike the enthymemes used so far, premises (29) and (30) and conclusion (31) constitute a fully explicit deductive inference, probably reflecting the father's intention of refutation. (33), the thesis in this narrative, is concluded from (31) and (32), and the negative statements such as *zettai nose rare hen* "[you] will never land it" and *muri ya* "it's impossible" also call attention to the proposition (33).

(29) If something makes a noise as it approaches, the father notices it.
(30) The drone makes a noise.
(31) The father notices the drone when it approaches.
(32) (If the father notices the drone approaching, then the drone cannot land on his head.)
(33) His daughter cannot land the drone on his head.

(33) can be interpreted as premise of (34). Proposition (34) is the parallel of (18) and reinforces the father's belief that he still retains a lead over his daughter in the story.

(34) (The father retains a lead over his daughter in the game.)

The rhetorical organization of the statement is summarized in Figure 27.4. As visually comprehended, there are two logical flows: One concludes that the daughter can land the drone on the father's head and another that she cannot do so. The former is argued from the perspective of a guardian with the emotional stance of an adult, as illustrated with pathos-oriented propositions (19) and (22). In contrast, the latter is viewed from the perspective of a competitor in the "game," and (34) reflects the emotional orientation toward a lead over the daughter.

Proof

083	honde=sono jiki desu.
	'And [it] was the period.'
084	de=boku nagoya de maishu, bangumi ni de sashite itadai teru ndesu kedo
	'I appear on a TV program [recorded] in Nagoya every week, and'
085	(0.2)
086	**rimooto** de shutsuen no hi ga a tta nsu yo.
	'one day, [I appeared] remotely [from my house]'
087 Tanaka:	hhhhh

The proof describes an episode that refutes (33), starting with introductory utterances expressing proposition (35) in lines 83–86. This episode is based on the father's preliminary

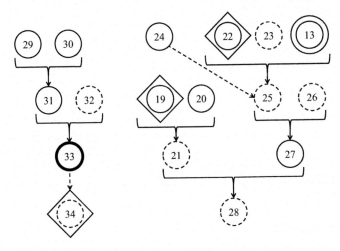

Figure 27.4 Rhetorical organization of the statement

ethos, that is, his job as a TV performer. (36) is a common premise to many people who have experienced remote meetings during the pandemic and entails (37), combined with (35).

(35) The father appears on TV remotely.
(36) (If one appears on TV remotely, one cannot move from there.)
(37) The daughter can land the drone on the father's head when he cannot move.

088 Hyodo:	nde asa, pasokon no mae de, doumo:: ((waving both his hands)) tte iute tara, 'and in the morning, [when I] was saying "Hello!" in front of the computer,'
089	funi [::::: ((imitating the flying sound))
091 Guest:	[hhhhhh
092 Hyodo:	kore **owa tta** na omo ta nsu yo. '[I] thought this [took me to] the end.'
093	zendaimimon [yan. '[This] is an unprecedented event.'
094 Guest:	[hhhhhhh ((The guests laugh at once))
095 Hyodo:	funi::: ((imitating the flying sound))
096	a =sou desu ne =po ((gesturing the drone lands on his head)) oh so COP isn't it po '[I said] "Oh, [that is] so, isn't it" [and the drone landed on my head]'
097	tte =**doroon** **noru** koto aru? tte natte QUOT drone land incident exist QUOT become '[I] thought, is it possible for a drone to land [on one's head like that]?'
098 Matsumoto:	u: [n. 'uh-uh.'
099 Hyodo:	[kore kowa omote, '[I] thought that's scary,'

Lines 88–97 describe a specific situation supporting (37). The flying sound of the drone *funii* has been repeated so far, so the sound works as metonymy for the drone itself such as line 89. The phrase *kore owa tta na* "this [took me to] the end" implies that (27) (i.e., the daughter can land the drone on his head) is the case. This further illustrates (38): Their positions were reversed in the situation.

(38) (The daughter retains a lead over the father in the game.)

In line 97, *doroon noru koto aru?* "Is it possible for a drone to land [on one's head]?" is literally a question, but it is interpreted as a rhetorical question, which implies that it is normally impossible to occur and undesirable, hence (39). (40) is the conclusion inferred from (27) and (39) and elicits fear toward the daughter because it leads to a real threat to his work as well as a defeat in the game.

(39) (If the drone lands on the father's head, then it disturbs his work.)
(40) (The daughter can disturb the father's work.)

100	>honde< boku=demo ko kkara ((pulling both his hands toward his face))
	'but I, from there,'
101	**pasokon no mae kara ((gesturing he looks at the PC)) ugoke nai kara**
	'I can't move from the front of the PC.'
102 Matsumoto:	un.
	'Yeah.'
103 Hyodo:	wa: te na ttara=ni: ga
	waa QUOT become COND=nii NOM
	'When [I was speaking] like this, *nii* [=the drone]'
104	funi::::: ((imitating the flying sound with a gesture that the drone approaches))
105	**mou=muccha sema tteru yan,** [tte natte,
	'I thought "wow, it's already there,"'
106 Guest:	[hhhh

Lines 100–105 tell that the father is in an impossible position because of (41), which reinforces (27), using the sound metonymy of *funii* and *nii*.

(41) The father cannot move.

Figure 27.5 is a visual representation of the proof, which provides a counterargument to the thesis (33). It is argued that given the setting of the remote work, (27) is the case, which entails both a defeat in the game as (38) and a threat in his work as (40).

Conclusion

---

107 Hyodo:	>honde<=koko nose raren no kana tte omo ttara,
	'and I thought [she] would land [it] here,'
108	mou **mechakucha** kawatte te, yarikuchi ga.
	'[but] her way was really, really strange.'

109	funi:::: ((imitating the flying sound with a gesture that the drone passes by him))
110	tte sudoori shite,
	'[The drone] passed [by me], and'
111 Matsumoto:	ho:
	'Oh.'
112 Hyodo:	daibu hanareta tokoro de kocchi mukete,
	'[she] pointed [the drone] at me, from a distant position,'
113	**hobaringu de ((gesturing the drone is hovering))**
	'[keeping it] hovering,'
114	**[boku zutto neratte kite ta** nsu yo.
	'[and she] was aiming at me'
115 Matsumoto:	[uwawawawawa
	'Wow, wow.'
116 Hyodo:	kowa:::
	[tte natte, ((with a terrified facial expression))
	'[I] thought "[it's] scary!"'
117 Guest:	[hhhhhhhh
118 Hyodo:	nose rareru yori kowa:::
	[tte natte, ((with a terrified facial expression))
	'[I] thought "[it's] more scary than landing [on my head]!"'
119 Guest:	[hhhhh
120 Hyodo:	mou housou go suguni **manga kai ni iki [mashi ta.**
	'After finishing my recording, I went to buy the comic book immediately.'
121 Guest:	[hhhhh

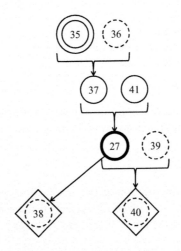

Figure 27.5 Rhetorical organization of the proof

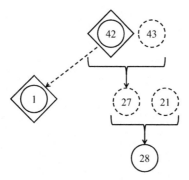

Figure 27.6 Rhetorical organization of the conclusion

The conclusion starts with a reminder of (1), just as the introduction. Lines 109–114 tell that the daughter does not land the drone on him but keeps it hovering at a distance. (42) takes three roles in the story: (i) when combined with (43), it is premise of (27); (ii) it arouses fear towards the daughter; and then (iii) it illustrates (1). The punchline in line 120 tells that the father accepted his defeat in the game and gave her a prize.

(42) The daughter threatens at the father as she keeps the drone hovering.
(43) (If the daughter threatens at the father by keeping the drone hovering, she can land it on his head.)

The conclusion is visualized in Figure 27.6. The episode of hovering primarily means that the father lost the game, and at the same time, it is interpreted as showing that the daughter is strange, which relates the conclusion to the introduction and gives coherence to the whole story.

Summary

Figure 27.7 integrates the four parts of the story. It visually shows that the whole story comprises two logical flows connected by enthymemes and examples, whose most highlighted propositions are (27) (i.e., the daughter can land the drone) and (33) (i.e., the daughter cannot land the drone). (27), the conclusion of the narrative as a whole, is supported by three enthymemes, which indicates that (27) is more strongly supported than (33). Since the narrative is intended to be entertainment, it is reasonable that we observed numerous elements of pathos. In particular, the reversal of the father and daughter's positions based on the contrast between (34) and (38) and the relation between (40) and the father's anxiety seem to structure the emotional orientation toward humor. Although ethos is not very salient in our case, elements of ethos build a basis of emotional propositions, such as (18) inferred from (10) and (13).

Our understanding of the rhetorical organization is closely related to cultural knowledge. Some propositions are provided by knowledge about the sociocultural setting in Japan. For example, the tacit understanding of (4) requires knowledge of the pandemic situation due to COVID-19 in Japan. (14) is accepted as a common opinion only when one knows of the history of Japanese toys. In addition, associations between propositions

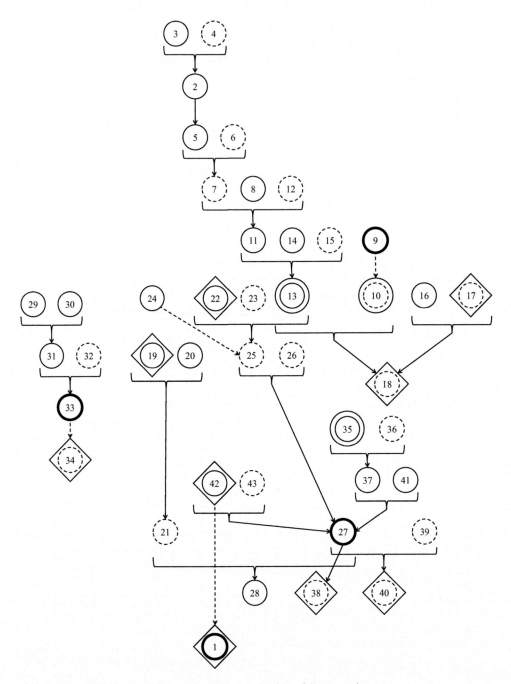

Figure 27.7 Visualization of the rhetorical organization of the narrative

and pathos might largely depend on the conventions of Japanese culture because it is cultural orientation that decides whether a description of a situation elicits sympathy with an emotion. The associations between laughing and superiority in (17), practicing and funniness in (22), or hovering and fear in (42) may be interpreted differently depending on the culture.

Conclusion

We showed in this chapter how the notions of ethos, pathos, and logos work effectively in describing rhetorical organization and probing the cultural elements underlying the propositions shown in the narrative. We also demonstrated how a visualization of analysis helps to understand the complicated rhetorical organization of narrative in an unfamiliar language, providing an analysis of a Japanese narrative based on a detailed transcript. Future work will examine case studies in other languages to determine whether the methodology proposed in this chapter is useful for comparative rhetoric (Lloyd 2021) in world languages and cultures.

Transcription Symbols

[	the point of overlap onset
=	no break or gap
(0.0)	elapsed time in tenths of a second
(.)	a brief interval without talk
X	some form of stress, via pitch and/or amplitude
::	prolongation of the immediately preceding sound, such that the more colons, the longer the prolongation
↑	shifts to especially high
.	falling intonation
?	rising intonation
,	intonation that sounds as if the utterance would continue
hh	an outbreath, which may indicate a laugh
°word°	the sounds are softer than the surrounding speech
>word<	the bracketed material is faster than the surrounding talk
<word>	the bracketed material is slower than the surrounding talk
((word))	transcriber's descriptions

Abbreviations

CAUS	causative
COP	copula
NOM	nominative
Q	question particle
QUOT	quotative

References

Aho, J. A. (1985) 'Rhetoric and the Invention of Double Entry Bookkeeping', *Rhetorica* 3(1): 21–43.

Amossy, R. (2000) *L'argumentation dans le Discours: Discours Politique, Littérature D'idées, Fiction*, Paris: Nathan.

Baumlin, J. S. (2001) 'Ethos', in T. O. Sloane (ed.), *Encyclopedia of Rhetoric*, pp. 263–277, Oxford: Oxford University Press.

Campbell, C. P. (1998) 'Rhetorical Ethos', in S. Niemeier, C. P. Campbell, and R. Dirven (eds.), *The Cultural Context in Business Communication*, pp. 31–47, Amsterdam: John Benjamins.

Comrie, B., Haspelmath, M., and Bickel, B. (2015) *The Leipzig Glossing Rules: Conventions for Interlinear Morpheme-by-Morpheme Glosses*, Department of Linguistics of the Max Planck Institute for Evolutionary Anthropology and the Department of Linguistics of the University of Leipzig. Available online at www.eva.mpg.de/lingua/pdf/Glossing-Rules.pdf (accessed June 17, 2022).

Connors, R. J. (1979) 'The Differences between Speech and Writing: Ethos, Pathos, and Logos', *College Composition and Communication* 30(3): 285–290.

Copi, I., Cohen, C., and Rodych, V. (2019) *Introduction to Logic*, 15th ed., London: Routledge.

Corbett, E. P. J., and Connors, R. J. (1999) *Classical Rhetoric for the Modern Student*, 4th ed., Oxford: Oxford University Press.

Demirdöğen, Ü. D. (2010) 'The Roots of Research in (Political) Persuasion: Ethos, Pathos, Logos and the Yale Studies of Persuasive Communications', *International Journal of Social Inquiry* 3(1): 189–201.

Green, L. D. (2001) 'Pathos', in T. O. Sloane (ed.), *Encyclopedia of Rhetoric*, pp. 554–569, Oxford: Oxford University Press.

Higgins, C., and Walker, R. (2012) 'Ethos, Logos, Pathos: Strategies of Persuasion in Social/ Environmental Reports', *Accounting Forum* 36(3): 194–208.

Hill, C. A. (2004) 'The Psychology of Rhetorical Images', in C. A. Hill and M. Helmers (eds.), *Defining Visual Rhetorics*, pp. 25–40, London: Lawrence Erlbaum Associates.

Hullman, J., and Diakopoulos, N. (2011) 'Visualization Rhetoric: Framing Effects in Narrative Visualization', *IEEE Transactions on Visualization and Computer Graphics* 17(12): 2231–2240.

Jefferson, G. (2004) 'Glossary of Transcript Symbols', in G. H. Lerner (ed.), *Conversation Analysis: Studies from the First Generation*, pp. 13–31, Amsterdam: John Benjamins.

Kirk, J. W. (2016) 'Mitt Romney in Denver: "Obamacare" as Ideological Enthymeme', *Journal of Argumentation in Context* 5(3): 227–248.

Kostelnick, C. (1996) 'Supra-Textual Design: The Visual Rhetoric of Whole Documents', *Technical Communication Quarterly* 5(1): 9–33.

Kostelnick, C. (2007) 'The Visual Rhetoric of Data Displays: The Conundrum of Clarity', *IEEE Transactions on Professional Communication* 50(4): 280–294.

Lloyd, K. (ed.) (2021) *The Routledge Handbook of Comparative World Rhetorics: Studies in the History, Application, and Teaching of Rhetoric beyond Traditional Greco-Roman Contexts*, London: Routledge.

Lyons, J. D. (2001) 'Exemplum', in T. O. Sloane (ed.), *Encyclopedia of Rhetoric*, pp. 277–279, Oxford: Oxford University Press.

Mshvenieradze, T. (2013) 'Logos Ethos and Pathos in Political Discourse', *Theory & Practice in Language Studies* 3(11): 1939–1945.

Phelan, J. (1996) *Narrative as Rhetoric: Technique, Audiences, Ethics, Ideology*, Columbus: Ohio State University Press.

Razuvayevskaya, O., and Teufel, S. (2017) 'Finding Enthymemes in Real-World Texts: A Feasibility Study', *Argument & Computation* 8(2): 113–129.

St.Amant, K. (2013) 'Culture and Rhetorical Expectations: A Perspective for Technical Communicators', *Communication & Language at Work* 2(2): 33–40.

St.Amant, K. (2019) 'Ethos Prototypes: The Intersection of Rhetoric, Cognition, and Communicating Health Policy Internationally', *World Medical & Health Policy* 11(4): 464–473.

Ting, S. (2018) 'Ethos, Logos and Pathos in University Students' Informal Requests', *GEMA Online Journal of Language Studies* 18(1): 234–251.

Walton, D. N. (2001) 'Enthymemes, Common Knowledge, and Plausible Inference', *Philosophy & Rhetoric* 34(2): 93–112.

Wells, S. (2001) 'Logos', in T. O. Sloane (ed.), *Encyclopedia of Rhetoric*, pp. 389–404, Oxford: Oxford University Press.

Wispé, L. (1986) 'The Distinction between Sympathy and Empathy: To Call Forth a Concept, a Word Is Needed', *Journal of Personality and Social Psychology* 50(2): 314–321.

Yu, N. (1996) 'Imagery', in T. Enos (ed.), *Encyclopedia of Rhetoric and Composition: Communication from Ancient Times to the Information Age*, p. 343, London: Routledge.

INDEX

accent 388
accentuation 183, 184, 188, 197
accountability 16, 17, 124, 176, 248, 271
accusations 10, 106, 107, 124, 225, 243, 245, 371
activism 128, 160, 224, 320, 323
actor-network 312, 319
adaptation 61, 159, 244, 252, 253, 321
adjective 78, 104, 223, 403
adolescence 154, 384, 406
adverbs 90, 93, 95, 184, 187, 353
advertisement 81, 240, 241, 350, 394, 398
advice 16, 31, 113, 150, 151, 352, 353
advocacy 93, 95, 160, 247, 248, 372, 373, 377, 378
aesthetics 95, 146, 151, 246, 387
affective 4, 168, 246, 248, 323, 357, 365, 396, 397, 399–401
affirmative 45, 73, 84, 156, 205
African–Americans 126
agency 159, 161, 285, 329, 372, 377, 398
aggressive 228, 254, 388, 416
alliteration 97, 155
allusion 49, 50, 157, 175, 399
ambiguity 26, 121, 139, 151, 153, 231, 277, 413
ambivalence 221, 230
amusement 121, 239, 243
analogy 26, 29, 38, 63, 107, 153, 170, 175, 256
anonymous 26, 113, 371
antagonism 181, 277, 278
Anthropology 247, 390, 460
anti-abortion 137, 224, 225, 228, 229
anti-communist 135, 140, 343
anti-democratic 220
anti-government 135, 227

anti-immigration 213, 235, 236, 242, 247, 248, 377
apologies 140, 182
argumentation theory 63, 113, 249, 250, 259, 260
Aristotle 20, 36, 42, 51, 70, 79, 86, 102, 110, 113, 158, 159, 161, 166, 177, 199, 213, 245, 246, 250–52, 260, 261, 325, 342, 346, 351, 352, 360, 393–96, 404, 407, 419, 441–43, 447
assembly 11, 101, 105, 108, 114
attenuation 182, 183, 196
Augustine 40, 167
authoritarian 19, 106, 112, 385

ballad 132, 136, 138–40, 145, 146
banners 137, 146
beautification 155
behavioural 204, 385, 386, 388, 421
biased 126, 274, 275, 429, 432, 435
Bible 150, 245, 247
biblical 64, 136
booster 183, 190
broadcast 392, 446
Buddhism 18, 108

canon 39, 66, 112, 141, 252, 309, 313
caricatures 244
cartoon 118, 128, 242
Catholicism 224
censorship 38, 136, 140, 142, 143, 169, 180
ceremony 114, 332
Chinese rhetoric 9, 10, 14, 16, 17, 20, 32
Christianity 19, 40, 58, 67, 108, 152, 153, 159, 199, 222, 224, 226, 228, 232, 233, 303, 308, 422, 426

Index

cinema 76, 120–23, 129, 130, 347, 355–57, 360, 378, 380–87, 389, 390
classical rhetoric 2, 3, 53, 54, 67, 102, 199, 201, 249–52, 312, 369, 460
collocations 413, 414, 417, 418
colloquial 3, 77, 82, 84, 93–97, 412, 414, 415, 418
colonial 108, 117, 118, 369, 439
Confucianism 20, 327, 328, 339, 343
consumer 49, 51, 240, 241, 246, 268, 344, 345, 347, 360, 390, 401
contradictions 327, 431
controversial 94, 118, 120, 139, 142, 150, 201, 238, 242, 286, 318, 326, 329
conventional 1, 40, 45, 89, 93, 153, 269, 279, 317, 345, 400
corpus 3, 4, 26, 29, 44, 46, 79, 165–67, 182–84, 190, 195, 199, 201, 202, 213, 260, 284, 287–92, 295, 297, 300, 303, 307, 308, 346, 349–51, 353, 357, 359, 362, 412, 413, 424, 425
counterargument 150, 334–36, 455
courtesy 65, 195
criticism 3, 42, 51, 55, 64, 70, 72, 77, 79, 84, 148, 149, 151–54, 158–61, 226, 312, 345, 347–49, 360, 361, 432
cross-cultural 20, 37, 149, 160, 284, 309

debates 9, 64, 81, 82, 96, 98, 123, 124, 214, 215, 219, 220, 250, 253, 254, 260, 272, 286, 307, 311–13, 315–17, 319, 323, 379
declaration 110, 138, 188, 248, 287, 332
deconstruction 269, 275, 349
decontextualized 36, 159
deductive 2, 70, 443–46, 448, 453
defend 39, 48, 170, 171, 180, 187, 201, 215, 217, 224, 225, 233, 249, 274, 313, 347, 356, 386
democratic 1, 4, 54, 58, 59, 65, 117, 139, 146, 168, 171, 173, 174, 176, 220, 221, 235, 278, 307, 312
depreciative 348, 351, 416
descriptive 2, 4, 5, 19, 36, 60, 71, 79, 87, 93, 96, 121, 124, 148, 149, 151, 153, 155, 157, 159, 161, 163, 174, 252, 324, 325, 334, 365, 422, 441, 446
dictatorship 135, 343
diglossia 77, 98
dignity 125, 128, 129, 222, 429
discourse analysis 3, 57, 58, 158, 160, 165, 167, 176, 179, 196–98, 213–15, 232, 237, 246, 247, 251, 252, 254, 260, 261, 346, 360, 379
diversity 2, 4, 85, 87, 92, 134, 156, 203, 207, 208, 231, 279, 284, 285, 290, 308
drama 60, 125, 141, 349, 354

egalitarian 359
embellishment 72, 95, 155, 156, 249

embodiment 120, 138, 395
emotion 124, 126, 142, 167, 172, 174, 241, 247, 320, 392, 396, 399, 401, 411, 415, 442, 443, 459
emotive 123, 189, 238, 360, 397
empathy 116, 127, 128, 167, 194, 203, 211, 212, 227, 308, 318, 368, 372, 383, 399, 461
emphasis 14, 41, 44, 49, 122, 158, 188, 189, 195, 199, 241, 285–87, 308, 312, 331, 425, 444
empiricism 70, 79, 80
empower 169, 286
endorsement 98, 257, 276, 425
entertainment 121, 122, 348, 350, 441, 457
enthymematic 44, 108, 159, 404
enthymeme 102, 114, 240, 241, 248, 404, 419, 443–46, 448, 450, 460
epistemological 28, 200, 238, 343, 421, 425, 431, 432
ethical 17, 21, 32, 127, 140, 144, 168, 212, 327, 340, 376, 387, 388, 395, 398, 399, 401, 421, 433, 436
ethnic 13, 106, 107, 214, 215, 220, 221, 247, 285, 378, 380, 383
ethos 4, 5, 14, 16, 20, 39, 63, 70, 135, 165–77, 179, 199–203, 210, 212, 213, 227, 236, 240, 241, 245, 271, 312, 321, 341, 345–49, 351–60, 393–401, 404, 408, 409, 418, 419, 440–42, 445, 446, 454, 457, 459, 460
evaluative 166, 194, 196, 347, 348, 351, 356, 416
expressive 58, 64, 90, 97, 349, 352, 409, 424

face-threatening 182, 193
fascism 132, 138, 214, 231, 384, 385
fiction 97, 116, 380, 389, 404, 410, 436, 460
figurative 39, 50, 57, 64, 90, 97, 153, 172, 443
first-person 204, 353
foreground 149, 271, 314, 394
forensic 28, 56, 158, 312, 314, 419
functional 57, 67, 151, 160, 174, 346, 347, 360, 400

genre 1, 2, 4, 39, 45, 48, 50, 51, 56, 60, 61, 63, 65, 102, 117, 122, 131, 132, 136, 137, 146, 150, 151, 220, 254, 267–70, 272, 274, 277, 279–82, 345–51, 353–63, 412, 423, 441
gestures 82, 160, 166, 397, 449
globalization 80, 118, 128, 143, 328, 416
grammar 54, 55, 58, 60, 61, 65, 67, 79, 90, 94, 99, 269, 272, 378, 382
graphic 76, 91, 127, 243, 289, 390

harmony 77, 84, 94, 150, 182, 191, 219, 383, 385, 411, 422
hegemony 85, 107, 121, 127, 181, 308

Index

heritage 3, 14, 33, 37, 76, 101, 129, 199, 208, 215–17
hermeneutic 5, 26, 34, 72, 162, 425
heuristic 25, 97, 253, 404, 405
hierarchical 108, 273, 278, 412, 413, 423, 436
hostility 42, 221
humanitarian 18, 166, 175, 372, 373
humiliate 75, 83
humor 63, 236, 243, 244, 246, 457
hypernym 112, 415

identities 29, 118, 120, 121, 123, 129, 146, 168, 185, 201, 214, 220, 221, 232, 235, 238, 284, 308, 309, 371, 380
ideology 2, 15, 16, 19, 54, 55, 86, 116, 120–24, 135, 176, 181, 215, 219, 222, 223, 225, 228, 230, 234, 242, 245, 278, 280, 284, 309, 343, 344, 368, 383, 431, 441, 444, 460
imaginary 349, 437
immigrant 176, 243, 284, 289, 290, 300, 379
inaugural 114, 176, 297, 331
inequality 117, 118, 124, 128, 129, 200, 373
institutional 44, 123, 220, 250, 254, 260, 271, 280, 281, 314, 395
instrumental 17, 18, 28, 93, 98, 181
intelligibility 28, 92, 357
intensify 128, 352, 359, 410, 434, 436, 443
intention 2, 38, 60, 63, 65, 110, 230, 315, 346, 359, 369, 393, 397, 424, 453
interdependence 41, 144, 248
intertextuality 70, 81, 84, 86, 138, 426
irony 64, 139, 140, 348

jokes 243, 246
journalism 45, 64, 238, 247, 249, 346–48, 351, 379, 412, 439
justice 35, 43, 70, 85, 130, 132, 140, 142, 153, 160, 166, 167, 173, 174, 219, 228, 249, 289, 308, 340, 427
justification 13, 124, 153, 189, 201, 253
juxtaposition 132, 142, 167, 308

karma 12, 18
keywords 166, 309
kingship 9, 17, 20

leadership 170, 175, 254, 320, 342
legend 32, 136, 150, 239, 394
legitimation 12, 221, 228, 243
legitimization 91, 213, 396
lexical 75, 84, 93, 96, 102, 105, 106, 110, 112, 155, 156, 192, 194, 202, 262, 357, 358, 412–14, 447
liberal 53–56, 65, 219, 230, 243, 287, 330
lineage 16, 17, 150

linguistics 5, 57, 58, 65, 66, 81, 85, 89, 99, 176, 196, 197, 215, 251, 260, 262, 345, 346, 360, 361, 460
literary 3, 14, 44, 53–58, 60–66, 69, 70, 72, 77–82, 84–86, 91–98, 118, 130, 136, 141, 146, 150, 158, 160–62, 173, 175, 179, 189, 403, 404, 411, 413, 418, 423, 424, 431, 432, 436, 439
loanwords 433

malicious 42
malignant 388
manipulation 19, 28, 33, 39, 44, 50, 125, 129, 154, 181, 197, 244, 249, 361, 421, 424
marriage 81, 218, 222, 224, 286, 290, 386, 406
memory 60, 79, 113, 135, 220, 232, 239, 246–48, 257, 383, 384, 396, 428, 438, 442
mentality 107, 286
metaphors 3, 37, 49, 50, 71, 74, 77, 79, 81, 84, 166, 172, 173, 175, 176, 206, 213, 214, 220, 228, 231, 312, 313, 316, 320–22, 352, 357, 360, 389, 418, 419
metonymy 49, 73, 74, 79, 155, 173, 175, 224, 455
migrants 165, 170, 199, 204, 206, 209, 373, 377, 379
minority 56, 126, 206, 220, 224, 285–87
mnemonic 60, 156, 245, 247
modality 102, 103, 107, 108, 112, 113, 169, 209, 314, 353, 354, 359
morality 9, 14–17, 21, 58, 218, 327, 406, 412, 421
multicultural 70, 216, 308, 309

narratives 24–30, 34, 91, 116–21, 124, 127, 128, 141, 160, 221, 226, 237, 245–47, 286, 287, 310, 311, 316, 319, 320, 323, 381, 387, 423, 438
nationalism 93, 213, 220, 231, 234, 235, 237, 240, 241, 245–48
neo-liberalism 328, 343
nomination 103, 200–204
non-Western 25, 28, 119, 127, 369
novels 96, 118, 141, 410, 411, 430

offensive 82, 83, 94, 209, 216, 330, 338
onomatopoeia 3, 89–91, 93–100, 443
oppression 138, 200, 257, 289, 307, 309, 374
orator 11, 12, 24, 40, 44, 65, 151, 162, 167–71, 173, 175, 261, 329, 341, 441
organizational 31, 196, 214, 343, 360
orientalism 369, 437, 439
orthography 101

pandemic 1, 125, 137, 165, 167, 238, 239, 245, 248, 391–401, 447, 448, 454, 457
parallelism 155, 190, 205

464

Index

paraphrase 110, 416

pathos 4, 5, 10, 63, 70, 135, 165–69, 171–78, 199–203, 211–13, 236, 240, 241, 245, 312, 341, 351, 392, 393, 395, 396, 399–401, 404, 408, 409, 418, 440–43, 445, 446, 457, 459, 460

patriotism 166, 203, 211, 328

pejorative 166, 418, 435

persuasion 1, 3–5, 10, 31, 32, 35, 39, 42, 43, 63, 64, 69, 72, 73, 77–81, 84–86, 102, 113, 146, 151, 158, 172, 175, 176, 178, 182, 187, 195, 196, 214, 220, 234–36, 243, 245–48, 250, 253, 259, 261, 311–13, 326, 341, 342, 345–49, 351–53, 355–57, 359–61, 363, 396, 401, 404–6, 408–10, 417–19, 423, 429, 431, 432, 436, 438–40, 443, 460

phraseology 416

plagiarism 276

podcasts 268, 317

poetry 53, 69–71, 78, 79, 86, 94, 96, 97, 135, 136, 139, 146, 161, 403, 411

postcolonial 118, 130, 423

pragmatics 2, 3, 54, 57, 58, 65–67, 113, 196, 214, 215, 220, 260

pronoun 109, 186, 204, 355

prototypes 124, 441, 460

proverbs 416

puns 155

qualitative 70, 174, 182, 201, 246, 346, 378, 424

quantitative 315

queer 154, 156, 157, 161, 285, 287, 290

Quintilian 39, 51, 393, 397, 405, 406, 409, 419

racial 120, 167, 177, 275, 290, 295, 297, 378

rapport 192

rationality 17, 126, 168, 312, 327, 337, 340, 396, 403, 410, 411, 418

readership 183, 186, 187, 189, 192, 194, 195, 350, 354, 357, 424, 426, 429, 436

re-contextualization 159, 238, 239, 242, 244, 245

religion 17, 19, 102, 109, 112, 113, 153, 199, 228, 231, 284, 289, 290, 292, 303, 304, 307, 308, 316, 409, 416

resistance 3, 131, 136–38, 209, 279, 309

revitalization 57

rhetorical analysis 3, 5, 43, 45, 46, 131, 132, 153, 176, 196, 236, 246, 249, 251, 265, 284, 285, 287, 289, 291, 293, 295, 297, 299, 301, 303, 305, 307, 309, 311, 312, 323, 351, 365, 383, 393, 396–98, 440

rhetorical devices 5, 48, 49, 69, 70, 73, 75, 79, 81, 82, 89, 91, 93, 95, 97, 99, 102, 178, 189, 191, 404, 421–25, 436

rhetorical figures 60, 63, 64, 74, 75, 85, 90, 95, 96, 155, 167, 249, 251, 259, 383, 412

rhetorical forms 51, 131, 154, 268, 269, 271, 272, 276, 282

rhetorical organization 5, 440, 441, 444, 446, 450, 451, 453, 454, 456–59

rhetorical potential 90, 91, 94, 97, 98, 135, 143, 415–17

rhetorical power 19, 29, 34, 35, 135, 142, 143, 238, 376

rhetorical processes 28, 29, 31, 34, 36, 267, 269, 271

rhetorical situation 40, 45, 113, 131–34, 139, 140, 142–46, 240, 241, 254, 272, 327, 330, 332, 340–42, 351, 397, 401

rhetorical strategies 4, 127, 130, 172, 178, 195, 221, 230, 239, 243, 249, 251, 259, 312, 314, 368, 371, 376, 377, 436

rhetorical structure 274, 326, 330, 334, 340, 345, 440, 441, 443, 445, 447, 449, 451, 453, 455, 457, 459, 461

rhetorical studies 1–3, 5, 7, 59, 76, 81, 87, 131, 213, 251, 259, 260, 310, 379, 444

rhetorical theory 1, 2, 24–27, 29, 31–37, 42, 54, 55, 64, 66, 158–60, 250, 251, 260, 270–72, 396, 419

rhetorical value 146, 274, 276, 277, 401, 415, 416, 434

rhetors 38, 50, 155, 369, 407

rhythmic 97, 149

Romanticism 139, 247, 411, 422

satire 64, 244, 247

semiotic 36, 234, 245, 246, 312, 378, 380, 381, 383, 386, 389

sensual 79, 409, 418

signifier 26, 28, 30, 116, 119, 121, 383

slavery 83, 275

socialist 135, 136, 218, 255

sociocultural 219, 247, 446, 457

statistics 123, 241, 290, 291, 334, 351, 379, 391, 418

stereotypical 118, 123, 126, 127, 239, 368, 369

storytelling 136, 311, 319, 381, 382

strategically 125, 181, 187, 235, 245

structural 28, 73, 90, 119, 181, 401, 404

stylistic 50, 55, 56, 61, 69, 72, 77–81, 85, 97, 98, 149, 151, 152, 154, 155, 157, 383, 413, 415, 444

subjectivity 128, 134, 186, 192, 229, 275, 357, 422

superstition 16

syllogism 70, 79, 102, 159, 252

symbolic 25, 28, 33, 34, 37, 42, 102, 119, 138–42, 162, 200, 234, 237, 240, 241, 245, 332, 380–84, 388, 392, 410

tabloid 222

tactics 116, 176, 287, 317

Index

tautology 327, 416
taxonomies 155, 183
terminology 1, 25, 26, 31, 34, 71, 77, 82, 83, 85, 119, 224, 421
textbook 4, 242, 284, 285, 292, 295, 297, 300, 307–9, 444
theology 40, 70, 71, 85, 148, 152, 158, 426
topic 3, 31, 44, 45, 61, 65, 77, 84, 116, 151, 158, 165, 175, 195, 198, 201, 219, 273, 275, 289, 295, 297, 308, 311, 315, 317, 369, 404, 405, 410, 432, 450
tragedy 117, 124, 130, 173, 215, 380
tropes 73, 90, 95, 123, 134, 149, 153–55, 220, 357–59, 369, 412, 413, 417

unbiased 271, 274, 275, 425
uncertainty 103, 183, 192, 193, 195, 216, 312, 314, 322, 323, 386

utterance 184, 189, 191, 195, 221, 415, 431, 446, 447, 459

vagueness 194
validity 63, 121, 143, 144, 431
valuation 143, 284, 286, 309, 393
verbatim 21, 314
vernacular 92–94, 96–98, 130, 430
vocabulary 76, 90, 269, 314, 341, 354, 358, 359, 370, 377, 412
vulgarisms 137

warfare 1, 31, 313
worldview 4, 124, 127, 158, 219, 221, 223, 230, 416
worship 16, 17, 83, 109

xenophobia 217, 377